COLLECTED ESSAYS

COLLECTED ESSAYS

BY

F. H. BRADLEY

OXFORD
AT THE CLARENDON PRESS

Oxford University Press, Ely House, London W. 1

GLASGOW NEW YORK TORONTO MELBOURNE WELLINGTON
CAPE TOWN SALISBURY IBADAN NAIROBI LUSAKA ADDIS ABABA
BOMBAY CALCUTTA MADRAS KARACHI LAHORE DACCA
KUALA LUMPUR SINGAPORE HONG KONG TOKYO

FIRST PUBLISHED IN TWO VOLUMES IN 1935
REPRINTED LITHOGRAPHICALLY IN GREAT BRITAIN
AT THE UNIVERSITY PRESS, OXFORD
BY VIVIAN RIDLER
PRINTER TO THE UNIVERSITY
1969

TO
THOSE WHO, LIKE THE AUTHOR OF
THESE ESSAYS,
FIND 'THE SEARCH FOR TRUTH A NECESSITY
OF THEIR NATURE'

PREFACE

THOUGH all but two of the essays included in these volumes have already appeared in print, it has not hitherto been in an easily accessible form. Both the pamphlets at the beginning of the present collection—*The Presuppositions of Critical History* (the author's earliest work) and *Mr. Sidgwick's Hedonism*—have long been out of print and difficult, if not impossible, to obtain; whilst the *Replies to Criticisms* and the great majority of the Articles have remained scattered, and more or less buried, in the various journals in which they first appeared. Their republication, therefore, seems necessary if they are to be rescued from oblivion; and is more than justified by their intrinsic value, as well as by the light they throw, when read in chronological order, upon the development of the author's views over a period of nearly fifty years.

The present collection also includes, at the end of the second volume, two hitherto unpublished essays, one on *The Treatment of Sexual Detail in Literature*, and an unfinished article, together with an explanatory appendix, on *Relations*.

A List of Abbreviations, by which it is hoped readers may easily find such references as they require, is printed immediately after the Table of Contents; and the order and date of all the author's publications are shown in the Bibliography on pp. 699–700.

We desire to thank the Editors of *Mind*, *The International Journal of Ethics*, *The Journal of Philosophy*, *The Philosophical Review*, and *The Fortnightly Review* for their courtesy in permitting us to republish articles which originally appeared in their Journals; and we are greatly indebted to Mr. G. R. G. Mure, Fellow and Tutor of Merton College, for the time and trouble he has devoted to the preparation of the Index.

M. DE G.
H. H. J.

1935

CONTENTS

CONTENTS

LIST OF ABBREVIATIONS

Ethical Studies $= E.S.$
Principles of Logic $= L.$
Appearance and Reality $= A.R.$
Essays on Truth and Reality $= T.R.$
Collected Essays $= E.$

(A Roman numeral following E indicates the particular Essay)

Mind $= M.$

(The Old and New Series in 'Mind' are indicated by o.s. and N.S., and the volume by a Roman numeral)

References to the author's works are to the latest editions, though references (preceded by the sign =) to the earlier editions are added for the convenience of some readers.

References by the author to the works of other writers have been retained without alteration.

I

THE PRESUPPOSITIONS OF CRITICAL HISTORY

PREFACE

THAT the following pages should not go before the public without an apology I am very sensible. Their matter I fear is unsatisfactory, and their manner worse; but no alteration that I could make would be likely to improve either. The reason why these reflections are printed at all is my wish and hope that they may be instrumental in leading some more capable person to clear up and dispose, once and for all, of a subject which ought to be disposed of.

The barbarous title of the following pages anticipates their method, and to some extent their conclusion. Their method consists in taking the existence of certain facts for granted, and in endeavouring to discover the conditions of that existence. These conditions by their absence annihilate the facts; and hence the facts involve them, take them for granted, presuppose them. And the conclusion is that, as the facts *have* presupposed the principle unconsciously, so now in judging we must proceed upon that principle consciously, and use it as a canon.

The subject of critical history is not so narrow as at first sight it might appear. There is no history which in some respects is not more or less critical. No one in the world thinks or could think of inserting into a history of the world *all* the events which have ever been handed down, precisely *as* they have been handed down. But if this is not done, if we exclude or alter or rationalize to the very smallest extent, then we have criticism at once, and we ought to know what criticism means.

That question being asked, it became obvious that

critical history must have a criterion, and the next matter was to find that criterion. It seemed equally clear after a time that the canon of history was—the historian. This result comes naturally from the consideration of particular historical practice (and in this respect as in others let me acknowledge how much I am indebted to Baur's *Epochs of Church History-writing*)[1] as also from reflection on the psychological aspect of the general question. The historian, as he is, is the real criterion; the ideal criterion (if such an antithesis can be pardoned) is the historian as he ought to be. And the historian who is true to the present *is* the historian as he ought to be.

This is the main thought in what follows, and, in order to reach such a conclusion, it was necessary to meet antagonistic doctrines at every stage, as well as objections which sprang up in my own mind continually. I have tried so far as possible to avoid wearisomeness, but have not succeeded; and, what is worse, I fear that I may not have succeeded, even at the cost of weariness, either in removing the objections I myself have raised, or in anticipating those which may occur to the reader. I think that in order to have attained a satisfactory result, the whole subject of probability and certainty ought to have been investigated. To this task I felt myself unequal, and my conclusions are hence to some extent precarious.

The preface is already out of proportion to the performance, but I am forced to say a word in conclusion on the application of anything set down here to religious questions. For what I have said I am answerable, but for nothing that any other person chooses to conclude. The view I have put forward is this, that every man's present standpoint ought to determine his belief in respect to *all* past events; but to no man do I dictate what his present standpoint ought to be. *Consistency* is the one word that I have emphasized. I cannot help it if any one thinks that the conclusions of this essay are reconcilable with only one

---

[1] I may mention here that von Sybel's *Gesetze des historischen Wissens* and Droysen's *Grundriss der Historik* are very brief and well worth reading, though they came to me too late to be of much use.

belief or disbelief. I can only say beforehand that such a man's opinion is not mine. These conclusions, I think, are negative only of a breach between the worlds of the present and the past; and to point out where such a breach exists was not my business, still less my business to express an opinion on the relative truth and falsehood of existing religious beliefs.

If we meddle in any way with the history of certain times, we must touch the element or a part of the element in which hitherto the Christian principle has brought itself home to the religious consciousness. And to a person who identifies the element with that which exists in it, or who believes that the truth of a principle is to be found at the beginning of its temporal development, such modification will doubtless appear an *all*-important matter. That it is important I do not question. I know that it is so. But I know this also, that the extent and generally the nature of the influence, which a modification of history must exercise on religious belief, is a subject on which it is remarkably easy to come to a conclusion, and extremely hard to come to a right one. Courage to express one's views has long ceased to be a virtue. Except where persons are concerned, there is no merit in possessing it, and it is on the fair way to become a vice. And, especially where religion is involved, there is one courage it is well to be free from, the courage to utter one's (mere) opinions.

All that I have left to say[1] is that whatever below may be of use to any one here does not belong to me, except in the sense in which a man's debts are his own. My debt is owing in Oxford, and my use of what I have borrowed is very far from the approach to a payment.

OXFORD

1874.

[1] I ought to mention that in Note A I have tried to bring the subject home to the general reader, while Note E is not meant for the general reader at all.

THE PRESUPPOSITIONS OF CRITICAL HISTORY

SUMMARY

Critical history involves two sides or elements, 'objective' and 'subjective' (7–8). False account of the relation of these two sides (8–9); refutes itself (10–11).

What is a fact for history? Not a simple datum of the senses (11–12); but a complex totality (13), a judgement (14), and more, a conclusion (14–15). This illustrated (15–17).

Testimony, as experience of others, rests for us on inference from our own experience (17–19). Illustration of this (19–20).

All history has a 'prejudication'. What is this? (20) Omnipresence and uniformity of law. History must assume this and so must science (21–3). Freedom of will no objection to it (23–4).

But what does uniformity in history mean? It means that all historical facts are subject to inference from the present world (24–5).

Objection to this. 'The present world itself depends on testimony' (26). Yes, but the critic's present world ought not so to depend (26–7).

Further objection. 'Then no testimony which goes beyond the analogous can be received' (28). Yes, it can; but only on certain conditions (28–30). Where testimony *must* fail to take us beyond analogy (30–2).

Is historical testimony of this latter sort? (32). What is *historical* testimony? Hard to say (33–4). We must take it to have three characteristics (35–7).

Once more, can historical testimony establish the non-analogous? (38) If it does not go beyond probability, No (38–9). Reasons why it cannot go beyond (39–42).

[Objection. 'This only applies to *existing* historical testimony. But history, as a science, is to rest on scientific evidence' (43). Why this will never be (43–5).]

Result at present obtained (45). Application of this result to historic material. Criticism must be partly negative (46–7), and absolute (47–8). Criticism stands towards tradition in four attitudes (48–51). Criticism not bound to explain everything on pain of retiring from the field (51–3).

THE PRESUPPOSITIONS OF CRITICAL
HISTORY

IN the world the mind makes for the manifestation of itself, and where its life is the process of its own self-realization, there the action and the knowledge of it are children, the hours of whose bringings-forth are never the same, and whose births are divided. Alike in the life of mankind and in the development of the individual, the deed comes first, and later the reflection; and it is with the question, 'What have I done?' that we awake to facts accomplished and never intended, and to existences we do not recognize, while we own them as the creation of ourselves. For a people only in the period of their stagnation, for a person only when the character and the station have become fixed for ever, and when the man is made, is it possible to foreknow the truth of the fresh achievement; and where progress has its full meaning, and evolution is more than a phrase, there the present is hard and the future impossible to discern. Unborn in the substance of the present there lies, it is true, and there lives that future: but the unborn is hidden as yet from the light, and the womb is secret, and the presage doubtful; and the morning of the child's naming is divided by many days from the darkness of begetting and the night of travail.

The sudden act of a moment is unveiled, it may be, to the gradual consciousness of advancing age; and there are seasons again when the slow drift of years comes home with a flash of sweet or sombre revelation; or it may be again that of these experiences neither is given for the time to humanity.

Neither the projection nor the recognition of reality are always the work of an hour; for there are periods when gathering tendencies and accumulation of changes copy their alterations in an altering reflection, when another day dawns through longer twilight, and another world more slowly steals on the sense, with its images so strange yet so familiar, and another man wakens through uncertain recollection to the same and yet to a new self-consciousness.

It has been thus with the growth of the critical mind. It fought in the name of another, and not in its own name; it has conquered before it set itself to the battle; and it was first in the making of its realm that it grasped the secret of its mission. The feeling of itself as power came before the knowledge of its purpose, and the passing of the power into act disclosed to it first its own nature. But the advance of its action was gradual, and the consciousness of itself was of equal growth, and with a tardy revelation followed the steps of a slow development.

Within the memory of to-day it has been that historical criticism has asserted and has made good an unabated claim; and with a sudden tide of success has risen to the consciousness of its unabridged mission. With the knowledge of itself it now knows also the purpose of its existence, and the reality which, in the field of its endeavour, belongs to itself and to itself alone.

Criticism has become self-conscious: but to be aware of its aims and the character of its work is one thing; it is another thing to attempt to comprehend the conditions of its being, and the justification of its empire. Such justification it is which historical criticism now mostly needs; for that criticism cannot, except by its actions, justify itself. Confined as it is to one limited sphere, to reflect on the grounds of its existence is for it to pass beyond that sphere; and the principles which regulate its practice are thus, because it cannot account for them, its presuppositions.

This is the subject of that which follows in these pages, and these pages will, so far as possible, be limited to this alone. Nor, however much at first sight it may appear so, will it be found an easy task to investigate the principles of critical history. It is a hard matter, because neither do we know at the outset what we mean by 'critical', nor shall we learn even at the end what history in general is, nor even assure ourselves of the fact of its existence. We here have enough, and, it may be, more than enough of considerations on history and on the 'science of history', with its actual or possible or impossible reality; but the question, 'When we use the word history what do we mean by it?' is, it would seem, too simple or too trifling a problem to stay the course of our 'advanced thinkers'. And yet the man who, feeling himself unequal alike to support that position or that title, is contented simply, so far as he can, to think, knows all too well that question, and knows it as involving the most difficult problems which philosophy can solve or discuss. Such a man, whatever may be his school, or whatever his principles, will not I know take it amiss in me that I confess at this point my inability, and seek to impose neither on myself, nor on his understanding, nor on the ignorance of the public. And so to begin——

It has been often remarked that, by whichever of the terms now in use we express it, history has still a double meaning. 'Geschichte' does not simply stand for 'Was geschieht', and ἱστορία would not merit its name were it nothing beyond the inquiries of the historian. Starting from different sides these words are extended, each to the same totality, by a broad or, if any one pleases, by a loose signification.

It might, I believe, be maintained plausibly, and perhaps even with serious conviction, that these two elements, that of events in time on the one side and, on the other side, that of recollection in the mind, were in history necessarily united; in this sense that a bare series of momentary occurrences cannot contain that without which history has no right to be named as history.

But such a discussion lies beyond our subject, and we must be content here both to assume an historical past of humanity, in the absence even of a recording subject, and to leave the assertion of a merely 'objective' history of Nature to stand or to fall untouched by us.

We do not question that history apart from the historian does exist; and contrariwise we must take it for granted that there is no such thing as history which is merely 'subjective', or, in other words, that whatever is 'created' by the historian is not in a proper sense history at all.

For that history as a whole has been so 'made', that in it we have nothing but a series of projections of present consciousness in the form of a story of past events, from time to time gathered up or abolished in a larger and more inclusive projection—this has, so far as I know, been upheld by no sober-minded man, nor could be: it is only the exceptional writings of particular periods of which such an account can be given, and scarcely even then without any modification.

But, be this as it may be, we refuse the name of history to such a production, and we assume that though history (Geschichte) may exist, where the writing of history (ἰστορία) does not exist, yet, where there is no real past, there also there is properly speaking no historian, nor any writing of history.

In what follows we have nothing to do with history as it is not for the historian: history presupposes, in its title of 'critical', the presence alike of the so-called 'objective' and the so-called 'subjective' elements; and it is only as involving both that we intend in future to use or to discuss the word.

In this sense (to touch at length on our proper inquiry) history stands not only for that which has been, but also for that which is; not only for the past in fact, but also for the present in record; and it implies in itself the union of these two elements: it implies, on the one hand, that what once lived in its own right lives now only as the object of knowledge, and on the other hand that the knowledge which now is possesses no title to existence save in right of that object, and, though itself present, yet draws its entire reality from the perished past.

Stated thus the facts would appear to force us to a grave consideration; but problems are hard to those alone who make them so, and to account for the conjunction of so diverse attributes has seemed (it is well known), and still seems to the earliest reflection, no difficult task. The explanation is simple. Knowledge is the reception of outward impressions, and it is but natural that the copy should resemble and reproduce the original. And if that which, independent of any act of judgement, was first learned be in like manner simply and honestly written down, surely this copy of a copy is still, undistorted by so transparent a medium, and true to the mould its original has shaped, the living imprint and the faithful though uncoloured likeness of the full reality?

Such is the view natural to the uncritical mind, and according to this history has no presuppositions, and indeed can have none: her province is to recall, and not to construct; she wishes to take the truth as it is, not to make it what it should be; and she demands from the historian the surrender of his judgement to the decree of the ages, not the projection of his desires and fancies into a region for ever passed from the limit of creation, dead to the action and the storm of life, whose tranquil expanse no breath of thought can ruffle, and where the charm is broken when the mirror is moved.

The theory is simple, and it may be pleasing, but it is no more than a theory; and could we, as we cannot, be blind to the difficulties which beset it from within, yet it is doomed to perish, for in its own practical application it exposes its own falsity and reveals its own illusion.

We ask for history, and that means that we ask for the simple record of unadulterated facts; we look, and nowhere do we find the object of our search, but in its stead we see the divergent accounts of a host of jarring witnesses, a chaos of disjoined and discrepant narrations, and yet, while all of these can by no possibility be received as true, at the same time not one of them can be rejected as false.

But the consciousness, for which testimony is the reproduction of a passive print, is at this point not resourceless. 'The pure rays of truth', we are told, 'are discoloured by the various media through which they pass, and it is the task of the historian to correct the refraction of one medium by that of another, and in this manner to arrive at the bare and uncoloured reality.' But the historian, if such be his mission, is not and cannot be merely receptive, or barely reproductive. It is true that he may not actually add any new material of his own, and yet his action, in so far as he realizes that which never as such has been given him, implies a preconception, and denotes in a sense a foregone conclusion. The straightening of the crooked rests on the knowledge of the straight, and the exercise of criticism requires a canon.

This is not the only difficulty which historical writing in its practice brings to the theory of passivity. There remains on the contrary another of equal weight. When the records of a bygone age have been all collected, and, so far as possible, brought into harmony, yet at this point the task of history does not cease. Writer after writer in rapid succession takes up the never-exhausted theme, and, where no new fact is left to discover, there still remains the ceaseless endeavour more and more thoroughly to apprehend the old material, the passion of the mind to be at home in its object, the longing to think the thing as it is in itself, and as all men have failed to think it before. With every fresh standing-ground gained by the growth of experience, with every rise of the spirit to a fuller life, comes another view of the far-lying past from a higher and a new level, and a fresh and corresponding change in the features of the object recognized. Impotent to deny the existence of these facts, and powerless to explain them, the uncritical consciousness refuses to advance, or advancing loses all hold on reality. It is forced to see in the place of its reproduction an origination, in the place of its witness a writer of fiction, in the place of its fact a theory; and its consistent issue is the barren scepticism which sees in history but a weary labyrinth of truth and tangled falsehood, whose clue is buried and lost in the centuries that lie behind.

An issue consistent, and indeed for a space necessary;

but inevitable to none except those alone who through helplessness and doubt have set their faces towards the truth. To the double-minded seeker, to the man who, though fain to win, has no heart to stake his possessions, in *this* sphere at least there is *no* inevitable conclusion. He justifies his belief in anything by his right to be convinced of nothing; yet for a present pleasure he forgoes his inheritance, and buys his immunity at the cost of slavery.

In view of the futility of such an outcome—not finding a solution in the metaphor of a crude reflection, ⟨and⟩ unable to remain in the doubt of scepticism or to sink to the dogma of despair—it remains to us once again to take up the question abandoned thus by the uncritical mind, and, with patience if not with hope, at least to attempt to exhibit it in a truer form. The heading, 'Presuppositions of Critical History', expresses briefly the doctrine which is the opposite of the uncritical, and anticipates the result that a history without so-called prejudications is a mere delusion, that what does everywhere exist is history founded upon them, and what ought to exist is history with true preconceptions consistently developed throughout the entire field.

But, to take up the problem from the beginning, we must return once more to the uncritical mind, and to its doctrine or its metaphor concerning historical tradition. The ultimate element in the field of history is, as before remarked, presented and necessarily presented to itself by that stage of reflection as a so-called 'fact', the imprint of which is on the part of the witness passively received and preserved: that which brought itself to the observation is subsequently repeated, or written down as so observed, and, in the absence of direct falsehood on the part of the narrator, remains as a simple and indecomposable material. This is the theory of simple reproduction, a view to be met with not solely in the world of common sense: the psychology of the people has made it its own, and consecrated it in the name and with the title of philosophy, and still we are assured with the complacency

of an absolute certitude that in perception the mind is
passive, and that the final elements of knowledge are the
facts conveyed through the senses.

Into the fullness of the problem raised by sensational-
ism, into the truth which underlies this 'metaphor now
hardened into a dogma', we are not prepared, nor indeed
is it necessary, to enter here. We will content ourselves
on the general question with the remark, that in the *act*
of perception it is no doubt true that the mind is at the
same time passive. But to say this is to say one thing,
and it is quite and altogether another thing to talk of
sensations (in the signification of bare feelings) as though
in themselves, and apart from the activity of the mind,
they existed as objects of consciousness. That is to *assert*
that a mere feeling is sufficient to constitute by itself the
minimum required for knowledge and reality; and the
proof of this assertion has been, is, and ever will be wanting. It *cannot* exist since the proof or even the assertion
is a sheer self-contradiction; and it is a self-contradiction
for the following reason. An assertion, and much more
so a proof, is intellectual; it is a judgement which implies
the exercise of the understanding; and the terms united
by the judgement must therefore fall within the sphere
of the understanding. They must be objects for the
intellect, and so, in a sense more or less entire, relative
to the intellect; in a word, intelligible. But the essence of
mere sensation was the entire absence of the intellectual,
and hence to make one single affirmation with respect
to sensation, as sensation, is to treat as relative to the
understanding that which is supposed to exclude the
understanding; and this is a contradiction.

To pursue with the reason an object which when found
is to be irrational, to think the opposite of thought while
fixed as opposite, to comprehend the incomprehensible
yet without transforming it—such is the task of that which
calls itself the 'philosophy of experience'. It is the pursuit
of a phantom for ever doomed to fade in our embraces,
a mocking shadow beyond the horizon of our grasp,
known to us as the unreality of all that we can hold, and

whose existence must perish at the threshold of human possession.

Yet let this be as it may. We are not concerned to ascertain the nature of that which may be regarded as the minimum of fact in general. The object of our inquiry is history, and specially here the ultimate material of the historical field; and we wish to know not what makes any fact, but what makes an historical fact, and what it is without which nothing can rightly be called by that name. We have to inquire in short what it is that in history and for history is required for the existence of its historical matter, and what it is that, be it what it may be in itself, yet can never enter as a member into the narrative of the past.

The facts which exist for critical history are events and recorded events. They are recorded, and that is to say that, although the work of the mind, they now at any rate are no mere feelings, nor generally the private contents of this or that man's consciousness, but are fixed and made outward, permanent, and accessible to the minds of all men. Failing to be thus they have failed to be for history, and history can never be for them. And they are events, and that is to say that each is no simple and uncompounded unit, but contains within itself a motion and a passage, a transition and a connexion between elements—⟨i.e. they are⟩ relations, the members of which may be distinguished though they cannot be divided. They are recorded events, and that means that, though fleeting in themselves, they are yet made stable; though divisible in time, they are regarded as wholes; and though the offspring of the mind, they are still independent and real.

Such are the characteristics of historical facts considered in themselves. We must regard them now in their relation to the individual witness or recorder. Let us view them as the objects of his consciousness, and ask what are they? and what function of the mind corresponds to them?

To solve this problem in a short space is scarcely practicable, and to ensure brevity we must be willing here to seem, it may be, contented with assertion.

They cannot be mere feelings. A chaos of sensations has no unity, and hence cannot properly be *called* a succession; nor, even when re-collected as a sequence of feelings in me, can it yet express an outward change in things. In a word, from feeling to the record of an occurrence there is, and there can be, no *natural* passage.

If we recall the characteristics of the narrated event, in the first place it will be clear that they presuppose in the mind both association and recognition of association: association, as that which separates (distinguishes), and at the same time conjoins; and recognition, as that which is aware of the divisible unity as a concrete whole. They require the action of that faculty which separates the subject from the object, and one thing from another thing, while it yet remains the bond of their unity. In a word, they testify to the presence of judgement. A feeling *is* at most; it is neither real nor unreal, true nor false: but every occurrence has or has not taken place, and every judgement professes, although it may fail, to express the actual.

The historical event (in our limited sense of the word history) involves in the first place a judgement. It is 'objective', it is distinguished in itself, and yet it is a whole.

But in the second place it involves much more than what we call a simple judgement. If we take the simplest historical fact, and reflect on the complex nature of the transition it attempts to express, it is clear to us that we are concerned with a number of judgements, the multitude of which wearies our attempts at analysis. And it is not less clear that these many judgements are united, and, as it were, resolved in a single judgement which answers to the whole event.

This one judgement comprehends in itself the many judgements; it must be looked on as their result, or in other words it is a conclusion.

The historical fact then (for us) is a conclusion; and a conclusion, however much it may appear so, is never the fiction of a random invention. We bring to its assertion the formed world of existing beliefs, and the new matter of a fresh instance. They are grounds for our position, and we know them as such, or at least we may know them. For everything that we say we think we have reasons, our realities are built up of explicit or hidden inferences; in a single word, our facts are inferential, and their actuality depends on the correctness of the reasoning which makes them what they are.

Such is (or seems to be) the constitution of the narrated event; and if its statement is a paradox, it is at least no new one. The evidence which the result lacks here will perhaps not be required by the reader; but in any case, so far as what follows is concerned, he must look for at most a further illustration.

To resume the discussion. In the case of the most straightforward witness deposition to the most ordinary circumstance contains in every instance the recognition of the previously known under fresh features and with new particulars: it involves inferential judgement; inferences of substance and attribute, of cause and effect; and, if the inference is false, the fact is unreal. It is matter of the most ordinary experience that the mediated and complex should appear immediate and simple. We see what we perceive; and the object of our perceptions is qualified by the premises of our knowledge, by our previous experiences. Not only to the child is the novel picture identified with a familiar image, but to each and all of us an uncertain shape is defined on a sudden as a particular object, or the tremor of a feature conveys the emotion of the soul—and all by what seems at the moment a mere communication of the senses.

Yet it is a proverb that in everything a man may be mistaken: and the reflection (when we do reflect) upon our errors brings home to us the conviction that we are wrong only because we judge, and that without this condition of both error and truth existence would be for us impossible.

If we go to the strongest facts, to the best attested events as they are proved in our law courts, we are forced still to admit that there are no facts as to which mistake is impossible; and in every case the mistake rests upon a mistaken inference. But, as we have said, it is the merest illusion to suppose that the entire abstinence from or the total removal of inference is a guarantee for certainty and truth. The best witnesses are those who from long habit have attained to comparative infallibility in their judgements; the testimony even of a child on familiar subjects is of value; but there may be events to which its deposition is worthless, not because it makes inferences, but because it fails to make them, or makes them wrongly, and not because we cannot trust its eyesight, but because we cannot rely upon its reasoning.

It is natural at this point to object that in cross-examination the lawyer has a means for removing the witness's conclusions and arriving at the sensible facts. This to a certain extent is true; a witness can be forced (in certain cases and down to a certain point) to recall and unwind the coil of inference which has made his events what they are. But to confine him to the facts of sense is to reduce him to a condition of impotence. If the man is to speak to anything, in the end the examination is confronted with a judgement, which cannot be called a sensible fact, and which yet defies its analysis; because, though there must be a ground, yet that cannot be recalled, since it never, as part of a conscious reasoning, was explicitly before the consciousness. Here the process must cease, and the existence of the fact rests upon the veracity of the witness in other respects, and the correctness of his judgements on general subjects. But with every precaution the best witnesses may be mistaken; there exists no testimony entirely secured from error; and the possibility of wrong evidence implies the possibility of false reasoning; nor in any case is it explicable except on the assumption that testimony to the simplest circumstance involves and is what it is by reason of an inference.

If it is thus where every safeguard exists, how will it

be where there are none? And if the ultimate legal fact
in its very nature is inferential, can we not say with
still greater truth that in the realm of history we have
and can have no facts whatever which do not hold in
their essence and depend for their existence on inferential
reasoning?

The correctness of the isolated event as recorded rests
upon a theory, and the recorded train of circumstances
which makes a narrative is a still wider theory, which must
depart yet farther from the fact as imagined to consist in
passive sensation, and must imply, together with its greater
possibilities of truth and falsehood, the increased existence
of active combination. We cannot recall accurately what
we have not rightly observed, and rightly to observe is not
to receive a series of chaotic impressions, but to grasp the
course of events as a connected whole.

It is a fact not to be lost sight of that our memories are
certain only because corrigible, and have become trustworthy solely through a process of constant and habitual
corrected recollection; the correction being in every case
the determination of an order by fixing its elements in
their proper relations, and its result a mediated sequence
of phenomena.

We have considered the primary historic material, both
as single occurrences and as series of events narrated by
an original eye-witness, and what we have so far seen is
this, that in the field of history it is impossible to free
ourselves from reasoning, and that in every case that which
is called the fact is in reality a theory. The identification
(so far and in this sense) of theory and fact is the end of
that stage in our discussion which we have just accomplished, but we are far as yet from our final result.

'Your conclusion,' it will be urged, 'be it never so true,
is far from justifying the historian in assumptions or presupposition. Let it be with the facts and the narratives
as you will; but they come to the historian as testimony,
as the experience of another, and, whatever they may be
in themselves, yet for him, as he has them, they are facts:

and in any case all further reasoning concerning them is frivolous.'

The doctrine might be stated with a show of plausibility. Will it bear the test of a practical application to our daily life? I think that to accord our impartial ear indifferently to things probable and improbable, to things true and false, and for no other reason than because we do not see with the eyes and hear with the ears of others, is, if we consider it, a strange and extravagant demand.

I am sure that we might search long and in vain through the lives of those who profess such a creed for any the smallest exemplification of it; and the reflection might occur to us that there are better illustrations of a belief that all things in general are equally credible, than the violent affirmation of the dogma that some things in particular are absolutely certain.

The common experience of reasonable beings bears us out in the assertion that we do not believe without a reason; that the fact asserted by another remains in its position, as an asserted fact, unless we have some cause to take it as true, and to make it a part of our own world: and further that this reason and ground is a reasoning (if not always a rational) judgement, from the possibility or likelihood of the event and the character of the witness. The distinction between our individual experience and testimony as the experience of others is not a distinction which can have the smallest tendency to modify the conclusion we arrived at above, viz. that all our history is matter of inference.

The distinction moreover is to a certain extent illusory. If to say that 'all knowledge comes from experience' is to utter no more than 'an empty tautology', then it must be but a similar tautology to assert that all experience is personal experience. The teaching that it is impossible for a man to transcend his consciousness is not unfamiliar to our ears; and we have learnt the lesson (important or otherwise) that we can only know the things which we can know, and that our world will never be wider than the world which will be ours.

It is a doctrine which often stands for no more than a ground for disbelieving and believing whatever we please; but here, as against the separation of testimony from experience, it has its significance. The experience of others has no meaning for us except so far as it becomes our own; the existence of others is no existence for us if it is not in our world that they live. If we know that other men are, we know it by an inferential judgement: and it is by a similar judgement that the matter of their testimony becomes ours. Both they and it can be nothing to us but parts of our experience; are made parts of it by an inference, and have no validity and no guarantee beyond that inference. To deny this is to state the opposite of a tautology, is to fall into a self-contradiction.

If nothing is ours which is not in our experience, then testimony, if known by us, must be so included: and at this point a familiar illustration may perhaps be excused as tending to throw some light on the preceding statements.

I have met, as I imagine, a friend in the street to-day, and I note it as a fact that A has been seen by me; but this is an inference, the theory on and of certain supposed recalled sensations. I am told on the next day by an eye-witness that A died yesterday; my inferences from the character of the witness, the recognition of a narrative of the death written in the handwriting of A's relatives, lead me to believe this. It is now a fact that A died yesterday; but this fact is again my inference: it is I that have made it a fact for me and, in case there has been a conspiracy to deceive me, it is not fact, but a false judgement of mine. What is now to become of the fact of my meeting with A? That depends on my reasoning, on my general beliefs, on my presuppositions. It may be a fact that I have seen an apparition, or the fact may be now an hallucination; but both one and the other are inferences. It would be possible to proceed much further. I might learn that a real man like A was present at the place and time. A mistake as to persons is now the fact. And it is useless here to urge that the visual sensation at the given time is the ultimate reality; because, in the present application, we have seen that, let it be never so actual, history can admit no such reality into its sphere; and in the second place there need not have been such visual sensation at all. For, if there were no reason to suppose the presence of any real man, and if an hallucination were hardly possible in my case, the fact might be that my memory was disordered, and that I dated too late a former meeting with A. In short, the fact varies with my judgement, and my judgement must always be based upon and fall within my own experience.

The history then (to proceed), which is for us, is matter of inference, and in the last resort has existence as history, as a record of events, by means of an inference of our own. And this inference furthermore can never start from a background of nothing; it is never a fragmentary isolated act of our mind, but is essentially connected with, and in entire dependence on, the character of our general consciousness. And so the past varies with the present, and can never do otherwise, since it is always the present upon which it rests. This present is presupposed by it, and is its necessary preconception.

History must ever be founded on a presupposition; and the scepticism which saw in the succession of historical writings a series of fictions, where the present was transported into the bygone age, was thus and so far justified: but the insight into the ground of the partial justification will exhibit, I hope, the source of the general mistake.

Paley protested against that which he called a 'prejudication'. We have seen the reason why every history is necessarily based upon prejudication; and experience testifies that, as a matter of fact, there is no single history which is not so based, which does not derive its individual character from the particular standpoint of the author. There is no such thing as a history without a prejudication; the real distinction is between the writer who has his prejudications without knowing what they are, and whose prejudications, it may be, are false, and the writer who consciously orders and creates from the known foundation of that which for him is the truth.

It is when history becomes aware of its presupposition that it first becomes truly critical, and protects itself (so far as is possible) from the caprices of fiction. But what, then, it will be asked, is the presupposition of criticism?

The answer is not far to seek. It is plain from the whole of what has gone before that the ground of criticism is that which is the justification of inference; and an inference, it will be admitted, is justified solely on the assumption of the essential uniformity of nature and the course of events.

Critical history assumes that its world is one, and that in that world it exists, and has but to demonstrate the existence of itself. Its demand is that the judgement which we found to be implicit in every historical fact become explicit, and that the whole sequence be consistently and rationally mediated. As intelligence, criticism seeks the object which already is in itself intelligible, and it realizes itself, if at all, in the form and the character which belongs to itself alone. In a word, the universality of law, and what loosely may be termed causal connexion, is the condition which makes history possible, and which, though not for her to prove, she must none the less presuppose as a principle and demonstrate as a result worked out in the whole field of her activity.

To this extent the characteristics of history are the characteristics of (natural) science, for both carry into the particulars an anticipation which the particulars have already realized in implication: and the reason of this is that for both the fact can exist so far only as already possessed of attributes conferred on it by virtue of the principle, and can oppose the principle by no means but its own self-annihilation.

'Science', we may be told in answer, 'is founded on experiment and not on a presupposition.' 'The fact of the existence of scientific experiment proves', we must return, 'the existence of an absolute presupposition, which it can be said to found, only because upon that itself is already founded.' We base our action on that which our action itself supports and testifies to. Unless upon the assumption of the exclusion of all interference and chance, no one could say that an experiment was of the smallest value. The man of science cannot prove his assumption beforehand; he knows that as a fact his science exists, and that there are certain conditions necessary to its existence, and he troubles himself little (if at all) with the possibility of the falsehood of his assumption.

Can science testify to a breach of the law which forms its presupposition? This would amount to a contradiction in terms; it would be an observation based upon a rule to prove the non-existence of the rule; it would be a deductive reasoning in which the conclusion would be a negative instance against the leading major premise. No experiment could prove that A (if isolated) was at one time followed by B, at another by C; because the very apparatus of the proof rests upon the absoluteness of the principle—that is to say, the judgements necessary to support the facts of the hostile experiment are self-annihilated in virtue of the experiment's supposed result. Science may retire from the field altogether, but while in its field it has no choice but to remain supreme.

That science should rule its facts seems disputable only so long as we suppose the facts to be something independent. But the truth is, on the other hand, that every scientific observation and experiment involves an inference true or false, and known to be true solely in virtue of the law. The simplest possible datum which is matter of science is no mere atom, but expresses and depends upon connexions in things to which the judgement, if true, must conform. But to know that relations of thoughts express relations in things is impossible except on the formal or virtual assumption of the absolute stability of these latter relations, and the consequent assurance that a false judgement is the result of a false inference in me, and not of a shifting connexion in the world. Science does and must control its facts, and an opposing fact is self-condemned because in every element the principle is already involved.

We find then that, as starting from a conception which it cannot prove, natural science is, in this sense, hypothetical, and exhibits in detail the truth of its hypothesis. Returning to history, we must ask if in this respect it corresponds to science.

That history and science (always in its English limitation to physical science) present no diversity, we are far indeed from suggesting. Unlike most branches of science history can create no experiments; and its subject-matter (we must take it for granted here) is not the same as the matter of science. The difference is wide, but, so far as the point above dwelt on is concerned, both science and history we find to be agreed, namely in this, that a fact which asserts itself as (loosely speaking) without a cause, or without a consequence, is no fact at all, and no better than a self-contradiction, for the reason that, while professing to exist, it abjures the sole ground of actual existence.

But there is an objection which at this point we are certain to encounter. We shall be told that the volitions of man are uncaused, and that hence the doctrine put forth above falls to the ground. Whether, strictly speaking, causation retains a meaning when applied to the will, we need not to inquire. 'Causation' we use throughout in the loose sense which it bears amongst us. And into the question of the relation of freedom to law we are not obliged here to enter. For our present purpose, however, we may thus dispose of the difficulty.

If the freedom of the will is to mean that the actions of man are subject to no law, and in this sense irrational, then the possibility of history, I think, must be allowed to disappear, and the past to become a matter of almost entire uncertainty. For, if we are precluded from counting on human nature, our hold upon tradition is gone, and with it well nigh our only basis for historical judgement.

We find, however, that the contrary is every day assumed as certain, and that where the weightiest interests are at stake, and as long as criminals are executed in many cases by right of what comes to a construction from the laws of human action, so long will there be at least no practical necessity for the discarding of historical evidence in favour of the doubts, or perhaps the dogmas, of any man.

Thus much at present then seems to be clear—that critical history must have a presupposition, and that this presupposition is the uniformity of law. And we have accomplished here yet another stage of the present inquiry.

But this, we shall be told and rightly told, is much too indefinite. No one now asserts the existence in history of events without a cause or a consequence, and the real point at issue is to determine more narrowly the character of the general principle. 'Uniformity', we shall be told, 'is an empty phrase; similar causes are doubtless followed by similar effects, but in the varied field of history there are causes unlike those which present themselves in our present experience, and which consequently imply the presence of unfamiliar results.' Upon this difficult point it is necessary to attempt to come to a clear understanding.

We have seen that history rests in the last resort upon an inference from our experience, a judgement based upon our own present state of things, upon the world personal in us; and that this is the sole means and justification which we possess for holding and regarding supposed events as real, i.e. as members in and of our universe. When therefore we are presented, as it were from the outside, with so-called 'historical facts', the like of which seem to stand in no relation to all that we have now in heaven or on earth; when we are asked to affirm the existence in past time of events, the effects of causes which confessedly are without analogy in the world in which we live, and which we know—we are at a loss for any other answer but this, that (so far as at present we can see) we are asked to build a house without a foundation, or with our instruments construct a work which can come into no connexion with those instruments. And how can we attempt this without contradicting ourselves?

When further we reflect upon the range and diversity

of our present experience, its width in respect to the different stages of development which it exhibits, and the continual and growing success of its attempt to find a unity in all that variety; then we find it still more impossible to accept, as the real past of our own real world, this riddle of an outer sphere, fallen amongst us down from heaven, and written in a foreign tongue.

Our difficulty is this—we are asked to affirm the existence in history of causes such as we can find nothing analogous to now in our present experience. On the other hand, it is only from our knowledge of what is that we can conclude to that which has been; and, this being so, how can we first infer from the world to the existence of historical evidence within the world, and then, starting from that, proceed out of the world, when all the time we are unable to stand except upon the basis of the world?

As we reflect, the conclusion is borne in on us (perhaps prematurely) that, upon the strength of historical evidence, to assert within the sphere of history the existence of any causes or effects, except on the conviction that there is now for us something analogous to them, is no better than a self-contradiction. And it is this conclusion which after the requisite explanation (and even, as it may appear, with certain modifications) we must in the end undertake to defend.

The statement seems at first sight a paradox, and is open to every kind of external counter-assertion. To these or to some of these we must in the end return, but in the meantime we have to encounter a serious internal difficulty.

Our present point of view is as follows. A critical position towards history in general implies that the mass of historical material is no longer one with ourselves, is not any more carried about in and with us as a part of the substance which we feel to be natural to us, but has, as a possession, been separated from the mind, and is held apart from and over against it as an object which presents a problem for the intelligence. This object, although a possession, has not yet been appropriated; though we have it, yet we have not made it ours; and though it is intrinsically rational, yet it has not been rationalized. We have seen further that, since all certainty with respect to the past depends ultimately upon present inference, the basis and foundation for the criticism of what has been is necessarily formed by the knowledge of what is.

The difficulty which first meets us at this point presents itself in the following question. 'Is not that which is to be the canon of testimony itself dependent on testimony?', i.e. does not the present knowledge of the historian rest to a considerable extent on what others have told him, and in fact consist of this in no small degree? 'The historian', it may be objected, 'does perhaps as critical divide the world of the past (as in the proper sense not yet known) from the present and known world; but the process is illusory, because this known world, which is the furniture of his mind, and the cosmos which forms the criterion for that which has not yet been systematized, is in itself largely built up of the communicated experience of others. Is it not then a flat contradiction to bring as a canon to criticism that which presupposes uncriticized testimony, and has absorbed it into all the tissues of its organism?'

The objection demands consideration, but its force depends on our supposing that the present experience, which is to be taken as the historical canon, is mere common experience, and it is answered by the reflection that the testimony which the present object involves is, or at least ought to be, no uncriticized material. The experience in short which is to be the foundation of historical criticism must itself be a critical experience.

The object of critical experience can neither be said to be given, nor, so far as the individual critic is concerned, to grow. It is made (or it makes itself); it is a creation, though not from nothing; it is the new-birth of an organism from matter organic but no longer in itself vital.

The contents which in early life are taken into and build up our consciousness, consisting as they do of our individual experiences blended into one substance inextricably with the experiences of others, exist in the uncritical mind as that which (for itself at least) is a confused and unsystematized world of consciousness. It is to such a world that the critical intelligence awakens, and its awakening is the sundering of its material from itself. It stands (so far as awakened) a self-conscious unity on this side, and regarding its matter as from the outside demands from it the same oneness, that intelligible unity which, as the world of an intelligence, it is to have and virtually has. The new object, which now for the critical mind is the sole and increasing reality, is the reorganization of the old world; it is true only because recreated, and can be recreated only because connected into a rational system. Every part here must live, and live in the life of the whole. The dead matter which was received on authority, and held true because it was so received, must render an account of its claims. It is true, if at all, now no longer as mere testimony, but because it has been examined and satisfactorily mediated with the critical object as at present existing.

This is the condition of its re-vitalization, that it can be subsumed under the present critical world. But what then is this world, which thus in its hands has sentence of life and death? It is the world of critical observation. The ultimate real object, the final reference and last basis, is constituted by that which has been, or can be, personally verified in our own external or internal critical observation. If we are asked for the reason of our beliefs we are sooner or later in the last resort brought back to this; and it is thus our immediate personal (though that need not mean our individual) experience, on which, by many steps or by few, all our certainty depends.

Our answer then to the above objection is this. Certainly our present world contains matter of testimony, but not *as* matter of testimony. What we stand upon is personal observation; and what we have ground to connect with that we will receive because of its connexion with that, and subject to appeal to that; and we will receive nothing else, but from that basis we will order our world.

But yet it is a matter of fact that our world is extended

to fresh cases which (roughly speaking) have nothing analogous to previous phenomena. And, this being so, we
are far at present from having established our contention
that history is incapable of attesting to events without
analogy in the present world. For why should not
historical testimony furnish such non-analogous cases?
Our answer must depend on the meaning we give to
'historical testimony'. *If* historical testimony implies more
than probability, *if* it is equivalent to scientific evidence,
then the above question remains unanswerable. There is
no reason why such attestation should not be possible.
But if we see cause (or choose) to oppose scientific to
historical testimony, and to confine the latter to the sphere
of the probable, then the question answers itself, so soon
as we have discovered what are the conditions of the above
extension to the non-analogous. What are these conditions?

That my real world can be widened by the taking in of
new facts, and that apart from any special analogy, is
indisputable. And in the first place (1) it may be so
enlarged by my own observation. Let us take as an
example the so-called 'mesmeric' phenomena. These may
be said (with accuracy sufficient for the present purpose)
to have possibly no analogy to anything in the observer's
world hitherto; yet no one could maintain that it was
impossible to know and to be certain of these phenomena
as real facts. On the other hand no one would assert that
these facts could be assured to us by the same amount of
observation, as would be enough for phenomena of a class
already recognized (wholly or partially) and capable of
subsumption under an acknowledged head as a similar or
subordinate case. In a word, if we are left to our own
observation, and have nothing analogous to support us,
we can indeed learn new facts with certainty, but on one
condition only, namely that of the most careful examination often repeated.

So far direct observation. Let us pass now to testimony
(2) and ask in the second place—Can I learn un-analogous
facts mediately with equal certainty, and if so, on what
condition?

Let us take once more the 'mesmeric' phenomena. These may have no analogy in our own private experience; and yet we may receive the facts, on testimony, as no less certain than those which we find for ourselves. They are received, and that critically, as attested: but, on the other hand (although not contrary to the conditions which make experience possible, nor yet in contradiction with the object he knows at present), they yet may be without any apparent analogy in the world of the individual critic.

Testimony rests on experience, and testimony goes beyond experience, and, as it would seem, without the support of experience. How is this possible? The answer is that in this, the strongest imaginable case, the testimony must be the strongest imaginable; it must be equal in validity to our own most careful observation. Nothing short of this is enough. The question then arises, 'How is such validity possible, if, as we have seen, testimony must finally rest on an inference from personal knowledge, and if personal knowledge is ultimately based on our own intelligent observation?'

The explanation is this—that by inferences, however complicated yet in the end resting on personal observation, we have so apprehended and possessed ourselves of the consciousness of others, that we are justified in assuming the identity of their standpoint with our own; i.e. we can be assured that the already systematized world, which was brought as a canon by the witnesses to the observation and to the subsumption of the mesmeric phenomena, was practically the same as that which we ourselves should have brought. We thus are certain that the men can see for us, because we know that they are able to think for us. And, having this entire confidence, we run no risk beyond that which our own experience is at all times liable to, viz. the error arising from individual perturbation.

Or, in other words, by an inference from that which I know already I certainly discover that the witness's mind is a universe, a cosmos, like my own and subject to the same laws; and hence, if I can conclude in addition to his integrity and his will to observe and judge, his judgement is to me precisely the same as my own. He may be right or wrong, but so may I; he is as likely to be right as I am; and I can only tell whether he is right by the same criteria which (apart from fresh observation) tell me that I am right. *If* I am able to apply a negative and positive criticism to his new fact, as I do to my new fact, then his fact is as good as mine. Our objective world is known to be the same, his subjective power of extending the object is known to be equal to mine, and the distinction of our individualities makes no difference to the matter itself.

We have seen that testimony, even without analogy, can be made part of our present critical object; but we have seen also on what condition. Testimony goes beyond individual experience, but not beyond *our* experience; or it takes us beyond our experience if it takes *us* with it. It is not uncriticized; it stands, if at all, on the basis of our world. It has been made subject to the laws and has been connected with and become part of our personal experience, not in its own right *as* testimony, not in the right of the witness *as* witness, but in the right of and on the guarantee of our own intelligence.

The question proposed above, 'Under what conditions is it possible to extend our experience to fresh phenomena, which (roughly speaking) are without analogy in what has been hitherto observed?', has been answered. Such enlargement, apart from our own observation, is possible only through the above-described identification of consciousness. This is the one and the indispensable condition.

The bearing of this result will be seen more clearly when exhibited in its negative form as an answer to the question, 'Under what conditions does testimony necessarily fail to establish a non-analogous case?' In the first place, we must say, wherever we are unable to verify the witness generally; in the second, wherever we cannot satisfy ourselves with respect to his particular procedure.

(1) In the first place, wherever the standpoint of the witness differs (wholly or in relation to the particular class of facts in question) from our own, or wherever its agreement is not known to us, there the testimony cannot stand

without analogy from our own experience. For, however possible any matter may be, yet we cannot on testimony receive it as real, unless we have ground to connect it with the real. Analogy is such a ground, but, failing analogy, there is nothing left but the inference to a strength of testimony which can exist only on the assumption of the identification of our own with another's consciousness (in general, or in relation to one particular division of the world); and this assumption, in the case supposed at present, we have no right to make.

To repeat—wherever the so-called 'fact' is made by subsumption under a view of the world different from ours, wherever we fail to make out that the judgement rested (consciously or unconsciously) on an ordered system identical with our own, there the 'fact' cannot be affirmed except on analogy; for, since the narrative is based on beliefs different from ours, the facts are affected by the beliefs, or, for anything we know, they may be so; we have no security that they are not affected. And the application of the above is, that any narrative of 'facts' which involves judgements proceeding from a religious consciousness or a view of the world which, as a whole or in respect of the part in question, differs from ours, cannot have such force as to assure us of any event un-analogous to present experience.

(2) In the second place, even where we are able to be sure that the witness regarded his facts from a point of view identical with our own, yet, taking this for granted, wherever we are not able to assume the witness's integrity, and wherever we have not firm grounds for believing that the amount of careful and intelligent observation was brought to the case which we ourselves should have considered necessary—there the identification of consciousness is still incomplete; the testimony is not equal to our own verification, and the matter of it must stand, if at all, on analogy, and apart from analogy cannot be received.

We have asked the question, 'Can our knowledge be extended by ourselves to embrace a fresh world of phenomena?'

And we have answered that question in the affirmative. We have stated the means, our own stringent observation. We have inquired again, 'Can testimony similarly enlarge our experience, where analogy fails?' And we have answered, 'Yes, where identification of consciousness is possible; but, where it is not possible, Never.' 'Never' for this reason, that to be critical we must stand on our own experience, that an extended experience is ours when we make it, and that the matter of testimony, where it does not become ours in such a manner as to be valid of itself and directly, must be valid and ours indirectly by an inference from the basis of our present knowledge. Such conclusion is an analogy, and by a mere analogical argument you cannot conclude to a non-analogous fact.

To this latter statement we shall have to return; but at present we have ended all that we have to say on testimony in general. We must pass to historical evidence in particular. We asserted above provisionally that in no case could historical testimony establish the non-analogous; that, for example, it could not attest the existence of 'mesmeric' phenomena. There seems at first sight no ground in the foregoing for such a contention. We must attempt, however, to justify it.

But such justification will be possible only at the cost of a considerable amount of assumption. What historical testimony can prove, and cannot prove, must depend in the end upon what we mean by 'historical testimony'. The answer to this question we must take to no small degree for granted.

What is historical evidence? It seems, till we try it, so easy to say; but the effort assures us of the presence of difficulty.

When we speak of historical evidence, and when we emphasize the 'historical', the accent is due to the contrast which, either disguisedly or openly, exists in our mind between 'scientific' and 'merely historical'. In general we imagine a distinction between the two sorts of testimony, but to put that difference into words is in any case arduous;

and to do so without the assumption of some point which is matter of controversy is, in the present state of opinion, I believe, impossible..

It is easy to bring forward a partial answer. We may say, if we will, that history is the testimony of the past to the past, while science is that of the present to the present, of the present in the sense of what *is* unchangeably: and this answer, if it is not the truth, must be said at any rate to have its truth. But for present purposes in its simple form it is altogether insufficient.

For in a certain sense we know *nothing* but the past. Scientific testimony, scientific observations are, like all things human, events in time, and while we grasp them as present they are gone. This is no psychological refinement: there is no one too sensible or too careless to apprehend at least that the present of to-day is the past of to-morrow, this week of next week, the last century of this century.

In a certain sense again we know nothing but the present. That the object of knowledge must be present is a truism; and historical evidence, to be valid for us, must be here and now before us.

And in practice the differences of time are of no more account than the differences in space. That a scientific experiment was made this year or last year may be in itself as utterly indifferent as the fact that it was made in England or America; the intervals are nothing to us. Historical testimony again may be what is called contemporary with ourselves; but in itself such a consideration does not necessarily lead us to belief or to disbelief. The orthodox Catholic of our day gets no hearing for his stories except from Catholics; and the tales of the uneducated concerning witchcraft or spectres do not find more favour from the fact that they belong to the present generation.

The distinction of past and present, as we see, will not help us from our puzzle; and our confusion is by no means lessened when we reflect that we cannot name one single event which, in certain quarters, would not be considered an object for science—'science' to be construed in the narrow meaning of physical science, and the event to be taken in the unlimited extent of its entire signification. On the other hand, the reflection meets us that, in the opinion of many, there is not one single 'scientific' fact which, as an event, can be excluded from history, if we allow ourselves the fullest use of the word.

In view of such complications, when we find that the objects attested to by history and science are apparently indistinguishable, and that the date of the attesters matters nothing in itself, we are at a loss to perceive any longer that distinction in kind we imagined to exist.

If further we confine this distinction to degree, and say history with its evidence is probable, while certainty belongs to the essence of science, we perhaps shall have stated what is altogether true, and in words at least shall have established our contention. For if history as a whole be probable, and if every probable detail be admitted to rest on an argument from analogy, then that the matter of historical testimony stands, if at all, on an analogical argument is an obvious conclusion. But it is in words alone that the assertion is made good, while the difference to be made manifest is simply obscured. We shall be found merely to have asserted that everything which is certain is matter of science, and that everything not provable is matter of history.

To identify the matter of science and history is not only in itself a serious assumption where the meaning of science is *natural* science; but it also for our purpose is practically useless. It is useless, because the terms 'scientific' and 'historical' will not help us in the least towards a result, but in this sense will merely express the result itself. They will be empty synonyms for 'certain' or 'probable'.

It is not worth while to linger over efforts at definition like the above. The attempts are hopeless. To maintain the distinction at all the sphere of history must be limited; and history can be limited only in the face of counterpropositions. To define historical testimony we must divide the whole which some think indivisible, and to do this by proof involves an engagement along the whole front of the position.

For our purpose here there is nothing practicable except to assume what we think is necessary, and to remember that it remains an assumption throughout.

We take historical testimony in the first place (1) to be *in* history, i.e. we confine it within the field of *human tradition*. Geological, geographical evidence, evidence from excavations, and evidence from language, we refuse to consider as properly historical. The reason is this, that they do not essentially lie within the period of human records; and history-writing is to count for us here as the limit of critical history.

Historical testimony in the second place (2) is *to* history. Astronomical or meteorological records, the whole account kept of natural events, are, as we understand it, not part of history. History for us too is a record of events, but the record of a single field, the tradition and the tale of the deeds and sufferings of *men*.

The theory which science may construct of the development of our system or of the planet on which we live; the story of the origin of animal life and the growth of its varied species, the account of the generation of humanity itself with its early stages and slow gradations—these we may accept (as we all do and must accept them) in some sense or other; but they one and all for our present inquiry must fall beyond the historical limit. Such evidence is not historical evidence.

We must go still farther. The records of the science of the day of its present human phenomena; the observations and experiments recorded by the physiologist or doctor, and even the narrations of empirical psychology—these in addition we refuse (so far as scientific) to consider under the head of historical testimony. Historical *material* they may be. (Is there anything human which may not be?) There is no human record which is not historical material, and therefore in a sense historical testimony also. It is not, however, the facts as attested which in such a case fall within the field of history. It is not the facts which are historical, but only the fact of their attestation, which latter belongs to a different world. To express the same thing more simply, scientific evidence is a human phenomenon which in itself is not scientific.

What is the ground of our refusal above? The following:—not only must historical testimony be in history and to history, but it also (3) must have its origin in an historical interest.

The interest of science is the discovery of the laws of what *is*, neither past nor present nor future events, nor events at all, but only the abiding. The interest of history is in the recalling of a course of events which *are not*, which neither exist nor will exist, but which *have* existed. The object of the one is 'the permanent amid change', the object of the other 'the changes of the permanent'; facts to the one are illustrations, to the other are embodiments; the individuals of the one are limited to be abstracted, of the other are incorporated to be realized.

In more simple language, the interest at the basis of scientific testimony is to use the particular case just so far as to get the universal *out of it*; the concretion of life is worth having solely for the sake of the abstract relations it contains. But the interest which gives birth to historical testimony is a human interest, an interest in the particular realization. Our common nature, which is personal in us all, feels in each one of us 'that nothing human is alien to ourselves'. Our interest in the past is our feeling of oneness with it, is our interest in our own progression; and because this human nature to exist must be individual, the object of historical record is the world of human individuality, and the course of its development in time. For scientific testimony the man is a mere example, for historical never: he is a new incarnation of the same felt substance, the manifest individualization, it may be, at highest, of a stage in progress (but on this point we wish to express no opinion). For the universal *as such* the historical witness cares not at all; at most it concerns him to see it embodied in a single person or the spirit of a nation.

It is possible, we admit, where matters are so complex and the tendencies of the mind so mix and meet, that the testimony of science may wander for the time to a merely historical field and interest; it is possible again that a record made for purposes of science may cover in addition the ground of history. In the first case the testimony is merely historical and not scientific; in the second case the testimony is both. It is primarily scientific and incidentally historical; it is more than historical, and in considering historical testimony we must be allowed to exclude it from our conclusion.

But in the vast majority of cases the three conditions we have just explained will be found sufficient to distinguish the testimony of history and of science. Doubtful cases will remain and must remain. The story of the plague at Athens might well have been told either from the point of view of history or from that of science; as it stands perhaps it belongs to both. The field of 'mesmeric' and similar phenomena, in the sphere between physiology and psychology, would afford a variety of evidence, passing by slow degrees from the scientific to the historical, and thence to a region which holds of neither science nor history. But these cases do not trouble our general distinction. Our rule must be this: we must first discover, as we can, whether the testimony is to be called historical or not; in the second place we must ask whether, being historical it is at the same time more, whether it is also scientific. This second class which is also scientific (i.e. such evidence as would be allowed to constitute the proof or part of the proof of a scientific generalization) we do not call simple historical testimony, and wherever it exists the following conclusions have no application.

We have narrowed 'historical testimony' to a limited field; and we have been forced to renounce the smallest attempt to justify our procedure. Arbitrary as that may appear it is not so altogether; and the result will I think accord with the beliefs of the majority.

Having attempted in some measure to define our terms

we can take up the question once more, 'Is historical testimony capable of extension to the non-analogous?'

We can now put that question in its other form, 'Is historical evidence probability or proof?' Into this general distinction it is impossible here to enter. It must be taken for granted, and wherever it is not allowed, wherever fact and probability are identified, there we admit the conclusions of this essay are without validity.

Is the matter of history probable or certain? We believe it to be probable; but this does not mean that about all its contents there is practically a doubt. It means that, be there never so many converging lines of probable reasoning, yet these never transcend the region of practical certainty. The result is never theoretically proved.

An historical 'proof' may be conclusive, in so far that we cannot doubt; a legal 'proof' may in many cases leave room for no possible hesitation; but neither the one nor the other is for us a scientific demonstration.

The matter of historical testimony is, we believe, not a certainty but a probability; the grounds of this assertion will be given below. But let us in the first place (1) suppose that it is admitted to be probable; then the conclusion will follow that it cannot extend to events without analogy in the sphere of present certainty.

Why is this? It is because in history we have a probable conclusion, which at the same time is required to stand as certain; an hypothesis which cannot be scientifically verified, but which nevertheless is to be taken as a fact; and the only means, the sole justification of such a result is in the accordance of the conclusion of the hypothesis with the known world. And that is the present world, the verifiable world, the world of to-day, or (in another application of the term) the world of science.

The propositions of science cannot be probable; the scientifically probable is not yet scientific doctrine. The theories of historical fact again are not probable in the sense that they are simply the statement of open questions. They are results; and where no result is possible, no history exists. But, resting on mere probable evidence, to come to a result beyond the limit of analogy—when we know in the present world no similar case, nor any tendency which makes in the direction—this is the procedure, we think, of no reasonable person.

And it should not be forgotten that, if the interest of history is not the enlargement of the territory of science, but rather the exhibition of the oneness of humanity in all its stages and under all its varieties; if it is ourselves that we seek in the perished (and is there anything else which we can seek?); if the object of our endeavour is to breathe the life of the present into the death of the past, and re-collect into this pantheon of the mind the temporal existences which once seemed mortal;—then, where we encounter an alien element which we cannot recognize as akin to ourselves, that interest fails, the hope and the purpose which inspired us dies, and the endeavour is thwarted. The remembrance of our childhood and our youth is the sweetest of pleasures, for it gives us the feeling of ourselves, as the self of ourself and yet as another; and the failure to recognize or the impossibility of interest in our earlier life is, to those whom it has befallen, the bitterest pain of the most cruel estrangement.

But to resume:—If historical conclusions are probable, they are subject to analogy.[1] Next we must ask if they ever are more than probable.

This question (2) we answer in the negative. If more than probable they must needs be scientific; they would be equal to the results of our critical observation, and for this, as we have seen, is required both identification of standpoint and assurance of sufficient integrity and carefulness.

To these the nature of historical testimony presents insurmountable obstacles.

In the first place (A) we must remember that historical testimony not only is *to* history, but is also *in* history. This addition prevents the identification of our minds with the minds of the witnesses. For history (i) (we assume it) is progressive, is a progress not only in the

[1] See on this point Appendix, Note C.

D

sense of that which increases in quantity, but in the sense of that which develops or evolves itself, is essentially the same in stages of growth which are diverse in quality, which differ from each other even more than the blossom from the bud, and the fruit from the blossom.

If the bud were self-conscious it would know of itself, but not in the way that the blossom knows it, still less as the fruit knows it; and as failing of the truth its knowledge must be said to be false.[1]

Still more is it so with history. In that ceaseless process which differentiates itself only as a means to integration, and which integrates itself only with the result of a fuller differentiation, the consciousness of the earlier stage of humanity is never the consciousness of a later development. The knowledge it has of itself is partial and false when compared with the epoch of an intenser realization. And when we reflect that for this highest development it is that history exists, we see that it is a hope doomed only to disappointment, when the present expects in the mind of the past to find the views and beliefs of the present.

If the stages of evolution were essentially diverse, the possibility of history is inconceivable; and if history were a manifestation of human phenomena where all but the accidental was simply the same, the interest it excites would in no respect be higher than the pleasure we take in an ordinary novel.

To proceed:—Not only is man's nature progressive, but (ii) history is concerned, so to speak, with the most human part of humanity, and hence the most fully progressive. The conscious deeds and sufferings, the instinctive productions, and unconscious destinies of men and of nations live most with the special and characteristic life of an individual epoch; and it is the time and the children of the particular time which alone are the past for which history cares.

And not only is the matter of history in progress, not only again does history select that element which progress affects the most, but thirdly (iii) within that sphere its

[1] This illustration is borrowed.

interest leads it to the most distinctive embodiment of the passing stage; not to those social relations which possess a limited permanence, but to the striking, the temporal, in a word the individual.

And as is the interest so is the subject interested. The historical witness is also the son of his time, and, in relation to that which bears most the stamp of the era, his mind is the reflection of the age in a mirror which shares its nature. It is thus that, in his character of recorder, his point of view when he relates phenomena dissimilar to ours will also itself not fail to be dissimilar.

For science it is true the observations of the one age are valid for the conclusions of another; and that, it may be added, where no present analogy is perhaps in existence. The facts of 'mesmerism' could be proved, we doubt not, by simple scientific testimony; and astronomical observations are accepted as facts, and doubtless would be so no less, in case they were supported by no analogy. The reason of this is, of course, that we are able so to reconstruct the observers and the conditions of their observations, as to possess ourselves entirely of their faculties, and use them as our own. And the possibility of this consists in the fact that science abstracts. It takes account not of all phenomena, but in each of its divisions of a separate and limited province, and it uses, so to speak, not the whole but a part alone of the observer's consciousness.

The object of science does not transform itself in a ceaseless progress, and the subject of science can separate itself from the concrete development of the historical mind, and can remain practically identical while coexisting with standpoints generally diverse. But this with history is impossible.

Not only do we fail to possess ourselves of the historical witness in such manner as to secure scientific proof, but secondly (B), even were this the case, to reconstruct the particular observation is well nigh impossible.

For the original fact of history is (i) an event which perishes as it arises. It dies and it can never be recalled.

It cannot repeat itself, and we are powerless to repeat it. And in addition (ii) we cannot prepare for it.

We may be ignorant of its approach; and if we were aware of that, yet to post ourselves in the fitting locality may be out of our power; or, given our presence at the time and place, still the fact is too complex for a certain observation. To fix you must isolate; and how can you isolate here?

And, given your power to isolate and to fix, yet too often you know not the important point. The moment which decides the movement of a complication reveals itself as such when the tendency is established; and then from our knowledge of the present too late we deplore our ignorance in the past.

And further there remains (iii) yet another consideration, which weakens still further (as compared with juridical) well nigh the whole of historical testimony. With the possible exception of contemporary evidence the historian is unable to cross-examine his witnesses. He can, by a critical analysis of the deposition, as a whole in relation to its parts, and of the relations which the parts bear to one another, and further by a comparison with other statements, to a certain extent make good this defect. But his procedure remains in the end but a wretched substitute, and a permanent source of weakness.

Such are the obstacles in the way of a scientific historical proof. The result of their consideration is this—that, even in case the historian should succeed in exhibiting identity of standpoint, yet the further reconstruction will never be complete enough to take him beyond a mere probability; and hence, since a probable conclusion must rest on analogy, that therefore the non-analogous is excluded for ever from the sphere of historical testimony.

This result we believe to be simply the theoretical expression of the best historical practice; and when there is one single supposed event in tradition, to which present experience can supply no analogy, which yet remains unchallenged by criticism, then and not till then will it be necessary to ask how such a condition of things can exist, and to attempt to reconcile with it the doctrine we have now put forward and endeavoured to defend.

This doctrine is at all events the reverse of sceptical. The present experience, which is open to our research, is so wide in its extent, is so infinitely rich in its manifold details, that to expect an event in the past to which nothing analogous now corresponds may fairly be considered a mere extravagance. And taking again historical testimony, as we have it now, there will be few, I think, who on reflection will find the above conclusions either forced on the facts or strained beyond them; or whose point of view will render impossible their general adoption.

But it will be urged that existing historical witnesses are no fair sample of historical testimony, that what may be or is does not mean what ought to be, and that first the conclusion has been fixed, and then a term has been narrowed to suit it. This in any case has not been done; but it is perfectly true that, if historical testimony be used in a more extensive sense, the above conclusion fails to apply.

History perhaps is a science to generalize what is, to discover the laws of phenomena. If it is this, then historical evidence not only may be but must be scientific; and nothing but scientific testimony has a right to be called historical. But in a world where all that we find in existence is so hard to understand, it seems idle to reflect on what merely is to be; and to speculate on a mere discounted possibility (or perhaps impossibility) is never, I think, a legitimate proceeding.

Let us suppose, though, that history is really to be a science, and one thing is clear from the first, that the mass of existing historical testimony is non-scientific, and well nigh (if not altogether) devoid of the smallest value. The necessary scientific evidence must be made.

'It is being made' (we shall be told of course) 'and that by statistics.' But to see the relations which the elements of particular societies bear to one another, or even to generalize laws, which apparently in all societies are likely to be more or less correct, is one thing. It is one thing to discover permanent relations in the stationary; and if history were stationary (if we could say of it that it was and is to eternity) in that case the science of history would be a far simpler expectation. But it is another, an altogether and an utterly different, undertaking to find the eternal laws which 'explain' the changes of an unending evolution, which is for us only so far as it has made itself, and each stage of which is the qualitative new-birth of an organic, and more than an organic, unity, which resumes its lower developments in a fresh integration, and informs its elements with its own distinctive nature. If the 'explanation' of the development of a man's individuality in every case presupposes the result it arrives at, and 'explains' in the end nothing that is individual—then it must be a more futile attempt for us who have not the result before us, mere children who have seen and known no more than the childhood of humanity, to 'explain' from that the future of its life, and to reach the laws which will evolve its character, through successive individualizations, from youth to manhood and from manhood to age. In this way to seize the 'red strand of necessity' in progress is surely impossible, and 'science of tendencies' is an amiable phrase, which sounds not much better than 'science of intentions'.

And if this science of progress is to be possible in itself, yet, where everything turns on recording, as they arise, the essential facts, there presents itself at once a new impediment. The essential facts are the determining element of movement, and the means to a fresh end; but to apprehend the means implies the knowledge of the end, to know the essential movement involves the knowledge of the terminus. But, confined as we are to a limited stage, with the heights above us hidden from our eyes (what we *are*, that we know), there remains to us nothing but either to secure the whole of the events, and this is impossible; or to run in imminent danger of recording those facts which are not essential, and hence are useless for the science of progress. It is a commonplace that the past has recorded too much that we could well spare, and too little of that we would most gladly know. Will it not be so always? What we think the important phenomena of 1870 and 1871 may perhaps have eluded our accurate observation, and in 1971 may with other things be a matter of controversy, while as for the interest of the historian of 1971, and the facts which bear most in his mind on progress, of these perhaps we have simply no notion.

So much in passing—but if after all there can really exist historical testimony which is more than probable, it must fall outside of and destroy our conclusion; and of course can assure us of non-analogous facts, since it is of such strength as to be valid evidence for a law of science.

We have ended the first and by far the largest division of our subject. We have found the principle of critical history, and have now to see its application to existing testimony. But let us briefly resume our present result.

We have seen so far that history is matter of inference; that every inference rests on a presupposition; and that this presupposition is formed by present experience. We have further shown that, although this experience is not always personal in the sense of that which we can immediately verify for ourselves, it yet is personal in the sense that upon the observation and judgement of our own mind it ultimately depends. We have shown that it is present, not in the sense of connexion with this or that moment, but in the sense of belonging to no moment in particular. We have shown that this character belongs alone to scientific testimony, that the material of history must hence be subject to analogy; and this distinction we have endeavoured to strengthen and defend.

Criticism is now left fronting the material, to recreate which it possesses and feels both the mission and the strength. And this may be considered an artificial position, in so far as the individual critic never does actually separate himself from the whole of his historical knowledge, but invariably brings with him to the work a portion of the traditional object, already rationalized and made part of his present and critical world. Nor is this apparent anticipation of his result unjustified in the individual, if that which he brings as a canon to criticism has been itself already confronted with criticism and rationalized by virtue of it—i.e. has been concluded to be actual fact from a critical standpoint which is essentially the same as the critic's own. For the true world is continually growing, and when part of history has been made real it at once becomes a means for the realization of the remainder. Artificial then as the complete separation of criticism from its material appears and moreover is, when we regard the individual alone, yet it is far from being so as soon as we consider the process of criticism in itself.

History, in the character of historical criticism, views its contents as lying outside itself, and its task is once more to contain them within itself. But to this the very nature of the contents presents an obstacle. The contents are records, which in a twofold manner claim to be received as real facts; first as the record of some particular age and author, and secondly in the character of recorded events. If now the whole mass were found to be completely mediated, subject to the conditions and according to the analogy of present experience; if namely the events narrated were consistent, were possible, and followed in a sequence, of which the causes and the results were in some measure known to us; and if further the dates and the general credibility of the writers were established by a satisfactory train of inference;—in that case criticism would have no task before it, save the work of verifying and reaffirming under its own guarantee the unchanged material in its original shape.

But how far, how entirely such a supposed state of things is removed from reality, needs not to be remarked. It does not exist, and the mode in which the matter of history is produced does not admit of its possible existence. It would indeed be strange if every record were authentic and trustworthy, if the judgements of a succession of witnesses scattered along the development of human progress were all secured from error, and without alteration could be harmonized into one connected whole. No one at the present time would dare to say that such is the case; and if such is not the case, then criticism, if it is to be criticism, must necessarily be to a certain extent negative.

So much is generally seen, but there is something more which cannot be said to be seen and generally admitted, namely this—that a negative criterion, if it exist at all, must be from its nature an absolute criterion, or be a self-contradiction. To the consciousness which never has risen to the critical point of view 'facts are stubborn things', and the most stubborn of all are those which the mind feels it has no share in, and which come to it with the weight of external authority. We have seen, however, what these facts are made of, and, at the point we have reached, it needs no lengthy reflection to justify the negative character of criticism.

Criticism from its very essence cannot be simply affirmative. The object which is to be criticized has ceased to be the real object, since for criticism it is the critical and that alone which is the real, and the uncritical object is consequently negated in its old and not yet reaffirmed in its new character. Criticism, if it be criticism, must in the beginning and provisionally suspect the reality of everything before it; and if there are some matters which it cannot reaffirm without falsifying itself, these matters have themselves to thank. If indeed it is so that this is their lot, that they cannot withdraw from criticism because in their very substance is involved and admitted that principle which in criticism becomes conscious of itself, and if yet to submit to criticism be for them to be transmuted or to be destroyed—this is no charge to lay against the arbitrariness of the critic. It is the contradiction implicit in the facts which to their own destruction has become explicit, and if they are denied it is only because they deny themselves.

If for history the fact means that which is real, and if the real means that which criticism has affirmed, it should not be forgotten that it is mere nonsense to talk of anything as 'an historical fact' unless criticism has been able to guarantee it as such.

There may be professed historical events, which in themselves, since they are represented without historical antecedent or sequent, contradict the conception of an historical fact (are the opposite of that which an event must be in order to exist for history) and, as they stand, history cannot even discuss their possibility.

There may be events which, though in themselves coming under the conditions of history, can yet be supported by no analogy from present experience, and, despite their testimony, they must wait for farther experience.[1] There may be events which, though both possible and analogous, are mediated with the real by no sufficient connexion, and until connected they are not yet rationalized. And lastly there are narrated facts which criticism can reaffirm as certain or probable. We must ask ourselves in what this process consists.

The historical material, as has been before stated, is twofold and presents to criticism two sides, on the one side the author, on the other the events recorded. Criticism must attempt on the one side to identify its consciousness, so far as possible, with that of the writer, by inference to establish his power and his will to narrate faithfully; on the other to find in the events recorded laws analogous to those which have been observed in present experience and in history so far as already rationalized. If the task be fully accomplished the facts are historically certain, if partially they are considered probable; but in each case they retain their original shape.

But these events thus reasserted by criticism form no continuous whole, the series presents gaps which a positive process is necessary to fill, and the process is an inferential re-creation according to law from a basis of present experience or of the historical certainty already attained. It is a sufficient answer to any difficulties which may be raised as to the construction of a past order to

[1] See Appendix, Note D.

point to the procedure of our police courts, where, in addition to the reconstruction of the witnesses by cross-examination, the sequence of events is reached by an active combination from present data. The inadequacy, however, of the historical material both in respect of quantity and quality makes the completion in this manner of the series of events an impossibility, and the persistent attempts to join the open links by the creation of causes and motives can lead to nothing but an overstrained Pragmatism, which fills the past with those fancies and opinions which only belong to the individual consciousness of the writer.

Thus far criticism has given an account of that portion only of its material which has been able to be realized because found to be already rational. There is still a remainder which has not been rationalized, which in other language, because incapable of forming in its own shape a part of the true object, must be considered as simply subjective.

Error is here presupposed, and the task of criticism is, by the removal of error, where possible to restore the truth. The process, as before, admits of a twofold method, namely the reconstruction of the supposed historical fact either from its inward or outward side, by inference on the one side from the mental character of the witness or on the other side from the course of events; and where the operation is successful, the fact once more takes its place in the world of reality, still as an outward event, but new-begotten and transformed.

It may be no unwarrantable digression to call attention once more to the view which in different forms we have so often encountered, according to which here the removal of mistake by criticism has for its result the 'original fact'. But in the present case the 'original fact' is primarily for history a fallacious inference, and if by the 'original fact' be meant again that which the fact should have been, still this for history is an inference, the theory of a theory, whose result is a double-distilled theory.

There is still an unrationalized material remaining for

history as a problem, alleged outward events which can be taken into the real series neither as unchanged nor yet as transmuted into other outward events. But even in this case criticism is not powerless; for, although the mistaken outward fact cannot be resolved into the real outward fact, we may none the less deal with the mistake itself, and the exhibition of those conditions which caused the wrong assertion of an outward fact is for criticism the satisfactory mediation of the alleged fact as a link in the historical sequence: the outward has now an existence, real indeed but inward, and assured to us only so far as inward.

These are the processes of criticism by which it makes its own the alienated material of tradition, whether in the form of outward occurrences or in that of inward events; but there must ever remain elements which it cannot reappropriate, and in many cases the testimony must be taken simply as testimony, the existence of which is historical, but the real fact or, in other words, the explanation of which cannot be given because we do not possess the data for its reconstruction.

The fact as attested may be possible, and in this case we lack the inference necessary to make it, as attested, part of history; or the attested fact may be historically impossible, and in this case we know that, as attested, it can never be part of history.

In neither of these cases can the testimony be explained as arising from the real existence of the attested. But it will be objected that we are bound to account for the testimony otherwise, or else accept the supposed fact. 'Testimony is a phenomenon,' says Paley, 'and the truth of the fact solves the phenomenon.' 'Testimony is a phenomenon'; that is indisputable, and as testimony it has its place in history. 'The truth of the fact solves the phenomenon'; that is equally certain, and we could wish that we had any means of knowing the solution. 'But', we shall be answered, 'it is the assumption of the existence of the attested fact which is this solution.' That, however, depends entirely upon the nature of the fact alleged. The phenomenon to be solved is an historical phenomenon, and its solution must be an historical solution, and to propose as this solution a fact which, when taken as historical, contradicts the very notion of history, and dissolves together with history both itself and every other certain event, this is a proposition which may indeed do credit to its author's zeal, but hardly to his prudence.

But if we are unable to accept the averred fact because it is either as yet without guarantee, or because it is an historical impossibility, are we then bound to account otherwise for the phenomenon of the testimony? Can it be urged against us that our theory contains within itself facts which contradict it, and that we must solve the facts or abandon the theory? By no means, for this is to confound that which is negatively with that which is positively irrational. These unrationalized recorded events are in contradiction with criticism only when affirmed by criticism, but now, in the character of objects which history does not yet know, they are nothing positive; they fall as yet without the theory; they are no foreign body taken up within the system, but are as yet an external and unassimilated crudity. The reproach, if such it be, that for history without the known there lies a still unknown, without the real a still unrealized, is a reproach not hard for history to bear, since she bears it in common with the whole of human knowledge.

No! It is no disgrace to be ignorant where the problem is recognized and the effort is made. And it may be that those who in some particular field have made that effort, and made it not in vain, may yet by trial and failure have learnt to regard perhaps one phenomenon, or it may be more,[1] as incapable of resolution. This for the individual

---

[1] I had in my mind here the two passages in Baur's *Kirchengeschichte* (B. i, §§ 39–40, and again 45) where he has expressed himself in a somewhat unsatisfactory manner. There are two points to be kept clear. (i) That Baur intended to exclude from the field of criticism *any historical event* is, I think, quite out of the question. That which 'lies without the sphere of historical investigation' is, he means to imply, not an event, not a fact for critical history at all: though it may be an object for a higher form of knowledge. Secondly (ii) when in both cases the spiritual process, which to Baur is the sole historical fact, is declared to be impenetrable by analysis,

may be inevitable, but absolutely to assert the insolubility of any one historical element is to give offence to the consciousness of criticism and to strengthen the cause of her enemies. Historically to *account* for a phenomenon may not always be possible; but it behoves us always to attempt to exhibit its historical origin as the result of known historical conditions; and in this sense its *possible* 'explanation' must be considered in every case as beyond a doubt. Every phenomenon has a possible solution, because as historical it must be the result of an historical antecedent; and the cause is a possible object of knowledge, because the result is known already as that which by its very nature is a member in a series of links, the essence of which is to be knowable. Historical events there may be which are destined to remain for us always problems, but problems they remain for us and ever will remain, and

surely in this there is nothing to call for any great amount of surprise. What Baur may very well have meant is that there are results for which no 'genetic development' will account, or give a reason, however much it may 'explain' them; and processes again (as we see, for example, in the case of many works of art) the elements of which defy distinction, because indissolubly fused within particular personalities by a flame, which mixes the substance of the elements with the nature of the vessel that holds them, and which itself is the new-birth of an individual soul. Hence they are not natural growths but creations; and if we like to call them miracles, we may. Sooner that, I conclude Baur would have added, than 'world-historical humbugs'; since the supposed reality of this latter phrase, however much it may (or may not) explain, will certainly account for nothing, and itself cannot be accounted for. It is a standing contradiction, a barbarous sideroxylon. If this is all that Baur had in his mind, it certainly involves no antagonism to critical history, but passes into a higher region. Concerning this region, however, it is altogether beyond our scope to say anything. Still Baur expressed himself in such a way as to make misunderstanding to the full as possible as understanding: and he was misunderstood. Strauss's criticism (as it appears in the translation of his second 'Life', vol. i, p. 398) seems to me to rest on a misapprehension of point (i). As to point (ii) Holsten (see the first two divisions of his *Zum Evangelium des Paulus und des Petrus*) has attempted in a striking manner the analyses Baur pronounced impossible. I think, however, that it is a serious mistake to imagine that by the success or failure of such attempts the *principle* of criticism is in any way affected. These remarks have become perhaps too long: my excuse must be that the man whose procedure they discuss is worthy of this and more, if it were only worthy of him.

their absolute insolubility, if we rightly consider it, involves no less than a contradition in terms.

We have reached the end set before us, and the title 'Presuppositions of Critical History' is, I hope, in some measure explained and justified. To have set in the presuppositions of history generally (or of history viewed as a whole) a larger task before me was once my wish. It was a desire too serious for accomplishment by me, but the truth of what has been done at present is perhaps, so far as it goes, independent of a wider result. For however humble the sphere of her rule, yet at least, while within that sphere, criticism is subject to no intrusion and oppressed by no authority. She moves on her path unheedful of the warning, unheedful of the clamour, of that which beyond her realm may be or may call itself religion and philosophy; her philosophy and her religion are the realization and the fruition of herself, and her faith is this, that while true to herself she can never find an enemy in the truth.

APPENDIX

Note A

If we wish to see with our eyes the material and the task of the historian, we must imagine a fresco representing in a continual progress the figures and the actions of generations. And this is not the work of a single artist. On the contrary the artists are many with the many generations, and at times there is more than one in a single division of the picture. But though they are many they are not all painters from the life; for some lived after the time when the figures they portrayed had perished. And of these latter some with their names have told us that they borrowed from copies now lost, and of others we do not know even this; while of some again we can see that they copied, and copied wrongly, from original drawings which we still have.

So the fresco is not simple, nor by any means one work; but in certain parts of it, representative of certain ages, we have many diverse pictures of the same figure, which all profess to be copied from the life; and over other spaces of several generations there are no drawings at all which profess to be original, but instead of them the painting of an artist of after years, who had only, if we believe the best that we can, the sketches of others to work from. And in some cases there may be one such secondary artist, but over other spaces there may be two, or three, or more; and these may not agree with one another.

Nor is this all—we have not only the differences of diverse primary painters in some spaces, and in other spaces the discrepancies of secondary artists, but in process of time the later painters have agreed in this, that the picture must be a copy of the reality, but as to the reality they have disagreed, all with the picture as it was before them, and each with one another. And wishing to have a copy of the original, they have all corrected the old figures or confusions of figures, and have remodelled and altered them to what they thought must be the life.

And the corrections of these artists have been themselves corrected by others who lived at the same time or after, so that at the first sight and to the careless eye the alterations only are to be seen, and not the underlying material. However, to the man who examines and searches, the whole chaos is visible, the drawings which call themselves original, the representations where there are no such drawings, and then, on and over these, the ceaseless corrections and re-corrections, combinations and re-combinations, of later artists.

But this mass is the picture, and the picture represents the original. So says the world, the present generation; but it adds, 'We cannot see the original, and the artist must make us a painting which will show us the men and the times as they were. The present picture is certainly a copy of the real persons; as they were, so have they been drawn; we will not have them altered, but we must see them. Make a picture out of them!'

Is this sense or nonsense? The new picture is to be a copy of the reality, or else it is to be no picture; and the reality does not exist, and so cannot be copied. 'Who thought of copying it?' will be the answer. 'We *have* the copy in the fresco.' Then why send for an artist when you only want a photograph? Or, rather, why copy at all? If you have one copy, which is already before you, what interest can you possibly have in reproducing that? 'But the artist is not merely to reproduce. Of course he is not to alter, much less to invent, but he must put the scattered materials together.' If, however, he copies every diverse representation, and encloses the collection in a single frame, whether it agree together or whether it do not—let him quote what precedent he may, he shall not prevent our asking, *Is* this a picture? A picture represents the real, and the real is one and is self-consistent; but here the figures of the real are many and are inconsistent, and only the frame is one.

'You have not understood us. The artist is to make a picture *out of* the fresco; and *because* the reality is one *therefore* the picture will be one, and so will answer to the real.' But the real is known only through the picture, and the picture is not one, nor self-consistent. If you know that the truth in itself is one, you know it apart from the picture and in spite of the picture; and you know *what* the truth is, *that* the picture is not. *How* do you know that as it stands the picture cannot be a copy of the real? Because you know *both* original *and* copy, and you compare the two together.

'That is part true and part false', will be the reply. 'It is absurd to think we know anything of the past apart from the fresco, for this reason, that the real cannot be invented but only copied, and the past is so perished that all that we have is the copy of it. But of course we know that what is real must be self-consistent because we can see that everywhere.'

Except in the fresco. 'Yes, but that is because the different sides and parts are so scattered; bring them together, and they will represent the real, and still be a copy.'

E

This is the imagined task of the artist. He is not to know the original except from the fresco; and yet he is to know that the original is homogeneous, while the fresco is heterogeneous. And this is not a consistent theory. But let us pass to practice: let us see the painter at work.

He finds that in many places his materials are in a state of the completest contradiction. He finds perhaps that A kills B and marries his wife, and that B kills A and marries his wife, and then he comes to the corrections, or the 'harmonies', or the rationalizations of later artists, some of whom represent both courses of events together, while most recombine or correct or simplify.

The artist has his orders. He is to make one picture or series of pictures, and he must not alter. He of course in fact both must and does alter; but let us suppose that he abides by his instructions; then he does nothing, or rather he returns to his patrons and informs them that their task is a sheer impossibility.

And so they are driven to reflection, and they see perhaps that it is because the fresco is *not* a copy of the real that the need for a picture has been felt; and it may be they assent at length to the alteration of the material. But they do not ask themselves the question, 'Is a picture a copy?' And they do not inquire, 'How is the supposed reality of the false copy to be denied at all, if we do not know the original?'

With their denial of the knowledge of the original they combine their assertion that the picture is a false copy of that original; and the result of their reflection is this, that the copy is a false copy because it is not a *mere* copy; and it is not a mere copy because it has not been *copied*, because it has not been taken from the life but altered and reconstructed.

But how are we to know what is a copy? 'There is no difficulty; we know *that* if we know that it has been copied.' And how in the world are we to tell this? 'We are sure of it because the drawings are contemporary.' Yet surely the *professedly* original drawings do not cover the whole space of the fresco, and even of these we find on examination that some are in a style which belongs to a later age, and in these cases we doubt the genuineness of the signatures. Are these copies too?

'No, not these, if you can show there are such, but the drawings of eye-witnesses reproduce the reality.'

This seems at first sight something more tangible; but in practice we are still assailed by difficulties. In the first place the professed original drawings leave great gaps in the space of the fresco; in the second we have in every case to determine whether the drawing is really contemporary and genuine, and for this at present we have no criterion; and in the third place we find drawings, which have to be taken all alike as copies of the reality, in irreconcilable hostility to one another.

We return baffled for further instructions. 'Of course,' we are admonished, 'it is not enough that the painter has been contemporary: he must also be willing and he must be able to copy accurately, and his relative value is to be found by study and examination.'

But by study of what? Of the fresco, or anything beside the fresco?

'Certainly you must not confine your attention to the fresco. There is painting going on all around you. You can see what are the signs of an honest copyist and an able copyist. You must apply these to the drawings in the fresco, and so will reach the reality by discovering where the artists have strayed from the right style. And as to the genuineness of the work, you ought by observation to know the marks of the truthful copyist, and the marks of the inventor and fabricator.'

Then it is not enough that the painter should be honest?

'No, for he can be clumsy; and so two honest painters can produce two contradictory copies. He must be able as well, and you must judge of this by the character of his work. If he is honest and able his work will be truthful and natural.'

But it is time to recall the original position of the artist's employers, and place it by the side of their present instructions. At first the figures of the fresco were to be reproduced without questioning or alteration, whereas now before reproduction we are to ask, Is this true? Is this natural? Have we a correct copy on the side of the artist? Have we a genuine fact for him to copy? And we find that we cannot ask ourselves these questions, till we know what is meant by a natural figure, and what is a faithful drawing of such a figure. Everything depends upon our acquaintance with this, and where are we to go to obtain information? There is no possible answer but one. To experience, to the originals of the present, for our knowledge of real objects; and to the different fashions, in which the artists of the day reproduce these, for our knowledge of styles and of peculiarities of painting, with their special relations to the object represented.

Then comes the question, Is the artist in making his picture to alter and correct the fresco? Is he merely to find out what parts of the fresco may be said to be drawings by good artists, or is he in addition to correct at pleasure and to re-combine features or figures or groupings?

And here the employers make one last stand. 'It is absurd', they say, 'to take the world of to-day, and to alter the picture from that. You simply invent a past which you take from the present, and you cannot tell but what the past was essentially different.'

And upon this point too the artist, if he be a wise artist, will refuse to yield. 'If I could do all that I could wish to do,' he will say, 'what you too wish should be done. But the question is not as to how much you want, but as to how much I can accomplish for you. You wish to see the real; but I know no reality save that which I see and study now for myself. You ask for truth; I know no truth but the accordance of the drawing with this my world. You wish for the removal of error; I know no error but departure from the life, as now after pains and sacrifice I see it. I am to find the causes of error? And how do I know them but by experience of the work of artists, which I compare with the reality, and so study their different styles and various deflections from the truth. It comes to this—I have no reality but one, you must have that or nothing. It may be things were different in the past; I cannot help that, I did not live then. If you object to a past brought into harmony with the present, you can have nothing from me at all.

'And I do not invent a past like the present. I see many types of reality, and many styles of copying that reality. I do not say, *because* I never saw a nose or an arm like that, *therefore* it was not so: but I do say, if any feature, figure, or position is neither like any I have seen, nor is a further carrying out of tendencies that I have observed, then I will never paint it so, or approve when any one else so paints it.

'And I must tell you that really there is no copying. Every man has his style, and cannot help having it. I have mine, but I have done my best to conform it to that which is true. Perhaps I have failed. You must take me or leave me.

'But you must not think I am going to invent. I have the fresco as my material. From my knowledge of the real I can tell from one part often what another is, and so reconstruct the whole. From my knowledge of bad drawing I can often tell what it is has made the style vicious and the features distorted, and so can arrive at the original.

'I can not do much for you. I can restore a great deal and clear away more. But again and again it will be my duty to tell you that I am powerless. Further experience may help, but after all, alas,

the result may be, that of the figures of one whom we most wish to
see as he was, we can accept not one as the likeness; and, after removal of vicious mannerisms and distortions, there is left some feeble
and colourless outline of him in whose soul the "world's broken
heart", it may be, was born again.'

NOTE B

The doctrine of the text supplies us with a means for judging the
maxim, 'Quod ubique, quod ab omnibus, . . . verum est.'

Now is there the smallest reason to suppose, merely because
the existence of a phenomenon or set of phenomena has been
asserted by writers in every time, that *therefore* the phenomena are
real facts? What is the *ground* of the inference? General consent
it cannot be: if there is one belief with a greater extension than any
other, it is the belief in the reality of supernatural apparitions, witchcraft, and sorcery. Yet the educated as a rule now reject this
belief.

The question is this, Why is the fact of continual assertion a
ground for belief? It is not because the *quantity* of the witnesses
precludes mistake—in these cases numbers are of little weight. It
is because the coexistence of the same observation with apparently
every variety of standpoint is a ground for concluding to *the quality
of the basis* of the observation. The various points of view cancel
each other, and the mutual obliteration of their differences affords
in general some presumption that the residue, which was that which
made the observation, is common to all, and therefore to us; is in
short an observation from our own point of view. This presumption
of course may or may not be justified.

Whether evidence of this sort can ever be regarded as more than
probable, or as valid for science, is a question which does not concern us here. For in any case the evidence would not be historical,
since it would demonstrate never the particular event at a particular
time; it could never reconstruct one particular observation, but
would be a general conclusion to the reality of a *class* of phenomena.

NOTE C

Unless the matter of historical testimony is subject to analogy
throughout all its details, the main argument of these pages is
broken; and I confess that, in my opinion, that part of the discussion
is the weakest. I will state the objection which occurs to me against
it, and will then endeavour to show that the objection is not really
valid, and to explain more fully the position taken in the text.

'What it comes to', it may be said, 'is no more than this. We have proof, and we have probability. Proof is scientific, a theoretical certainty; probability is not scientific, but it may be a practical certainty. Probability we admit must depend on analogy; but we utterly deny that the probable and the analogous are convertible terms, so that hence the non-analogous means the improbable.

'Can analogy[1] lead us to the non-analogous? Yes. It is only in the conjunction of the words that there is anything paradoxical. The real paradox is to identify the probable and the analogous, so as to be forced to assert that no non-analogous scientific fact can ever be probable.

'If we assure ourselves that the standpoint of an inquirer is the same as ours, we can receive as probable what he thinks probable, and without specific analogy from our own private experience. Or, taking his proved facts as certain, we ourselves may conclude by inference to a probable fact both new and non-analogous. In the field of science such results as these must be considered probable.

'And again in science, where I cannot be sure of the precise standpoint of the observer, I may yet take the facts, which are certain for him, as possessing at least probability, and these facts again ⟨are⟩ not subject to analogy.

'Turning now to history, why in the world, if I partially possess myself of the witness's consciousness, may I not regard his facts, when apart from analogy, as certainly probable? To refute me you must maintain that I cannot get a probable proof by a partial identification. And this you maintain in the teeth of facts.

'And if my conclusion is probable, and if history does not go beyond probability, why is my conclusion to stand outside when others no better are admitted?

'So much for the facts, and now for the reasoning. Analogy is not to affirm the non-analogous? Nothing is easier. You start from your private experience, and you argue by analogy to a consciousness probably right in the matter of its non-analogous testimony.

---

[1] I have throughout used 'analogy' in the ordinary sense, which prohibits our applying the term to personal observation. But, if we look closer, in the extension of our experience we use what may be considered as analogical reasoning. In observing an altogether new sort of fact, the parts of the fact are brought into the mind by subsumption under certain known heads. If it were not so we could not observe the fact at all, as it would come into no relation with our minds. This process might improperly be called 'analogy'. The fact as a whole is of course not accounted for so. It requires to be made one object by a synthetic act of the mind.

You get the fact of a man, whose evidence, even apart from analogy, is probably right; and then you receive as probable his testimony *en bloc*, though supported in detail by no analogy. To the particular facts you have nothing similar, but to the main fact which contains them you have; and this main fact rests upon analogy and makes its particulars thereby probable.

'(And, briefly to illustrate, there may be supposed events in history which, though not in contradiction with my notion of the Divinity, may yet involve attributes supported by no analogy from that idea and experience which I have. Yet on evidence I am bound to believe in these attributes, unless the others exclude them; and why cannot history prove them probably by a partial identification with the consciousness of the witness?)'

Thus far the objection. There is in it little that we cannot adopt, except the particular application to history.

The problem is as follows. Let us suppose a man in the past whose point of view is equal to our own. Let us suppose that he testifies to an event in history, and further to a non-analogous event. His evidence is not scientific, because we cannot assure ourselves of the conditions of his observation. Yet his evidence amounts to a high degree of scientific probability. This case is certainly conceivable. Why then, the question arises, is that which is probable enough for science actually not probable enough for history?

I answer that I do not deny the mere amount of probability. I admit that the case in question may actually possess a greater probability than most of the events, than all if you will, which I make part of history; but none the less do I say that I will never receive that event as historical, except upon analogy from the present.

We must make a distinction. For science there is proof and there is probability; there are likely but uncertain facts, and probable but unverified hypotheses; but for science there is no such thing as a probable *conclusion*. The conclusions of science, which it takes for certainties, are never, while science is true to itself, anything short of fully proved. Science recognizes theoretical but not moral probability; and it cannot do this latter, because practical probability may amount to certainty.

The conclusions of history are never proved; they are first theoretical probabilities, and secondly they are more, they are moral certainties. In history the conclusions are moral certainties; but, as history is not practical, its results must be theoretical, and hence while probable are still received as theoretical certainties.

A theoretical certainty must be taken as certain, i.e. as more than a probable conclusion. One of three things must be done then. We must habitually consider the events in history either (i) as theoretically probable, and that means uncertain; or (ii) as morally certain, whether with or apart from analogy; or (iii) as morally certain only when supported by analogy.

The first course (i) simply means that you have no history at all. For history you must have facts, you must have something you can believe in, and say of it 'this was so'. The mind must feel itself at home in the past; and it cannot do that when the past is represented by nothing but a present of doubtfully-weighed probabilities. History here is a word without meaning; yet history there ever must be and, let it be a delusion or not, we at least assume that it is not so.

If history exists it must be more than uncertain. We pass to the second question (ii) and ask, Is history to be considered as (morally) theoretically certain, and that independent of analogy? The historical order is here an hypothesis or theory which is taken as true. Let us reflect on the result of receiving as true a conclusion in history apart from present scientific analogy.

This conclusion is not scientific, for it is not proved but only probable. For science the facts and the conclusions from the facts are not admitted as realities; and yet for history these same facts are certain. This means that what is true, what you believe, what is a fact, what really has happened, at the same time is not true, may not be believed, is not yet a fact, and cannot be said to have happened. The collision is inevitable, since the facts are the property of both spheres alike. The theorist of course may keep up the distinctions, and may never forget the saving clauses; but for the practical historian or man of science this is simply impossible. The whole interest of history is to have one truth, one reality, then as now, and now as then. One course or another must be taken. Either against the scientific conscience, and to the loss of science, the historical reality must become the scientific reality; and that means that the un-analogous hypotheses and traditional facts must be received into science as verified certainties, with their consequences developed in every direction, to provoke a collision at each new discovery—or else (and this must be the better alternative) scientific evidence is made the criterion, and historical testimony subjected throughout and in all its details to analogy from that. This is the real interest of history, to find what it knows under other aspects. This is the method, and this alone, by which to avoid the struggle of truth against truth and reality against reality—a collision intolerable to the oneness of the mind which bears the distraction. The third way (iii) is thus the only course possible to save us from scepticism in history or from credulity in science. It is the one path open to the practical critic; and this is the justification of a suspension of judgement in presence of even more than a sufficient probability. Suspension of judgement is, however, exclusion from history.

Long as this note has become, there are yet two points which deserve our attention. The first is merely an illustration from legal proceedings. Let us suppose in a criminal case that, to prove the theory of the prisoner's guilt, an attested fact must be taken as true, though the judge and the jury are aware of nothing analogous. Speaking as one who is ignorant of law, I venture to think that on no common evidence would the prisoner be convicted. Scientific witnesses would be required; and if their testimony was insufficient for an actual enlargement of the experience of the jury and the judge, I do not see how a conclusion could be come to. Yet, while legal is stronger as a rule than historical evidence, still legal are weaker in one way than historical conclusions. A verdict is an opinion of particular persons on a particular case; a fact in history is a past reality. This difference comes from the difference of the interest.

The second point is what seems an inconsistency in historical practice. The probability, which actually itself would not be taken into history, nevertheless is used as the basis of an analogy for theorizing tradition into an historical fact. For instance the probable evidence of past stigmatization (which would not, in default of present analogy, prove the historical fact) would perhaps and by some persons, if it were present, be made to justify the affirmation in history of the existence of stigmata. I must doubt whether this course is critical; but it is important as showing the interest of history, which moulds the past after the present, and for which the present probability is at once a canon, simply because it is present.

NOTE D

It would be a serious mistake to suppose, because at a certain time criticism is not justified in considering an event historical, that *therefore* criticism will *never* be able to affirm it. There are several instances to the contrary.

Herodotus records the account of the circumnavigation of Africa (iv. 42), and does not believe it, because it contained a fact which to him seemed incredible, since utterly without analogy (as he thought) in the astronomical world (ἔλεγον ἐμοὶ μὲν οὐ πιστά, ἄλλῳ δὲ δή τεῳ, ὡς περιπλώοντες τὴν Λιβύην τὸν ἥλιον ἔσχον ἐς τὰ δεξιά). This very circumstance, as the commentators remark on the passage, is the best evidence for the truth of the Phoenicians' story.

The accounts of stigmatization furnish another example. It was clearly impossible for the critical historian to receive this testimony in the absence of any present scientific analogy. But if (as seems likely) such analogy exists, if the possibility of the phenomenon can be scientifically proved, the case as to the medieval stories is at once altered; and their possible reception becomes a mere question of the amount and quality of the historical evidence.

Again, in the face of admittedly strong historical evidence, Gibbon (cap. xxxvii) declined to believe that the African confessors spoke without tongues. Gibbon was unquestionably right, since he had before him nothing analogous. It turns out now to be the fact, however, and is said to be proved by repeated scientific experiments, that speech is possible after the total excision of the tongue. The attitude of the historian to the supposed miracle must now of course be different, and the testimony may be received and weighed.

The rule for the critical historian is always to keep on the side of safety. It is better to suspend the judgement and be wrong, than to be right against reason and in the face of science.

Note E

Everything, we have said, depends on personal experience. And this means that, when pressed, we must come to and must start from that; must from the ground of that connect our self with past selves, so as to know what once on a time was fact for them; and so as to know that it also is fact for us now, because in respect of the class of phenomena in question their consciousness is identical with ours. In critical history we either perform this operation ourselves, or we take it for granted that it has been or could be done.

And with the phrases of 'personal observation' and 'experience' we have said enough doubtless, if that were our object, to satisfy most persons, or at least to stop their mouths. But a man who inquires will wish to go farther.

'I know well', he may say, 'that fresh observation and facts are supposed to give the basis from which to correct or make valid the old material. But what I do not see is how on your standpoint such a position is possible.

'You say that all is inferential. This must mean that, as are the premises of the inference, so also are the conclusions. To get beyond your premises is surely impossible; and as for correcting them, that is nonsense.

'Come to the facts. It is notorious that a man may be quite incapable of receiving essentially and vitally new facts in their essential
and vital meaning. He *will* subsume them under his own categories;
he must make them members of his world, or not take them in at all.
As is the man, so are his facts. Uneducated persons and children transform to their own likeness all they assimilate: and savages are in many
cases literally unable to take in what to us seem simple impressions of
passivity, for this sufficient reason that they have no internal world
which answers to them, no premises under which to subsume them.

'What it comes to is this. A man has a certain world to start with,
and he doesn't know how he has got it: this world contains every
sort of matter, historical and otherwise. *"Personal observation!"*
What on earth does *"personal"* mean, when the contents of his person, his personal world, are already traditional and decidedly not his
in particular? And what sense is there in sending him to "observation", when that only enlarges but cannot correct or innovate, for
the simple reason that what is not in harmony excludes itself from
observation? This "personal experience" is a mere superstition, for
nothing is more personal to any man than the traditional world
already personal within him.

'You have used "inference" to knock down "fact"; and now
from "fact" you want to start to get a basis for inference. But all
facts are alike in being inferential, and therefore alike in this, that
they issue from and are based on the given.'

The objection is well worth considering in itself, and comes to
this, 'How are critical observation and experience possible?' This is
a somewhat wide question, and we make not the smallest profession
of discussing it here. And we are not obliged to discuss it. It may
seem that we are so: it may seem that we have rested on critical
experience, and are therefore bound to explain its possibility.

This is quite wrong. What we wanted to show was this, that
given the existence of history, it must be critical; and that *if* it is
critical, *then* it must rest on present critical experience. That is
our whole conclusion; and if any one chooses to argue, 'There is
no *critical* experience and therefore no *critical* history', we shall not
contend with him, but merely add 'and therefore no history at all',
and treat his subsequent historical dogmatism with silent contempt.

Not for the sake of our argument, then, do we feel bound to consider the objection we have developed; but entirely for the sake of
the subject of the objection itself are we willing to say something;
not much, but not much less than what we have learnt.

In the sharpest form of the difficulty it comes to the old crux, 'knowledge implies previous knowledge', or 'subsumption previous subsumption', and is directed against the possibility of any beginning, and hence against the existence of knowledge at all.

It is impossible to attempt to deal with this here. Nor does it touch the particular case. We are not treating of the beginning of knowledge and experience in general, but find ourselves on a problem in the middle of the stream.

As it touches us the problem is this. 'Since you start from the given, and rest on the given, which at all events *may* come to you as uncriticized and uncritical—*how* are you to criticize it? How *from* what is given get to that which is critical, when the source and instrument vitiates the outcome, when the unsurveyed foundation damns the edifice? If you tell a superstitious man to observe *personally*, do you really think that he will observe critically? Only the critical mind is capable of critical observation, and a mind full of uncritical matter cannot possibly be critical.'

It is a hard question, but we must try to answer. We must bear in mind that in the growth of knowledge there are two sides. On one side we have the given whole, the world, or the consciousness, or the self—briefly that which is *so far* the real. And now under this we bring fresh facts. We subsume them under that which we have and we are; and this means that they become a part of the whole, which *therefore*, and as over against the *former* world, is a fresh whole.

But we shall be cut short here. 'This is not to the purpose. What you want is to get a split between fresh observation and the old world, and you can't do it this way. You forget that the facts not already of a piece with the system are *not* subsumed, and hence the whole may be overlooked but is never criticized. It only grows like the lower forms of nature by accretion and not by evolution, by simple addition of new material and not by a process of differentiation and integration.'

We resume. And it doubtless is true that in some individuals, and in some countries and times, to a certain extent this is the case. If it always were true, then there would be no criticism nor any critical observation. But as a matter of fact humanity does not grow in this way and it cannot. And what is the reason of this? Where is it that the description of progress as growth by accretion is incorrect? When is a split between new and old a possibility?

When the old involves a contradiction; i.e. when, supposing itself to be a system, it in reality is not consistent. Then that which is subsumed under it will also be inconsistent, inconsistent with the old and also with itself. The contradictory elements will be exhibited in their freedom and, by the particularization of fresh subsumption and by growing divergencies in consciousness, will contradict the unity of consciousness. The uneasiness will cause reflection on the object or stage of consciousness (both are the same), and then an alienation and rejection.

'But in this what about the new personal observation? Are not the system and its particular subsumptions all negated alike?' They are; and it is possible that, turning away from both old and new, the mind may suspend itself dissatisfied, and here again the critical experience be wanting.

But the mind is such a unity that it holds a contradiction in itself until the divided elements cohere, are solved and blended into another consciousness, a fresh system, a new world—new, and which contains the old in a transformed shape.

And this is why (to begin with 'personal') the personality is wanted; for that is no less than the principle of synthesis which makes this new world.

'Let all this be true,' it will still be rejoined, 'you have got a split between the reflecting person and the old world. But what of experience and observation? What have they to do with your new synthesis, your new object, your re-systematized world?'

Patience! I reply. The new synthesis is not yet a world, but an embryo world; and further, the new principle, which has resulted from the negation of the old, may either be itself an object *for* consciousness, or may be merely a consciousness which is not yet aware of itself; i.e. it may be a new doctrine that we are aware of, and go forth to realize against the old, or may be the changed attitude of mind that knows itself as yet only as the denial of the old world, and must have a new world to know what itself is.

In the former case it is a conscious principle, but abstract and undeveloped; and it is a new object, but still subjective, not yet evolved or known in its determinations. You want to know what this new world is in the concrete? You must see for yourself. Subsume particulars under it; fill it with matter, and you will see. Realize it, and you will find what it is you have realized. That is why personal observation is wanted.

The old matter of the old system is vitiated throughout, because vitalized by a defunct theory. You want sound matter, and you get it by subsuming under principles which you feel to be true. Thus you make a system, the principle and details of which are both known to you. And now you can re-systematize the material of the old world. You could not do it before because the old world was so particularized that nothing abstract could reorganize its details. You wanted a principle truly particularized into the concrete; and now you have that, you can proceed, remembering that the new object is the real object, and the old powerless before it.

Or, in the second case, the new consciousness is not aware of itself. It knows itself only as the self, for which the old world is inadequate and alien; it feels the impulse to find itself anew in another world; but it has no principle under which it consciously subsumes; the self which subsumes is not, as self, an object of consciousness. It *finds* a fresh object, it *sees* a new world grow up before it, and it thinks of itself as the passive and reflecting mirror. By observation it gets its new world, and from that it learns the nature of itself. It gets the consciousness of the principle which was the unknown agent at work, and then from that basis it can proceed to re-include the old rejected elements.

So far we have considered that progress which involves a breach with the existing world. But we have yet the case before us where it is the finding of new facts which seems to overthrow a hitherto unsuspected creed, and premises sound in themselves.

We must go back for a space. We first saw how the mind, as a world or system, finds itself in an object of like nature; we saw how it was a contradiction involved in the consciousness which made the subsumed object contradictory; and next how the mind, as unity, rose above its own contradiction, and reflected on and negated its former stage of consciousness or world.

But such conscious reflection is by no means the normal process of empirical development; and, as often as not, the old is not negated till it is found existing peacefully side by side with a new state of things, which has got there Heaven knows how. How did it get there?

It is the unconscious reflective action and systematization of the mind which has made it. The proceeds of experience are contradictory, and the mind is a principle of unity. It feels the contradictions and, without knowing it, is more or less alienated from its contents, but comes to no downright breach with the world. On the contrary it imagines itself to be bringing all new details faithfully under the old world or old self; and it does not know that *itself* is the active principle of subsumption, and that it no longer is one with the former self. From that old self it separates itself more and more, develops and partially solves its contradictions, critically corrects its one-sidednesses, rules out its inconsistencies with unconscious but incessant activity; and all the time is subsuming new matter under this innovating and perpetually growing self.[1] The assimilated details, it is obvious, no longer will bear the character and form the counterpart of the old self, but show more and more in their development the results of the mind's unconscious work; and, being subsumed into the new self, react powerfully upon it to increased separation from the former stage of consciousness, and to the production of fresh facts which are still less in harmony with the old system of belief.

All this time, however, the subsuming self, as in a succession of fresh individuals it gets farther and farther removed, still thinks itself loyal to the ancient creed, which really is rapidly becoming (or may even in parts or altogether have become) a traditional mass, a semi-effete stage of consciousness, an organism from which the life has been drawn by a younger organism to feed itself, a dead or half-dead self existing in and alongside of a new world and a new self. At this epoch the smallest shock—any extra-contradiction between the two lives, a sudden discovery, or in short any accident—will force upon the mind the consideration of what it really is, and the startling and appalling revelation that it has two selves and a double world. Whether a contest ensues will depend on how far the soul has been withdrawn from the elder organism, and how far the younger has appropriated to itself all sides of the reality. But in any case the victory will lie with the new (though the new may be forced in the struggle to extend and modify itself), since it is the self which pleads and judges its own cause; and, after vehement reaction (it may be) and violent rejection of the old, the traditional mass, the effete organism will itself be assimilated, and live once more in the new and reintegrated body.

If the further question be put 'What necessity is there for the given world to be self-contradictory?' this note must certainly be kept within bounds; but briefly an answer might be given, which appears the best to give. The universe seems to be one system; it is an organism (it would appear) and more. It bears the character of the self, the personality to which it is relative, and without which

---

[1] We may consider the process as taking place in one and the same mind, or series of minds; but in reality the differentiation of the old system of belief is accelerated by the diversity of individualities. In an inconsistent substance the inconsistencies are explicated by being more or less fixed, in different individuals, as one-sided personalities. The collision of these is an instigation to the general mind to recover and re-collect itself from them into a consistent centre of integration.

for us it is as good as nothing. Hence any portion of the universe by itself cannot be a consistent system; for it refers to the whole, and has the whole present in it. Potentially the whole (since embodying that which is actually the whole), in trying to fix itself as itself, it succeeds only in laying stress on its character of relativity; it is carried beyond and contradicts itself. Or more briefly thus. Evolution is necessary because the mind is actually limited, virtually unlimited; and the object lives in the life of the mind and varies with it.

To sum the result. 'Go to *experience*' does not *here* imply respect for one class of facts alone. You go to experience to know what facts in general are, since the only way to realize your principle, to know what your premises are, what your system is and is to be, is to subsume matter under it. And 'Go to *personal* experience' is essential, not because, as this or that man, you are better than anybody else who is or has been; but just as experience is necessary to get facts for your principle, and tell you what it is, so *you* must form the matter by subsumption in order to know that it has been subsumed under *your* principle, and is therefore *a fact for you*.

No facts but my facts; and only through my facts do I realize myself, and know what I am. Personal observation does not mean that this or that sensuous matter comes into relation with this or that sensuous individual. To imagine that in this is to be found the smallest guarantee or test of truth is a wretched superstition, a proof of the most utter philosophical uneducatedness, and that completest blindness to the experience of everyday life which is possible only to a vicious *a priori* dogmatism. 'Experience' means the verification in the concrete, and the bringing to consciousness (formally or in detail) of our known or unknown actuating principle and presupposition; and 'personal' means that our world is to be a unity answering to our oneness—it means the emphasis of the idea of system in a new man.

II

MR. SIDGWICK'S HEDONISM

An examination of the main argument of *The Methods of Ethics*

PREFACE

THE following pages are intended to supply, not a general review or estimate of *The Methods of Ethics*, but an examination of the main argument of that work, the thesis it supports, and the steps by which it goes to its conclusion.

The position which Mr. Sidgwick's book has taken in the literature of the day fully justifies the length of this examination. The remarks which I found space to make in my *Ethical Studies* were, I fear, too brief and condensed to express my objections. And I think that a discussion of the subject in detail can hardly fail to be of use to the student of Moral Philosophy.

From the first I have found Mr. Sidgwick's book not easy to understand, and it is probable that in some points I may have misapprehended his meaning. My own belief is that Mr. Sidgwick's argument is in itself not clear, and that the obscurity arises from the omission on his part of any serious attempt to arrive at an understanding of the fundamental preconceptions with which he operates. In this the reader may find I am mistaken; but I cannot doubt that the inquiry, if it does not prove the edifice unstable, will at least bring more clearly into light the nature of the foundation. And this will be a result well worth the labour.

What I have tried to do is first of all, at the price, I fear, of a great deal of tediousness, to help the reader to master the most prominent conceptions of the book, and to bring to light the obscurity and ambiguous nature of the leading terms and the equivocal character of the main thesis. Then, in Part II, I have entered on the proof of the thesis which is offered, and have endeavoured to show that it is unsatisfactory. Lastly, in Part III § 8, I have tried to exhibit the real nature of the author's proposed Ethical Science, and to point out some of the objections to which it lies open; and in § 9 I have discussed the problem, partly moral and partly theological, which is raised at the end of Mr. Sidgwick's work. Some general remarks on the 'objective' character of morality have been excluded from want of space.

MERTON COLLEGE, OXFORD.
1877

PART I. THE DEFINITIONS

§ 1. *Reason*

NO one, I think, who reads *The Methods of Ethics* can fail to be struck by the recurrence of the word 'reasonable'. Plainly it is a term we ought to understand, for the Right, the Good, the End, the Desirable, all seem to fall under it[1] and to depend on it for their meaning. It

[1] There can be no doubt that 'reasonable', 'right', 'ought', all stand for the same idea (29), and as little doubt that 'preferable', 'desirable', 'the end', are equivalent. True, 'good' can be distinguished from 'right', but for our purpose the distinction seems to be of no importance, and (as applied to conduct) they 'coincide substantially' (98). Indeed (80, note) we hear

---

TABLE OF CONTENTS

PART I. THE DEFINITIONS

[This Table of Contents followed the Preface in the original edition. The pages now given in it are those of the present volume.]

is scarcely saying too much when we say that Mr. Sidg-wick's main thesis stands and falls with his view of the 'reasonable'. But when we ask, Has the word been ex-plained with sufficient clearness? I think the answer must be, No.

What is reason? It is defined (27) as 'a faculty which takes cognizance of objective truth'. We shall have to ask hereafter what 'objective' in general means, but here 'objective truth' seems opposed to 'purely subjective phenomena', 'the sensations of the sentient being' (23), and is 'the same, whether recognized or not, for all Minds or Subjects' (182).[1]

But in what way does reason apprehend truth? Is it merely 'discursive'? No, 'it seems . . . to belong to reason not merely to judge of the relation of means to ends, or of the consistency of maxims: but also to determine the ultimate ends and true first principles of action' (26). This 'operation' is 'intuitive'.

Reason, so far, is not merely discursive but also 'intui-tive'; and the question which remains is as to the nature of the 'objective truth' which it apprehends. For—

'we do not say, in physics, that individual facts are apprehended by the Reason: we consider this faculty to be conversant in its dis-cursive operation with the relation of judgments or propositions; and the intuitive reason (which is here rather in question) we restrict to the apprehension of universal truths, such as the axioms of logic and mathematics. Now, as I shall presently notice, it is not uncom-monly held that the moral faculty judges primarily of individual cases, applying directly to these the general notion of Duty, and deciding intuitively what ought to be done by this person in these particular circumstances. On this view the moral apprehension is more analogous to Sense-Perception than to Rational Intuition (as

of 'right' and 'reasonable', and the equivalent phrase 'what ought to be' (done or aimed at). I am not sure whether 'good' and 'reasonable' are ever coupled, but the end is the 'end of reason', and the good is the rational end or ends. It would tend to clearness if we were told at the beginning which of these terms are convertible, or at all events whether we have to do with one, or more than one, 'fundamental notion'.

[1] It is right that I should say here that I cannot reconcile with this Mr. Sidgwick's view as to Egoism being reasonable. See below, p. 102, note, and pp. 116–17.

commonly understood): and hence the term Moral Sense has been preferred by many, who did not mean to suggest thereby any scepticism as to the reality of moral (as distinct from psychological) truth. But it is so important to avoid this suggestion, that it seems better to use generally the term Reason: provided it be not supposed to mean anything more specific than "a faculty which takes cognizance of objective truth" ' (26–7).

We find, however, that it does hereafter mean something more specific. We find (85) that, in speaking of 'the popular view of Conscience', our writer says:

'This view may be called ultra-intuitional, as it recognizes simple immediate intuitions alone and rejects all modes of reasoning to moral conclusions. But it may equally well be called ultra-empirical as it emphasizes the authority of particular moral experiences in comparison with universal rules or axioms. This then we may describe as one phase or variety of the Intuitional method, involving really a negation of method, and excluding what is more strictly called Reason from moral decisions.'

And then comes this note to the word Reason, 'i.e. the faculty of apprehending universal truth'.

It would appear then that in future we have to deal with a strict and a loose use of Reason, but I cannot find that in the sequel, when Reason comes in, we are clearly told *which* Reason is meant. On this point I have found Mr. Sidgwick very hard to understand, but I will try to put before the reader what seems to be his doctrine.

I think that Reason stands for the faculty which apprehends 'universal truth' (85), 'general rules', 'abstract moral notions', 'moral axioms' (87), and further that it includes as well the *reasoning* to particular cases from 'general moral maxims', whether these latter are 'universal moral intuitions' (190) or not. The word *may* cover more, but I doubt it.

Now (this is an important matter) is 'conscience', in the sense of a judgement on particular cases (85), irrational? I think not. 'Even when the decision of the moral faculty is felt to relate primarily to some particular action, we cannot really exclude generality from the notion of the action thus judged to be right' (86). 'The moral truth apprehended will be intrinsically universal, though particular in our first apprehension of it' (ibid.). And (189) we find that all moral judgements have a 'potential universality'. The result seems to be that 'conscience' is not irrational; but it certainly is 'unreasoned'. 'Reflective conscientious persons' are 'inclined to bring' each case 'under some general rule' (ibid.).

In both cases, of the immediate and the reflective conscience alike, I take it that reason gives, or at least apprehends, the general; but the latter case is 'reasoned'; there is an explicit reasoning which brings the particular as an instance under the universal rule. Then what are we to say about the former case? In what sense is reason present in non-reflective conscience? Does reason here give a product in which both elements exist but are not distinguished? Is reason here in a 'potential' or 'intrinsical' or 'latent' state in which it gives an individual intuition? That is one view. Or are we to say that this intuition in which the two elements are not made explicit is not really reason at all? That is another view. On this 'potentially universal' would mean that you can by reflection separate the two elements implicit in the individual judgement, and then the universal element, when explicit, is apprehended by reason, though not before.[1] But which view is our author's I cannot say.

I am afraid that this discussion may appear to the reader mere verbal trifling, but he will find, I think, on reflection, that the subject of 'potential universality' calls for a clearer explanation than it has received, and again that it is a most important matter to know whether reason apprehends the individual or only the general. When we come to argue from the nature of reason to the nature of the end, this difference must seriously affect our conclu-

[1] I fail to understand Mr. Sidgwick when (27) he speaks of a view which holds that 'the moral faculty judges primarily of individual cases, applying directly to these the general notion of Duty, and deciding intuitively what ought to be done by this person in these particular circumstances'. His language here implies that the general notion is explicit, and that to some extent the judgement is reflective; but this can hardly be what he means to say.

sion. But for the present all we can say is that what is
true for reason seems in the main to be that which is true
in general or in the abstract.

§ 2. *Practical Reason*

So far we have had to do with reason as cognitive; and
now we are come to practical reason, the light grows
dimmer and dimmer, and we see little more than that we
are encountered by at least some of the difficulties of
Kant's ethical dualism.

'The real end of Reason' is the same as 'the absolutely
good' (391); but how can *reason* give an *end*? 'The Moral
Reason is a Spring of Action' (x). Reason 'dictates'.
'Reason prompts us to a certain kind of action' (29–30).
Reason has ' "a categorically imperative" function' (24).
So far there seems to be no doubt.

'Acting rationally' is acting 'from an impulse in harmony with an intellectual apprehension of an objective
rule, or intrinsically desirable end' (43). 'That in us which
claims authority is never a mere sentiment, but always
a faculty cognizant of an objective rule or imperative
which exists independently of its effect on our feelings,
and such a faculty is what we must mean by Reason' (62).
'There actually is found in man a certain impulse to do
what is reasonable as such' (x). There is a 'central desire
to do Right as such' (347).

But what does all this mean? I confess I cannot say.
Reason seems to be 'a spring of action' in this sense, that
when reason says, Something ought to be done, then
there goes with that a desire to do what reason orders. So
much seems clear, but it does not tell us how reason can
order.

Are we to say that in practical reason thought and will
are united in such a way that the object of this faculty is
no mere *fact* which we recognize, but an *end*, an idea
which in us calls for its reality? Then what need for an
adventitious desire to turn reason into a 'spring of action'?
Are we to say that practical reason is *made* practical by
this desire, that the addition of this desire to theoretic

reason constitutes practical reason? This does not seem to be our author's view. For—

'It is enough if it be granted that there exists in all moral agents as such a permanent desire . . . to do what is right or reasonable because it is such: so that when our practical reason recognizes any course of conduct as right, this desire immediately impels us with a certain force towards such conduct' (27).

Clearly then, even apart from the desire, reason is still practical, though not perhaps 'a spring of action'.

But then how can reason give an *end*? How can it 'prompt' or 'dictate' or be 'categorically imperative'? Is there, besides the desire which makes it a 'spring', *another* desire which makes it practical? If so, what is it after all which gives the end? If not so, how can reason 'prescribe' and order, as well as perceive? Is to be 'cognizant of an imperative' the same thing as to give an order?

It is possible that our author's view may be that desire gives the end, while reason qualifies it. *What* the end is reason does not know, but, *given* the end, it further determines its nature, and so brings into play a third element, the 'central desire to do Right as such'. If so, the end is hardly the 'end of Reason', and reason is no more categorical, but hypothetical, or at best, with co-ordinate authority. But I do not think this is what Mr. Sidgwick means.

The following questions I think need an answer. Is reason nothing but 'the slave of the passions'? Does desire give the end and reason calculate the means? Certainly our author does not hold this. Does reason desire or will? This again he seems reluctant to affirm. But if it does not desire and will, how can the end be the end of reason? If reason is no more than 'cognizant of an imperative', how is it practical? Is my reason practical when I read an Act of Parliament? Does my sight 'prompt' or 'dictate' when I see a police notice on the wall? When I hear the word Forward, are my ears 'categorically imperative'?

Does reason tell you what to do, or does it tell you only what you are told to do? Does it give orders, or do no more than carry them? And then *whose* orders does it carry?

To explain our *obedience* to the order by bringing in a desire for the reasonable does not help us at all. The question is not, Does an emotion attend the *recognition* of a mere fact? For in morality we have not to do with a mere fact, with this or that command which is prescribed from without, seen perhaps by reason, and then obeyed by desire and will: nor, I think, does our author hold this. In morality we prescribe to and dictate to ourselves. We do not perceive that there *is* an order, we *give* that order, and we *put* an end before ourselves to be done. And how can reason do this? If we abstract from desire and will, what is left of 'end' and 'ought' and 'imperative'? Has 'This is my *end*' any sense when desire is kept out, or comes in but to say '*And* I will do it'? Does not end mean will, and my end my will?

I can find no answer to these questions in *The Methods of Ethics*. It is not fair to our author, I admit, to ask him for a psychology which he does not undertake to give. It is fair to point out that the psychological doctrine, which (whatever it may be) he most undeniably does put forward, is either wholly obscure, or else labours under well-known difficulties which are not met, but which, if not met, must gravely affect his thesis.

The question of this section, if we put it from the other end, is, What is the relation of desire to the desirable? and that word leads us to the following section.

§ 3. *The Desirable and Pleasure*

I am afraid the reader will be tired already by these questions about words, but we cannot go on until we have asked what 'desirable' means. In ordinary English it is the same as what 'is to be' or 'should be' desired, but it *may* also stand for that which simply can be desired, or does excite desire. The latter usage, I believe, has no place in our spoken language, and even in literature perhaps is obsolete, but still it exists. How does Mr. Sidgwick use the word?

When it appears in his writing apart from its connexion with ethical questions I think it *always* bears the first sense. But what is its more technical meaning? Passages (at the foot of pp. 137, 318) show that it is not equivalent to 'desired'; and (93 note) we find ' "Good" = "intrinsically preferable or desirable" ', and again (391) we hear of 'the real end of Reason, the absolutely Good or Desirable'. Clearly then desirable or preferable = good or end (cf. 60, 133, 183).

Nor can the phrases 'intrinsically', 'absolutely', 'objectively', 'ultimately', 'in itself', be taken to differentiate desirable and good, for they are applied to both; 'the ultimate end, or entity, regarded as intrinsically good and desirable' (66; cf. 369, 391, 392 note). And moreover we find 'good' and 'desirable' coupled without qualification (95 last line; cf. 94, 369), and (9) 'desirable' is used as one notion with 'intrinsically good', or 'end which Reason regards as ultimate'.

So far we see that 'desirable' = 'good' or 'end'.

'Let then pleasure be defined as feeling that is preferable or desirable, considered merely as feeling' (118). 'Pleasure being defined as "feeling judged to be preferable or desirable considered merely as feeling" ' (xii). 'To mean by Pleasure only Preferable or Desirable Feeling of whatever kind' (372). 'Happiness, or the sum of such feelings as, at the time that they are felt, are immediately known to be intrinsically desirable' (368). Mark here *intrinsically*. 'The kind of feeling which is most pleasant or preferable as feeling' (162).

What is all this? The end of the argument being to show that pleasure and good are the same, is it possible that here at the beginning we have 'good' and 'end' inserted into the definition of pleasure? I think we shall find this really is the case. The audacious *petitio principii* which commended itself to Mr. Mill (365) is perhaps more veiled in our author's pages, but through its thin disguise we recognize the old cause of our errors, the unconscious equivocation by which desirable means indifferently, What I like, or, What I ought to like, just as the conclusion suggests.[1]

I think the reader will search in vain for any passage in which Mr. Sidgwick discriminates these two meanings of 'desirable'. In his argument it is the second which is prominent, but in his definition of pleasure he has the first in view; if, that is to say, he really does in his own mind distinguish between them. Let us see what the definition of pleasure is.

Pleasure is 'the kind of feeling which pleases us, which we like or prefer' (114).[2] In short, it is 'agreeable sensation' (33, 41) or 'agreeable feeling' (x).

So far we have seen that desirable or preferable can pass either for pleasant or good, and so is a ready means for identifying these terms. And now we must ask more narrowly as to this pleasure which is the end for Hedonism.

Pleasure we saw was feeling that is desirable as feeling, and now what is feeling? That question must be answered before we can proceed.

We hear (76–7) of a 'certain state or quality of the consciousness of the agent which we call Pleasure or Satisfaction', and this leads us to doubt, first, whether pleasure be a feeling or the quality of a feeling,[3] and second, whether feeling is the same as consciousness. The latter point is of great importance because, as we know, there is no psychical phenomenon whatever which 'consciousness' has not been used to cover.

---

[1] It is interesting to see that, in his remarks on Mr. Mill's proof of Utilitarianism, our author calls attention to the fact that in this 'desirable' = what one 'ought' to desire (365), and instructive to notice that he seems unaware of Mr. Mill's equivocation. He understands the latter writer to make an *inference* 'from the universal desiredness to the desirability of Happiness' (366); against which interpretation I will simply refer the reader to the passage as Mr. Sidgwick himself quotes it (365).

[2] I am anxious not to disturb the exposition by avoidable criticism, but I must point out that to insert the conception of *preference* into the definition of pleasure seems wholly indefensible.

[3] See below, p. 82, and p. 96, note.

Pleasure (389) is 'to include the highest and most refined kinds of preferable or desirable consciousness'.
Happiness is 'the most pleasant consciousness conceivable' (19). 'Happiness was explained to be preferable or
desirable feeling or consciousness' (369). And (78) we see
'a pleasure' may mean 'a whole state of consciousness
which is only partly pleasurable'.

Of course if our author likes to identify consciousness
and feeling he has a right to do so, but then we have a
right to ask him to be consistent in his usage. This I think
he is not.

We find (52; cf. 164) that 'passive' and 'active consciousness' are distinguished, and the former identified
with 'pleasure or pain or desire or aversion'. 'Changes in
the train of ideas and feelings that constitutes our conscious life' (52). 'Conscious existence, the stream of action
and feeling' (102). 'Conscious life includes besides actions
the whole range of feeling' (103). And (179) action and
feeling are distinguished. Again (131–2) 'cognitive' consciousness is distinguished from 'presentative consciousness', and further the latter from feeling.[1]

In short, while on the one hand feeling and consciousness seem convertible, on the other hand consciousness is
by far the wider term, and covers the whole self. We find
(171) 'life or consciousness'; and the result of this somewhat loose terminology is that instead of 'agreeable sensation or feeling' we can write if we please 'desirable
conscious life'. And this is no mere inference of our own,

[1] I am not sure whether it has any bearing on the subject, but in fairness
I should say that (164) Mr. Sidgwick distinguishes 'our faculties' from 'the
mental phenomena which result from their exercise', of which latter alone
we are 'directly cognizant' (cf. 193). The faculties I take to be the same as
the 'possibilities' or 'tendencies' (whatever they are) which, in addition to
the actual existence, i.e. 'particular states', constitute our being (102–3).
I give this view because I feel so little at home with Mr. Sidgwick that
I cannot say whether it may not be relevant here. But in any case the confusion would remain. For while we saw on the one hand feeling = consciousness, we have again 'the transitory phenomena' (which appear to be
the 'effects' of the 'possibilities') described as 'actions or feelings' (193). So
again 'feeling or cognition' (23; cf. 102–3, 170).

but, as we shall see, Mr. Sidgwick does actually do it in the
very crisis of his argument (373). Must we not say then
that as in 'desirable' we had a *petitio principii*, so now in the
wavering phrase 'consciousness', which is the same as feeling, and yet includes thought and action, and which
enables us to write Life for the sake of life, instead of
Pleasure for pleasure's sake, we have a considerable
ignoratio elenchi? I think we must say this, but we must
add that the confusion slides in in the argument, and that
in the definition our author avoids it.

Returning now to the subject of pleasure, let us ask in
what sense is this defined to be the end? The vital point
is this. Is *the pleasant* the end? Or is *pleasure* the end?
The former question we may answer in the affirmative and
yet be not one step nearer Hedonism. But if we say, The
end is pleasure as distinct from that which is pleasant, then
that is Hedonism. And our author does answer the question so. He does not say clearly whether mere pleasure is
a feeling or only the quality of a feeling, though the latter
seems to be his doctrine (76–7); but this distinction is,
I think, of little importance here. Mr. Sidgwick is perfectly clear on these points that 'Feeling cannot be conceived to exist otherwise than as it is felt—its manner of
existence is its being felt' (117). 'The pleasantness of the
feeling is a purely subjective fact' (116). We are to
'separate in thought any state of consciousness from all its
objective circumstances and conditions . . . and contemplate it merely as the transient feeling of a single
subject' (ibid.). 'All pleasures are understood to be so
called because they have a common property of pleasantness, and may therefore be compared in respect of this
common property' (78). The end is 'the sum of pleasures
valued in proportion to their pleasantness' (xi). And from
p. 116 we see that pleasantness is the one preferable
quality of any state of consciousness when considered as
mere feeling.

The end is the pleasantness of pleasant feelings, and
the greatest surplus of that to the whole creation, 'the
innumerable multitude of living beings, present and to

come' (373). The end is not the pleasant merely; that which is pleasant is only a means to the end and, strictly speaking, nothing is the end but pleasantness, and the maximum surplus of that.

This is the thesis which our author has to maintain, and before I go on to criticize it I should like to point out that we have already got the means of proving something very like it. If we write 'an end' for 'the end', and leave out 'maximum surplus', we can demonstrate thus.

Happiness or pleasure is desirable feeling or consciousness, and what is desirable is good or end; therefore pleasure is end or good. And the desirable or good must be reasonable, which means universal or at least objective, hence pleasure is an end as universal or objective, i.e. not as the pleasure of this or that man but as pleasure in general. So far we demonstrate from our definitions. And to prove our whole thesis we may add, Is there anything desirable but conscious life, or even life? But pleasure is that, and that is pleasure. So pleasure is *the* one end. Further, since you cannot distinguish pleasures by quality, you must do it by quantity, and hence maximum of pleasure is the end. Q.E.D.

And the moral of this section is that a good definition saves argument.

§ 4. *The End*

The end is 'the sum of pleasures valued in proportion to their pleasantness', and we have now to criticize this. For further remarks on the subject I must refer to my *Ethical Studies*, but there are two main points which I cannot pass over; one the possibility of comparing the pleasantness of pleasures, and the other the nature of the greatest sum.

I. And first it would appear that the abstraction of pleasantness from the pleasant, in order to the pursuit of a maximum of the former, is impossible to execute. You cannot abstract and compare so as to arrange the world of pleasant things in an order of quantitative pleasantness.

The question, I take it, is *not* whether by abstraction

you can have a science of quantity in general, nor again whether in particular you are *ever* able to say one feeling is more pleasant than another. There is no dispute between me and Mr. Sidgwick on either of these points. The facts are obvious. The question *is* (1) whether you can compare *all* pleasures in this way, and (2) whether you can compare *any* pleasures, so as to express them as quantities of units of pleasantness, reduced to the same denomination. Can you add and substract pleasures, and say, This lot will be greater, and so much greater, than that lot?

If you cannot do this latter, if you can only, taking any two pleasures, say, One is greater than the other, but can give neither the quantitative relation of one to the other, and still less the quantitative relation of one imagined lot to another lot, what then, I would ask, becomes of the 'calculus', and, with it, of scientific Hedonism? And, secondly, to come to the first point, if it is not true that all pleasures can be compared as degrees of pleasantness, if the ideas of past pleasures are seldom exact copies of the reality, if they are too heterogeneous to be always compared, and if this holds *a fortiori* of pleasures in prospect; if, again, the changing mood of the subject conditions the quantity of pleasantness in a way not always to be calculated;—then once more the 'calculus' is seen to be an impossibility.

It is unnecessary for me to enter on these objections, since partly they speak for themselves, and, in addition, I can refer to Mr. Sidgwick's book (pp. 120–30) for a discussion which in the main confirms them sufficiently. So that when we hear from him (*M.* o.s. ii. 36) that 'we can perfectly well compare a pleasure felt under any given conditions with any other, however otherwise conditioned, and pronounce it equal or unequal; and we surely require no more than this to enable us to take "amount of pleasure" as our standard for deciding between alternatives of conduct', we may content ourselves with remarking that his assertion is not only in direct contradiction with the facts of life, but is also irreconcilable with his own more sober views.

II. And, to come now to the second main head, the 'greatest sum of pleasures' is open to very serious objection.

(i) The cardinal point in my opinion is that the Good must be a whole, and that hence a mere aggregate is not the Good. The true End is not put together out of counted units, but the Hedonistic End is a mere addition of particulars. 'Irrelevant metaphysic' as any such consideration may be for our author, I hold it to be fatal to the greatest-pleasure doctrine in any form.

(ii) The next point is that, if by greatest sum we mean an infinite quantity, then that is a self-contradictory idea, which can indeed be aimed at, but by no possibility can be realized (vide *E.S.* 70, 89 = 76, 97–8).

(iii) Neither in his book nor in his article does our author tell us whether for him the sum is infinite or finite. A definition of happiness[1] (*Methods*, 19) points to the former view, but there is no certainty. If I knew that Mr. Sidgwick held to the infinite sum I would at once leave the matter here, remarking at the same time that he gives no hint of a solution of the problem of approximation to an endless sum.

But I do not suppose our author is prepared to say that the sum is infinite; and, though left in darkness, I must point out some difficulties which meet us when we take it as finite.

We may consider the sum either (*a*) as a series in time of units or groups of units, or (*b*) as a coexisting collection. I will take the series first.

(*a*) If a man is to have an end he can realize, then he must be able to say, It is mine, I possess it. And so with humanity, or the sentient creation generally; if there is a realizable end for them, there must be some time at which this end can be realized. But a sum of successive feelings is not such an end; for these pleasures do not exist as a sum, and to have the sum at any moment is impossible.

---

[1] The definition of 'greatest happiness' on p. 109 tells us nothing. I think the reader will find (on such a minor point I will not burden him with references) that Mr. Sidgwick is somewhat wavering in his use of the term 'happiness'.

Well but, I shall hear, is it not possible to go through the pleasures to the last, to sum the series, and to say, I have had them all? And have we not here an end which can be realized?

Taking first the case of the individual man, I answer, Yes, doubtless, if you think that a man's end can be realized after he has ceased to be, and that it is enough that some one else, when he is dead, should say, He has summed the series, and attained the end. For myself I hold that a man's end is not realized at all unless during his existence, and that a good which my whole life long I must be without, and which comes to me only with my extinction, is no good for me and not my good at all.

But Mr. Sidgwick does not hold *my* sum of pleasures to be the end. For him the end is the sum of the pleasures of the sentient creation, or, at the least, of humanity. But if this sum is a series in time I do not see how it ever is complete as a collection, so that any one can say humanity has realized the end by having had the sum, and I do not see who is to say it, and in fact I see only that I am using words which to me have no meaning.[1]

(*b*) Dismissing then the sum as a series, let us take it as a finite coexisting aggregate. Then the end will be that at any time the sentient world should be having the greatest possible quantity of pleasantness. In this case the realization of the *sum* lies open, I think, to no logical objection.

But *greatest possible* sum at once lands us in difficulties. What does it mean? When and in what sense can we say that I and the sentient world are having a greatest possible sum of pleasure?

I suppose the answer must be that the actual is that which under all the conditions was possible. One of these conditions is the direction of our energy towards increase of pleasure, and the total result (if the energy is so directed) we call the greatest possible sum, an end which can logically be realized wholly, and is really gained approximately. And I think, if it is clearly understood that we are dealing,

[1] See more in Appendix, note A.

not with an indefinite, but with a limited sum, that this answer so far may stand.

But if this is Mr. Sidgwick's answer, as perhaps it may be (I can only guess), yet, though it is true that not everything I have urged elsewhere (*E.S.* 89, and note = 97–8) is applicable to our author, since he rejects the Hedonistic determination of the will, for all that we are by no means at the end of our difficulties.

The end is to get as much as we can. The realization of that is the *summum bonum*. If we suppose that, at a given period of the world's history, energy has been so far as was possible directed towards gaining pleasure, then the *summum bonum* is now realized, whatever the amount of the pleasure gained. Perfect virtue thus is and must be perfect happiness, and every failure to get perfect happiness is so much vice in oneself or others. An edifying conclusion, if reached by a somewhat strange road. But Hedonism, if it accepts this result, collides at once with ordinary notions of happiness. To say, If all had done and did their duty we should all be perfectly happy, no matter how small our surplus of pleasure—happiness at the next moment may be increased or diminished, but if all do their duty, the greatest possible sum of pleasures is at every moment realized, whatever be the fractional surplus of pleasure over pain—is surely a somewhat paradoxical assertion. But if we refuse to accept this hypothetical conclusion, then we fall back upon the unlimited quantity.

I have shown elsewhere (*E.S.* 95 note = 104) that it will not help us if we take mere increase of pleasure as the end; and our result so far is that, even if the common Hedonistic psychology be dropped, and the end be taken neither as an infinite sum, nor as a successive series which must be summed before it is realized, we are in sharp collision with ordinary notions, though not at present in contradiction with ourselves.

But if we keep to Mr. Sidgwick, it seems to me that we shall have to contradict ourselves. He has not merely rejected the Hedonistic determination of the will, but has betaken himself to 'Freedom'. What he means by Free Will he has (as usual) not told us; yet, so far as we can see, in the sphere in which it holds it is the same as pure chance.

If this is so we are at once in trouble. The realization of the greatest possible sum had a meaning when we could say, Here was a complex of conditions, concurring causes (or whatever else you like to call them), and this, which is actual, is the greatest possible result from that complex. The actual is what was possible. But when Free Will is brought in can we say this any longer? In the complication we are considering, acts of will are an element, and if (as I understand our author does) you decline to say, This result which did follow *must* have followed, then you leave a reserve of possibility in the will, and the actual no longer is all that was possible. Hence 'greatest possible sum' becomes a phrase without meaning. You never can say we have got that, because pure chance is admitted into the matter, and there is no telling that the wills of the agents might not, under all the conditions, have produced something else and something more; nor do I see how any exact limit can be put to the quantity of their action. Greatest possible actuality ceases in short to have a meaning when pure chance is once let in. It is a fiction, and a fiction is not an end which you can realize either wholly or, I think, approximately.

And here I will leave the subject. It would be an endless task to attempt to anticipate every sense in which the sum of pleasures can be taken, and it is probable that much of the above may be beside the mark. It is hard to discuss a man's opinions when you do not know what they are; and if our author has ever asked himself the meaning of 'the sum', he has at present not imparted his answer to the public.

The questions which call for a discussion are these. Is the sum limited or unlimited? If limited, is it to be taken as a series or as a coexisting aggregate? If the latter, what is the exact meaning of greatest possible sum? If it is to be considered as a series, has not the series to be completed before it is realized? And, if so, when and how is it completed? Is the end mere approximation? and again, Can you be said to approximate to the impossible? Is once more the sum infinite? And, if it is so, is it not a fiction? No Hedonist, I think, can fairly refuse to enter on these questions; and then there remains the 'irrelevant' metaphysic, which I do not ask Mr. Sidgwick but do ask the reader to consider, Is not the end a whole, and, if so, can it be a mere collection or aggregate or series?

And now after this wearisome discussion, for the length of which I do not think that I am responsible, let us leave the criticism of the 'greatest sum of pleasures' and try to see how this sum can be a 'real end of Reason'. We did not get very clear on Reason, and so must not wonder if this point too remains somewhat obscure. Does Reason give the mere abstraction of pleasure in general? Then pleasure of others and amount of pleasure both fall outside it. Does it give us the intuition of a collection of pleasures without reference to this or that subject, and is 'so great' or 'greatest' included in this intuition? That does seem a great deal to ask of Reason. And then is the intuition universal or individual? Does, once more, Reason not give the end at all but only qualify it? Is both 'pleasure' and 'sum of pleasures' given as the end apart from Reason, and does the latter merely add 'objective' to this ready-made end? Then, as we have said, the end is hardly the 'end of Reason'. Does, again, an intuition of Reason tell me that my greatest sum of pleasure is the end, but tell me at the same time that my end is 'objective' and the same for all subjects? Perhaps. I cannot say.

But what is meant by the objectivity of the end? In one sense it is not 'objective', because all pleasures are merely subjective. Nor in another sense is it 'objective', because it ought to be and therefore is not.[1] It seems to be objective in the following sense. We get somehow the notion

---

[1] There are some noticeable sayings on the opposition of 'ought' and 'is' on pp. 3, 92, 94. If Mr. Sidgwick had not qualified this statement on p. 5, he could hardly have avoided the conclusion, Nothing which is, ought to be, and might even be taken to hold, Whatever is not, ought to be. I do not think this is a mere matter of verbal accuracy.

of pleasure and greatest sum of pleasures as the end of our being, and, whether reason comes in or is there already, the result of reason is that the end is objective and right. And objective seems to mean this. Strip from sum of pleasures all reference to myself, and it ceases to be *my* pleasure. Strip from its pursuit all reference to any one in particular, and it is a pursuit for no one in particular, and that means (*how?*) what is imperative on all alike. I cannot venture to assert that this is our author's doctrine, and so will not risk a mistaken and wasted criticism. All I will say is that, *if* this is his doctrine, then 'objective'[1] means 'abstract', and, with the abstraction from the desiring and willing individual, there is no more possibility of the objective being a goal to all, or imperative on any one. If it is not the end of any one in particular, then it is not the end in general or at all.

The question of the 'reasonable' as 'objective' will return on us when we try to understand Mr. Sidgwick's view of ethical science. But now we have partly realized the doubtful nature of our terms, and seen some of the psychological and metaphysical difficulties which beset our main thesis, it is time to ask, What proof have we got that it is true? How are we to show that the greatest surplus of units of pleasantness is the end?

PART II. THE ARGUMENT

§ 5. *The Intuition*[2]

We have seen what the Hedonistic end is, and we have now to prove that this is not merely *an* end but *the* end, that nothing else whatever is strictly speaking an end at all.

The method is simple. First, we show that nothing is ultimately good unless it enters into relation to conscious-

---

[1] I have been forced to ask myself the question what 'objective' means in *The Methods of Ethics*; but as it is not *necessary* for the reader to follow this inquiry, I have printed it in the Appendix (note B).

[2] Throughout this I presuppose in the reader an acquaintance with the chapter on the 'Summum Bonum'.

ness of some kind. Then we separate what is left into
'objective' and 'subjective', and finding the former is not
the end, we lastly put the 'subjective' as the end and accept
that.

Against the first step I have nothing to say, provided
that consciousness is taken to mean (as we have seen it
does mean) life, or mind in the widest sense. But against
the rest of the proof I will make at once two preliminary
objections.

(i) It must be shown (not asserted) that the alternative
of objective and subjective is tenable. Failing this, the
proof goes. (ii) It is a logical error to argue, Because A is
not desirable without B, therefore B by itself is desirable;
or again, Because A +B and B (by itself) are both desirable, therefore nothing but B is desirable. In other words,
however correct it is, having both A and B isolated, to say
B is better than A, and A is not worth having, yet you cannot possibly go from that to, Therefore B is as good as A
and B together, and B is the only good. We shall see the
application of this directly.

To proceed. We accept the first proposition that consciousness (= life) is the end of life; but we at once demur
to the alternative of subjective and objective. We say,
first, that this is a false alternative, and next, that it does
not carry the required conclusion. What our author has to
show is not merely that pleasure is *a* good or a *better* good,
but that it is *the* good and the *only* good.

To the falseness of the alternative we shall return, but
first of all we shall take the question (as we have a right to
do), Apart from alternatives is pleasure for pleasure's sake
the good? Is it even by itself good or desirable at all?

The appeal I understand to be 'to the intuitive judgement of each reader' (371). In what sense it is to his
intuitive reason I hardly know.

We know what the Hedonistic end is. It is 'the sum of
pleasures valued in proportion to their pleasantness'. It is
in short Pleasantness as the one end, all else as means.
And now I ask the reader to put this before himself as a
moral agent, and say not Do I like it?, but Is it the end of

my being, the ultimate good, the real end of Reason? Is it for me and for others the one thing worth having for itself?

That I submit is the only fair way to put the issue. How does Mr. Sidgwick put it?

'But now, when we have so far limited the application of the notion Good to conscious life, it may seem that our result is really identical with what we call Happiness. For Happiness was explained to be preferable or desirable feeling or consciousness: and if we say that all other things called good are only means to the end of making conscious life intrinsically better or more desirable, is not this saying that they are means to the end of happiness?' (369).

Now I think the reader will see why we spent so much time over 'desirable' and 'consciousness'. But it is not fair to Mr. Sidgwick to stop here. The passage goes on,

'On the other hand, it seems clear that in ordinary thought consciousness, active and passive, is conceived to be preferable on other grounds than its pleasantness.'

Our author now proceeds to the alternative we shall discuss hereafter, and puts the question, Are mere 'objects' desirable?

'But can this, on reflection, be maintained? It seems to me that it certainly cannot. Here I can only appeal to the intuitive judgment of each reader, when the question is fairly placed before it. For my own part, if I have any intuition at all respecting the ultimate ends of action, it seems to me that I can see this: that these objective relations of the conscious subject, when distinguished in reflective analysis from the consciousness accompanying and resulting from them, are not ultimately and intrinsically desirable: any more than material or other objects are, when considered out of relation to conscious existence altogether. Admitting that we have actual experience of such preferences as have just been described, of which the ultimate object is something that is not Feeling: it still seems to me that when such objects are conceived to come, not apparently or transiently, but really and finally, into competition with Happiness, we cannot maintain the rationality of such preferences' (371–2).

All I shall say at present on this passage is that it plainly does not carry the required conclusion, i.e. 'a mere pursuit

of universal happiness'. Admit every word of it, and yet
it gives us no right to say the end is nothing but the subjective. 'Better' does not = 'the only thing good'. Nor
again by showing that an element by itself is not *the* end or
an end can you prove that it is *nothing but* a means.

After accounting for the aversion 'we find in Common
Sense' 'to admit Happiness (when explained to mean a
sum of pleasures) to be the sole ultimate end and standard
of right conduct'; and after again defining Pleasure as
'Preferable or Desirable Feeling of whatever kind' (372),
where the reader will not forget the ambiguity of the
terms, the Hedonistic end is once more presented to us
for our acceptance.

'But Universal Happiness, desirable conscious life for the innumerable multitude of living beings, present and to come, seems
an End that satisfies our imagination by its vastness, and sustains our
resolution by its comparative permanence and security' (373).

I am very far from accusing Mr. Sidgwick of intentional unfairness. But I must leave it to the reader to judge
whether this is the right way to put the question. The
ambiguity (for a time removed), as at the beginning (369),
so now at the end wraps the issue in a cloud. No one,
I am sure, who himself kept the problem in view could
state it in such a way; and the crowning phrase 'desirable
conscious life' combines *petitio principii* with *ignoratio
elenchi* after a manner not easy to parallel. The thesis to be
proved is that mere pleasure is the end. Mr. Sidgwick
writes conscious life for pleasure, and adds desirable
(which *means* end) to the definition.

Whether our author feels secure in the position which
so far he has taken I can hardly tell. At all events he does
not remain there, but moves to what he evidently considers the decisive point.

'If we simplify the question by supposing only a single sentient
conscious being in the universe, it then is surely evident that nothing
can be ultimately "good" for such a being except his own happiness'
(374; cf. 378, 360, 392 note).

Mr. Sidgwick, as I understand, appeals here to 'Common

Sense', and I am quite ready to go before that tribunal; but first there are one or two questions to be asked. *Can* we so 'simplify the question'? Have we a *right* so to simplify it? And on our author's theory *do* we simplify it so?

(i) The supposition of one finite conscious being in a material universe, which Mr. Sidgwick introduces so modestly, is an utter impossibility, not only according to at least one half of philosophical theory, but also according to current religious belief.

(ii) It is simple dogmatic individualism to assume that the end for all is the mere multiple of the end for one, which therefore can be found by isolating a unit. Here again we must say that an author has a right to make what assumptions he pleases, but surely not to introduce them tacitly.

(iii) The supposition is so far from simplifying the question that it at once involves Mr. Sidgwick in contradiction with himself. The words 'ultimately and intrinsically good or desirable' (392 note) mean the same as 'objectively good' or 'reasonable'. But this was valid not for one individual as such, but was 'the same for all minds'. Is it not then a contradiction, given but one conscious individual, that his end should be objective? But, if not objective, then not ultimately good.

But if this does not hold, and if one individual may consider *his* pleasure to be objectively desirable, then the argument against egoism (see below) will be shaken if not destroyed.[1]

The only way that I see out of this dilemma is to suppose the single sentient to have an intuition of Reason, which tells him that pleasure in general or in the abstract is the end of his being: whereon he proceeds dutifully to pursue *his own* pleasure simply for the sake of pleasure in general. But I do not understand Mr. Sidgwick to maintain this.

---

[1] Notice on p. 374 the wavering view of the reasonable, according to which one's 'own happiness seems to be a rational ultimate end'. This will meet us again.

Now I think if we pleased we should after this have a right to refuse to go before 'Common Sense' with Mr. Sidgwick's supposition. Nevertheless we will not refuse. Figure yourself then, reader—your imagination, not like mine, may keep pace with our author's—figure yourself as a single sentient being in a non-sentient universe, and tell us, would you not believe in 'a real end of Reason, the absolutely Good or Desirable'? Would you not say, I can reach my end; there *is* something I *ought* to live for, and that is my pleasure?

The reader must answer the question, for I confess my fancy is too weak to realize the position. So far as I can do so, I answer it in the negative.

And now that we have put the Hedonistic end, let us look at the alternative, the true alternative, which involves no 'hypothesis unverifiable by experience'. But we must come to this through two one-sided statements of the issue:—

(i) Let us first understand by the 'objective' end something out of relation to the mind. Is this the end? I think we may say it is not.

(ii) Next let us suppose (I think this is what Mr. Sidgwick means) certain relations of our wills to other wills or, more generally, certain relations of our minds to something not our minds (371, 375), and this in entire abstraction from pleasure. Let us distinguish these 'in reflective analysis' from all feeling, and ask, Is function, apart from pleasure, a human end?

Elsewhere I said Yes to this question. I think that was rash. I can say neither Yes nor No, for I am sure now that I cannot perform the analysis required so as to bring the residuum before me practically. When I try to think what I should be like without pleasure or pain, I can find no certain result. Abstracting from these, I find the relation of my will to the universal will to be so unreal an abstraction that the words mean nothing at all, or, at least, nothing practical. I must leave the reader to answer the question for himself; and, so far as my views are concerned, he is most welcome to answer it in the negative.[1]

But there is another way of putting it which I think *is* intelligible. Given maintenance or heightening of function on one side with the same or less pleasure: given on the other side lowering of function in qualitative excellence (I have said elsewhere what I mean by these words) with the same or more pleasure—which is your end? Not which would you like best, but which *ought* you to take? Given even (for argument's sake) the possibility or cer-

---

[1] In *M.* o.s. ii. 36 Mr. Sidgwick says, 'He (the Hedonist) is only concerned to maintain that, when in a mood of calm reflection we distinguish these ideal objects (such as the pursuit of truth, &c.) from the feelings inseparably connected with them, it is the quality of these latter which we see to be the ultimate end of rational desire.' The passage illustrates well our author's loose terminology. It is much the same statement as we quoted on p. 92 from *Methods*, 371–2. There we had 'consciousness', and here 'quality of feelings'. I will try to define the issue.

(1) Does Mr. Sidgwick mean by *quality of feelings* the mere pleasantness of them, entirely distinct from every other quality they possess? If not, his conclusion disappears.

(2) Does he mean that in the pursuit of truth, &c., we can distinguish, first the feelings from the activities, and then, next, the pleasantness of the feelings from their other qualities, and bring these things severally before our minds as distinct objects of choice? If not, once more his conclusion vanishes.

For that conclusion it is necessary that, taking the idea (e.g.) of the pursuit of truth, I should be able to separate in my mind, first, the feelings from the activities, and, next, the bare pleasantness of the feelings from every other quality they have, in such a way as to be able to contemplate, as several objects, first this mere pleasantness, and then the residue of feeling and activity; and to be able to say the element of pleasantness is the one end, and all the rest is not an end at all, nor goes to make the end an end, but is a bare means or accompaniment.

I do not believe that any one can perform this operation: and for myself, so far as I can make any approach to such a choice, it does not appear to me that the pleasantness, in its abstraction, is even *an* end. Still less does it appear that it is *the* end, and that all the rest of the feeling and activity is a bare accompaniment or means. But the reader must judge for himself.

The alleged fact that we can compare all pleasant things in respect of the amount of their pleasantness, does not show (as Mr. Sidgwick seems to think it does) that we can put bare pleasantness on one side, and everything else on the other, and, bringing these as several objects before the mind, make our choice between them. And besides, the alleged fact is contrary to experience (see above, pp. 83–4).

tainty that what we call progress might entail, not mere loss of pleasure, but actually a less amount of pleasure than pain to the creation or to humanity—which is the *right* course? Hedonism tells us (this follows from p. 384) that progress is here an absolute evil, because the surplus counts and the surplus is pain. The issue, I think, is fair and tolerably intelligible, and I will leave it to the reader. Hedonism falls if the question is answered in the way I answer it.[1]

(iii) But I deny the right of any one to compel us to such a choice, unless he first proves against us what Mr. Sidgwick does not attempt to prove, nor even asserts. We do not separate 'objective' and 'subjective': we do not say, Virtue *or* pleasure, and Pleasure *or* virtue: we say *both*. The true issue is virtue + pleasure as the end, against mere pleasure as the end. To say, Function is the end, is by no means to say, Pleasure is not good. It is to say, Pleasure is an inseparable element in the human end, and in that sense is necessarily included in the end; and higher life implies pleasure for the reason that life without pleasure is inconceivable. What we hold to against every possible modification of Hedonism is that the standard and test is in higher and lower function, not in more or less pleasure. *If* any one can prove that higher life means less or no surplus of pleasure, *then* he can fairly ask us to face the alternative. We are ready to do this, but against Mr. Sidgwick we certainly need not do so unless we please.

I have been forced to repeat a good deal of that which I have said elsewhere: it would be little more than a similar repetition did I enter on the remaining difficulties of the chapter; and as Mr. Sidgwick (in his article on Hedonism[2]) brought forward nothing against the doctrine I advanced, I must consider that it stands. The result of this section, in my judgement, is that our author has not shown the greatest surplus of pleasure to be *the* end, or even an end at all.

[1] In the passage quoted from *M.* o.s. ii. 36 Mr. Sidgwick appears to deny this; but I may not understand him rightly.

[2] 'Hedonism and Ultimate Good', *M.* o.s. ii. 27–38.

§ 6. *Unconscious Hedonism*

The latter part of the foregoing section has, I think, removed by anticipation the argument from the latent or unconscious Hedonism of common morality. Indeed, as an independent proof this seems to have no weight at all. To go through the virtues and to show that they all bring pleasure establishes the thesis, Virtue in general is pleasant, and it establishes no more. To conclude from Virtue is pleasant to Pleasure is the end and virtue merely the means is surely a logical leap of some width. If you could show (and Mr. Sidgwick has not done so) that the greatest surplus of pleasure comes from what we call virtue, i.e. that no other way of life we call not-virtuous could have produced a greater, even then you have not proved one step towards the Hedonistic thesis. The argument may hold against asceticism; that is for the ascetic to dispute. Against us it does not hold. If the end is the fullest life for each with the most harmonious life for all, the most harmonious life for each with the fullest life for all, it is not very hard to see why virtue should in general be pleasant, nor need it stagger us to be told (though neither we nor Mr. Sidgwick affirm this) that what we call the most virtuous life is, when the whole is considered, also the most pleasant. I am unable to see how, if this is so, it goes to show either that one element of the whole is the end and the other nothing but a means, or even that the element of pleasure is to be used as the criterion for the element of virtue. The reason for placing the criterion in function rather than pleasure (even on the hypothesis that greatest pleasure must coincide on the whole with highest function) is that the function is definite and the pleasure indefinite. I have stated these points elsewhere, and Mr. Sidgwick has advanced nothing against them.

§ 7. *The Suppression of Egoism*

We come now to one of the most characteristic parts of *The Methods of Ethics*. It is always interesting to study the position of the Hedonist towards Egoism, particularly to those who, like myself, feel sure that consistent Hedonism must be egoistic. We will first see what Mr. Sidgwick's attitude towards Egoism is, and then try to understand the reason of it.

Our author's Egoist is the man who pursues the maximum of his own pleasure; and since, as we have seen, right and wrong are 'objective', and reason apprehends the universal, it is natural to think that for Mr. Sidgwick it would have been plain at once that egoism and morality are irreconcilable, and that to show this by 'argument' was not only superfluous but impossible.

No doubt there is a method of arguing with the Egoist in the sense of the man who takes his self for his end. Argument is possible as to the nature of the self; and the Egoist may be convinced, perhaps, that he has made a mistake. But in Mr. Sidgwick we find no hint of the kind, and indeed anything of the sort would be for him, I suppose, an 'hypothesis unverifiable by experience'.

Failing this, I should have said the only course left was to call attention to the immorality and 'irrationality' of Egoism, and so leave it. Mr. Sidgwick does not do this: he approaches the Egoist with 'argument' (391, 392 note) or 'proof' (461). And in this 'argument', which I have done my best to understand, I can see no more than one or two tautologies.

We have first two 'self-evident truths', of which each seems to be 'an indubitable intuition of the practical Reason' (371; cf. 470). These are the Rule of Equity and the Rule of Benevolence.

The first is 'Whatever I judge reasonable or unreasonable that another should do for me: that by the same judgement I declare reasonable or unreasonable that I should *in the like case* do for him' (358).

With all due respect for our author's opinion, this Rule seems to me to be a pure tautology. The right, the objective, the reasonable, is, by the definition, what holds in abstraction from 'the mere fact that I and he are different individuals' (358) or 'the mere individuality of different individuals' (183 note) or again 'the mere fact that *he is he*' (391). The meaning of 'reasonable' is what holds in abstraction from the individual, and hence is the same in all individuals. If we really wish to be 'reasonable' we must write X for 'me' and 'him', these being unreasonable distinctions, and then the Rule is, Whatever X judges reasonable or unreasonable that X should do for X: that by the same judgement X declares reasonable or unreasonable that X should *in the like case* do for X. That, as soon as we know that reasonable = universal, is surely a bare tautology.

The second Rule, without any doubt 'an indubitable intuition of the practical Reason' (371; cf. 468, 470, 472), is the Rule of Benevolence.

'Here we are supposed to judge that there is something intrinsically desirable—some result which it would be reasonable for each individual to seek for himself if he considered himself alone. Let us call this the individual's Good or Welfare: then what Clarke urges is, that the Good of any one individual cannot be *more* intrinsically desirable, *because it is his*, than the equal Good of any other individual' (360).

'I cannot regard the fulfilment of my desires, or my own happiness, as intrinsically more desirable (or more to be regarded by me as a rational end) than the equal happiness of any one else' (364).

Mr. Sidgwick proceeds:—

'But now, of these two propositions, the first is a necessary postulate of *all* ethical systems, being an expression of what is involved in the mere conception of objective rightness and wrongness in conduct, while the second is the fundamental principle of that particular system which (in Book I) we called Utilitarianism.'

The first of these propositions, I remark, is not an expression of what is involved but of what is explicitly stated in 'objective rightness'; and here again in the second the phrases 'desirable' and 'rational end' postulate abstraction from 'the individuality of the individual'. In respect of the rules we have no right to distinguish one individual from another, and this second proposition comes to no more than 'X cannot regard his own happiness as more desirable than the equal happiness of X ', which seems to me either tautological or nonsensical.[1]

As Mr. Sidgwick says, 'This seems to be as much a self-evident truth as the principle of Equity' (360). I agree with him on this point. My objection is that it is *self*-evident in the sense of having the self-same subject and predicate, and that, in short, in a different form it is the tautology we had before.[2]

We think then that our author not only 'may seem to have laboriously executed one of those circles in reasoning before noticed' (366), but certainly has done so: and when he proceeds, 'We seem to have done nothing; and in fact we have only evolved the suppression of Egoism, the necessary universality of view, which is implied in the mere form of the objective judgement "that an end is good", just as it is in the judgement "that an action is right" '—it is impossible for us not to answer, You really have done nothing, and have 'evolved' nothing but that which long ago you explicitly postulated.

So far our only way with the Egoist has been to reiterate the postulates which he denies, and if the argument is to proceed we must do more. We must make him accept them, and on paper it is but to ask and to have. The Egoistic Hedonist, who holds that absolutely nothing but his subjective pleasure is the end, advances 'the proposition that his happiness or pleasure is objectively desirable' (391), and having thus admitted that his own doctrine is

---

[1] In plain words, these rules are, What is good for X is good for X, and what is right for X is right for X. They cannot mean, What is good and right for *one* X is so for *another* and a *different* X. Right and good are the same for each, and each is the same for right and good. The 'difference' Mr. Sidgwick supposes to be constituted by 'individuality' falls outside the 'universal' and 'objective'. In saying 'reasonable' we postulate indifference to 'the individuality of the individuals', and hence the words 'one' and 'other' are irrelevant. By introducing them you mean to add nothing to the universal at all, or, if you do, you flatly contradict our author's view of 'objective rightness'.

[2] It ceases to be a tautology only if it postulates absolutely that pleasure is *an* end or *the* end. Then it becomes a mere assumption and, if any argument is meant, a glaring *petitio*. But I do not understand Mr. Sidgwick to put it forward in the above sense.

false, naturally is at once confuted and ignominiously
suppressed.

It is hard to discuss this matter with gravity. I will
merely remark that the Egoistic Hedonist who could admit
the above proposition would show that he simply did not
know what he was saying. 'Objectively desirable' means
desirable *not* for me in particular, and the Hedonistic
Egoist is the man he is by holding that *nothing* is 'objectively desirable'.

He would laugh if you said to him of his happiness that
'the mere fact (if I may so put it) that *he is he* can have
nothing to do with its objective desirability or goodness'
(391). 'I pursue my pleasure, my dear Sir, not because
I am I, nor for the sake of any other tautology, but because
I feel it and like it, while yours I can neither feel nor like.'
Would not this be his answer to our author's 'argument'?
And Mr. Sidgwick fully admits that argument is here of
no avail (391).[1]

But let us turn to the more interesting question, what
has led our author into this position against Egoistic
Hedonism. The answer is in a word that Mr. Sidgwick
dares not break entirely with this view for fear his own
ground should give way beneath him. He not only, as we
shall see hereafter, has doubts whether Egoism be not
'reasonable'; but, if his own thesis is to stand, it is of the
last importance that Egoistic Hedonism should *not* be
suppressed wholly. His tactics (I use the word in no
offensive sense) are, standing on Egoistic Hedonism to

[1] But even here he makes the Egoist say 'that he ought to take his own
happiness or pleasure as his ultimate end'. This too is surely inaccurate.
'Ought' for Hedonistic Egoism refers only to the means. Cf. *E.S.* 116 =
127–8. On the whole subject of Egoism, as treated by Mr. Sidgwick, I
have failed to find a consistent view. He not only (374) allows that Egoism
is reasonable, but on p. 391, when he formulates the Egoistic first principle
in two ways, and says that against the second the 'proof' holds, while against
the first (as just quoted) it does not, I cannot see the vital distinction. If
'ought' = 'reasonable' (80 note), and 'right' = 'reasonable', and is 'the
same, whether recognized or not, for all Minds or Subjects' (182), surely
the moment the Egoist says he *ought* to take the end he does, he contradicts
himself, and the proof holds just as much as when he says his happiness or
pleasure is 'objectively desirable' or good. Where is the difference?

universalize that into Utilitarianism. Of *my pleasure* he
wants to keep one part (pleasure) and drop only the *my*.
And to do this the Egoist must be won over—hence the
'argument'. But even if the Egoist ⟨should⟩ become an
ally, I think this movement cannot be executed in the face
of an enemy. What it comes to is, as I have said elsewhere,
Take from Egoistic Hedonism pleasure as the end, take
from morality the 'universal' and the 'reasonable', and
then argue, *My* pleasure is not a reasonable end, pleasure
in general is not mine, therefore pleasure in general is a
reasonable end. This of course is futile; and the only way
left to separate the 'my' from 'pleasure' is to postulate in
a single sentient an intuition of my pleasure as pleasure in
general, which seems to be an untenable position (I cannot
say if it is our author's). It naturally leads to the doctrine
that the 'my' and 'your' are an illusion, and that mine when
viewed under the light of reason is the same as yours.[1]
This result (substantially the same as Schopenhauer's)
could I think be deduced from our author's doctrine of
the 'reasonable', but, apart from the objections we entertain to the premises, the strict result would seem to be that
not only the differences of 'you' and 'me' are illusory
because irrational, but that also, and on the same ground,
pain and pleasure are both illusions.

In our last section we shall come once more upon
Egoism, but now we must turn to Mr. Sidgwick's view of

---

[1] The reader will find it instructive here to develop a doctrine of non-
hedonistic Egoism. Suppose the law of the universe by which it progresses
to be the struggle for existence, the reckless self-assertion of each against all.
Suppose that the individuals are aware of this law, then is it not both the
'objective' and 'subjective' end of the individual to assert himself against all
to the uttermost? By making himself his sole end, is he not fulfilling the
objective end, the intrinsically desirable, &c.? Against this position (not
mine) what form would Mr. Sidgwick's 'reasonable' take? The fact that
I am I, if I have most force, is a vital difference to the end of the universe,
and to get that end by getting the strongest to the front, there is (*ex hypothesi*)
but one course, that we should struggle recklessly. I do not know whether
any enthusiastic follower of Mr. Darwin has clearly developed this view.
It is much to be wished that some one would. If the reader will carry it out
for himself and bring it into collision with our author's 'argument' against
Egoism, I think he will find that it throws light on the subject.

Ethical Science, which seems vitally connected with his doctrine of Reason.

PART III

§ 8. *Mr. Sidgwick's view of Ethical Science*

Ethical Science does not yet exist; but it is possible. What is its nature? The end we know. The study of the means to the end is Eudemonics. This, plus 'the acceptance of the end as absolutely prescribed', is Ethics (8). It treats of the ideal to be realized and the actions which are to realize it. Hence 'its affirmations are also precepts' (2, 3).

'The science of Ethics, therefore, necessarily treats of action which to a great extent *is* not: action therefore which (we may say) *ought*[1] to be! Its affirmations are also precepts: indeed if it were not so, the distinction just drawn between Ethics and Psychology would vanish' (3).

The end, as was said before, we know. The means are the actions of men.

The object or scope of the 'science' is practical. It is to direct us to 'externally and objectively right' conduct (381). It is to tell us what to do, not merely in general, but in particular. It is to be no mere outline but a scientific code.

'For instinct varies and is uncertain, and sometimes gives no clear guidance at all: and yet we are convinced that the right course must be the same for all, and ought to be determined upon universal principles; and it is for these that men appeal to the moralist' (217).

'Its aim is rather to show a natural transition from the Morality of Common Sense to Utilitarianism, somewhat like the transition in special branches of practice from trained instinct and empirical rules to the technical method that embodies and applies the conclusions of science: so that Utilitarianism may appear only as the scientifically complete and systematically reflective form of that regulation of conduct, which through the whole course of human

---

[1] We have already noticed that this view of 'ought' is open to serious criticism. A minor point would be the question whether 'science' is the proper term to use.

history has always tended substantially in the same direction' (395–6). 'In the more technical parts of practice we prefer the judgment of a few trained experts to the instincts of the vulgar' (434).

In one word we are to have a system of Casuistry.

'For if the particular case can be satisfactorily settled by conscience without reference to general rules, "Casuistry", which consists in the application of general rules to particular cases, is clearly superfluous. But then, on this view, we shall have no practical need of any such general rules, or of a science of Ethics at all' (85; cf. 295, sub fin.). And 'we study Ethics . . . for the sake of Practice' (191).

May the rules of this system collide? Certainly not.

'In order to have a complete theory of Ethics, we require not only to make our maxims perfectly precise, but also to systematize them completely, in order that no collision of precepts may remain possible' (200). 'Such a collision is absolute proof that at least one of the formulae needs qualification' (320). 'In conclusion, then, we must admit that while we find a number of broad and more or less indefinite rules unhesitatingly laid down by Common Sense in this department of duty, it is difficult or impossible to state even the most certain of these with such clearness and precision as would enable us to determine exactly the extent of duty in any case. And yet, as we saw, such exactness seems to be required for the perfection of practice no less than for theoretical completeness, in so far as those duties are liable to come into apparent conflict with each other, and with other prescriptions of the moral code' (235; cf. 388).

For an act to be right we see it must come under one head or clause of the code, and that this cannot be at variance with any other.

'One may hold that duty varies with the individual and is so far relative, and yet maintain that it varies on rational grounds, capable of being explained, systematized, and reduced to principles' (6; cf. 377 sub. fin.).

Briefly then, we see, Mr. Sidgwick's conception of Ethics is wholly jural.

It is at this point that an interesting question, the relation of morality to law, is opened. My knowledge of the subject, I am sorry to say, even did space permit, would not enable me to enter on it. I do not know how far, as a matter of fact, any code of law can be made so systematic as not to contradict itself. But there are two obvious points which present themselves here. First, no modern code makes the smallest attempt to regulate our whole life in accordance with a leading principle. And secondly, a most important point, all law abstracts and must abstract, while morality may not do so. In morals we take a case and we ask, Is this morally right or wrong, and how far? Here we can refuse to consider no single item of the whole complication. The previous life of the man, his difference from other men, the combination of circumstances in its general character and then in its relation to *this* man, all have to be admitted in a moral judgement. You cannot say 'such and such an act is wrong, and wrong to such an extent', and then bring the man under the law as such and such a case of criminality. But, on the other hand, is not law obliged to do this? Is it not from its very nature compelled to keep to the 'universal' and to treat the whole case as an abstraction, i.e. as a *mere* instance of the law, which the case really *never* is? Is not the best administered and best law possible compelled either to leave such liberty to the administrator that practically it ceases to be law, or else obliged seldom quite to coincide with morality, and too often to come into a collision with it, which, though unavoidable, is none the less painful?[1] I submit these questions to the judgement of the reader, and if we are obliged to answer them in the affirmative, then I would put one more question, Does not this nature of law raise a strong presumption against the jural view of Ethics?

Turning now to the question of a moral code we see an alternative awaits us. Either you are prepared to give up your code at a certain point, or else you must attempt to get every possible complication within its clauses.

To accept the former is to throw the code over. Ethics is no longer 'a complete method for determining right

[1] I do not mean that Law can never try to judge the whole case morally; but I think I am right in supposing that it does not do so except in considering the amount of punishment, and again of damages in civil (are they really civil?) actions of a certain sort.

conduct' (217). Our judgement is no more 'a systematic deduction from rules' (85). And even then we are left with the question, Do not the rules collide? The opinion which I have put forward elsewhere is that they both do and must.

But I understand our author to accept the second proposition. All complications, I understand him to say, are to be anticipated in the code, or at least so provided for there that the act will come without collision under some one head.[1]

What we are going to try to show is that this attempt to get every qualification inside the code leaves in the end *nothing* outside, so that the objective criterion becomes merely subjective, and will justify *any* action whatever. In short, just as in metaphysic we see abstract individualism and abstract universalism turn round the one into the other, just as in Kant's Practical Philosophy the categorical imperative covered in the end anything or nothing, so in our author's Hedonistic casuistry we shall find that 'objective rightness', just because he has made it *so* objective, becomes in fact merely subjective. It is an old story that extremes meet, and Mr. Sidgwick has illustrated it once more.

'One may hold that duty varies with the individual and is so far relative, and yet maintain that it varies on rational grounds, capable of being explained, systematized, and reduced to principles. So much relativity, indeed, is admitted to some extent in all moral systems. But if it be maintained that two men may act in two different ways under circumstances precisely similar, and yet neither be wrong because each thinks himself right: then the common notion of morality must be rejected as a chimera. That there is in any given circumstances some one thing which ought to be done and that this can be known, is a fundamental assumption, made not by philo-

---

[1] The teaching that we should act sometimes on impulse, the 'self-limiting' power of Reason (323-4), together with what is said as to tact (202; cf. 206), merely means, I think, that we in our practice may find the clause best sometimes by not thinking of it. That the *moralist* not only may, but must, draw his code so as to exhibit every right act as a deduction from it, will be seen from the passages quoted and referred to above to be Mr. Sidgwick's doctrine.

sophers only, but by all men who perform any processes of moral reasoning' (6).

That there is some *one* thing right is false, if ever in any circumstances there can be two courses *either* of which is right. Certainly common opinion holds that this is possible, and how on Mr. Sidgwick's view it is impossible that two courses might equally conduce to the greatest surplus I cannot see. But if this is so, then the proposition 'that two men', &c., must be reconsidered.

This is not perhaps an important point, but it is as well not to set down at the beginning an inaccurate statement as a 'fundamental assumption'.

To proceed, at all events 'Right and Wrong are really objective: that is, the same, whether recognized or not, for all Minds or Subjects' (182–3). But what does this mean? That what is right for you must be right for me? No.

'If then I assert any action to be right, I imply that it would be right for any other person in my circumstances: or (for obviously that the circumstances are *my* circumstances cannot make it right) for all persons in precisely similar circumstances' (183).

This sounds well; and hearing further 'that the rightness at any rate of *most* actions is altered by a *material* alteration of circumstances', we naturally now want to know what circumstances may be 'material'. Some of these we shall see hereafter, but we find a decided answer to the general question in the note to the above page.

'It should be observed that difference of circumstances must be taken to include difference of nature and character—in short all differences beyond the mere individuality of different individuals.'

So much is certain. But what is 'the mere individuality of different individuals'? Ah, that is the sort of question no modest inquirer tries to answer. We keep to experience, and use these categories so far as for his practical purposes every one must. To ask what they mean, what *we* mean when we use them, would it not be to discuss 'hypotheses unverifiable by experience'? Indeed, in too many cases I think so; or shall we say not 'unverifiable by experience', but there most verifiable as the fictions of a one-sided theory?

We must take it, I suppose, that this 'mere individuality' is what you have left after you have got a variety of men and abstracted all the differences of nature and character. The residue of myself, after my nature and character are removed, is my individuality.

Let us take it so. But then the result which *must* follow is that everything beside this residuum is objective. The circumstances of nature and character will *not* be '*my* circumstances'. They will be material to and will qualify rightness, and rightness is objective. The act is right because it is an instance deducible from the code. We have seen the extent of the circumstances which may enter into the act, and it is now obvious that *either* we must give up the idea of deciding right and wrong systematically from a code, *or* we must provide in the code for all these complications, not only for all combinations of outward events, but also for the differences of nature and character. Otherwise we shall have only a 'subjective criterion'.

It is much to be wished that Mr. Sidgwick would express himself more definitely on this point. As it is, I cannot understand him to do anything but accept the second proposition. Let us proceed, however, to the practical application of the code.[1]

'We must observe that the admission of an exception on general grounds is merely the establishment of a more complex and delicate rule, instead of one that is broader and simpler: for if it is conducive to the general good that the exception be admitted in one case, it will be equally so in all similar cases' (448).

We see so far that 'exceptions on general grounds' are allowable, since they are not really exceptions at all, but additions to the code. How simple and how workable that code will be the reader may stop to consider. Or rather let him wait until he has read the following:—

'There is, however, another kind of exceptions, differing fundamentally from this, which Utilitarianism seems to admit: where the agent does not think it expedient that the rule on which he himself acts should be *universally* adopted, and yet maintains that his in-

---

[1] I must earnestly beg the reader to go through the whole chapter, bk. iv, c. 5, not only to check me, but to convince himself.

dividual act is right, as producing a greater balance of pleasure over pain than any other conduct open to him would produce' (449).

Here, most persons would have thought, is an end of the code altogether. But no:—

'Here, however, we seem brought into conflict with Kant's fundamental principle, that a right action must be one which the agent could desire to be done by all persons under similar circumstances: and yet it was argued (Book iii, c. 1, and c. 13), that this was a necessary truth involved in the very idea of right conduct. And it certainly seems to me such: only (as was noticed in Book iii, c. 7, in the particular case of veracity) we must admit a qualification of this rule, which importantly modifies its practical application: we must include among relevant "circumstances" the belief (supposing it to exist) that the action will not be widely imitated. In short, the Kantian principle means no more than that no act can be right for me "because I am I": if right for me, it must be right on general grounds and therefore for some class of persons: but there is no reason why this class should not be defined by the above-mentioned characteristic of believing that the act will remain an exceptional one' (450).

We are not surprised after this to find that

'the Romanist view of the economy to be observed in the distribution of truth, seems to be strictly in harmony with Utilitarian principles' (452).

And, to continue the quotation:—

'So again, in so far as the harm of an act consists chiefly in its bad example, it may on Utilitarian principles be right if it can be done with perfect secrecy, but not otherwise. On both these points Utilitarianism is manifestly at issue with Common Sense: for the very notion of the latter involves the repudiation of an esoteric morality, differing from that popularly taught: and an action which would be bad if done openly is not commonly thought to be rendered good by secrecy' (ibid.).

'Thus the Utilitarian conclusion, carefully stated, would seem to be this: that the opinion that secrecy may render an action right which would not otherwise be so, should itself be kept comparatively secret: and similarly it seems expedient that the doctrine that esoteric morality is expedient should itself be kept esoteric' (452–3).

I suppose all this is to be inserted in the code, and at

this point I will put it to the reader whether what it comes to is not in plain language this, that, taking the greatest surplus of pleasure to the creation as the end, you may and ought to use your private judgement as to the means: that *any* act, no matter how seemingly immoral, is moral for you if you have a sincere opinion that it will increase the surplus. I will use no illustrations to help the reader to understand this doctrine; but I will venture so far as to ask him to make them for himself.

All that is left of the 'system of objective rules' is this. Having judged an act to be the means to the greatest pleasure, you add to your judgement the superfluous, if not senseless, formula, And if any one else were I, it would be right for him to judge and act as I do. Then you may call the act Right and Duty, or (perhaps) even more than Duty (456). If this is so, and follows necessarily from Mr. Sidgwick's teaching, then it may be no more than an idle fancy that once and again has made us think of the Probable Opinion; it may be wholly unfair to see the doctrine that the moralist tells men what they ought to think (352), and that Ethics is practical Casuistry, take the practical form of the Spiritual Director;—but I think it is fair to say that Utilitarianism, when carried out, comes to something not unlike Jesuitry.

I have no reason to suppose Mr. Sidgwick to be more friendly to that cause than I am. But what he teaches, and what must follow from his teaching, we must take on its own merits. And at this point he may say he is treated unfairly, that these casuistical doctrines are valid only in the present transitory stage, where the morality of 'common sense' still lingers, and where the moralist has not yet (with the assistance of the sociologist) succeeded in constructing the full code. But I do not think this is what he means. Let us go on to the next paragraph:—

'Of course in an ideal community of enlightened Utilitarians this swarm of puzzles and paradoxes would vanish: as in such a society no one can have any ground for believing that persons in circumstances similar to his own will act in a manner different to that which he adopts' (453).

Now I think we have a right to suppose that our author must maintain one of these two things. *Either* he holds that a time is coming, or may come, when the means leading to the maximum of pleasure will have been systematized with all the above qualifications in one harmonious code, and further believes that the community will be so enlightened as not merely to have mastered this code, but to be able by private judgement to bring each action under the fitting clause—*or* he does not affirm this, but thinks that the relative distinction of the 'enlightened' and the 'vulgar' may or must continue.

If he accepts the first alternative I withdraw my objections. But I shall leave it to the reader to judge whether argument is any longer possible; whether we are not in the realm of fiction and apocalyptic literature; whether, after having emptied the contents of each human being into this monstrous code, Mr. Sidgwick has not been forced to postulate something like omniscience in 'the individuality of the individuals' which is left to execute it.

But if he accepts the second, then does not all that I have urged hold good? When we look things in the face, is it not moral for any one, who likes to call himself a moralist, to use and act on his private judgement as to the means which will produce the maximum of pleasure in any and every case in which he chooses to do so? And has not so far the result proved mere individualism, and the objective criterion turned out 'subjective'?

'Ah but', I may hear, 'Mr. Sidgwick distinguishes objective and subjective Rightness. Have you forgotten that?' Indeed I almost had. But let us see what 'objective rightness' means.

'By Utilitarianism is here meant the ethical theory, first distinctly formulated by Bentham, that the conduct which under any given circumstances is externally or objectively right, is that which will produce the greatest amount of happiness to all whose interests are affected' (381).

The end is the maximum surplus. The means are the actions and rules which necessarily lead to that end, according to Mr. Sidgwick in *one* way, but for argument's

sake let us say in one or more possible ways. In any given
circumstances there is one course of conduct (or several
courses) which are externally and objectively right. And
now I ask, How can this course be known? The science
of Ethics does not exist; what can take its place? The
science of Ethics, I make bold to say, while man is man
can never exist. Even if the world never altered, to have
a complete knowledge of the laws of life, and to be able to
judge correctly the enormous complication of detail so as
to say, This act will increase the surplus and that act will
not—goes beyond the human knowledge that we find in
experience. And if the world alters, then the idea of knowing beforehand the laws of that alteration and of calculating
existing data accordingly, is the mere dream of a doctrin-
aire which omniscience alone could make real.

'That there is in any given circumstances some one
thing which ought to be done, and that this can be known,
is a fundamental assumption' (6). But if that thing be
'objective rightness' it cannot be known. To say of past
conduct, This *was* objectively right, is to say, No other
course would have produced more pleasure on the whole.
To say of present conduct, This *is* objectively right, is to
say, No other course will produce a greater surplus of
pleasure to humanity or the creation. Such knowledge
seems to me so plainly beyond the reach of our minds that
I think it is not worth while to dwell on the point. Once
more I must leave it to the reader.

But if such knowledge is, I will not say too high for us,
but clearly impossible, then 'objective rightness' *is* what
we *think* objective, and we are left with 'subjective rightness'. And, in the teeth of his own doctrine, Mr. Sidgwick
himself accepts this conclusion.

'Thus upon any theory of Ethics we require to distinguish *real*
from *believed* or, as is now commonly said, "objective" from "subjective" rightness. Indeed this distinction sometimes involves us in
a practical perplexity, not as regards our own conduct (for we
obviously cannot distinguish what we believe to be right from what
really is so) but in arguing with others' (182).
'For a Utilitarian must hold that it is always wrong and irrational

for a man to do anything else than what he believes most conducive to
Universal Happiness, and it is not possible for him to do more' (456).

The difference in the end is between what *we* think
right and what others think it, and, on our author's view,
what is that more than a 'subjective criterion'? 'But no
subjective criterion of duty, however important it may be,
can help us to construct a system of objective rules of
conduct' (184).

This is what we wanted to show, that a one-sided view
has proved fatal to itself, that the attempt to make right
'objective' in abstraction from the individual, has issued in
the confession that right is 'subjective', and individual
judgement the practical criterion.

And now a word in conclusion. The reader may say,
Then *is* not right merely subjective, and is not that contrary to the moral consciousness? I think it is contrary,
but it is not my doctrine. For me, though right is subjective, it is none the less objective; but rather it is one
just so far as it is the other. It is *both*, not in the sense that
this or that man or set of men, as such, *make* it, nor in the
sense that what *is* objectively right is simply taken up by
the subjective side, and so *becomes* also (formally) subjective, but that right is a whole which is determined by
both elements, and apart from either is not itself. I cannot
further explain this here.

And again if I am asked, But does not the doctrine you
hold admit of collisions of duties and exceptions to rules,
and is not that Jesuitry? Would it not in fact be pernicious in practice?—my answer is very simple, that for
me Ethics is not practical, but is a purely speculative
science. I do not for one moment wish to blink the fact
that in my opinion Ethics must teach that whereby the
moral consciousness may be offended, and I have never
attempted to blink it (see *E.S.* 143 = 158). *But* a practical
collision between Ethics and morality is for me a sheer
impossibility, because the former has nothing whatever to
do with practice. The question for me is solely, 'Is moral

science *true*? Has it or has it not succeeded in understanding the *facts* of morality?'

The truth or falsehood of this science is not to be
decided by a direct appeal to the moral consciousness.
This is supreme in its own sphere, as the experience which
gives facts, but it cannot leave that sphere without altering
its nature and losing its authority. Theory stands and falls
by the theoretical text alone, i.e. its agreement with the
facts and with itself. It is to start from and be verified in
experience, but it is *not* mere experience. It is reflection
and interpretation; and when mere experience pronounces
on the abstract conclusions of science, then it ceases to be
experience and, becoming theory, must itself stand and
fall by the theoretical test.

But when science ceases to understand and proposes to
alter the facts, then common experience has a right to be
heard, and the more loudly it speaks the better for all
parties. For Mr. Sidgwick moral science is practical
Casuistry which, if it does *not* alter the facts of life, has no
title to existence. And here, in my opinion, the province of
non-theoretical morality is invaded, and it has a right to
speak. Science (to repeat it) is absolutely free while it is
theory, while it keeps to the ὄν, and what is called 'common sense' is simply out of court. But when it becomes
art, and applies itself to γένεσις, then it must answer for
itself and not fall back on the privileges of theory. Thus
in morals against a theoretical dissection or construction
of morality, however abhorrent to our feelings, we can
properly claim no right but that of scientific discussion;
but against any practical proposal we have a right to speak
as practical moral agents.

I hope the reader will not go away with the idea that I
wish to represent our author as a revolutionary character,
or his book as 'dangerous for young persons'. I do not
suppose there is any serious or, I might say, any difference
of opinion between us as to what in particular is right and
wrong, for we both substantially accept the doctrines of
ordinary morality. The difference is one of principle, not
detail. I object not to the things he teaches us to do, but

to the spirit and the way in which he teaches us to do them. It is not the particular conclusions of his Casuistry, but the whole principle of it, that seems to me both false in theory and corrupt in practice.

And if we consider not our author himself but his main doctrine, we must say more. Deduced by a man of practical good sense, the conclusions of the Hedonistic Art of Life would never seriously conflict with common morality. There are good psychological reasons for that. But once admit the principle, and what is to happen if men with no sense nor hold on real life, but gifted with a logical faculty, begin systematically to deduce from this slippery principle? Is this not a danger, and is it a wholly imaginary danger?

§ 9. *The Final Difficulty*

'And yet we cannot but admit . . . that it is ultimately reasonable to seek one's own happiness' (473). I confess that, prepared as I was by a passage on p. 374, and though I saw that our author was but half-hearted in his attitude towards Egoism, I did not expect this. Here it is, however, and there can be no doubt about it. But 'whatever I judge to be Good, I cannot reasonably think that it is abstractly and primarily right that I should have it more than another' (366). 'In fact I have defined "reason" so that "reasonable" conduct must mean "right" or what "ought to be done"' (29), and right is 'the same . . . for all Minds or Subjects' (182). This again has been the constant theme, and the nerve of the main argument. How did we suppress the Egoist but by this? And now why did we knock down the Egoist at all if we meant to set him up again? I must suppose that Mr. Sidgwick holds that 'reason' gives us two contradictory reports; and having used one through-out his book[1] he now brings forward the other. The previous argument then rests on a thesis the contradictory of which is no less true. If that is so, it may perhaps not be presumptuous to suggest that we might have been clearly

---

[1] There is an exception on p. 473. Cf. *supra*, p. 73, note, and p. 102, note.

informed of it before. It looks very much as if our author, after all his efforts, finds the egoistic position too strong for him, and is willing, if only it can be accomplished, to avoid the 'conflict between the two kinds of reasonableness'(374) by subordinating everything to the selfish end. The reader must judge whether, if this is so, a large and important part of the work must not be seriously modified, and whether at last 'practical reason' means anything at all.

Well, so much seems pretty clear, that it is reasonable to seek *both* one's own maximum pleasure *and* that of the creation; and the problem is to satisfy both desires at once. The question seems not so much about what ought to be as about the consistency of the Practical Reason (470–1). If the Good (sc. pleasure) of the individual is not ultimately identified with Universal Good (sc. pleasure), then the universe (471) is 'fundamentally irrational' and morally chaotic.

In other words, it is 'a matter of life and death to the Practical Reason' (371) to show that the only true selfishness is morality, and morality the one best selfish policy.

The solution of the contradiction, which brings order out of chaos, is that certain quantities of pleasure and pain should be attached to individuals, that they should be adequately rewarded for obeying the rule of duty and punished for violating it (470).

The difficulty is to show how this attachment of pleasure and pain is to be effected. Humanity, we find, cannot wholly carry out the task, and hence something external to humanity is required. What remains then? Surely, surely it is our old friend the *Deus ex machina*,[1] and anxiously we sit awaiting him: the crisis is at hand, the actors at a deadlock and we on the stretch. Vain expectation, for the days of Paley are gone by. The machine is grown old, and the god will not come to the

---

[1] Mr. Sidgwick wishes to justify both selfishness and morality. The way to do it is to show that they are one thing from different points of view. He fails to effect any union from the internal nature of each, and so requires them to be brought together from the outside. That is a purely mechanical expedient.

front, and the stage is in confusion, and the curtain falls hurriedly in the middle of the fifth act.

As to the moral and religious character of Mr. Sidgwick's doctrine I have said what I thought necessary elsewhere. What I think he should make plainer is whether he thinks the above hypothesis removes evil from the universe; how this is possible while human beings remain on the one hand so stupid, and on the other hand so impulsive; and, supposing moral evil is not removed, whether 'Practical Reason' is satisfied with that. Next, what does he mean by *adequate* reward and what does he mean by punishment? Is the pain merely to be threatened? Will that serve? Surely we are much too stupid. Is it to be inflicted? Why? What good does that do? Is not that *immoral*? And what reward is adequate? We know what coin the 'Wages of Virtue' are to be paid in, but the amount surely matters, and the rules of payment for work; for may we not after all be dealt with unfairly? I do not know what our author's answer to these questions is, or whether he thinks they need an answer. I am of opinion that, if Hedonistic Moral Theology is to stand, they must be answered, and also that they cannot be answered.

And yet we cannot in fairness leave the matter here. We should wrong our author if we took him at his word, and judged him to mean no more than he says. His difficulty, we must believe, is other than he thinks it, and it is the old puzzle, How can morality be reconciled to the world?

The hardest form of the question, the problem of evil and the moral ought, is, I think, not what Mr. Sidgwick contemplates, nor again that of the general coincidence of happiness and virtue. What he has in his mind we take to be the familiar stumbling-block that in the world we know each man *is* not happy according as he is virtuous, and that he *ought* to be so because he deserves to be so. This is a knot which more than one philosopher has called on God and immortality to loose or to sever, and we think this was the real *dignus vindice nodus* with Mr. Sidgwick. It is indeed no matter to treat lightly, but a serious and difficult problem. I do not pretend to give a satisfactory solution, but, even though I overstep the limits of my undertaking, I will offer some remarks.

First of all, it is necessary to remember that in healing an evil there is a risk of 'healing it by another', and that this is specially the case in a doctrine of rewards and punishments. Seeking to satisfy morality we may postulate that which itself is morally offensive, and I think this has certainly been done in some forms of the doctrine of rewards and punishments,[1] though I am far from suggesting that it is so with all. But I am not going to enter on this point.

I think the simplest plan is to go to the moral consciousness and ask the question, Do I deserve a reward for doing my duty? Do I deserve punishment for moral offences? If punishment and reward are taken to consist in mere pain or pleasure attached to me from without, I cannot find that morality tells me I deserve *either*. But if they are taken to mean the lowering or heightening of my private life, then I understand it to say that I do deserve punishment, but not that I deserve reward.

My bad will is what ought not to be, and the negation of that will is demanded, though mere feeling of pain is not. But the assertion of the good in me to the suppression of the bad entails lowering of my private existence, contradiction and pain. It may entail, *supposing* that to be the only way to assert the good, even my extinction, and so this may be demanded.

The heightening of my existence as *mine* I cannot see that morality does demand necessarily. Calling for the assertion of good in me it does call for the assertion of my existence. But I cannot find that it says to me, Your existence *ought* to be increased with increase of the good. On the other hand it does say, You must assert the good to the extinction of your existence, *if* that is the way to assert the good.

---

[1] Here is a specimen: 'I shall therefore dismiss my reader with this maxim, viz., our Happiness in this World proceeds from the Suppression of our Desires, but in the next World from the Gratification of them.' *Spectator*, No. 634.

So much seems fairly clear; but then the real question is, I think, not, Does morality say this? but, Does it not *also* say something more, and something perhaps not agreeing with this? Do we not feel when we see wickedness flourish and virtue in rags, This is not right, or good, or just? No doubt we do. And then must we not say that it is just or good or right that advantage should go with virtue, and disadvantage with vice, not merely on the whole but in each individual agent, and that a world where it is not so is not governed morally?

It would no doubt be possible, taking a position of extreme rigour, to call in the name of morality for the suppression of these sentiments: but that we feel would be a one-sided and unsatisfactory view of the case.

There can be no doubt that the demand for rewards as well as punishments rests on a true moral judgement ('instinct' or 'intuition' if you will). But I think it is a mistake to suppose that this demand is absolute. The error of the moral or theological doctrine we are discussing is, I think, first that it maintains in an unqualified manner that which is nowhere true apart from a higher truth, and secondly, that, by a false or uncertain analogy, it asserts the conditions of life as we know them in human society to be valid beyond that society. But this is to anticipate the conclusion.

Let us ask then, Is it just that unequal happiness should go with equal virtue? The preliminary answer to that is, *If* there is a law which assigns advantage and disadvantage in proportion to virtue and vice, then you deserve both, and it is unjust if you do not have them.[1]

---

[1] I must ask leave here to correct a mistake I have made elsewhere (*E.S.* 191 = 211–12, note). I denied that getting one's deserts and getting justice were the same thing. Of course in real justice they are not the same, but then in ideal justice they are, and I cannot now understand how I failed to see this. In fact, one's desert is what is due to one by law: it is advantage or disadvantage necessarily connected with our acts by virtue of a law. The execution of such a law is justice, and hence 'what is just' and 'what I deserve' are two names of one thing. It follows that there is no desert where there is no law; and it follows again that, *if* the highest moral law is *not* a law providing for the distribution of advantage and disadvantage, then

This is not much more than a verbal answer, and I give
it to call attention to the meaning of justice. The real
question is not, Is it *just* that there should be a moral
law for assigning advantage and disadvantage?, for that,
I think, has no meaning at all. It is, *Ought* advantage and
disadvantage to be assigned? *Is* there an absolute moral
law to that effect? And if so, does it not remain un-
executed? If you or I were the ruler of the universe, should
we not think it *immoral* to govern it as it is governed?
That is the real question. Should we not have a law to
reward virtue and vice, and should we not act on it?

I think we make a mistake if we affirm this, and the
mistake, as we said, consists partly in an unfounded
analogy, and partly in an incomplete analogy. We take
the analogy of human society, and then we emphasize one
moral law which holds there, forgetting wholly the highest
law. I will take the latter point first.

(1) If you or I were the ruler of a finite human community, should we feel morally bound always to assign
disadvantage and advantage in proportion to moral evil
and good? Should we feel bound always to reward virtue?
I do not think so, but for the present let us say, Yes, we
will reward virtue and punish vice proportionably by an
absolute law. Now I ask, *Why* should we do this? And
for myself I answer, We do this because by doing this we
realize the greatest amount of good (not pleasure).[1] But
having said this, I begin to perceive that this law cannot
be absolute. We are the servants of the law in one way; in
another way, by identifying ourselves with the highest
law, Do the most good, we override all lower laws and
become their masters. Human life being as it is, we do
most good by having rewards and punishments generally;
and again, for the sake of the good, we are obliged (for
obvious reasons) to go by a law. But then, all that being

the conceptions of justice and desert are inapplicable there and must be
overruled.

[1] Mr. Sidgwick does not yet (*M.* o.s. ii. 32) seem to be aware that a man
may be 'prepared to accept "Common Good" as the ultimate end for which
moral rules exist' and yet reject Hedonism.

admitted, it does not follow that we may never go by another law which overrules the former.

And now I put it to you, if you were ruler, whether you would have an absolute law to reward virtue proportionably, or whether you would do it without a law. If the latter, how do you justify it? If the former, then are you not speaking of what *might* be best if the world were not the world it is, but rather what you wish it to be? Does not experience show that such a law would not be moral as things are, because it would do more harm than good?

I think we can easily see that we might have a state of society in which, if the ruler tried to distribute advantage and disadvantage by merit, he would produce on the whole less virtue and more vice. If so, what is it moral to do? Surely to go on the absolute law to do good, and to override all relative laws. Surely the law of retribution is one of these relative laws.

Morality, it seems to me, not only can but does approve of such a proceeding. No rational community tries to go by an absolute law of rewards and punishments. They all exercise for instance the right of pardon, because they do not believe that justice is the highest moral law. And morality sanctions what they do.

It is the old matter of collision of duties. For morality I am sure no law is absolutely imperative except the law, Realize the good; and *all* other laws must in theory be subordinate to this. In practice I do not say *all* are, because a collision may never be able to take place, but in practice again I am sure that this law of rewards and punishments is subordinated. In fact the highest moral law, before which all others must bow, is not justice; it does not directly distribute advantage and disadvantage to the individual, and stands above such a consideration.

Of course it must be understood that I am speaking of the world and morality as we know them. I recognize no other criterion. The world of our fancies and wishes, the home of absolute categorical imperatives, has no place in legitimate speculation.

What it comes to then, so far, is this. In human communities it is unjust not to reward and punish where there is a law to do so. It is right to have such a law where by doing so you realize most good. Otherwise it would not be right to have such a law. And where you have such a law it may be right to override it. Yes, I will say it, there *is* a duty to be unjust.

(2) If this is true, then the analogy as we had it was left incomplete. And moreover, in the second place, it is unfounded. I do not see how we have the means of judging from that which we do in human communities for the sake of the good, to that which is good and right to be done in the universe. We do not, and (is it sceptical to add?) we cannot, fully know the conditions there. If any one wishes to maintain that, *because* advantage and disadvantage do not coincide with virtue and vice, *therefore* the government of the world is not moral, he must be prepared to show that, if he were in power, he could produce less evil and more good than there is, by going on a law of rewards and punishments. In other language, supposing that in all cases the self-realization of each man as such were proportionate to the identification of his will with the will of the whole—would the will of the whole system be more intensely realized in fuller individuals? I do not see how any man is to say, Yes; and, if he will not do that, his objection must fall.

The mere moral consciousness cannot pronounce on such questions as these. It sees its good and goods, and it knows its duty. Give it an hypothesis, an 'if', and with care you may extract something from it; but it is a delicate matter to do so, for, if you put your case in the least one-sidedly, you are sure to get a wrong answer. And to turn an 'if' into an 'it is' is wholly beyond it. Let me remark in conclusion that the reader who wishes to fall back on Omnipotence will find a good answer in Mr. Sidgwick, p. 469.

But from this theological discussion we cannot shut out religion. And, when we get there, it does seem that the notion of claiming reward for our merits and standing on our rights with God is a pre-Christian point of view, I had almost said an anachronism. We all know that one of the leading doctrines of Christianity is that not one man has any desert before the law, or can be justified except on his abnegation of every sort of claim. No one can deny that this is an important phenomenon of the religious consciousness, and I think it is not harsh to say that a theological discussion which overlooks or refuses to consider this fact as a fact, is a strangely one-sided account of the subject.

It is natural at the end of our examination to ask ourselves what we think of the argument as a whole. It would be idle if I said anything else than that, as an argument to prove a thesis, I believe it has no value. I can find no unity of principle which holds its parts together. Rather I seem everywhere to have seen an attempt to unite irreconcilable points of view, which has failed because the criticism, which should first have loosened their opposition, has been wanting. Hedonism and Individualism on the one side, and abstract Rationalism on the other, have met but have not come together, and the result is a mere syncretism, a mechanical mixture of both.

I make no pretence to estimate the worth of *The Methods of Ethics* as a whole, but I may say this much, that, as we have found an absence of criticism in its leading ideas, so it is far from being a complete collection of opinions on the subject of which it treats. And this failure to take account of the views most opposed to traditional English doctrine has been at least one cause of the uncertain handling of leading conceptions, and the confusion in the result. On the other hand, there is no doubt that the work is valuable; and it is obvious that there are two things in it which for some time will keep their place—the examination of popular morality and the discussions on English thought. No book, it is safe to say, has been published for years which has done so much to stimulate ethical speculation amongst us, and in more senses than one to point to a reform in our moral philosophy.

APPENDIX

Note A

Whether the sum is to be realized as a summed series I do not know; but in *Mind* (o.s. ii. 37)[1] Mr. Sidgwick writes as if this might be his opinion. In this article he subjects to 'summary treatment' the objection against the sum of pleasures as stated by Mr. Green. I shall not presume to say anything on Mr. Green's behalf, who is far better able to defend himself than I him. But as Mr. Sidgwick has mentioned my name in the matter, I may point out that he has not made any attempt to meet the objections I raised in my book. He may please himself as to doing this, but he should not write as if he had done what he has not done. I asked, Is the sum finite or infinite? He has not answered. I asked, Is the end realized in life or after death? He has not answered. He is silent on the question of approximation as the end; and if he answers the question whether the sum is a series in time or coexistent, it is impossible to say what his answer is (vide *E.S.* 88–9 and note = 97–8). If our author wishes the issue to be clear, he must first take the trouble to find out what he means by greatest sum of pleasures as the end, and not leave to a critic the task of conjecturing his views before he examines them.

So far as what Mr. Sidgwick has said bears on the general question I will endeavour to say what is required, though I can do little more than repeat the remarks in the text.

And first let me say that the question is whether we can *get* the Hedonistic end, *not* whether we can *aim* at it, and that it is time our author realized this distinction rather more clearly. Next, if Mr. Sidgwick means by 'greatest' an infinite sum, I refer him to my book (70, 89 = 76, 97). If he means a limited sum, then what he has to say seems to come to this. 'A finite greatest possible series in time can be summed, and hence greatest sum of pleasures may be gained, because the pleasures are had, though not all at once. And, again, the sum is a whole with parts, and you can have the whole by and in the parts.' (These of course are not his words.)

Now the question here is *not*, Can any finite series in time be considered as a whole with parts? The question is (i) What does greatest possible sum mean? And (ii) If the end is the realization of a series, can the end be realized *before* the series is summed? And if it is realized not before, is it realized at all?

[1] [See 'Hedonism and Ultimate Good', *M.* o.s. ii. 27–38.]

(i) Mr. Sidgwick says 'we can aim at living as long as possible, without any regard to the manner of our living; and if we turn out centenarians, we shall commonly be thought to have succeeded in our aim' (37). This shows that our author has not even seen the difficulty. The assertion that A has lived as long as possible means, I should have thought, that under all the conditions, his will being one, a certain finite length of life was possible, and that he has lived it. The amount in comparison with other men is surely irrelevant, unless what is meant is that he has lived as long as it is possible for any human being to live, i.e. that there is a fixed maximum (say 100 years) which he has reached. If Mr. Sidgwick means this latter, and will also fix a maximum of pleasures, then I am quite ready to discuss such a view. But at present he has left us in the dark.

(ii) Next, if we make an end of living as long as possible, or an end of realizing the greatest possible amount of pleasure, can we attain these ends; and if so, how?

The end of living as long as possible is surely not gained until we die. The summing of the series is our extinction; and in and by that alone can we gain our object. So with the sum of pleasures. It may be said of a man, He got the sum of pleasures; but it cannot be said till all his pleasures are over. If a man said, 'I want long life', when he was old he would have got it. If he says, 'I want a great sum of pleasure in my life', again a time may come when he can say, not 'I have it', but 'I have had it'. But if he says 'longest' and 'greatest', he is foredoomed to disappointment.

But the Good must surely be κτητὸν ἀνθρώπῳ. Surely it must be that which I can say I have now, not wait for until I am dead. Surely, again, to have had as much pleasure in life as possible is an object I never can say is mine. And is it not a mockery to tell us, You shall have the end of your being when you have ceased to be: the end is not to have but to have had; and when that comes you are gone?

Does it help us if we bring in the conception of whole and parts? Not in the least. It is the same thing over again. To say of a limited number of pleasures or days, This is part of the whole and so I realize the whole in this, is simply suicidal. For *any* number of moments or pleasures, no matter how small, are a 'part' of the sum, and the dilemma we are left with is as above. Either the end is realized in a part of the series, or it is realized only in the whole, which is not a whole till the series is summed. If the first is true then the end is *not* the sum; if the last is true *we* never get the end.

If this is not plain I am afraid I cannot make it plain. Let us say once more, The object of my life, my object in my life, is to live the greatest possible number of days. Do I, can I, ever get for myself that object? Is it not to turn my life into the aim for a success which cannot come, to make life 'Death's fool', a perpetual dying, where there is loss in every gain, and the end we live for, once gained, means in that moment the loss of all?

It is so with the pursuit of pleasure. If you will not put a limit to that which you want, you never will get it. You never will be able even to say, I have had it. If this is not to aim at the unattainable, what is? And if good is unattainable by me, is it good at all?

And now when we leave the individual, as we must if we are to follow Mr. Sidgwick, does not every difficulty become still more difficult? The series of the pleasures of the sentient world is to be a whole with parts. If the end is to get a part, then *any* part is the end. If the end is to get the whole series, the series of the pleasures of the sentient world must be summed. Then I grant you the end has been, in one sense, attained; but I should like to ask, When does the time come? And who is it that gets, or has got the end?

The end as a coexisting aggregate has been considered in the text; and in ending this note I will ask the reader to believe that it is not for my own pleasure that I have wearied both him and myself with the subject.

Note B

What does *objective* mean for Mr. Sidgwick?

(i) It is opposed to 'the sensations . . . of the sentient being which may vary from A to B without either being in error' (23; cf. 24). A judgement is not objective when you cannot raise the question of error (183; I abstain from criticism). But this so far tells us only what the objective is *not*.

(ii) There is a comparatively rare use by which it = that which I perceive as *not* my feeling self. 'Attitude of our minds' may be 'objective, extra-regarding rather than introspective', i.e. directed not on pleasures but 'external objects and particular activities' (133). It is opposed to the 'emotion that accompanies his cognition of this relation', i.e. to some law or ideal represented as objective (371; cf. 24). In this sense, however, the objective seems indifferent to truth or error.

(iii) The next sense is 'what is valid for all subjects': and at first it seems as if we might say 'what I judge to be so valid' (cf. 366), 'The objective judgement "that an end is good".' But here if I am wrong my judgement would be subjective merely, and we see that the true objective = what *is* valid for all subjects, and in this sense it seems = the subjectively necessary or normal. This perhaps is Mr. Sidgwick's most common usage.

Ought is objective; and 'this notion of "ought" . . . we may perhaps say, is a necessary form of our moral apprehension' (93). So beauty and 'the so-called secondary qualities of matter' are objective (24) because error is possible. In this sense the objective is opposed to what *we* like. It is 'an object of knowledge and as such the same for all minds', and so has 'objective existence' (5). It is a 'standard' (96; cf. 187).

And in this signification of necessary or normal we could 'distinguish *real* from *believed* or, as is now commonly said, "objective" from "subjective" rightness' (182; cf. 190 note); and understand 'that Right and Wrong are really objective: that is, the same, whether recognized or not, for all Minds or Subjects' (182). But Mr. Sidgwick means more than this by the term.

(iv) It = what is real apart from consciousness. It is the 'external aspect and relations' of an act (182); 'objective relations of the conscious subject, when distinguished in reflective analysis from the consciousness accompanying and resulting from them' (371); 'the relation between the mind and something else, which is whatever it is independently of our cognition of it' (370); 'objective constitution of the relations of conscious beings' (375). And so we have 'Objective Good' *v.* 'Subjective Good or Happiness' (377).

We see, from p. 381, that this is the meaning of 'externally or objectively right' conduct: and must so interpret the opposition (182) of 'real' and 'believed', and the objective character of Right and Wrong. This again seems meant when it is said (184) that 'no subjective criterion of duty, however important it may be, can help us to construct a system of objective rules of conduct'. And the 'objective rule or imperative' (62) may be something which is, whatever it is, out of relation to the mind.

I think it would have made things clearer if Mr. Sidgwick had been more explicit as to the meaning of this term. May I venture to refer him to Mr. Wallace's *Logic of Hegel*, p. 73?

III

IS SELF-SACRIFICE AN ENIGMA?

[*First published in* MIND, o.s., viii, No. 30, 258–60. *April,* 1883.]

I AM venturing to offer a few remarks on a very old subject. It is not that I have anything fresh to say, but I should like once again to point out a very common and injurious mistake. Mr. Leslie Stephen, in his *Science of Ethics*, has spoken of the association between misery and virtue, and of the general existence of vice and suffering, as a puzzle and an enigma. I should be sorry to appear anxious to weaken the authority of Mr. Stephen's views, since in the main I sympathize with them, and in some of them I even permit myself to feel a personal interest. On the contrary, it is because I believe rash assertions about evil to be fatal to the cause which we both have at heart, and which I may call the *liberation* of Moral Philosophy, that I wish to submit some rather obvious reflections.

When I say that I deny that there is any mystery or puzzle or enigma of any kind which attaches itself to the general existence of suffering and crime, or is involved in the misery of virtuous failure and in the reality of self-sacrifice—I may appear in the light of a presumptuous dogmatist. But my object is to point out that dogmatism and presumption belong to the man who proclaims the enigma, much rather than to myself who deny it. For the assertor does not mean merely that evil is a fact which, like other facts, in the end is inexplicable, and so is a mystery. He must mean that evil is *specially* puzzling, and he implies by consequence that he has some reason which would lead him to expect the absence of this evil. For surely if, like myself, he knew of nothing whatever which conflicted in his mind with the presence of evil, then, like myself, he would cease to find any special mystery in the matter.

Well, if so, the difference between him and myself is

that, aware or unaware, he commits himself to a statement which I find to transcend the powers of my understanding; and the question is whether I am obstinately blind or he presumptuously dogmatic. I naturally am forced to adopt the latter view.

Why should evil *not* exist, and why should *not* this or that virtuous man be wretched? You may say that it conflicts with a moral government of the universe. But, if so, you *assume* this moral government of the universe, and (I must be allowed to add) you assume *very much more*. For you feel that self-sacrifice involves injustice, and that a Moral Governor would not be so unjust. But here you quite forget that justice is one duty amongst other duties, and that a Divine Ruler, like his human counterparts, might at times find a duty which overrides bare justice. Thus, assuming that the universe is morally governed, you assume besides that the rule of justice can have no possible exception in favour of another and a higher duty. These assumptions are assuredly not so self-evident that to deny them should entail the charge of presumption.

But I shall be told that the Governor of the universe is *omnipotent*. Perhaps; but, as I could never find out what that means, I can hardly be expected to admit it as true.

If, however, the person who finds evil so puzzling is willing to give up the Moral Governor who never can be more than barely just, I do not see after this how he will succeed in defending his puzzle any longer.

He may say: But all evil, and with it self-sacrifice, are surely undesirable. Yes, perhaps so, I reply; but do you dare to assume that the desirable must be real and the real desirable, and that, if I hesitate to follow, I am presumptuously diffident? And, suppose that I do follow and do assume with you that the desirable must be real, then how am I to know that pain, crime, and self-sacrifice are really undesirable? I do not see how to affirm this, unless I am prepared to say that the world as it stands is worse than nothing, or unless again I have reason to judge that another world, better and more desirable than ours, really is a possible alternative. But for myself I do not possess such knowledge. For anything that I can tell, every possible alternative (if any alternative is possible) might turn out in the end to be *less* desirable. Of course, if you know better, you are right in speaking otherwise; but I should be glad to be shown the foundation of your knowledge. If you wish me to agree that a change in the character of our world is really desirable, you must show me first that the change is possible, and next that it would not bring on some other alteration which we all should regret. And I think I may say that you will not find it easy to perform this task.

And if I am further pressed with the objection: But possible or not possible, desirable or undesirable, you can fancy a change that you do desire; then I answer: Yes, I can fancy a great deal, spring without winter, eternal youth, and the first flush of passion always at its height. But how can I desire these unless for the moment at least they seem possible, and possible without an overbalancing result of loss and misery? And is this seeming possibility anything better than an illusion? Are you prepared to make our irrational fancies the measure of the universe? If so, you may be right, but once more I must ask to be excused from following you.

Of course I, like other men, do look upon evil as something which, we may say truly, *ought* not to exist; but then I try to find out what I mean by this phrase. What I mean is first of all that human wills *ought* with all their strength to endeavour generally to make evil non-existent. And in the second place I mean that it is *one* of our special duties (though not our sole duty, nor even our chief duty) to aim at the putting an end to injustice and to the possibility of self-sacrifice. In this sense we may say that, from a moral point of view, evil and with it self-sacrificing virtue are both undesirable; we must look on them as things which ought not to be. And so far we are agreed. But if you then propose to rush straight away from this moral duty of finite beings to the general nature of the universe as a whole, if you find courage to assume that *our* moral struggle is in the universe a rent and a conflict—a conflict which we have reason to think cannot really be there, and so find puzzling—well, if so, I admit that you have justified your enigma, but you must allow me to add that the limits of my intellect seem no limits to yours. You seem first of all to know that the whole is a harmony, and then to be sure that the presence of anything that to us seems a discord must of necessity make that whole discordant. I admire, but cannot follow you.

I am afraid that, when some readers hear a poor 'ontologist' like myself uttering warning cries about the limits of our knowledge, they will think of Satan mighty in the Scriptures or rebuking sin. And yet I feel bound to submit to their attention that very rule which first made me an ontologist, still keeps, and will keep me one: *Where you find a puzzle you are making an assumption, and it is your duty to find out what that assumption is.*

IV

IS THERE SUCH A THING AS
PURE MALEVOLENCE?

[*First published in* MIND, o.s. viii, No. 31, 415–18. *July*, 1883.]

THIS question is one of a number of important and interesting topics which Professor Bain has discussed in *Mind*.[1] He combats on this point the opinions of Professor Grote and Mr. Stephen, and maintains against them the existence of pure malevolence. And by this I understand him to mean that malevolence is not a derivative passion, but has been from the first, or at least is now, one of the original elements of our nature. The subject is one of very great importance. As Professor Bain has pointed out, the consequences of such a view reach very far. And when we consider the weight which in matters of psychology deservedly attaches to the writer's opinions, I cannot but think that on this ground also an answer is due. I could have wished that some person more qualified than myself had attempted a reply; but, in order that silence may not seem an admission, I feel called on to give a reason for the faith that is in me, and for my entire disbelief in Professor Bain's conclusion. It will be, I think, more convenient if I treat the general question and do not reply controversially on every head.

Let me say first what I take the issue to be. The question is *not*, Is there *real* malevolence? That exists and is a clear and palpable fact. It is impossible to deny that cruelty can give pleasure even when there is no ulterior object and aim. And this fact can certainly not be explained *away*; but then that is not the question. The question is whether it can be explained and derived from known laws and elements of human nature.

I must begin by confessing that my mind is biased. Even if I did not see how to account for malevolence, I do

[1] *M.* o.s. viii. 48–68. For Bain's reply see o.s. viii. 562–72.]

not think I could conclude that it was original. The double presumption that weighs against it would force me, I think, to suspend my judgement.

The first ground for suspense would be my inability to give this passion its place in human nature. It entirely declines to pair off with benevolence founded on sympathy. For we not only see that, as a matter of fact, the perceived pain of others is painful to ourselves, but we also see how and why this *must* be so. The fact follows from the first principles of psychical life. But pure malevolence would seem a thing quite by itself, a foreign germ dropped from outside into our system.

This consideration makes me biased, and there follows another which carries great weight. If a human passion claims to be original, it should show itself present in the lower animals. But what animal is cruel for the sake of cruelty? The accusation has indeed been launched against the cat (Romanes, p. 413), but in this one point that guilty animal is innocent. There is not the smallest reason to credit it with a knowledge of the pain it inflicts, or with the idea of prolonging life to lengthen torture.[1] Add the desire for play to the appetite for slaughter, and all is explained. And if further the monkey is included in the charge, then I should see, in the appearance of the passion so very late in development, a proof that it was developed and hence presumably explicable.

But I do not feel obliged to fall back on these presumptions, since the passion can actually be analysed and explained.

I do not wish to reproduce in detail the excellent remarks made by Mr. Stephen and Professor Grote, but will briefly set down the chief materials that are offered for an explanation, and will then enlarge on one important point. We have in the first place the feeling of wrong, the identification of my comparative failure with another's happiness,

---

[1] A case was reported to me of a cat, otherwise effective, who was useless as a mouser because his habit was, having played with his mouse until weary of the pastime, then to let it go unhurt. Was this animal malevolent? And, if not, why any other?

and the consequent wish to remove the latter. And under this head we may set down envy and jealousy. We may add that, if anything is a source of pain to me, that may generate hate and the desire to remove this source of pain by retaliation. Then we have the latent self-gratulation on our own security, which tends to make pleasant the view of others' disaster. And again we have another origin of pleasure in the excitement of the senses and the imagination which comes from violent sensations. Mr. Stephen has done well to lay great stress on this fact (cf. Horwicz, *Psychologische Analysen*, II. ii, § 322), and I do not see how it can be called in question, or itself in every case reduced to malevolence. When the vessel is among the breakers and the life-boat in the surf, who but hastens to look on, and yet who wishes ill? What malevolence underlies our fearful delight in the supernatural, our passion for adventure, and our love for the perilous contrasts of gambling? At least among human beings we find a genuine 'hunger for change and emotion'; and, whatever in the end we may think is the truth of it, it seems as if, within limits, all heightening and expansion of our 'self-feeling' were pleasant. Nor is it any answer to reply that pain becomes predominant when those limits are overpassed, or when *other* conditions are added.

These known affections of our nature do clearly all contribute to make malevolence, and yet there is another point which I think is essential.

We shall all admit that there exists a love of power. And by this I do not mean the mere pleasure which comes from energy put forth, but the delight in self-assertion and the wish to increase the area of our control. I am not offering these phrases as a theory of the passion, but as a description which may point to an evident fact. There is a desire in human nature to widen the sphere which it can regard as being the expression of its will. And this desire has no boundary. Now the mere existence of another man's will, which is independent of ours, is a limit to this desire, and in consequence we aim at the removal or diminution of that check to our sovereignty. How remove the limit? The limit is removed by the subjugation of the other. We must make him a material for our self-assertion, in other words, we must work our will on him. But how be sure that we do this? His submission is not enough, for his submission may be willing and he still keep in reserve an independent choice. We work our will on him when he struggles ineffectually, and when we force him to that which he most dislikes. In this way we efface him as a boundary to our power. But why not kill him? Well, perhaps he is useful; and, apart from that, killing must make an end, and the end of him is the end of our mastery over him. We have our will of him most by keeping him in the state which he most longs to escape from. In this devilish extreme of wanton cruelty we have, I presume, got as far as malevolence. We do desire the other's pain, because only by his pain can we make an utter sport and plaything of his will. But even here we do not desire his pain simply and as such. Even here there is a positive ground for our cruelty, and our malevolence is never and could never be *pure*.

This explanation may be confirmed by the reflection that torture inflicted by a third person, who is not our agent, lacks a great element of pleasantness. No doubt we here may sympathize with the torturer, and so get pleasure; but a tyrant, speaking generally, would care little to see the cruelties of a neighbouring tyrant. The malevolence which would take delight in the quiet and passive starvation of the unoffending would be an abnormal product.

Still even that disease could be readily explained. The misanthrope, to whom the sight of abject misery would bring joy, would be a man who for some reason hated his race, was aggrieved by it, and in its misfortunes felt his own depression repaired and his self-assertion restored. Where I hate, I desire the diminution of that welfare which pains me by expressing the source of my pain. And my hatred may lead me to the cruelty of desiring the constant recovery from a constant smart, and the luxurious alternations of a morbid appetite. But even here we have not got *pure* malevolence.

With the above principles in our hands we might confidently approach the pathology of the subject, but I prefer to call attention to an additional source of pleasure in evil. We are said to be gratified by our friends' misfortunes. That is true, but we should make an important distinction. The lingering disease of a friend would not be pleasant unless it called forth self-felicitation. What is pleasant is a sudden and exciting mischance. The excitement falls under a principle we have described, but the suddenness appeals to our sense of the ludicrous. Now even if we follow Professor Bain (as for myself I cannot) in reducing the comic everywhere to a perceived *degradation*, that is very far from establishing malevolence. For the degradation must imply a degrading *power*, and our pleasure would lie in thus feeling our own self-assertion increased. I think that Professor Bain would find it difficult to verify the presence of malevolence in *every* species of the ludicrous. When we laugh, for instance, at an absurd child's doll, do we do so from a latent *odium generis humani*? And, if malevolence is to be imported into the sense of the comic, are we to find it at the root of our joy in the sublime and of our pleasure in resignation?

I would add one word more on the delights of angry temper. Where this is not retaliatory and *therefore* remedial of our own wrong, it can easily be explained by our love of excitement, and explained again by our desire for making ourselves felt, and for swelling at the expense of those around us. In something of the same way we all cling to our wrongs, for they keep us for ever in mind of our rights, and we hug our hatreds since without them how little would be left to some of us. Our positive self-realization, whether normal or morbid, is still the end of our being. The devil that but denies, the malevolence that is pure, is no mere ethical monster. It is monstrous too psychologically, and, despite Professor Bain's warnings, we must take heart to say that it is not possible.

The reader, I think, can now judge for himself how I should deal with the remainder of the instances adduced; and, while admitting the difficulty of some special applications, I venture to think that the origin of malevolence can be satisfactorily explained.

V

SYMPATHY AND INTEREST

[*First published in* MIND, o.s., viii, No. 32, 573–5. *October*, 1883.]

DOES our interest in others come solely from sympathy, and is sympathy a mere consequence of intellectual progress? In the following remarks I shall try to show that these questions must be answered in the negative. They suggest a simplification which the facts will not warrant, and they would press a truth till it becomes one-sided.

Taken broadly, it is true that the idea of others' pleasure or pain must itself be pleasant or painful to my mind. It is true that I am led to promote or to remove this source of my feelings, and it is true that, in the main, I do so by a benefit to the person concerned. It is true once more that mere want of perception is a sufficient cause of defective sympathy, and that a very large part of immorality can be fairly reduced to perceptive stupidity. But I think that these truths are not the whole truth. Instead of saying that interest comes from sympathy we might say that sympathy depends upon interest. And the second statement, I believe, would be as true as the first. In what follows I shall not aim at a complete view of the subject, but shall point out that to some extent we do first perceive because we happen to love, and do not love merely because we happen to perceive.

It cannot in the first place be said that sympathy by itself *is* interest. In rudimentary sympathy the expression of a feeling by another person produces in my mind the feeling which I have similarly experienced. But this feeling contains no reference to another person, nor in itself is it even an active desire. And when it leads to desire I need not aim at the benefit of the person who thus affects me (cf. Stephen, *Science of Ethics*, p. 243). Like some gregarious animals I may turn against the being, the sight of whom gives me pain.

Thus sympathy is not interest; and on the other hand we can have interest without any sympathy. The condition of something other than ourselves may be pleasant or painful, although we do not sympathize. Let me endeavour to explain this.

We are sorry when we see the daisies mown or the trees cut down, and we take an interest in many inanimate objects. But do we sympathize? For trees and flowers we to some extent do feel, but can most of us feel for a book or a house? The illusion is possible, but does it always exist? When the bird cleaves to its eggs and the cat to its den, when the child bewails his broken toy, and the workman groans over the spoiling of his work, when the loss of common articles, if long-possessed, can vex us, and when the mere alteration of places that we love makes us wish for the old scene—is there everywhere here a latent sympathy? Such an explanation would surely in the end prove over-strained. But if so, we may have interest when sympathy is absent.

Is this fact inexplicable? So far from being so, it is even a psychological necessity; and, if we could not love without sympathy, our whole nature would have been changed. We shall agree, I think, that to feel pleasure in one's own welfare, and pain at one's own loss, is possible without sympathy. Well, what is this 'self' in which we take an interest? Is it confined to the sensitive parts of our body? May not rather our idea of that which is our 'self' include anything which is immediately connected with our well-being? We might say that the 'self' in which we feel interested is the world of our habitual sources of pleasure. And when anything we regard as such a source is damaged, we feel that our personal existence is lowered, and are at once concerned to protect or recover. I cannot indeed see how this fact should be otherwise.

Thus interest precedes sympathy, is possible without it, and does not always rest on it. But when we pass to our interest in animate beings, then sympathy will come in. For we cannot have regard for the feelings of others unless we perceive those feelings, and we cannot perceive them unless in some measure we ourselves feel them. And here at least it may be contended that perception comes first, and that the process is primarily intellectual. Here at least, we may be told, it is defective understanding that is the cause of our deficient sympathy.

But even this contention I cannot admit. I do not doubt the validity of the process described. The mere intellectual apprehension of another's pleasure is assuredly an actual emotional fact, and that emotion must in the main cause an interest in the welfare of the other person. This account will cover a great part of the phenomena, but it will not cover them all. For the interest need not come from and depend upon the perception, while on the other hand the perception may depend upon the interest.

The first point I have explained. When our pleasure or pain is identified with an object, we desire the continuance or cessation of that object; and our desire is so far free from sympathy. The mother is an object of desire to the child before he can know that she feels pleasure or pain. And when this knowledge has come in, I see no reason to suppose that it makes such a simple affection impossible. But if so, speaking broadly, our sympathy might more depend on our attachment than our attachment on our sympathy. And we may remember that selfishness and defective sympathy are not *always* concomitant, nor again do their opposites always go together.

But—to come to the second point—even where they coincide, and where our interest in others seems proportionate to our intellectual apprehension of their state, even here I must pause and must raise a doubt. You tell me that I sympathize because I perceive, but *why do I perceive?* When C is in pain, why does A's mind dwell on this, while B remains blind or inattentive? Can we say that it is simply because B is stupid? Is it true that the most clever persons are the most sympathetic, and the most sympathetic the most clever generally? Experience shows the opposite. Take, for example, our present interest in the lower animals as compared with that felt by our fathers and grandfathers. The change is striking, but I do not see how it can be simply set down to general growth of intellect. It would be as true to say we are now less obtuse because our sympathies are wider, as to assert that these are wider because we are more clever. And if in answer I am told 'not more clever *generally* but in this *one* respect', that reply is an admission. Why in this one respect if there is no special reason, and what is this special reason?

Let us state the question thus. Granted that, if my attention is fixed upon the misery of others, that will lead me (speaking generally) to regard them with an active interest in their welfare—granted this, why does A's attention keep fixed while B's fails and wanders? Is it not often because A takes an interest while B takes none? And what is this interest? Is it purely theoretical? We cannot say that. Apart from the doubt (which I do not entertain) as to the existence of *any* pure theoretical interest, it is certain that at first the direction of our mind is wholly practical. At an early stage there *is* no attention save practical interest. But if sympathy, to be active, involves attention, while attention itself comes from practical feeling, is it not clear that our regard for others' welfare does not *always* in the end depend upon intellect? If so, the doctrine we criticize has proved one-sided. It is a simplification which would shut out of view one great part of our nature.

We might learn something on this point by considering the development of the lower animals. Are sympathy and affection proportional to intelligence? Are 'clever' and 'affectionate' inseparable qualities? The example of ants and bees would not support an affirmative answer. Co-operative societies perhaps may exist before intelligent sympathy is even possible. But at any rate it is clear that in sympathy we have not got the sole root of morality. If it is right to affirm, Without sympathy no interest, it is as right to affirm, Without interest no sympathy. I believe *neither* would be accurate.

A further consideration of these points would, I venture to think, make the instructive discussion in Mr. Stephen's pages still more instructive.

VI

CAN A MAN SIN AGAINST KNOWLEDGE?

[*First published in* MIND, O.S., ix, No. 34, 286–90. *April,* 1884.]

THERE is an old paradox which at some time we must all have encountered. That no one sins willingly, and that vice is ignorance, must at some time have been offered to us all as gospel. And most of us, I presume, have long ago concluded that a truth has here been pressed into a falsehood. We naturally reflect that, as for the artist beauty rules the universe and is the dominant reality, so for the reasoning philosopher reason is the king and master both of the world and of the soul. And we have persuaded ourselves that such prepossessions lead to conflict with fact. For not only may the ruler at times be absent, but even if he is present, yet appetite defies him, and, with no cloak of ignorance, sins wilfully and knowingly in the master's sight.

I cannot think that our persuasion is false. For me, too, the old gospel has joined the museum of one-sided growths, and, with 'the practical reason', has been placed on the shelf of interesting illusions. I would not seek to revive them; but, on the contrary, my object is to remove a hindrance to their well-earned repose. There is a psychological doubt which remains unsatisfied, and serves as the foundation for a serious mistake. Our experiences seem discrepant. For myself, and in my own mind, I am able to verify the presence of wrong-doing in the face of and despite the voice of conscience. I feel sure of this fact, but others are not certain, while others again within their experience are certain of the opposite. They assure me that never until conscience has slumbered, never until for the moment they have forgotten the quality of their act, are they able to give way to an immoral impulse.

It is not likely that any of us are quite mistaken about the fact. When an observer tells us that with him bad action never coexists with present knowledge, that an actual consciousness of its immorality is incompatible with the victory of any desire, we may be sure that he is not wholly in error. He has observed a fact, but observed it wrongly; and our task is to show that his mistake has come from a view that is partial, and an interpretation that is erroneous.

Perhaps the most convenient way of pointing out the root of the error will be for me to invent a defence, which will show what I think is the source of the delusion. And if I dwell upon truths which we all understand, I may excuse myself by observing that, if all of us understand them, nearly all of us make mistakes because we disregard them.

What defence can we find for the doctrine that knowledge excludes wrong action? We are not forced to invoke the obsolete primacy of the 'practical reason': we may move to the ground of a saner psychology and may rest upon fact. For we may urge, 'No one knows an act to be wrong unless he has an idea of the wrongness. But if this be admitted, observe what follows: the *idea* of wrong implies the *feeling* of wrong. And this consequence is certain; for our ideas, we know, are representative signs, and to perceive the signification without the presence of the whole sign is quite impossible. Thus when you have in your mind the idea of a horse or a cow or a bad action, you possess a present image, part of which you neglect, and part of which you take as your meaning, and use as the idea of something not present but represented. But now what is it that could represent a horse but something present in the form of a horse-image? And what is it again that could be the idea of a moral or of an immoral act, unless it were something present to the mind in one of these qualities? But to be present to the mind as moral or immoral implies a feeling of right or wrong. What represents, and is used as the idea of the act, must therefore imply a corresponding emotional element. If so, however, the conclusion seems proved; for since what represents right or wrong is emotional, it therefore, because it is emotional, will work. It will not indeed work as the idea of something else, but it will work as the actual present state. It will be the badness that is *felt*, and not the badness that is *thought*, which will have power to move us. In other words, it is the whole sign that is active, and not the mere signification. But this will make no difference. Since you cannot represent the wrong that is signified without the present image which is felt as wrong, the knowledge of vice must thus be *per accidens* a dislike of viciousness, and this felt aversion, psychologically implied in all ideas of immorality, will fetter the will, until, with the knowledge, the feeling disappears.

'And we may support this defence by an appeal to the general theory of motives. A motive, if that means the *object* of our desire or aversion, must be the idea of something pleasant or painful. And thus (I have argued in my *Ethical Studies*), if the motive is the end and is so an idea, then what moves is never the motive as such. But on the other hand the motive will move *per accidens*. For an idea implies a representative state of mind, and that state of mind must have present existence as a psychical phenomenon. The state which represents something pleasant or painful must furthermore itself *be* pleasant or painful. The idea will thus indirectly imply a feeling, and in this indirect way a motive will move.

'And by this we may not only support our paradox, but may prop up, besides, another doctrine. To suppose that what promises to be most pleasant must always move us, we know is a mistake, because the promised is an idea, while the mover is feeling. But since the future prospect of the most pleasant could not be represented to us in idea, unless there were a feeling which served as the sign, hence, through this feeling and *per accidens*, the promise will move, and, *per accidens* again, the promise of the most pleasant will move us the most.'

Such is the defence which we may place in the mouth of our failing paradox, and this defence, though erroneous, still is based on a solid foundation. The reader may refuse to follow us through these psychological subtleties, but I am sure that any one who is not at home in them is threatened by errors from every side.

The defence we have put forward amounts to this: an idea not only represents something else beside itself, but is in itself an existing phenomenon, and in this capacity does psychological work. And hence the idea of immorality will be felt as an actual painful fact, and so will repel; while, again, the idea of the greatest pleasure will be felt as most pleasant, and so must attract.

The mistake that is made here is tolerably simple. It is true that the idea of a pleasure or a wrong act must imply a feeling, and that this feeling will do *some* work. But it is not true that the feeling need determine the will to avoid or pursue the object of the idea. This is perfectly obvious, and our experience of the contest of discrepant impulses puts it beyond doubt. What is felt pleasant or painful will determine us or not, according as it stands to our whole state of desire. We need ask no hard questions about the nature of desire, but may state the matter thus. Admitting that pleasure and pain are what move us, it is still not mere pleasure nor again mere pain, that determines the movement. It is the greatest felt pleasure, or the balance of pleasure or pain, that will succeed. And hence obviously, when we ask if a feeling will *work*, the question is a question of that feeling's intensity, and a question of its *comparative* intensity.

We shall agree, I hope, that the above is obvious; but it gives us a key to the puzzle before us. When an observer maintains that he cannot act against a wakeful conscience, what happens in his mind, I think, is this. He has fixed his attention upon the wrongful quality of the act, and that fixing of the attention has important results. In the first place it is exclusive; that is, it keeps out *other* ideas, and so removes the conflicting influence of *their* feelings. In the second place (I do not ask how these two functions are connected) the attention strengthens; that is, through attention the idea becomes clearer, and the images and feelings involved in that idea become also stronger; so that to resist such an isolated and heightened prompting is now impossible. Hence, if our observer were to say, 'When I realize with vividness the immorality of my act, I cannot, while I do so, go on to commit it', I think that his statement would be quite correct. It would be in accordance both with sound psychology and with the evidence of fact.

But such a modified statement would fail to carry the required conclusion. It would not show that, when my conscience is aroused, I am unable then to oppose it and defeat it. For, in the first place, when we have before us the idea of a bad act, our attention need not be concentrated upon this one element of our whole state of mind. On the contrary, we may try to observe indifferently all the discordant factors of our complex condition; and, if we do this, our idea of the immorality of the act will not gain any *relative* increase of strength. And again, and in the second place, there is a very great difference between ideas. Some are highly *symbolic*, and in this case their effect on the imagination and feelings is comparatively weak.

I will try to explain this second point. Suppose, for example, I have thought of something pleasant, and then am asked to think of something *twice* as pleasant. I am able to perform this in more ways than one. I may retain the pleasant image which I already have, and which has furnished me with my idea of the represented pleasure; I may increase the pleasantness of that pleasant image, and may use this increase as a sign of something that is twice as pleasant. In this case we might roughly and inaccurately say that what *represents* twice the pleasure is itself actually felt to be doubly pleasant. But I may take another course: I need not try to double my pleasant image, but may qualify it from outside by another and a foreign image of quantity. That is, I may call up an image of something *not* pleasant, which is increased twofold, and I may use this as a sign to stand for *twice*; and adding this from the outside to my idea of something pleasant, I may so indirectly acquire the idea of what is doubly pleasant. In this case I do not say that the effect on the feelings and on the imagination will vanish wholly, but I am sure we shall agree that it will be much diminished.

The point is so important that I perhaps may be allowed another illustration. I have the image of a horse before my mind, and I want to think of a hundred horses. Now, to do this, I need not try to have before me a hundred horse-images, but may apply the idea of a hundred from else-where. No doubt, this idea of a hundred times must rest upon *some* present image, but there is no sort of reason why it should rest on the obscure image of a hundred horses. In the same way, if I desire to think of a horse one hundred times as large as the first, I need not struggle to magnify my present horse-image. I may employ some *other* obscure image, take from that the idea of hundred-foldness, and employ this to modify my idea of a horse.

And we may strengthen our position by a familiar experience. We all know that as a rule it is impossible to recall either vivid pleasures or vivid pains. But it would be wrong to say that I have not the knowledge that my pleasure or my pain was very great. I do know this; but I know it discursively and by the intellectual addition of the idea of intensity to my idea of the feeling. And hence the effect on the imagination and emotions may be very weak; it may serve in temptation but to sour the pleasure without preventing the sin. In a corrupted state, where the passions are enfeebled and where cruel experience has opened the eyes without changing the heart, we may find the condition described by Lamb, 'the sin and the suffer-ing co-instantaneous, or the latter forerunning the former, remorse preceding action'.

The result of this is that the idea of a greater pleasure need not in itself be felt as more pleasant, nor the idea of a greater pain as more painful. The increase of feeling, if it takes place at all, need take place in no proportion to the increase thought of. This again must be true of the idea of wrong-doing. I may qualify my idea of a certain act by the addition of immorality, but I may transfer that addition from another and wholly separate image. In this case my knowledge that an act is bad does not rest on an image of the act as bad. It consists primarily in the intellectual use of a symbol, and the secondary effect on the imagination and the feelings may be almost inappreciable.

Our ethical paradox, if true at all, will be true only of a mind which is confined to intuition; and such a mind is not known to exist, except at an *early* stage of evolution. But any mind, which can abstract and reflect and reason discursively, will be able to think of an act as being wrong, and yet the feeling of that act's wrongness may not pass beyond an ineffective minimum. It is only where the attention is concentrated upon the quality of the act, and even then it is only where the act in its wrongful quality is present as a vivid imagination, that the conscience will be irresistible. It is not knowledge, it is a relative degree of feeling excited by a certain kind of knowledge, that coerces the appetite.

This, I think, will furnish us with a partial justification of our paradox, and it also may serve as its final refutation.

VII

SOME REMARKS ON PUNISHMENT

[*First published in* THE INTERNATIONAL JOURNAL OF ETHICS, April, 1894.]

THAT the doctrines connected with the name of Mr. Darwin are altering our principles has become a sort of commonplace. And moral principles are said to share in this general transformation. Now, to pass by other subjects, I do not see why Darwinism need change our ultimate moral ideas. It will not modify our conception of the end, either for the community or the individual, unless we have been holding views which long before Darwin were out of date. As to the principles of ethics I perceive, in short, no sign of revolution. Darwinism has indeed helped many to a truer conception of the end, but I cannot admit that it has either originated or modified that conception.

And yet in ethics Darwinism after all may perhaps be revolutionary. It may lead not to another view about the end, but to a different way of regarding the relative importance of the means. For in the ordinary moral creed those means seem estimated on no rational principle. Our creed appears rather to be an irrational mixture of jarring elements. We have the moral code of Christianity, accepted in part and in part rejected practically by all save a few fanatics. But we do not realize how in its very principle the Christian ideal is false. And when we reject this code for another and in part a sounder morality, we are in the same condition of blindness and of practical confusion. It is here that Darwinism, with all the tendencies we may group under that name, seems destined to intervene. It will make itself felt, I believe, more and more effectually. It may force on us in some points a correction of our moral views, and a return to a non-Christian and perhaps a Hellenic ideal. I propose to illustrate here these general statements by some remarks on Punishment.

Darwinism, I have said, has not even modified our idea of the Chief Good. We may take that as the welfare of the community realized in its members. There is, of course, a question as to the meaning to be given to welfare. We may identify that with mere pleasure, or again with mere system, or may rather view both as inseparable aspects of perfection and individuality. And the extent and nature of the community would once more be a subject for some discussion. But we are not forced to enter on these controversies here. We may leave welfare undefined, and for present purposes need not distinguish the community from the state.[1] The welfare of this whole exists, of course, nowhere outside the individuals, and the individuals again have rights and duties only as members in the whole. This is the revived Hellenism—or we may call it the organic view of things—urged by German Idealism early in the present century.

Now this conception of the end, it seems to me, is not affected by Darwinism; but the case is altered when we come to consider the elements and means. For Darwinism has much to tell us about the conditions of welfare. We are all agreed that the community, though it may have grown naturally to be what it is, should now more or less consciously regulate itself, and deliberately play its own Providence. As to the manner and the amount of this interference we are not at one, but as to its necessity in principle there is no real disagreement. But, if the survival and progress of the race have been due to certain causes, these same causes can hardly now have become not worth considering. If, that is, a foreign Providence has led us, so to speak, hitherto by a certain rule, when we are our own guides and masters are we forthwith to ignore its method? So far as there is a presumption, that surely points to a very different conclusion. I do not mean that it is right for us now consciously to adopt unchanged the old unconscious mode of progress. For it is not possible to

---

[1] The above view, in my opinion, is not wholly true. It is, however, true enough, I think, to serve the purpose of this article, and so far as any corrections are required in the conclusions, the reader can introduce them.

return to an unreflecting condition, and again no community could allow within itself an unchecked struggle
for existence. But when we modify and depart from the
workings of natural selection, I urge that we ought at least
to proceed on some kind of principle. We ought not
thoughtlessly to disregard the old conditions of welfare,
but where we supersede these we should know what is to
operate in their stead. The laws of past progress must, I
admit, be qualified through progress itself, but it is not
likely that these laws have become wholly invalid. And,
at any rate, to assume this without ground seems plainly
absurd. But in our morals and politics this absurdity is
dominant. We do not deny that progress has been made
largely by natural selection, and we must admit that in
this process the extinction of worse varieties is essential.
It is clear again that with this struggle and this extinction
the community now interferes. Thus the method which
in the past *has* succeeded is more or less modified. But if
we ask on what principle it is changed, and what is to
serve in its place, we find no rational answer. The competition *à outrance* has been checked, and under artificial
conditions we seem to sanction a struggle between rival
fertilities. We compel the higher type, it may be, to stand
by helpless and to be outbred by the weaker and lower,
and we force it to contribute itself to the process of its own
extrusion.[1] We lay an irrational stress on the education of
the individual, we emphasize the less important and the
more doubtful teaching of Darwinism. But on the main
point, the suppression of undesirable types, we appear
ready to entrust our destinies to Providence. Yet we are
called on, we know, ourselves to be a Providence to our-

---

[1] It is no good answer to urge the infertility of the criminal class. The
only good answer would be to show that the higher type is everywhere so
much the more fertile that this superiority alone ensures its prevalence. And
such a contention surely would be ridiculous. I certainly include Mr.
Spencer among those who irrationally interfere with natural selection. The
limits he would set to competition seem arbitrarily fixed. The old metaphysical doctrine of the individual's rights—a doctrine which became
obsolete early in this century—can hardly to-day be considered a rational
principle.

selves. And we ourselves deliberately, we know, make frustrate the old providential working.

What has succeeded has not been merely superior fertility. The stronger in other points has used his strength to drive the inferior out of existence. He has certainly not been forced at his own cost to protect that inferior from the natural doom of its defects. And surely the presumption is that what has prospered will continue to prosper. But where is the view of politics which fails to interfere with these past conditions of success? And where is the view which interferes on any consistent principle? But, if so, on perhaps the supreme problem of politics our general frame of mind must be called deplorable. It is full of blindness, cowardice, superstition, and confusion unspeakable. Indeed, one's main consolation must be that perhaps in practice after all things have got to go blindly. But, however that may be, it is not the concern of this paper to deal in general with progress. Assuming here that the welfare of the community is the highest end and law, and assuming that selection among varieties is necessary to that welfare, I intend briefly to apply these ideas to the subject of punishment.

Darwinism, we may presume, should modify the view which we take of punishment. This does not mean that any of our old doctrines need quite be given up. The educational, the deterrent, and the retributive view may each retain, we may rather presume, a certain value. But all of these, it seems, must be in part superseded. They must be made subordinate to another and a higher law— what we may call the principle of social surgery. The right and the duty of the organism to suppress its undesirable growths is the idea of punishment directly suggested by Darwinism. It is an old doctrine which has but gained fresh meaning and force. And its principle is the old principle and the one ground for any sound theory of punishment. The moral supremacy of the community, its unrestricted right to deal with its members, is the sole basis on which rational punishment can rest.

But, if so, how does Darwinism alter our views and

threaten moral revolution? It tends, in a word, to break the connexion between punishment and guilt. This connexion, clearly or obscurely, confusedly or explicitly, is still maintained by well nigh every theory of punishment. The union of these ideas is in fact so rational and strong that in the end perhaps we have no choice but to respect it nominally. While widening the idea and the thing, we might confine the name of punishment to that surgery which seems retributive. But the retributive principle, the absolute restriction of punishment to crime, is the very centre of the position threatened by Darwinism. We have here the main root of that confusion which now obscures the subject. And in passing on to consider some current doctrines I need pay little or no regard to any other principle. Hence I shall at once criticize the retributive view under two forms, a normal and a diseased growth. Guilt and punishment in both of these doctrines are connected necessarily. The first accepts and justifies this essential connexion, while the second attempts to reject it. But rejection and acceptance in the end stand on precisely the same ground. Crime by the perverted view is regarded as *mere* disease, while disease itself is still treated as *only* disease, and therefore to be respected (as hitherto) because it is *not* criminal. I will proceed to explain this statement.

Let us first examine the normal form of the retributive view. We must here distinguish two aspects, a positive and a negative. The first of these declares punishment to be essentially the supplement of guilt, while the second asserts that apart from guilt individuals are sacred. Now, on its positive side I still hold to the retributive principle. The doctrine that punishment is moral reaction, the reaction of the moral organism against a rebellious member —this doctrine, so far as it goes, seems quite satisfactory. And there is little of what I urged years ago,[1] whether in its favour or against its inappreciative critics, that I would scruple to repeat. But then this retributive view pure and simple will not work. For practice, if taken by itself, it is too narrow, and even in itself it labours under intrinsic

[1] *E.S.*, 1876.

difficulties. These latter (to take them first) arise from the doubtfulness of every moral valuation. If you are to estimate morally, then, in proportion as the moral standard grows more inward, the genuine facts become inaccessible. And it becomes less and less possible anywhere to measure exactly moral responsibility. But with a more external standard again you are threatened from the other side. You are left in doubt if your estimate is genuinely moral.[1] And in particular you have to struggle with the task of drawing in each case a line between wilful badness and unwilled disease. Such internal difficulties are a serious hindrance to retribution. If you can acquire the right to punish only by proving moral crime, it seems hard to be sure that this right is really secured. Thus the principle is good, but its application is seriously embarrassed. And partly for this reason we do not usually attempt to apply the principle pure and simple. In practice having secured, as we believe, the right to punish, we give weight also to other considerations. We modify our sentence with an eye to the general good. We make an example, or, on the other hand, we let mercy or policy more or less abridge strict justice. But with this the retributive principle has ceased to be absolute. Punishment has ceased to be essentially an affair of justice, and we have been forced to recognize a superior duty to be unjust. We have not, indeed, given up the idea of retribution and desert, but we have made it secondary and subject to the chief end of the general welfare.

And the negative side also of retribution must suffer the same fate. To punish any except the guilty was wrong because unjust. But how will it be when justice is but an inferior and subordinate duty? It is obviously unjust to remove members not morally culpable on the simple ground that their removal is good for the organism. But then it was unjust before to punish any one in any degree more or less with a view to secure the general good. We cannot, in short, play fast-and-loose with the supremacy of

---

[1] On this difficulty see some further remarks in my *Appearance and Reality*, pp. 381 [= 431] et seq.

justice. And having once set that down to be an inferior and subordinate principle, we cannot then attempt on any point to take it as absolute. To remove the innocent is unjust, but it is not, perhaps, therefore in all cases wrong. Their removal, on the contrary, will be right if the general welfare demands it. The negative side of justice proves, in short, no stronger than its positive side. And the sacred rights of innocence have become a thing conditional. They exist, so far as the rule of justice is not overruled, and they are intact, if anywhere, there where punishment corresponds to desert. But, where the good of the whole may call for moral surgery, mere innocence is certainly no exemption or safeguard. We may doubt if such cutting-off without crime can fairly be called punishment, but, the thing being justified, I will not pause to consider the name. It is better to ignore a question which does not seem to affect our main result.

We have now considered the normal form of the retributive view, and we have found that its validity is merely relative. Justice, in other words, is but a subordinate principle of Ethics. And on its negative side also the principle is not absolute. To remove the innocent may everywhere perhaps be wrong, but you cannot urge this barely on the ground that their removal is not merited.[1] Let us go on to see the diseased growth from our normal principle.

There is a way of thinking and feeling about punishment, not uncommon in our days, which exhibits a high degree of inconsistency. It more or less explicitly accepts the doctrine that crime (all of it or some of it) is mere disease. Or, rather, crime is taken as a natural deviation from the type. And rightly from this ground a protest is made against such unwilled defects being imputed and judged of morally. Now, with this protest no one can fail

---

[1] The retributive view again on its negative side is inconsistent, because, apart from punishment, individuals are in practice not sacred. The community is forced to inflict more or less relative disadvantage, and therefore injury, on its members without regard to moral desert. The state is forced to be unjust, and against this injustice the retributive view does not utter any protest.

more or less to sympathize. But here is the beginning of
blind and thoughtless confusion. For, protesting against
the principle of the retributive view, or at least partially
against its application, and thus, at least in effect, with-
drawing part of life from that principle's sway, these moral
innovators stand at the same time on its absolute supremacy. Justice on its positive side is restricted, but on its
negative side is to retain unlimited sovereignty. Criminals, some or all, are diseased, and are therefore innocent,
and the innocent, of course, are by justice proclaimed to
be sacred. They are to enjoy therefore that treatment
which was assigned to mere disease, when mere disease
was not taken to include and cover crime. And surely such
an attitude and such a claim are most inconsistent. This
insane murderer, we may hear it said, is not to be destroyed.
Justice is the assignment of benefit and injury according
to desert; but this man is not a moral agent, and hence it is
unjust to injure him. But, if he is not a moral agent, I
reply, surely what follows is that justice is indifferent to
his case. What is just or unjust has surely nothing to do
with our disposal of his destiny. And hence, so long only
as we do not pretend retributively to punish him, we may
cut him off, if that seems best for the general good. For
justice, we have found, is but a subordinate and inferior
principle. It can hear no appeal from the tribunal of the
common welfare. And to take a view of crime which seems
to abolish all accountability, to make in this way everywhere impossible any application of strict justice, and then
in the name of justice to claim protection for ravishers
and murderers, seems really preposterous. The claim is
rational only as an appeal to us to modify our principles.
It is a confused request to us in the name of justice to
dethrone justice. But when justice (as it must be) is de-
throned, and when Darwinism (as it will be) is listened
to, there will be a favourable hearing for the claims of
ethical surgery. And we may now dismiss both forms of
the retributive view.

But against the unlimited right of the moral organism
to dispose of its members is there anything to be set?

There is nothing, so far as I see, but superstition and pre-judice. The idea that justice is paramount, that, with the individual, gain or loss must correspond to desert, and that, without this, the universe has somehow broken down —this popular idea is, after all, the merest prejudice. It seems to rest either on the assumption that there is no principle above justice, or on the common error as to the absolute validity of principles. But the necessary collision both of rights and duties, their mere conditional force, and the subordination of all else to the one principle of general welfare, are truths not to be refuted. And, dwelling no more on this crude popular superstition about justice, I will pass on to consider an opposite error. There is a belief that (not animal, but) human life is sacred. The former prejudice as to justice is, I suppose, anti-Christian; but the sacredness of human life seems largely a Christian idea. And I exhibited the root of this error in a former discus-sion.[1] The individual in the next world has an infinite value; the things of this world, our human ends and interests, are all alike counted worthless, and the rights and duties founded on these interests, of course, bodily disappear. The good of the whole, worthless in itself, can therefore confer no right to interfere with its members; and each individual, on the other side, is, so to speak, the preserve of Providence. Violence, immoral in itself or, at least, immoral for us men, is forbidden us, and is left in the hands of the Deity. Now to criticize this view, otherwise than by stating it, seems here not necessary. Once admit that life in this world is an end in itself, and the pure Christian doctrine is at once uprooted. For, measured by that end and standard, individuals have unequal worth, and the value of each individual is but relative, and in no case infinite. And the community, we have seen, is itself its own Providence, and therefore against its rights the individual is not sacred. With this we may pass from the Christian error, and may proceed to consider a fresh form of delusion. The individual may be taken, as such, to have positive and negative rights, rights not derived from

[1] Unpublished.

another world, but still inhering in him independent of his place in the community. But both the individual and his rights, in this sense, certainly do not belong to our human world, and hence, unless they exist in some other world, they are existent nowhere. They are survivals, in short, from obsolete metaphysics, and about their vital principle I do not intend to speak further. But the rights of these supposed individuals, once placed in a community, must necessarily collide, and all attempts to avoid this collision are idle. And to find a rational ground on which mutual interference is here legitimate, and there unlawful, is once more impossible. This question is one which called for discussion a century ago, but at the present time it can be considered a question no longer. The rights of the individual are, in short, to-day not worth serious criticism.

What is the result which, so far, we have gained? The welfare of the community is the end and is the ultimate standard. And over its members the right of the moral organism is absolute. Its duty and its right is to dispose of these members as seems to it best. Its right and duty is, in brief, to be a Providence to itself. And what went counter to this doctrine we found to be mere superstition.

Darwinism, on the other side (if we may speak for Darwinism), suggests a further conclusion. It could not tell us anything new concerning the end, but about some of the means it spoke decidedly. It urged on us that a condition of welfare is the selection of the more fit, and it added emphatically that selection means the rejection of worse varieties. And, since we now are Providence, it begged us in the name of Providence to reflect. And we found on reflection that we do much to thwart and very little to further the necessary conditions of our welfare. Then, as to punishment in particular, Darwinism showed us a strong presumption. Punishment should, it concluded, in the main be governed directly by the principle of moral surgery. The removal of diseased growths, of worse varieties, Darwinism insisted was obligatory. And it urged us, on this ground, to reform and make consistent our doctrine of punishment. This is our result; and as to punishment, we have to ask if the conclusion drawn by us in the name of Darwinism is sound.

The conclusion might be unsound as containing but a partial truth. It might be false, in other words, because one-sided. The welfare of the community is the supreme and paramount end. No objection possibly can be based on any ground but this. But on this ground it may be urged that there are other interests, other elements in the moral end, other conditions of welfare. Darwinism unrestricted, we may be told, cannot even exist in social life. There are spiritual conditions of that life, we may hear, more essential than the removal of worse varieties. And the ethical surgery, if so, might cut deeper than Darwinism perceives. It might in the end sever that moral bond by which the community is made one. This is a fair issue; but let me endeavour to make it more clear. Let us ask what Darwinism teaches and what it does not teach. The reader must bear with me if I dwell on what seems self-evident.

Darwinism, rightly interpreted, does not teach a return to nature. Given a community aware of itself in its members, we have, with this, gone beyond any stage of mere natural drift. For such a community, less or more, aims consciously at an end. It more or less has become its own Divinity and Providence. Further, Darwinism does not fix a hard limit to the community's rights. It does not suggest their confinement to the protection of person and property. Indeed, to start with mere competition as a first principle, and then to exclude competition in the most characteristic form of violence, would not be rational. But if, on the other side, the state may repress violence, clearly the state may also suppress other forms of the struggle. Darwinism, again, does not teach the supreme value of education. Certainly education works as a means for getting the best to the front, and as a means for obtaining the full use of the individual's powers. But Darwinism hesitates to ascribe to it greater efficacy. And in comparison with the suppression of unfavourable varieties, the importance of education in any case seems not great. And further, Darwinism assuredly does not teach universal selfishness. It neither proclaims it as a fact nor does it inculcate mere self-seeking as a moral duty. Mutual assistance, on the other hand, action in common, with more or less of self-sacrifice, is shown to be a condition of higher well-being. Darwinism, in fact, teaches us that within the whole the principle of competition has become subordinate. It has ceased to be absolute, and is over-ruled less or more by the main principle of general advantage.[1] Help for the helpless, benevolence, charity and mercy, are proclaimed by Darwinism to be conditions of social welfare. They are hence principles, principles once again not absolute, but once again secondary and subject to the general end. And thus, in pressing on us the claims of ethical surgery, Darwinism would indignantly deny a neglect of benevolence. It would urge that true benevolence is unflinching pursuit of the general good. There is no one (it might retort) so remorseless as the humanitarian, no one more ruthless and bloody than the sentimentalist, no one so pitiless as the rider on Christian principles. And it is not a rational world where the surgeon is charged with cruelty.

On another planet, if you like, it may all be quite other-wise. But on our planet, so far as we know, some hardship is inevitable. And if we are to play at Providence, as we must, then we must by commission or by neglect ourselves inflict hardship. Surely, then, the least cruel, the most merciful course of conduct—the best means in our power to diminish suffering—is to regard nothing but the con-ditions of general advantage. And as to these conditions Darwinism offers a positive doctrine. It teaches, in a word, the necessity of constant selection. It insists that the way to improve—the way even not to degenerate—is on the whole unchanging. That way consists in the destruction of worse varieties, or at least in the hindrance of such

[1] Darwinism does not teach the principle of tribal or national selfishness. Regard for a whole beyond my social group, for humanity, and indeed for all sentient beings, is certainly not opposed to Darwinism. I have omitted these points in the text because I found it best for the sake of argument to simplify the question.

varieties from reproduction. Merely bring the fittest in each generation to the front—do nothing to secure that the next generation shall come from these fittest—and, in short, you are trifling with your mission as Providence. This is what Darwinism teaches, and it adds that society at present sins grossly by commission as well as by neglect. Not content with inaction, society works directly in the very interest of evil. It secures artificially the maintenance and the propagation of the unfit, while the fit are even injured in order to contribute to this general injury. And against such ruinous perversity Darwinism protests. It insists on the necessity of social amputation. The wholesale confinement or, again, the mutilation of worse specimens is not a satisfactory substitute. For it seems wrong to load the community with the useless burden of these lives and, in the second place, there is a consideration too often ignored. To maintain in existence a creature, while depriving that creature of the conditions of happiness, is surely to inflict on it the direst suffering. Now, to pass such a sentence worse than death would, of course, be right if it were necessary and an ultimate resort. But in any other case it would be the extreme of indefensible cruelty. To remove from the social organism, as it were, by ligature a member sentient and miserably conscious through life of its own protracted dying, seems a most barbarous device. And by comparison clearly there is more kindness and mercy in the knife. To my mind this question of imprisonment has been often a cause of indignant surprise. That a man should hate capital punishment is not surprising. For, apart from religious and metaphysical superstitions, we must admit that such punishment is a terrible necessity. But that the same man should on another side feel no compunction, that he should cheerfully sanction a long, or even a lifelong, imprisonment, that to bury alive a fellow-creature should, in plain words, seem a matter of course—this, to me, I own, is disgusting. It illustrates glaringly our moral confusion and blind sentimentality. For to shrink from an evil because we cannot ignore it, and to forget every horror not inconveniently forced before our eyes, is too characteristic of our morality. And too often we drape with the clothes of mercy the detestable idol of stupid cruelty. But human nature everywhere is prone to avoid fundamental issues. Life is a thing beset on all sides by hard necessities, and of these to choose the least is the one rational way of kindness. To face a problem in this spirit is, however, not possible for the sentimentalist.

Now against this claim and this plea for ethical surgery I do not suggest that no rational objection can be urged. For our remedy clearly would bring some amount of evil. It would cause a shock, not merely to superstition, but to a large body of genuine moral feeling. It would certainly neither prohibit nor discourage works of true mercy, and it would entail no degree of physical cruelty. But still our remedy would have to utter and to enforce this sentence, 'You and you are dangerous specimens; you must depart in peace.' It would probably add, 'There are some children here over and above what we want, and their origin, to say the least, is inauspicious. We utterly decline to rear these children at the public cost and, so far as we can judge, to the public injury.' Now such an attitude plainly would outrage a large mass of moral sentiment, and it would undeniably therefore be a source of suffering and evil. But on such points our sentiments to some extent are conventional, and therefore, so far, might very well be changed. And in any case to avoid as long as possible any moral shock is not the end of our being. The real question is, on which side lies the balance of harm? Measured by the good of the community, is moral surgery the less or the greater of two evils? We have to choose, in brief, between the complex results of alternative courses, and I do not propose to attempt a detailed estimate. I wish not to advocate any result to which my mind has been led, so much as to press for a serious consideration of the problem. I am satisfied if I have shown that the claim of moral surgery, however inconvenient it may be, cannot at least be ignored.[1]

---

[1] It is no good answer to urge that, after all, we have progressed so far in spite of neglect. For the conditions certainly have not remained the same.

'Then, on an ethical subject too, you really offer no practical suggestion?' No, in an ethical discussion I even venture to think that practical proposals are out of place. And then for myself I make no claim to be a practical man. I am sceptical as to the value for such a purpose of any moral philosophy, and I am sure that my small energies would not be decently expended in the field of practical reform. I am a theorist, in short, but yet, I hope, not anything of a projector; and if I am to make myself ridiculous, I prefer at least some manner which suits my tastes. But what advice could I offer beyond general platitude and well-worn commonplace? It is the part of a wise man to consider carefully the 'for' and the 'against', and before accepting an operation to weigh critically the worth of the diagnosis. But it is the part of a fool blindly to suffer evils to take their course. We may be right to wait and to observe, but there is a thing still which it cannot be wrong to remember. Radical plans of reform, if we suppose Darwinism to be right, are very certainly for the most part not radical at all. They may alleviate, or again they may aggravate, the symptoms, but most assuredly they cannot touch the real disease. And Darwinism, if it cared to quote Greek, might remind us of what everywhere is still the mark of the quacksalver and the mountebank,

θρηνεῖν ἐπῳδὰς πρὸς τομῶντι πήματι.

But, for myself as a bystander, there are some feelings which I am not careful to hide. I am oppressed by the ineffectual cruelty of our imprisonments. I am disgusted at the inviolable sanctity of the noxious lunatic. The right of the individual to spawn without restriction his diseased offspring on the community, the duty of the state to rear

They are changing every day, and in great part unfavourably. The positive checks to population, in the shape of hardship and disease, acted as a selection of stronger varieties; and these checks every day are lessened. It is far easier now for weak and diseased specimens to survive and to breed. The struggle again, if we retain free trade in reproduction together with protection of the results, is becoming largely a mere struggle between rival fertilities. And from this competition the morally superior more and more refrain. I do not think that in the past such conditions have ever prevailed.

wholesale and without limit an unselected progeny—such duties and rights are to my mind a sheer outrage on Providence. A society that can endure such things will merit the degeneracy which it courts. More and more on certain points we seem warned to return in part to older and to less impracticable principles of conduct. And there are views of Plato which, to me at least, every day seem less of an anachronism and more of a prophecy.[1]

[1] Since this article was written, I have read a criticism on myself by the Rev. H. Rashdall in this *Journal*, October, 1891. Mr. Rashdall appears to me to misunderstand the view which he attacks. He takes me to hold an 'intuitive theory of punishment' (p. 22), by which (so far as I can judge) he means a view based on some isolated abstraction. I find this strange, and what is perhaps stranger is that he treats me as teaching that punishment consists in the infliction of pain for pain's sake. At least I am unable otherwise to interpret his language. Now, I certainly said that punishment is the suppression of guilt, and so of the guilty person. But I pointed out that negation is not a good, except so far as it belongs to and is the other side of positive moral assertion (*E.S.* 27 = 25). Pain, of course, usually does go with the negative side of punishment, just as some pleasure, I presume, attends usually the positive side. Pain is, in brief, an accident of retribution, but certainly I never made it more, and I am not aware that I made it even an inseparable accident. If a criminal defying the law is shot through the brain, are we, if there is no pain, to hold that there is no retribution? My critic seems, if I may say so, to hold an 'intuitive theory' of my views.

Starting, as it seems to me, from such misapprehensions, Mr. Rashdall's criticism does not appear to myself to hit the mark; and I will therefore not attempt to meet it in detail, but will merely add a few remarks on punishment by the state. Punishment does not rest on an abstraction, but is the reaction of a moral organism, and this organism in every case has a particular concrete character; and what is punished is, of course, always a revolt of a special and concrete nature. Surely, therefore, the varying amounts of the reactions required will follow naturally in accordance with the general principle. It is the welfare of the special state which, of course, decides the amount of ill-desert. And I find, again, no difficulty in the increase or diminution of the penalty by considerations other than those of desert. But, since the welfare of the state is used in punishment as the criterion of desert, I would remark that such increase or diminution may be less than is imagined. Still, I admit it, as for example in the case of pardon, and I consider that it occasions no real difficulty. It is a mere instance of the collision of rights and duties, and of a superior duty and right to be here unjust. All that is required is that (if pressed) we should admit that such a modified penalty is not strict punishment.

In short, I should have little to correct in the old statement of my view except a certain number of one-sided and exaggerated expressions.

VIII

THE LIMITS OF INDIVIDUAL AND NATIONAL SELF-SACRIFICE[1]

[*First published in* THE INTERNATIONAL JOURNAL OF ETHICS, *October*, 1894.]

WHAT are the limits of self-sacrifice? How far and on what principle is a man or a nation to give up welfare or existence? I will try first to state the principle of self-sacrifice, I will point out next some prejudices which obscure this principle, and will then show the general mode of its application.

I shall here assume that self-sacrifice can exist and also may be right. And the question is on what principle is self-sacrifice right, and is there a limit at which it becomes wrong? The general principle is perhaps not hard to lay down. To sacrifice one's self is to destroy or diminish one's personal existence, and this by itself is not good. Mere self-destruction, whether partial or complete, is not desirable. Self-sacrifice is right if the loss is sustained with a view to a greater gain, and otherwise it is wrong. We must assume that what I forgo is of value, for, if it were worth nothing, it could not be a sacrifice. Supposing, then, that I lose it for something worth no more, my action is not right, and if I lose it for something worth less, my action is wrong and may be immoral. This is the principle, and to this there will perhaps be no objection. The conflict of opinion arises in part from difficulties in the application, but it comes mainly, I think, from the interference of moral prejudices. There are one-sided points of view not subordinated to the governing principle, and we must next proceed to see what these are.

I will begin with the self-styled 'Christian' party, who profess to base their morality on the New Testament. But

---

[1] This paper was written in 1878 or 1879. Apart from abbreviation it has been left much in its original form. [Note by the author.]

whether it is really more Christian to follow or to ignore the teaching of the Gospels I shall not discuss.

Let us then examine this 'Christian' point of view, and ask if there is here any limit to self-sacrifice. There is no limit whatever. The soul of every man is worth so much that they are all worth the same. They have cost the same price and their value is equal. And there is no end for the individual but to avoid the torment and to gain the bliss both for himself and others, and these two objects emphatically are not two but one. My interest is indivisible from the interest of others, for I can save myself only by seeking to save also my brother. Hence competition disappears; for if I struggled merely for myself, I should lose myself certainly.

This theory is simple, but it is fatally defective. Self-sacrifice seems unlimited, but it really is impossible. A man cannot give up his good where he has no good to give up. The temporal existence which you sacrifice you declare to be worthless; indeed, you naively urge that as a reason for sacrificing it. But apart from this existence you sacrifice nothing. What is the living self-development of an individual or nation? What is the beauty and the good of human being? You have made it all dross, or stumbling-blocks, or means of probation. The end is in the *other* world, and that means it is taken out of this world; and that means that life is worthless or immoral.

Where the self is worth nothing, self-sacrifice is surely impossible. And, again, it is only where no man has any value that all men have equal value. When there is an end and a worth in this world men become unequal, for they must realize the end in different degrees. Hence Christianity in the above sense cannot be reconciled with morality; and let us proceed to examine another false point of view. We may call it the doctrine of one-sided patriotism, or national morality.

Worldly existence is here in itself desirable. The life of the individuals in the community and of the community in the individuals, the development of humanity in the organism of the state, is the end. Self-sacrifice of the member is demanded and limited by the good of the body. If the body requires it he develops himself, and if the body requires it he suppresses himself. Thus, self-sacrifice for the good of the state is right, and for any other end is wrong. Outside the state there is no moral self-sacrifice, because outside there is no good. And there is, of course, no international morality.

But human duties cannot be limited to the sphere of the state. And hence this view, like the 'Christian' view, is one-sided and false, nor could either be consistently followed. And yet both creeds to-day own their thoughtless adherents. There is a 'Christian' party and a party of 'British interests'. But the 'Christian' politician never asks whether, if war is contrary to the gospel, politics also are not contrary. And the man who denies international right, and preaches tribal morality, can hardly be consistent. Neither party is in earnest with the principle on which it orders us to act.

But these doctrines are combined and confused in a third view more common than either. I must now examine this, but I confess I do not know what to call it. For the name of 'Humanitarian' is too good to be more than lent for the occasion.

The elements which enter into this creed are (1) the idea of personal and national self-development, (2) the doctrine of universal love and self-sacrifice, and (3) the principle of the value of the individual. It may be said to start with the morality of the state, to widen this so as to take in humanity, and to qualify it further by the idea of unlimited self-sacrifice, adding also a notion of the infinite worth and equality of all men. And the practical conclusion is that nations, like men, all have equal rights, that they should all be governed by law, and none selfishly struggle for advantage, and that neither peoples nor individuals may be exterminated, but in any case must be respected.

This creed is identified with much that is noble; but it is inconsistent, deficient, and in part downright false. It approves of self-development, but it condemns self-assertion, the struggle of competition without which there is no development. It extends the range of state morality, but leaves out one factor of that morality, and it transplants others beyond the conditions of their existence. And, borrowing from religion the value of the individual, it seeks to use that value falsely elsewhere. I will go through these points, and will begin with the worth of the individual.

The equality, or, again, the absolute value of individuals, is not a principle which holds between man and man or nation and nation. On the contrary, the end being the development of human nature, those who have the force, and who judge this course to be conducive to the end, may exterminate or make any use of both men and nations. For the end is superior to the individual, and it is right to act for this end to the best of one's judgement. And, if so, the conclusion must follow as above. The end *does* justify the means, and cannot fail to do so, unless either the means are not essential, or the end itself not desirable or at least not paramount. But the end we are speaking of here is absolute.

There is a sense in which all men have equal and incomparable value, but this sense falls outside the world of morality. The inner moral values of men may not be comparable, but you cannot from this conclude that they are equal. It is only before God that men become equal, and even thus their equality is but partial. As ideally one with the Divine Will they all are equal, but as diverse functions of that Will they become unequal. Where there is a performance there are degrees, and where men come into relation there is an outward performance which can be compared. And religious equality is here no truth, but has become a superstition.

And leaving these abstract considerations, if we take the case of criminals within, or savages without, the community, it surely may be right to abolish their existence. The principle we act on no doubt can be misused by the immoral. It can furnish a pretext for blind persecution or selfish aggrandizement. And the progress of humanity being furthered by the diversity of its elements, it is desirable in general that individuals should develop their natures. And this shows a presumption against the extinction or hindrance of man or nation. But it does not prove that in some cases we are not morally bound to accomplish it.

The early Christians were right to insist on the sacredness of life and on the equality of all men, but for us now these ideas have a subordinate position. To the Christians men were equal, because in the other world their value was infinite and in this world nothing. For the development of human nature was not to them desirable. But for us that development is a good thing and an end in itself. And, this being so, we have left the one ground on which individuals are sacred. In getting a *temporal* value they have acquired a *relative* value, and that relative value, measured by the end, may demand their suppression. It thus, for practical purposes, is wrong to maintain the equal or absolute value of individuals unless we are prepared to hold that human nature in itself is worthless. And with this we pass to the remaining elements of 'Humanitarianism'.

This, we saw, extends national morality to the world. The relations of states are to be those of men in a state; and here we have at once false analogy. This creed, again, ignores the principle of self-assertion which is sanctioned by the state; and here is defective analogy. And, in preaching unlimited self-sacrifice, it runs counter to sound morality.

Beginning with the false analogy, and considering the moral relations of citizens and of states, I will recall some familiar points of difference. In a nation the law is supported by force. There is a sovereign, which by its executive carries out the laws and compels the unwilling. But there is no international sovereign now, and there may never be any. And a nation has courts for the settlement of differences, while international courts seem hardly possible. The absence of an executive would make them idle, and this is not all. A national court is presumed morally to represent its citizens. It stands on the common morality

of the litigants, and has no selfish interests. But an international tribunal could not be presumed to be always
representative or even disinterested. And it is doubtful if
international law can be said really to exist.

I shall be told, no doubt, that the absence of a sovereign,
and judicature, and executive, makes no difference to our
duties. But surely that must depend on what our duties
are. Unless we believe in some *a priori* rights of human
beings as such, it is the conditions of our lives which make
our duties and rights, and if you remove the conditions the
duties are removed. To take men's goods without their
consent, we are told for instance, is stealing, and stealing is
stealing whether with individuals or nations, and whether
you have laws or none. But this is all erroneous. Stealing
is an offence against property, but there is no absolute
reason why property should exist; and in a communistic
state it might not exist. It is in the end the state which
decides whether I am to have property, and fixes the conditions on which I am to hold it. And to say that the
removal of these circumstances leaves things where they
were seems really irrational. Mine is mine, no doubt, and
yours is yours; but then, *what* is mine and yours, and how,
where there are no laws, can that question be answered?
I am not denying here the existence of right between
states; but to take the moral rules we find existing between citizens, and, turning these into abstractions, to
apply them recklessly everywhere and anywhere, I urge, is
indefensible.

Thus we cannot argue in general from civic to international morality, and in particular we cannot transport
the duty of self-sacrifice unaltered into the world at large.
A man owes a debt to his country, but a nation may feel
it owes nothing to some other nation. Duty to one's
neighbour remains, but then who is one's neighbour?
Within the community he is another representative of
the same ideas, and I can believe, when I sacrifice myself,
that my life survives in the whole, and that the common
spirit gains by my loss. Can a state say this of a neighbour alien in race and alien in ideas? Or may not self-

sacrifice bring here no advantage, and but result in fruit-less waste?

In such points the analogy from citizens to nations is false. But this analogy, we have now to see, is also deficient. Within the state there is a principle opposed to self-sacrifice; and reasoning from men to nations, we could not say that self-sacrifice is unlimited, for the self-assertion of the citizen is a moral duty.

The welfare of another, just because it is another's, is not better than mine, and the consequences which would follow are grossly absurd. Nor is it much less absurd to teach that self-sacrifice should stop nowhere, or that the well-being of any one is as good as that of any one else. Doubtless, the mere fact that he is he, and I am I, ought to make no difference, and it is foolish indeed in any one to suppose that it could. But if you mean that *the kind of man he is* should make no difference, and that he may not, because of this, get in front of another, you have passed from verbiage to falsehood. The good of the whole is the end, and the competition of the individuals is a means, for if the best do not come to the front there is general loss. And so the community sanctions self-assertion, and it lays down the limits and conditions of self-seeking. You may not kill or steal, but you may struggle against one another for existence. To empty a man's till is forbidden, but to bring him to beggary by competition may often be laud-able. 'Unto him that hath shall be given' and 'reward for merit' are not principles of self-sacrifice, but, within limits, they are principles approved by the state.

And the rule of self-assertion must also hold between nations. Our 'Christian' free-traders forbid us to take the goods of a nation by force; but to undersell it in its markets, and to drive it out of its trade, seems one more illustration of the precepts of the gospel. For, 'this is not selfish, and it will be better for all in the end. In the pacific contest of free-trade my gain or loss is still one with my neighbour's, and *we* need not raze the commandment "Thou shalt not covet", for coveting is impossible.'

But even if competition in trade is ultimately for the

good of humanity, it is hard to believe that the advantage must come to every man. Men and nations take time to find the better trade they have been compelled to seek. They suffer in the process, and they do not always survive it. And while their competitor is gaining, he surely sometimes must gain what they lose, and after all has sought his own at the expense of his neighbour.

Thus, within limits, self-seeking is desirable among nations, and the question is solely about these limits. It is easy to talk of law, and to assert that war between states is to be judged like violence within states; but this is merely to fall into the old false analogy. The state sanctions the principle of self-assertion, and qualifies it to suit with civic conditions. But, conditions being different, the principle of competition may have a different range. If a nation narrows that range and excludes itself from foreign commerce, why should it not do so? But if, again, it carries self-assertion beyond the limits allowed in civil life, once more, is this immoral? It may sound fine to say, 'Competition is one thing and war is another', but it is not easy to draw a distinction in principle.

Selfishness is not wicked, for the state encourages its citizens to be selfish; and violence is not wicked, for the state is violent towards its citizens. War is not *illegal* violence if there is no law which condemns it, and we might even say that such a law must be founded on war. It is here that our 'Humanitarians' make a terrible mistake, for if international law is ever to be real, it must have an executive. But an executive must mean force, and force between nations is war. When a majority have become agreed that on certain points they will compel refractory states, the law of nations will be a reality. And thus, if war goes out, it will surely be by way of war, by an irresistible armed consensus with force in reserve. But what, if so, shall we say to the 'Humanitarian' who cries Peace at any price? Shall we answer, There is but one Humanitarian and one friend of peace—the man who is for war in the name of Humanity?

We have found that the equal value of individuals is an

illusion, and that the analogy from the citizen to the nation is invalid. The end is general perfection, and for this end, certainly, self-sacrifice may be required. But duties within the state being specially determined, to extend these beyond their conditions is indefensible; for, like other general truths, the general truths of ethics are conditional. And beside this mistake we found also another. The analogy from civil life does not show that self-sacrifice is unlimited, but it shows, on the contrary, that within limits self-assertion is valid.

But our 'Christian' party, I suppose, will have a word for us. 'You have proved', they may say, 'that self-assertion is recognized by worldly morality, but the morality of the Gospel is the ultimate standard.' And on this point I think we should understand one another. If 'Christianity' is to mean the taking the Gospels as our rule of life, then we none of us are Christians and, no matter what we say, we all know we ought not to be. If Greek morality was one-sided, that of the New Testament is still more one-sided, for it implies that the development of the individual and the state is worthless. It is not merely that it contemns victory over the forces of nature, that it scorns beauty and despises knowledge, but there is not one of our great moral institutions which it does not ignore or condemn. The rights of property are denied or suspected, the ties of the family are broken, there is no longer any nation or patriotism, and the union of the sexes becomes a second-rate means against sin. Universal love doubtless is a virtue, but tameness and baseness—to turn the cheek to every rascal who smites it, to suffer the robbery of villains and the contumely of the oppressor, to stand by idle when the helpless are violated and the land of one's birth in its death-struggle, and to leave honour and vengeance and justice to God above—are qualities that deserve some other epithet. The morality of the primitive Christians is that of a religious sect; it is homeless, sexless, and nationless. The morality of to-day rests on the family, on property, and the nation. Our duty is to be members of the world we are in; to be in the world and not of it was their type of perfection. The moral chasm between us is, in short, as wide as the intellectual; and if it has been politic to ignore this, I doubt if it is politic any longer. We have lived a long time now the professors of a creed which no one consistently can practise, and which, if practised, would be as immoral as it is unreal.

Self-assertion, we have now seen, is as right as self-sacrifice, and at this point we may notice another mistake. It is no true deduction from Mr. Darwin's views if any one maintains the morality of mere national selfishness. For the mere fact of self-assertion and the acting on the principle of self-assertion are, in the first place, not the same. And, further, in the beginnings of morality among gregarious animals this fact of self-assertion itself has visibly suffered a change. The struggle of the community against outsiders plainly holds a place by the struggle of the individuals within the community. And how can we consistently set up tribal morality and a mere struggle between states as ultimate, when within tribal morality the principle of selfishness is not paramount? If there the law of self-assertion has ceased to be supreme, its supremacy, where states are concerned, is the merest assumption. The progress which has limited the struggle of the citizens will limit, we may rather suppose, the struggle of states, and self-assertion will everywhere be reduced to an element in a higher morality.

And here we may take leave of the one-sided ideas we have criticized. The end we take to be the development of human nature. This principle necessitates self-sacrifice, since its way may be through the loss of individuals. And it necessitates self-assertion, since only thus can the end be reached at all. It subordinates both, and their limits can be stated in general. It is possible that a man or a state can develop self best by serving others most, and here the question disappears. Again, a man or state, by giving up private good, may do most for the end; and here self-sacrifice becomes a duty. But if by self-assertion, to the loss or even extinction of others, a man or a state considers that it most profits humanity, there self-sacrifice is immoral.

These truths seem too obvious to require explanation, but they are so constantly misunderstood that I venture to dwell on them. Suppose, first, that we have one single nation; the perfection of human nature within that nation will be the end. The good of each man here for the most part should coincide with that of others, but wholly it cannot and should not coincide. For without competition the community grows effete through the loss of vigorous individuals. The worthless are not pushed aside, and the fittest do not come to the front. And hence, if I am the fittest to have advantage, it is my duty to take it. But on the same principle there are cases where self-sacrifice should be welcomed. Self-sacrifice is an end in general where it results in a greater gain, and it is an end to the loser so far as he identifies himself with that which gains. But in itself self-sacrifice is an evil, and there is always some presumption against it. To give up life or possessions or talents for the sake of others may be immoral.

And the same thing holds between nations. Each gains generally, but not always, by the gain of all. Some competition, and hence self-assertion to the loss of another, may thus at times be right. And at other times, for the sake of humanity, a nation should deny itself. National self-sacrifice, as compared with civic, has a wider object but a narrower exercise. It is hard for a state to judge that its loss is balanced by general gain. And nations differ in value, and there is no organism to ensure that loss of one shall advantage the others. The influence of example is weak where public spirit has hardly an existence. And (sophistic as it may sound) the readiness in a nation for self-sacrifice would be an argument in favour of its self-assertion.

The general principle seems plain, but does not carry us far. A nation must aim at the good of mankind and at peace in the end; but, as things are, this principle will in some cases justify violence, and even extermination. For, beside the principle which establishes the end, there can be no absolute law; and the means to this end cannot be fixed beforehand. And such means certainly need not always consist in abstinence from war or even from aggression. Our first hope at present is an international executive enforcing the morality of the best; but, if that is to exist, then the best must agree, and must be the strongest. And strength means war in reserve. We may look beyond this possibly to a better state of things, but the first seems the only road to the second. The meek will *not* inherit the earth, and a nation which claims morality must be ready to use force in defence of right.

It is idle to denounce this view as the trumpeting of a bellicose policy or the glorification of blood and pillage. This view necessitates the belief that a war begun thoughtlessly or selfishly is a crime. It is hostile only to the reckless application of one-sided principles. We remind the party of 'British interests' that a cynical self-seeking is immoral, and that a nation which adopts it may lose one source of strength. To the peace-at-any-price manufacturer we remark that a thing may be worth more than what it fetches in the market; and we say to either the 'Christian' politician or the covert Quaker that, while on other points he ignores the teaching of the Gospels, he is a hypocrite if he tries to teach us our duty on this. And we beg the sentimentalist to remember that, after all, force rules the world, and that self-assertion, after all, is a condition of welfare.

It would be a good day if in England we could gain some clearer ideas about selfishness and patriotism; if we could learn to abstain from insincere professions and from sickening cant. We might then, perhaps, remember that, when trade is gone and manufactures perished, the memory of a nation that has strengthened itself, and dared to risk something in the cause of humanity, is not so easily lost.

IX

ON THE ANALYSIS OF COMPARISON

[*First published in* MIND, o.s., xi, No. 41, 83–5. *January*, 1886.]

THE interesting paper on 'Comparison', which Mr. Sully has published in *Mind*,[1] suggests some fruitful lines of inquiry. And there is one point, and that one of capital importance, on which I should be glad to add a few remarks, fragmentary and, no doubt, in other ways defective. This point is the *analysis* of the comparing function.

Mr. Sully has, of course, not omitted this question. He has pointed out certain features in the act of Comparison; but I do not find what can be called an attempt to resolve the product into its elements. I will, however, not criticize where it is probable that I do not understand, but will pass to Mr. Sully's description of the act.

'The term Comparison may be roughly defined as that act of the mind by which it concentrates attention on two mental contents in such a way as to ascertain their relation of similarity or dissimilarity' (490). 'Comparison is a mode of intellectual activity involving voluntary attention' (498). 'But it is an act of attention of a very special kind' (492). In this description there are two points which call for remark. In the first place I should doubt if *voluntary* attention is essential to comparison. This is a matter of observation, or perhaps only of wording; but the second point is one connected with principle. Comparison is called 'an act of attention of a very special kind', and this at once suggests a difficulty. If the special essences of the various intellectual functions are to be referred to differences in the kind of attention, then these kinds of attention should be described and enumerated, and, if possible, developed from the simple form. But if the differences in attention come rather from the different objects we attend

---

[1] *M.* o.s. x. 489–511.

to, then the speciality of the various intellectual functions must be looked for in themselves, and cannot come from varieties in attention. But I should confess that on the subject of voluntary attention, and of the position it holds in mental development, I am unable to understand Mr. Sully's teaching.

I will now offer the remarks which I have to make on the analysis of Comparison. We may say that the mind acts on two data in such a way as to ascertain their similarity or dissimilarity. Well now, what is this way? The mind passes of course from one object to the other, but then *how* does it pass and *what* crosses in the passage? If we use technical terms, we may answer as follows. Comparison is the (unreflective) subsumption of one datum under the other reciprocally, or the apperception of each by the other in turn. Having data A and B, we pass from A to B with A in our minds as our leading idea, and then return to A with B in our minds as the idea which predominates. The result is that the diversities are brought into collision and so into notice, and that the identities are both reinforced by blending and also set free by the struggle of their competing differences. The process is either general or special. We may use, that is, the whole content of A or B, or but one special feature or aspect of each.

Now what operates in the above is the suggested idea of the identity in diversity, or diversity in identity, of A and B. This idea it is which (by redintegration) causes the process which brings about its own reality. If the comparison is intentional, the idea will have been there and have led from the first. But it may arise accidentally. Having A and B before me and casually passing from one to the other, I may perceive an identity or difference. This may interest and, becoming a dominant idea, may set up the process of alternate subsumption.

Thus in Comparison proper we have two data A and B, we have an idea of their identity and diversity which interests, and an ensuing process of alternate subsumption. We may have in addition an idea of this process. But before Comparison proper is developed the process cannot be set up by the idea of its result. We have then simply an identity felt in our data, which seeks in vain (by red-integration) to particularize itself in one as it does in the other, and so causes a collision.

It will, I hope, tend to clear up this rapid sketch if I try to show how Comparison is developed. Let us suppose that a child, or some other animal, has eaten a number of lumps of sugar. The result will be that, when a hard white lump is presented to its sense, that lump will be qualified by the idea of sweetness. But the lump now presented is a piece of salt, and what follows is a shock of discrepancy and pain. The question is whether this shock will subside and pass away, or be retained and lead to an advance. Let us suppose that it is retained. The suggested idea of sweetness is so strong that again and again the whiteness of the salt leads to attempt and disgust. But in this way a new connexion of whiteness and saltness will be formed in the mind.

Let the salt still remain, and let us offer beside it new pieces of sugar (while constantly changing the local positions), and let appetite be urgent. What will happen now may be a passage to the sugar with a certain idea of saltness, and to the salt with a certain idea of sweetness, and in each case a failure. The identical white leads to both, and the last presentation to sense in each case fills up the idea, and the result is perplexity. I think the issue may be as follows.

We are to suppose that in the sugar is a glittering appearance which is absent from the salt. These differences may not have been perceived, or at least noticed, and may have so far remained inoperative. But as attention grows through desire and pain, let this attribute become more prominent, and let it pass into the idea with which the animal goes from the sugar to the salt. On this a fresh collision will take place. And another discrepancy will be felt when the idea of the dull salt collides with the sensation of glittering sweetness. The two pieces now, while held together by their identical attributes, are forced apart by their differences, and in this passage between them the diversities become explicit.

This I believe to be the way in which Comparison is developed. Its result, the perception of mixed identity and diversity, becomes, as an idea, the means for setting up the process which has yielded it. The chance result of groping is what gives the source of voluntary movement.

There are doubtless objections which will be taken to this fragmentary outline, but of these most will, I think, be founded on errors. I have dealt with some of them in my *Principles of Logic*, but there is one I may point out here. It will perhaps be said that my explanation is circular, since classification and comparison exist from the first and are implied in the earliest form of recognition. But the facts, as I find them both in general and in particular, are irreconcilable with this view—a view which, I believe, rests much less on observation than on preconceived ideas. And if an objector replies, But the comparison is yet 'latent', it is 'virtual', it is 'nascent', it is only 'potential'—that moves me not at all. I must be allowed to say openly that such ambiguous phrases have, until they are explained, no right to exist in a scientific psychology, and that if they were explained their attraction would vanish. I have found that an assertion of 'potential' existence often stands for a 'nascent' perception of error; and in that sense it is welcome.

But I trust to meet with the general approval of psychologists when I say that in analysis there is still much to be done.

X

IS THERE ANY SPECIAL ACTIVITY OF ATTENTION?

[*First published in* MIND, o.s. xi, No. 43, 305–23. *July*, 1886.]

THE question I have placed at the head of this article may serve to define its subject-matter. Is Attention, so far as it is *psychical* activity, an original element, and is there any specific function of attention? The strict result of the English analytical school would give a negative answer to both these questions. With that denial I agree, and I have not been able to find sufficient reason to doubt its truth. Active attention is not primary, either as being there from the first or as supervening, but is a derivative product. Nor again, I should add, is there any one special activity at all, but various activities, if they lead to one result, are called attending. This is the doctrine which this paper is written to defend, or rather to press upon the reader's notice. The whole subject is so difficult and is so implicated with other branches of psychology, that to treat of it fully is not possible here, even if in my case it were possible anywhere. My chief object is to record a kind of protest. I observe a tendency to break up the life of the soul, to divide it into active and passive factors, or to suppose a passive beginning with a supervening activity, the latter by some identified with an irreducible act of attention. I believe this tendency to be a serious obstacle to psychology, and there is another tendency not less injurious. Attention may be given such a position that the reader cannot tell if it is primary or derivative, or, if primary, whether it is an original element or something that supervenes; or, again, whether it is one of a class of activities, or itself a class of different activities, or one function exerted on different objects. And my purpose is first to ask why we should desert the conclusion that attention is a product; and, if we must desert it, to urge that the alternative should at least be stated distinctly. The attention I am to speak of is *active* attention.

Attention (whatever it may be besides) at any rate means predominance in consciousness. Some element or elements, sensational or ideal, become prominent from the rest and seem to lower them in strength, if they do not entirely exclude them from notice. That which we attend to is said to engross us. 'The expression means that a sensation tends more or less strongly to exclude from consciousness all other sensations.'[1] Not theorizing but applying descriptive metaphors, we may call attention a state which implies domination or chief tenancy of consciousness. Or we may compare it to the focusing of an optical instrument, or to the area of distinct vision in the retinal field.[2] Now in active attention we produce this condition (there is no doubt of that), and the question is how we are able to do this, or what is the machinery which effects the production. In order to answer this question, we must first make a general survey of the facts.

A flash of lightning by night, the report of a firearm, the sudden prick of a knife, or a violent internal pain, all these for the moment so occupy our notice that everything else becomes feeble or is banished. I shall not ask *how* it is that these intruders prevail, whether there is one cause or various ones, and, if so, how they are related.[3] Nor shall

[1] Abbreviated from J. S. Mill on James Mill's *Analysis of the Human Mind*, ii. 372.

[2] Hamilton, *Met.*, i. 238, Lotze, *Med. Psych.*, 505, and (later) Wundt, *Phys. Psych.*, ii. 206. I may take this opportunity of saying that I have considered Wundt's doctrine of Apperception and am unable to adopt it, perhaps because I have failed to understand it.

[3] There is mere strength, pleasure and pain, and habit, including under that head inherited predispositions as well as the attractions of familiarity and change. How these stand to one another is matter of controversy which does not concern us. Stumpf, *Tonpsych.*, i. 71, is inclined to doubt the fact of attention's always strengthening, partly on the ground that in that case it would falsify observation. But, in the first place, since strength of course is relative, the observed relation might for more than one reason remain unaltered. And, in the second place, there is a most important point to be considered, to which it seems to me that Stumpf has hardly done justice. This is the distinction between the strength of a perception as a psychical

I inquire if we here can be said to attend or are active in any sense. I think no one would say that we ourselves *produced* the tyranny of these assailants. Let us then go on to the states where we are certainly somehow active. When the ears are erected or the eyes opened or moved, and these reflex acts increase the power of one sensation against other mental elements, I do not know if we properly are said to attend. And, though there is a kind of 'activity', yet assuredly there is here no active attention. For no psychical activity at all is present, or in any case none which produces the dominance of one mental element. Still, if the reader objects, I will not at present insist. He will agree that these reflexes are but one amongst other sorts of attention, and I will therefore pass on.

We come next to a class where the activity is still muscular, a muscular activity exerted upon a percipient organ directly, or indirectly as by turning the body. But in addition we have here a preceding idea and (according to one view) a feeling which moves. A visible object for example suggests, indirectly or directly, ideas and feelings which lead to our fixing it, and that fixation makes the perception of the object predominant and steady. There are many stages in this class, and we shall all agree that in some of them we have an active attention. There is a question in fact whether attention is much *more*, and to that question we shall be obliged to return.

We come next to a number of cases of attention where muscular activity seems not essential. But in all of these state and the strength which is perceived by means of the perception. If we consider ideas, it seems hopeless to contend that the idea (e.g.) of a strong or weak pleasure or pain must always itself *be* a strong or weak state of mind. Such an example as the tranquil recollection of a tooth-drawing would at once confute us. And if this is so with ideas, it will, I think, be so still when we come to perceptions. The difference between the state and its ideal content will hold good there also. It will be possible to have a perception of violence which itself is not violent, and of feebleness which itself is not weak. The degree will be a character distinguishable from and contained in the whole state of perception, which latter may in some other way vary in strength while the degree remains the same. But how this can be possible is a most difficult question with which I do not feel myself at present competent to deal.

N

an *idea* must be present and appears to operate. A simple instance is the appearance in sensation or perception of an element not striking in itself but with which a dominant idea is associated. If an idea or a mass of ideas are so interesting that they are able to engross us, then the elements connected with them, whether sensible or ideal, may engross us also (cp. J. S. Mill, loc. cit.). Whether perceptions and ideas that attract us by their strangeness belong to this class I shall not inquire, nor for the present shall I ask what 'interesting' means. What must engage us is the doubt if in this class we have everywhere *active* attention. When a thought, as we say, is much in our minds, and we dwell upon everything that suits with its presence and supports its rule, we do not know of any *act*, since all comes of itself. 'If I am active,' we should ask, 'what is it that I do?', and it is better therefore to go on to clearer instances. When I retain an idea or keep watch on an object, and still more when I investigate, I am supposed to act and also to attend, since my thoughts are confined to one main subject. But is this active attention? When for example at this moment I write about attention, I am active, no doubt, and I presume attending; but if you ask me whether I actively attend, I hesitate for an answer. For, if I am well and not distracted, attention seems of itself to wait upon my other activity, and, if it does not come because of it, seems to come spontaneously. It is otherwise where I have resolved to attend to some matter and still persevere. We have here the attention that proclaims itself active, and there is more than one variety. I may simply intend to occupy my mind with a certain subject, or may resolve in particular to be active upon it in such or such a manner.

Let us enumerate the results of the above survey. In the first place (1) we may have resolved to attend, or (2) to effect some mental operation which involves attention. We may also (3) perform the same act without intention or resolve, and again, where we are not conscious of action, (4) a dominant idea may lend its force to a connected element. Once more (5) a muscular act, itself the result of idea (and perhaps feeling), may cause the predominance of sensation or idea; or (6) a sensation may be fixed by a simple reflex; or (7) lastly some element may predominate by what seems its own superior energy. The last two varieties, I think, must now be dismissed. They have of course great psychological importance, but it seems evident that they are not *active* attention.

I shall go on to attempt a clearance of the ground by dealing with the claim of muscular action; for if this contained the essence of active attention, our task would be shortened. The 'Will', it may be said, controls the voluntary muscles (and them alone), and the voluntary muscles by acting on the organs control sensation. And when we attend to an idea, and when the muscles do *not* move, yet the Will still controls. For in the idea attended to is 'a muscular element', and this 'mental, or revived, image occupies the same place in the brain and other parts of the system as the original sensation did' (Bain, *Emotions*, 370). Hence the Will is enabled to direct itself to the idea, and so to control it; and in this way the activity of attention is explained.

But this view will not bear an impartial scrutiny. I say nothing about the physiological hypothesis on which it seems to hang, and I will not ask whether, if the facts were as alleged, the explanation would be sufficient; for the facts are largely otherwise.[1] I attend to various visceral sensations, I attend to a single instrument in an orchestra, I attend to the several components of a smell, I attend to colour and not shape, and I attend in one colour, such as greenish-blue, to the blue or to the green; but it is needless to go on. There is according to the theory 'a muscular intervention' in all these cases. And this cannot mean merely that in all there exists *some* 'muscular element', for this (if true) would be perfectly *irrelevant*. The fact to be explained is my attending to A or B and not to C or D, and unless there are special 'muscular elements' *a*, *b*, *c*, and *d*, the fact is not explained. But, if such elements are everywhere postulated, then I think I may say that, when the

[1] Cp. Lotze, *Med. Psych.*, 509.

physiologists and the anatomists have been converted, it will be time enough for the psychologist to inquire. On the other hand, if, as I presume, Professor Bain makes no such postulate, then I am unable to see how the theory can touch the fact to be explained.

Active attention does not consist merely in muscular innervation, and, if so, we must go on to look elsewhere. But I should like to say first that it seems to me most doubtful if attention *must* have even a muscular concomitant. I do not deny that early in development this is so, and I do not deny that, if attention reaches a certain degree of strength, there is some muscular accompaniment, such as frowning. But in my actual experience, when I pass from inattention to a direction of my thoughts, I cannot verify the *universal* presence of a muscular element; and I know no good *a priori* proof of that presence. I should add that to me this question seems to be merely one of fact, and to have no other psychological importance.[1]

We have now surveyed, and to some extent have cleared, our ground, and the best course will, I think, be rapidly to go through the rest of our cases, and to ask in each if we require a specific activity of attention. After this and in conclusion we will deal with some particular difficulties.

Let us first take the case where a sensation engrosses us, though not directly, and where yet we are not conscious of any activity. What operates here will be a connected idea; for the idea engrosses, and what goes with it will therefore engross us also. We, I presume, are all agreed that ideas and that groups of ideas may interest. In what interest consists is a difficult question. It is, I think, quite certain that it consists to a large extent in pleasure and pain, but that it always consists in nothing else, or that pleasure or pain *must* always be present, seem both to me improbable.

---

[1] Some psychologists appear to be so taken by the idea of our voluntary muscles that they seem at times to forget the existence of such things as glands and skin and mucous membranes. I would refer the reader specially to those chapters in Dr. Tuke's *Influence of the Mind upon the Body* which deal with the action of the intellect upon the involuntary muscles and the organic functions; or see Carpenter's *Mental Physiology*.

But for the purpose of this article I shall assume that what interests does so by means of pleasure or pain. Then, if an idea is pleasing, that idea may engross us, and if an indifferent sensation suggests the idea, the idea on its side will affect the sensation and cause it to dominate (cp. J. S. Mill, loc. cit. 372). How it does so is again a question that opens a somewhat wide field. We must content ourselves with the answer that it works by redintegration and also by blending. It is blending when, if two mental elements have got the same content, the intensities of both are more or less combined with a total or partial fusion of the elements. I should say that this process cannot wholly be reduced to redintegration, and whether its existence is compatible with the strict principles of the English school of 'association', I do not know. It of course presents some difficulties in general, and raises a number of interesting problems. But, without dwelling on these questions, we may lay down the result that, if an idea engrosses, then any sensation which is connected with that idea may in consequence engross. And attention so far has appeared to consist in interest, either direct or transferred; an account which, we shall find, will hold good everywhere (cp. Waitz, *Lehrbuch*, 634–7).

Let us pass on to the cases where we feel an activity. In the first class of these we make no resolve, but, performing an operation, we are occupied with our performance. We are writing or reading, and the subject engrosses us. We, I presume, attend, and we certainly seem active; and the question is, What is such active attention, and does it simply once more consist in interest? I have no doubt that it does. The subject may predominate because of the activity, but the activity itself is produced by interest. Why am I active? Because the function of itself is interesting, or because the idea of the result is dominant. The main idea of the subject favours those activities which further its existence, and it lends them its strength. It naturally selects them. Or the idea of an answer to a question which interests creates uneasiness and a coming up and maintenance of any function which serves to relieve.

The attention is caused by an indirect interest, for that produces the activity whose subject predominates.

There are some objections which, perhaps, before we go on, should be considered here. It may be said first (*a*) that no intellectual activity exists, and secondly (*b*) that the dominant idea could not work. The objections have perhaps not been made in this form, but it will serve to bring out the points of difficulty.

(*a*) If no intellectual activity exists, and if yet there is *some* activity present in intellectual functions, this activity, it would seem, might be attention. It is not possible for me here to discuss the question of intellectual activities, their existence and their origin, and I prefer to reply, If no activity of intellect, then none whatever; for psychology deals simply with psychical processes. I shall return lower down to this general question, but here will assume that the intellect is active.[1] And if so, its activity upon a certain object will (as was said before) result from interest. The objection, however, may be pressed as follows. Let that be the case, it may be said, where the intellect does something; but what where it does nothing and where yet I am active? In the *retention* of an image or in the *watching* of an object I am certainly active; but where is the intellectual product? The product appears to be mere attention and, if so, the activity must be attention also. I must meet this objection by attempting to show the nature of retention and of observation. The feeling of activity I will deal with hereafter.

What is active *retention*? The image of a person will not stay before our minds, or in reflection we fail to keep hold of an idea or maintain a process. We make an effort and succeed, but where is the machinery? The machinery, I answer, consists of an idea which is able to dominate and so fixes an object connected with itself. This idea may be simply the idea of the presence of the idea required. Again it may be some other idea which implies the first and makes a whole with it, a process familiar under the name of Con-

---

[1] I should say that I decidedly reject the doctrine that active attention consists in comparison. See Lotze, *Metaph.*, 540, *Grundzüge d. Psych.*, 26.

tiguity. This idea will retain partly by means of Red-integration. It has a context which perpetually suggests the idea to be retained as often as that wavers; and this context again is more or less extensive, and therefore self-supporting or self-restoring. And secondly, the idea (as was mentioned before) will strengthen by blending, and so tend to retain. These I think are the means employed for retention; and if so, there is no specific activity. Let us pass to *observation*. When we watch, say a trap, or perhaps a rabbit-hole, or the proceedings in a law-court, what is it that we do? The last example suggests an instructive distinction. When we observe we must do it in a certain interest; but we may either want to see what happens in this or that special way, or generally to see whatever may happen. And the explanation seems simple. The idea of the object changing itself in such or such a manner is an interesting idea, and so naturally causes retention of this object in prominent perception. And where we are said to watch simply, the idea is the same, only now indefinite. If I am told to keep my eye upon anything, the idea of my seeing some change is suggested, and my observation is a case of motived retention.[1] We may say then that either there is no activity or that the activities (mental or physical) are *not* a specific attending. Attention will be everywhere a mere example of the common processes of mind, and will consist in the influence of a dominant idea.

(*b*) Or if it is said that this dominant idea could not influence, the answer is easy. It must be admitted that, by what has been called 'Contiguity', the idea of the end both prompts and selects the means which produce it. And the dominance of that idea is surely indisputable. It may not contract the muscles, and may fail even to produce 'a nascent stage of the process of innervation' or 'a tendency

---

[1] We should avoid the mistake of treating these phenomena as cases of Comparison. They *may* involve Comparison, but cannot do so from the first, since they certainly precede it. At an early stage there are not two things held before the mind, and so Comparison is impossible. They belong to the same class as elementary Recognition, where we find a sameness or difference without knowing what that is.

to strive' (whatever that may mean), and if the reader is committed to such ideas I cannot hope to persuade him. But I would ask others to reflect that we have been willing to suppose that the idea prevails through pleasure and pain, and (if you must say so) through desire. All that is wanted so far for a common understanding is the presence of the idea and the denial that its influence consists in a discharge upon the muscles, whether actual or potential.

'Still,' the objection may come, 'in an act like retention we fix ideas that waver, and we even recall an idea that has vanished. And we are said to do this by "the idea of the idea". But an idea must either be there or not there, and cannot be both, unless somehow "potential". So that an idea of an idea is not admissible.' I confess that the phrase has a certain obscurity, and I do not know whether any one has worked out the detail of its various meanings. But it is not hard to make a sufficient reply.[1] It is plain that we have the idea of an idea. We may be asked (e.g.) for our idea of a statesman, and may be answered, 'I do not call that an idea.' 'Tell me then,' we might reply, 'what is *your* idea of an idea of a statesman.' And that means, Give me the general character which such an idea should have. This account will hold good everywhere. The idea of an idea is a psychical state, the character of which is used representatively and contains the feature of being an idea of a certain kind. We may distinguish two varieties. In the first of these the absent idea which I think of is the idea pure and simple, while in the second it will include my psychical state as I have this idea. For example, I possess a general idea of the solution of a problem, and that in the first case contains merely the general character of the answer required, or the principal feature of the necessary process. But if (as in the second case) I think of myself as having the solution or as performing the process, I must represent also the psychical presence of the whole event, of course again only in its general aspect. Thus, if we realized the first idea we should have simply to fill out

[1] I think that Professor Bain has given to a kindred question an answer that is somewhat confused, in a note on James Mill's *Analysis*, ii. 358.

its logical content, but the reality of the second would give us its actual psychical existence. And with this passing notice I must leave an objection which depends upon a vicious theory that would destroy logic wholly and cripple psychology.[1]

To resume then, ideas of ideas are possible, and such ideas can dominate, and the presence of these ideas can produce their own reality. And so far attention has been fully explained as an instance of the working of ordinary laws. But we have still another class of our facts to consider. The cases of attention which so far we have surveyed are in a sense involuntary. In them we had not a resolve to attend. We must now deal with the class where I say 'I will attend to this matter' and do so, or where at all events I resolve to perform such an act as implies attention. At this point, it may be said, our explanation breaks down, and here we have a specific and original activity. All before was automatic, but this is volitional and gives us a direct revelation of energy.

'But an energy that does what?' is the natural reply. I suppose an energy that fixes and strengthens. Well, if so, I am led to remark at once that the presumption is in favour of our old account, because fixation and strengthening was what it explained. If, when I simply attend, that function results from an indirect interest, is it likely that when I resolve to attend we should have to import a wholly new factor and bring upon the stage a supervening agency? Let us examine this more nearly.

When I readily attend to the details of a subject and perform the operations (both physical and mental) that lead to a view of them, or when in general I pursue the means to some end, that, we saw, did not involve any other attention than was explained by the normal working of interest. We must now take the case where, prompted to such application, I am solicited elsewhere, and return to my task after wavering and struggle, perhaps in addition

---

[1] The unsatisfactory way in which internal volition is dealt with (or ignored by) the mass of psychologists comes in part from an inability to distinguish clearly between the idea of and the reality of an idea.

saying to myself, 'I am resolved to mind my business.'
And there is a suggestion, it would seem, that in these
cases we are met by a difference of principle. But, we ask,
where is this difference? In the struggle of ideas and feelings in my mind, and in the inconstant result, there is
nothing surely which calls for special explanation, nor
most assuredly is there a consciousness of special activity.
And if it is the act of resolve upon which stress is laid, then
I fully admit that this function must be recognized as
differing from others, but I see no reason to think it one
kind by itself or anything but an instance of our general
principles. We have seen that what interests occupies our
minds, and that it does so directly or indirectly. We have
seen that in the latter class we have the working of an idea,
and in some cases also the help of an action, physical or
intellectual—such action not being an activity of attention
in any specific sense. We saw in short that attention,
whether we understand it as the state of our being engrossed, or as an action which brings about such a state,
was nothing unique, nothing else but a result and an
illustration of more general laws. Thus, if we take interest
to mean liking, attention comes from liking, my liking for
the thing or for something that implies it, the idea of some
person to whom I am attached, or of some pursuit or principle more or less abstract. These interests are ideas which,
in the normal course of psychical events, work out their
detail by a transfer of liking and support that detail against
invasion. We shall see that *resolve* does but illustrate this
process.

I am to say 'I will attend', and am then in consequence
really to attend; and on the other hand in our account
attention consisted in indirect interest—interest, that is,
in a further idea. But here where is the idea? It is not far
to seek. If I resolve to attend, I of course have the idea of
myself attending. That is, I have either an idea of myself
doing this or that work, which work in fact produces
attention, or I have an explicit idea of myself attending
to something to which the work is in fact a condition.
This idea of myself in such a character dominates by its

pleasure, or its implication with pain, or its force, or its associations (we have agreed to leave this matter unsettled), and it produces in the common psychological way the means to its realization. Where is then the difficulty? I have an idea of myself doing this or that, and such an idea may surely be interesting. Or, if it is not so in itself, there are further ideas of myself accomplishing a whole performance which includes it, pursuing (e.g.) the greatest possible sum of pleasures, or acting upon some other principle of virtue. In short, give me the idea of myself somehow engaged, and let that idea give me, indirectly or directly, a feeling of satisfaction or success or self-approval, or in some manner interest me, then, if this idea is connected with means that lead to its reality, it surely will produce them in the ordinary way. The result of attention will follow the resolve without any mysterious 'act' which intervenes, and the phenomenon is explained by indirect interest. It may be said that the idea works *because* I fix it, and that this fixation *is* attending; but the answer is of course that another idea, a still more remote interest, fixes the first one and sets up the process. And if some arbitrary force proceeding from the self is suggested against me, I can only reply that I do not know what this means. I cannot well discuss phrases which convey to me nothing I can find in fact, and which I am compelled to believe are simply unintelligible.

We have now traversed the field which we set before us, and have offered an account of its main phenomena, defective no doubt, but I trust sufficient to answer our purpose. We have found nothing in attention that is not derivative, nothing which could justify our placing it among the primary elements of mind. In attention there is either no activity at all beyond the common processes of redintegration and blending, or, if the activity exists, itself *is* not attention. Any function whatever of the body or the mind will be active attention if it is prompted by an interest and brings about the result of our engrossment with its product. There is no primary act of attention, there is no specific act of attention, there is no one kind of act of attention at all. That is our result, and through the rest of this paper I shall consider some objections and attempt to remove some remaining difficulties.

I will first make a remark on the nature of Resolve. When I determine to act, either now or in the future (and perhaps again only in case an uncertain condition is fulfilled), I am aware of a peculiar state of mind. I do not act and yet I feel myself asserted, forefelt (so to speak) in an unreal action. But this state admits of an easy explanation. Apart from its actual realization an idea may possess very many degrees of particularity. Now when the idea of an action is opposed by other states, they prevent it from filling itself out with detail in accordance with the reality at present perceived or imagined in the future. But, as the obstacle is from any cause lessened or removed, this idea will in proportion grow more particular, and, if it cannot lead to action, will be largely filled out by ideal detail. This detail will of course contain feelings the same in character as those which would be present in the real act; but there is no need to explain this by a hypothetical physiology, or to raise a mist with vague phrases such as 'tendency' and 'nascent'. The fact is merely that of these feelings the greater part (if not all) will be less intense than they would be in the action, and a varying amount of them will be wholly absent. Still, enough will be there to give a sense of expansion, such as we feel to accompany our real actions; and this is mistaken for proof of an inner energy, not derived from common sources, but to be referred to a specific act of attention or some other faculty. I should like to work out this point in greater detail, but I have only room to suggest that any intelligent adherent of arbitrary Free-will should do it for himself.

I will pass next to a kindred source of difficulty. 'In attention', I may be told, 'we feel that we are active; we are aware of energy, and we know this directly. In the account which you have given this factor is omitted, since attention comes there as a result from elements that are not active. And we object that the essence of the matter is

omitted since the essence is just this revealed activity.'
But I should reply that, if attention is *not* derivative, the
right course is to show my mistake in its derivation. If I
have either accounted (or am able to account) for every
single thing which your 'energy' *performs*, you will hardly
persuade me that the feeling you speak of is really effective,
or is anything but a concomitant, more or less constant
and more or less obscure. And I think that I might fairly
leave the matter so. But, since the consciousness of force
has been given an importance which is paramount (and I
might add transcendent and absolute), it is better to add
some further remarks.

I would first suggest that a revelation of activity or of
force or of will or of energy (or indeed of anything which
answers to a phrase of this sort) is open to dangerous metaphysical criticism. If these ideas can be shown to contradict themselves, then the revelation could be met by an
admission of its existence, but also by a denial of the truth
of its message; and in England at least I am sure that this
criticism has (to speak in general) been merely ignored.
I mention this in passing, and I lay no stress on it, since
in psychology I do not think such a criticism would be
relevant any more than it would be in physics or physiology. But, confining myself to the field of psychology, I
utterly deny the alleged revelation. It gives us not a fact
but an intellectual construction, and (I should add) a
thorough misinterpretation. In the first place I should like
to be told *what* it is that the message conveys. Does it tell
me of my body or of my mind or of both, and what precisely does it tell me? I have supposed (perhaps wrongly)
that psychology is a science which deals with psychical
events and the laws of those events, and that the phrase
'activity', whenever used, should be explicable in those
terms. But though others no doubt may have had better
fortune, my own experience is that in our leading psycho-
logies it is difficult or impossible to know what 'active' or
'energy' means. And since apparently these words stand
for something important, I cannot but feel that we have
a right to complain. If I may say what I think, the present

use of these phrases is little better than a scandal and a main obstacle in the path of English psychology. If one cannot employ them with a definite meaning, why use them at all? For a psychology that could not get on without them would most assuredly pass its own sentence. And (to apply what I have said to the present case) if the activity which is revealed tells me something about the origin and the nature of those events which we call attention, then, until its message is translated into clearness, we cannot regard it. But if it is meant to be a feeling which gives no message at all, and the question is whether this fact is essential to the process of attention, and again whether and how far we are able to decompose it, then it seems to me that the language applied to this feeling has been strangely misleading. For suppose that a psychical event which we cannot analyse is a necessary link in the process of attending, then from this it will follow that attention so far cannot be explained. But from this there is no passage to a statement about activity, which (whatever it may be) seems certainly complex and largely to be built upon inference from experience.

But on the assertor of such a link in the process of attention lies the burden of proof. Even suppose that a feeling of activity is present, yet we have explained the fact of attention without it, and so we deny its efficacy. And in the second place we remark that a feeling of energy can hardly be asserted in *all* attention, and that it is difficult to say at what stage (if at any) it is always a concomitant. And where it is concomitant, perhaps there we go on to call the attention 'active' for no reason but the presence of this delusive feeling, which (so far as we have gone) seems not active at all but an accompaniment more or less superfluous. And if it is said, 'But you have not explained this feeling', I might reply that I cannot be called upon to do so. If I do not, does it follow that my account of attention is incorrect? Or, if so, would it follow that *therefore* attention reveals activity or energy or will or any other tidings of the kind? But if this could not be maintained, then perhaps, with a view to make good my case, I should do better to deny the claim of the feeling and to rest on the denial. Still, to throw light on the subject so far as I can, I will offer some remarks on the nature of this much-misused phenomenon.

First let me say that by calling a feeling 'derivative' I do not mean that it comes *simply* from the union of other psychical elements. I do not mean that an emotion *is* simply those conditions which we say produce it. The conditions, the presence of certain psychical elements, must often, if not always, produce other states before the whole is present which we call the emotion. Of course *how*, for example, given certain ideas, certain internal sensations follow upon them is an open question; and it is an open question, when those sensations have followed, what part of this mass of sensations and ideas and feelings *is* the actual emotion. I have not to resolve these doubts, but am to point out conditions through which we get, and without which we should not get, the feeling of activity.

This last phrase recalls a shocking ambiguity. A 'feeling *of*' has at least three different senses. It means feeling simply felt, and that never as yet has been interpreted by and combined with ideas, or feeling recognized as that which is *of* something else, or feeling not now recognized but modified by the results of past recognition. In the first of these cases the 'of' does not belong to the feeling. It belongs solely to an outsider who adds ideas true or false, but in either case derived from other experience. And to predicate these ideas directly 'of' the feeling is a serious error. Now if we take activity at the stage where it is recognized and is felt as such, we can see at once its composite character. It contains the idea of myself changing something opposed, and it contains still more. If I suffered a change from which something else followed, that by itself would not be taken as activity. The change must come from me, that is, I must have an idea of it (if not also a desire), and this idea, or end, must lead to the change. Now I think no one can deny that to be conscious of all this is possible only through a liberal interpretation of much experience. But on the other hand what sense, when these constituents are removed, is left to my consciousness of energy put forth? If there is a feeling which goes now together with this complex and has gone before it, that feeling is *of* energy in much the same manner in which relief from the pains of hunger and cold is a feeling *of* swaddling clothes and *of* milk, or a metaphysical proof of their absolute reality.

But what is the feeling which becomes by experience the feeling of activity? Or for the present let us ask what are its conditions. I think its origin lies in the feeling of expansion that follows upon the enlargement of the self. I have to assume the doctrine that of our psychical contents a certain group is closely united, and is connected in a very special manner with pleasure and pain, and that this group is the first appearance of our self. I have to assume again that this psychical mass, with its connexions, is perpetually growing larger and smaller as against other elements. And I must assume once more that the expansion gives *in general* a feeling of pleasure, while contraction brings pain, and that we may call these the two chief modes of self-feeling. I must assume all this here and pass over the difficulties which of course beset it. Now the expansion is *not* the consciousness of activity, nor is it a consciousness of the self or the body or a consciousness of anything at all. It merely is and is felt in a certain way. Not till after a considerable growth of the soul (which we cannot here deal with) does there come the perception of a self and a not-self with what is called consciousness. Then when we get to know from repeated experience that changes ensue upon modes of our self (as a body that is conscious, and later as consciousness along with a body), we acquire the notion of activity or will. We are active when the not-self, consisting in external or internal sensation or perception or idea, changes on the presence of an idea and (I will add) a desire of that change within the self. This expansion of our area beginning from within gives a certain feeling, and it is interpreted as a putting forth of a something from out the self into the not-self—the something being energy or force or will, named in a variety of phrases all equally delusive, and in fact of course being nothing at all. Where the group of the self is contracted by the not-self and a pleasant idea of expansion is suggested, there is a feeling of pressure. When in addition the limit of resistance wavers, and the ideal expansion is realized partly, with a further advance of expansion in idea and perhaps an oscillation of actual retreat and actual advance, there is wavering and a consciousness of tension and effort.[1] In all this there is a happening—a happening of events; there is nothing beside facts coexistent and successive, with the result of other facts. And I think in this way we could give throughout psychology a definite meaning to action and passivity.

I cannot dwell on this outline, but must hasten to consider a point of interest. There is no doubt that in getting from experience (as we must) the idea of self-expansion, the muscular element is most important. But it would be wrong to say that our sense of tension and effort must always come from muscular feeling. In the resistance of an idea that will haunt or escape us, and in the tension of waiting for the issue of a crisis, the origin of the feeling is clearly not muscular. And if it is urged that at any rate the feeling has elements which must have arisen from muscular experience, that, if true, would not be relevant. It would not show that these elements originate the feeling, and it ignores the distinction between a total emotion and its producing conditions which we mentioned above. I have not said that from self-expansion, however strong the ideas and sensations concerned, and however intense the pleasure and pain, would come the entire emotion of activity, strain, effort, and success. Not only do the kinds of the elements involved make important differences, but there is a fresh result of internal sensations. This result—take, for instance, the sense we have of fatigue or elation—is exceedingly hard to decompose. It seems an obscure confusion or blending of organic sensations from a variety of sources, and I confess that at present I should not feel able to discuss it. I have mentioned it to point out that it does not

[1] Cp. Waitz, 301 ff.; Nahlowsky, *Gefühlsleben*, 86 ff.

concern us, for it is clearly no more than concomitant with, or sequent on, what we call activity. If we have hitherto found no revelation of energy, we need hardly look for its original message in this residual oracle of organic sensation.

I have now said all that within present limits I can say on the psychical origin of our sense of activity, and of the meaning we might give to the term in psychology if so disposed, and I must hasten to bring these remarks to an end. But there is one point as to which I may fear misconstruction. It might possibly be said that physiology proves attention to be active, and that this settles the matter. Now of course I am not competent to speak physiologically. I have the sincerest respect for physiologists. I believe them to be men as a class superior in ability to psychologists and surpassing them in devotion, and engaged on a subject to whose difficulties (it seems to me) those offered by psychology are in comparison trifling. But such a question as the existence of a psychical activity is a matter which falls outside physiology. We might get from that science instruction valuable and, in some particulars, even necessary; but suppose that we knew (as I presume we do *not* yet know) the physical side of the psychical process, is it certain that about the main question we should not be precisely where we are now? For in the first place the existence of this or that feeling could hardly be deduced from physiological premises if actual observation were unable to find it. And in the second place between a process in the brain and a consciousness of energy there is really a gulf which is not to be filled up. You may know from experience that they are found together, but, given the first, you could never have got to the second, and they remain in the end quite heterogeneous. And so I venture to think that, whether the incoming current stimulates the centre, or the centre discharges on the motor nerves, or the central motor organ puts forth energy also upon the sensory centre, or whatever else may happen, is as regards the main question entirely irrelevant, and, so far as I can judge, seems likely to remain so. And if any one replies, Here is physiological activity with a psychical feeling, and *therefore* of course the latter must be a feeling *of* activity, I will not gainsay it. I will merely ask him not to vary the meaning of his phrase without giving us notice, and somewhere to set down as clearly as he can what he means by a physiological activity. He should then give us a list of the psychical states where this condition is present, either according to the doctrine of physiologists in general, or of perhaps two or three, or of perhaps himself only. And in this case we may avoid that disastrous muddle of the body and the mind, which may appear 'scientific' but can advance no science.

We have now seen that from physiology no evidence can be brought to settle our main problem, and we have already attempted to exhibit the origin of our sense of expended energy. If that account is correct, then a specific activity of attention is no fact observed in the mind, but is a construction more or less fictitious and misleading. And if our account is not correct, that result still remains. We shall have shown that in every stage of attention we require no intervening event, and that a sense of energy (supposing it to exist) would be therefore not essential and probably not effective, but a more or less constant concomitant or result. And, if so, we have accomplished the task we undertook. There are two features however in the process of attention which deserve a passing notice.

Is attention negative, and is it so directly or always indirectly? I think the latter view the right one. When we are engrossed by one thing we lose sight of the others (why this must be so I shall not inquire), but the attention seems positive. And when an idea is painful and perhaps suggests also a prospect of pain, and when because of this character it is weakened or banished (I shall not ask through what means), there is in no case a negative activity of banishment. The attention which banishes is the dominance of an interest exclusive of the first and with a possible dominance of the idea of their conflict. In the latter case the positive interest will be strengthened by a powerful contrast, and attention to the pain will increase its strength and may hasten its disappearance. Further, when we attend to the absence of a certain idea in the sense of attending to the prevention of its presence, the influence is positive. We have the idea of a certain element being suggested and being found in fact to be incongruous with reality, and we have also (let us say) the desire that this should be so. Hence, when the idea arises, we have (apart from the weakening action of pain) a strong suggestion of its expulsion from the field. And the first chance mental element that suits with this suggestion attracts our notice and is used as the positive side of expulsion. But if the idea of what ought to be expelled is too dominant, the process renews itself and defeats its own purpose. There can be no attention which is merely negative.

Finally we may ask how attention is fixed. We resolve to attend, and we persist in that attitude though the object is not in itself engaging. This is easily explained. In resolving to attend we had, as we saw, an idea of ourselves, and we have in the sequel a constant perception or feeling of ourselves (based no doubt upon our internal sensations) as being here and now and in this or that disposition or attitude. It is this more or less particular perception of self which recalls the resolve, and, in the absence of attention, produces a conflict between the idea and the fact of ourselves. In the same way any obvious external object or internal condition, once connected with the idea of myself engrossed in a certain way by such or such an object, will more or less continually suggest that idea with the usual result. The principle in these cases is one and the same, and the detail of its various applications would hardly serve to make it much clearer.

XI

ON A FEATURE OF ACTIVE ATTENTION

[*First published in* MIND, o.s. xii, No. 46, 314. *April*, 1887.]

I SHOULD like, in consequence of Mr. Ward's article (*M*. o.s. xii. 45–67), to be allowed a few words on an essential point. To Mr. Ward's objections in general I cannot reply, because the only answer I could make would be to confess that I have failed entirely and throughout to convey to him my meaning. I am sorry for this, because otherwise I should have valued his criticism. All I wish to do here is to attempt to clear up one point as to active attention—namely, the manner in which it may intensify sensations. The account which I adopted (*M*. o.s. xi = *E*. x) was that the result is caused by a transfer of strength from an idea through blending.

If we take for example a composite smell, one of its elements may engross me directly by its strength. Again, resolving to observe and bringing the idea of one element, I may find the answering component in sensation strengthened. Or again, that component may excite ideas, its own forming the centre, and upon this we may find the sensation grow stronger. In all these cases I think the idea blends itself with the sensation, so adding strength thereto. No doubt much happens besides, but I think thus much to be essential, and I tried (as I believed) to say so (*E*. x. 186–9).

Nor need any one who holds that the working idea interests through pleasure be, I think, at a loss. If he should be so misled as to doubt that there are ideas of pleasure, he need not therefore cease to believe that ideas may be pleasant. Nor need he doubt that an idea, like every other psychical event, has a force which is not the same as its pleasantness. He will say, I think, that the influence of this pleasure on the sensation is another and a further question, but that here the essential point to his mind is a transfer of strength as distinct from pleasantness.

But, for myself, I do *not* hold that interest must consist in pleasure, and I really did my best, though it would seem not successfully, to say so (ibid. 186–7). I ought, indeed, to have mentioned, when, for argument's sake, I treated the interest of ideas as their pleasantness, that I did not intend that to hold good, for argument's sake, of sensations also. This, in fact, did not occur to me, and so I omitted to issue any warning to the reader.

I will only add my regret that my paper should have appeared to be a criticism of Mr. Ward individually. Nothing in it referred to him, and when the manuscript left my hands I do not think that I had read one word of his writing. I have had that pleasure since, and can assure Mr. Ward that, though I think the view of attention which he has adopted is quite inadmissible, this is far from blinding me to the solid value of his work in general.

XII

ASSOCIATION AND THOUGHT

[*First published in* MIND, o.s. xii, No. 47, 354–81. *July*, 1887.]

THE intention of this paper is to show in outline how Thought comes to exist. Its method, I trust, is strictly psychological. It has to do solely with psychical occurrences and their laws. The facts immediately experienced within a single organism or soul,[1] and those facts regarded merely as events which happen, make the object of psychology.[2] The word 'Association' has been used to express my

---

[1] Not *subject*, because at first there is no proper subject, nor Ego, for the further reason that in abnormal states we may have more than one Ego or none at all. If we do not define by the organism, as for some reasons is undesirable (I do not discuss this), we must use the word 'soul' or 'mind'. In psychology I should define the soul as 'a totality of immediate experience, possessed of a certain temporal continuity of existence, and again of a certain identity in character'. 'Totality' is used to exclude partial states. 'Experience' is not definable: it can only be indicated. 'Immediate' negatives and excludes phenomena so far as their content is used beyond their existence: truth, e.g., *as truth* is not merely psychical. The amount of continuity and ideal identity required to make a single soul is matter of opinion, and mainly, I should say, of arbitrary opinion. The above definition is of course open to metaphysical objections, as are the conceptions which *must* be used in all empirical science. The objections are therefore irrelevant. It would be as idle to urge that the soul (as above) is not a real thing as to say the organism is not one real thing because its matter has changed. At any given time the soul *is* its phenomenal contents *plus* that past which is taken to belong to it.

[2] On the object of psychology see an article by the Editor, *M.* o.s. viii. 1–21. Mr. Ward, *M.* o.s. xii. 45–67, in objecting to the above position, has invited me to define a psychical fact or event. A metaphysical definition I of course decline to give in an empirical science (*L.* 339–42 = 315–18). A definition in psychology is for me a working definition. It is not expected to have more truth than is required for practice in its science; and if when pressed beyond it contradict itself, that is quite immaterial. With this understanding I will state what I mean by a psychical event, first giving an incomplete definition and then correcting it. A psychical fact must (1) be immediately experienced (see above). (2) It must have duration: what does not exist through a succession of moments is not a fact. (3) It must have quality: there must be sense in asking 'of what sort', quality being here

agreement with the English school at its best. With it I am convinced that thought proper is a product, and that,

taken to include the aspect of pleasure and pain, though usually it is convenient to separate quality from 'tone'. (4) A fact has intensity. (5) In reply to the possible objection that duration *has* not duration, &c., we must say, Any one of the above aspects *is* a fact, so far as it is a mere aspect of that which has all the rest. So far, I hope, the definition is not very obscure. But, further, (6) it is necessary to include relations, even where no one would say that they are immediately experienced. Is the reappearance of some traits of childhood in old age not a psychical fact? But are these relations of succession and identity immediately experienced either by the soul or by the observing psychologist? We see here the impotence of empirical science to justify its principles theoretically. We have to amend our definition of fact; and yet, if amended, it threatens to let in metaphysics. But we meet this practically by the proviso that the above relations are not facts, save and except so far as they exist between facts as previously defined. That, I hope, answers the purpose; and the definition will run: 'A psychical fact is anything which is immediately experienced and has duration, quality, intensity; or is any one of these aspects, as a mere distinguishable aspect— so far, that is, as one aspect is taken as belonging to something which possesses the other aspects also; or, again, is any relation existing between any facts as previously defined.' If we leave individual states and go on to the general, and ask if laws are facts—that is, to some extent, I presume, a matter of taste. I should say that, to speak properly, they are not so, though it may be convenient to call them so. The laws, of course, are confined to the region of facts.

It must be, of course, understood that our science does not disregard *other* aspects of psychical states, e.g. logical or ethical. But it looks at them merely with a view to deal with them as appearing in and as influencing the course of psychical events. And a reply to the objection that 'an unanalysable element in every psychical event' is not itself an event (l.c. 66) seems hardly wanted when we know what we mean by an event. Obviously the whole life of a man is an event, is a piece of new duration, though no event to the man. And, apart from that, changes in the intensity of the element would, of course, be events; as would be also the changes in the relation of that element to others. Mr. Ward, I presume, has argued from some meaning which he attaches to fact and I do not. But my object is merely to find a plain way of barring metaphysics out of psychology, and I am far from asserting that another way cannot be found, though an 'individualistic standpoint' is, I am sure, no solution. Unless this end is reached somehow, the amount of metaphysics to be introduced is limited merely by the inclination or the knowledge of the psychologist. I say advisedly that I do not know a single metaphysical question which can be ruled out of psychology on principle, if any single one is let in; and I would call upon every English psychologist to face this problem without reserve, and to come either to an understanding or at least to a clear issue.

starting from what is presented, and keeping wholly to that field and to the laws of its movements, our science can trace Thought's probable generation. And if at any point we fail, then that point must be marked as 'at present unknown'. Nothing can warrant our importation of a faculty or faculties, or a subject and its functions, or an activity, or an energy, if we mean by these more than some law of phenomena, some way of happening among psychical events. Our sole remedy is to reconsider our data and their laws, and to refuse to bring shame upon our honest nakedness by scraps of physiology and rags of metaphysics. It is to mark my entire adhesion to this principle that I have used 'Association', but I dissent from very much that has been joined to the word. The English school, in my opinion, has failed to show the origin of the higher phenomena, because in its starting-point it has been seriously mistaken. Both the elements and the laws, into which (like all science) it has analysed the given, have been formulated in such a way that successful advance from them seems not possible. And the main cause is to be found in that dogmatic Atomism, which (whatever it might be as a statement of first principles) had no right to interfere with an empirical science. But I will not repeat a criticism which elsewhere I felt bound to urge to the extreme, and perhaps urged too harshly. I would rather feel that, in helping (so far as I can help) to modify the starting-point and to make progress easier, I am endeavouring at least to work in the spirit of the best English tradition.

For more reasons than one I cannot pretend to offer here the satisfactory treatment of so large a subject. I shall attempt in the first place to mark out the ground by pointing to the main characteristic of Thought; I shall then try to show rapidly how this feature has arisen, from what foundation, and by what laws; and in the third place shall deal with some difficulties. I shall have everywhere to be so brief as to require the utmost indulgence of the reader, and will at once begin with the first of my tasks.

What is the chief characteristic of Thought? I shall make on this point a very short statement, and must be allowed to refer to my *Principles of Logic*. The main feature is objectivity, and this means a control proceeding from the object. That which suffers control is the entire psychical process, so far as it does not subserve the development of the object. Sensations, emotions, fancies, volitions, are suppressed or modified to suit this end. I may, of course, will to think, and to think this or that, but the way in which this or that shapes itself in thought is independent of my liking. To interfere would be to vitiate or wholly destroy. But now what is the object? That it is not mere sense-experience should be a commonplace. Nor is it simply whatever is excluded from the self, because the self is also an object of thought. And to say it is that of which we are conscious would throw no light, if we may be conscious where we do not (strictly) think. The object is any portion of the psychical process, so far as it bears and subserves a certain character. It must in the first place have a meaning, an ideal content which is distinct from its existence as a psychical occurrence. And further, this content must preserve its identity. It must from beginning to end be a self-same whole which keeps together without any foreign assistance. We must be able to say that from the beginning it has been and still is merely itself, and is therefore in the end because of its beginning. This claim may be invalid, but it is involved in our beliefs as to what thought must be if it keeps its character. The standard is, in short, to include all the facts and to get them consistent, but to do this merely in an ideal form. The end in other words is individuality, which in the attempt to be perfect must try to be complete, because its autocracy is not possible if its empire is limited. I believe that what follows will make this more clear, and I have stated it that we may realize the task before us. This goal has to be reached by a natural development from the lowest beginnings of psychical life.

I have said that Association in its usual sense has failed to account for this development, and has failed at the end because wrong at the beginning. We have now to modify its principles and make them more effective; but I will first repeat how entirely I accept their main tendency. Psychology is concerned with nothing beyond presentation and its laws, with nothing but the process of given events and the modes of their happening. It is from these elements that we must explain the generation of all else, for at all events no *other* explanation is admitted within our science. I shall state lower down what I mean by presentation, and will now point out the changes to be made in our ordinary doctrine. First, the Atomism must go wholly. We must get rid of the idea that our mind is a train of perishing existences, that so long as they exist have separable being and, so to speak, are coupled up by another sort of things which we call relations. If we turn to what is given this is not what we find, but rather a continuous mass of presentation in which the separation of a single element from all context is never observed, and where, if I may use the expression, no one ever saw a carriage, and still less a coupling, divided from its train. You may urge that your doctrine is the absolute truth in the light of metaphysics. That may be so, but in psychology, because it will not work, it must not be let in. And to the Associationist, as to the Herbartian, we must reply that in our science their metaphysics are irrelevant, and that in other respects we can accept wholly the principles of neither, because (as they are used) they do not seem to work successfully, and because without great inconsistencies they would not work at all.

Hence the Atomism must go wholly, and the 'associative links' must be connexions of content, not conjunctions of existences; in other words, Association marries only universals.[1] I of course do not mean that bare universals are psychical facts. These connexions in strictness are not facts at all, although at times it may be convenient to call them so. An actual fact works so or so because of such or such a connexion when its content has one of the features connected; and it is then a case or instance of the law. But the association by itself is the law by itself, and no actual event that can ever occur. Lower down I shall have to say

[1] I must refer the reader here to my *Principles of Logic*. I do not think I should be justified in occupying the pages of *Mind* with a reprint of my work.

more on what are called 'dispositions', and must now advance rapidly. Atomism being rejected, the Law of Similarity goes with it. This of course expresses truth, but a truth which is derivative and a consequence from others. Its importance rests on the objection to sameness, but psychology (like other sciences) has a right to call phenomena identical so far as they have the same content. And if the sameness is a fiction, none the less it means to use it. We are therefore left with Contiguity, and it is necessary to re-state this so as to make it depend always on identity of content, not of existence. 'Every mental element when present tends to reinstate those elements with which it has been presented.' The meaning of 'tends' is that it does so unless prevented at the time, or unless something in the meantime has happened to prevent it, and that according to circumstances a greater or less force is required for prevention. The 'element' means any distinguishable aspect of the 'what' as against the mere 'that'. And we must remember that these connexions, being independent of the 'this' of mere presentation, hold good everywhere, at all times, and with every context. This has most vital consequences. Psychology should, of course, not assert that its elements in truth and really do work in abstraction and apart from a presented context, and, if it is wise, it will remember that its separation of one part of the soul from the rest, or even again from the universe at large, is made wholly on sufferance. But to any one who brands this assumption as falsehood we must reply, 'If a fiction, it deals with the facts. Let psychology mind its own business.' Whether this altered law of Contiguity should keep its name or have another, such as Redintegration, depends on those who have earned the right to dispose of it. I shall use the term if they permit me.

We have so far reduced the laws of Association to a single principle, and so far I have been able to refer the reader to my *Principles of Logic*.[1] I must now proceed

[1] Professor Bain in *M.* o.s. xii. 161–82 has criticized some points in the account I there gave. I am sorry that the amount of space here at my disposal compels me to say merely that my opinions have not been changed

more slowly. Beside this improved law of Contiguity or
Redintegration, there is a law of Blending or Coalescence
or Fusion. Where different elements (or relations of
elements) have any feature the same they may unite wholly
or partially. The more wholly they unite the more their
differences are destroyed, with a transfer of strength to the
result. And where they unite partially, they may or may
not bring before us a new relation. There is no doubt that
these laws of Contiguity and Blending work so closely
together, that in many cases we hardly know which we
have to lay stress on; but I do not think that one can be
reduced to the other. Unless we extend blending beyond
events (to this point I shall return), it will not cause reproduction, since in that only one of the elements can be
present, and what is absent cannot blend. And, on the
other hand, though with blending we have usually reproduction, yet we also have effects which that will not explain. I must pause to illustrate this latter point. Take the
cases first where strengthening is produced, where, e.g., an
idea makes intense a sensation. You may say that the sensation has its content enlarged by ideal recovery, and that
doubtless is usual; but to say that it is necessary and
that it explains the phenomenon seems quite untenable. In
instances such as those where attention strengthens sensations in the extremities or elsewhere, I cannot *always* find
an enlargement of content, and, if there is ideal recovery,
I am sometimes at a loss to say *what* is reinstated. Take
the cases again where distinctions are produced in a perception or idea.[1] I see a blur in the sky, and because I know
it is a constellation, I then perceive that it is so. Again,
I am thinking of an Englishman and then see a host of
ants, which makes me think of an army of Englishmen. In
the first case we may be told that it is all reproduction, and
that the interstices are recovered by ideal contiguity. But,
I answer, if the idea already was there when I did *not* perceive, will its further reinstatement effect the perception?
Or again, if the idea was not present, and there really has

[1] I have got considerable assistance here from Fortlage, *System der
Psychologie*, 1855. Cp. Volkmann, *Lehrbuch*, § 93.

been an ideal reproduction (or, again, an external suggestion), does that by itself explain sufficiently my altered
perception? We must remember that, having two objects
apparently the same, after an idea has been suggested we
may go on to perceive the suggestion as a fact in one case
and *not* in the other. This must point to a strengthening
as distinct from a recovery. And when I thought of an
army, if the idea of an Englishman was already there, it
could hardly be recovered; and where through association
it was brought in by the ants, yet how was it altered and
turned into an army? Was it not by a transfer through
blending following on the reinstatement? We must say
then that fusion, the importance of which will appear in
the sequel, is not a case of reproduction.

Can we go on to find a principle which underlies the
two laws we have just set forth?[1] I think we can, though
we must not say that these laws can be deduced directly
from it. Every mental element (to use a metaphor) strives
to make itself a whole or to lose itself in one, and it will not
have its company assigned to it by mere conjunction in
presentation. Each struggles to develop itself by the
weapon of identity, which gives strength by coalescence
and enlargement by recall. And this effort to succeed by
association with like characters may bring loss of life to the
single member. To speak more strictly, each element tends
(that is, moves unless prevented) by means of fusion and
redintegration to give itself a context through identity of
content, and in the result which is so made the element
may not survive in a distinguishable form. It is also a fact
that the collision, which results in great part from this
movement, causes pain and unrest; and I think we may see
that the unrest cannot cease as long as the elements given
are unable to form a whole possessed throughout of such
a content that it suggests nothing out of harmony with
anything else. The reader may dismiss this statement as
mere 'transcendentalism'; but until my error is shown me
I shall believe that it is strict empirical psychology, a mere

[1] The process which Wundt calls 'Assimilation' I take to be subordinate
where it is not fictitious.

general statement of the way in which events do happen. We may call it, if we please, the law of Individuation, and we should find that thought and will are each one case of it, made distinct by the different fields in which particularization is worked out. But we must remember that our law perhaps to some extent uses a scientific fiction. It is convenient to speak of the movement of each element, but we must not assert (or deny) that in reality the element can do or be anything—unless, indeed, we are prepared to make psychology a battle-field for metaphysicians.

We have so far seen that Association can be reduced to the struggle of each element towards an independent totality by means of sameness in content, and that this principle works by coalescence where the conditions are given, and, again, by redintegration made through the establishment of connexions superior to time. And if we like to call the movement an *ideal* process, this may distinguish it from what is by comparison *mechanical*, the basis upon which alone it exists and to which it has to suit itself. I must now point out this machinery, though, I fear, without completeness. There is first the incoming of fresh sensations, external and internal, partly new and in part the same. There is the disappearance of old ones, caused I will not here ask how. There is the limit to the amount of what can come to us at once, a limit varying but effective. We see here the conditions of another kind of struggle, a struggle for existence among actual facts, alongside of the former struggle through identity, but crossing it at times and blending with it inextricably. In this more mechanical conflict what favours individuals? We must mention first habit, aptitudes produced by repetition, or got by heredity, or again in some way not known. Elements suited to these are strengthened, and in some cases also enlarged, and so tend to dominate. Where these aptitudes depend on ideal connexions they are instances of association, but where or so far as there is no psychical revival this is not the case. I think that psychology must accept this fact as an ultimate, unless it will venture on Herbart's startling assumptions or deviate into physiology. Passing by this, we come next to mere natural strength of presentation. If we wish to get this *bare*, we must look for it in 'disparate' sensations, those which possess no *special* common character.[1] Strength will here amount simply to prevalence or domination. That which occupies more mental space than or, again, totally or partially excludes something else is said to have more force. And it has *bare* force when it prevails, not by virtue of aught else (such as habit or pleasure), but in its own right and simply.[2] Turning now from these conditions to one not mechanical, though hardly ideal, we reach the influence of pleasure and pain. That these work seems certain (though of course not demonstrable), but the way in which they work is still matter of controversy and I shall pass it by, and for the same reason shall do no more than mention Contrast.

But there is one point which, before we go on, I must notice—the nature of 'traces' or 'residues' or 'dispositions'. Associations are set up, and we say that these exist, but how can that be? Do the elements continue as psychical facts, and if not, do their relations remain somehow apart from them? Or what is the real nature of a general tendency? This is a problem which, in my judgement, falls outside psychology. To ask what a law is belongs to metaphysics, and such a question elsewhere can bring nothing but mischief. There are, so far as I know, four courses we may take, three bad and one good. We may follow the line laid down by Herbart, and force out an explanation by

---

[1] All sensations, in my judgement, do possess some common character. This will hold good whether we do or do not accept the view that the special sense *continua* have been differentiated from one primitive *continuum*. See Horwicz, *Psych. Analysen*.

[2] When we get sensations possessed of a special community we can say of the stronger, It is the less *plus* some more. On the vexed question of 'units' I can say nothing here. The feature of domination in consciousness, or superiority general or special, becomes of course an idea, and we can so get the idea without the reality of strength. The reader will see that I dissent partly from Lotze's view as to strength (*Mikrokosmus*, i. 229, *Metaph.*, § 262). The whole question is very difficult, and would require a long discussion. The reader should consult Mr. Ward's remarks (*Encyc. Brit.* xx. 58), which, however, good as they are, still leave much to be desired.

audacious assumptions and complicated fictions. And then we know where we are; as we may think we do, again, when we deny that a disposition is really psychical, and leave psychology for a region which I assuredly would not venture to call physiology. We clearly do not know where we are when we take a very common third course, and use phrases which may mean anything, to hide the fact that there is nothing distinct that we mean. But there is only one scientific course, to say plainly that what a disposition really may be we neither know nor care. We have in science to do solely with events and their laws, events not being laws, and laws not being events, and we mean by a disposition that, because something has happened, therefore something will happen, *suppose that* something else happens and nothing interferes. And for this reason we cannot talk (except by a licence) of the blending of one disposition with others or with presentations. If no element is there in existing fact, blending has no proper meaning.

We have now glanced at the field in which our improved Association has to develop the various faculties of the mind, and we have seen the motive powers used by the various combatants, and the heterogeneous conditions of victory. We have seen the cause of that disorder which at every moment can be found in the most regulated minds. We have now shortly to describe the beginnings of soul-life, and to exhibit roughly the means by which Thought in the proper sense comes to exist.

To give a picture of the earliest psychical condition, whether in man or the lower animals, is not my intention. Nor is this necessary for my purpose, which is to show merely in outline those steps which connect the origin and the end. The nature of the earliest stage of soul-life must be largely conjectural. It is likely that in some points our knowledge will be much increased; but we shall always be left with certain given limits, within which we must construct a sketch that is probable but which we cannot quite verify. What we can be sure of is that any theory which begins with a derivative function, such as choice or memory, cannot possibly be true. The short account I am to give avoids, I hope, such sheer barbarisms. It is, I trust, at least psychologically possible.[1]

In the beginning there is nothing beyond what is presented, what is and is felt, or rather is felt simply. There is no memory or imagination or hope or fear or thought or will, and no perception of difference or likeness. There are, in short, no relations and no feelings, only feeling. It is all one blur with differences, that work and that are felt, but are not discriminated. Hence to the question, Is this life discrete or continuous ?, our answer is ready. It cannot (for the soul) be discrete, because that implies distinction. There is not only no good evidence in favour of discreteness, but there is this argument against it. Suppose that for an outside observer sensations, as a series or as a collection of series, happened in the mind, yet, for that mind at the outset, the separation and succession would not as such exist. If the whole were not unbroken, it would at least so be given to a feeble mind, because the machinery required for the perception of succession, and of relations in general between sensations, is not yet at work and could not be at work. And, if I am told that this perception is entirely simple and wants no machinery, I am afraid I must pass on, until my objector shows at least that he is not barbarous but has some acquaintance with the question at issue. There are, then, no several sensations for the early mind, and, whatever efficacy we may assign to relation and to change (a point which I omit), there is no change and no relation which comes as such to that mind. For itself it is not discrete, and hence also it is not explicitly continuous.

If now, turning from this point, we ask *what* is presented, that inquiry may have a good many senses. Do special sensations exist, and, if so, in what sense and how many? How do quantity and quality stand one to the other, and can we say that either, as such and specifically, makes itself felt? I intend to pass by these questions, and glance rather at the doubt as to pleasure and pain. Do

---

[1] I must be allowed to refer once more to my *Principles of Logic*. Mr. Ward's excellent article (cited above) will be found in many points to support the view I have adopted.

these exist from the first, or must we say they come later? I do not know any way of deciding this problem. In the first place, I am not sure if sensations are *now* ever entirely indifferent—if, that is, they are ever more than relatively neutral; and, if so, whether they are neutral as being wholly bare, or as having in them a resultant both of pleasure and pain. Again, if we suppose that some sensations are to us now indifferent, either in normal or again in pathological conditions, can we go from that to the conclusion that it ever was so when the mind was a simpler whole? Is there, in short, any good argument for the absence (partial or total) of pleasure and pain (or one of them) from the earliest soul-life? If I had that knowledge about pleasure and pain which some psychologists possess, I might per-haps settle these questions. But, as it is, I must conclude that it is safer *not* to suppose that at first pleasure and pain may be absent from sensation, or for the mind are attached to parts of the whole; and so I shall assume their presence. How then will these two sides stand to one another? In the first place, a pleasure or a pain is not anything by itself. It is always something painful or pleasant, and that some-thing is sensation (or sensations).[1] And in reply to the possible objection that pleasure and pain are not given at all, I must point to the facts. If we take 'given' or 'pre-sented', not as implying a donation or even a relation to an Ego, but rather for that which is simply, and comes as it is, then in this sense pain and pleasure must be called presentations.

[1] This is the place to take up the question of reproduction by pleasure and pain. Are they exceptions to the law that *all* elements move towards redintegration? In the first place, though I cannot show that they do act merely as pleasure or pain (because I do not know how to make the abstrac-tion required), yet, on the other hand, I do not see how to deny that a mere difference in bare pleasure (supposing that to happen) might make the essence of revival as against no revival. It seems probable that pleasure in general may as such have associations, and still more probable that pleasures in their union with qualities may have special associations, and may recall where the qualities alone would not recall. And the evidence seems in favour of pleasure and pain being recalled by qualities sometimes and not being *always* recreated. That being so, I feel bound to include them under the law.

But the objection leads on to a further discussion. Is there anything at the start beyond mere presentation, that is feeling with the distinctions of quality, quantity, and 'tone', which *we* abstract from one another, but which at first come within one blurred whole which merely *is*? I feel convinced that there is nothing. I do not think, in the first place, that there is at the start any aspect of *self-feeling* ($L. 503 = 456$). True, the whole that is given, however poor that may be, does expand and contract, and feels pleasure and pain; but to *be* a felt expansion, and to feel it as such, are not the same thing. Until a core has grown together, against which the alteration can come as an 'other', I cannot see how the aspect of self is possible. And I find no reason to suppose that at the beginning this internal group does, even in a rudimentary shape, exist. If the early soul is rich enough to afford this variety, yet the distinction is not a thing which requires no making, or can make itself at once and without machinery. Hence there is at first no self-feeling, even though we mean by that merely one aspect of the whole; and still less is there anything like a subject and object. I observe much confusion on this head. The distinction, we may hear, is not to be transcended. Now, if this is meant metaphysically, it is utterly irrelevant. Whether really and in the end all the contents of the universe, my self included, are or are not relative to some subject, is a question on which psychology has nothing, and cannot have anything, to say; while to stop short of this question is to make no advance at all. But, remaining within psychology, I remark, in the first place, that in verifiable experience we occasionally have states where this relation of subject and object wholly ceases to exist. Still, this is not the main point. For where experience does give us a reference to self, that self is not naked form. It has always a content, a concrete filling that varies but never is absent. Now, I would urge, if this reference exists at the start, what is the content of the subject? Is it likely that experience, at its poor and blurred beginning, does divide itself into two parts with a relation between them; and, if so, what fills each part, and what machinery can at once effect this distinction? Until these questions are fairly met, the introduction of a subject into the early mind is not merely perhaps false, but is not scientific. The mere form of a subject could do nothing, and indeed for psychology is nothing; while to give the Ego a concrete, super-sensible character would hardly serve better. For if this character comes into given experience, then it becomes mere presentation that is mixed with the rest; and if it somehow stays outside and touches only, so to speak, with the end of a relation the presented datum, then it falls outside empirical psychology. And with respect to Attention, or Apperception, or Activity, I have said something before (*E.* x) which I will not repeat. I should be loath to criticize the doctrine as, for instance, it has appeared in the writings of Wundt; and, maintained as it is by Mr. Sully and, to a still wider extent, by Mr. Ward, it has become to me no clearer. Not only to my mind does it fail in part to be intelligible, but I find no adequate information as to the basis on which I am to suppose that it rests. The main point, I think, is this: if attention is not an event or a law of events, has it a right to exist in empirical science? Is it not simply a revival of the doctrine of faculties? And I am afraid to go on until I have pointed out the vice of admitting faculties. It is not merely their number which makes them objectionable, and it is a very serious mistake so to look at the matter. The principle is the same with one as with a hundred. In its worst form the faculty is a something outside that interferes by a miracle with the course of phenomena. I need not say that in this sense it is embraced by neither Mr. Sully nor Mr. Ward, for with both of them Attention has a law of its working. In its more harmless form the faculty acts by a law, but the objection to it is that in this case it is idle. If it is merely an expression for a way in which things do occur, or if it is used further to mark a condition of their happening which is not yet known—then at its best it is a bad way of stating a law. And it seldom stays at its best. It becomes a phrase offered in explanation of phenomena beyond that field from which it has been drawn, which phenomena the mere law would at once be seen *not* to explain. I feel no doubt that Wundt has used his Apperception in this way, and little less that Mr. Ward has partly followed the same line, and that Mr. Sully is at least somewhere on the brink of doing so (cp. *M.* o.s. x. 490). And I have thought it right to speak plainly because, if I am wrong, that may lead to the explanation of a doctrine which assuredly needs one, and which, from the character of its advocates, cannot be ignored.[1]

We have so far concluded that in the beginning there is neither a subject nor an object, nor an activity, nor a faculty of any kind whatever. There is nothing beyond presentation which has two sides—sensation and pleasure and pain. And for the mind there is no discretion, or even discrimination. All is feeling in the sense, not of pleasure and pain, but of a whole given without relations, and given *therefore*

---

[1] The appearance of Mr. Ward's article (*M.* o.s. xii) since this was written has not led me to modify it; but I will add a few words. Mr. Ward appears to me hardly sufficiently alive to the necessity of defining a term like 'activity'. If activity were wholly simple, then, of course, it could not be defined, but only pointed out. The question is, however, first, whether such a simple element does exist, and next, whether, if so, it answers to what we call activity. But Mr. Ward, I gather (l.c. 66), considers that activity contains a relation. If so, I would invite him to say more explicitly whether the terms of the relation are psychical facts, in the sense of being immediately experienced and having quality, duration, and intensity; or, if not that, what else they are. If Mr. Ward will do this, he will, I think, be convinced that the question is about more than words. I may be allowed to add that the question is hardly so much about the reality of activity as about its nature; and that my contention is hardly (as suggested on p. 66) that, *because* our perception of activity is composite now, *therefore* in attention there cannot be an unanalysable element. Activity has, it seems to me, a complex meaning now, and I have tried to show the psychical development of this complexity. Let that derivation be false and my contention is still this—Activity in its general use seems to have *some* meaning, and the man who uses it in psychology is bound first to say with what meaning he uses it. If he makes it an original constituent, he is none the less called upon to state its content; or if he holds that it admits of no more than bare pointing out, he is bound to state this explicitly. And, in the second place, he should say *why* he applies to this unanalysable element the term Activity rather than any other word. Meanwhile I feel called upon to repeat that in general the present way of treating this word is little better than a scandal.

as one with its own pain and pleasure. So far as it is possible to experience this after contrast has done its work, we do so most of all in organic sensation. From this basis, the machinery we went through above has to bring out subject and object, volition and thought.

I am entering ground that should now be more familiar, and shall hence advance very rapidly. The first point we have to notice is the formation of groups. The condition of this is that in the flux of sensations there should be regularities. Without some identity in the given our experience could not start, and no Ego or faculty could give us any help. These groups will consist mainly of the sensations conjoined by reflex action on the environment; but of course the salient connexions in those points of the environment, which have thus become emphasized by pleasure and pain, will enter into the groups. The way in which these unions come to be made may, I think, be assumed, and what I wish to urge is that at first they are neither subjective nor objective, nor have aspects distinguished. They are felt wholes in which the features all run together. The next point is the formation within these groups of features accidental and essential. I, of course, do not mean that they are known in that character. What I mean is that connexions have degrees of strength. When in the struggle of the elements repetition of the pleasant has sometimes led to pain, when the object and the movement (sensations A and B) have had one sequel CD and another EF, then what has been uniform coheres and defies competition, as the variable and occasional hardly can do. We have therefore some groups weak throughout, and within every group we get aspects connected strongly, while others are attached feebly. This point is of importance.

If we leave these formal considerations and look at the content of our groups, we find a striking difference. There is one of our groups, or one set of features in our various groups, which bears a special character. In the first place it is always (more or less of it) there; in the next place it is connected with pain and with pleasure as no other group is. It is thus permanent, essential, and emphatic, against the variable and that which in comparison is accidental. First, what are its contents? The core of them is formed by that bundle of feelings which always is given, and which later we know as internal sensations. And (to anticipate) round this core, and identified with it, comes the whole body-group of sensations. This (still to anticipate) becomes the representative of the group we call self. And (anticipating further) let us ask what distinguishes the body from foreign objects. It is this mainly, that any alteration whatever of my body (whether regarded as antecedent to or as sequent on other events) is connected with pain and pleasure. It is not, I should say, strictly true that any change of my body-group must be felt as painful or pleasant. What is true is that the exceptions are too weak to affect the force of the association. And further, the changes of the body-group bring pain or pleasure *immediately*. It is not so with other groups. These are painful or pleasant when in certain relations, and in others their character is turned to the opposite, or fails altogether. Hence the pain or the pleasure becomes something not essential. Fire burns, warms, and does neither; an approaching body hurts or pleases, or again is indifferent. These other groups are not yet distinguished from the feeling they cause in me (this comes later); they are still one whole with my enjoyment or my suffering from them. But in comparison with the body-group their connexion is weakened. Because indirect and inconstant, it has failed to dominate. The body-group, upon the other hand, has grown together with that core of internal sensation, which has been indifferent either never, or too seldom to affect the strength of the connexion.[1]

[1] In order to simplify, I have dwelt solely on pleasure and pain, because I think this the main point. If we may suppose them absent, I do not deny that a distinction of subject and object would be developed, but it would hardly be the same as that given now in experience. A complete account of the growth of our knowledge of our bodies would have, of course, to consider other points. The alteration of outer objects is not regularly a cause of further sensations (other than pleasure and pain), while the change of the body is so. This is illustrated further by double sensation, when two parts

Returning now from our digression we may have brought back some light. The foundation of the group which grows into the self is, and remains, those sensations which continue to be feeling in the sense of being one with pleasure and pain.[1] The real question is by what steps and in what degree and to what extent other groups are dissociated from this feeling-mass and qualify it by their contrast, and, on the other hand, what features are in various degrees connected with it. We have seen the way of dissociation. It lies in those repeated variations which by collision must loosen the feeling-aspects of some groups. On the other hand, we perceived how the direct and unceasing conjunction of the body-group with pleasure and pain made it inseparable from that aspect and one with its core of internal sensations. But at this point we must be cautious, or we shall fall into an error which is far too common. The feeling-mass is in the first place *not confined to the body-group*. It will contain more or less of *whatever in the environment has not been dissociated from itself*. The sensations from our surroundings, inclusive of other animates, are, certainly at first and probably afterwards, more or less inseparable from our self-group. This is a conclusion which follows from our principles theoretically, and in

of the body touch. Again (at a much later date), change of the body is found a condition of the perception of fresh phenomena. From another side the body is controlled directly and regularly by the feelings and thoughts; and outer objects, if at all, indirectly. I cannot pretend to deal here with the question fully and systematically. The problem of localization I omit wholly, and, as to the perception of the extended in general, all I can say is that I do not think it essential to the distinction of self from other objects, though now it colours all relations. As to its originality, I think that clearly in its origin it could not have borne the *relational* character it now has, and could have been neither discrete nor (properly) continuous. But all the attempts which I have seen made to derive extension from what is quite non-extended in my opinion break down. The problem is unfortunately mixed up with metaphysical preconceptions, both as to the discrete nature of the elements, and again as to the intensive, not to say simple, character of the soul. On the subject of discrimination and the perception of relations, I shall be able to say something when we deal with voluntary Analysis.

[1] This is the main key to pathological states of the Ego.

practice certain facts are inexplicable without it. Nor is there anything to urge against it but the metaphysical prejudice of individualism. And, in the second place, the outlines of this group are not fixed, and they never become fixed. If I ask what is myself, what are in general those habits, those ways of feeling, thinking, and acting, which make me what I am, the answer would vary with years. And it would vary in particular as from moment to moment the self contracts or expands with failure or satisfaction, and suffers from or possesses itself of the external; and at its limits I should not know what was part of me and what foreign. So that in putting forward the body-group as identified with, and representative of, the group one with feeling, we must remember that the body, neither at last *nor at first*, includes all the self; and that at its limits, and again later through nearly all its extent, the body becomes dissociable from self.

We have so far reached the stage where in the one mass of feeling (the unbroken whole of sensation and pleasure) groups are more or less connected, and where the greater part of these groups have been dissociated more or less from the feeling-nucleus, the core specially connected with pains and pleasures. We are still below the point at which consciousness,[1] with its subject and object, has appeared. This is fully reached first when a relation is perceived between the group identified with feeling and some features not identified. But this perception is led up to by a long course of hardening among cohesions and of collisions in the felt between the discrepancies. And, when consciousness is reached, it is not constantly maintained. It must come spasmodically and at intervals, with lapses between them, before it grows into a normal attitude of mind. The perception of the relation as such I will deal with lower

---

[1] I think, on the whole, that this is the best sense to give the word. But we cannot get rid of another, in which 'to be conscious' means 'to notice' and 'the unconscious' is that of which we are not aware. We may obviously be 'unconscious' of sensations which, for all that, make part of the object-group. Again, we must remember that in those states where the subject and object disappear, almost if not altogether, features of the object may sink back wholly into the stage of mere feeling.

down, when I touch upon discrimination in general. But what calls it forth is the practical collision between the feeling and a non-feeling group. After experienced satisfaction the object is approached with an expansion and excitement caused by ideal suggestion. If it resists and causes pain, there is a violent collision between the sensations, due (directly and through movement) to redintegration, and the discrepant outer group. And when both persist, the alternate expansion and driving in of first one group and then the other, with the strong pleasures and pains which mark the struggle, tears in half,[1] so to speak, the mere unity of feeling which formed the battle-ground. What we have called the feeling-core has had to identify itself at once with its own contraction and expansion in regard to the outer group, and the task is impossible. Before experience and association had brought up and fixed expansion on the presence of the object, the task did not exist, because the self was driven in and there was an end of it. Now it *must* go at once two ways which are divergent, and from this effort supervenes, not the cessation of the struggle, but the first perception of it. I do not mean that consciousness could have been predicted as a result apart from specific experience. I mean that, feeling sure it has emerged, we can to some extent see how that emergence must have happened. We can feel the problem that pressed hard upon the struggling mind and understand how the result has partly solved it.[2]

I will, in passing, glance here at the origin of our ideas of activity and resistance; and as the latter at all events

---

[1] It does not, of course, really tear it, or we should get two selves indifferent to each other.

[2] I do not intend to consider here the influence of society and the collision with other selves, nor to date the origin of that perception. The discrepancy of the symptoms of pain and pleasure in another body with the feelings in mine no doubt operates strongly as soon as it does operate. It is, however, possible to exaggerate the importance of the social environment. To say, Without other selves no self *at all*, is surely going too far. It would be, perhaps, as true to say, If other selves did not exist, we should certainly invent them. But it is not necessary, and I think not permissible, in psychology to make either assertion.

implies the former, I will keep to activity. The general idea, I presume, is that of an alteration of A not taken as belonging to anything outside, but as a change of something beyond A which realizes something which in A was ideal. This may be quite indefensible, but it is, I think, what we mean generally when we use 'activity'. And when we come to the soul and the perception of our own activity, it is perhaps going too far to say that without an idea of the change no rudimentary form of that perception would come.[1] But, in seeking for the minimum that must be apprehended, we cannot postulate less than a concrete and limited self-group, and a following alteration of this as against its limit. Further, the origin of this change is not to be referred to an other, nor do I think the mere absence of such a reference would be enough. The origin, as well as the process and result, must be felt to belong to the self-group, and for this the change must ensue, not only from the permanent character, but also from a present occasional feature. Now I do not deny the theoretical possibility of an ultimate state of mind holding all these constituents and so yielding the idea of activity on reflection. What I deny is the presence of one shred of evidence for the existence of such a state. That 'motor' feelings of any kind should supply such a complex seems to me quite preposterous. And what I cannot understand is how, without some apprehension of a concrete self with limits, and its change in time as arising from itself, anything like activity can exist *for the soul*.[2] And with all due respect for those who hold to (and some of whom build I know not what upon) the ultimate character of activity or resistance, I am left to conjecture that either they attach no definite mean-

---

[1] The account of this matter (*E*. x), to which I must refer, should be so far modified. Further, I did not mean to convey that I myself took *desire* to be essential. My own view is opposite to this. I must excuse myself from entering further into Mr. Ward's criticisms (*M*. o.s. xii. 45–67), on the ground that they seem based upon misunderstandings which a comparison with the present article may remove.

[2] The soul may, of course, have been 'active' long before *for the outside observer*. So used the phrase is harmless so long as it is felt to be unnecessary, and is merely *used*. See above, pp. 195–6.

ing to these terms, or else some meaning which is foreign to them, or else that they have never made any serious attempt to analyse that which they set down as irreducible.

We have reached the knowledge of an object other than my self and in relation with it. We have to advance to the idea of something real by itself and independent of its connexion with my feeling-centre. We may deal with this briefly. The object recurs often and, in itself and in its environment, is mainly the same, hence it seems permanent and identical. But, on the other hand, it is variable; and of its features some depend upon foreign relations, while others, because more constant, are not seen to be relative. And the relative part, because discrepant, belongs not to the thing; the thing (what is left of it) exists out of relation. The result of this advance is, of course, inconsistent, and raises problems which psychology has not to take up. There is no need to exhibit its progress in detail. There are emotive attributes which the object palpably has and has not. A sword hurts when it cuts me, but when it cuts something else it may give pleasure or nothing. What then has it got, and what does it give? Further, when at rest it certainly does not cut, and yet we call it cutting. Again, not only do things vary, but they vary and persist in spite of my pleasure and action, and, at least to some extent, are not changeable by me. To that extent, then, up to which my changes do not alter them, they are real altogether apart from my existence. And, where language comes in, because for others as for me, and again because in some points *not* for others as for me, the object becomes partially free from us all. What is discrepant collides and sets at liberty the remainder which has not come into collision.

It is now easy to advance to the distinction between things and my thoughts about them. Disappointment reflected on brings knowledge of error, and language of course co-operates largely. Desire and expectation have to yield to the thing. They cannot alter it, and it decides whether they succeed or not. Whatever they may be, and whether they exist or do not exist, and when one man

thinks this and another man that, the object is, and becomes, what depends on itself. If our expectations, then,
are not to fail they must depend upon things—things
not merely now and here, but in the distance and in the
future. And the fact, more or less invisible, controlling our
thoughts which without it end in failure, has now been developed. This is the theoretical object, though the interest
we take in it is still mainly practical.

But in thinking, it may be said, I am aware that I act; I
make an alteration, and this is a difficulty. And for metaphysics, without doubt, a grave problem arises; but not
for psychology. Objects are found to possess qualities
regularly though not always; take, for instance, colours.
Hence an object may be changed, though not in itself, and
therefore only for us. Again, the thing for me is altered
when I change my position, turn my head, close my eyes,
or cease to touch with my hands. But it comes again as
before, and changes regularly on my movement. Still, my
movement did not change it, because I find it as before. It
could not change it, because in the interval the thing acts
as it would act if its qualities were there. And for others
again, independent of my movement, the changes take
place, and are no change for me. Hence these movements
do not alter the fact, but ourselves. It is the same with the
invisible object of thought. That develops on my action,
but I do not control it, as baffled expectation at once makes
manifest. And so here, as before, there are actions about
the thing which change only me. As the light shows us
colours or darkness conceals them, while the colours in
themselves remain what they are, so thought gives us, like
true light, the nature of reality, or like twilight and mist
presents us with appearance, or like darkness with ignorance. But the object is what it is, and, so far only as in
action we suffer its control, does our thought remain true.
As to the nature of the control our early reflection has
nothing to say.

We have seen how thought is objective, but we have
not yet reached the goal which, at the beginning, we set up.

The object was not that which excluded my self, for we saw that my self is also an object, and we have to find how it becomes one. It is easy to see the way in which my body, first in some aspects and at some times and then altogether, can be distinguished from my self. And it is an object which obviously we are interested in knowing. So, too, my internal states, and my self as the thing which possesses these qualities, come naturally to be thought of. The one process, that combines and sunders through individuation amid discrepancies, goes on working to the end. The feeling-core with its early and its acquired constituents is a hard thing to reach, but the interest is unceasing. If this and that cannot really be the thing itself which feels, what in the end can it be?

Thought has an object and subject, but these are not fixed compartments or parts in the self. Any process, as we saw, which preserves identity of ideal content is thought and is objective. But why an *object*, we may insist, since this means *not* subjective? It is an object, we reply, because it is distinct from and regulates other psychical movements, and these by contrast are subjective. Even in the highest self-consciousness, where my self is the object, the distinction persists. It is not possible to have a state where, beyond the content of the object, there are not psychical elements which exist and interfere and need constant control. Pure self-consciousness as a state where perceived and perceiver are psychologically at one, and where existence no longer jars and struggles with content, is no actual condition. There is always something to control, and in this sense thought remains for ever objective.

But, we shall be reminded, not only does thought exercise control, but it does so consciously. It has an end and a standard, and this calls for explanation. We may ask first how thought comes at all to be critical or 'normative'; next, in what the standard consists; and in the third place, *why* it is thus and not otherwise. (*a*) Since control by the object is found satisfactory, the idea of that control, of course, interests and moves, whether always as the object of desire I will not ask; and the character of this control of course comes to be generalized, and so moves in a more and more abstract form. (*b*) What in the end is this character, cannot be discussed here at length. We found it to consist in identity or individuality of content. (*c*) Why it is thus and not otherwise, is a difficult question. We can see at once that, if the object is either changed for another or taken incompletely, there will be practical failure. And the mind, it will be urged, has simply followed this line of most pleasure and least pain, and its experience has cohered and is perceived as an axiom. On this I wish to say first that an axiom or a postulate, or a criterion in general, if we regard its *validity*, falls outside psychology. For that science it is merely a general character which moves, which brings rest when successful and unrest when defeated. We are confined simply to the origin and nature of an axiom as it comes into the course of psychical events. Now, if this standard has been produced merely by what has happened to succeed, it seems strange that its principle should be precisely what operates at the start and in the earliest association. Is that only a coincidence? Or shall we suppose that the type of our first rudest movement has also somehow resulted from natural selection? Perhaps so, but I would remark that, unless we will be resolute and make the nature of things result from a struggle and a survival among bare possibilities, then an account of this sort cannot go back for ever; and psychology, I should have thought, has to make its start from *psychical* ultimates. We must begin then without anything like mental association, and try to show (I suppose) how its laws have been made by conjunctions of presentations, which gave pleasure and pain (or at any rate succeeded or failed) and somehow led to these laws. I cannot here criticize such a doctrine, and will say only in passing that if it understands itself it will make psychology an appendix to physiology. I am contented with the view that for psychology the law of individuation is an ultimate, and that this law has suc-ceeded, because it answers to external events in a way which to psychology is itself once more an ultimate; and that, thus succeeding, it becomes an end and a standard for thought and feeling and will, according to the special conditions of these processes.

If we ask further as to its connexion with pleasure and pain, and raise the doubt whether our 'norm' satisfies directly and in its own right, or has now got pleasure conjoined with it because circumstances connect pleasure with success, and *it* has somehow happened to succeed, I cannot here answer fully. But I see no reason to doubt that the realization of our principle is pleasant directly, just as much as when our self succeeds against the environment. And I think an inquiry into the conditions of pleasure would show that in the main those results please which are the same in character with the result of our principle. It will be the feeling in both cases of one self-realization diversely produced.[1] To ask a question beyond this would be to enter metaphysics.

We have now pointed to the essential feature of thought; we have seen the machinery which works in all psychical processes; and we have hurriedly shown how from a basis of mere feeling this machinery develops the function of thought with its subject and object. And, did space permit, we could easily complete and verify our explanation by exhibiting volition and emotion, in their contrast to thought, as other developments by the same machinery from one single foundation. But there are theoretical activities which have not been explained, and I must endeavour in what remains to indicate how these confirm our previous account.

There is a difficulty which kept me for some time at a stand. Thought is certainly a function of analysis and synthesis, and the synthesis is plainly an application and development of Contiguity. But what is the origin of analysis? True (as I have pointed out in my *Principles of*

---

[1] The conditions of pleasure can, I think, be reduced to harmony (including pureness) and expansion, answering to consistency and completeness in knowledge. But whether, as in knowledge, the two will fall under one head is not a simple question, and I shall reserve my opinion for another opportunity.

Logic), the synthesis must analyse, since the competition of different redintegrations forces elements apart while holding them together. But take a case where I set myself down to discriminate, where I say to myself, I will investigate this object or analyse this sensation. We can indeed see how synthesis largely assists us, but in the end there will be something which cannot so be explained. And the true explanation is that the idea of discrimination works further by blending. I will exhibit this briefly, beginning first with the involuntary perception of difference, and then dealing with analysis.

As I have remarked above, discrimination is in one sense inexplicable. We are unable to make the transition from the fused to the relational condition of mind, in such a way as either to see *how* this particular result did come, or to feel simply that it must be so and that no further explanation is required. But the result is explicable in this sense, that we can retrace the collision which goes before it and see how it contains the warring elements in solution. There are two thoughtless extremes against which we must guard. In the first, sensations are different, and that is distinction. In the second, distinction supervenes, and that somehow makes difference. Each has one side of the truth that (explicit) difference implies distinction, and distinction rests on (undiscriminated) differences. The first error forgets that my sensations may be different and I not know it: while the second does not reflect that the very best faculty wants some machinery; and that, if without due cause it wildly throws out relations, then it explodes at haphazard and its missiles stick by pure chance.

If we had discrete presentations in series or together, that would not give even the faintest beginning of distinction. If there is to be a change, it, I hope, begins to be a truism that something must change and, if so, *therefore* must endure. If we are to feel change, then in feeling some element must be continuous. It is of no use to bring in the Ego, for the mind in general can do nothing in particular or at all. If the identity is to work it must be determinate and special; but this offers no difficulty. Our presented whole from X(*abc*) becomes X(*abd*), and gives identity with diversity. How will this go on to work? For mere shock and collision, we must remember, may shatter wildly the contents of our mind and cause pain and unrest; but to have collision in one's mind, and to feel it as such, are hardly the same. Mere invaders that seized on us and dropped us in turn, that fought furiously in our precincts and well nigh pulled us asunder, would be nothing to the purpose. We feel the struggle that we make, and by *we* I mean simply our presentations. The collision is made when, with X(*abc*)–X(*abd*), the persisting X(*ab*) has two differences, *c* and *d*, either of which it can restore by Contiguity[1] against the presence of the other. Itself, therefore, when one of these elements is banished, reacts, and bringing in the other produces a collision located in one point by a basis of identity. Again, if the two groups are there together, their identities, X(*ab*)[1], X(*ab*)[2], blend, and so force *c* and *d* to struggle for existence. It is this conflict of the soul against itself which begins to be felt as difference.

The very lowest perception of change implies a basis of identity with incompatible differences, in and through which that struggles against itself and so gets for a moment the feeling of relation. The same process, developing itself under special conditions, results in the perception of various relations in which the two elements in their connexion come to consciousness at once. These special relations present us with a number of difficulties, made more difficult by the fact that our space-perception now qualifies and overlays the whole field. I can but emphasize in passing the essential point. There are *no* qualities which in themselves are incompatible. They may be naturally incompatible in the sense that our machinery is not able to present us with both of them together, under some con-

---

[1] Where there is an after-sensation the mind has a little less to do. But to take the existence of an after-sensation as being by itself a solution is, of course, quite thoughtless. Not what it is, but what it does, is the point to consider, and, if it acts, it acts by ideal redintegration on the basis of partial blending.

ditions or at all.[1] They are *all* again ideally incompatible, if we try simply to identify them (without blending); and *all*, on the other hand, reconcilable, if we distantly couple them by means of relations. They are not really reconciled because the differences are all there, and the relations are not a harmony of these opposites, though they enable us to get round and to ignore the collision of unity and diversity. And if thought is a faculty of relations, it is thus for ever condemned to inconsistency and makeshift. But what I would emphasize is this, that the one law of Individuation brings on the conflict, and then (practically though not theoretically) disposes of the problem by means of a relation. This is why 'contraries' are most hostile, because the more special the identity the severer the struggle, if that struggle arises. But these forms of relation, which make experience what it is, are not (so far as I see) to be deduced from first principles. We are unable to reconstruct their specialities, though the necessity for them and their main character may be understood. And what we find everywhere, when elements are held apart and in relation, is a basis of identity which ideally connects them—even though that basis be not special and now appear to us no more than their co-presentment as members of one total given state of the feeling-centre.

In discrimination we get a result of variety in unity, and when we go about to distinguish or purposely analyse, what happens is this. The result of distinction becomes an idea,[2] and, when we will, we have that idea over against a presentation. I have an object A and the idea of variety, the latter present now as the idea of a variety in A, call it

---

[1] I cannot enter here on the difficult question as to the part played by quality as distinct from quantity. The view that in *all* presentations there is a common basis admitting of degrees would have considerable bearing here.

[2] Cp. my remarks on Comparison (*M*. o.s. xi = *E*. ix). Mr. Bosanquet criticized these (*M*. o.s. xi. 405–8) in a way that I found very interesting, and I admit that I was wrong in making alternate subsumption *always* necessary. In some cases we do without it, but in others I think this is certainly not possible. We cannot always go from A to B with a point of comparison. We may find that first in returning from B to A.

A(bc). And this variety may be general (we may want to make any distinction that we can), or it may be more or less special, call it Ay(bc). Now, how will this idea work? It will work first of all obviously by means of Contiguity. Striving to particularize itself, the idea of itself accomplished will restore anything connected with that accomplishment. This is the way in which Contiguity is known to find means for an end, and there is no need to dwell on it. The idea of A somewhere exhibiting variety leads to restless movement about the whole field of it; the idea of its showing this or that variety leads to particular search, as when a beast surveys a region for its prey or its enemy. And so far the idea of distinction working by contiguity explains analysis.

But there is another side which we noticed when, above, we spoke of blending, and which this latter process alone, I think, will make clear. When I scrutinize the object of sense or of thought, I find that, on my attention and the presence of my idea, its features grow diverse. It is as if, so to speak, my will had served as a microscope, as if I were turning the screw and the detail were coming out. And here doubtless, working side by side with contiguity, we have the process of fusion. In the first place the idea gives strength to answering elements (E. x and xi) which were there and were not noticed, or which come there on fresh presentation when their supports are strengthened. We may think here of the perception of obscure sensations, or again of the action of fixed ideas and moods on the environment. But we have a second case where the variety is *produced* by our wills. We may illustrate this by the play of our thought or imagination. I think of a man, and then of a hundred men, and then further I group and divide these hundred men at my pleasure and, as we say, quick as thought. We have blending here which (with contiguity) transforms the picture before us. The suggested features, it is true, do not strengthen given detail, and so far there is no blending. It is the *basis* of the suggestion which is presented also in the picture, and, by blending, that basis overpowers what is given, partly drives off its detail, and substitutes in part or altogether the detail of the idea. I am far from wishing to underrate the work done by redintegration, but though that work is essential, yet in some respects, and particularly when volition comes in, it is not enough. In the use of blending we must, of course, see that there are elements to blend; but with that precaution our psychology would, I think, find it a key to unlock several puzzles. The failure of psychology with regard to the creative imagination can, I think, in part be so removed. And at all events, in my judgement, blending explains the origin of voluntary analysis.

There are other difficulties which, no doubt, will occur to the reader. If I had space I am confident that I could deal with most of them; but in conclusion I can do no more than sum up the distinctive features of thought. Thought is, first, not the whole psychological process. There are always other elements which compete with it for existence within the subject. And so thought is objective, not because its content excludes the self, but because it has to control tendencies, which fall outside itself and solely in the course of my psychical events. Thought is 'normative', because its process has a standard and end. The result produced by that movement becomes a principle which itself moves, first unawares and then with slowly increasing self-consciousness. And this end struggles both for room to exist within my mind, and strives also against its own defects and failures. Thought once more is 'necessary', because its end is able to compel. Within itself one element is because of another, and outside itself it can force competing tendencies. And it is 'universal', assuredly *not* because always abstract, nor again because *always* possible for more men than one, but because its connexions are independent of this or that man's private liking, and transcend the immediate deliverance of sense. And it is an obvious 'activity', because succeeding it expands the group of the self, and that expansion in its origin and its result is attributed to the subject. Its end, Individuality, must gain all its material from the flux of presentation, but from the very start it ignores 'thisness'. Irrespective of the moment's confused deliverance, the content it takes up is applied to qualify every other context. That what is must be and is eternal, is the principle of all our psychical movement; and this builds up not thought only, but emotion and will. Thought, however, in its character diverges from these. It cannot make presentation, and, where thought is volitional, where its idea, that is, produces its content particularized in psychical existence, still thought and will are different. To the thought, realized as thought, its mere psychical existence is something necessary, but still *per accidens*— while the essential end of will is reality within the series of psychical events. And, as thought cannot make phenomena, it contents itself without them, and is therefore symbolic and not existential. And, aiming at a totality which events never give, it converts their degradation to ideal uses, while it builds its own world out of them, and lives both in them and apart. And building piecemeal, as it must, it becomes relational, and is free to choose its own relations. Its individuality could not be perfect until all its distinctions were harmonized in one system; and it is therefore driven to an infinity of analysis and synthesis, striving to include all variety within one identity.

Thought, we may say, is the process which aims at and is controlled by individuality, an end, however, to be realized not in existence but solely in content. And, as against will and feeling and the perpetual flood of incoming sensations, it is the process controlled by the identity of the *object*. But, if we ask whether thought is wholly self-satisfied, if it feels not only its internal defects but its estrangement from existence and from feeling and will, if it does not long for a fuller, a more concrete, completion, in which *as thought* it would no longer survive—we must go elsewhere for an answer.[1]

---

[1] I feel it right not to omit the 'Law of Duality'. I made its acquaintance some years back when engaged on Logic, and was quite content to ignore it. Now that Mr. Ward has endorsed it, I think I ought to say briefly why I have never accepted it. (1) In the first place I cannot see how the Law comes from Apperception or Attention. The derivation may have been

accomplished, but I am quite unable to follow it. (2) The arrangement of thought's content into pairs, and into wholes whose materials throughout are subordinated by couples, is, I think, not always fact. I have elsewhere (*L.* bk. iii, pt. i, cc. 1 and 2) pointed out cases which I at least could not reconcile with this Law; and, until I see that done, I must be allowed to doubt if it is possible. (3) So far as the Law expresses fact, it seems to me obviously secondary, plainly derivative. Thought is compelled to be relational, to move by the aid of relations and piecemeal; and, as with relations the minimum is one with two terms, we may say, if we please, that thought's process, *so far as it is confined in its movement and its result to relations*, is in this sense dual. (4) I think that, if we must have a faculty, one of Discrimination would be far more useful than Attention is. The attempt to explain, not Duality by Attention, but Attention by Duality (as Distinction or Comparison) has, I should say, been the more successful of the two. I can, of course, accept neither. (5) Duality *might* mean that in the end thought is ruled by the category of subject and attribute. If so, that statement would require a thorough explanation.

XIII

WHY DO WE REMEMBER FORWARDS AND NOT BACKWARDS?

[*First published in* MIND, o.s. xii, No. 48, 579–82. *October*, 1887.]

TO the reader who is new to this question it may wear the appearance of a paradox. He may reply that to go forwards is obvious and natural. But if I ask why should my memory go only one way, why should memory move never from the present to the past—he may find that what seemed obvious seems now merely false. Still, if he attends to the subject and confines himself to bare memory; if he discounts, that is, the cases where we reach the cause from the effect, or in general reconstruct a whole from its inter-dependent parts;—he is likely to admit the existence of the problem. And he may accept the conclusion that the re-production of a series has but one possible direction, from the earlier to the later. Whether with Professor Bain he will add this tendency to a long list of 'ultimates' (*M*. o.s. xi. 469), or will try to find some explanation, I cannot foretell. For myself, though I of course accept the fact of this general tendency, I am not sure that it has no excep-tions. I do not believe in the *impossibility* of remembering backwards, and even doubt if sometimes that does not happen in fact. And, so far am I from accepting our habit as an ultimate, that I venture to find no difficulty in seeing how it was acquired, or at all events may have been so.

I ought perhaps to begin by attempting to explain how it is possible to reproduce a time-series at all. This would be a far more serious task, and I cannot here undertake it. And so the question must be simply as to the direction of the recall. 'Yes,' a reader may suggest, 'the problem is, why, when time itself goes forward, memory is tied also to that direction.' But this is not the way to put the question, and we must begin by purging ourselves of such ideas about time. The stream of events does not really run from the past into the future, and it is easy to see that this flow is our own construction. We find, on reflection, that we really do not perceive the future and the events past and present streaming onwards and into it. What we think we see, upon reflection, is a succession of events, in which what we call the present constantly, in part at least, becomes new, and in part slips away backward into what we call the past. And this construction, by which time flows backward in a stream, bringing new things from the future, and carrying old things to the past, is more natural than the former one (Lotze, *Metaph.*, §§ 138 ff.). Indeed the reader at this point may define the problem thus—Why, since events go backwards always, does our memory of them always take the other direction?

But further reflection shows us that this question still has failed to see the point to be explained. In speaking of a stream of time, we forget that a mere stream, if regarded by itself, cannot have a direction. It does not flow towards one point rather than another, or indeed towards any point at all. And hence, until we have more than a mere stream, until a qualitative point is taken as an end, there can be no meaning in direction. Again, a stream, if it is to be a real stream, must possess an identity of what flows. If we did not have the same water in different positions, if we had always other waters, then to speak of a stream would be to use words without a meaning. We must try to apprehend more clearly what is implied by such a phrase as a current of events; and let us help ourselves with the following scheme:—*abc—acd—ade—aef—afg—*.

In this we may regard *a* as being constantly increased or continually diminished. We may look on the original position of *a*, with its earliest possessions, as receding backwards with each change, or, on the other hand, as going forward and as gaining constantly. And the difference comes from the way in which the new is considered as standing to the old in the different cases. But again, if we please, *a* may be stationary, and the stream may flow past it, as—*bc—cd—de—ef—fg—*. What then is the direction of the current? It may be running for ever into an ideal reservoir, say on the left hand beyond *bc*, or going forward continually to a point on the right hand beyond *fg*. Thus, if the stationary *a* be one of the Egyptian pyramids, it may seem grounded and left behind while events have flowed forward, or the survivor of a tide which has swept all else back into oblivion. And since all motion is relative, the stationary (we must remember) seems in certain conditions to take on an opposite movement.

But I fear the reader has had enough of these formal reflections. It is not a stream in general which we have to do with, but the stream of *our* events. And here we have the essence. It is our psychical states which furnish both the flood and all the matter which flows or which stands against the stream. In the succession of these states it is the group of self, more or less unvarying, that has the place taken by *a* in our scheme. And it is the attitude of this group towards the incoming new presentations on which everything turns. It is this relation which gives a meaning to *direction*, and shows the essence of our problem. Why is it natural for us to look upon Time as running forward? It is because *we* go forward with it, marching willingly to our increase or dragged captive to our decay, but in either case going to meet fresh experiences. Or why does Time run backward from the future? Because *we* do *not* go back, but still hold our own against change, and force the incoming to minister to our constant identity. And time goes backward once more when our life slips backward with it, when what we are appears a stone that marks the growing space beyond which our self for ever recedes from us upon the ebb. But again we may be stationary through some blessed hour, anchored in some quiet backwater, a still eddy beside the torrent of things, out of the world—so we feel it. Here, if events hurry forward to the future, or are whirled backward into the abyss, it is all one to us, since we ourselves *are*. But we are stationary once more, when all we have fails to interest and when the new seems merely old. It all (we feel) makes no real difference, is all the same thing over again; *we* do not move; and if events go forward still as they did before, or if, on the other hand, it is nothing new that is coming from the future;—this is a question that is indifferent. Time has here again hardly a direction.

Let us turn now to our problem about the order of reproduction. We have seen that the direction of mere Time does not help us even to ask the question rightly. And we can see now better how to ask it. Why is our memory directed towards our incoming sensations, and towards the side from which change comes? It is so (we may say, in the first place) because our thoughts in general naturally take this road. And why they take it appears to me almost obvious. The answer, in a word, is practical necessity. Life being a process of decay and of continual repair and a struggle throughout against dangers, our thoughts, if we are to live, must mainly go the way of anticipation. This, when we attend to it, seems quite evident and a mere commonplace. In a creature placed low down in the psychical scale no such thing as memory can even exist. And, though to say that its thoughts are occupied with the future would be barbarous psychologically, still the ideal qualifications of its sensations correspond in the main to future changes of its state by approaching sensation and action. And, if this were not so in the main, of course the creature would be destroyed. And hence, when after a long time memory is developed, it naturally takes the habitual mental direction. We are like a boat anchored on a tide, a boat that ceaselessly decays, and that, to maintain itself, must gather material from what comes floating down; and not only this, for there sweep down impending masses which threaten it. Now if, in order to gather material and to ward off destruction, we turned habitually towards the wrong end of our vessel, how, if such a thing were possible, could it fail to make an end of us? And then, when after a time we get strength to rest, and to recall some great benefit secured or great danger avoided, what is more natural than that still our thought fronts the same way, and, fixing an ideal point behind, goes on forward to meet again past experiences face to face? We have no practical interest in the mere course of events, and merely to drift with it can be nothing to us practically even in imagination. We are concerned practically with what meets us and what we go to meet, and this practical concern has formed the main habit of our thought. This, I think, is the real solution of our problem.

And we must remember also that a backward direction in thought is the road away from our present selves. These present selves interest us most, and in the main we tend to see the past in its relation to them, and so to take the path forwards from the past that brings us home to them. But if we felt that our selves were lying in the past, we should so far tend to go back. Thus in old age or under abnormal conditions, where the present interests us little, we are said to live in the past. But here recurrent natural wants must still keep up in the main the acquired habit of our minds.

Our thoughts seem really to go back when the exclusive object of interest is placed far behind us, and we retrace towards it every unwilling advance that has carried us away. Each event adds a link, but our mind moves from each later link back to the earlier; we are interested in each solely as a thing to be passed by, in the order which carries our thoughts home. And, I apprehend, memory may here travel back from the later to the former, because for our interest the earliest is the end. Thus, when we steam against the sea from our native shore, if we thought of ourselves we should go forward against the waves. But as our hearts are left behind, we follow each wave that sweeps backwards and seems to lengthen the interval. And, in remembering objects passed by upon the waters, I think, contrary to our main habit, our memory might take the road that leads to our desire. But nature here, not less than elsewhere, soon effects a change in the course of our thought.

XIV

ON PLEASURE, PAIN, DESIRE, AND VOLITION

[*First published in* MIND, o.s. xiii, No. 49, 1–36. *January*, 1888.]

THE object of this paper is to indicate briefly the
nature of Pleasure and Pain, Desire and Volition. Its
limits and its methods are those, I hope, of strict empirical
psychology,[1] but within these limits it will be understood
that I cannot even touch upon all parts of the subject. And
for this reason I must give to points of disagreement a
space out of due proportion. Those who know the subject will know both the amount of substantial agreement
among psychologists, and again how very little in what
follows is specially mine. I must first very rapidly sketch
the main features of Pleasure and Pain, then go on to
Desire, and in conclusion try to seize the essence of Volition. And I am forced to warn the reader that my present
limits compel me to count upon a greater effort from him
than I ought, perhaps, to expect.

I

To say that what we call sensations in *every* case must be
coloured by pain or pleasure is to go beyond our knowledge; but without sensation we never have pleasure or
pain. Not a pleasure, but something pleasant is what we
experience, and the actual fact is an event which, together
with duration, has quality and tone, and an intensity of

---

[1] I have tried to define these in *M*. o.s. xii. 355 [*E*. xii. 205, note 2]. There
are two main errors to be avoided. The first makes the soul a mere serial collection of states. The second treats it as a thing somehow outside psychical
phenomena, which can be acted on and can react. The second mistake
becomes aggravated when this thing is called the Ego. I will use this opportunity to thank Mr. Ward for the space which (in *M*. o.s. xii. 564–75) he
has given to a refutation of my views. I regret that inability to identify myself with the doctrines which he has criticized has deprived me throughout
of any profit from his labours.

each. If we like to apply the term aspect, or side, or moment, these are all open to objection, as metaphors must be. But what they try to say is that, as a sensation is not, as a matter of fact, a thing given separate from its psychical context, so pain and pleasure do not exist apart from sensation, any more than duration or intensity are ever discovered by themselves. They are all alike presentations,[1] as being elements within the presented whole. They are all of them distinctions, and we might call them, all alike, the creatures of our attention. Indeed pains and pleasures have no qualities of their own. It is the quality of the sensations, or arrangements of sensations, which we place to their credit. The kinds of pain which have been urged in disproof of the above, the feelings that shoot or that burn or gnaw, are each due to the special sort of sensation, or again to the temporal and the spatial orders of sensations, together with the rhythm of intensity in the pain. Thus pain and pleasure are mere aspects of mere psychical fact. They exist and they say nothing. Like sensations they are at first neither objective nor subjective. If I say that they are given simply, a subtle critic may object that given means sent to an Ego with another Ego's compliments, and that, if I were capable of knowing what I meant, I should inevitably mean this. Still I shall use the word, and for myself must decline the interpretation. That pleasure or pain, as they come first, have, in any sense whatever, a reference to the Ego is a fundamental error. It takes the products of development and places them at the starting-point, where no Ego (conscious or unconscious, whether for the soul or for the observer) exists except in false theory. In addition I would remark that even now there is no reference to the subject in some of our aesthetic pains and pleasures, and that there may never have been one. I would add further that in moments of

---

[1] I know of no argument for refusing this name to pleasure and pain which does not rest upon some dogmatic preconception. Suppose (e.g.) that they are not *essential* to presentation, does that go to show—when their (physical or psychical) conditions produce them—that they are not presented? Are warmth and cold not presented?

agony (as happens too before unconsciousness in swooning
and under anaesthetics) it is most doubtful if Ego or non-
Ego exists. Of course the phrases we *must* use imply what
exists at our phrase-making level, but these implications
are no argument against the existence of lower levels. To
say 'I felt myself all one pain' is perhaps an attempt to
deny the self which it asserts; as in—

> 'First 'twas fire in her breast and brain,
> And then scarce hers but the whole world's pain,
> As she gave one shriek and sank again.'

In short, of themselves pleasure and pain merely *are*;
they have no meaning and no reference; they are at first
certainly mere aspects of sensible quality, just as sensible
quality, where their conditions exist, is a mere aspect of
them.[1]

If we go on to ask for their physical conditions, they are
taken to be connected one with physical benefit and one
with injury. Whether they should be called accompaniments or results I shall not inquire; but whether the connexion is without exceptions must be considered. First,
however, there are mistakes which we must place on one
side. Pain and pleasure are not the feelings *of* anything at
all, in the sense that they report it or in any way convey it
(*E.* x. 197). Again, they clearly cannot go *always* with a
general heightening and lowering of our vital forces, actual
or even potential. Nor, further, is it possible to connect
them with the *general* advantage or the *general* injury of the
creature which feels them, unless that connexion is subject
to most serious exceptions. We have to ask, then, if in
any sense pleasure always goes with benefit and pain with
injury. Lotze[2] has pointed out a way of answering in the
affirmative. If the advantage and the harm are momentary
and local, the exceptions might disappear. For example,
a sweet poison does not injure by its sweetness, it rather
locally so far benefits; and thus contrariwise with pains.

[1] I include *uneasiness* under the head of pain. As to the Ego, cp.
E. xii. 216–17 ff.
[2] *Med. Psych.*, 1852, pp. 237–9.

And Feeling, like the thermometer, tells what *is* now and not what will be hereafter. If this is true, then the law would be valid universally. What would remain unexplained would be the want of correspondence in some cases between the quantities of pleasure and benefit, and so again with pain. But I must leave this matter as it stands; and, again, the possible genetic derivation and development of the law cannot here be discussed.[1]

Can pleasure and pain (at least with regard to mere sensations) be connected simply with the quantity of the stimulus?[2] Certainly too much of anything might always be painful, but whether with everything there is a too-much is far from certain, nor is it certain that the painful, if one only could have less of it, would always become pleasant before it wholly ceased to be. And, without discussing views which I have no room to state, I will say simply that (so far as our knowledge goes at present, and without prejudice to the future) we cannot avoid connecting pleasure with sensible *quality*.

If we pass now to the *psychical* conditions of pleasure, all the result, which so far we are able to take with us, is the connexion of pain with damage and of pleasure with the opposite. We must see if on the psychical side more is visible. Can we say that pleasure is the result or the attendant of activity, and does pain again go with a hindered energy? First, I must remark that I do not know, and that I still am not ashamed of not knowing, what 'activity' means; but, speaking subject to that ignorance, I find the assertion not verifiable. There are surely pleasures and pains where to find what we should commonly call psychical activity is out of the question. And if the faculty

---

[1] Mr. Spencer appears not to be acquainted with Lotze's view. I understand Mr. Spencer to hold that pleasure may attend that which is in no other sense whatever good for the individual. He seems also to deny the existence of an intrinsic connexion between advantage and pleasure, and to believe only in a conjunction made by circumstances. If so, I think he much underrates the amount and kind of evidence wanted for such a conclusion.

[2] On this see Wundt. Horwicz (*Psychol. Analyses*) seems to me to have shown Wundt's failure, but to have also failed himself.

of Apperception or Attention, or again the Ego, is appealed to, I cannot say that I am shaken. Such a thoroughly retrograde step will hardly take us to anything beyond baseless assertions and illusory explanations (*E*. xii. 2 19). But if we are to keep to what we observe, and take an instance where we pass suddenly from a pleasant warmth to a painful heat, we cannot see that the hindrance of psychical activity makes the transition to pain. The pain appears to come given to us by a physical cause; there seems neither to have been nor to be a particular psychical activity in the case; and to take the activity as general (if there is general activity) would not account for the special seat of the pain.

I shall assume, then, for the present that the conditions of *some* pleasure and *some* pain are not psychical,[1] and, leaving mere sensible feelings, shall examine those which attend psychical movements or dispositions. The two main conditions appear here to be harmony and expansion, and we are at once led to ask whether, as was the case with the intellect, these two characters will fall under a single head.[2] I will begin the inquiry from the side of pain. There it seems to me that discord is the one constant feature. Mere loss, mere contraction of psychical existence, never pains us by itself. It does so only when some element feels itself thwarted or diminished, and for that we must have positive reaction and tension. If from the world which is dear to me you could isolate one fraction and extirpate it wholly, with all its memories and connexions, then I should never feel the loss of it. It is where the element with its connexions is left in part, and so reacts, that it becomes the seat of pain. Wherever we have pains whose origin does not seem physical, there we find a collision and a struggle of elements; and wherever we make a collision which is not rapidly arranged or subordinated, there we can always find pain. It is true that pains and pleasures, not of psychical origin, may enter into and even occasion the tension, as when the idea or the remaining smart of a wound makes the tension of fear, or the removal of some dainty

---

[1] The assertion of the opposite would in my opinion rest upon mere dogmatic preconception. [2] [Cf. *E*. xii. 208, 230.]

the struggle of disappointment. It is quite true that a collision often goes with pleasure on the whole, because the state, taken on the whole, is not a state of struggle, but contains the discord as an overpowered element. But it remains true that, so far as pain is not in its origin physical, it arises with tension, and that, wherever you have collision, you so far must have pain. And I cannot think that Professor Bain is right in setting down surprise as a neutral state, even in the special sense which he assigns to the word 'neutral' (*M*. o.s. xii. 577). It may of course be even pleasant, but if you take it as bare surprise, that is, apart from any supervening apperception and expansion, it seems certainly painful. If we then accept the result that the psychical origin of pain is tension, can we extend this view to cases where the origin seemed physical? It seems possible, first, that in such pain there is an unconscious psychical conflict, a collision of psychical states, an inroad and a resistance. But the objection is that, though possible, such a view lacks evidence. The existence of the unconscious struggling element would be a serious assumption and one not called for. It is far otherwise if we say that *all* pain comes from tension, either physical or psychical, and in the former case from the alteration and the resistance of a physical condition. So far as I know, this is a view which physiology can sanction, and, if so, pain in all cases may be set down to discord.

Passing now to the conditions of pleasure, we may expect to find the opposite. I do not say that we *must* find the exact counterpart of discord; but, if we did not, we should be discouraged. Pleasure, we said, seems to accompany both harmony and expansion, and there is a question whether both will fall under one head. Let us try first with expansion. There is no doubt that in general a mere increase of the psychical area seems pleasant, and no doubt again that as a recovery the increase is usually more pleasant. Can we say, then, that pleasure *always* comes from an expansion, or from a maintenance which against an opposite is really an increase? If so, harmony, as the removal or the overpowering of discord, would fall under expansion. To go so far as to call pleasure pain's mere negative would be an obvious absurdity. But, for all that, a precedent or a suppressed element might always be essential, and pleasure be dependent because a counter- if not a re-assertion. Or, if not that, yet perhaps the conditions, which would have gone on to pain, must be in part there for pleasure. Considered psychically, we may urge that every incoming sensation is at least to a certain extent an attack which necessitates reaction, and physiologically the stimulus required for the pleasant discharge may be taken as an invasion. Hence in both cases the positive will be really an expansion. In harmony too the variety is still negative against the unity. And in the mere 'relativity' of pains and pleasures an unanswerable proof seems found, for there a pain, because a recovery, becomes actually a pleasure. Briefly then, if pain is felt hindrance, a pleasure is felt furtherance against defect or opposition, and in either case is expansion; or, if you prefer a modification, it is always a counter- or a re-assertion. Is such a view the correct one?

I am not prepared to deny this, but, as before with activity, it is necessary to make assumptions quite beyond our real knowledge, or else to put an indefensible strain on the facts. It is not possible to find always a sense of defect as the condition of pleasant expansion. Again, in some pleasures, e.g. of smell, it is often impossible to verify a tension. Further, pleasures and pains are not wholly relative. And lastly, if expansion *per se* were pleasant, then mere contraction should be painful, which assuredly it is not. I shall return to these objections, but will first attempt to state a view which, though not free from difficulty, seems to interpret the facts with the use of less force. If pain is discord, pleasure may be taken as the opposite. But, if the opposite is harmony, then harmony is ambiguous, since it may imply either the overpowering of collision or its simple absence. And if the latter is an improper use of the term, let us by all means drop the word harmony. Let us say, pleasure is the feeling which goes with presentation when that has not got the conditions of pain. A sensation is pleasant when not psychically or physiologically discordant. Pleasure thus will be the result of such positive conditions as imply the absence of pain. It will be the attendant either of *all* normal sensations, or of merely those where its (unknown) conditions of quantity or quality are present. The absence of hindrance does not constitute the pleasure, pleasure is essentially positive; but there would be no *inconsistency* in adding that its conditions must contain a variety—which *is* not painful but might become so if altered in character through quantity or quality.

Such a view seems to me to include all the facts, and it explains at once the pleasure of expansion. For, if mere positive sensation is *per se* pleasant, then more of the same will be naturally more pleasant. Expansion will make more of the same where the state was pleasure, or turn the scale where pleasure and pain were balanced. Just as increase of sugar is not sweet as mere increase but as presence of more sugar, so will it be with sensation; and expansion will be reduced to the head of mere position. And the same principle explains the pleasure of harmony proper. This enables us to have more of what already is pleasant, or to have without tension and with a balance of pleasure what would otherwise become painful. And we will now weigh our objection against the view that expansion *per se* is pleasant. We said that, if so, contraction should be painful *per se*, and *per se* it is not painful. It is painful only through repression and the tension of what is forced in. If we take the state where in full comfort a creature falls asleep, there its psychical area is progressively diminished, but it feels no beginning of pain. You may say that in repose other functions are set free, other sensations and also ideas come into being, while others are intensified, and that the change adds to the pleasure, so that in repose the soul might even be fuller than before. I admit all this, but if we keep to our crucial example of an animal which normally falls asleep after a healthy meal, it is all too little for the purpose. With every possible admission, it remains still a monstrous paradox to say either that the psychical contents do not diminish or that the animal suffers pain. And, if so, contraction is not painful *per se*. It is painful where the removed survives still in idea, or is recalled and struggles for existence. And I admit further that this is usual. But where the idea fails, there contraction is not noticed. It becomes *bare* contraction and ceases at once to give pain. And I would press this strongly against the doctrine that expansion *per se* can be pleasant.

But our view that pleasure arises from unhindered position has to meet greater difficulties. We shall be told that pleasure is never pure, but that pain is of its essence, either as precedent or ingredient. I reply that, even were there no pure pleasure, yet the impurity might be external, like insoluble dirt in water. And secondly I deny the fact. I repeat the classical example of pleasures without want, where, if we keep to what is verifiable, we cannot find pain. And the fact again that in infancy (according to Preyer) pains come before pleasures seems to be without relevance, even if it were shown (as it is not shown) that in each case the special pain comes before the special pleasure. If we next go on to compare different levels of psychical life, we cannot find that the different balances of pleasure are merely in proportion to the contrasts which those lives contain. That a life monotonous, but without pain or care, could not at a low level be pleasant, seems to me a mere paradox, the offspring and again the parent of error. And I think such mistakes bring no real danger to our view. Its main difficulty arises from the pains of mere contrast and the pleasures of relief. It will be urged that one and the same state may be pleasant or painful because of its relations; that in pain, if I remember my yesterday's torment, my state becomes pleasant, and that my pleasure, if I think of all that I once hoped, may be turned to pain. How, if pleasure comes from what is positive, can these facts be explained?

The explanation is not easy, but still I think it is practicable, and there are three points to be considered. In the first place, the physical conditions may be so altered as to give an opposite result. In the second place, in the result we may have new positive sensations. In the third place, we must allow for the influence of ideas. I will apply these considerations to the case where the commonly painful is now pleasant. (1) In the first place, our physical state may be so changed that the conditions of pain are in consequence not present. Where there is no discord there will be no pain. And this is true again psychically; for what was painful because it jarred, may by the suppression of its antagonist have lost its painfulness. (2) In the second place, though the pain remains actually present, it may be overbalanced by new pleasure. In partial relief we may still have pain there: but its *diminution* has set free those normal sensations and ideas, both from a physical and psychical source, the conditions of which were suppressed before by the greater pain.[1] The state may on the whole therefore be pleasant, and the fact that, if the pain were being increased rather than diminished, it would overbalance the pleasure though the amounts were the same is on our view quite normal. For it is the *newness* of the pleasant sensations, as they rise, which directs attention upon them, so that they preponderate and depress the rest which is painful. And, if the pain were increasing, its novelty would for the same reason overbalance the pleasure.[2]

These principles will explain a large part of the facts, but they do not explain everything. For, if we take a case where the state of relief continues, it may cease to be pleasant. Habituation to pain has limits, and on the other hand our healthy sensations lose freshness and get feeble. We become depressed, and the balance of our state is pain. Yet even here, if we remember a worse pain behind, our state once more may be pleasure; which, if pleasure is really positive, seems inexplicable. (3) Here we must fall back on our third principle—the influence of ideas. The idea of pleasure is itself a positively pleasant fact, and can so turn the scale. I will explain this briefly. It should be

---

[1] Volkmann, *Lehrbuch der Psychologie*, §§ 70, 71.

[2] Why novelty attracts attention, whether from a psychical or only a physical cause, I cannot discuss.

a commonplace that ideas are psychical realities, and we cannot represent without using a psychical fact. Further, what represents a pain must be a pain, and so again with pleasure. It is not true that the idea of the greater pleasure or greater pain must itself be a stronger pleasure or pain (*E.* vi. 146), but to think of a pain or a pleasure without *in some degree* feeling them is quite impossible. That is the first point. The second point is that, though pleasures and pains are not 'relative', our ideas of them are largely so. We think of feeling as a series, a scale which rises or falls from agony to delight; and in this scale more or less of pain or pleasure stands for less or more of the opposite. This way of thinking is to some extent a downright illusion, but it comes inevitably.

In our experience we pass frequently from pleasure to pain and from pain to pleasure—and, where this happens, the circumstance is usually one to which we attend. Beside other reasons for this which we noticed above, we must remember that, if pleasure removed survives in idea, this produces discord, and that in desire satisfied pleasure often comes after sharp pain. From all this comes a tendency to place pleasure and pain on one scale. Further it is familiar that, in passing from one sensation to another, the first is used in idea to interpret the second, so that our standard may be nothing but our last experience. Hence, judging by the difference which separates two sensations, and not remarking that the former was far removed from the average, we constantly exaggerate. And so the relief from pain which really in itself is still painful, is, because so far from what we suffered, figured as the opposite of that, and not as its mere absence. It seems the other extreme, and that in our experience has been pleasure. Taking this into consideration, I hope the reader will agree that our ideas become comparative, though our bare sensations of pain and of pleasure are not so.

But if the idea of relief is the idea of a pleasure, and if the idea is also fact, we can solve the problem of a painful condition which is pleasant. The idea of past pain is painful, but its degree, as a fact, is here inconsiderable. On the other hand, in passing from what it represents to our actual painful condition, the divergence is so great that our present state is judged to be something opposite. It thus (apart from hope) is thought pleasant, and the idea or thought, as we saw, is an actual pleasure. Now this idea at once works both in proportion to its detail and also its degree.[1] It not only in itself is an ingredient of pleasure and tends to neutralize pain, but it acts positively in setting free what pain was suppressing, and again in intensifying the sensations which agree with its content.[2] In this sphere what *seems*, *is*. And it is idle to object that to mistake a pain for a pleasure is impossible. For the question is not of a simple pleasure or pain, the question is as to the balance in a mixed state; and there an error is both easy, and in addition goes on to make itself a truth. We need not appeal to cases of enthusiasm or mental weakness. We may see every day persons who feel well and happy when they are led so to think themselves, and who feel the opposite as soon as the opposite is suggested.[3] And it is, I think, clear that in the lower animals, where ideas can act less, the relief from pain affords also less pleasure. In short, our opinions may be relative when the facts are not so. And I venture to offer this with the foregoing as a solution of our problem, and in defence of the doctrine that pleasure is positive.

Finally, if the extreme doctrine of 'relativity' is brought in, and I am told that all sensation must depend on change and contrast, and that what is not relative (or even a relation?) is nothing, in that case I still refuse to allow, apart from special evidence, that pleasure is dependent on pain. But I shall admit that its conditions involve an opposite, in this sense that they contain a reassertion or even an expan-

---

[1] Lotze (*Mikrokosmus*, i. 231) is, I think, wrong here.

[2] The idea creates its reality by blending with a *basis* in sensation, and then forcing the rest (*E*. xii. 235–6).

[3] Preyer (*Seele des Kindes*, p. 76) has verified the fact that children can be made through suggestion to take a disagreeable taste for an agreeable one. He very properly illustrates from hypnotic states in the adult. There is of course error here, but so far as the idea has altered the sensation, there will not be a mistake about the sensation itself.

sion. But mere expansion will still not be pleasant *per se*. It will still be a principle that is subordinate to harmony. And harmony will be taken, not as simple position with the absence of discord, but as the positive unity which contains and overpowers opposites. I venture, however, to think that our former view explains facts with less setting up of our ignorance in the place of knowledge.

If we pass now from the conditions to the results of pleasure and pain, the first doubt which meets us is whether they exist. Just as it may be denied that pain or pleasure is ever produced by sensations or their relations, so it may be maintained that what at first seemed to be their effects is really due to other causes, and that the connexion is indirect. I do not think that in either case a disproof is possible, but probability is on the side of the doctrine that pains and pleasures can be produced, and also do react. But how they react, and what is the character of their influence in general, is open to doubt. I shall first state the opinion which seems to me most true, and shall then try to defend it. Mr. Leslie Stephen's view[1] is that pleasure represents equilibrium, a state in which there is a tendency to persist, and pain tension, a state from which there is a tendency to change. That is, I believe, substantially the view to which I had before been independently led, and which (in MS. only) I had expressed thus: 'The generalization nearest the facts would seem to be (1) Pleasure is conservative of rest or motion (2) Pain alterative.' I should now prefer to put it thus: The action of pleasure is to make the pleasant both dominant and steady, while the action of pain is to excite change away from what is painful—a statement which will require considerable explanation. I must call attention at once to an important distinction. In the action of the pleasant, and again of the painful, we have to separate the specific from the non-specific influence. *Every* incoming mental state can first act as a shock, and produce mainly a suppression of our existing state of mind and a lowering of all functions. Again, it may act as a stimulus, and call forth indirectly a current of new sensa-

[1] *Science of Ethics*, p. 51.

tions and ideas. And, lastly, intensity or duration may lead to exhaustion, either local or general. None of these effects, to say the least, is *always* specific. They need arise neither from pain nor from pleasure as such; and I will go on to point out what in my opinion does so arise and really is essential. If we take a psychical state and then suppose it to become pleasant, we observe that this state seems to usurp more mental space. It drives other states out, and lowers the relative intensity of those which remain. It weakens again the attack of fresh incoming states. Certainly to say that pleasure is intensity would be to me a mere paradox, and to say that all their effects are identical would be little better. But, so far as causing both persistence and dominance, pleasure seems to work like strength. And for this reason pleasure causes both motion and rest. Where the sensations or ideas are those which would produce motion, if sufficiently strong, pleasure takes the place of intensity and effects its result (see below). It does not move at all *per se*; it moves, or it prevents movement, on one and the same principle and merely *per accidens*. Once more, pleasure seems to produce movement by raising the whole tone, and by thus rendering the subject, so to speak, explosive; in such a state, that is, that on a stimulus movement follows with ease and plentifully. But this again involves no new principle. For in the first place the pleasure is to some extent a symptom, and is itself the effect of the general bodily condition. And, where it is the cause, it acts merely as intensity might act. It supports first of all the suggestions or the actual beginnings of change. In the next place, by adding strength without bringing collision, it causes an expansion of our general area which by itself is excitement. To this point I would direct the reader's special attention. The ordinary effect of any strong incoming psychical state is to produce a movement, and this tendency is not dependent on the pleasantness or painfulness of the state. What is true of the infant is true of every living creature, that every strong feeling tends to bring on a motor discharge.[1] Hence,

[1] Preyer, *Seele des Kindes*, p. 93.

where pleasure produces movement, its action is indirect. For, where the states which it emphasizes are connected with repose, by the same action it supports them against suggestions of movement, and its indirect effect is rest. Finally, where the pleasant exhausts and so decreases change, the same principle holds good. Either its action is not specific and it works simply as an intense and enduring state of mind, or else once more its specific action produces a particular effect, the same as that which would result from mere quantity of a particular suggestion.

If now we turn to pain, we must be careful still to discount those results which are not specific. Avoiding these we find its effect to be change and restlessness. It appears to move us *per se*, whatever may be its quantity. To the apparent exceptions I will return, and must attempt first of all to get clear on the principle. I said that pain excited change away from what is painful, and I must try to state this accurately. What seems most probable is that pain, coming from discord and conflict, reacts to make that more intense. The restless movements, in which the elements (physical or psychical) press and struggle against each other, become more violent, and that which reacts is stimulated to movements stronger and more extended in range. Hence a change which may result in the suppression of the source of disturbance. The line taken by this change will be either, so to speak, mechanical, or furnished by remedial associated movements. I see no good cause to suppose that pain has a direct negative action upon its source. The point to keep in mind is this, that if the changes fail to remove the pain, the disturbance is continued and extended and intensified; while, if the stimulation is removed, the movements die away, and the resulting condition is stable. Pain may on the other hand indirectly increase its cause and itself. For, if the reactive movements are unsuccessful, the tension grows as they are strengthened and by consequence the pain. Our domination by these movements forces attention upon that which is directly connected with them, and this, together with contrast, makes the pain more intense. That the general action of pain is to increase the conflict that occasions it, is a view that works satisfactorily; the objection to it is that it seems to go beyond our knowledge in making pain arise always and everywhere from discord. But if for this reason we cannot accept it without some reserve, we may modify it thus. We may say simply that the general action of pain is to set up disturbance about the seat of its origin, a disturbance which continues and heightens itself until a result has been produced which removes its source. Pain on this view will not always cause tension and reaction; but it will cause local agitation, and continue that and widen it, until some change has brought relief. Upon neither view, so far, has pain a direct negative action; but if we choose to add that pain works directly towards lowering that which pains, so that change in the other direction has more chance of domination—that would be a tenable doctrine, but one I think quite uncalled for by facts. If, on the other hand, we can adopt the view that both the cause and the effect of pain is discord, that gives a unity to our doctrine, and is confirmed by the positive reaction of pleasure on its positive source.

And, so far as I know, all the facts would harmonize with this conclusion; while, on the contrary, that pleasure promotes and pain essentially checks action seems quite contrary to experience. Pain checks action when its continuance produces exhaustion—that is certain, and I do not doubt that its wearing effects are specific; while pleasures probably exhaust us not because pleasant but because intense. But the direct action of pain here is still to excite change, and its opposite influence through exhaustion is indirect and accidental. And it prevents motion again indirectly by suppressing those feelings which would otherwise produce it, and indirectly once more when by experience we have learnt that to move is to increase pain. But restlessness here takes other forms, or is diverted into some kind of restraining effort. Nor does fear paralyse because painful, but mainly because it otherwise prevents the feelings and ideas which are necessary for activity; and when the dreaded evil turns to real pain, the

260 ON PLEASURE, PAIN, DESIRE, AND VOLITION

creature struggles all too late. Restlessness, bodily and mental, is the chief effect of pain; the remainder comes accidentally. But as to the action both of pain and pleasure, we shall be clearer when we have got some light on Desire.

II

Pleasure and pain are not desire, nor does either of them necessarily involve it, either originally or even at our stage of development. 'If' (as Mr. Spencer recommends, *Psych.*, i. 280) 'we substitute for the word pleasure the equivalent phrase—a feeling which we seek to bring into consciousness and retain there, and if we substitute for the word pain the equivalent phrase—a feeling which we seek to get out of consciousness and to keep out,'[1] we are confusing consequence and condition, and are making a serious psychological mistake. If we take pleasures of repose and simple pleasures, as of smell, where no want has preceded, I at least am unable there to verify desire. And with pains the same conclusion, though less obvious, is not less certain. In dull constant pains, to assert that desire is always present would be surely a paradox. To be restless is not necessarily to *desire* a change. And if it is urged that pain means tension and tension desire, I reply that *psychical* tension is not always the cause, or even *always* the effect of pain; and that, if it were so, yet mere tension (as we shall see lower down) is not the same as desire. Nor, to pass to another error, is desire the idea of a pleasure or the pleasant in idea. For it is not true, in the first place, that you can have desire without tension; and, apart from that, in the second place, it is not true that pleasure in idea must be the object of desire. I intend here to treat these two errors as refuted,[2]

[1] This erroneous doctrine is held far too widely. The further substitution of 'desirable' as another 'equivalent phrase' for pleasure has led to further errors on the part of J. S. Mill and Professor Sidgwick.

[2] My justification is the fact that, so far as I am aware, no attempt has been made to deal with the objections which have been urged from various sides. In my *Ethical Studies*, 1876, if I may mention my own contribution, I discussed the question of desire and in the main, I still think, satisfactorily. Volkmann, whose acquaintance I have made much later, must be referred to (*Lehrbuch*, § 143). The only thing like an argu-

and to pass to something which I at least find more interesting.

Desire is obviously a state of conflict and of tension, and there is a doubt whether this tension is not the whole of desire. If we have an idea of a state of ourselves, which is impeded by our actual condition, and which struggles against it to become a reality—can we call this desire?[1] On this view pleasure and pain are accidental to desire, and the tension of the idea against fact is its real essence. Is this doctrine a true one? It will be seen lower down how far I can follow it in respect of volition, but as an account of desire I cannot assent to it, for I still believe that pain and pleasure belong to the essence. And it seems to me clear that we have thoughts, and thoughts of our own possible future, which try to come in and are impeded, and where yet desire is plainly absent. Among other states one is led naturally to think of expectation. Now, if the tension of an idea against fact makes desire, then all expectation must be desire, and this is maintained.[2] But, as I observe the facts, one can anticipate one's own neutral future without any desire; and even a misfortune, when one is resigned and is fully prepared, may be awaited without either fear or hope. And again, further, we may expect what we know *we* shall not see, and, surely sometimes, may do this without any desire. 'No,' I shall be told, 'there is always uncertainty and unrest and a desire to have an end of it. We want the removal of the tension through the victory of something expected.' But, I reply, we must

ment that I have found since is in Waitz (*Lehrbuch*, p. 421) who, to the objection that an idea of the pleasant may exist and yet not be desire, replies by an attempt to deny the fact. He says that, if the idea is not desired, it also is not thought of, and does not appear, *as* pleasant (now). But this rests on an ambiguity. To appear (*erscheinen*) pleasant may mean simply to be felt as pleasant, or to be thought of as pleasant. The former is beside the question, and to the latter I reply by asking: How could I have a doubt or a denial as to pleasantness under present conditions unless I entertained the idea? But is that doubt or denial a desire?

[1] Drobisch, *Empirische Psychologie*, p. 222; cp. Volkmann, § 139. Waitz, p. 418, dissents.

[2] Drobisch, p. 98; cp. here Wundt, ii. 334.

distinguish. All tension may set up desire, and, if prolonged, usually does so—that is certainly true, while to say that it essentially *is* desire is not true, and it will repay us to dwell on this distinction. Why, in the first place, does expectation tend to pass into desire? We have an idea which tends to particularize itself (*E.* xii. 212–13) and, in the present case, not to complete itself ideally, but sensibly in presentation. What is presented on the other hand is now in some point discrepant, and hence a conflict which so far is neither desire nor expectation. It is so far not desire, because (to anticipate) the idea is not felt to be pleasant; and it is not expectation until the idea in its content has a reference to a subsequent and modified presentation.[1] Now, in expectation, the idea, *as* an idea, is not discrepant with the presented, but, as a mental state, it is so; and again, the time-relation (which makes expectation) has a tendency to drop out, and so to give rise to conflict. Further, disappointment may come in, and, while weakening expectation (proper), establish and aggravate the discrepancy. Hence, in all expectation may come a discord which produces pain, while, on the other hand, the idea is felt (and perhaps also expected) to relieve. At this point, when the idea is felt to be pleasant against an actual pain, desire has been created. We may illustrate this by the case of an expected operation. It is first looked forward to with sinking dread, but, if it is deferred, so much mental unrest may be produced that we find our present state intolerable. Quite apart then from any hope of an ultimate benefit we desire anything that will free us from present anxiety. Fear may thus, through its own pains, be turned to aversion against itself, and on the same principle with greater ease a neutral expectation, through its tension, may be transformed into desire. For this reason the view that *mere* expectation already is desire cannot be accepted. Nor do I think the pleasure from gratified expectation would be an argument in its favour. That is caused naturally by the expansion which comes when the idea is particularized, and which also comes at times from an access of fresh

[1] We see here how incorrect it is to say desire implies expectation.

sensations, where no idea has preceded, and no desire could have been felt. We must bear in mind further, with a view to avoid confusion, that there are many intellectual states which really do involve a strong desire for a result; but these states are not mere expectation, and pleasure belongs to their essence.

Our result so far is this. Desire is not mere pleasure or pain or the mere idea of pleasure, and it is again not the mere conflict of idea with presentation. We must add that want or craving or the pain of defect is not desire, unless these are taken to imply the idea of what is wanted. But from this mistake we may collect the positive truth that not only does a mere idea of pleasure fail to be desire, but, even when that idea is felt as pleasant, still desire may be absent because want is not there. Thus we may remember past delights and take joy in the remembrance, but feel no present wish to re-experience them because we are satisfied as we are. And unless an uneasiness precedes, or is developed, no desire arises. Thus for desire we must have three elements—an idea conflicting with reality, that idea felt to be pleasant, and the reality felt to be painful; and these elements[1] felt as one whole state make up desire (*E.S.* 266 = 239). Whether the whole is pleasant or painful depends upon circumstances (ibid. 290 note = 259). The moving element in desire is twofold—first the pain of want leads to change, and in the second place, apart from that, the idea tends to realize itself, mainly by Contiguity. The pleasure does not move except so far as it reinforces the idea, and adds, on the other side, to the pain by contrast. There are questions as to the *object* of desire to which I shall return; but I will first deal with some remaining difficulties as to pleasure and pain.

[1] I do not use 'feeling' as equivalent to pleasure and pain. I could not in a short space explain what I think the proper sense of the term. But the 'felt' answers roughly to the 'immediately given'; and, since this is one with its pleasure and pain, and, since these aspects are emphatically immediate and also prominent, they tend to usurp the word 'feeling'. This usurpation is, in my opinion, not justifiable, and, against the constant stress of language, can hardly be maintained consistently. Cp. Prof. Bain's remarks, *M.* o.s. xii. 376–9.

There are some points in what follows where I have to express my dissent from Professor Bain's views. I do not intend to criticize his law of Self-conservation either in principle or in all its details. My position towards it as a whole may be readily gathered, and I will use this opportunity to remark how much the psychology of the Will has been indebted to Professor Bain, and how much I feel that I have learned from him. But I cannot agree that pleasure tends in general to excite activity and pain to check it, and I will show how in some cases such a doctrine is incorrect. When on this view an animal approaches the fire, the pleasure of warmth excites the motion until the pain of heat checks it. But we have seen that, quite apart from pleasure or pain, an idea realizes itself (through Contiguity mainly). The idea of approach, once suggested, tends to call up the associated ideas and feelings, and they again the physical movement—and this apart from pain or pleasure. Professor Bain for other purposes has laid stress on this tendency of an idea to realize itself,[1] and I must direct attention to the same point here. If now we add the action of pleasure, as we understood it above, this idea of movement is supported and strengthened, just as it would be if it were *not* the idea connected with activity, but were another idea connected with repose. And I must go on to point out that the pleasures of repose have been somewhat strangely dealt with. If we take such an instance as rest in a warm bath, then upon our view we could truly say that the pleasure reacts to increase the special bodily functions, and again the sensations and ideas that are soothing our mind. But that would not satisfy Professor Bain's doctrine, and, if I do not misunderstand him, he is driven into surprising paradoxes. He states first that pleasure produces the activity of maintaining a *rigid attitude*, and secondly that, as we are, we *must be* active because we *should be* so [under altered conditions] if disturbed.[2] But the necessity surely for such paradoxes is a refutation of the doctrine.

[1] *Senses and Intellect*, p. 342; *Emotions and Will*, p. 390. Cp. the tendency of mental movement to persevere, *Senses, &c.*, p. 426.
[2] *Mental Science*, p. 324; cp. *Emotions, &c.*, p. 317.

And the same conclusion is forced upon us by the inhibitory action of pain. We saw above how and why pain, apart from exhaustion, does check action by stimulating change. The stimulation, however, according to Professor Bain, is wholly non-specific, and the pain simply lowers. But surely the necessity, which led to the conclusion that pain, as pain, does not cause movement, could have led far more easily to the same denial as to pleasure, or even to the assertion that pain, as pain, always heightens vitality and that its lowering action is not specific. And when, in particular, unpleasant taste is asserted *not* to set up facial movement, the theory comes into rude collision with fact; as it does once more when it maintains that in satiety eating stops only when 'we have run up to the bristling point of some pain'.[1]

If we are willing to enter further into the detail of desire, we shall see the workings of pleasure and pain more clearly. Let us take the case where an animal moves, or attempts to move, nearer to a dying fire. Here the actual state is felt to be disagreeable either because simply felt as chilly, or because hostile to the idea of greater warmth, which has survived and strives to realize itself, and which also by contrast works on the actual feeling. Or again the idea of more warmth through approach may be suggested by association as a relief, or once more a chance movement may bring it in through sensation. Hence comes desire, and in this there are several moving elements. The pain of chilliness in this case moves to produce a change; next, the idea of warmth moves to realize itself; thirdly, that idea is felt to be pleasant and has its own action increased; lastly, by contrast, the original pain is also increased, and, if the original state had been neutral, would now be created. The whole result is the felt tension which we call desire, and we can see that the source of movement is not single, and cannot be set down to mere pain and still less to mere pleasure. It is true that relief from pain is an idea which is pleasant, though it assuredly is not always the idea of a pleasure. It must always be felt as pleasant, so far as it

[1] *Emotions, &c.*, pp. 330, 316; contrast Preyer, pp. 74 ff.

goes, and its pleasantness most certainly adds to its activity. Through such an idea of relief it is that in pain we are able to keep ourselves from moving. The movement or attitude that lessens pain becomes a working idea which keeps down restlessness, and to a certain extent does work because it is pleasant. But we falsify this truth when we transform it to the paradox that the whole of the activity comes from the pleasure.

The great importance of this question will perhaps justify further detail. Pain, it may be urged, must check action, because at least in some cases the pleasant activity could not otherwise cease. But this objection would forget that, as the pain of want goes, the pleasure loses its assistance; and that again, further, with physical change the positive conditions of pleasure may disappear. The mere tendency of the idea to realize itself survives, but in its weakened state this can be driven out by the ordinary competition of other ideas and sensations, and that without pain. And when further we are asked how, if pleasure does not move, a half-tasted satisfaction can intensify desire, it is not hard to make answer. In the tension of desire the idea of the movement is struggling and unsteady. Hence doubt may weaken desire and certainty may inflame it, not because desire implies expectation or belief or even clear consciousness, but because it does in some ways depend on the strength and steadiness of the idea. Now increase of pleasure does go to support the idea. And further in partial satisfaction the idea will probably be reinforced by sensations which have come in. And both of these influences again will cause excitement by expansion. Secondly, by the same influence, the pain of want will be increased and so the tension aggravated. And the natural result of the whole is that desire becomes more violent and moves more violently. We see the other side of this when the cup raised to the lips removes thirst before the drinking. That is not only because the pain of uncertainty is removed, but mainly also because the idea overpowers the reality. This is now viewed, not as thwarting the idea, but as itself passing into its process, and so the tension, and (possibly) the pleasure, disappears. Where ideas are weaker, as in the lower animals, this seems to happen much less. And where we are active it happens seldom, for there usually to the last there is something which resists, and the last obstacle is often most vigorously attacked. Thus a port in view makes the idea of wreck doubly painful, and adds to our striving unless the sight of danger disappears. What is called the effort of despair comes on the other hand mainly from the pain and the extraordinary excitement which its tension has generated; the pleasant idea of escape must of course be an element, but the whole state is clearly painful, and pain the chief mover.

Turning now from the inquiry, What *moves* in desire?, let us once more inquire, What is the *object* desired? That the object is always pleasure we have seen is a mistake, and it would be another mistake to introduce muscular activity into its essence. Indeed even in some sensuous desire, as for warmth, there may be no essential relation of the object to our muscles. Nor can I see any good reason to doubt that a creature might have desire even though it possessed no self-movement. But, passing by these prejudices, let us raise another question. What is desired seems to be always the realization of our idea; and it has been argued that this reality must be a reality for us. But that, it is further urged, must be our state of mind. If so, what is desired will be a presentation to ourselves.[1] But this is clearly not the case. We may desire what we know it is impossible we should see, as the fortune of our descendants and a good use of our legacies. And to call this an illusion, and to argue that our desire is here really for certitude, or else for the impossible, would be to me a mere paradox. 'Oh! to know he is safe!' implies a wish for his safety, and we want the knowledge of that usually as something *per accidens*. Desire of course cannot be satisfied unless the idea is both realized and realized for me. But the idea, the *content of* the desired, as distinct from the psychical state of desire, need not include any kind of

---

[1] Drobisch, p. 220; Volkmann, ii. 397; Lipps, *Grundtatsachen, &c.*, p. 610.

relation to me. That relation must exist in my actual satisfaction, and my desire can, therefore, in some cases, never be
followed by satisfaction. But I fail to see how that shows
that the object of my desire must be other than I think it,
or why, in general, desire *must* imply a possible satisfaction.
Again, I have of course a natural tendency to imagine myself there where I know that I cannot be. But this tendency
is very far from always qualifying the object of desire.

I will now glance briefly at a point far too negligently
handled. What is the nature of *aversion*? First the object
of aversion, like the object of desire, is always an idea. We
may indeed *seem* to desire the sensations that we have, but
our object is really their continuance or their increase, and
these are ideas. And so it is with aversion.[1] The mere
incoming of the painful is not aversion, nor is even the fear
of it, if fear is confined to mere contraction or again to
aimless shrinking back. To me aversion seems positive,
what we call 'active dislike'. It implies a desire for negation, for avoidance or destruction. And hence its object,
to speak strictly, cannot be reality, since it implies negation, and that is an idea. But desire for negation is still not
aversion, until painfulness is added. The object to be
negated must be felt to be painful and may also be so
thought of. Aversion then is the desire for the negation of
something painful. It is not a negative kind of desire over
against a positive kind, and I myself could attach no meaning to a negative desire. Aversion is positive, but its true
object is the negation of that which is commonly called its
object—a confusion which has arisen from taking dislike
to be mere negative liking. Aversion has a positive character, or it would not be desire; but its positive side is variable. There may be a definite position whose maintenance
we want, as when we are averse to the injury of something

---

[1] Mr. Sully, *Psych.*, 582, should not have spoken of 'the assertion of
Waitz that aversion involves a belief in the reality of the pain'. What
Waitz says is that its object must be thought probable and *expected*, a very
different view. Even this, however, is contrary to fact. All that is true in
it is, that, where we can, we suppress groundless fears because their nature
is essentially painful, while that of our desires is not so.

we love; or again, the positive may be left blank—something, anything, is what we want if it will serve to rid us of the painful. But again we may positively desire the act of destruction, with the agencies of its process, and so depend for the pleasures of life on our aversions. I hope this brief sketch may throw light on an obscure corner of our subject, and I will, in passing, advert to another mistake. Desire and aversion have been taken to be aspects of desire, since that is tension,[1] and (we may add) is to that extent painful. This is mere confusion, for all aversion has an ideal object. Now the (painful) tension of desire is not an object at all. It may be made one, and so may give rise to an aversion. But this will clearly *not* be an aspect of the original desire, but will be a new desire supervening. I may remark further that (as was the case with desire) the *object* of aversion (as distinct from the *state*) need not contain any sort of reference to the self. It is no illusion by which I am now averse to the ruin of my country after my death.

The subject of desire offers other interesting questions, but I must go on to *volition*, and will do so by the discussion of a necessary problem. How far is an *idea* required for desire? It may be truly objected that, if idea is to mean image, then, when desire is directed on an object of sense, there need be no image, distinct from that, present to the mind and, if so, no idea. But my reply is that idea is no more equivalent to image than it is to sensation. With me the opposition here is not between external sensation and internal image, for both of these are mere psychical facts. The difference between them is doubtless psychologically important and also interesting, and it would be a pleasure to me elsewhere to discuss its difficulties. But here it is irrelevant. Sensation and image are psychical facts of different kinds, still they are mere facts. Their content is not alienated from and indifferent to their existence. But an idea is any part of the content of a fact so far as that works beyond its existence. It does not work apart from, but it works more or less independently of, its starting-place. It is of course a psychical event, but that side of it is

[1] Volkmann, §140; Lipps, p. 604.

accidental. It is what later becomes a *meaning*. And for this reason we may have an image without an idea, and again an idea without any image, since a sensation may supply us with a content used beyond the sensation. Now the result of the idea's working need not be separated from its basis, as when I see a man, and through association then see him as an Englishman, and do this without any image. Here what we say is 'called up' (and which is *not* an image) may be said to coalesce with, and to be modified by, the starting-point.[1] But again the element brought in may be discrepant with the presentation, as when the sight of a fruit gives me feelings of taste, which cannot, while that is out of my mouth, be identified with it. The result here may be an image, a psychical fact known not to be in outward existence. But there is an intermediate state where the presented is qualified ideally so as to collide with itself, and where this discrepant content is desired without being a separate image. A common instance of this would be desire for (the continuance of) a feeling which exists. And it was when sensation had been overpowered by its idealized self, that desire, as we saw, almost ceased before the moment of possession. This again is how we can have a desire without knowledge, a dim desire with no clear object—as in the usual example of the sexual impulse. It is not that we have *no* idea, for, if so, our state would be something lower than desire. But the idea is a common element, a something in a number of psychical states, which pleases and is not in harmony with these states as they are, and its increase is felt to lead us beyond, we know not where. We desire the presented, but we desire it with an ideal qualification. We need have no image, and yet even here we want to realize an idea.

To take idea merely as existing psychical fact is everywhere to be driven into a deadlock or a fiction. For instance, desire, we all know, may be for internal fact; we may want, e.g., the existence of an idea. But, if so, we

---

[1] This is only a mode of statement and is really incorrect. Since in the present case nothing comes into existence in separation from the starting-place, there can be no coalescence or modification proper.

must have the idea of an idea. Upon this, James Mill, a man whose courage rose higher as facts grew more opposite, presents us with a dilemma. The idea is there *or* it is not there (*Analysis*, ii. 358). No, we reply, when we desire, it must be there *and* yet not there. We must have a psychical fact containing features out of harmony with its existence and pointing beyond. Suppose I desire to go through a proposition in Euclid. I have a psychical fact which contains both the general character of this process, sufficiently for recognition, and also the feature of the existence of the process as my psychical fact—and this is not in harmony with what I have. No doubt to say what the basis of an idea is may be very difficult indeed, and I am not discussing that (*E.* vi. 146, x. 190). What I must insist on is that, when we desire, we have already what we want in recognizable character; and, if an idea is an image, this leads to difficulties which, in my knowledge, have never been met. Suppose that we are trying to remember, for example, a name, what is there in our mind? This question was forced on his editors by James Mill, but the answer is unsatisfactory. 'We have some collateral or something to determine our search for it', is Professor Bain's answer (*Analysis*, ii. 358). If we had a mere collateral, I reply, that is not the idea of another collateral at all; nor again, if it were, should we desire this particular one, for the mere collateral would be satisfied by anything else which turned out to be collateral. And if Professor Bain means more than this, will his theory account for it? 'We will to remember the Greek name of the god, called by the Romans, Bacchus. We have in mind the name Bacchus, and the knowledge that the Greeks had a different name for the god' (*Analysis*, ii. 359). Yes, but the idea of a name qualified by the general feature of belonging to a god with a certain character—how is this going (apart from the grossest of fictions) to be translated into the existence of mere psychical images?[1]

[1] And what is the image of 'a blank in our present ideas'? J. S. Mill has tried (*Analysis*, i. 99) to answer the question: What is the idea of the absence of anything? And his failure is again instructive here.

The importance of this point in regard to Volition compels me to refer to another mistake. I cannot admit that mere completeness, and the filling out of detail, is the essential distinction of the real from the desired. It is usually a concomitant, but it may be absent. The main feature which is desired is existence within the context of the outer or inner world of presentation—and the detail certainly *need* not be greater on the whole, though there is commonly some new feature which is also compulsory. If I am looking for the solution of a complicated intrigue, when I first see this, it need not be richer than what I previously possessed, except in one feature, and on the whole it may be poorer. And suppose I long to see if my horse is at night in the field, I may have an image far more special than the dim form I can make out. But my desire is satisfied if the bare essentials are perceived within the context of the given outward space. Particularization of an idea's content is in some cases what I desire, and its existence even in psychical fact is here to some extent accidental (*E.* vi. 146). But this is far from being the case everywhere.

III

From this point we may pass straight to the essence of Volition. It is will when an idea produces its existence. A feature in present existence, not in harmony with that and working apart from it, gives itself another existence in which it is realized and where it is both idea and fact. And will is not a faculty or a separate kind of phenomenon. It is merely one special result of general laws and conditions,[1] the main law of Individuation with its branches, Blending and Contiguity (Redintegration). If an idea works itself out ideally and subject to identity—the process is thought. If, on the other hand, it produces fact in which its character and existence are no longer discrepant, the process is will. And the other kinds of phenomena could be easily shown to arise from other workings of the same laws and elements. But here, confining myself to

---

[1] Both here and in what follows, I suppose the reader to be acquainted with my articles in *Mind* [= *E.* x and xii].

volition, I will first state broadly the main principle, then defend it against objections, and add at the end a modification. We shall see the essence most easily if we begin with *internal* will. Now mere thought need not be will in any proper sense of that term. If I begin with an idea, and its logical consequences develop themselves in my mind, it is true that this process is a series of new facts, and we may say, if we please, that these events are produced by the activity of thinking. But still the process is not will, because the result is not the existence of the original idea and, throughout the process, the side of fact is merely accidental. Suppose, e.g., first, that my wandering thoughts come on one of Euclid's theorems and that they are led to trace the argument; and suppose, secondly, that in addition I have at the beginning the idea of going through the argument;—the second of these cases is volition, while the first is not. For in the second we have a general idea of the proposition over against a psychical state with which at present it collides, and then we have in the result a process where the existence is the existence of, and proceeding from, this idea. But in the first case, there being no idea of the result, the result does not give to the idea existence. Or take the will to recollect—here I have first an idea of the thing wanted, but not its existence (what exists is discrepant with the content required), then the result gives me psychical fact containing my idea. But if, without being required, the thing, as we say, had come up, the result would still be a fact containing an idea, but this idea would not be one that has gone before and has gone on to produce its own existence, and therefore it would not be will. Thought must alter the phenomenal sequence, no doubt, but so also does mere emotion and again sensation. The question is whether this sequence has an ideal character, which, going before, has thus made its own existence in fact. And where this is not the case, the process is not will. Thought is not will except so far as there has been a will to think. But if we go on to ask *how* an idea can produce its own existence, the answer is—by Contiguity and also by Blending. By the first the end

suggests the means, and by the second it reinforces whatever in psychical fact is already its own existence. I will
not dwell upon this point, but pass on further to difficulties.

When we go on to volition where the end is not a
thought but an outward event, there it may be said that
our view comes to shipwreck at once. For there a bodily
state is (or is implied in) the existence of the idea, and to
make a bodily state we require a new agency. But I do
not think so; I think we require merely the recognition
that Association extends to the bodily side of mental states;
and I assuredly could not call such an agency new, or anything but what I at least have always presupposed. I cannot even attempt here to lay down accurately the relation
in which body and mind stand to each other, but shall
assume that every psychical state has two aspects, and that
these aspects once conjoined may redintegrate each the
other. I am aware of the view that looks on mind as a bare
effect, or at the most as a mere dependent concomitant.
And I am aware of the view which denies wholly the interference of body with mind, or even goes on everywhere
to make the 'cause' a mere occasion upon which something else supervenes. And, considered as deductions from
metaphysics, these views might be respectable—though
the first of them (as we find it) comes usually from the
coarsest and most ignorant dogmatism. But I decline to
enter such an atmosphere. To demonstrate the influence
either of body on mind or of mind on body is obviously
impossible; but there is evidence enough for each, and no
more for one than for the other, and I am going to assume
that this is so. But I do *not* suppose that bare mind ever
works upon bare body. I assume that in a psychical state,
which has both sides, the mental side may be the chief
determining condition of a bodily result, and I cannot
undertake here to define this further. Now, on this
assumption, when we pass from internal to external volition, no new principle will come in. The one principle that
we require is that Association in its working should not be
limited to bare mind. And since it has been clearly understood that the laws of psychology do not pretend to be

ultimate and absolute truths, I see no ground for hesitation. The law will be that, if a state of body A^1 and a state of mind B^1 have occurred together, any one state with the quality of A or B (call it A^2 or B^2) will tend to bring in the other. How this law is to be interpreted, if we press for final truth, I refuse here to discuss.

I will deal now with volition directed externally, and shall at first keep to cases not dependent upon the so-called 'voluntary' muscles. The reader must understand that I am saying nothing about the *origin* of the will,[1] but am aiming at its essence. And that its essence is not to be found unless in connexion with these 'voluntary' muscles seems to me a mere prejudice. An idea of a state of my salivary glands or sexual organs will produce its existence in fact. We hear of those who can blush, shiver, sweat, or shed tears (Lotze, *Med. Psych.*, p. 303), if their mind is set on it. And if we think of various sensations in parts of our bodies, we can produce them at will, and can induce at our pleasure other bodily alterations through emotional excitement. Now on the one hand, I believe, the view could not be sustained that our striped or voluntary muscles are here the necessary agents; and on the other hand to deny that these changes are volitional would be to confess oneself refuted. With the nature of the process, considered physiologically, I am not concerned; but, as will, it is merely a case of our law. Where we have had a bodily state A^1 with a psychical state B^1, then, when B^2 comes in, A^2 tends to appear; and, if an idea of A is what produces the result, that result is volition. Blending too will supplement Contiguity; not that psychical and physical can be said to blend, but, where we have a local sensation of any kind whatever, there the idea of local change will assimilate itself with the sensation through their common basis, and, by strengthening that basis, will increase the bodily result. And, when we pass from these states to alterations produced through our voluntary muscles, the main principle is the same; and, abstracting as before from the question of origin, we can state it at once. Whenever

[1] On this difficult question see Sully, *Psych.*, pp. 593 ff.

any kind of mental state has been associated with a condition of our muscles, that state tends to reproduce that condition, and (as before) Blending may assist. Hence an idea of muscular movement, or of some end which implies it, will, given the proper associations, produce its own existence; and this without the invocation of any faculty such as Activity or Attention. With the physiological machinery I am not concerned, except to say that I should welcome with humble thankfulness any kind of finding from a jury of physiologists, if it confined itself to physiology.

This is the essence of volition, and, before I proceed to add a needful proviso, I will explain it further by considering some hostile doctrines. Professor Bain, who perhaps has thrown more light on the Will than any other psychologist, would, I presume, reject the conclusion I have adopted. As to the connexion of the will with the 'voluntary' muscles Professor Bain's doctrine is not clear to me, either on the side of body or of mind, and I will therefore not attempt to criticize it. And, where I feel that it is impossible for me to pass on in silence, my state is still one of a respectful inability to comprehend. What Professor Bain seems to teach is that the will must be selfish, and that, for all that, disinterested actions exist. Such actions do exist, but, as I understand it, are not volitions, but proceed from the intellect. When a mother deliberately sacrifices her life, the good old fashion was to call this an illusion, by which the mother aimed at her own pleasure and hit something else. From this Professor Bain dissents, and he holds the act to be unselfish. It is a disinterested action, but it is not will; on the contrary it is irrational, and comes from the intellect. And to the objection that the act is most palpably a volition, the reply, I suppose, is that, if this were the case, the will might be unselfish, which is not possible. But this strange confinement of volition to self-seeking action, so far from appearing axiomatic, and a thing the opposite of which can call for no discussion, strikes my mind as in obvious conflict with fact. Indeed, I should have ventured to consider it the plain refutation of any principle from which it comes.

And, since I certainly cannot attribute this to Professor Bain, and as certainly cannot find what else I should attribute, I must leave the matter as it stands with an expression of regret.

But, to pass on to another problem, it may be objected that desire is essential to volition, and that, unless the idea is felt pleasant, though it works, we have no will. This objection is defensible, and it was long before I ceased to consider it valid. But if we take acts from 'fixed ideas', from mere suggestion, from imitation and obedience to the word of command—not to add hypnotic phenomena—I cannot see that desire is always present in volition. If an act is suggested or ordered, and I do it, as we say, without thinking, it is a paradox to deny this in every case to be will; and the presence of desire is, by me at least, often not discoverable. Nay, on the contrary, the idea of the action may be painful.[1] We can indeed argue that, there being a general desire to act or an uneasiness during inaction, the idea of acting must be pleasant, or again that, by setting up a tension and then suggesting relief, the idea becomes pleasant. This is legitimate, but quite insufficient to prove desire in every case. In the first place, a tension and a readiness to act certainly need not be present before the idea comes; nor, when it comes, need the idea first be felt to be pleasant before it can move; and, again, if the idea *makes* the tension and so becomes pleasant by suggested relief, then the idea is acting already apart from its pleasantness, and we are trying to explain the cause by its effect. Nor, where tension is set up, does the idea always become pleasant at all. Further it is not true that in all cases a tension exists. In a sudden act not only may we fail to be aware of it, but there seems to be no interval long enough for its origin. We can, of course, postulate that which we fail to observe, but why should we do so? Why should the idea working itself out *not* be a volition? If we deny this, we should stand on something better than a

---

[1] I would remark here that, if we intend to make means and end essential to volition, we need to lay down that doctrine with more limitation than is usual.

mere preconception as to the necessity in all cases of pleasure and pain.[1]

Let us go on to consider other possible objections. An idea, we may be told, is not in all cases required, since the act may proceed direct from a perception. But I answer first that, if the perception is qualified ideally (as we explained on desire), and then produces the existence of that qualification, this is the working of an idea; and secondly, where this fails, the action is not will, and I think no one apart from theory would dream of so calling it. And with this reply we may pass on to more serious questions. It may be objected that our account is not too narrow but too wide. If an idea realizing itself is will, then the result of expectation, being a realized idea, will come from volition. But not so, I reply, if the result is produced, *not* by the action of the idea, but by quite other agencies. If the idea is realized by something else, it does not realize itself. And this leads us to consider a point of importance. In the result of the idea, whether external or internal, there are always circumstances which fall outside the idea's content. Where these are usual and normal, they are held to come from the idea and themselves to have been willed. But where in the result elements appear which are not normally connected with the idea's realization, and again where the normal result of the idea is interfered with from outside, we have not got will. There is, of course, very great uncertainty as to the detail of this principle; and as to the features which, for this or that subject, are and are not normally connected with the idea, there is also confusion. But I am here simply concerned with the *psychological* principle. I will illustrate briefly. If I resolve to think out a problem, do I will everything which turns out to be required for its solution? And so again with the external. When I kill trying to cure, has the result been willed? We should say that any excess beyond what I believed normally connected with the idea is not my will at all. Suppose,

[1] The attitude of both Mr. Sully and Mr. Ward is to me somewhat puzzling here. They seem to consider the question scarcely worth discussing; but I cannot understand why.

on the other hand, I were thinking of a result, say the finding the amount of an unrighteous gain, and without any operation I got the answer required; or say that I wished to steal a jewel and then found it in my hand. In these cases we should deny the existence of volition, because the normal working of the idea, however intense, could not have so brought out its reality. Part at least of that reality is referred, not to the idea, but to something else of some kind. And, though the limit and the detail are certainly vague, I think this principle is certain, and I will carry it on further. Suppose the memory of the disgusting causes us to vomit, suppose we blush because we think we may, or yawn, or itch, if the ideas of these are suggested—are we to call this volition? I think the answer will confirm the principle we laid down. If the connexion between the idea and the result is thought such that the idea was held with the expectation of its reality following, then, unless something happened abnormally, we should call that volition. Because I am able to yawn at pleasure, if I entertain the idea and so yawn, then I have willed it, unless I can show interfering conditions. But I cannot blush at will because the idea does not produce the reality, unless indeed by going round through emotion, upon which I, personally, cannot count. Hence my blushing is accidental in regard to the idea, though that idea really was a condition which acted.

But this, of course, leads us on into still greater difficulties. Take a case where the idea produces its reality, but where we say that the idea is forced on us and not resistible. We need not go to hypnotism for examples, for these, so far as I know, are only one kind among others of the action of ideas.[1] A morbid idea becomes dominant, and perhaps recurrent at intervals,[2] and produces an action. Is this volition? A painful suggestion, to which we are averse, by

---

[1] The idea that psychology is to be revolutionized by experiments in hypnotism could hardly have been entertained by any educated psychologist. But it is easy to startle the vulgar with the pathology of a science. To learn its principles is another thing.

[2] See Knop, *Paradoxie des Willens*, for examples.

T

its mere strength and persistence carries us away. We fear to fail because fear unsteadies us; we fear to fail because of fear, and that anxiety produces the object of its aversion. This is not will, and yet the idea seems to make its own reality. Nor would it avail us to attempt to fall back upon desire and to make that the criterion; for, even where we desire, we do not call it will if the result seems abnormal, as when above I desired a conclusion without the operation. Desire shows will only if we desire what is under our control; and, if it is under our control, we should call it volition even if desire were absent. And in all these cases, I presume, our control is the criterion. If the idea is not controllable, we refer it to the outside and deny our own volition. If I could not help it, I did not will it.

But can we give a definite meaning to our inability to help? I am not asking as to our moral responsibility in general, nor as to the particular limits and detail of our control. I am asking simply for the principle on which we call, or refuse to call, our actions volition. We saw that will was an idea producing its own reality; but we saw also that the connexion may be merely apparent. The result may show an element forced out or thrust in by something abnormal, and which therefore we hold external to the process of the idea. And since the idea does *not* here produce *its own* reality, these actions fall outside our definition of will. But we have to deal now with cases where the strength of the idea is said to prevent volition. We seem here to go upon the principle that an idea has a normal, absolute or relative, strength, and that anything beyond may therefore be referred to something external to our wills. And at first this degree of strength seems purely arbitrary; but it is, I think, not wholly so. A criterion seems to be found in the presence of an opposite idea. If I have an impulse and the idea of resistance is not present, the action is will, unless we save ourselves by the further (unexplained) assertion that resistance *would* have been present if the conditions had been normal. But, given the presence of a resisting idea, then I think we should disown the result of the impulse. For, if that impulse had been normal, we feel a counter-idea would have restrained it, and therefore its strength and its result may be looked on as foreign. And where the result is desired, the same tendency may still be noticed, and extreme force in the idea may be referred to the supernatural.[1] I think this aspect of self-control is one reason why the will has been (falsely) confined to the 'voluntary' muscles. The connexion of the idea with the result is there both far more direct and more regular, but this is not quite all. The opposing muscles give us a power of resistance and control, because they supply us with an idea which works wholly counter to the first. Apart from these muscles the simple definite counter-ideas fail, and control is more difficult. We cannot banish an idea by the mere general idea of its expulsion, and the special banishing element is often hard, or even impossible, to find.

Hence the conclusion I would urge is not that popular usage is quite consistent with our definition of will, but I would insist that, where it is not so, it is also quite inconsistent with itself. And, I think, through all its inconsistency it clings unconsciously to the principle that, where an idea realizes its own content, we have the essence of volition.

I am compelled to add, before closing, a few words on the feeling of Activity. I may be told that this belongs to (if it does not constitute) the essence of will, and is at all events a criterion of the presence of volition. Now, if this means that in all cases by applying that criterion we are delivered from doubt as to the presence of will, it is obviously false. For it is no easier to answer the question 'Was I active?' than the question 'Did I will?' But, dismissing this, let us ask if a feeling of activity is essential. On this I should like to say, first, that we may experience this feeling where will is not clearly present, and where the self-expansion does not seem to be produced by an idea of

---

[1] I am keeping here to formal considerations. The material want of correspondence in the idea to our character would be of course another important reason for accounting it foreign.

the result. In such cases the question arises how far an idea must always in some sense be presupposed; but I must pass this by. I will here (for the sake of argument) admit (what I do not hold) that with the feeling of activity we must have will, just as with will we have a felt activity; but the question will be as to the nature of their connexion. For me the feeling of activity will be merely a result, or at most a concomitant symptom. Wherever we have self-expansion attributed merely to self, there we feel ourselves active; and where an idea causes its own existence, there, normally, we have felt self-expansion. And it is not true that the presence or absence of this feeling is always the cause why we own or disown the idea. It is often true that the independent impression of foreignness is what makes this feeling fail. Normally any idea which realizes itself expands my self as a consequence,[1] and, because mine, will produce the feeling of activity. And where the idea is felt to be foreign through its material want of agreement with my self, there the contraction of the self and the failure of my activity is not a cause but a concomitant effect of the foreignness. Finally, where the working idea

[1] That is, of course, expands it *so far*. If, e.g., I will to narrow my psychical field, and succeed, that is still so far self-expansion, and since the idea is felt to be mine, I am aware of activity. I will repeat here, however uselessly, that in my opinion *mere* expansion of self can *not* give activity. Of course, therefore, some expansions of self may be passive; and indeed some are so. Of course, again, some may be painful. Of course, once more, even where the expansion is attributed to the self, the whole mixed result may be painful, though even here the element of successful activity is always pleasant. A difficulty may seem to arise when (unsuccessful) effort appears to give activity without expansion. But in such effort there will be unsteadiness and oscillation and the beginnings of that which, if it went further, would become complete success. This so far will be expansion, and without this, and if all were stationary, I am convinced that we should have no feeling of activity, nor indeed of effort. And I suppose that it may be my duty to state that I have made the distinction between activity of the soul 'for the soul' and 'for the outside observer' (*E*. xii. 226), and have even expended italics to mark the fact that I have done so. On this whole question I fully admit that the view which I have adopted requires further working out. On the other hand I am as sure of its general truth, as I am convinced that no one will understand it who approaches it from a basis of hardened preconception.

appears for other reasons external, or its results to be in any way due to outer interference, there the absence of the feeling of activity is caused by the independent perception, or again, partly and in some cases, is a joint effect with it. Throughout psychology we may feel sure that a consciousness of activity is a thing to be explained and not a thing to explain by. And with these hurried remarks I must bring this subject to an end.

But in conclusion I am forced to say something on the *normative* character of the will, and shall allow myself here on some points to travel outside psychology. Just as with thought we saw the law of movement become self-conscious and an end (*E.* xii. 229–30), so it is with volition. The end of both is Individuality, self-realization as the unity of harmony and expansion; but for will this end must seek existence in the series of events. My end is to realize this perfection in my psychical being, yet not in mine looked at by itself, but regarded as an element in a higher system. And, as with thought harmony and expansion fell under one head (ibid. 208, 236–7), so it is again with will. If positive self-realization is the end and is essential, that end, given plurality, becomes negative of discord. It means a harmonious individuality that, because it finds opposition, is forced to expand. This end is not quantitative in itself; but, since perfection can never be reached by us wholly and yet is approached in various degrees, morality becomes approximative—though, if the end were attained, there would be no more quantity. And, since thus there is a scale of higher and lower, these aspects of harmony and expansion may diverge, and their seeming discrepancy may give rise to difficulties. For one life may be wider and another more harmonious. An end may bring greater loss to, or of, individual beings, while at the same time it seems to realize a higher system. Hence in a given case it may be hard to distinguish higher and lower. We have the same difficulty with knowledge. That may concentrate itself into a general view, or may scatter itself into details, and it is often hard to discover which movement best deserves the epithet of progress. We assume usually that differentiation, whether in science or in life, will not lead mainly to distraction, but will result sooner or later in a higher unity. But where this assumption is not well founded (or at least seems hard to justify), a real difficulty arises.

If we turn now to pleasure and pain, and the relation they bear to the End and Standard, we may be asked if it is possible to justify their exclusion. But certainly they are not excluded. I do not suppose that facts exist, or ought to exist, merely in order to realize a form, or generally for the sake of any abstraction. When we say that our end is to realize a principle, we mean that the reality of that principle is our end. But this again should mean the existence of fact having the character of our principle. It ought not to imply that the reality has another character, which is connected with the end merely *per accidens* and externally. This, it appears to me, is an assumption which would go beyond what we know. And thus, if pleasure is the feeling of positive self-affirmation, and pain again of discord, these feelings most obviously cannot be excluded from the idea of realized Individuality. To say that without pleasure the end would still be the end, is to transcend our knowledge; as it is even to assert that with a different sensible character the end would still be desirable. So far as I see, every one of its aspects goes (or may go) in reality to make the end what it is; and I do not object to use the existence of pleasure and pain as means to know about its realization.

But, if so, we must deal with the objection that the end has characters which may diverge. It seems as if, to progress towards a higher individuality, we might be forced to increase pain and to sacrifice pleasure. But I cannot accept this possibility. We must bear in mind that, as we saw above with harmony and expansion, the sacrifice of one aspect may simply be relative, may be temporary and local. And, secondly, I feel sure that on some points we should reconsider common views as to progress. A one-sided, distracted life, even if distraction proceeds from advance of the intellect, is not really higher than what, taken intellectually, may be beneath it, and may perhaps be destroyed by it in the struggle of life. And I think that the habit we have got into of believing the opposite has come partly from the assumption (rational or otherwise) that such a distraction is but relative, and must really be a means to some higher unity. And further, when measuring high and low by the test of self-dependence and individuality, we are too likely to fall into blind individualism. The psychical creature is not one thing actual by itself, nor is its spiritual relation to a higher individuality another thing that falls (I know not where) outside its being. Duped by such prejudices, we may set that down as poor which in truth is most rich. And I think that, if the reader will take these points into consideration, he may hesitate to say that development of individuality can bring greater pain. For myself, if that were shown to be possible, I should admit it as a difficulty which I was unable to solve.

Nor, further, will the implication of pleasure bring quantity into the end. Perfection will imply pleasure and the absence of pain; and we may add (I presume) that pain neutralized by pleasure, so as on the whole to lose its character, is not to count as pain. To make the end to be realized consist in increase of pleasure, or in an infinite sum or series, or in anything else which would exclude absolutely the possibility of its own reality—may be left to those who are metaphysically incompetent. To hold that of two pure pleasures one cannot be better than the other may seem at first sight paradoxical, but it is another side of the truth that a harmonious individual would be perfect and could not be more perfect. And, just as the end apart from pleasure becomes approximative, so, when pleasure is included, the end becomes neither more nor less approximative, to those who understand. My space does not allow a fuller explanation.

I will add merely that our conclusion has not led us to Hedonism. Hedonism I understand to abstract pleasure and pain from life, and to make of everything else a mere external means to the getting of one and the avoiding of the other. Hedonism holds, in short, that every other aspect of the world is absolutely worthless. Now I can say (speaking broadly) that what is not pleasant is worthless, but I cannot add that it is worthless merely because it is not pleasant, and that the same thing (mere pleasure added) would, simply for that reason, once more be valuable. I dissent wholly from such a one-sided abstraction; and that the universe, or our life, exists for the sake of one of its elements seems to me most indefensible. I at least know no rational way of arriving at the worthlessness of any single aspect of the world. This is the main point, and I must venture to doubt whether any one can agree with us here while still remaining a Hedonist in principle. Our Hedonism has, however, begun to purge itself of a mass of inherited errors. Its barbarous psychology of motive seems now quite optional. And its attachment to the reality of the mere individual and to the ultimate value of his private claims—a dogma neither based on nor assailable by reason —has begun to be challenged. How much Mr. Stephen has done for our moral philosophy, by breaking away here from the highest authorities, has, I think, hardly yet been appreciated. He should have gone far towards making it possible for those who disagree to argue.[1]

[1] How far in what precedes I may have changed the position which I took up ten years ago, I have not thought it necessary to inquire. The divergence would be found, I think, on the whole to be inconsiderable. But I have not ventured to suppose this a question likely to interest.

XV

ON PROFESSOR JAMES'S DOCTRINE OF SIMPLE RESEMBLANCE (I)

[*First published in* MIND, N.S. ii, No. 5, 83–8. *January*, 1893.]

IN Professor James's *Psychology* (vol. i, p. 532) there is a doctrine and an argument with regard to simple Resemblance. Both the argument and the doctrine, I venture to think, are open to criticism, and perhaps some discussion on this point may prove of value. I would much rather express my general admiration for Professor James's brilliant work. And since the argument, if not the doctrine, is derived from Professor Stumpf, I am sorry again to criticize a writer whose book on Space, years ago, taught me much. I have thought it better to confine myself to Professor James's statement.

There is such a thing, he holds, as simple Resemblance.

'Any theory which would base likeness on identity, and not rather identity on likeness, must fail. It is supposed, perhaps by most people, that two resembling things owe their resemblance to their absolute identity in respect of some attribute or attributes, combined with the absolute non-identity of the rest of their being. This, which may be true of compound things, breaks down when we come to simple impressions.'

We seem bidden here to make a choice. We must either accept resemblance between what is simple, or we must hold

'that the difference between two objects is constituted of two things, viz., their absolute identity in certain respects, *plus* their absolute non-identity in others.'

Now I wish to point out at once that this alternative seems incomplete. A man may be sure that resemblance between what is quite simple is quite unmeaning; and yet he need not believe that the one alternative to 'simple' is 'composite', if 'composite' means made up of separable parts. The view that sameness and difference are everywhere inseparable aspects most certainly exists. But its existence is not included in the dilemma in which the argument consists. And, in the second place, while holding resemblance, not indeed to *be*, but to be based always on, partial identity, one need not in consequence hold that this identity is explicit. If, that is, in things before my mind, which to me seem like, I do not distinguish, and perhaps could not specify, the identical point, this does not prove that no perceptible identity is there. But on these false assumptions Professor James's whole conclusion seems to rest.

The arguments employed make use of the instance of a series. Such an instance entails this very grave disadvantage. One cannot fully deal with its complication unless one attacks the general problem of the unity and order of a series. And to touch such a difficult question by the way is hardly possible. Certainly if Professor James's view of resemblance got rid of this problem, the inconvenience (he might fairly urge) lies all on one side. But this, I imagine, can hardly be said to be really the case. I must therefore warn the reader that the instances used in the arguments involve a serious and (so far as I see) an irrelevant complication. I am hence forced to treat merely that part of them which seems to me to be essential.

I. The first argument (I state it in my own way) is this. Take several sensible qualities which form a series. These qualities may have resemblance without identity. For, if identity, then an identical part; and if so, then a part which can be specified. In at least some cases one is unable to specify the part, and therefore, so far, there is no identity. Hence the resemblance is simple.

This argument appears to be thoroughly unsound. Resemblance I take, not to *be*, but to be an impression based upon, experienced partial identity. This, however, does not involve a perception of the identity, as such and discriminated. I may call things alike or different, and only afterwards discover the point which impressed my mind, and on which my judgement was founded. This is common experience, and, so far as it goes, is adverse to

the assumption that what I cannot distinctly indicate
is therefore absent or ineffective. And then, again, some
sensations seem to possess a common feature. They have,
to me, a general character, of which I can be vaguely
aware, though I cannot isolate it, or in any way (as we say)
'bring it out'. You cannot, e.g., point out what general
colour is; but, on this ground, to deny that particular
colours have for your perception anything in common
appears not reasonable. 'Yes, but', I may hear, 'you have
not considered the series. The colours are not more or less
alike as being colours. They are more or less alike, for
example, in being darker or lighter. Will you not deal
with that point?' Well, I should have thought that darkness and lightness most assuredly were characters of
which we are aware; and so, again, with bitter and sweet,
and high and low, and dull and sharp, and (when you
come to space) with up and down, or right and left. And
to tell me that these characters in and for my mind do not
exist, because I cannot make them explicit and distinct,
appears quite arbitrary. And Professor James, it seems to
me, is himself concerned in denying such a doctrine. For
how can we have a consciousness of uniform direction
(p. 490) if there is not some one element common
to all the degrees? How are we to speak with any
meaning of 'more' and 'less', if it is to be a 'more' and a
'less' of *nothing*? To choose the instance of a series, in
order to disprove identity, was, I venture to think, indeed
suicidal. You may perhaps urge that we have a series of
resemblances, and that in this resemblance in the end
consists the identity. But the resemblance, I reply, is not
resemblance at large, or in general; for the series, we are
agreed, has a particular direction. It moves to more or less
of high or low, or soft or loud, or light or dark, or sweet or
bitter. But a particular kind of resemblance, degrees of
which make the unity of a series, seems to me to imply
resemblance in and through a particular point. But, if so,
with that we have a resemblance based on identity. Professor James has scarcely made it clear how he would deal
with this obvious reply to the first argument. And I do not

think he has supplied any adequate information at all as to the unity of his series. How far this information is supposed to be given in Chapter xxviii I am unable to say.

II. The second argument I must quote in full, as translated from Stumpf.

'We may generalize:—Wherever a number of sensible impressions are apprehended *as a series*, there in the last instance must perceptions of simple likeness be found. *Proof:* Assume that all the terms of a series, e.g. the qualities of tone, $c\ d\ e\ f\ g$, have something in common—*no matter what it is*, call it X; then I say that the differing parts of each of these terms must not only be differently constituted in each, but must *themselves form a series*, whose existence is the ground for our apprehending the original terms in serial form. We thus get instead of the original series $a\ b\ c\ d\ e\ f \ldots$ the equivalent series $X\alpha,\ X\beta,\ X\gamma \ldots$ &c. What is gained? The question immediately arises: How is $\alpha\beta\gamma$ known as a series? According to the theory, these elements must themselves be made up of a part common to all, and of parts differing in each, which latter parts form a new series, and so on *ad infinitum*, which is absurd' (p. 533, note).

This is the argument which I presume contains the abstract principle, and for myself I cannot call it 'conclusive' or even 'acute'. It is a dilemma based (if I understand it rightly) on a vicious alternative, and a dilemma certainly not reduced to its simplest form. I will endeavour to state its principle.

A thing is simple or else composite, and, if it is composite, its parts in separation retain each its own proper character. Resemblance, hence, if composite, is made of two parts, identity and difference, and these parts in separation, and taken bare, must still be identity and difference. Otherwise resemblance must be simple.

Now in certain cases of resemblance try to find the difference which is nothing but bare difference. You find only a difference which still contains some part of the identity. The attempt to get rid of this identity, and to bring out the difference bare and pure, can never succeed. And therefore difference is not separable, and therefore resemblance is not composite. And therefore it is simple, Q.E.D.

Now apply—if you think it worth while—this principle to the concrete instance of a series. If the steps of a series are not simple, you must be able in each case to separate the difference and the identity. And the differences themselves clearly must not have any serial character. For, if so, they would contain identity, and not be pure differences. They would be the series itself over again, and not the bare differences *of* the series. Thus in a series *ex hypothesi* the constitutive differences (if they exist) *must be* serial, for otherwise we are left with bare identity, and the series has vanished. But if, on the other hand, the differences *are* serial, still the series is gone, because its differences now do not exist. They are taken in connexion with and not apart from an identity; that is, they are not pure differences and so not differences at all. But the effort to find pure differences leads to the infinite regress and fails. Therefore the differences do not exist; and therefore the steps of the series (and I suppose the series itself) are simple. Therefore resemblance must be simple.[1] Q.E.D.

Now if the object were merely to disprove the view that resemblance consists of two 'parts', would it not be better simply to urge that identity and difference, if so taken apart, have each forfeited its character? That is the way of disproof which I should have thought was as plain as it is old. And then to argue from the proof that resemblance is not thus composite, direct to the conclusion that therefore resemblance is simple—is (I should have thought) to offer us an equally plain and familiar fallacy. Hence, probably I have not understood the argument which has gained Professor James's applause.

I am myself better acquainted with this dialectical way of reasoning when used to arrive at a very different result. I know it better when employed as a means to prove that

---

[1] I have here perhaps proved too much, but this may be all the better. So far as I see, a dialectical argument, the same as Professor Stumpf's, might be used to destroy Professor James's view of a series—if, that is, for him, in any sense, the perception of a series contains a common element and a diversity. As, however, I have no clear statement as to what Professor James understands by the unity of a series, I cannot offer a criticism which would have to be conjectural.

we have not separable parts, but inseparable aspects. But then it has not been picked up and applied for one particular end, but has been worked systematically and in all directions. Professor James would be invited, e.g., to exhibit a simplicity which was barely simple and not qualified, at all or in any way, by complexity. And then the same infinite process would be forthwith set up. But as this is all the common property of philosophical students, I must once more presume that I have not understood what, as I understand it, has no value. But I doubt if the fault can be entirely on my side. And with this we may perhaps pass from Professor Stumpf's dialectical argument.

At any rate, I may be told, in fact there *are* simple impressions, and these decide the case. What precisely they would prove and disprove, if they *were* anything real, would be a rather large inquiry. It would be a question certainly not confined to one special problem in psychology. But as this matter is (if I may say so) somewhat old ground with me, I may perhaps refer to what I wrote some years ago. I had been urging that association by Resemblance could be in all cases explained by Redintegration. And I then went on to say:—

'It may be objected, in the first place, that, if the sensation is simple, this theory will not work. I admit it, and I should be sorry if in such a case it *did* work. I would rather that any theory which I adopt did *not* explain impossibilities. And that any actual presentation should be simple is quite impossible. Even if it had no internal characters, yet it must be qualified by the relations of its environment. And this complexity would be quite enough for the purpose.'[1]

Simple impressions, in short, are mere abstractions, falsely taken to be facts. And I venture with great diffidence to add that this elsewhere seems to be the view held by Professor James himself. By simplicity he on other topics appears to mean a character which excludes not diversity, but only separability and partition. A whole in

---

[1] *L.* 332 = 307. I would venture to refer the reader to the rest of this discussion on Resemblance.

this sense would still be simple, however complex it might be, so long as it were integral, and contained inseparable diversities. But if so, Professor James's argument against identity bodily disappears. It holds as a disproof only of *one* untenable view of identity. And if so, obviously the further dilemma with its conclusion is vicious.

There is a view (Professor James must be well aware) which holds that identity and difference are complementary aspects, that the one aspect may be emphasized here, and the other aspect there, but that an attempt to isolate them leads everywhere to an infinite regress. And, of course, this view insists that identity and difference depend always upon content. They are both—to use Professor James's expression—'qualitative', or else nothing.[1] Now certainly a view may exist, and yet be so contemptible as to be treated fairly as non-existent. But then a man who holds that view is curious to know something of the ground for such contempt, at least in the case of a writer whom he has been led to respect. And therefore I turn for further information to Professor James:—

'The vanishing of all perceptible difference between two numerically distinct things makes them *qualitatively the same*, or *equal*. Equality, or *qualitative* (as distinguished from numerical) *identity*, is thus nothing but the *extreme degree of likeness*' (p. 532).

Well, but *of course* we want to know if likeness implies any difference—Yes or No—and again, further, if an *imperceptible* difference will do. We want to know this, because the extreme degree of likeness, if difference *is* necessary, will surely not be likeness at all. And if there is to be *no* difference—I wish Professor James would help me to answer the question, how things in that case can be distinct. Because suppose (as I cannot) that things distinct possess no other difference in quality, yet it seems to me that you must either qualify them by their relations or not.

---

[1] Identity can be taken *also*, in some cases, to involve continuity, but here qualitative sameness is, of course, still essential. Suppose it gone, and then see what identity is left. And mere continuity itself—does not that in the end imply an identity of content? Where otherwise lies the unity of temporal duration?

It must be Yes or No—which you please; but, so far as I can perceive, not both at once. If it is Yes, I can see no way to deny that the things are now *perceptibly* diverse. If it is No, I cannot understand, for the life of me, how *they* are now different at all—at least to human beings. In short, a distinction without any difference, and a series involving degrees, but degrees of nothing—are to me hopeless difficulties. If these things are plain to Professor James, I cannot believe it would be a misemployment of his powers to make them plain to us others—for I need not say that I am not alone in my unwilling blindness. And if I have fallen myself into some vicious dilemma, I have been waiting for years for some kind hand to help me out. But, if again a psychologist is not called on to vex himself with these idle problems, then perhaps also he need not entangle himself in dialectical subtleties which, if they are good at all, seem only good when one carries them through. But who am I that I should dare speak to Professor James of the dialectical method?

I should like to end this Note with two or three remarks. I would plead first that, if it has seemed unduly long, the issue involved is one of very great and wide-reaching importance. And next, with regard to the perception of a series, I would repeat that I have not attempted to explain this in passing. It is a problem in any case delicate and difficult, but, if we once discard identity, then I think much worse than difficult. Our one chance lies in maintaining the vital, the inseparable, connexion at every point between identity and difference.[1] But I certainly cannot end without another expression of my great and sincere admiration for Professor James's work. If it is not free (and how many books are free?) from lapses, those lapses leave its level something very much above the common.

[1] And suppose that we find that a certain perception is inexplicable and ultimate. Are we from this to conclude that it is therefore simple? If in what is ultimate we find diversity of aspect—where is the inconsistency?

XVI

ON PROFESSOR JAMES'S DOCTRINE OF SIMPLE RESEMBLANCE (II)

[*First published in* MIND, N.S. ii, No. 7, 366–9. *July*, 1893.]

I FEEL that some reply is due to Professor James's remarks in the last number of *Mind* [N.S. ii. 208], and I will begin by recalling the original issue. Professor James contended 'that any theory which would base likeness on identity, and not rather identity on likeness, must fail'. He argued not that there *might* be, but that there *must* be simple resemblance not resting on identity.

In proof of this thesis he adduced arguments which I endeavoured to meet. These arguments, as they were stated, are withdrawn, and Professor James now relies on a simpler form of one of them. He argues that identity not based on mere resemblance is untenable, because it leads to an infinite regress. And I will try to deal with this contention in its present shape.

The attempt is difficult for this reason, that, desiring to examine the proof adduced, I am unable to find any. The series of degrees, not degrees of anything at all, is no longer urged, and Professor Stumpf's subtleties are no longer before us. But I can discover nothing which is to stand in the place of these. There is an assertion that identity must lead to an indefinite regress. But the ground of this assertion seems not stated explicitly.

And hence in the main I have to repeat that a view of identity exists which, so far as I see, wrecks Professor James's thesis, and which, it seems to me, he throughout, and from first to last, ignores.

Identity and difference on this view are inseparable aspects of one complex whole. They are not even 'discernible', if this means that you can separate them in idea, so as to treat one as remaining itself when the other is excluded. And the whole is emphatically not a 'synthesis', if that means that it can be mentally divided, and that its elements then still keep their characters. The 'Hegelian commonplace' suggested by Professor James (p. 210)[1] is therefore, to me at least (whatever Hegel would have said of it), in principle erroneous. It seems to contain the root of Professor James's own doctrine.

Let us take, for example, the different kinds of our sensations. In each kind I should say that there is something the same. Colours or smells differ among themselves, but there is a point in which, as coloured or as odorous, they are identical. But to call this or that colour a 'synthesis' would in my view be mistaken. For the uncoloured differences on one side, and their colour in general on the other side, are the products of false analysis and vicious abstraction. You may of course consider and attend to either the sameness or the differences in colour; but you must not use language which implies that either aspect, if not qualified by the other, is consistent even in thought. You cannot, in short, separate them even in idea; you can only lay stress for the moment on one side of an integral whole. It is as it would be at a far lower degree with, for instance, the inside and the outside of a sphere. Whichever of these you consider, you have also the other along with it. And to speak of their 'synthesis', as if they were Indian boxes one inside the other, would be in principle vicious.

And the view which I advocate is so far from seeming to me subtle, that I am prepared to hear that it is even trivial. But let us see how it applies. With colours and smells, and other kinds of experience, we have not reached the end; for these again are all alike and have something in common. They are all alike in being experienced or felt. Sentience, being, or experience (these are all the same to me) is a character in which everything is finally identical. And let us see if this doctrine is destroyed by Professor James's indefinite regress.

We hear that analysis, if we pursue identity, takes us to one of two conclusions, each untenable, and that therefore

[1] [References to Professor James's article will be found in *M.* n.s. ii.]

simple resemblance is true. Whether simple resemblance itself is tenable seems a question not directly faced. An attempt is made to prove that thesis indirectly by setting out and refuting all other possibilities. But I hardly see how it can be assumed that we *must* possess *some* tenable view. And in particular I cannot find that the above view of identity is recognized at all. But, if so, the proof is obviously unsound. I am ordered either to accept the 'Mind-dust theory'—a thing I venture to consider not worth the least notice—or else to affirm 'the postulation of point after point, encapsulated within each other *in infinitum*, as the constitutive condition of the resemblance of any two objects' (p. 208). But these alternatives surely do not include the view which I hold. To me it seems strange that colour should be encapsulated within colours and general sentience within sensations, and that my own life should be felt the same only because somewhere it has, or is, a box with something in it, and that otherwise my life is one because of one (?) simple immediate resemblance, resting, I suppose, on no constitutive condition whatever. But what to me is strange too is that any one, thinking so about Identity, should incline to banish it only at a certain point and not wholly and altogether.

And this idea of 'encapsulation' is, so far as I see, no mere metaphor. It seems the whole argument, and it contains the entire essence of Professor Stumpf's superfluous subtleties. The view which, if not refuted, ruins Professor James's thesis is this, that identity is always one aspect of an integral whole, and that if you abstract it, in the sense of ideally putting it in a box by itself, you have made it inconsistent with itself or reduced it to nothing. Experience or being is the last term in my regress, and is where I stop. And I am told that I am bound in reason to go back further still. And asking for a reason all I get is this. We have, say, a, b, c, d, all with one ultimate aspect m. And I am ordered to encapsulate m and then to see what happens. But I was taught what happens years ago when I learnt too imperfectly from a great master who saw into these matters perhaps as far as Professors Stumpf and

James. And I remember enough to recognize in this order
to encapsulate the merest attempt to beg the whole question. And I say that I will neither take *m* as abstract being,
and so make it nothing, nor will I take it as a 'synthesis',
and so within it set up an infinite regress. I will take it
rather as one aspect in vital connexion with another aspect,
and, if this is absurd, I ask at least that some one will try
to tell me why. For my part, since in experience identity
and difference seem indissoluble and since otherwise the
entire world of our knowledge seems dissipated, I will take
them in this union, though certainly I cannot explain it.
For I have always supposed that explanation must stop
somewhere. And if any one urges against me such questions as how quality makes itself and how relations are
engendered, I submit respectfully that all this is the
merest irrelevancy.

So far as psychology is concerned, I have tried elsewhere
to make my view clear. The question between Resemblance and Identity, I have urged, is there one of relative
efficiency. I have protested and I do protest against
attempting in psychology to judge of ultimate truth. If
Resemblance *were* the ultimate truth I would not use it in
psychology, because I am sure that there it works badly.
And when I hear from Professor James that he cares
about it as a thesis, that a little surprises me. For where,
I ask, in psychology is this thesis to be *used*? Professor
James, I thought, had broken with that insane mythology
which Resemblance begets. I thought that the doctrine
accepted from Professor Stumpf was a thing out of connexion with his actual work. But if he cares about it, then
clearly I am somewhere mistaken.

Or is the thesis idle psychologically, and is it as a piece
of ultimate metaphysical truth that Professor James contends for it? I wish, if so, that point had been clear; for,
if so, from the first I could have been much shorter. The
question is, I presume, the fundamental problem about
the One and the Many. Can these features be held apart,
and again is there any way of intelligibly taking them together? What opinions I have on this matter are in print

and ready to appear. But I will say at once that, in the full sense of the term 'intelligible', I do not think the union of these aspects of the world is intelligible. I think that in the end *each* (not merely one) shows inconsistency when apart, and that taken together they fail to satisfy the ultimate demands of our intellect.

But there is something else I think also. So far as the world or any part of it is to any degree intelligible, so far as there is any knowledge which to any extent goes beyond the barest feeling, this is the case solely because Identity, as I hold to it, is fact and truth. Deny this principle and the world, as we have it, is destroyed. And immediate Resemblance without identity seems to me, on the other hand, sheer nonsense. As a principle of knowledge it is useless and worse than useless, and in itself it is a mere heap of staring inconsistencies. And if I am invited here to a metaphysical discussion, I will make Professor James this offer. If he will state the principle on which he objects to identity (a thing which, let me remind him, he has not yet even attempted to do), I also will take the same principle, whatever it is. And I will show that, judged by it, Professor James's thesis as to Resemblance (p. 208) is indefensible. But I should add that I venture to provoke this conflict only because I feel sure that any appeal to principle would render it unnecessary. And if I am asked, Since all at the end may be unintelligible, why not at the beginning say, All is simple, and so have done with it?—I feel the force of that inquiry. But I would suggest in answer that not to trouble oneself at all might be even simpler.

If, however, we may remain on the firmer ground of psychology, I would end these remarks by stating how the case seems to stand. The contention against Identity was that at a certain point it breaks down and must give place to Resemblance without identity. So far as I have been able to understand this contention, I have tried to answer it. And the point I would urge is this. If in psychology such Resemblance is wanted, then (true or false) by all means let it be used in psychology. And if Professor James could show me that in his own admirable work he has found it useful, that to me would be an argument of very great weight. And if by the help of it he could solve the problem of the perceived unity of a series, I would confess that these remarks have been largely mistaken. But if, in psychology at least, the principle will not work—if it merely lingers with the lingering survivals of the old Association mythology—why not banish it from psychology? Why not let it reign, if it can, in the distracted realm of metaphysics?

XVII

ON PROFESSOR JAMES'S DOCTRINE OF SIMPLE RESEMBLANCE (III)

[*First published in* MIND, N.S. ii, No. 8, 510. *October,* 1893.]

I SHOULD be glad to accept Professor James's conclusion [*M.* N.S. ii. 509] that the question between us is
about a word. But to me both Resemblance and Identity,
as he advocates them, are mere self-contradictory ideas.
Resemblance without identity, and again 'stark self-same-
ness' without difference, seem counterpart pieces of nonsense, nonsense unwarranted either in psychology or logic.
And surely Professor James does deny Identity in the one
sense in which I admit it. But with regard to Resemblance
I would once more solicit attention to certain points.

Is Professor James prepared to maintain that, where the
point of sameness is not explicit, it does not exist? Does he
hold that in the end we have resemblance, though there is
no point in which the things are alike and on which the
resemblance is founded? Or, if not, will he explain why
this point is not to be called one and the same? Does he
teach that in a series you may have degrees of more and
less which are more and less of nothing? Or, if not, will
he tell us why this one something, of which there are
degrees, is not to be called the same? And, when a series is
perceived as one, is its unity to lie in resemblance without
sameness? And, if so, may we be informed whether there
is only one such resemblance or several? And, if there are
several, where are we to hold that the unity lies? And, if
there is but one such resemblance, will Professor James
say how the serial differences in resemblance remain themselves, so long as through all there may not be any point
of sameness? This last question cannot be troublesome to
one who has understood and applauded Professor Stumpf's
dialectical exploit. But if the objection is verbal and applies
not to 'same' and 'sameness', but only to 'identity' and
'identical', may we have that stated?

It is easy to discredit such questions as idle conundrums asked in the interest of some obscure and foolish mysticism. It is easy to disregard them and to stand on inherited dogma. That is all so easy that in the present case I looked for something more interesting. But I leave it to the reader to judge whether these inquiries do not fall within psychology, and whether some answer to them should not be supplied by any satisfactory treatment of psychological principles. I am confident that Professor James, if he could be induced to deal with these problems, would not fail to throw light on them. He would certainly find that our difference involved much more than the mere meaning of a word.

XVIII

ON THE FAILURE OF MOVEMENT IN DREAM

[*First published in* MIND, N.S. iii, No. 11, 373–7. *July*, 1894.]

THERE is a question about dreams to which at present I have not found a good answer. Why, when we strive to move in dream, do we not always move? I am hardly parodying the average account when I represent it thus: In dream we do not move, and, when we do, it is called somnambulism. And, though many psychologists of course stand far above this average level, I have not seen a satisfactory discussion of the question. And I thought that some reader of *Mind* could perhaps direct me to such a treatment, or would himself perhaps throw some light on the matter. I will in the meantime venture to set down such ideas as I have acquired.

That we move in sleep is clear, and every one knows it who, for example, keeps a dog. And how far such movements may go, either without a dream or again with one, seems difficult to say. The nature of common somnambulism and its relation on one side to normal dream, and on the other side to hypnotism or again monomania, seems a problem certainly not solved. But my question here is a narrow one. When in dream we think of moving and desire to move, why *usually* do we not move? The fact, I believe, is thus, and it calls for some explanation. And though I can adduce two reasons for this fact, I doubt if they are sufficient.

(1) We may give as a reason, first, the comparative weakness of psychical states in dream. Ideas of movement will, apart from hindrance, always, we may say, produce movement. But always on the other side there is hindrance to a certain degree. There is at least the inertia of existing physical and psychical states, as we may verify when lying awake in the morning before we rise. Ob-

viously, therefore, if in dream the ideas of movement are weak, they may fail to move altogether or to move enough. We may not get beyond the easiest beginnings, such as movement of the tongue or the extremities, and, if the ideas grow stronger, we tend to become awake. Normally we must wake because, through redintegration, the ideas strive to fill themselves out to their usual context, and because that enlargement normally must bring waking and orientation. Otherwise we pass into some abnormal state not to be considered here.

This is the first reason, and it is open to objection as follows. It is not true (we may be told) that in dream all psychical states are weak. External sensations in part are absent and for the rest in general are weakened. And though some sensations of pressure and cold may be exceptions, we need not here take account of them. But with internal sensations and with ideas the case is altered. For ideas and emotions may in dream be unusually strong, as is evidenced by certain physical effects. And we may compare with this the strength of ideas and of emotional states in hypnotism. So that on the whole it is not true that in dream motor ideas are weak.

To this objection we may reply that 'strength' and 'weakness' are to the last degree ambiguous. A very 'weak' state, when hindrance is removed, may dominate mentally. And it is this absence of inhibition which explains the physical effects of dreams, and makes the 'strength' of the emotions very doubtful. So in hypnotism the extreme mobility of the subject seems hard to reconcile with the asserted depth of the feelings. And in hysteria again the self is dominated by moods and ideas which in themselves would seem rather to be weak than strong. Hence the general weakness of dream-states (we may say) has not been disproved by the objection.

Still for our purpose such a general weakness may be inapplicable. For if ideas of motion can dominate our minds in dream, then (it may be pressed on us) this domination should be enough to move. We may reply that in the position of our limbs there is physical inertia, and, so far as that position implies feelings, there is psychical inertia too. And a certain degree of strength as against this inertia may be lacking to the idea, and so after all no motion need take place. And, as was remarked above, we may verify this when we are reclining and idly entertain the idea of movement. I will, however, not attempt to decide how far in this way the objection is met, but will pass to the second and, I think, the better reason for absence of movement.

(2) If an idea of movement is to move it must not remain general. It must (to speak broadly) be the idea of a particular movement, and that means it must be specified in more or less detail. If the detail is absent, then, in general, no movement will follow the idea. Now as to the extent to which a motor idea must be specified *psychically* there is difference of opinion, and that question I wish to avoid. But what I will assume, and what seems enough for my conclusion, is this. If an idea of movement is to be effective, we must have some perception of the position of our limbs and perhaps also of their relation to the environing world. If I do not know where the ground is and where my legs are placed, my idea of running will probably not carry itself out. And to strike an object which has no given relation to my arm, when I also have no idea of that arm's position, seems an idle endeavour. Hence, if from any cause in dream the idea has to remain vague, the action on its side will remain in abeyance. And in dream it seems a fact that ideas of active movement do remain vague, and the reason of this fact can, I think, also be given.

As to the fact, so far as I know, there is little doubt. When in dream I vainly desire to run or to strike, I have not a specified idea of movement proceeding to a certain point and there stopped in a particular way. It is always *somehow* only that I am prevented from acting, and it is only *somehow* that I intended to act. The idea, in brief, remains general, indefinite, and vague.

And for this vagueness we are able to assign a cause. The information necessary to complete my idea in dream is wanting. The content of my dreams usually has no relation to the actual situation and position of my body. It is unusual even for any one to dream that he is lying in his own bed, the mind turning to other scenes which interest it more. And we may perhaps lay down as certain so much as this—if into my dreams there entered a perception of my actual bodily position in its relation to outer objects, then we should have passed beyond ordinary dreaming and beyond the subject of this paper. For in normal dreams our eyes are shut, and sensations from our skin and muscles in part are absent from consciousness, and are present in part to a very small extent. 'Muscular sensation' in general is reduced to such a point as to have always little command, and usually none, over the course of our ideas.[1] And this failure in dream of a stable world in relation to our bodies seems a sufficient reason for our want of self-control. Our ideas wander partly at least because there is no perceived outer object by which to steady them. And for this same reason—for lack, that is, of incoming sensations—ideas of active movement fail, even as ideas, to complete themselves in dream.

Suppose that, while awake, I desire to strike some object. We may all agree that this action is a complicated affair, though we shall differ as to how far the complication is psychical. But at least I must know my attitude and my relation to the object, and to reach my end I must set in motion a train of means. Now part of this train consists in actual movements of my limbs and, more or less, in sensations coming in from these. And if such steps fail, the series is not carried out to its end. If no sensation of any kind tells me that my arm is raised and bent, rather than hanging by my side, I cannot, I presume, go on to strike and to strike in a particular manner. But in dream this defect is normal. The sensations required to carry out the

[1] So far as the sensations from breathing are an exception, they are an exception which seems in accordance with our main thesis. For they tell us nothing or little, I presume, as to the position of the body. I am not here seeking to pronounce on the question how far self-control even in waking depends on a stable sense-world. To a considerable extent it clearly does so depend.

series do not occur, and the idea remains in consequence general and suspended. It is opposed by the body because, so to speak, it is out of relation with the detail of the bodily machinery.

This account seems confirmed by the fact that, where the required perception of the position is less complicated, dream-movements are easier. Thus, for example, it is common to move the lips and tongue and fingers. Wherever the idea happens to agree with the actual position, movement, we may say in general, results. Moved by an idea we can turn the body from discomfort or rub an irritable spot which is near to our hands; and there are other examples, in some of which movement seems to follow an idea. So far as in dream a motor-idea can keep in relation with the actual position of our limbs, so far, given a certain intensity in the idea, movement seems to take place.

And if the idea is strong enough it will, I presume, always produce movement, not the movement required but still movement of a certain kind. But with this it will cause waking or at all events cessation of normal dream.

I have suggested, as some explanation of the absence of movement in dream, first the weakness of ideas, and next specially the vagueness of ideas of active movement. And the cause of this last seems to lie in the failure of corresponding sensations. But at this point we must consider a serious objection. For, while awake, one can imagine active movements in detail and with vividness, and yet no motion of the limbs need really take place. And, if the fact is so, it may seem to have destroyed our explanation. But I venture on the other hand to think that the explanation is confirmed.

As to the fact I shall say little. One can imagine active movements, I believe, in considerable detail though no movement of the limbs takes place. The amount of the detail and the presence, conscious or unconscious, of some change in the muscles do not concern us here. For one can certainly fancy oneself playing at a game with some particularity, and yet no changed position of the limbs need result.

But between such imagination and dream there is a most instructive difference. For in dream the 'real' body is not present to consciousness, while always in imagination it is more or less perceived and its perception guides and controls us. We have there two worlds, one the world connected with our present real body, and this world, however dim, never ceases to be experienced. And beside this we have the other world which is called imaginary, a world which we merely behold or in which we may also be actors. And, if we act there, we must possess there an ideal body. Now within its own world of course our ideal body can move, but its movements in the main are confined to that world. For the perception of the real body, incompatible with and repelling such movements, forces them to develop themselves wholly in this other world of imagination. And the field of consciousness being thus marked out into two or more provinces, the feeling of defect and of collision is avoided. We may remember bodily movements that are past, or plan others in the future. We may hold ourselves passive spectators of a combat in which our all is at stake, or we may follow a struggle on the boards of a theatre or in the pages of a book. In all these waking states there is some mental orientation and, with that, self-control. And the perception of our real body is in the end the point which serves to give us our bearings.[1] It is that which enables us to distinguish and to live in the various spheres which may be called 'ideal'.

Now whether our waking images have a force and detail, which in dream is wanting, we need not seek to decide.

---

[1] Of course in these cases (among which falls the more complicated instance of the actor's consciousness) we may, and sometimes do, fail to keep in mind the whole position. We 'forget ourselves' and, if so, a bodily movement may happen at once. But with this lapse we have also passed beyond mere imagination. By a bodily movement I here mean that which would be commonly called an action, as distinct from a mere expression of emotion. In the case of the actor, where real bodily movement takes place, that happens within limits prescribed by the real and not merely by the represented situation.

The main point is that in dream the perception of our real body is absent. And this absence leaves ideas of movement free to develop themselves practically. They blindly struggle to complete themselves in and by relation to the hidden real body, and with that attempt comes failure and a sense of inability and of coercion. While dreaming we, in other words, have no means by which we can distinguish one world from another;[1] and our images thus move naturally to realize themselves in the world of our real limbs. But this world and its arrangement is for the moment out of connexion with our ideas, and hence the attempt at motion, as we have seen, for the most part must fail.

In the above suggested explanation I have not attempted to deal with abnormal dream-states. And how far with regard to normal dreams the account is satisfactory I do not know. Perhaps a psychological explanation of dreams may be impracticable, but it seems not certain, if so, that any other will ever be forthcoming.

[1] There is also a state of half-waking, half-controlled dream, not, I think, experienced by me personally. This state seems to be consistent with and to confirm the above account.

XIX

WHAT DO WE MEAN BY THE INTENSITY OF PSYCHICAL STATES?

[*First published in* MIND, N.S. iv, No. 13, 1–27. *January*, 1895.]

IN this paper I have no special conclusion to advocate, nor, so far as practice goes, do I know what conclusion it suggests. I have found the intensity of psychical states a most ambiguous term, and I have seen no discussion of its sense which has satisfied my mind. And my aim in these pages is to endeavour to re-open the subject. I will attempt first to remove what seem to myself to be some errors and prejudices, and I will then go on to inquire into the meaning of psychical strength.

We may begin with the question whether psychical states are at all comparable in quantity. This has been denied, and psychical states, it has been said, are by their essence not measurable. It is not merely that in practice *we* cannot measure them, it is not merely that we cannot find and state their amounts in common units, but the contention is that in principle they have not degree and in principle do not admit of comparison in quantity. Now this denial to my mind seems based on confusion, and I will try to show that it is not tenable.

It seems evident generally that everything which exists has a quantitative side, but I am not going here to do more than notice this in passing. And the admitted fact that, rightly or wrongly, we do ascribe degree to psychical states, and speak of one toothache and one flash of light as felt to be more than another, I will at present also pass by. But I will meet the denial that mental states are in principle measurable by the question, If so, then what is measurable? If, that is, you cannot compare anything psychical in quantity, is there anything left which could possibly be compared at all? And when this question is faced it surely admits of but one answer. Either you compare what is not psychical, and such a process seems meaningless, or else the psychical must *somehow* admit degrees in quantity. But, if so, the point to be discussed is merely the 'how'.

And this possibly may be all that was meant by the denial of quantity. Our perceptions are psychical states and, whatever else outer things are, we seem to know them only by and in our perceptions. But certain aspects of the perceived both persist and recur and have a special nature. Time and space, in other words, are content of a sort which admits of measurement in quantity, though the perceptions themselves as wholes (it is urged) are not measurable. For, when we measure, it is not the perceptions which are compared but only their aspects, and only the aspects of space and also of time.[1] Yes, I reply, but if this is all you meant, the ground has been changed. For you first denied wholly that psychical states are comparable in quantity. But you now agree that they may possess aspects which are so compared, and all that you deny is that *otherwise and in other respects* they can have comparable quantity. And with this clearly you have deserted your abstract principle. Clearly you have allowed that psychical states may in principle be measured, and your addition 'but only some states and merely in one respect and not in any other', whether it is true or false, is merely an affair of detail. The principle at all events has been abandoned.

Then do you admit, I may be asked, that psychical states *as wholes* are not commensurable? But *as wholes*, I would reply, are they comparable at all? Or rather let us attempt to find out what we mean. In order to compare things—no matter whether they are psychical or not—you must compare them in some respect or not compare them

---

[1] While agreeing that space in the end is required for accurate measurement, I would point out a feature in time which has been sometimes overlooked. It seems possible, at least theoretically, apart from space, to compare two durations which coexist and start together, but which may differ because one goes on when the other has ceased (cf. Bosanquet, *Logic*, i. 178). This remark has, however, so far as I am aware, no practical bearing.

at all. That seems obvious, and there is something else
perhaps not less evident. Things cannot be compared
at all unless they are more or less definite, unless they are
taken, that is, as circumscribed groups of content. But
if so, they must be abstracted and to some extent *not*
treated as wholes. If I am to compare two objects, let
us say two stones, the stones first must be objects. But
this means that they are content more or less abstracted
from its sensuous setting. It means that the vague
totality of the 'this-now' is ideally mutilated, and that the
'given' is emphatically not taken as a whole. And, if you
object to this, of course all comparison is precluded. Then
having so got your objects, in order to compare them, you
must abstract once more. You must consider them from
an identical part of their content neglecting the rest. And
if you will not do this, all comparison and measurement is
impossible. Your cloth and yard-stick, for example, as
wholes are incommensurable.

These remarks seem evident, and let us see how they
bear on psychical states. Plainly here we want to know
first what 'a psychical state' means. If without abstraction
it is to stand for a total 'this-mine', then of course, all
comparison being excluded, such a sensuous given is
incomparable, and we must be careful how we venture
even to call it a 'psychical state'. But if you are willing
to distinguish and to abstract, psychical states are at once
comparable. We may regard, for instance, my whole
condition viewed at two different times. Here by an
abstraction we have taken two groups of content, and these
groups, the same in some respect or respects, will differ
in others. They may thus be compared, and, so far as
abstract principle is concerned, their quantity may serve
as a point of comparison. For their quantity may be one
of the respects in which these groups are the same and
different.

Thus psychical states, if they mean the varying conditions of my whole self, may at least in principle be compared and compared in amount. But the term 'psychical
state' can have a different meaning. Everything that in

any sense however ideal is present in my experience may loosely be called my psychical state. For every ideal object must also have its side of psychical existence, and that distinction of content in which it consists must happen in me. I see the rose and smell its perfume, and all this content and all its synthesis is thus a fact of mine. Every element and feature in this ideal whole must modify my being, and therefore from this side it can be called my state. But I am not the rose, nor am I odorous, nor do I bloom. Such syntheses in their proper character and in their own internal distinctions, while you rest on these, are not my adjectives. They form part of my psychical facts only so far as you do not stand on their abstracted meaning, only so far as you do not take that except in one with its aspect of psychical event, its bearing on me. And however we formulate this distinction of existence and content, and on whatever principle in the end we take it to rest, to neglect it is everywhere to fall into confusion.[1]

'One rose measured with another may be double in size, but their two perceptions, as my states, are not comparable in quantity, and therefore psychical states are incommensurable.' But in this objection psychical existence and content are confused. For the content of my perceptions is measurable, and (as we saw above) no one could otherwise measure any object. And again my two perceptions, as two additions to my present psychical being, can obviously more or less increase that in amount; and in principle therefore they each must have a quantity. And if all you mean is that the quantity perceived in and by the two ideal contents is not the same quantity which is given in the two psychical facts, that hardly proves that this second quantity is nothing and nonsense. But if again you mean that two psychical states, as two mere sensuous wholes, cannot be compared in amount, that remark surely is irrelevant. For everything taken merely as it is given is of course in a sense unique, and, as we have seen, it is then incomparable even in quality.

[1] While insisting on the vital importance of this distinction, I should perhaps long ago have warned the reader that it should not be credited to me.

'But psychical states after all are not contained the one in the other, and therefore no relation of quantity is possible.' But here once again there seems to be some confusion. Is a yard-stick contained in a roll of cloth? Are two donkeys contained in a horse, or so many horses in a steam-engine? Is a measure in every sense 'contained' in what it measures, or are not such questions misleading? Surely in measurement one does not ask whether one given fact takes in another fact bodily. One asks, since two things have a certain same aspect, how in regard to that aspect they are related. And if the objection asserts that two perceptions, say of a foot and of a yard, are in respect of their content not identical so that the second contains the first—that is to maintain that no measurement anywhere exists. But if it is meant that these two perceptions, as two psychical facts, do not add to my existence, and that my existence is incapable of more and of less— that once more surely would be preposterous. And hence from both these separate aspects it seems quite clear that my perceptions have quantity. And to urge that these two respects are two, and not the same, would be irrelevant. They are not the same, but for all that they both are present, and on their connexion I shall have something to say hereafter. In the same way we might also speak of the relative breadths or thicknesses of a yard-stick and a yard of cloth, or of their relative degrees of weight or tenacity, or odorousness or brightness. And what should we reply to an argument that, because their smells did not contain the same linear units, the smells therefore were not contained the one in the other, and could therefore have no degrees of odorousness at all? Should we not answer, Certainly I do not yet know how to measure these degrees, but you certainly have given me no cause to doubt their existence? Two perceptions of space in respect of that one common content, we agree, are measurable. Does it follow that these perceptions can be quantitatively compared in no other respect at all? Even if that conclusion is true, it is true merely as a matter of fact, and it cannot be deduced from any abstract principle.

'But no,' I may be told, 'for extensive quantities are in principle all that is measurable, while psychical states by their essence are (some or all) merely intensive. And the intensive is either not comparable in quantity at all, or is so only by concomitance with another scale, the distinctions of which are not qualitative.' The whole of this objection, so far at least as it makes any appeal to principle, seems to rest upon error and false assumption. It ignores apparently or forgets doctrines which when recalled remove its basis. For there is really no such thing as quantity *merely* extensive, or as quantitative differences without quality. Because anything is qualitative, that is no reason why it should not also have quantity. And to speak of a scale of degrees, which do not in any sense rest upon units, seems utterly unmeaning.

A perception of quantity involves not merely a diversity of units, but a diversity which also is taken as a single integer. At least otherwise the whole meaning of quantity seems vanished. But this integral aspect must surely imply a quality. A three or four of anything, though not counted, may be a distinguishable plural whole, and, when these wholes are counted, still as wholes of units they possess each a quality. And without this qualitative side it appears impossible to see how or why we should ever have begun to count or measure. For if uncounted totals did not feel different in a certain way, and if this way did not give the feeling of more and less, I cannot imagine how a distinction and summation of units could ever have happened. Quantities are perceived first, I presume, not as being quantities at all, but as differing merely in quality. They are perceived next as also more or less of some quality or thing. They are seen next to arise and to consist in the addition of units, and to have a qualitative side which varies as these units are more and less. The commonest experience shows us, I imagine, that groups of units feel different as wholes, and that, without counting, such felt differences are every day used in estimating quantity. And to speak of quantities as being barely extensive without any intensive aspect, and to talk of numbers as being merely discrete and not also continuous, is surely to set one-sided and false abstractions in the place of facts.[1]

And what in the end are qualitative states that possess no quantity? Certainly at a low level one can perceive things as being merely Yes or No, or simply again as being 'this' or 'so' and as being not 'that' or 'thus'; but as soon as one has advanced as far as any perception of degree, one has plainly at once both quality and quantity. So that either you must contend that no psychical states have in any sense degree—and that is to set yourself vainly against fact—or you must allow that in principle psychical states can have a quantitative aspect. For that degree means quantity becomes obvious as soon as we reflect. Wherever things are arranged in a scale so that you speak of them in that respect as being more and less, these things so far are quantitative. There is an identical element in these things, and there are diverse amounts of that element. This is what we mean if we mean anything at all by degree, and if we have no such meaning how and why do we come to speak of degree at all? In brief, the attempt to evade this conclusion must lead either to the denial of degree, or to the meaningless assertion of degrees which are not degrees of anything. Nor by bringing in the word 'direction' do we succeed in avoiding this result. Certainly we have qualitative ends which we more or less approach or recede from, but we have here still an identity and difference in quantity. For if the end is a state, more or less of which we already are or possess, the conclusion is evident. And the conclusion is still certain even if the end itself has, as such, no degree. For the road towards that end or away from it contains more and less of some element, and degree consists in the varying amount of this element between our position and the end. The top of the mountain or an extreme right or left may be taken as in themselves without degree; but the road by which we reach them, a road which in some sense belongs to their being, shows units and units. And in a blended colour or taste

[1] I naturally am not pretending here to deal properly with the relations of quality and quantity.

the actual quality of the ends is already present less and more throughout the scale. In short, gradual movement in a certain direction has no sense without identity and quantity. And to take the quantity of the states as the distance 'between' them would give us no help. For a scale of relative distances of course itself implies a more and less of the same something within these distances. And the qualification of the states themselves by the distances (for in fact they are so qualified) adds one difficulty the more to our unsolved problem. But if a serial perception of degrees is to be 'simple', one wonders first what simple means. For if the phrase denies *separability* of aspects, that denial is merely irrelevant, while if it denies their *diversity* it is merely false. And if a perceived series of degrees is not to possess both identity and diversity, by what miracle we take it as a series our phrase does not explain.

'But where there is quantity', it will be objected, 'there must be units many or few. In psychical states, on the other hand, the units cannot be given, and quantity therefore is not predicable.' But, I reply first, there are no units anywhere if not in psychical states. And hence the objection can apply solely to some psychical states, or again to psychical states viewed as such or merely as my adjectives. Now these states, we may admit at once, cannot truly be called measurable, if measurement implies the statement of so many identical units. Such units exist, we may be sure, but we are not able in fact to discriminate and fix them. On the other hand, their discrimination is not required for the perception of quantity, nor is it wanted for measurement, if that term is used in the widest sense. For I can tell that this sheep is larger than that sheep and a third sheep larger than the first, though I cannot say that their amounts differ as say 17, 15, and 18. And water is known by my hand to be hotter or colder, though I must fetch the thermometer to tell you how much. Yet without scales or a thermometer my perceptions have degree, and in a sense they are measurable, though not precisely. For wherever I can say 'more' what I really must say is 'This—and'

or 'This and this—and'; and clearly here we have a
difference in which I find the same again together with
something else the same. And if so, I must use at least
my first object as a unit.[1] I am taking two things
together and I find that the second is the first and also
something else the same. And when I go on to consider
the internal volume and plurality of both my objects,
other units are employed. For I perceive that each thing
repeats more or less the self-same element. And because
I cannot analyse so as to make explicit any ultimate units,
you cannot conclude that such underlying units are absent.
Such an argument indeed would end in absurdity. It
leads to the scale of perceived degrees which are degrees
of nothing, and to the similars which in no respect whatever are the same, and to the numerically distinct which
in no way whatever is different. And it rests on the
superstition that there can be no feature or aspect of things
unless we can abstract this and, so to speak, when called
on, produce it by itself. But we know that things are the
same or different before by comparison we have found
where they are identical or differ, and if our comparison
fails to find this, our knowledge none the less may remain.
And where psychical states are arranged in special scales
we must admit units of each scale, though certainly we
may be unable to produce them. And since psychical
states, where disparate, can still be perceived as diverse in
quantity, we must in the end assume units of psychical
extent in general. We have at least so far found no argument to show that such units are impossible.

And the attempt to find a scale which is not qualitative
at all is in principle irrational. For (a) in the first place
no units can be distinct unless they differ, and this difference implies in the end a diverse quality. The 'before'
and the 'after' in succession, for instance, are not reversible, and this difference certainly colours the successive
units. And in space diversity is not thinkable as a fact
apart from 'right' and 'left' and 'over' and 'under', and
these differences, essential to distinct units, are surely

[1] Cf. here Mr. Bosanquet's *Knowledge and Reality*, pp. 88–9.

qualitative. So that varying extents of muscular sensation apart from local qualities, except as an abstraction, appear to be meaningless.[1] And (b) in the second place such total extents (as we saw above) have a qualitative side. Each is a whole which has degree and an intensive character. And the ability to count units and to measure, far from removing this feature, implies it throughout as a corresponding and integral aspect. And from another point of view muscular wholes themselves are not commensurable. For every such whole as a concrete psychical state has a particular quality. And such qualities in themselves are not comparable in quantity, nor indeed if you take each as a mere 'this'

[1] In the text I am referring to Münsterberg's doctrine, *Beiträge*, Heft III. He speaks occasionally as if muscular quantities were more and less only through different durations. But it seems clear that this is not meant, and that for the purpose in hand such a difference would not suffice. For with two sensations I should have to wait till one had ceased, in order to know which is the stronger. It would, I presume, be impossible to have muscle-sensations of the same duration but differing in strength, and this, so far as I know, would be contrary to fact. So that extent (as Münsterberg seems occasionally to state) has to be considered as well as mere prolongation. But with extent must come in local differences in quality. Further, the connexion of certain muscle-sensations with certain groups of other sensations seems not treated with clearness. They are connected in such a way that amongst contemporaneous groups the more and less of one feature is perceived without confusion as more and less of the other. And whether the links of these connexions are physical merely or psychical also, seems a question to be raised and answered. But I am not undertaking or venturing to criticize a view which I may not have understood, and I will not even suggest that in its main result—if what that result implies were recognized and the doctrine were modified accordingly—this view is untenable or worse than unproved. A perception of more and less might everywhere, I presume, depend in some sense upon muscle-feeling. But wholly unproved on its negative side the view apparently is. For, in order to exclude all units save those of one sort, surely it cannot possibly be enough to select and cover one part of the ground. All that I would remark on the experiments otherwise is this, that in going from one ratio to another it is not evident that the passage need be direct. For since diverse quantities and ratios have each a general character which can be learnt by experience, it seems possible that such a general impression might unconsciously serve as the intermediary. But I am very far from asserting this to have been the case. I must end with an apology for offering the remarks of one who is scarcely at all acquainted with experimental psychology in general, or specially with the controversial discussion of this point.

are they comparable at all. In short, the objections to the measurement of psychical states apply in principle also to the measurement of muscular sensations. These objections, however, we have so far seen, are founded on confusion.

But I must enter further into a point which I have noticed already. Some perceived wholes, we are informed, are mere multiples of their units, while other wholes are in no sense multiples or contain units at all. Both the assertion and the denial, I answer once more, if so stated, are mistaken. No whole even in space or time is just nothing but its units, or would be a whole at all, if, as a whole, it did not possess a quality. And on the other side, because a whole cannot be regarded as a mere sum, from this you cannot argue that it owns no quantitative aspect, does not contain any units or have any numerical value. It is not true that a difference in kind entails the absence of every corresponding difference in degree, or that this latter difference is not in principle measurable. Indeed, to take for granted that no degrees are possible unless in fact we can measure them, and are able to show and specify the units involved, seems, I venture to repeat, quite arbitrary and indefensible.

On the other hand, these objections enforce an important truth which we are bound to recognize. The relation between the units and the whole is in different cases extremely different, and a question is opened here with which I cannot pretend to deal satisfactorily. That the units should not differ at all in quality seems in principle to be irrational, and that the mere units *make* the whole seems in every possible case to be false. But the characters of various wholes must be taken as connected with their quantitative aspect in various ways and in varying degrees of directness and intimacy. Every whole has a quantity, but except in certain spheres that quantity is not its true expression. From that quantity you could never recover the quality of the whole, you cannot see *how* its character demands a certain quantity, or show how it arises from the conjunction of any units. It is otherwise with space and time, for, if we consider any portion of space, we may view this as resulting from the synthesis of certain parts. These parts, lying outside each other, can still be recognized unchanged in the whole, and as units they can be identified with other units falling outside this whole. As separated and combined in various ways these units differ, yet in one respect they all remain identical. Thus all parts of space can be regarded as integers, which each possess a quality, and yet come from and are the various multiples of identical units. And hence for us they are commensurable, and we may conclude further that only such wholes as these, if taken in and for themselves, are measurable in fact. This conclusion I think true, and I am in no way endeavouring to dissent from it. I agree that it is only where the parts lie perceptibly outside each other that the whole is able, in itself, in a proper sense to be measured.

But it is another thing to conclude that everywhere else there cannot be quantity or any units or degree, and that measurement is in principle meaningless. The perception of more or less did not begin with numeration. And where a scale, say of blueness, is observed, though the units cannot be separated and shown, it seems impossible either to deny here the presence of degree or to show that it consists in the external synthesis of spatial units. And as there were units of space before by analysis we had found them, so, I presume, there may be units elsewhere which we by no analysis can distinguish. Units may be combined in manners, I suppose, which more or less we cannot follow, and they may be connected more or less unintelligibly for us with the qualitative character of their totals. We cannot in brief deny that wholes may possess necessary numerical ratios, even when we are able neither to identify and count their units, nor to show *how* causally the quality of such wholes is connected with their quantity. Hence, though it is true that only spatial (or temporal) wholes 'contain' perceptibly their components, and that therefore only the spatial aspect of things can in fact be measured, that does not prove either that psychical units which are not spatial are nothing, or that everywhere else but in space and time more and less have no meaning.

In every perceived series of degrees the second member can be seen to involve the first *plus* something else of the same sort. All psychical states, apparently without exception, stand to one another as greater or less or again as equal amounts of my personal being. All psychical states therefore (it would seem to follow) must contain a certain amount of common units. It is only in spatial and temporal wholes[1] that the components fall asunder and are visible side by side. And, apart from this, measurement in the proper sense seems to be impracticable. But, apart from this, measurement does not appear in principle and in the abstract to be impossible.

Up to the present I have been engaged in the attempt to dispel prejudices which have obscured the subject. There is no such thing as quantity merely extensive, or as intensity without quantity. Degrees not resting on units in the end are meaningless. Quantity without an essential qualitative side, and a qualitative object with no quantity, are not conceivable. These are all abstractions falsely supposed to have individual existence. And it is a superstition to hold that in the soul is nothing except that which can actually be abstracted and ideally sundered. Further, we saw that psychical states can be considered in various ways. And it does not follow, because in one way they are not comparable in quantity, that they cannot in quantity be compared at all. And psychical states viewed in a certain manner we found were not comparable even in quality, and the same result holds also with those outward things which no one doubts are measured. Abstract objections of this kind possess no value, and to meet them by looking for a psychical scale, which is quantitative solely, we found was the attempt to combat one superstition by means of another. Further, our inability in fact to measure does not prove the absence of all units. And you cannot argue that, because only what is extended in

---

[1] I abstain from raising the doubt whether and how far, entirely apart from spatial perception, temporal wholes would retain their character. That every kind of distinction depends on such a perception is an opinion which seems defensible, though I think it is incorrect.

space or time can be counted, therefore more and less consist solely in degrees of that extension. And all psychical
states, we may conclude, if not measurable in fact are at
least measurable in principle.

And now, having tried to remove a mass of erroneous preconceptions, we must enter on the definition of
psychical strength. I will point out first the essential
ambiguity of that term; I will go on to state some of its
meanings and will endeavour to explain them; and I will
ask in the end what is the relation of strength, as actual
amount, to psychical force, and what these ideas can be
taken in the end to signify. The reader must bear with me
if anywhere I dwell on what seems trite and self-evident.

There is nowhere such a thing as absolute strength, but
all strength is comparative and relative. Things again
are not compared save in a certain respect and through
a feature of their content which is the same. And 'more'
means more of something in which two things are at once
identical and different. It is the more and less of this one
feature which gives the direction and the scale of degrees,
and without this the word 'degree' would be simply
meaningless.

Now where anything is complex and in its content has
various features (and certainly all psychical states are complex), this thing may enter into various scales, and it may
therefore possess at once a variety of strengths. And since
its features perhaps are more or less indifferent to each
other, the thing may thus alter independently its various
strengths. And then degree or size, we know, is in a
sense external and arbitrary, and a thing, while itself unchanged, may thus acquire an altered quantity. For the
thing may enter into a different whole and a diverse scale.
Thus in a foot-rule each inch, as regards that whole,
would remain of the same size, though the whole rule
were lessened itself to an inch or enlarged to a mile. And
so the inch is (if you please) of various sizes at once.
Hence, from the other side, you cannot by any change
alter a thing's quantity if you at the same time alter
correspondingly its scale; just as, while the thing itself

remains unchanged, its quantity by a change of scale can be altered. These trite remarks perhaps will not seem idle when we consider their application. They show that the intensity of a psychical state may possibly be increased by the mere defect of other states. And it is utterly useless perhaps to argue the question whether attention increases intensity, until you have stated the scale which is concerned, and have asked if attention may not possibly alter that too. For the attention which doubled at once both my rule and my object, would for the purpose in hand double nothing at all. One must beware of arguments from which one would be forced to conclude that no relative size could possibly be observed under a microscope.

Let us pass on from this ambiguity to notice another. Are the intensity and the force of psychical states the same or different, and, if they differ, how is one related to the other? Now, taking a 'state' to mean some limited constituent of consciousness or sentience, we observe that it may seem to prevail or dominate not merely by its own strength. Accompaniments and reactions, intellectual and emotional, and in general the connexion with habits psychical and physical, seem factors here to be considered. And how far the prevalence of a state can be attributed to itself and to its own proper force, and how far such force is identical with mere intensity, becomes at once a problem. But this for the present I must quite disregard. I must provisionally abstract from pleasure and pain and every kind of reaction, and ignore for the present this question of force. I must, that is, at first confine the inquiry to the actual strength of a state when taken by itself. Let us begin then by asking what such strength can mean.

(1) My whole psychical condition at any time may be taken as a limited amount or extent, and some constituent state, say a perception, may be viewed as occupying a certain part of this area. And to this no one, I think, would object save in the interest of some theory. Now by a fiction let us take my whole condition to remain the same in amount, while the perception itself is increased and covers more of this same field of psychical existence. Such

relative quantity, or more or less ground possessed by a state, we may call its varying strength. A state is strong in proportion as it is more relatively to the unchanged amount of my being. But that amount is again itself a relative quantity. For a man's mind contains more than does the mind, say, of a mouse or a butterfly, and once more no one apart from prejudice would call this in question. But if so, we have got the idea of general psychical quantity. We have first of all an amount of myself which is taken as normal, and we have then the minds of other sentient beings compared in quantity with this and viewed as standing towards it throughout in some ratio. So that my perception, regarded as a certain fraction of my normal mind, is expressible also as, and also *is*, some fraction or perhaps some multiple of other minds. We have, in other words, accepted the principle of psychical units. Everything psychical is related in quantity to everything else psychical, though to specify exactly the relation may be out of our power. Any psychical fact (to put it otherwise) must contain a certain number of normal units. This is the sense of strength in which, if we pleased, we might call it absolute. And this meaning, to my mind, is but the expression of good sense and of everyday reason.

But psychical strength can be taken also in another and subordinate sense. The constant quantity of my whole condition was but a useful fiction, and my psychical area is obviously in itself a changing integer. My mind is full and then empty, my feelings are dull or acute, and I am active variedly or seem to sink to a mere passive residuum. So that let a perception itself keep up a uniform strength, let it contain the same amount of any psychical area we take as average or normal, yet to me from time to time it will become less or more. Its sum of psychical units, we may say, remains identical; but since my total state contains a fluctuating number of like units, the relation of the perception to that whole must fluctuate also. Thus the ticking of a clock, forced at one time into the background and with a quantity we neglect, may at another time become the main constituent of our minds. The sensation is more to me and it is more of me because I am less, and my decrease has bestowed upon it a relative intensity. And though the perception's constant quantity independent of my change is an assumption often untrue, yet the presence of two strengths and two scales appears undeniable. My normal area and my fluctuating area are divergent amounts of psychical units, and they naturally give two different measures of strength. And however much in practice these two strengths may influence and even imply one another, it is clear that, to some extent, they are different and also diverge. Hence we have already two scales and two strengths which may vary independently.

Strength has so far been regarded as quantity of psychical existence, psychical existence measured by (*a*) a fixed, or (*b*) by a fluctuating scale. And without pausing to deal with difficulties, some of which must engage us later, I will proceed to a different meaning of strength.

(2) When we speak of a sensation or perception or idea as being more or less than another, we often fail to be clear as to the scale we have in mind. But 'more of what', 'measured by what scale', and 'relative to what whole'—if we cannot answer these questions, we are speaking to some extent at hazard and blindly. Now two senses of more and less we have noticed already. A perception or idea, viewed as something which has psychical existence, we have seen can be more and less in two different ways. But beside its psychical existence a perception or idea has a reference to an object. And a more or less of some character thus referred may be what we meant when we spoke of the perception's degree. This fresh meaning of strength differs from what we had before, and it once more is able to vary independently. And this meaning itself may be developed in a number of divergent applications. I must endeavour even at some length to make this plain.

A perception or idea, even if you consider that apart from its psychical context and conditions, is never a simple piece of existence. Its character is complex, and of that complex character we use for a certain purpose some feature or features. I am not attempting here to explain

the fact of attribution, but am insisting merely in something implied in that fact. When an object is qualified
it is not qualified by that whole state which we call a perception or idea. It is only one or more aspects of that state
which become the adjective of our object, and the state
itself may hold an indefinite amount of unapplied features.
But from this follows at once an important result. The
more or less of an idea or of a perception may mean the
more or less merely of one aspect employed as an adjective,
while, taken as a whole, the perception or idea will not
vary in the same ratio. I perceive a foot and I perceive
two feet, and in one aspect and character my second perception is the double of my first. It contains, we may say,
twice the units *of a particular kind*. But as a mere psychical
fact my second perception does not stand in that ratio.
It will not on the whole contain a double amount of
psychical units, but will be doubled merely with regard to
one part of its area. And how that part stands to the rest
will depend upon other conditions. The perception of two
feet will, to speak in general, occupy more psychical area
than the perception of one foot. But you cannot conclude
even in general that the second psychical fact is twice the
first, or that in any special case it is even greater at all.
For you are using scales which are not the same, and which
in part may diverge. Your increase or decrease on one
scale may therefore with regard to another scale change its
ratio, or it may even become indifferent wholly and quite
irrelevant, or even actually be inverted.

I take in my mouth a solution with at least two flavours
and of a certain temperature. Then at the next moment
my perception is changed, and changed in quantity. Its
warmth is doubled, or, if you please, its coolness halved.
It is twice as sweet, or half as acid, as it was before. And
the perception itself—is that double now, or now half what
it was, or is that question not, rather, ambiguous and
absurd? As psychical facts the two perceptions have (we
have seen) a relation in quantity, but as to that relation
you can here draw no inference from your data. For the
constituents of a perception may vary each in its own scale,

while the whole perception keeps its quantity or varies independently. A perception certainly is more of a fact so far as it is hotter, though whether it is less of a fact so far as it is cooler seems not quite so plain. So far as it is more acid it has more psychical existence—to that I agree. But how if with more acidity goes less sweetness, and if the variations of temperature, or again of viscidity and of volume, have ratios which are more or less indifferent and independent? Surely then to ask at large about more and less, without specifying the element and the scale or scales to which one refers, is to put oneself at the mercy of that blind fortune which does not always smile on the blind. The perception of twice anything is *to that extent* twice the perception, but the perception for all that might be decreased to say one-half or one-tenth. And this is not because mental states have no quantity at all. It is because they have quantity in an indefinite number of senses, and because to some extent these different scales seem independent or may even be related inversely. And where the scales generally correspond the special case is never simple, so that other conditions can affect and may even in the result destroy that correspondence. And if you answer 'but this does not apply where the states are simple', I admit this readily. But I pass it by as being itself wholly without application.

These considerations gain force when we pass from perceptions to ideas. I do not mean that with ideas we find any new principle at work, but the distinction between applied content and psychical existence becomes more palpable. All content of course has psychical existence, and more of that content, we have seen, is *so far* more of psychical existence. But in an image the aspect which we consider may form so small a part of the whole image, and that aspect may also in amount be so inversely related to other aspects, that in the end no conclusion can possibly be drawn. I perceive a light and am to imagine it twice as large. But suppose that the perceived light is the noonday sun. Must I imagine this not only increased in area, but also maintaining a character in proportion to its size? And if I cannot do this, am I prevented from think-

ing of it as doubled? All that is wanted, surely, is for a
perception to be so taken in one character as in that respect
to be identifiable in other contexts. And if this is done,
and if with regard to that character internal consistency is
preserved, surely everything else may be taken as freely variable. The intensity of my doubled sun-image in heat and
light is wholly irrelevant. Nay, its actual area as measured
by my perception is irrelevant also. It is the ratio of the
imagined sun to an imagined sky with which I have to do,
and the absolute size of my scale does not matter. My
image must preserve identity with my perception, or else
I do not think at all; but the identity here does not consist
in absolute area or intensity. The quantitative ratio therefore between the perception and its doubled image is here
wholly irrelevant and may be unknown.

And when without using concrete imagery we form
ideas of our sun, the same conclusion is more glaring. I
am to think rapidly of my perceived object being changed
so as to be larger, brighter, redder, and hotter, and let us
now say not twice but, if you please, ten or a thousand
times; or again let each attribute, if you please, vary
diversely in increase. What happens here, I suppose, is
that I possess the idea of a general or abstract scale of
quantity, and that I identify a place or places on this general
scale with a feature or features of my perceived sun. And
where I think rapidly there seems to result no individual
modified image, but a mere putting-together of two or
more abstract and sundered characters. We may realize
perhaps even more clearly what this means, if we imagine
ourselves to think of our perceived sun's total disappearance, and then carefully reflect on what that thought must
imply. But, without pausing to consider this, we perhaps
may take our conclusion as made good. At the point we
have reached psychical intensity can be seen not to be
meaningless, but to have acquired an indefinite number of
divergent meanings.[1]

[1] It should now be evident that I can have an idea of psychical strength,
and that I can have that idea either strongly or weakly. The aspect of a
certain amount or of a certain place on the psychical scale can be given

The result we have so far reached may be briefly resumed. (1) Everything psychical has an intensity, first, of psychical being. It occupies an area and contains units which are more and less in amount relatively to my passing state, or more and less measured by some fixed scale of psychical existence. And, because my passing state has a quantity which varies, these two psychical intensities partly diverge. (2) But superimposed on and parallel with these two degrees of psychical existence, we have also a variety of scales of special content. In regard to one or more of their features psychical facts are related in amount, and they give us degrees of this or that special quality, such as heat, smell, or colour. Now increase of one feature means increase, so far, of psychical existence, but the ratio of increase in special quality has no fixed relation to the increase of psychical existence. Suppose, for instance, my psychical condition now = 1000 units, and that in this total my perception of colour = 100. Now suppose one feature of this colour-perception = 10, what is the intensity of this feature? It is clearly one-tenth or one-hundredth as you measure it by each total. And my present state, we must not forget, is really a fluctuating amount. It contains now, let us say, 1000 standard or normal units, but it may later contain say 1200 or again say 750. Here is a new sense in which also my special perception has got intensity, and the reader, if it amuses him, may find the fractions.

Thus more and less on any special scale must mean also more and less of psychical existence, but how much more and less cannot in general be decided. And this truth in an ordinary complex case is quite irrelevant. For gain and loss within the whole psychical fact may balance each other, and the total amount may remain the same while its factors are changed. Thus a perception may in one respect be more and in another respect less, while as a psychical quantity it remains the same. And with the psychical facts called ideas, though no new principle is

itself with varying amounts of unemployed detail and so of psychical existence.

introduced, the multiplication and involution of divergent scales becomes more glaring. The former meanings of intensity all remain, but other scales and other meanings are superimposed on the ambiguous complex.

But in principle, I would add, this result is not sceptical. It would be sceptical if it showed that there were no scales at all, or that in themselves scales varied unworkably. And how far in practice amounts can be measured I do not inquire. But to insist that quantities all are relative to some scale; that one thing in various ways can be relative to various amounts; that, so long as in any total the internal ratios do not change, other changes may be irrelevant; and that before you ask about degree you should know first what scale is in question;—such conclusions seem dictated by ordinary reason. And from another side our result is hostile to scepticism. For all psychical phenomena, it urges, can in principle be measured. They can all in principle be taken first as various amounts of existing psychical content, and then also as special amounts on diverse scales of content variously specialized. And everything psychical in the end must be taken as in principle somehow commensurable. This conclusion I will proceed to defend against several objections.

An objection may be urged first against the idea of measurable psychical existence. Quantity, it may be said, is predicable only of content made the adjective of an object, and psychical existence, whether by excess or defect, cannot possess this character. But the objection would rest on a mistake. The merely 'given' taken as such, we saw above, is not comparable, but the merely 'given' is not the same as psychical existence. Psychical existence implies the construction of a soul-substantive enduring in time and owning adjectives which through change preserve a basis of identity. Such an arrangement clearly transcends any deliverance of sense, since it involves the construction of a soul-object qualified by content. And of such an object quantity can in principle be predicated. And to urge that my experience is not throughout perceived and treated as my adjective—that,

when I am self-conscious, what I perceive must be less
than what I am—would be irrelevant. For everything
that I am, though not perceived, is in principle perceptible. In its general character and in the mass it can
thus be taken as adjectival content, and can be predicated
of the ideal construction which I call my existence. Nor
is there anything in me which is unable so to be
predicated.

In these inquiries, while distinguishing, we must not
divide. The higher and more specified state of mind does
not banish the lower. It is superimposed on, it still implies,
and from one aspect it still is at the stage of the unspecified
basis. Everything in experience is felt and is given first
as a 'this-now'. Then the content of experience separates
itself into groups, a 'me' and a world of 'not-mes', ideal
objects to which all is referred as adjectival. And the
same felt content, we must never forget, is used at once
to qualify both the self and the not-self. There is first
the feeling-green, then the sensation of something-green
and of my so perceiving it. But if these two groups and
their adjective and their relation were not felt, they would
not be experienced at all. And, from the other side, the
feeling which precedes, and which also underlies and contains the distinction of me and not-me, can, when reflected
on, be taken as the adjective of either of these objects.
The history of my whole experience is an adjective which
has its place in universal existence, and is also itself the
private existence of my soul. And whatever advance in
further distinction and ideal development takes place, the
aspects both of feeling and of psychical existence still persist and are essential. But where there is existence, there
also we must have more and less. And with these brief
remarks I must leave the subject of psychical existence.
Objections urged against it may seem subtle, but will be
found in the end to rest on confusion.[1]

I pass from these refined doubts to dwell on the idea
of psychical units. I do not contend (I may repeat) that

[1] The question, whether for psychical reaction something more than
existing content must be assumed, will be touched on hereafter.

such units can be fixed and used in practice, but in principle their existence must be assumed. Psychical states of every kind can as against one another seem more and less, a toothache, for example, can appear weaker or stronger than an exercise in logic. And if in these different things were nothing in which as amounts they were identical, and more and less of which they possessed, I do not see how they could come as members in one scale. It is here with quantity as it is with quality. If smells or if colours have no common quality, why do I treat each class as if it possessed it? And if the quality of all psychical states had no one common feature, how could I feel them as entering into and making up my being? To reply 'then show your quality, and show your units bare' is surely irrational, for, by the hypothesis, as bare they do not exist at all. They could be shown only as abstractions, as single features specially noticed in concrete wholes, and how far in each case the abstraction is definite and useable, is of course a further question. I have two greens which are the same in green, I have a green and a red which both are colours, I have a colour and a sound which both are sensations, and I have a colour and a toothache which are both the same as being felt and as being mental states. I have two blue-greens in which the green is more and less, and two greens the same but more and less in brightness or in area, and a colour-sensation fluctuating as more and less against an invading sound, and, when the sound is removed, at once becoming more of me. There are differences specifying a lowest basis of sameness, and then these differences themselves are further specified, and as identities they underlie higher distinctions. And against this essential and all-pervasive evolution to object, 'But show me the identity bare, and then I will believe', is surely blind irrelevancy. For a bare identity or difference is just that which, if the view objected to is true, is *ipso facto* impossible. In other words an identity or a difference is by its essence relative. Thus two perceptions are related first as quantities of general psychical existence, they are related next as fractions of my present condition, they are related next as two perceptions of length, and so on indefinitely. In each respect they contain relative amounts of one common something, and these identities persist whatever more specified identities are superimposed. Thus units of psychical existence, we may admit, cannot be distinguished and fixed, but they seem open for all that to no rational doubt. Let us go on to another point.

There is an instructive, if obscure, discussion by Lotze[1] on the strength of ideas, a discussion which no German writer at least might have been expected to ignore. Into this as a whole I regret that I cannot here enter, but on one point I will comment. Ideas, Lotze seems to tell us, themselves cannot be stronger or weaker. For ideas are not what they mean, and they may signify strength, but, it seems, themselves cannot possess it. Now this distinction of existence from meaning I gratefully endorse, but from the conclusion which seems based on it I have to dissent. For in the being of an idea I find always psychical matter extraneous to its meaning, and this unemployed content, I must insist, can vary in quantity, while the specific meaning of the idea remains identical. And though one aspect is able to react on the other, they need neither have the same quantity nor preserve the same ratio. In something of the same way in a perception of heat, volume and degree may be confused, but for all that each aspect possesses its own proper amount. Now, like every other state, an idea must have its quantity of psychical existence, measured by a normal scale, or measured also by my passing condition. Nay, we have seen above, that, in order to mean more or less, a state must, in that one aspect and merely so far, have more psychical being. And right as it is to say with Lotze that ideas are not what they mean, it is also true that ideas can mean nothing but that which they are. For unless a thing has, and to that extent is, a quality, I cannot myself understand how it goes about to show

[1] *Mikr.*i. 229, *Met.*§262. The meaning and position given to *Erregung* strike me as obscure; nor do I perceive, again, how far Lotze realizes that any alteration of anything in degree is, in itself and merely so far, a certain change in quality.

it.[1] The idea of the extended has extension,[2] the idea of the heavy has weight, the idea of the odorous has smell, and the idea of pleasure, beyond all controversy I should have thought, exists and is so far pleasant. But the specific aspect of the idea, though not destroyed, can be utterly overborne, the truth and the existence of that aspect fall in different worlds, and their intensities, though weighable and not mere shadows, are not weighed merely in one balance.

But, I may be told, you are avoiding the point of the objection. For with ideas we have relational activity, and of this activity there are no degrees. And though the product has degrees, they are not degrees of psychical strength. My desire, I reply, is not to avoid this point, but, if that be possible, to discover in what sense I am to take it. Naturally I cannot enter here into the special nature of the relational consciousness, nor ask with what meaning or what absence of meaning 'activity' may be used.[3] But if I am to understand that relations and distinctions are not psychical facts, I answer respectfully that I find it quite otherwise. But, if they are facts, then at once I presume they have psychical existence. And if you tell me that I can have an idea or perception which contains a relational complex, and that this complex can *ad libitum* be made more complex, while its psychical existence is not thereby increased, and while the whole perception occu-

[1] The existence of conventional and arbitrary signs, and of mere accredited representatives, forms no valid objection. For, unless the meaning is *somehow* there and belonging to the sign, the sign would be no sign. The question is merely as to *how*, within the whole actual sign, the meaning and the existence are in each case connected—whether, that is, they are connected indirectly and through external association and credit, or directly and through an internal property. But, for the purpose of the text, this question of *how* the sign possesses the content it signifies seems quite irrelevant. Here (though not everywhere) the above distinction has no importance.

[2] I hope in a future paper to return to this point.

[3] The doctrine for instance advocated by Brentano, *Psychologie*, pp. 157 foll., as to the relative intensity of Vorstellen and Vorstellung I could neither affirm nor deny. For all I know, it may be plainly tautologous or again plainly false. For I at least, until I am told, do not know what an 'act' is to mean. And I must be pardoned if from time to time I repeat this, and repeat also that I am not yet ashamed of my ignorance.

pies no more room in my mental area—I reply that once more you seem to be in collision with palpable fact.[1] And I am curious to know the principle on which more is to happen *in* me, when it is not to happen *to* me. But if all you mean is that a whole relation is both more than its terms and also is less; if you mean that the terms, taken either without the relation, or taken again not in that aspect in which they are related, have psychical strength, and that *this* strength is irrelevant to the essential content of the relational whole;—your conclusion has vanished. For you started with denying that the ideal whole has any psychical strength, and what you now deny of it is merely the psychical strength of, in short, something else. Because the strength of a related complex is not that of its unrelated factors, nor of its factors so far as they possess unrelated aspects—you assert that it possesses no strength at all. And this conclusion, false in principle, in practice collides with facts.[2]

In brief, a perceived or thought relational whole must be a psychical state, and whatever other aspects and scales of quantity this perception may develop, it must through all from one side still remain a psychical state. It must be measurable, that is, in the scale of psychical existence. And with this I must pass on to another branch of the inquiry into strength.

Strength has so far been used in an arbitrary sense. I have taken it as equivalent to extent or actual area of psychical being. And a 'state of mind' again has been understood arbitrarily, for I have treated it as something with an existence clearly circumscribed. But these assumptions have now to be discussed and corrected.

[1] I am not here denying all difference between clearness and mere strength. But I am urging that increase of the first must *so far* mean increase of the second.

[2] The same principle is involved in the objection that a stronger idea or perception is a different state, that it has a different content and not the same content to a different degree. Yes, I reply, but if some part of the content is always irrelevant, the idea or perception, increased and so different with regard to that aspect, may in respect of its essential aspect remain the same. And if so, the same idea *will* have different strengths.

In a particular state of mind, say a sensation, perception, or idea, what is the state itself and how much is mere accompaniment or result? Can you exclude the latter element and, if so, where and how can you draw the line? States are, for instance, painful and pleasant, but what is here the conjunction or connexion? Have we adjectives or have we accompaniments or once more mere results, and, if results, to what precisely are the results to be attributed? And a state also has irradiation, physical and psychical; it spreads in itself and it spreads in its effects; and whether this spreading is to qualify the state and, if so, how far, is a question not easily answered. But since 'irradiation' is an idea perhaps not wholly clear, let us pass from it to consider what is implied in 'reaction'. A sensation is qualified by reaction, and how is the reaction provoked? Is it due to the mere strength of the sensation or to its quality or to both? And, when the reaction is there, in what sense does it belong to the sensation? Exclude the case of general shock, and confine your attention to special responses to a special stimulus. There is a 'disposition', physical merely or psychical as well, and this latter generally at least, I presume, is acquired and has the form of a mental habit. Now if the sensation (to speak in general) has a quality which corresponds to the habit, a reaction takes place which qualifies the sensation. But what is here the sensation itself, and what are mere results? And beside the 'strength' of the sensation, has it got an independent 'force' to produce such results?

A state, we may reply, only is that which at present it is. And what it may become, or what it has become, is, so far, a different state potential or actual. But this answer, it is clear, does not dispose of the problem as to force, and even as regards the individual being of the 'state' it offers no solution. For the question was as to the boundaries and limits of this being. So suppose that the state is distinguished from what it causes and becomes, yet even then can you divide it now from what it is not? For any sensation, perception, or idea is surely the product of abstraction. It is a special distinguished content which has also a psychical existence. And the difficulty is here not to distinguish merely the 'what' from the 'that', but rather to draw a line between the existence and its conditions, between the 'that' and the 'how'. And this ideal partition of an undivided psychical whole is always more or less arbitrary, and it tends more and more, as you descend, to become even impracticable. For if you pass from an idea, and again from a perceived quality referred to an object, and come down to a sensation which is merely given as a certain something—the 'that' and its 'how', as you descend, become steadily perplexed. And to separate at the lowest level the existence of this somewhat from its connexion with my total state, and from its colouring of pleasure or pain, becomes in practice impossible. The individuality of a psychical fact is thus always an abstraction, it is always to some extent arbitrary, and it tends in part to become an idea which in practice is inapplicable. But within limits the use of this abstraction seems possible and legitimate.

We are however met by further troubles when we consider the relation of strength to force. For we have taken strength so far to mean extent of psychical area, the occupancy of so much ground or the possession of so many units. And this idea we found clearly to be legitimate and even necessary. But we must beware of misunderstanding, and there are cautions which I must be allowed to repeat. There is no psychical empty space in which psychical states contend. There is merely a common underlying substance or quality which all such states contain and which each further specifies. It is on the basis of this indwelling identity, and it is only by virtue of it, that states are able to struggle at all. And this quality, regarded itself as specified into a plurality and into distinctions of more and less, affords units and degrees of psychical amount. And because our whole psychical condition, taken at an average or at any one time, is a limited quantity—the ground or area occupied by a partial 'state', and the units of existence which it usurps, can be thus in principle defined. Whether in practice such units can be shown, and can be used for exact measurement, is a question I pass over. But in any case I repeat and I would insist that the units and the underlying quality are merely abstractions. To regard them as capable of existence barely in their own character, and to demand their production and their exhibition naked, I must consider ridiculous. But I urge on the other side that to deny the existence of an identity, when naked, agrees perfectly with the assertion of its existence when clothed. Or (if you prefer the metaphor) the soul keeps no stuff not worked up into garments, but because of this to deny the sameness and the more and less of a common stuff would be quite irrational. Or the soul, we may say, can let no building-land wholly unbuilt-on. But such a condition does not exclude its power to afford an indefinite amount of area and for any kind of superstructure.

But if strength is the same as actual extent or amount of units, then strength is a narrower term than force, and it will not cover all the facts. For if a state is strong it should dominate, it should hold its ground, it should repel and more or less extrude what attacks or even does not attack it. And, without acting thus, it must be ready, when called on, to maintain itself. Its strength in brief seems to be extension not actual only, but also potential.[1] And if it maintains itself by an extraneous help, are we to call that its strength? The position of pain and pleasure, we saw above, gives rise to questions. And again a state apparently may dominate by its relation to other existing states, and also by its correspondence with 'dispositions' physical and psychical. And it may even be said to dominate not merely through actual support, but by help which is indirect and even conditional. An idea, we may say, is strong when it itself is constantly suggested, and when any opposing elements, as they arise, provoke a reaction which excludes them.

We have therefore to introduce here the idea of potential

---

[1] In what follows we are on ground which is covered by the term 'interest'. It is in my opinion a mistake to try to limit the use of this term to denote pleasure and pain.

energy. It is of course mythological, but its employment seems forced upon us. A state which corresponds to 'dispositions' has a key which fits the wards, and so this state can unlock energy, which, being unlocked, it then harnesses to its cart, or astride of which it gets and calls this its own strength. It is perhaps well to use metaphors which confess themselves absurd, if we desire wholly to escape from domination by mere metaphor. However, every man here must follow his own taste. And some writers prefer to speak of a 'functional disposition' as if they knew what that was, when perhaps any one can see that they have never faced the question. To me a 'disposition' is a convenient but clearly a mythological way of stating a general fact or law, a way of psychical happening which I do not pretend to understand. When certain things, physical and psychical too, have happened already, then, given something else under certain conditions, a certain result will take place.[1] And in the present case this conditional result is the addition of strength, and a psychical state therefore can 'have' potentially the energy which, when become actual, it appropriates.

But when this all has been admitted, our difficulty remains. For (a) the strength thus produced seems hardly to belong to the state itself, nor (b) does the state act as a stimulus by reason of its mere strength. (a) If a state has force to set free energy under certain conditions, the issue of this energy, we may admit, in the end is increased psychical area. Thus force is not strength, if strength means actual area or existing quantity, but force is so called only because it means potential strength, and because, given the conditions, it passes into amount of psychical units. And all so far seems tenable. But why, on the other hand, the state is credited with all the strength, which conditionally it provokes into being, seems not intelligible. The stimulus may itself be destroyed by that explosion, the outcome of which you desire to place to its credit. And if this has a sense, surely in the end that sense is arbitrary and useless. Even where the stimulus survives as an element in

[1] Compare *E.* xii. 214-15.

that increase it has provoked, even where the conditions are ascertained, and where in the whole result the stimulus is so placed that that whole is regarded as its adjective— even here to credit it beforehand with the incoming amount is an evident liberty. Even here its force will be its credit merely, and not its actual possession of existing units. And otherwise the force of a state is but the fact that conditionally it may act as a stimulus, and so conditionally produce some increase of some psychical extent. But by what right that conditional extent is to be called *its* strength is not apparent at all.

(*b*) Nor even as a stimulus does the state act by virtue of its strength. To act it must indeed possess some strength, a minimal amount that will vary with varying conditions. But its special act is certainly not the effect of this mere general strength. For we take the state to be acting not as a bare shock, but by reason of and through its special quality. And if it has the quality required, the degree of that may within limits be irrelevant. But this quality on the other hand cannot be resolved into amount of psychical units. You cannot say that the state stimulates thus or thus, simply because its strength is so much. You may by a legitimate abstraction consider that strength, that number of psychical units, without regard to any quality. But you cannot derive the qualities and their effects from a mere number of units and show them as its result. And to speak of a special arrangement or grouping of these units would be, so far as I see, to use words without a meaning. We have a general quality, and within that quality we have strengths that vary, and we have special qualities, and within each of these we have again varying strengths. And the second set of distinctions we regard as superimposed on the first. They specify the underlying substance, and to their specific natures a certain amount of this substance in each case corresponds. But to deduce the qualities from the units of common substance, or to make an equation between these terms, seems out of the question. Given a certain quality you have somehow implied a certain quantity, but, given the same quantity, the same quality is not necessarily implied. And, if so, the force by which a state maintains or increases its ground will in the end diverge from the extent of its actual occupancy. And by the use of the term 'potential' we make no real advance in understanding. For the force which potentially is strength, in the sense of occupied area, either cannot be taken as belonging at all to the actual state itself, or belongs to it not as an amount but as a special quality.

If there are any results from this inquiry it is time we gathered them. (1) The force of a mental state is a phrase which is most ambiguous. It seldom, if ever, means the same as its actual quantity or area. (2) Psychical strength, taken as an amount of psychical existence or a number of its units, is a conception valid and perhaps useful. Its scale may be relative to my varying condition, but again is average, normal, or absolute. (3) The units of this scale probably cannot be shown, and certainly cannot exist bare; but as an abstraction we seem forced theoretically to assume them. (4) Everything in the soul which in any sense becomes more or less, has *so far* a more or less of psychical existence, but only *so far*. Every 'state' is complex, and the whole state therefore may have a quantity which bears no fixed ratio to any one aspect. (5) Within our psychical content there thus fall scales indefinite in number and more or less independent and able to diverge. Hence a single state may vary quantitatively in various respects, as well as in respect of psychical existence. And to a certain extent these respects may diverge in quantity. But the practical outcome seems merely this, that before we talk of intensity and before we predicate degrees of strength, we should first of all define its kind and the scale we are to employ. Otherwise may come discoveries where no one knows what is discovered, and controversies where in the end no one understands what is in dispute. But others must judge to what extent this reflection has practical bearing. My object in this paper has been to raise some doubts on an interesting question, the difficulties of which, it appears to me, are not sufficiently recognized.

XX

ON THE SUPPOSED USELESSNESS OF THE SOUL

[*First published in* MIND, N.S. iv, No. 14, 176–9. *April,* 1895.]

THE following considerations must not be taken as quite expressing my own beliefs, nor again are they offered as original. But they will perhaps bring some thoughts together in a way which may be useful.

There is a view as to the connexion between body and soul which seems to grow every day more in fashion. On this view the bodily sequence is wholly independent of mind. It goes on as it would go on if nothing psychical were there. The soul is somehow an adjective which makes no difference to its substantive. It is the whistle of a steam-engine which has no effect on the engine's movement; for the soul is somehow that kind of whistle which expends no steam.

Now, though this view is respectable, it seems none the less ridiculous, but my first object is rather to show its connexion with another prevailing doctrine. I refer to what we may perhaps call Darwinian teleology. Everything which on a certain scale persists must be taken as useful. It was not made to be useful, but, if not useful, it would by now have been unmade. So that whatever on a certain scale has arisen and has persisted must certainly be useful. Now, if this doctrine is good, I do not see why we should not apply it to the soul, unless we are prepared everywhere to make the soul an exception to everything except disadvantage; and no one, I believe, has as yet openly contended for that principle. But when the Darwinian view is applied to the soul, the soul apparently must be of service. Pleasure and pain, volition and thought, must after all be there for something, and must after all do something. For otherwise by this time they would surely be no longer there at all; since, if so, they would be varieties useless and yet persisting.

The above reflection is obvious and, I presume, must be answered as follows. The soul is useless, but on the other side the soul costs nothing. To be pleased or pained brings no good, but brings also no harm. And thus the soul, being something which with regard to advantage or hindrance is nothing, falls wholly outside the Darwinian doctrine. But this answer can hardly stand unless we are ready to accept the old wives' story of the whistle blown and blown by nothing.[1] And if we hold to the belief that something comes from something, and that from nothing nothing comes, we shall have to seek for a less irrational proof that the soul may be useless.

If we consider that, on any view, the soul covers a large area of fact, if we decline to believe that this mass of existence is produced from and costs nothing, if we reflect further that fruitless expenditure is disadvantage which (it seems) must eventually destroy itself—we shall find it impossible to take the soul as being of no service at all. The soul must be useful, but it may be useful perhaps in a qualified sense. It may afford an advantage perhaps which is but conditional, provisional, and temporary. The soul in other words, though of service now, in the end may become useless. And in the end (we must add) having become useless the soul will cease. We can find also some further reason to expect such a supersession of the soul.

Every organism, we may anticipate, will become perfect. They will all in the end be adapted to their environments, and will be internally free from defect and jolting. But, if the soul is consciousness, the soul in its essence seems to involve imperfection. For consciousness consists in a process of distinction and relation, and it implies some collision. That which later we know as choice between incompatibles is at first certainly not present, but at the very dawn of consciousness we have some struggle between suggestion and fact. And if it were not so, and if we felt nothing of a baulked attempt, we never, it would appear, should become conscious at all. But consciousness, so

[1] Surely we have not got to take *this* as one of the 'fairy tales of science'?

living through friction, through delay and wavering, tends, as defects are removed, itself to pass away. Thus habits of action and of perception, acquired haltingly and with painful prominence of each struggling detail, become automatic more and more and, with that, unconscious. From which we conclude that, when on the whole adaptation has grown perfect, consciousness will have become superseded wholly.

This conclusion, if correct, seems the solution of our difficulty. Consciousness, though useless (we may say) both in principle and in prospect, will none the less be at present of service. Or at the least it will be the necessary accompaniment of what is useful. It will be that crying of an imperfect machine which arises from friction. This friction is expensive to the machine, and in principle it is not useless merely, but positively injurious. But because inseparable from the machine at a certain stage of its development, the friction must be taken as an advantage to what owns it. But when by Evolution machines grow perfect and friction gradually is reduced to nothing, consciousness then will meet the destiny assigned to it by principle. It will have become useless wholly and, with that, will cease to exist. And, with that, the world will have become perfect and purely physical.

There are, however, some objections which this view perhaps too much ignores. (i) For it has assumed, first, that the soul is the same as consciousness. But consciousness, with its distinction of subject from object and of objects from each other, is perhaps after all not so wide as sentience. But if the unconscious may be psychical, perfection after all need not be physical merely, but may be a sentient whole in which the oppositions of consciousness are transcended. And this psychical fact cannot be proved as above to be useless even in the end. (ii) Further, even if the principle were not unsound, the detail seems refractory. Without a process in time it is hard to see how any machine is to work and go. But with a process the door seems opened to accidents and jars, and so to outbreaks of consciousness. And since new machines have, I presume, to grow, and since old machines will, I suppose, wear out, perhaps after all perpetually there must be infantile and senile relapses into soul. And in short the Evanescence of Imperfection seems little better than the craze of a theory-monger. The facts rebel, and the principle seems mainly prejudice. The sentient machine of the Universe, though perfect, may by its essence involve collisions and friction between its parts, together with an outcry of consciousness. And what is above consciousness may still contain it as a necessary factor, while consciousness thus always, and yet never, is superseded.

The view of the soul as the result of friction seems in every way untenable, and to be oneself the self-awareness of jolts in a half-finished machine would be too stupid altogether. The distinction we draw between friction and work depends after all, I suppose, on a selected point of view. And if we wish to insist that the harmonious movement of a physical machine is by itself the one work, and that all beyond this is injurious or at least superfluous—perhaps we might begin by asking whether our point of view is rational or arbitrary.

Living once near a quarry on a hill, I was persecuted by a strange noise. It came from a wooden brake screwed against the wheels of descending and loaded carts. And listening to this noise, I fancied it the cry of some soul forced at intervals out of matter by too rude motion. And I tried to imagine the thoughts of such a soul and the views which it might take of its own meaning and destiny. It would perhaps at first feel sure that its own feeling was an end in itself, and that except for the sake of that or something like it nothing existed. But after many vagaries this soul might come to very different results. It might reflect perhaps how its self was engendered by accident and defect, and how a perfect cart would admit no friction nor be liable to any soul. A perfect cart would be motion unhindered, harmonious, and silent. Or this soul might think itself in any case but parallel to the physical motion. It might consider itself to be certainly in a sense dependent on the cart's movement, yet not so as to be produced at its expense, or as in any way to make any difference to it. But it struck me then that this last view was perhaps the most foolish of all. For that something could come from nothing and lead to nothing, or that something could happen with no expense to anything, remains always irrational. And I should dare to repeat this though I had thrown at my head some word longer even than 'psycho-physical'.

XXI

IN WHAT SENSE ARE PSYCHICAL STATES EXTENDED?

[*First published in* MIND, N.S. iv, No. 14, 225–35. *April*, 1895.]

THE question asked above may be met by a general
denial. Psychical states, we may be assured, are not
extended in any sense or at all. But this denial, if taken
absolutely, could not be sustained. It seems open to an
objection such as the following: If what is psychical is not
extended then nothing is extended, for in the end everything must be psychical. And at least in some quarters
it appears doubtful if such an objection could be met. But,
to pass by this argument in its more sweeping and more
assailable form, I will go on to urge it in a shape which to
me seems conclusive. The psychical existence of extension may be wholly denied, yet the idea and the perception
of extension must at the same time be affirmed. And any
such position, I would submit, is inconsistent with itself.
For the perception and idea are admitted themselves to
be psychical and, if this perception and idea in no sense
possessed extension, in what possible way (we must urge)
could they represent it? And since to this question I
have not yet found a reply, I must conclude that in some
sense the psychical can be extended.

But ideas and perceptions, I shall be told, are not what
they signify. It is true, I reply, that their meaning and
their existence are different. But if this difference is taken
to preclude sameness, the statement would become false.
For a thing, though the same, becomes different also when
diversely applied. And a feature of content, which makes
the meaning of an idea, must, I presume, in order to do
this, be present psychically. Thus, for example, the idea
of my horse in a sense has extension, and this idea also is
a psychical state. And when you ask me to believe that a
psychical state may have somehow extension, while in no

sense whatever it is extended, I cannot follow you. For how far and in what sense that which has extension itself is extended, I propose to discuss. But to deny extension wholly and altogether I find to be unmeaning. And if I am asked whether the extension of my horse exists also in my soul, that inquiry in no degree tends to stagger me. These extensions are different and they must be different since, and so far as, they belong to and qualify what is different. But for all their differences, they are also and as well most assuredly the same extension. And if they are not to be the same, I in my turn ask how my idea can be a true one. Nay, without extension in some sense, how could a false idea even succeed in looking like truth? For to appear with something or as something which one in no sense has or is, if we admit it to be possible, is at least a thing which calls for some explanation.[1] And in default of this explanation we must assert that psychical states in some sense may be extended.[2] Let us endeavour further to define the sense of that extension.

There is an obvious difference between extension as it is in the soul and extension as it is in the physical world. For the movement and the collision of material things is not present in the soul, or rather is not present in its full and complete nature. And we find this at once if we endeavour *a priori* to demonstrate about matter. So far as mere space is concerned we appear to possess its nature inwardly, and hence to be able within ourselves to control and to develop its essence. But clearly no such claim could be upheld with regard to body, and to anticipate or even to demonstrate the various qualities of nature seems quite impracticable. Observation and experiment have taught us connexions which internally we can repeat, and which partly we can combine and can rearrange. But we are not able (as with mere space) to experiment internally, for we do not possess the complete nature of the

---

[1] Compare here *E*. xix. 334–5.

[2] Whether extension is a primitive or an acquired perception seems a consideration not relevant. For in any case it exists, and that existence is all that need here concern us.

physical process. Thus by sheer hallucination we may even actually perceive a physical world, but no mere hallucination would supply us with fresh physical facts. We should be dealing always with but our old acquired material, and presumably we could not, apart from accident, gain from a sheer hallucination new information about nature.

On the other hand to deny that in the soul we have at all the extension which meets us in nature would be mistaken. We certainly have this same extension and can repeat the process of its happening, but we can do this only within limits, partially, and up to a certain point. For when we perceive a sequence in nature, we perceive in this but one feature of a whole. The result observed does not follow really and in fact except from the complete conditions, and to experience these complete conditions is quite impossible. The essential process, so far as known by us, is gathered piecemeal, constructed ideally, and put together in the abstract. And hence our essential process, as such, is not that actual process which produces the perceived result. Or rather it is the actual process, but so incomplete as to be actual no longer. In this sense we may deny that the physical extended moves and happens in a soul. For it happens there not integrally but merely in certain fragmentary aspects. And we possess it not bodily but only in schematic outline.

Now to object that in the psychical world also we, sometimes or always, have sequences, the full conditions of which we cannot experience, would be irrelevant. For in any case in the soul we find no world or order of spatial happening such as we ascribe to nature. And however many psychical sequences may remain incomprehensible, our conclusion remains. We are right to deny that the physical extended in its full process has psychical existence. Let us pass from this to another doubt which concerns us more.

One may reasonably deny that the physical extended essentially consists in its extendedness. The properties of the physical world follow, one may contend rather, only in part from its mere extension, and from its mere extension, however well you knew that, you could not comprehend the process of nature's happening. But hence the extension of nature, and the order of nature so far as it follows from that extension, can (it may be held) after all be possessed by the soul and, in a word, be psychical. This is a grave question on which I must again touch lower down, but its full solution cannot be attempted here. And for our present purpose we may be content to leave the question unanswered. We may either say that psychically we cannot possess the complete nature of physical extension; or again we may conclude that, while we possess this, the physical extended has also an additional aspect, an aspect essential and beyond our psychical experience. In this latter case we must allow no essential difference between extension physical and psychical, and we must hold that the process of the physical extended, so far as extended, also happens partially in the soul. But in the former case physical extension itself will not be experienced by the soul except as defective in its essence. Psychical extension, in other words, will lack an integral feature owned by the extension which is physical. But with such refinements we perhaps need here concern ourselves no further. For it will be true in any case that up to a certain point we have psychically the same extension which qualifies nature. In any case the two will have some identity, and the doubt attaches merely to the point at which they diverge. Psychical and physical phenomena, in other words, to a certain extent will in any case share the same extension. But in one case the physical world will have that extension less fragmentary and more complete, while in the other case the physical world will, besides its extension, necessarily possess an additional factor not owned completely by the soul.[1] With this we

---

[1] I of course cannot raise here the question of the ultimate nature of the physical world, and ask whether and how far it exists outside souls. And whether in the last resort unperceived nature is even actually extended I again cannot here discuss. For the purpose of the text I have felt bound to assume that unperceived nature is extended.

may pass from a distinction which for our present purpose seems barren.

But if psychical states are extended, I may be told,
absurd consequences will follow. For these states will
then collide, if not with outer things, at least with each
other. Nothing of the kind, I reply, need really take place.
For even if we can assume of physical extensions that
they all are comprised in and form parts of one extended
world, such an assumption evidently becomes false when we
carry it further. The extensions in the soul need have no
spatial relation to the physical world, nor again amongst
themselves need they be spatially related to one another.
When any phenomena are related spatially they are *ipso
facto* parts of one spatial whole—so much is certain. But
that all things spatial must be spatially related to each other
is not certain, but false. It is in fact a prejudice without any
rational basis. The worlds of the *Arabian Nights* and of the
Pilgrim's Progress have no spatial connexion either with
each other or with the room in which I write. These
worlds have a common unity, that is certain, but they are
not contained in one space. And whatever may be the
case with nature, in the soul there is an indefinite number
of extensions, between which no spatial relation exists.
Each of these states so far, we may say, has a world of its
own. And to urge objections based on the infinite or the
finite character of space would once more here be idle.
For the assumption of spatial unity would not help us to
dispose of any one of such difficulties.[1]

The soul contains extensions and it contains many
extensions, but the soul is not extended. We have here
in principle, I believe, the answer to our main inquiry.
For a thing may have qualities that are spatial and yet
itself need not enter space, and the denial of this truth once
more would rest on mere prejudice. Certainly, to be extended cannot mean merely to own an unrelated spatial
adjective. It must mean on the contrary to have a spatial
relation beyond oneself, and hence oneself to pass into and

[1] On all these questions I may refer the reader for some further discussion to my *Appearance and Reality*, chapter XXII.

belong as a part to an extended whole. But, this being admitted, the question is whether, without itself being extended, a thing cannot possess extension—whether, that is, we cannot say of a thing that it is extended in certain respects, though not extended as a whole. And the answer, I presume, must turn on the position which in the thing's essence we have assigned to extension. If, that is, we make extension predominate in the thing's nature, and treat the other qualities as subordinate to, and as following from, this special aspect, the thing itself clearly will have to enter a spatial world. But if on the other hand extension had no privileged or primary rank, if the thing's other attributes are in no way secondary or subordinate to that, but on the contrary perhaps superior in amount and in value—then clearly the thing itself will not be extended. The extension will qualify one or more aspects and adjectives of the thing, and these adjectives certainly will become parts each in its own spatial whole. But the rest of the thing's nature will remain aloof. You cannot so attach this outstanding nature to the extension as to carry it, and with it the whole thing, into a spatial order. The whole as a whole therefore will *have* extension, but—except in relation to one or more of its adjectives and just so far as they go—the whole will not *be* extended. If any of its states are spatial, then, in respect of these states and so far, the thing must be spatial. But whether it is spatial otherwise, and taken as a whole, will depend on the conditions. And the question is decided in each case by the relative importance of the thing's adjectives and by the position amongst these which extension occupies.

Now in the physical world, rightly or wrongly, extension may be taken as primary and predominant. And, if so, nature will all be extended, and also, perhaps, will have to be viewed as enclosed in one space. The position of such qualities as, say, smells and sounds will remain irregular, for, though localized, they are not properly extended. Still extension, rightly or wrongly, has been given a superior standing. It is not one adjective on a level with others, nor can its connexion with nature's essence be taken as mediate and conditioned. Nature *has* odours and tastes—here and there and under such or such conditions; but you can hardly say that nature *is* odorous or savoury in the sense in which you say it *is* extended. For every distinct partial aspect within a whole is possessed by that whole, but they cannot, each alike, be said to qualify the whole directly and simply.

But when we pass to the soul the position and rank of extension is altered. It cannot any longer be taken as predominant or primary, but has on the contrary to accept a secondary, if not an occasional, place. It is, we may say, undermined and overpowered by other adjectives. And hence the psychical whole *is* not extended. It merely has extension here and there, indirectly and as a quality of some of its states, between which states there need be no spatial relation at all. The psychical field of struggle is no space except by a metaphor, and the weapons of the contest are not velocity or mass. Nay, the extended itself, so far as psychically it competes, does not compete primarily by means of and through its relative extension.[1] It struggles, as all psychical elements struggle, by intensity, by pleasure and pain, and by the associative force of content. The soul has extension (we have seen), for it has 'states' which are extended. And as a whole the soul possesses the adjectives owned by its partial states, and, in these respects and so far, the soul itself *is* extended. But to omit 'here and there' and 'in this and that point', and to predicate extension of the whole soul without condition and at large, would be gravely erroneous. It would in fact be as absurd as it would be to call the soul sapid or odorous.

And this distinction between what the soul has and that which it is—the distinction between what the soul is itself, as a whole or directly, and what again it is indirectly and merely in respect of its parts—this distinction I take to be the solution of our chief problem.

[1] So far as they are related spatially, extensions in the soul can struggle for the same place. The basis of the struggle is here the partial identity of their content. It is in short a case of 'contraries'.

I will notice finally some minor difficulties connected with the subject, though, as it seems to me, they do not affect our main conclusion. Not all extensions in the soul, we saw, are related spatially. But where they are so and are combined to form one space, is this unity itself extended? Now, if the several extensions really are imaged as coming together, their unity clearly has also become spatial, and as a psychical state the whole perception is so far extended. But where we think not in concrete imagery but abstractly, this result must be modified. Having the idea of several spaces we then may think of them as combined and as one, and we may do this without properly representing their union as spatial. For we may apply to them an abstract and extraneous idea of unity. And, if so, the resulting synthesis may itself not actually be spatial, though always tending to become so.[1] Let us go on to consider another minor problem.

Let us suppose that, besides perceiving the place where I am, I think of other extended objects both present and past, objects some real and some imaginary. Now I may have several of these objects, I presume, at once, and may also consider them together. But where things in any sense are taken together, that unity is of course a psychical state, and in the present case the question is whether we are to call this state extended. It is probably not extended always, but, with some persons at least, it always tends

---

[1] Even if the idea of unity which is applied is spatial, it remains doubtful how far the several extended objects become parts of one extension. If, for instance, I am asked to think of a number of bodies each of a different colour, these bodies being scattered in space or divided also in time, and then am asked to think of these bodies as close together in space—what, I suppose, happens is this. I apply a more or less abstract spatial scheme of diversity in unity, and I identify the coloured bodies with the diversities of this spatial scheme. Now, if my thought is rapid and remains abstract, need it imply the mental juxtaposition of the various colours? And if not, how far and in what sense have the coloured objects become parts of one new extended state? We must reply, I think, that so far the bodies have not become parts of such a state, for they have come together spatially only from one side of their being. On the other hand, this abstract unity tends naturally to become more concrete and to pass into actual mental juxtaposition of the colours also.

to become so, and all objects thought of together tend to become parts even of one visual field. But the whole question, however interesting, has no bearing on our principal result. For the unity and synthesis of these several objects certainly will not consist always in their presence within one visual field, but that presence rather may be itself a symptom and consequence of their unity. And my whole psychical state at any moment is of course never extended. The background of feeling, before which every object must come, consists largely of elements which not in any aspect are extended. And the unity of feeling is of course itself not spatial. With these brief remarks I must pass from problems which seem here not in place.

The result of our whole inquiry is briefly this. The unity of the soul is not spatial, nor as a whole is the soul extended. But here and there, without any doubt, it has features which are extended. And the soul is extended in respect of these features, while you consider it merely so far and regard it fragmentarily. But to predicate extension of the soul, when the soul is taken together and as one, is quite impossible. That is no better than it would be to term the soul acid or salt or fragrant. For in the soul extension is not a universal head or law, under which adjectives fall; and, as an adjective, it is not all-pervasive. It is really but one among a number of predicates, its position is partial and its rank is secondary.

I may be allowed perhaps to append some remarks on 'Extensity' and on my difficulties with regard to it. I was long ago convinced of two things. (a) We cannot, I believe, understand how the perceived spatial world arises (if it does arise) from what is quite non-spatial; and (b) the spatial perception, however it arises, cannot have at first the relational character of developed space (E. xii. 222–3, note 1). Hence it seems to me proper to postulate a mode of perception which gives, on the one hand, more than mere volume and, on the other hand, less than space. And yet extensity, as it is offered me, I cannot accept for the following two reasons. (i) I am not able myself to find extensity in observation anywhere as a fact. (ii) I cannot identify everywhere volume with extensity, so as to deny all volume which is not 'extensive'. On the contrary I take extensity to be a specialized volume. And, though I probably have failed to understand the position of Mr. Ward or of Professor James, and though I am aware that with regard to extensity they seem, at least in part, to differ very seriously, they appear to me to agree in what perhaps are two mistakes. Both seem to me to deny in effect all non-extensive volume, and to claim also to observe extensity as a fact.

(i) Whether extensity can somewhere be observed is perhaps a question of little moment, and on my own failure I should certainly not venture to stand. But since my own difficulty may be more than personal, I will endeavour to state it. And my experience is this. Whenever I observe I either get something which seems to imply space right out, or else I get something which seems not to have even extensity. I can find volume everywhere—that I do not doubt —but not all volume appears to me to come possessed of side-by-sideness, or even to have features joined and divided by any fixed order of relations. When on the other hand I dwell on my perception, it tends to become distinct spatially, without, so far as I see, becoming merely extensive. And my perception thus grows not spatial merely, but spatial even visually. A compound smell or a confused organic sensation, nay, any kind of diversity and every possible distinction, in the end, when I dwell on it, becomes localized somehow in a visual field. And in short, while I observe, I find no way from an awkward dilemma. I must hold that all observed diversity and every distinction involves a character which is spatial right out, and in my own case visually spatial, though the elements themselves (e.g. smells) need not be extended. Or else, if I may take this character as but imposed by the process of my attending, and if I may deny that my mere perception of volume possesses it, then extensity itself seems gone with this justified removal. Or at least, while I keep to the observed facts, I myself cannot find it. I start with something which appears to be not so much as extensive, and I end with something which seems to imply what is fatally more, and during my progress I cannot make the required observation. And hence I should prefer to accept extensity as a postulate, if it were correctly formulated so as to fill the void stage in the development of space.

(ii) From this I pass to the second objection. Extensity, it seems to me, is a special kind of volume, nor could I deny the existence of volume without extensity. To such a denial I am in principle perhaps not opposed. Nay, if I had to assert that no diversity could be anywhere perceived without the help of spatial marks of distinction, that would make but little difference in principle to any views I entertain. But I think such a doctrine is mistaken, and in the same way I must decline to identify volume with extensity. If I take for instance my whole condition at some one moment, or if I take some group of organic sensations, or again for example some complex smell, I am led to a very different result. In these cases I am aware of volume, of an uncounted plural whole, I certainly perceive a muchness, but on the other side I cannot predicate extensity. I cannot find side-by-sideness, nor can I find a fixed interrelated arrangement of any kind. There are qualitative differences within a whole, but these differences seem not, even as qualities, to have an ordered position and situation among themselves. They are neither continuous in this sense, nor are they continuous again as showing indefinite internal divisibility. They are no serial field, in and on which motions, if only they could supervene, would find positions and so generate space. I at least cannot observe these characters given everywhere as fact, and I am therefore forced to suspect one of two things. Either these characters have been transferred from elsewhere into the facts, or I, as is likely enough, have not understood what extensity is to mean.

And since, where one does not understand, it is better not to insist on criticism, and since some obscurity seems to beset the use of 'volume', I may perhaps do best if I attempt to indicate what I myself mean by it. In the first place 'massiveness' seems not synonymous, for, if I imagine myself a balloon or a cloud, I am voluminous but not massive. 'Oppressiveness' again would refer to a certain effect on me, and the more oppressive (a fur rug) is not always the more voluminous (a down coverlet). These terms may be dismissed as being clearly not the same as mere volume. It is volume where (a) positively I have a whole containing a diversity felt as a many and much of one somewhat, and (b) negatively it is *mere* volume so far as here I do not count any units or pass discursively through any relations. Again, to have *mere* volume strictly, I should not view my 'much' comparatively and as being or as having more than something else is or has; and further, although the 'much' has a quality, I must not take that quality as a degree, with a place, that is, on a qualitative scale dependent on quantity. There are comparative volumes of course and there are of course degrees in volume, but these are special developments of the two undeveloped aspects of mere volume. Mere volume has a manyness which neither is counted nor compared, and it has a quality of muchness which is not taken on its own scale as a more or less of itself. The aspects of volume, which we might call its intensiveness and its extent, are present and given, but are not distinguished and developed. And after that result has taken place, I have still mere volume so far as I disregard the development and distinction.

Now it does not seem to me that this mere perception of an uncounted plural whole need imply side-by-sideness or fixed interrelation or serial arrangement or, in any proper sense, continuity external and internal. Space, in short, has volume, but volume need not be spatial or even have 'extensity'. And if I am wrong in this, yet the question calls, I think, for some inquiry.

With that inquiry perhaps might go a more careful treatment of the connexion between amount and degree. And as a possible help, and by way of supplement to a former paper (*E.* xix), I will venture to add some remarks not original nor perhaps all relevant.

Psychical states must all from the first be more and less of one somewhat, but the perception of quantity is rightly placed later than that of quality, if, that is, quality is taken at its rudest stage. The sense of something other and different comes, I believe, before that of more and less. But I certainly am not here attempting to derive or in any way to explain the origin of quantity. Quantity (however it comes) is another kind of change within the quality. When somewhat grows more or less, it becomes otherwise without ceasing to be the same quality or thing. If red changes to green that is an altered quality, though I do not deny that quantity may also be involved in the change. But when red changes to more of red or redder, while remaining red, that is what we call quantity. And we are led to distinguish further because 'more red' is ambiguous. It may stand for merely more of the same red, or it may mean that the red, while still red and while so far still the same, is also changed within itself and is now more or less as red. The redness itself here is opened to contain the diversity of an internal scale. Thus the more and less affected first only that which is red, but afterwards we have a more and less within redness itself.

Now it is not uncommon to speak of intensity and of extent as being aspects quite diverse. And when a greater extent of a quality, such as warmth, is in fact taken wrongly for a higher degree, we are told that volume and intensity are here confused or are not distinguished. But this explanation, though not untrue, seems partly incorrect. The real mistake lies, I think, not in failure to distinguish between extent and degree, but in failure to distinguish between two degrees or two amounts of different kinds. And I will endeavour briefly to make this clear.

Every perception of quantity, whether it is a perception of amount or degree, must possess the two aspects of extent and intenseness. Even in the case of degree the perception must contain an internal plurality, and even in the case of extent it must have as a whole a special quality (E. xix). There is a difference in the two cases, but the difference lies in the 'that', of which we have amount or degree. If you take red and increase its degree, preserving the same spatial area, you gain more units, but more units of red and not of spatial area. If you keep the redness the same, while the spatial area is increased, you have a higher degree not of redness but of area which is red. And hence—since in each case there is an increase both in intensity and in extent, and since both increases come to us alike as a moreness of red—a confusion between them seems only natural. Nay, the distinction between these aspects is presumably a late acquisition. But in theory this distinction can be turned into a hard division with erroneous results.

Volume itself is most certainly capable of degree. If you have a coloured surface which is red, that, even if you disregard its redness, has volume, and corresponding to that volume the surface as a whole has a quality. And if the coloured surface is increased by an addition which is not red but green, you will have an increase in volume and also in quality. Your perception will grow in intensity as it grows in volume, though neither this volume nor this intensity will belong specially to red or green. And then, coincident with and superimposed on this double growth, may come an increase in redness or greenness also two-sided. And all these changes, which partly are independent, partly must influence one another and result often in confusion or even in positive mistakes.

I do not know how far such remarks are relevant to the question in hand. They may serve at least to suggest that the connexion between quality, quantity, and degree is not simple, and cannot be disposed of easily. On the positive nature of extensity I have indeed said almost nothing. It has to be postulated and is not observed, and, while less than space, it is certainly more than mere volume. I have said no more because I doubt if I have more to say. And with what class or classes of sensation we have to postulate this character, is an important question which I have not touched. Nay, even that which I have laid down I am prepared to find mistaken. Every sort of diversity, after all, and every distinction may imply space proper, or, if not that, may imply something more or less spatial; and this last character again may be given in actual observation.[1] Volume without extensity may in short turn out to be an error. But whatever conclusion on these points may prove true in the end, the way to it, I am sure, is not short or easy. The introduction of extensity, in brief, I think has been useful, but extensity would be more useful if it were more thoroughly explained and discussed. By such an explanation I at least should expect to profit.

[1] Professor Sully (*Human Mind,* i. 95) seems to accept extensity only as hypothetical. If so, I do not understand what position he gives to volume and massiveness. In rejecting extensity wholly (*A.R.* 30 = 35) I had in mind solely the fact as supposed to be observed. The remark was not intended to exclude a hypothetical form of space-sensation (cp. *E.* xii. 222, note 1).

XXII

A DEFENCE OF PHENOMENALISM IN PSYCHOLOGY

[*First published in* MIND, N.S. ix, No. 33, 26–45. *January*, 1900.]

THE object of this paper is to defend 'phenomenalism' in psychology, and to defend it mainly by endeavouring to fix its true sense and by clearing this from mistakes and perversions. That phenomenalism is the one rational attitude in psychology I am as convinced as I am convinced that in metaphysics it is senseless. And phenomenalism I may here provisionally define as the confinement of one's attention to events with their laws of coexistence and sequence. It involves the complete abjuration of any attempt to ask in psychology for ultimate truth or consistency, and it involves the adoption as relative truth of whatever serves best to explain the detailed course of facts or those particular ways in which things happen. And, though I am well aware that I have no right to speak for any one but myself, I believe that the great body of psychologists desires and is anxious to accept phenomenalism in this sense and to relegate other inquiries about the soul to metaphysics. For, if we do not accept phenomenalism, I can perceive but one alternative. There will be in principle no division at all between psychology and metaphysics. One will be unable, at least on any principle, to limit the scope of an inquiry into the nature of the soul, and to refuse to be distracted by never-ending discussion of first principles. However anxious a man may be to confine himself to the mere observation and explanation of psychical events, he will be liable at every point to objections based on the question as to ultimate truth. And apart from phenomenalism we have nothing to justify us if we refuse to answer and to defend ourselves on this ground; while, if we do not refuse, the consequences at once are disastrous. You in particular may be sure that in metaphysics you have the truth, but then another man may not think so, and experience shows that the one probably will not convince the other. And the only reason, it seems to me, why things have gone as well as they have gone, is that psychologists have in practice, but as a rule upon no clear principle, confined to a large extent the scope of their inquiries within the limits of phenomenalism. To lay down and to defend a principle of such limitation is the object of this article.[1]

[1] I must notice here an attempt to limit the scope of psychology by defining its standpoint as 'individualistic'. I have remarked elsewhere (*A.R.* 273 = 309) that this attempt is in principle mistaken. It would be absurd to suppose that metaphysical questions cannot be raised from an individualistic standpoint. Hence, whatever the phrase may be meant to mean, it as it stands is useless. And I cannot think that Dr. Stout is successful so far as he adopts this formula, or generally in his definition of the sphere of psychology (*Analytic Psychology*, i, pp. 1–12). He, in my opinion, fails to demarcate psychology from metaphysics, which latter he defines in what seems to me an erroneous manner. It is indeed possible that Dr. Stout's view and mine may be really the same, but, if so, I cannot think that his view has been clearly formulated. Psychology, he says, investigates the history of the individual consciousness, and it is not concerned with validity or worth, but with existence, and with what appears to the individual mind. But I cannot see how that by itself is enough to divide it from metaphysics. The real question surely is as to *how* it is to study the history and processes of the individual mind. Is psychology limited to phenomenalism in the sense which I have given to that term, or may it go beyond this, and if so how far? Dr. Stout, it seems to me, fails altogether to answer this vital question.

I will briefly illustrate my meaning. I may wish, for instance, in studying the history of the individual mind, to ask fundamental questions about the relation of its plurality to its unity, and also to discuss the ultimate reality of its time-process. Is anything of this kind to be permitted in psychology? Or I may wish to maintain the doctrine that the history of the individual is in a sense explained by a fundamental underlying volition or conation. Are we as psychologists to debate this? One man again may propose to reduce all Association to Redintegration, and another may seek to stop him by arguing that really there is no identity in things but only resemblance. Is this plea to be admitted in psychology and discussed there, or, if not, on what ground? Now to reply that psychology is not concerned with the validity of cognitions would, it seems to me, be idle. If you mean by cognitions the cognitions of that individual consciousness which we are studying, that surely would be irrelevant, for we are not, I presume, supposing that this particular consciousness is entertaining these

The presumption in favour of that limitation seems to me, I confess, to be so overwhelming that my best course will be simply to try to defend the doctrine of phenomenalism against objections and misconceptions. But let me first attempt to state its nature more accurately.[1] Psychology is to be concerned with psychical events, and such an event is whatever is immediately experienced, either as a whole or as an integral aspect of a whole, and is not for the purpose in hand taken otherwise than as an adjective happening to and qualifying a particular soul. These facts are events because they happen in time, each with a place in the order of the 'real world' in general, and of this one soul in particular. On the other hand, by their 'happening' is not meant that they have no duration, for, to be events at all, they certainly must have some duration. But further psychology is not confined merely to these several events and aspects of events, and it has also to study them in their relations of sequence and coexistence within one soul. These relations, so far as they fall outside immediate experience, are of course themselves not events in the sense of facts immediately experienced, and again their laws are not events at all. But the scope of these laws on the other hand is strictly limited, and they are and remain special cognitions about itself. But if on the other side you possibly meant that psychology is not to judge of truth at all, that would be obviously untrue, and certainly no one could maintain it. It is quite true that psychology has not to investigate the truth of the cognitions of the mind which it studies, as such, but I wholly fail to understand how, with this, we have divided it from metaphysics. But I should add that I probably have not understood what Dr. Stout means by metaphysics.

The vital question seems to be this: Does Dr. Stout mean to confine psychology to events and the laws of events? Does he mean to assert that, since psychology is not concerned with more than this, it is at liberty to use fictions, and that the question of truth is not to be raised in it except so far as truth means whatever serves best to explain the course of mere events? I cannot understand how it is that, if Dr. Stout really holds these doctrines, he should not have expressed them more clearly. But if Dr. Stout does not hold them, what alternative does he offer? To me it remains unintelligible, and I must therefore persist in repeating that there is no alternative between accepting the view which I advocate and having in principle no boundary at all between psychology and metaphysics.

[1] Cf. here *E.* xii. 205–7.

mere laws of the bare coexistence and sequence of events. With regard to the meaning of one soul or subject, that, so far as I see, must be fixed arbitrarily. In the psychology of man and of the higher animals I myself think it would be most convenient to fix it by the identity of the organism, and to treat a plurality of souls within that—if indeed a plurality ever really happens—as the adjectives of one soul. The mere course of psychical events, as such, happening within a single organism, and the laws of coexistence and sequence between these events, will then be the object of psychology. And within psychology no further question, and in especial no question about ultimate truth, is to be entertained.

I will at once endeavour to explain this further by defending it briefly against a series of objections. I will not try to take these in a systematic order or to keep them wholly distinct, and I shall for the most part state them in my own way.

(i) It may be objected, first, that the soul really is one, and that on the view of phenomenalism it has no unity. To this I reply that it has all the unity which is wanted for our purpose. I do not indeed say that its continuity in time is unbroken, nor is there any need for me to say this; and again the history of the soul as a whole is of course not immediately experienced by it. But the soul has certainly an identity in quality which appears in the series and the nature of which can be studied.[1] And besides qualitative identity it has relations of coexistence and sequence which phenomenalism takes as real,[2] and it has also laws of those relations. And with so much the soul certainly has a real history. The question of its ultimate real unity is not recognized by phenomenalism, but I cannot see that this prevents us from treating its history as one.

---

[1] The possibility of an entire defect in this I do not discuss. I do not myself care what answer psychology gives in this case to the question of unity and identity.

[2] Under this head of relations will fall any piece of psychical duration, beyond what is immediately experienced, that psychology may have occasion to consider.

(ii) 'But in the soul, then, at any one time there will be for phenomenalism nothing but what is experienced at that time.' Not so, I reply, and this is a sheer mistake. For phenomenalism the soul is at any one time what is experienced at that time, but it is also more. For it is qualified also by the past which really belongs to it, and that past belongs to it not merely as what it has been, but as what it now is. The soul in other words *is* the dispositions which it has acquired.[1] And if it is objected that with this we have gone beyond phenomenalism, I reply that once more the objection rests on a mistake. For the dispositions are simply statements about the happening of events within the phenomenal series—assertions as to what will happen, or rather would happen, under certain conditions more or less unknown. They, in other words, are tendencies or individual laws. Certainly if phenomenalism professed to know the ultimate truth about these dispositions, and in the end really to understand them, it would end in failure and would also be quite false to itself. But, on the other hand, professing entire ignorance and the completest indifference as to their real nature, it uses these tendencies as facts, and in this it follows the example of every limited science. The dispositions are not phenomena, but they are legitimate fictions used to explain the happening of phenomena.

I will try to put the same thing in a different way. In

---

[1] If we recognize native psychical dispositions, a point on which I wish to say and to imply nothing, these again will qualify the soul. They will be something, the real nature of which psychology does not discuss, but which it expresses as tendencies—statements as to what will happen under certain conditions. It is better to understand that these are not to be taken to exist before there is a beginning of actual psychical fact. Anything before this will be not a psychical but a physical disposition. It is, I should say, not convenient to assume a soul there, where there not only is (as we assume) nothing psychical now, but where that has not existed and may not be about to exist. The inconvenience is less in a case where we suppose a temporary but complete 'suspension' of psychical life. But even in this case, if any one insists that we have no right in psychology, during such a suspension, to speak of an actual psychical disposition, I cannot say he is wrong. At any rate, if we do this, we should not forget that we are making use of a certain licence.

metaphysics I recognize in the end no distinction between the experienced and experience, and any attempt to draw such a distinction I consider to be in the end mistaken and futile. And hence there is naturally no readier way of proving my metaphysical views to be absurd than to assume dogmatically that this distinction holds good in metaphysics. But in psychology, since there we are not concerned with what is true in the end, I consider that this distinction is both justifiable and necessary. Beside that which at any one time is experienced, you have also the thing to which the experience belongs. And far from deny-ing this, I have always taken it as a matter which is even obvious.[1] But for psychology this thing is nothing beyond the history and the group of tendencies which have just been mentioned. For more is not wanted, and therefore more is not admissible at least within psychology.

(iii) 'But in the experienced', it may be said, 'there is more than events, for there are ideas and judgements about objects, and these surely are not events.' But we must, I answer, here distinguish. To say that ideas and judgements do not happen at a certain time, and that in this sense they fail to be occurrences, seems clearly con-trary to fact. And again it would surely be once more contrary to fact to say that, when they happen (since they do happen), they are not also felt to happen in the soul and are not experienced as my states. But so far clearly they are events. The reality to which the ideal content is referred, that ideal content and its reference—everything in short is present in my feeling. Everything is thus so far an event which has a place in my history and is pre-dicable of me. That which is not so predicable is the mere connexion of the ideal content with the reality, so far as that connexion is taken by itself, and so far as abstraction

---

[1] I think that it is perhaps best to call this thing the soul, but I have no objection to the use of 'subject' or even of 'self' so long as it is clearly understood that you are not at once from these terms to draw certain conclusions, which I think quite false, about 'object' or 'not-self'. Another kind of mistake would be to refuse to recognize any psychical subject other than the body.

is made of any other aspect. Certainly, then, I agree that, so far as this abstraction is maintained, we have not to do with an event in my soul, but I add also that we have to do with something which falls outside of psychology. On the other hand, the idea or the judgement, if you take it in any fuller sense, is assuredly a psychical event. You may go on to urge, if you please, that at any rate cognition proper is not explicable; but that is a point to be discussed within psychology, and at any rate here it is perfectly irrelevant.[1] However much a thing is inexplicable, that hardly proves that it does not happen and is no event.

A truth, we may say, is no truth at all unless it happens in a soul and is thus an event which appears in time. As it there exists, and as by existing there it influences the future history of that soul, it is a matter for psychology, and for the psychology that confines itself strictly to phenomenalism. But as anything less than this or anything more than this it does not fall within psychology, that is, if there are to be any limits set to psychology at all.

'But', it may be further said, 'let us take such a case as the following: A mind may make the Deity its object and may so, as we say, be "converted". Now the Deity is not an event, and is not so thought of, and does not in that character influence the mind. But yet this influence, whatever else it may be, is clearly psychological, and at the same time falls outside your psychology.' But no, I reply, this is once more nothing but misunderstanding and confusion. The Deity is not a mere event of course, and of course the Deity is really present in the mind that makes

---

[1] If I speculate psychologically about myself, it may be said in this case that psychology is concerned with my judgement in every sense, both as it exists and as it is true or false. Certainly this is so, but this once more would be irrelevant. Psychology is indeed interested here in the truth or falsehood of my judgement, as well as in its personal history and existence. But, so far as concerned here with truth, psychology is concerned with it not as mine, but abstracts wholly from that side of it. And the truth therefore will so far not be a fact or object to psychology at all, but part of its own impersonal attitude towards its object and part of its own way of dealing with that.

it an object, and it is really present not as an event, and it really exercises in this non-temporal character psychological influence. This is all true, and yet it does not prevent something else from also being true. The presence in the soul of what is more than an event is certainly an event in that soul, and it is just because it is more than an event that in this case it is also more of an event in the history of that soul. And it is from this side of event that psychology has to do with the matter in its origin, and in its content so far as that qualifies the soul and also influences its future history. And all this falls within psychology as I have defined it. Psychology in short abstracts one side of the living whole and considers that apart. And its abstraction is the opposite of that abstraction which considers reality and truth apart from its appearance as event in the history of finite souls. And at least the abstraction made by psychology is both legitimate and necessary.

(iv) But a further objection has been made that there may be 'an unanalysable element in every psychical event', and yet that this is not an event. I must confess that I do not know what this objection means. It seems obvious that any aspect of any event will itself happen in time and will occupy time, and will thus itself, whenever it happens, be an event, however identical and however unanalysable it may remain, and whatever may be its duration. And, as I have replied elsewhere, 'changes in the intensity of the element would of course be events, as would be also the changes in the relation of that element to others' (*E.* xii. 205, note 2). And without attempting further to understand I must leave the matter thus. If this 'element' comes into the experienced at all it is certainly an event; but, if it is not in this sense an event or a phenomenal relation between events or a law of events, then it has no place within psychology. Let us pass on to a new objection.

(v) 'On your understanding of it,' it will be said, 'psychology is not true. We want to know the real truth about the soul, and we do not want to be put off with a series of events which are abstractions and laws which in part are fictions.' Well then, I answer, by all means betake yourself to metaphysics, and gain of course what you seek there. But why, I urge, beside metaphysics may there not be a phenomenal psychology for persons like myself? 'But it will not be a science', you reply, 'if it does not give or seek the real truth.' I on the contrary should maintain that, if it gives or seeks the real truth, it is not a separate science at all. The very essence of such a science everywhere, I should say, is to employ half-truths, in other words to use convenient fiction and falsehood. And if you deny this in general, I will urge that at least it is so with psychology. Do you really mean to tell me that I am not to use and work with such ideas as a law of association, or a disposition, unless I can state these in a form which is ultimately and utterly true? It seems to me that such a question, when once raised and once understood, can only be answered in one way, and with this I will pass on.

(vi) 'But psychology cannot', I may be told, 'be a separate science, because these sciences each study separate compartments in the nature of things. On the other hand psychology has no such compartment, since there is nothing which falls outside the mind, and psychology therefore is not and cannot be a limited science.' Now what conclusion really should follow from the premise, if that were true, I will not discuss, for the whole premise in my opinion is radically false. A limited science is not in principle made what it is by having a compartment to itself, but by studying whatever it studies with a limited end and in a limited way. If you ask for instance unconditionally what are matter and force, that is a question for metaphysics. It becomes a question for phsyics if you ask what they are for a certain limited purpose and in a certain limited sense. And exactly the same thing in principle holds with the science of mind. If you ask about the soul unconditionally, what is the truth about its nature, the inquiry is metaphysical. But if, on the other hand, you confine yourself to a limited kind of question about the soul, that limitation keeps you within empirical psychology and is the boundary of your science. And this in principle seems as clear as it is evident and visible in practice. It is evident in practice, I will venture to say, to any one not biased by theory that both practical and theoretical knowledge of the human soul is in fact actually possessed and used by those who are not metaphysicians. And an objection which would disprove the existence and possibility of this fact can hardly be well founded.

(vii) I will consider next a further objection, which possibly may be raised, in order in my reply to it to define my position more clearly. 'We admit', it may be said, 'your contention as to the object and scope of psychology. Its object, we agree, is to study the mere course of psychical events as such. It has to observe facts and to classify them, and then to seek to explain them—to explain, that is, not their ultimate nature, but their origin and the course which they take. It has to find, so far as is possible, the reason why they happen as they happen, and not the truth as to what they are. It seeks to discover the reason why we find this one rather than that one, and it does not study the real nature of all or of any, but only their nature so far as they qualify the history of the soul. But,' it may be added, 'agreeing with you so far, we are then driven to dissent very widely, for we think that more than mere phenomenal laws of happening is admissible, and is necessary for explanation, and we do not see on what principle you should object to more if it works.' Now, I reply, if this were said, and if this really were meant, I should be satisfied on the whole, because I think that the issue once raised in this way must be decided in favour of the cause which I adopt. But I will venture to add a few words in order to make the issue still clearer. If the end and scope of psychological explanation is defined as above, I do not object to *anything* that is offered, so long as and so far as it works, and so long as it is offered merely as something which works. But I must insist that nothing does work except so far as and so long as you use it as a mere law of happening. And hence I object to your 'more' because it is most certainly useless and almost certainly hurtful. Even if you had the absolute truth about the soul you could not for our purpose, so far as I see, use it as the absolute truth, unless indeed we take the absolute truth to consist in mere laws of empirical happening. For it is only these laws which you can use here, however much more you may possess. And hence, if you will produce your 'more', I will undertake to show of it one of two things. It is useful in psychology just so far as it really is *not* used as more than, or as anything else than, a law of phenomena. Or otherwise it is really not useful in psychology at all, but is a false and mischievous pretence of knowledge.

The question of 'dispositions' will furnish, I think, a good illustration of my meaning. A disposition, I should say, in psychology is a mere way of stating that, when some things have happened, there will be a 'tendency' for other things to happen—we may expect them to happen, that is, under favourable conditions—and, so far as these tendencies are reduced to rule, they are used properly to explain the occurrence of particular facts. On the other hand, a psychologist may think that he knows what a disposition really is, and may be prepared with a more or less elaborate theory of its nature. Or again, without asserting knowledge, he may propose to use an avowed fiction. In either of these cases the test to be applied is the same. So far as the 'real truth' or the fiction serves as a law to explain the phenomenal sequence, it is admissible within psychology, and beyond that it is illegitimate.[1] A disposition for instance may be identified with a conation.[2] Now if and so far as by this identification we can better bring the particular facts under their laws of happening, the use of conation would be an explanation and would there-

---

[1] This attitude of avowed ignorance would of course by some psychologists be considered improper. Professor Ward (*Psychology*, p. 48), for instance, appears to assume it as self-evident that a disposition is an actual mental state, into the nature of which as psychologists we are bound to inquire. The account which he himself seems to give of it I have never found to be really intelligible. Mr. Stout (*Analytic Psychology*, i. 24–6) has criticized this account, but I could not say whether he has understood it rightly or not.

[2] A conation, that is, which is not actually experienced. To reduce a disposition to an actually experienced conation would of course, if practicable, be perfectly legitimate.

fore be justified as a working fiction. But otherwise its employment would be at best useless and would probably be hurtful. It would be hurtful because it tends to suggest that we understand and have explained facts, where we do not understand them and where no explanation has been given. But in this way attention may be diverted from the real problems to be solved.

You can only explain events, I would repeat, by the laws of their happening, and it does not matter for your purpose, so long as these laws work, whether they possess ultimate truth or are more or less fictitious and false. And anything other than these laws is useless at best, and therefore probably mischievous. And if the object and scope of psychology could be agreed on, and could be limited explicitly to the mere study and explanation of phenomena, I believe the rest of this conclusion would be readily evident. What in short we want in psychology are explanations that truly explain, and above all things we do not want true explanations.[1]

I have now tried to state in general what is to be understood by phenomenalism in psychology, and I have replied to certain objections as they have been made or as they have occurred to me. But there remain two other objections, more or less connected, which I will now proceed to notice. These objections are directed against a false view of phenomenalism, and themselves seem based on a radical misunderstanding of that term. They in fact rest in great part on doctrines which I should regard as wholly indefensible. These objections may be stated as follows:—
'You have taken', it will be said, 'no account of a fundamental difficulty. In the first place mere phenomena are quite discrete and lack all continuity; and in the second

---

[1] I was glad to see that Wundt, in the fourth edition of his *Physiologische Psychologie*, ii. 283–4, appears to state definitely that his 'Apperception' is to be understood in psychology merely as the name of a class of psychical phenomena with its laws of happening. How far, so understood, Wundt's doctrine is tenable, and how far again his practice has been wholly consistent with his present statement, are questions I do not discuss.

place they at any rate are all mere perceptions merely given to the self. This, it is true, is not the case with regard to pleasure and pain, and as to whether these are or are not phenomena, we have our own view which you seem unable to understand. But at any rate, to speak in general, phenomena are mere objects, and the whole life of the self cannot be resolved into objects without a self, even when the laws of these objects are added *ad libitum*. And with your educational advantages,' it may even be added, 'it seems strange that you should not see this.' But I would reply that not only was I, if I may say so, brought up to see this, but I was brought up also to perceive something else as well. And the result is that I reject both the doctrines on which the objections are founded. Phenomena are not merely discrete nor again are all of them objects, and in short the true phenomenalism has been completely misunderstood and perverted.

1. On the mere discreteness of phenomena I need say very little, since truer views seem now steadily making their way. What is immediately experienced is not a collection of pellets or a 'cluster', as it used to be called, of things like grapes, together with other things called relations that serve as a kind of stalk to the cluster. On the contrary, what at any time is experienced is a whole with certain aspects which can be distinguished but, as so distinguished, are abstractions. Now each of these wholes is an event, and each of its aspects is an event, but that does not make them discrete. Every whole and its aspects as experienced has a certain duration and so some continuity in time, and it has some qualitative identity through different times actual and possible. And the duration that is experienced at one time is continuous with that which is experienced after it and before it. For, without our entering on any difficulties here as to the outward limitation of the experienced,[1] the identity of its content

---

[1] I refer here to the difficulty of drawing a line at which it ceases. The immediately experienced of course has limits, and it has very narrow ones. It is the same as the 'present' in the sense of what is directly felt in any one 'now'. To confuse this with the 'present' which is formed by any ideal

forces us to take it as continuous from experience to experience. In short, phenomena are legitimate abstractions, but they are not discrete reals.

And if they were merely discrete in and by themselves, then on the other side I would urge that the disease could have no possible remedy. The idea of a self or Ego joining together from the outside the atomic elements, and fastening them together in some miraculous way not involved in their own nature, is quite indefensible. It would be the addition of one more discrete to the former chaos of discretes, and it would still leave them all discrete. The idea of anything being made wholly from the outside into something else, whether by an Ego or by God Almighty, seems in short utterly irrational.

2. And as phenomena are not discrete, so phenomena are certainly not all objects.[1] This is another mistake, or in some cases it is another aspect of the same fundamental error. If all phenomena were objects or mere perceptions, and were confined to what in any sense is before the mind, then of course phenomenalism would be untenable. So understood it becomes a gross error which, if not now in

content, so long as that is taken to endure unbroken, would be a very serious error. Cf. here *A.R.* 463–6 = 523–6.

[1] If 'object' were understood in abstraction as *mere* object, then we may say that in strictness no psychical phenomenon would be an object. But this point need not be considered here. If I am asked what we are to call the experienced so far as it is not the object of a perception or cognition, I should say that the words 'feeling' and 'to feel' are obviously suggested. If we take the words in this sense we follow both the common usage and the literary associations of the English language. We violate both of these if we try to confine feeling to mere pleasure or pain, and a violation of this kind in the end must produce confusion. I think it was certainly ill-judged when instead of 'feeling' I used 'presentation' (*E.* xii), for that term tends, I presume, to suggest the presentation of an object. In fact, in *Mind* [o.s. xii. 564–75, 'Mr F. H. Bradley's *Analysis of Mind*', by James Ward] a laboured criticism of many pages was produced mainly to show that, presentation being so understood, what I had written was something like nonsense. If, on that understanding, it had not been nonsense, this would have been certainly something like a miracle, and certainly nothing to my credit. But in the present unsettled state of our terminology to assume of any writer that he uses words in the sense which we think the proper one seems likely to lead to waste of time.

principle exploded, will I imagine never be exploded, and far from maintaining phenomenalism in this sense, I consider it a thing with which one need hardly trouble oneself. But really phenomena are not all perceptions, they are not all objects given to a self, they do not all come before the mind, and to regard them so is, I venture to think, a radical mistake. And this mistake is, I venture also to think, very hurtful and a serious obstacle, wherever it exists, in the path of psychology. I will state the doctrine briefly, or I will rather state the manner in which I am forced to understand or perhaps to misunderstand it.

We have (according to this view) on one side the experienced, and that, if for the moment we disregard pleasure and pain, consists in the perceived, in objects given to and before the self. This forms the whole content of the experienced. The experienced in short is but one aspect of experience, and the other aspect consists in the activity of the self. This activity is itself not perceived and does not itself enter into the experienced content, and is not and cannot itself be made into an object. But beside these two sides of experience, one experienced and the other not experienced, we have also feeling in the sense of pleasure and pain. The position of this is to my mind so obscure that I cannot venture to state it. It is not an object, and cannot possibly be made into an object, it cannot be remembered, nor can we have an idea of it. Whether we are to say that it is not experienced I, however, do not know and must leave uncertain. Now this whole view, or any view which is like it, I venture to consider quite untenable and even absurd. Far from thinking the worse of genuine phenomenalism because it conflicts with such a view, I regard that conflict as a sign of truth and as a point in favour of phenomenalism.

The view (i) in the first place is in my judgement contrary to plain fact, and (ii) in the second place it refuses wholly in the end to work. (i) The position of our original awareness of pleasure and pain, for we somehow are aware of them, is to me so lost in obscurity that I can but point to it and pass on. But, when I am told that I cannot make an object of a pleasure and cannot attend to it, I must reply by a flat contradiction. So far as the pleasure is felt merely, it is, I agree, so far not an object and does not come before the mind, and to urge that, in being made an object, it must to some extent be modified is at least a reasonable contention. But to insist that beside being felt it cannot also be made an object at all, seems in plain collision with fact.[1] And it is again in plain collision with fact to make the whole of what is at any moment experienced consist in objects before the mind. If you take a cross-section through that of which at any one moment we in the widest sense are aware—the whole way, I mean, in which we come to ourselves and feel ourselves at any given moment—you will hardly find that everything experienced there has the form of an object over against and given to the self. For the self feels itself, and it feels itself as something concrete, and it feels the presence of an object or objects given to this self which is so far not an object and yet is experienced. Against my objects I surely may feel myself to be passive or active, nor does this feeling consist in the mere presence of one or of two meaningless sensations. But how I can so feel myself if I am not aware of my self as something over against my objects, and how I can be so aware of my self if my self is itself not experienced, seems an insoluble puzzle. And to assert generally that in an emotion I experience nothing but objects together with pleasure and pain, and not my self otherwise at all, would seem even ridiculous. And in desire and conation the felt presence of a self, which is not experienced wholly as an object, seems really, when we reflect, to stare us in the face. Or rather it would do so if we had not blinded ourselves by a preconceived theory as to what is possible. And in short this whole view is a construction which for certain purposes may seem convenient, but which from first to last is really in sharp collision with the facts.[2]

[1] There are some remarks on the question of ideas of pleasure and pain at the end of this paper.

[2] For some further remarks I may refer the reader to *M.* n.s. ii, No. 6 [*TR*, 192–8].

(ii) 'But what does that matter', I may hear it said, 'so long as the view works?' Yes, but, I reply, it does not work, but from the very first is in difficulties, and at a certain point it breaks down visibly and utterly. And, to omit the other difficulties, it breaks down finally in the following way:—The aspect of self has by this view been turned out of the experienced, and yet no one on the other hand can deny that self-consciousness is a fact. We rightly or wrongly, then, are in fact aware of a self, which self on the other hand cannot be experienced. But how in that case we can become aware of it, and by what process the idea or the notion, or whatever you prefer to call it, is ever to enter into our minds, seems impossible to discover or at least to exhibit intelligibly. And this is not a small matter and it is not a failure to explain some point of detail, but it seems on the contrary to be a cardinal and vital defect. Here is a fact—a very large and most important fact surely—which on a certain theory seems inexplicable, and which, so far as we see, would on that theory be impossible. And apart from other considerations, which here appear to be wanting, I submit that with so much any theory must be taken as disproved.[1]

I would venture to illustrate the above by a reference to a late work by Professor Andrew Seth. In his interesting volume, *Man's Place in the Cosmos*, Professor Seth takes up a position against phenomenalism in psychology, and I should like to point out that in that position he finds it impossible to maintain himself. The phenomenalism which he criticizes appears to involve the view that phenomena are all objects or perceptions. Now this view Professor Seth himself appears to endorse, and he does not seem to find it, so far as it goes, in the least mistaken. In fact I understand him to insist himself that all the content

[1] I was taught early that there was a most important test to be applied to every doctrine. Supposing a doctrine true, is the fact of its truth consistent with the fact that I know it to be true? This test I have always found, whether in metaphysics or in psychology, to be one which should never be neglected, and I do not hesitate to urge that in these studies its importance is really vital. On the other hand I readily admit that I am not competent to give any opinion as to what is to hold good within 'Epistemology'.

and matter of experience, all the experienced in short, does thus consist of objects, and that phenomenalism, not in the least mistaken so far, is mistaken only in ignoring other aspects of experience which are themselves not experienced. And 'feeling' I understand Professor Seth to identify here simply with pleasure and pain, and in respect of these to endorse wholly the position we have sketched above, and in the teeth of fact to deny that pleasure and pain can be made into objects or attended to or remembered. And, in short, so far and up to this point Professor Seth's position does not seem to me to call for any special remark.

But the second part of the article becomes to me very interesting and instructive. In this Professor Seth is concerned with the positive knowledge which we have of our own activity, and the conclusion at which he arrives seems to me to introduce a wholly different principle. Feeling becomes now for him no longer mere pleasure or pain, but it is the immediate awareness on the part of the self of its own being and activity. And this view of feeling, so far as I can judge, is in radical discrepancy with the first view, or at least would be so if its meaning and its bearings were developed. For this deliverance of feeling now surely cannot be denied to be matter which is experienced. You can surely no longer refuse to reply when you are asked as to the nature of its 'what'; and when inquiries are raised as to the variety of aspects within its content, you can hardly treat them as unmeaning. In short, the identification of content with the 'object' side of experience seems to have been tacitly given up, and with the abandonment of that prejudice the way has been cleared for quite another kind of doctrine. But I do not understand how Professor Seth himself fails to perceive that he has here two different views as to feeling, and that, if he accepts the second of these, he can no longer make use of the first.[1] And I will

[1] I do not know on what view of feeling Professor Seth stands in that portion of his instructive review of my book in which he touches on the subject (pp. 168, 213). I should like to say once more here that the essence of the view which I adopt—whether that is right or wrong—is that feeling does give us a positive manifold content.

venture to add that, if Professor Seth would throw the first view over wholly and entirely with all the false prejudices which belong to it, and then without any *arrière pensée* would commit himself to and would develop the second view, he would produce a work which, whether they agreed with it or not, would be of the highest interest and advantage to students of philosophy.[1]

It is only for a false view, then, that phenomena consist merely of objects. The experienced contains in itself very much more than these. And it is the whole content of the experienced which, when regarded in a certain way, becomes a coexistence and succession of events and forms the subject-matter of empirical psychology.

I should like to append to this paper some remarks on a point which I have noticed already, the question, that is, as to whether there are ideas of pleasure and pain. And, since a separate question may be raised about pain, it is better for us here to confine our attention to pleasure. My object in what follows is not to attempt in passing the full discussion of a large subject, but to mention some difficulties which, so far as I have observed, have not been properly recognized. I shall say no more here on the strange paradox that I cannot attend to a pleasure; and the general doctrine that Association holds only between 'objects' I of course do not accept. I follow here the more

[1] 'With the elimination of real causality from the course of things', Professor Seth remarks, 'the world is emptied of real meaning' (p. 125). But, without raising here any discussion as to the sense in which causality is to be taken, I should like to emphasize a question which Professor Seth, it seems to me, too much ignores. If you eliminate something, as he seems only too ready to do, from the *experienced* world, have you not in fact banished it from the world altogether? Is there in short any other world in which it could exist?

Since the above was written I have had the advantage of consulting Dr. Mellone's *Philosophical Criticism*, but I cannot see that his position is really in advance of that taken by Professor Seth. It appears to me that what is true and what is false are still left standing side by side. But why the true view is not from the first laid down and without scruple worked out, while the false view is thrown aside, I am quite unable to understand. But Dr. Mellone, I trust, will do this some day.

established view, and judge that there is reason to think that Association holds everywhere. I think also that, if any one maintains the separation in a concrete product of the aspect of pleasure from the aspect of sensation, and asserts the activity of one side only—the burden of proof should rest upon him. But, without entering here on these points, I wish very briefly to call attention to some difficulties which result from the view that we have no ideas of pleasure.

This view considers that we have ideas only of that which was pleasant, but that its pleasantness is in no sense recalled in idea. The mutilated residue which actually is recalled may create a fresh reaction of pleasure or not, according to the conditions now present. And as the residue provokes or does not provoke this reaction, it becomes or does not become what we commonly call an idea of pleasure.[1] This view seems a paradox and I think that it is certainly a mistake, the result of a previous error in principle, but on the other hand I do not see how its falsity could be actually demonstrated.[2] It has, however, in its working to encounter, it seems to me, the following difficulties.

(1) The memory and thought of a past pleasure may in fact now on the whole be pleasant or be indifferent or be painful, while it yet may remain in each case the actual and positive idea of a past pleasure.[3] If indeed we con-

---

[1] I may perhaps be allowed to mention that the reader will find this view stated in my *Principles of Logic*, 442–4 = 408–10.

[2] I do not think that it is 'almost impossible' to produce a conclusive instance of 'purely affective memory' (Ribot, *Psychologie des Sentiments*, p. 170). It seems to me that from the nature of the case such a thing could not exist. The required abstraction cannot be made, and hence any proof or disproof of this kind seems out of the question. The issue must be decided in one way or the other according as one view or the other is found in the end to strain the facts more or less, when all the facts are considered.

[3] I am forced to dissent from much in the following passage from Dr. Stout with regard to association in the case of pleasure and pain. 'In order to see that the law of contiguity does not apply to pleasure-pain as it applies to presentations, we have only to recall some very common experiences. The sight of food awakens pleasure before eating; but after we have eaten to satiety it gives rise only to indifference or disgust. This is

sider what the idea on the whole *is* now with regard to pleasure and pain, and distinguish this existence from what the idea means, we must, I quite agree, call the idea a new creation. But we must also add that this new creation does not necessarily, as we have seen, qualify the meaning of the idea, for that meaning in each case, we have seen, remains an idea of past pleasure. Now this ordinary instance raises, I submit, serious if not fatal difficulties. inexplicable by the law of contiguity. If the pleasure of eating became associated with the sight of food by repetition, it ought easily to be revived whenever we concentrate attention on a well-furnished dinner-table. The pleasure depends on the satisfaction of an appetite, and when the appetite has disappeared it disappears also, and cannot be revived by mere association' (*Analytic Psychology*, i. 271–2). On this I would remark first that the facts are not quite as Dr. Stout has described them, and in particular I would call attention to one point among others which he has here ignored. In the clear absence of appetite or in the clear presence also even of disgust, I still may remember that I *was* pleased. And an apparent fact of this kind is surely something to be reckoned with. And in the second place Dr. Stout's remarks seem to rest on the assumption that, wherever there is an association of which one member is present, the associated element must under all conditions come up, and perhaps even come up easily. But does Dr. Stout himself really accept this principle? His argument, if I understand it rightly, would prove of the ideas say of mastication and deglutition, or say again the idea of vomiting, that, unless these *always* are aroused by the sight of some food, they cannot be associated with it at all, but in every possible case, where they arise, are fresh and further resultants. But is not, I would ask, such a principle false, and does not the application of it bring us into collision with fact?

Dr. Stout's general view as to pleasure and pain is, I think, on the whole stated admirably, and it is perhaps in consequence of this that he is driven at times into a fatal *impasse*, and, as it seems to me, tries to extricate himself by arguments that will not bear examination. In illustration of what I must be allowed to call the paradox that all pleasure involves conation, he adduces the fact that if a cat is resting comfortably, it resists interference (ii. 304–5). But this seems precisely the old fallacy about pleasure and activity which I once before tried to refute (*E.* xiv. 264) in the form in which it was offered by Dr. Bain. You surely cannot, because under altered conditions a thing becomes this or that, treat it as actually being so now and without those conditions, except of course by a licence. And it is, I would venture to add, one thing to postulate, on what rightly or wrongly seems sufficient evidence, the existence of conation everywhere where we find pleasure, and quite another thing to undertake actually to verify the presence of this conation everywhere in fact. But on this point I may probably have failed to interpret Dr. Stout rightly.

One way of meeting these would be, I suppose, to argue that the present reaction has stages and at all events is mixed, and that the various stages, or generally the various ingredients of this general mixture, somehow distribute and arrange themselves rightly without the operation of association, and thus not only belong, but are recognized as belonging, to their several excitants. I cannot think that such an account would prove satisfactory, and it seems to lead to complications, and to call for elucidation which I could not supply. But another way of explanation would of course consist in the denial of the fact to be explained. One might assert that there is not in fact any such thing as a pleasant idea of past unpleasantness or an unpleasant idea of past pleasure, and that it is only by an illusion that we think that we possess these things. But for myself I am unable to see how such a position could be maintained. And hence the above difficulty appears to myself to call for very serious consideration.[1]

(2) The next question I should like to raise is a difficulty about the requisite lapse of time. In ideas of the

---

[1] There is a difficulty here, I admit, which attaches itself also to the view which I think the true one. In order to have an idea of pleasure I consider that we must *to some extent* have an actual pleasure, for I accept it as a principle that to some extent an idea must be what it means. But on the view which I adopt we have here an associative bond to unite specially the two elements, in addition to whatever original union there may be apart from that bond. And I consider this to be a very great advantage on my side.

An interesting but very difficult question arises here as to our perception of the different strengths of pleasure and pain. We indubitably in fact do perceive these degrees, and we at least seem to have ideas of them. In fact I should say that we can without doubt actually have a strong idea of a weak pleasure or a weak idea of a strong pleasure. A question, however, must be raised as to whether we can perceive different strengths of pleasure *as such*. It is necessary, I think, to say that we can even do this. I do not of course mean that we can have a 'more' of pleasure without a 'more' of what is pleasant, but that we can, beside a 'more' of what is pleasant, actually have a moreness of and in pleasure. If we follow the facts we must, I think, suppose a scale of degrees in pleasure as such, a scale which can be attended to and made into an idea. On this ground again the paradox that we cannot attend to or have an idea of pleasure would seem not easy to maintain.

pleasant the pleasantness at least *seems* to be an integral part of the meaning; and, if it is not so, and has to be on every occasion freshly made, is there always enough of time, when we think rapidly, for this new creation to supervene in each case? Or if there is not time enough, are we to be said here to think only in words and without a genuine meaning? To one who like myself considers pleasure to be an essential element in beauty it seems hard to suppose that, when we use aesthetic ideas, this element of their meaning is in each case a fresh effect of the other elements. But even apart from this special instance of aesthetic ideas, how is the general difficulty about this lapse of time to be dealt with?

In asserting the law of Association to hold of pleasure we must of course remember that, unless there are distinctions in pleasure of such a kind and to such an extent as most certainly seem wanting, the connexion cannot be taken to hold from the mere aspect of pleasantness to this or that pleasant thing in distinction from other things. The bond will hold from the side of pleasure but generically. On the other side, however, from the thing to the pleasure, the special association will hold. But such a one-sided arrangement does not seem to me to be really exceptional or to create any real difficulty.

These points which I have mentioned may perhaps have been discussed satisfactorily and may very well, I admit, have been so discussed without my knowing it. But if this is not so, I venture to think that we have difficulties here of which some serious account should be taken.

XXIII

SOME REMARKS ON CONATION

[*First published in* MIND, N.S. X, No. 40, 437–54. *October*, 1901.]

IN the following paper I intend to remark on certain aspects of conation. I hope to supplement it with others which will discuss some further questions about volition and desire. But I cannot even in the end attempt to treat these subjects completely, and in these pages especially my object is very limited. I find myself with a view more or less definite about desire and conation, a view which in the main I accepted long ago, and which I have seen no good reason to abandon. I find on the other hand certain doctrines taught by some writers whom I sincerely respect, doctrines which at least appear to be incompatible with that view which I have adopted. And I am confident that none of us has ideas so absurd that, when understood, they should have no truth. Hence I am going to set down about conation some things which to myself appear to be true, in the hope that some one will explain how and why to him they are not true, or how being true there is perhaps no one who in the end holds views in collision with them.

The main contention of this paper is that conation is something which we experience, that it is complex and has in itself some inseparable aspects which therefore are experienced, that apart from these experienced aspects conation has lost its true meaning, and that the use of it in another meaning, if not illegitimate, is in psychology at least dangerous. Certainly I do not deny that there is experience below the level of conation proper. And I do not deny that this experience has features which survive at a higher level, though in part more or less transformed there, and that these features go to constitute that which we call conation. An inquiry into the nature and limits of such a lower experience would in its own place be important and even necessary, but it falls beyond the narrow scope of this article. We are to ask here about the minimum which can be taken to be contained in conation proper. How much of that minimum can exist, and under what precise form it exists, where conation is not reached, is a question which cannot be considered here. On the one hand, to repeat, I should agree that below conation there are certain aspects or elements which we also find in conation proper. On the other hand I must not be taken to admit that any one of the aspects of conation exists outside of it exactly as it exists within it. And I fear that with due regard for the limited purpose of this paper I could make no attempt to be more explicit.

Confining ourselves then to conation where it exists at its proper level, we discover there in every case some inseparable characters. These essential features are the aspect of a 'not-myself' and of a 'myself' hindered by this, together with an idea of a change containing the removal of the hindrance, an idea with which the 'myself' feels itself one. And all these aspects must be experienced at once if conation is to exist. The appeal is of course made to the experience of the reader, and it would, I think, be useless to attempt a long exposition.

The first question is whether we can experience conation at all. I am not concerned here to define conation accurately and to ask whether, for example, we could properly apply the term to all desire. But taking conation here as a general head under which fall desire, striving, and impulse, our question would seem to admit of but one answer. When I strive or desire I certainly can feel and be aware more or less distinctly that I am striving or desiring. This seems plain, and no one, I believe, could deny it except perhaps in the interest of some theory, nor indeed do I see how to make it plainer. Whether we may ever use conation as the name of some state of which I am not at all aware as conation, is of course another point to which I shall return. But for the present I shall assume that conation can be experienced as such, and it is about this conation of which we are aware that I am at present to speak. When we experience this, what is it that we feel and experience?

When I am conscious of striving, there is an existence, a 'not-myself', to be altered, and I find that I am aware of this existence. The point is to me so clear that I cannot try to make it clearer. But the objection may come that what I strive to change may at times be my own self, and therefore that this existence cannot properly be called a not-self. I however reply that whatever is felt as an existence opposed to the self is for this purpose a not-self, and that in conation such an opposition is always experienced. And, as I shall come back to this point, I will at present deal with it no further. But in conation I am not only aware of a not-self, but I am aware of it also as something to be changed. In conation I therefore must possess and use an idea of the change. I have in other words an end, however vague, and I have it also in my knowledge; and if so, I must have an idea of a 'to be', and without this idea there is no conation. This second point once again seems to me almost too clear for exposition, but it is necessary here to guard against two fatal misunderstandings.

(i) It will be objected first that we may have conation, and may even experience conation, without any idea of an end. There are impulses (it will be said) instinctive and acquired which are indeed directed on an object and directed to an end, and yet in these no idea of the end need be present to the mind. And there are again the facts of felt need and dim desire where want and impulse are experienced, but where we certainly do not know the goal in which we seek satisfaction. Now (it will be urged) there may fairly be a difference of opinion here as to what and how much we in each case experience, but in some of these cases at least it is clear that we have no idea of an end, and on the other hand it is equally clear that conation is present. And the existence of blind conation, it will thus be said, cannot possibly be denied. But in answer to this objection I must insist that if there is a conation it is not wholly blind, and that where we have real blindness we have something which is not really a conation.

In some of these alleged blind states there in fact is certainly a vague and ill-defined idea, a point which I shall soon attempt to explain, while in others on the other hand I agree that no idea of an end is present in fact. In the feeling of want, for example, I may be aware of pain and uneasiness and of restless movement, and yet in some cases at least there may be no idea of what would satisfy, and therefore, I should add, certainly no conation at all and no appetite proper. And of course in some 'impulses' I should agree that the subject is impelled to be active, and that the activity is directed to a certain end, and I should agree also that while active he may have no idea at all of this end. But then I should deny that such 'impulses' are cases of conation, for I should insist that in these no conation is experienced. Something is experienced there, I should say, which also enters into and is experienced in conation proper.[1] What are present there are certain aspects of conation proper, and these aspects, given another element, really are transformed into and become an actual conation, and they normally in fact are developed into it. And so *you*, standing outside, transfer covertly this wanting element from your own experience to the mind of the other subject. Hence through confusion you call the fact by a name which belongs to the complete state, a state which in fact and actually is not being experienced by this subject at all. Or else, perhaps, you knowingly for the sake of convenience apply the term in a mutilated sense. In either case I consider your procedure indefensible, and the issue, it seems to me, may be raised in the following way. Take an instance of conation where the idea of a 'to be' is present, then take another state of mind without any such idea or, to avoid objection, let us say another state of mind so far as it is without the idea.[2] Be sure that

[1] I would once more here remind the reader that I cannot in this article attempt to explain how much of conation in the proper sense can exist outside conation. My object here is merely to insist on certain features without which there is really no conation.

[2] I am not attempting in this article to show where conation is and is not experienced as such. I will only say here that there are assertions about

the idea has been removed wholly and utterly and is not covertly supplied. Then see whether, in passing from one of these experiences to the other, you do not feel an essential difference between them. If you do not find this difference I confess that I cannot proceed, though I am unable to believe that you have properly performed the operation. But, if you find it, I urge that this difference is essential to conation, and that where it is wanting conation is not present. For the conation of which I am now speaking is, I would remind the reader, experienced conation. And if you reply that this essential difference is not essential to conation, I ask for the name of that state to which really it is essential. So far as I see you give no name to what I call conation, a state which, as we have now recognized, essentially differs from what you call by that name. We will not argue about names, and I will leave you to find that which you think suitable. And then I should repeat, conation involves the idea of an end, and without this there is no conation at all in the sense of experienced conation. And whatever name you substitute for conation my contention will remain unaffected. It will be simply a question of writing one word for the other and of employing probably a bad name instead of a good one. Only I must insist that you do not pass tacitly in future, wherever it pleases you, from one meaning to the other.

(ii) 'But', it may be said, 'there remains a difficulty about the *idea*. If we admit that conation cannot be experienced without an awareness of something "to be", yet in many cases where really this genuine feeling exists you cannot show an idea. We may for instance have a perceived thing and a desire for that thing, and may yet have no image at all.' This objection, however, would rest on a common prejudice about the nature of ideas.[1] It is

the omnipresence of this experience which I am quite unable to reconcile with fact. Cp. *E*. xiv. 260.

[1] I am here taking no account of those who, while more or less assenting to the substance of what is urged in the text, would nevertheless wish to confine the use of the word 'idea'. This is a difference merely with regard

believed that, in order to have something ideal which qualifies an object, we must have an image or images existing
separate or at least separable from that object. I say
nothing here about the further possible question as to the
alleged necessity for words, except to dismiss it as here
certainly not worth discussing. But this identification of
the ideal with images is surely a mistake. If, to have ideas,
we had to wait till we possessed such images, assuredly,
I should say, we never should get any ideas or could ever
begin to think at all. And this is a point to be insisted on
everywhere and generally, and not specially with regard
to desire and conation. The first form of the ideal is a
sensible existence modified in its content so as to be incompatible with itself as merely perceived. In intellectual
perception a suggested modification of this kind is usually
accepted by the perceived object, and the object is thus
altered accordingly and so ceases in its old form to exist.
There is hence no awareness here of anything ideal at all.
But under other circumstances, and always we may say
in desire,[1] the case is altered. The perceived existence
there is qualified in a way incompatible with itself, and yet
it cannot simply accept this new qualification and so cease
to exist as at first perceived. On the contrary it persists
as before, and yet is modified also in an incompatible
manner. And in the awareness of this qualification of the
perceived fact, a qualification discordant with the perceived fact, we gain our first experience of the nature of
an idea. An obvious instance is a perceived fruit which I
cannot reach, while yet I feel it, as we say, in my hands or
in my mouth. The fruit itself is qualified here at once
actually and ideally. The ideal qualification does not or
need not consist in separated images, and yet it is an idea
and is the end which is desired by me. If I may be allowed

to terminology. It seems to me all-important to extend the application of
the term 'idea' and to keep any restricted use under the general head. I
am, however, far from denying the value of distinction here.

[1] If our wants could be satisfied at once as they arose, should we know
what appetite means? I do not discuss this question, but I think it turns on
what we mean by 'at once'.

to quote a passage from a former article, we have here a 'state where the presented is qualified ideally so as to collide with itself, and where this discrepant content is desired without being a separate image. A common instance of this would be desire for (the continuance of) a feeling which exists. And it was when sensation had been overpowered by its idealized self, that desire, as we saw, almost ceased before the moment of possession. This again is how we can have a desire without knowledge, a dim desire with no clear object, as in the usual example of the sexual impulse. It is not that we have *no* idea, for, if so, our state would be something lower than desire. But the idea is a common element, a something in a number of psychical states, which pleases and is not in harmony with these states as they are, and its increase is felt to lead us beyond, we know not where. We desire the presented, but we desire it with an ideal qualification. We need have no image, and yet even here we want to realize an idea.'[1]

It is by this principle that we can distinguish between appetite and the mere feeling of need or want. In the last phrase I must be permitted once more to remark on the fatal ambiguity of the word 'of'.[2] If the need or want is felt as such, we certainly possess an idea, however vague and general, of that which we want, an idea which, we have seen, need not be separated from the object as perceived. With such an idea we have, normally, also appetite. But without that idea we have but more or less localized feelings of discomfort and restlessness, and these sensations are not feelings *of* want except for a further knowledge and recognition existing in an outside mind or coming to our own by later reflection.

---

[1] *M.*o.s.xiii. 23 [*E.* xiv. 269]. I would refer the reader further to the context of this passage, and again to my *Appearance*, 547 = 606. It is possible to object to the presence everywhere of an idea in conation and will on the ground that, if this were so, we could not will to have an idea without already possessing it. But the objection is met by insisting in these cases on the genuine presence of an idea of the idea. I have referred to this point on p. 270 of the above article, and had previously discussed it, *M.*o.s.xi. 313 and 319 [*E.* x. 190 and 197].

[2] Cp. *E.* x. 197.

We have seen that in conation we experience a not-myself together with an idea of its alteration, and I will now proceed to point out a further aspect of our experience. In conation and desire I feel that *I* am desiring and striving, that I am being hindered by the not-myself, that I am something and yet that I am not what I would be. In brief, in conation the self is experienced as itself qualified by the idea of the altered object. It is thus felt to be in collision with the object as not-altered, and without this experienced aspect there is once more no conation at all. The appeal is again to the observation of the reader, and nothing, I think, would be gained by a lengthy attempt at exposition. I will, however, try to remove some misunderstandings.

How, it may be asked, can this hindered self be experienced unless it is experienced as something concrete, and how can it be anything concrete when, as we saw, the self can even oppose itself in desire to its self? Where the self is experienced as a concrete hindrance, how can we also there have a concrete experience of the self as hindered? But the self, I reply, never can make an object of its whole self at once. It can at any one time so attend only to certain elements of its content. These are distinguished from it and so being distinguished make a not-self, but the whole of feeling from which they are distinguished remains and still is felt. This whole is concrete, and only because this concrete substance is actually experienced is it possible ever to experience a self or a not-self at all. I at least do not know what is meant by the experience of an object or a not-self, unless the self is also at the same time experienced inseparably with it.[1] And I do not know what is meant by such an experience of the self, unless that self is something concrete and is so actually experienced. The same remark applies to our state when we merely perceive an object as given to us. Unless the 'us', the self, is here experienced as a concrete content, I cannot myself imagine

---

[1] I do not mean that the self must be experienced at the same level, that, e.g., as against a perception the self must be perceived. This would be a very serious error.

how we are to go about to feel it as passive. And with regard to conation and desire the case seems to stand as follows. We have before us a not-self which is an object, and we have before us an idea of a 'to be' which again is an object. We experience further our self in collision with the not-self, but that self, though experienced, is (so far as the conation goes) not before us and it is not an object, except so far as, and to that extent up to which, it enters into the content of the idea of the 'to be'.[1] On the other hand, our self must be felt as a whole and felt also as one with the idea of the 'to be'. And if the self is not so felt, there is at once an end of what we experience as conation. And I would appeal on this point to the judgement of the reader who has no theory to save.

'But', it may be further objected, 'my self is something which goes beyond the moment. It is the unity of my life, and how can this be felt as the mere content of one experience? It is more than one single experience and therefore it cannot really be felt within one.' But it seems possible, I reply, so to feel it when a man stakes here and now his entire being on the accomplishment of some end. And the whole objection seems in fact to rest on a misunderstanding. Certainly it is desirable to ask about the real nature of that self which goes beyond the moment, and to inquire how far and in what sense it is identical, and is felt to be identical, with that which at one time is experienced. But this task, necessary in its own place, is here not necessary, and, however important these questions are, I may pass them by. For my contention was that in conation the self in fact is experienced against a not-self, and by urging that the self is more than this experience and goes beyond it, you obviously do not disprove that contention. You do not disprove it unless you are prepared

---

[1] Usually and, perhaps it might be contended, even normally, the self to some extent does thus enter in. I have an idea of myself for instance as already touching or eating the fruit which I desire. The more prevalent doctrine, I believe, is that in desire this *must* always be the case. I am not, however, able to accept this view as correct (see *E.* xiv. 267). I hope in a future article on volition to return to this matter.

to insist that, because the self is more, it must therefore be less and in fact does not enter into my experience at all. On a doctrine of this kind I shall lower down have something to say, but at present I will meet it by an appeal to fact. I find my self in fact so experienced, and if upon any theory that cannot happen, so much the worse for the theory.

'But', I may further be asked, 'may we not have an outbreak from some tendency in the subject or self, and may not this outbreak produce a characteristic experience? May it not be directed to a certain end, and yet, as experienced, not contain the element of a hindered self?' Yes, I should reply, in the main I agree that this contention is sound. But, on the other hand, I must urge that it is irrelevant and a mere return to the confusion which I have already pointed out. Such an experience is not a conation for the self which feels it. It is not experienced as a conation, and therefore it is not properly a conation at all. For, I would repeat, it is conation as experienced which at present is in question.

We have seen that in conation or desire we have the aspects of not-self and self and an idea of a 'to be'. I wish now to insist that all these aspects must be experienced together and must be felt as one whole, and that, failing this, the experience of conation is destroyed. I have not to ask here if any felt state can precede and can be experienced without any consciousness of a not-self or self, nor have I to ask whether the practical attitude is prior to the theoretical attitude, if indeed either is prior. Such questions, however important, may here be disregarded. I am urging that as soon as conation is experienced, whenever that is, it must contain certain features and must also be felt as one whole. Now 'feeling' I use for experience, or if you will for knowledge, so far as that experience or knowledge does not imply an object, and I should myself give as a very obvious instance a simple pain or pleasure, or again those elements of our Cœnaesthesia to which we do not attend. I am myself averse to the use of the term 'knowledge'[1] here, because that term naturally tends to imply that there is an object before me and a distinction experienced between the knower and the known. But within feeling there is no such distinction between the experience and the experienced or between the known and the knowing. If it is knowledge, it is that form of knowledge which does not contain a not-self as opposed to the self.

But everything that in any sense whatever we know or experience must, so far as it enters into our experience, be felt as ours. The most abstract thought, for instance, of the most remote thing must also and as well, while I have it, be an element in my felt self. The thing is not a *mere* feeling of course, and, so far as you regard its content as referred to a subject (so far, that is, as it is thought of and is taken as a thing), it is so far not a feeling at all. For you have got it now as abstracted from that immediate whole into which, taken otherwise, it enters, and enters as a mere feature. And an experience or knowledge of any kind which is not thus felt as now and mine, is in my opinion a mere illusion. Everything, we may put it so,

[1] A difficulty is caused here by the ambiguity of the term 'knowledge'. This is used on the one hand as equivalent to 'experience' or at least to 'familiarity' in the widest sense of these terms, and on the other hand it is restricted to a theoretic state and to what may be called the cognition of an object. I cannot of course ask here in what cognition consists, and whether beside an object it does not also involve an idea and judgement. But, passing this by, we may say that knowledge is used either in a very broad sense for experience or in a narrower sense as limited to knowledge *of* or *about* an object. And hence on the one hand it sounds absurd to say that we do not know pleasure and pain or conation, and it sounds absurd again to speak of these states as being states of knowledge. The fact is that we naturally pass from the state in which we merely, for instance, feel a pleasure or pain to the state in which we feel it and also make it an object. The view that we cannot make an object of a pleasure or pain, I may remark in passing, is to my mind quite indefensible. Hence, because I can and do make these things into objects (as indeed I am able to do in the end with everything), and because there is a natural tendency to confuse our state when we do this with our state when we merely feel, it sounds absurd to deny knowledge in the case of an experience of pleasure or pain. But when we speak strictly I think it is better to deny, and, when we realize what we mean, the absurdity disappears.

that in any way whatever comes within our experience, is a feeling, though in our experience there are some things which also and at the same time in certain aspects are more than felt, and, if taken merely so, are not felt. Thus in conation the not-self which is an object is also felt as an element of my whole state, and the idea of the 'to be', which is an object, is once more felt as another element there. And the self, to which the not-self is opposed and which finds itself at one with the idea, is both felt as mine in the same sense in which the object is mine, and it is felt as mine again in a further and a higher sense.[1] These several aspects are all felt, and they are each not felt as separate but together in connexion with one another as

[1] I do not discuss this last point here. It will be taken up in other articles. It is a matter which in one sense I agree is inexplicable, but at the same time I may hope to convey to the reader my meaning with regard to it. This may be done, perhaps, briefly in the following way. We find in conation both the theoretical and the practical relation of self to an object. And for the purpose of this article we may take these relations as existing and as really inseparable, and we need raise no question either as to any priority between them or as to anything that may have preceded one or both. But while taking them here as really inseparable, let us by an abstraction separate and consider first the theoretical relation by itself. In this experience there is an object for me, let us say a fruit. This object is in the first place (*a*) felt as mine, as an element, that is, in my whole felt state, and it is also in the second place (*b*) felt as something other than myself. And my self, so far, it will be understood, is not an object at all. Let us now, however, add and restore to our abstraction the practical relation and let us note the difference. There will be here also an idea, let us say of eating the fruit. This idea is itself an object beside and against the first object, or more correctly, perhaps, we may be said to have a new complex object containing both. Now the idea, being an object, is like the first object felt (*a*) as an element in my whole state, and (*b*) again, like the first object, it is felt as a something not myself. But the idea is also (*c*) as against the first object felt as mine and one with me. My self feels that this idea (which, so far as it is an object, is an other) is in its opposition to the first object not an other to myself. On the contrary, the idea is felt as the expression of my self against the first object, which is now in two senses something alien to me. If the reader will consider this brief statement with attention, he will I hope realize the meaning of that special sense in which in conation the idea is felt as one with myself. I will add that even in the practical relation I do not myself consider that the self necessarily enters into the content of the idea and so becomes an object to itself. This is, however, a point to be discussed in a future article.

integral features in one whole. This whole is 'known' and is experienced, though as a whole it is not an object. We may of course go on to make it an object, but, so far as we do this, we have induced a new state of mind. We have got now a new felt whole with an added element, but we have still a whole in which everything on the one hand is felt as mine, and where on the other hand the feeling of my self is not and cannot be an object.[1]

We have seen that conation is experienced and has a complex content, and we have noticed the elements of that complex. We have further seen that conation must be felt as one, as a single whole with certain aspects, all of which must be experienced if conation proper is to exist. And I would recommend this result not as a theory but as a fact to be observed by the reader, and I am even confident that, if the reader will observe disinterestedly the thing for himself, he will find it to be very much as I have described it. He may consider that what I have set down has been more or less mal-observed and misinterpreted, but I think that in the main perhaps he will agree about the facts, if, that is, he does not come to the work with a theory to save. And since the result which I have stated is on the whole not mine and is far from being novel, it seems to me strange that some psychologists should treat this result, altogether or in part, as being something unknown or non-existent. And yet the outcome of a failure to notice such an apparent fact as we have described, and the outcome of a further insistence perhaps, on the part of some, that the self itself is not experienced at all, and itself does not enter as an element into the content of the known—seems not satisfactory. Any such doctrine seems not only in itself contrary to fact, but in its working also it appears to break down. For in the end no one, even to save a theory, can

[1] So far as the conation remains a conation, it still must be felt as such. So far as it is made a mere object it is not a conation, and the making it an object may under some conditions destroy it. To make an object of a conation may even be said, if this is taken in the abstract, to tend to destroy it. But, the conditions being complex, the result will of course always vary with them, and the general effect may be to intensify the conation. I cannot, however, discuss this subject here.

deny the fact of self-consciousness. Somehow the self as a reality or as an appearance is known, and in the end somehow the self, whether truly or falsely, does get into our experience and knowledge. But how, if it does not itself enter into the experienced, the self could ever be known, or ever in any way could be thought of or imagined, remains an insoluble problem. We have here a question that may be asked or may be ignored, but will never, I think, be answered intelligibly.[1]

We have seen that conation, if experienced, must possess certain aspects, and that apart from these it is not experienced conation. And taking this as shown, I will go on to deal shortly with a further point. Why, it may be asked, even if conation is not in fact experienced except as you contend, should we not for some purposes employ the term when taken otherwise? Now if this question is asked with respect to metaphysics I wish to say nothing here. And if the question were asked with regard to some branch of natural science I should not venture to say anything, because all that I could say would be that whatever ideas, however fictitious, best work there I believe to be best and right. But if the same question is raised about psychology I may answer briefly as follows. If you take a term like conation which stands for an experienced fact, and apply it to something else which is not so experienced, you clearly so far are making use of a fiction.[2] And about this fiction we must ask a twofold question which is vital. Is it in itself a good way in which to explain some psychical facts, and does it when so used entail mischievous consequences? Now I would not deny that this fiction can

---

[1] In much of the above I am once more urging what I had to urge long ago in my *Ethical Studies*. I have always, I hope, been at bottom faithful to that cardinal truth which I was so fortunate as to learn early—the truth that what matters is the self that is experienced, and that there is nothing else whatever which matters. Between a self outside the experienced and no self at all there is in the end really no difference.

[2] I am not objecting to the general employment of fictions in psychology. On the contrary I think them necessary, and justifiable so far as they are useful and not injurious.

serve as a legitimate way of explanation, though when it is taken on the whole I venture to think that it does not work successfully. But on the other hand its use seems open incidentally to a very serious objection. For psychology surely has to observe and to study psychical facts, and among these facts, we have now agreed, is conation in its genuine form as something experienced. If therefore in psychology you will insist on employing conation in another form also, you will have two meanings of conation which you will be bound throughout and everywhere to keep in mind and to distinguish. Your working fiction must not be allowed to distract you from the attentive study of the genuine fact; and the full nature of the genuine fact, when you apply your fiction, must be kept resolutely out of view. This has to be done within one and the same study, and any failure is liable to make mischief. Now if you can yourself perform this feat, you must be different I think from the majority of psychologists,[1] and further, if you did yourself perform this feat, it is almost certain that your readers would not follow you. If then we admit that the feat, if actually performed, may in some ways be useful, on the other hand the attempt to perform it on the part of your readers and yourself would probably result

---

[1] I find it hard to believe that a writer clear as Dr. Stout usually is distinguishes always between an experienced conation and what he would call a 'quasi-conative tendency'. I venture to think that he is himself at times thus led into ambiguity. We may agree to his statement (*Manual*, II. viii, §§ 5, 6) that 'a pleasing process is a process which tends to maintain itself'. But when we hear that 'it will not be denied that there is at least an unconscious tendency to continue a pleasing experience until we have had enough of it', we may be forced to protest. It is far from certain that these two propositions are the same. I should myself agree to the first, though as to its meaning there is much to be said (*E*. xiv). But I must deny the second until at least I have been told what it does and does not involve. I cannot admit the assertion that pleasure is *always* the result of a satisfied conation, or even that it *always* implies a conation—if, that is, conation stands for what we experience as such, or even for an unconscious striving of our whole nature. But if on the other hand the unconscious conation is that of a mere element in our selves, Dr. Stout's language concerning it would hardly be defensible. If in short conation is used for an unconscious tendency, I think ambiguity will most probably follow.

in more or less of confusion. And in this confusion the genuine fact to be observed would tend to become lost to view. But in any case I would end this paper with the appeal which it has been its main purpose to urge. Let us at least begin with an attempt to observe in its entirety the experienced fact of conation. Let us endeavour to find out what it contains, and, if that is complex, let us seek to analyse it and to set out its aspects; and, if in the fact there is nothing complex, let us try at least to point to the fact and to distinguish it more or less intelligibly from other facts or elements or aspects of fact. And if what I have contended for here with regard to conation is really incorrect or superfluous, still I must think that it would be better if its incorrectness or its superfluity were shown, and that from that exhibition there would at least result some gain in clearness.

It may naturally be asked whether the objection, which I have raised to the use of 'conation' in any sense other than that of experienced conation, applies equally in the case of a term like 'activity'. Is this term to be confined in psychology to the activity which is apprehended? I have long ago stated that in my opinion it need not be so confined.[1] We commonly speak of the activity of a volcano or of a drug, and may even talk of an effort or a struggle on the part of some material object, just as again we also may speak of its passivity. I am very far from condemning

---

[1] See E. xii. 225–7, and E. xiv. 281–3. I have also more recently touched on this distinction in $A.R.$ 545=604. I was led to speak there of 'the question, What is the content of activity as it appears to the soul at first, *in distinction from it as it is for an outside observer*, or for the soul later on?' I observe that in making an extract from this passage for a controversial purpose Professor Ward (*Naturalism*, ii, p. 244) has made his extract end before and short of the words I have now italicized, and has thus himself actually caused the passage to ignore a distinction which it really contains. Professor Ward, I must presume, was not aware of the meaning attached to the above words, and indeed his misapprehension with regard to my meaning may be described as general. With regard to this extract the reader may perhaps agree with me that the result, if unfortunate, is instructive.

this language even when applied to a material object, and it would surely be absurd if I condemned it when applied to what is higher. We are right, I think, in using these terms either of the soul or again of the self as a whole, or again of any element in the self or soul. A fixed idea would of course be an instance where we might be almost compelled to apply such terms to an element or a group of elements. On the other hand we must distinguish such activity, which is, we may say, only in itself, or in other words only for an outsider, from the activity which is also for that which is active—the activity which is experienced (*a*) properly in the sense of being apprehended as activity, or (*b*) improperly in the sense of being attended by some feeling which is not itself an apprehension of activity. Whether, however, in the last case we can properly say that the activity is for the mind must certainly (to say the very least) be questioned.

If we observe the above distinctions, and if we do not try to transcend the region of psychical events and their laws (cp. *E*. xxii), I think we may safely use the term activity within psychology. On the other hand I do not see how psychology can rightly ignore the question of the origin and nature of our apprehension of ourselves as active and of course also as passive.[1]

The term 'conation' is however, I think, in a different position. Its application to the state of a thing which is not aware of any striving, though not new, is, I presume, not established in psychology. And 'conation' does to my mind suggest naturally an actual awareness of the fact of striving. If, however, we cannot abstain from a different use, we should at least attempt in some way to guard ourselves throughout from ambiguity and confusion. We should, I submit, have some way of distinguishing clearly a conation which is not experienced at all, or not experi-

---

[1] A question naturally may be raised as to the minimum which is involved in such an apprehension, and as to whether we can be aware of activity and of passivity in a lower sense, a sense which does not involve agency proper. I have discussed this question at some length in a later article of the present series.

enced as a conation, from a conation which is really experienced in that character. To confuse these three distinct meanings must surely upon any view be inadmissible.

The great importance of the matter on one hand, and on the other hand my apparent failure at least in part to convey my meaning, may perhaps excuse my offering some further desultory remarks on the topic of activity. Some writers wish to build on this as an ultimate fact, and this is the position taken (as I understand) by Professor Ward in his book on *Naturalism*. I recognize, as we all must, the great merit of Professor Ward's work, but with regard to this fundamental point I am unable to see that he has made any serious attempt to explain and to defend his view. I venture to think that he has even failed at least in part to understand the objections to which it is exposed. And though I readily admit that there may be some misunderstanding on my side, I cannot suppose that Professor Ward's position does not call for further explanation.

(*a*) In the first place, however much activity is 'a fact of experience', a question may still be raised as to the ultimate truth and reality of activity. Apparently Professor Ward would consider that any question of this kind is inadmissible, but I have been unable to ascertain what his position on this point really is. He does not of course say that activity, having no sense or meaning, therefore cannot have a meaning which is unsatisfactory, and that we therefore cannot be called upon to state the sense in which the term is used. Professor Ward does not again (as I understand) claim that the content of activity is simple, and that in this it is like, for instance, the aspects of mere pleasure or mere sensation, and is a simple experience which we define not by internal analysis but by designation. And in short with regard to the objection raised against the internal inconsistency of activity I am unable to find in what Professor Ward's answer consists. On the other hand I have been unable to discover how, if such an objection is not met, his doctrine can be sustained.

(*b*) And the objection which can be urged from the side of our apprehension of activity has not, I venture to think, been met by Professor Ward. If against a 'Naturalist' it is argued that the 'Naturalist' is in possession of an idea, which possession, if his own theory is true, is in fact not intelligible, Professor Ward, I understand, is prepared to endorse this argument and to agree that such an objection, if made good, is fatal. But he seems hardly to realize that the same kind of objection with the same possible consequence has to be answered by himself with regard to activity. If a man is in possession of this idea and if he cannot account for the possession, his doctrine must somewhere, I submit, be fatally defective. This is why even beyond psychology our apprehension of activity must be dealt with and gives rise to a most important problem. And a writer can hardly (it seems to me) get rid of this problem by insisting that he at least distinguishes the fact of activity from our consciousness of the fact—for such an answer would not, at least to my mind, appear to be relevant to the issue. The real issue to my mind is whether Professor Ward being in possession of the idea of activity —a fact which I presume is admitted—can give an answer to the question how he has become possessed of that idea, an answer, I mean, which judged by his own view is intelligible and consistent. And I cannot find that Professor Ward has even addressed himself seriously to this question.[1] The reader, I take it, is not helped by the assurance that activity and passivity are 'facts of experience' and that we have an 'immediate experience' of them. For no one until otherwise informed can know what such

[1] I presume that I should be wrong in taking the footnote on p. 44 of the article on 'Psychology' to be an attempt to deal with the subject. In the *Journal of Speculative Philosophy* for October, 1882, p. 378, Professor Ward has himself noticed the above question as one which requires an answer, and has gone on to indicate what that answer might be. But if in the year 1900 I tried to show that the brief indication was unintelligible or untenable, I might well be accused of serious unfairness. It is to be presumed, I imagine, that Professor Ward must have modified his opinion as to the objection's force, or as to the answer which could be produced to meet it. I at least understand him now to proceed as if his foundation were no longer threatened by any such objection which, if not met, would be fatal. In fact, if this were not so, the reader, I submit, would have just ground for complaint.

ambiguous phrases are meant to convey, and I may perhaps be allowed to illustrate this by a familiar example.
If an unknown drug is administered to me without my
knowledge I may next day have an immediate experience
of its effects in my feelings and thoughts, but if I said,
'This is why I talk and am able to talk of this drug', my
assertion might be criticized. And even if I insisted perhaps that nothing else in my experience ever felt like that,
I should hardly by this addition have made myself consistent. 'What you call your experience', I should be told,
'is one thing and the knowledge of this drug is another
thing. We fail to see how from the first you can arrive
at the second. Either your knowledge comes from elsewhere or it is no knowledge at all.' And the same thing
surely may be said about an experience of activity. If we
assert this experience to be in any sense an apprehension
of activity as activity, then, it seems to me, we are bound
to reply to the question, What is contained in this apprehension? If on the other hand what we experience does
not contain in itself, and so reveal to us, activity as activity,
we surely cannot refuse to reply when asked whence comes
the knowledge we possess. And if we cannot answer
intelligibly our account has surely broken down and as
a whole is ruined. And though one might be very wrong
in supposing this to be the case with Professor Ward's
doctrine of activity, yet until he has applied himself
seriously to meet the above objection, his position, so far
as I see, must be regarded as hypothetical or even as
precarious.

(c) It is, at least in the interest of philosophy, a matter
for regret that, before attempting to build Theism or anything else on such an ill-defined principle, Professor Ward
should not have given us a serious inquiry into its nature.
It is unprofitable surely to assert of the subject that it 'only
is, as it is active' (p. 245) when not even the meaning to
be given to such a formula is accurately fixed. It would, for
instance, be one thing to affirm that there is no being as
apart from activity, and another thing to attempt to deny
the distinction between them. To assert the mere identity

of being and activity does to my mind, after some attempts to avert this result, really end in what is not intelligible. But this, so far as I understand, is not the doctrine which Professor Ward adopts. And yet even the assertion that apart from activity there is no being at all is to my mind, if not clearly false, at least highly questionable, and on this point my state of mind is surely not exceptional. In short, whatever may be the view adopted by Professor Ward as to the relation of activity to being, there will I submit be difficulties which call for discussion and which cannot be disposed of by unexplained assertions. And at the risk of showing prejudice I will add that an inquiry by Professor Ward into these fundamental matters would be far more interesting than any attempt to build on hypotheses, or on assertions, or on the ruins of Naturalism.

XXIV

ON ACTIVE ATTENTION

[*First published in* MIND, N.S. xi, No. 41, 1–30. *January*, 1902.]

MY object in this paper is naturally not to attempt a complete treatment of its topic. I was led to write it because, in endeavouring to make clear the essence of volition, I found myself embarrassed constantly by the claims of attention. And rightly or wrongly I resolved to remove beforehand this recurring obstacle. I am therefore going to try, so far as I can, first to fix the meaning of active attention in accordance with the ordinary usage of language, and next to deal with a certain number of questions concerning it. That the usage of language to some extent varies I readily admit, but this variation is on the whole, I think, consistent with one central meaning. And in psychology to employ words in a sense opposed to their everyday signification is surely most ill-advised. It is difficult to suppose that the established use has no reason behind it. It is hard to imagine that the reader and the writer could ever wholly free their minds from the influence of association even if that were irrational. And in short, if we cannot employ terms in something like their ordinary sense, it is better to make new ones than to abuse and pervert the old. In the case of attention the abuse has even been carried to such a point that attention has been used to include and cover what every one does and must call a state of inattention. Such an attempt must naturally be short-lived, and we need not trouble ourselves to discuss it. It will repay us better to ask what is the ordinary meaning of our term and what that meaning implies. In this article I shall take attention always (unless the reader is warned) in the sense of *active* attending.[1]

[1] In this and in some other points I am departing to some extent (it seems not worth while to ask in detail how much) from an article in *M.* xi. No. 43 [*E.* x]. I must beg the reader also not to forget that throughout the

And I do not mean by this merely a state in which in some sense we may be said both to be active and to attend. I mean by it a state in which the attention itself is involved in and follows from an agency on our part.

I will at once proceed to consider the facts in the light of ordinary language. If I am sitting at ease with my mind not dwelling, as we say, on any subject, but wandering aimlessly as I regard some well-known scene, I am what every one would call inattentive generally. If we keep to ordinary language I am not attending here to anything at all. I am occupied by no one object, and even that mode of sensation and feeling, which may be said to predominate, is both diffused and feeble. Let us suppose now that a sudden and acute pain shoots through me, or that without warning a gun is fired close by, my state at once is altered. These things at once occupy me—there is no doubt of that—but am I to be said at once therefore to attend to them? If we use attention strictly for *active* attention we are unable to say this unconditionally. My state becomes attention if I go about consciously to get rid of my pain, or again if I begin to wonder what it is; and the same thing holds, of course with a difference, in the case of my hearing the shot. And I naturally and probably under the conditions do so go on to attend. But suppose that at once, recognizing the sound as the report of a gun, I throw myself flat on the ground, have we, with merely so much as that, got active attention? I should deny this, and I should deny it again even if my act has proceeded from the idea of escaping danger and has thus been a real volition.[1] For attention in the first place, if we follow the usage of language, must have an object, and in the second place it must involve some dwelling on and maintenance of that object, and so by consequence some delay. If an

present article I am assuming that volition consists in the self-realization of an idea. There is obviously no space in which to discuss this question here. I may refer the reader provisionally to *M*. xiii [*E*. xiv], and again to *M*. n.s. x [*E*. xxiii]. But I propose to deal with the question in future articles.

[1] For the justification of this see the references given above. The arbitrary limitation of volition to acts of choice is in my view quite indefensible.

animal hearing a sound pricks its ears and springs at once, and, as we say, by one action, we should not call that attending. But if it pricks its ears and then pauses, we at least perhaps have got attention. There must in brief be an object and its maintenance, and hence we must proceed to inquire about the meaning of these terms.

The mere having of an object or objects is by itself not attention. If I am sitting listlessly, as described above, it cannot be said that I perceive no object. For I certainly have objects before me though I attend to none of them. There may even be some prominent object in my visual field, or there may be some predominant object of hearing, such as the sound of a machine, and yet I need attend actively to neither. And I may be assailed by ideas which are certainly objects, and which maintain themselves, as we say, even actively, and yet I need not attend to them. I may succeed in not attending to them if and so far as, whenever they recur, I do nothing to maintain them but turn instinctively to something different. Thus to treat attention as the state generally where I have an object would be at least to come into collision with language. I do not attend by the mere perception or thought of an object. I begin to attend when in a further sense I go on to make this my object.

To attend in the proper sense I must by my action support and maintain an object in myself, but we have attention only so far as I maintain it theoretically or at least perceptively. Attention alters something, that is clear, and it is so far practical, but in the sense of altering the existence of the object it is not practical at all. If I turn a handle and so keep up a sound, that by itself is not attention and it need not even in any way imply it. If I turn the screw of a microscope, my act is not in itself attending, and it need not involve attention to the object, though in most cases in fact it does so. If again I move my eyes or my hands and so gain knowledge about an object, that action in the first place need not involve attention. And in any case, so far as I alter the actual thing, that alteration will fall outside of the attention itself. So far as in general my act can be said to create the existence of the object, we have so far not got attention at all. My act is attention only so far as it supports and maintains the ideal presence of the object in my perception. Thus attention is practical, but it is not practical except as altering myself and as so causing the object, unaltered by me, to maintain and to develop itself before me and in me.

In more familiar language we may say that my end in attention[1] is to maintain an object before me with a view to gain knowledge about it. My aim is thus to develop the object ideally for me as it is in itself, and so to know it. But in saying this we must be on our guard against a possible error, and we must not confine knowledge to a purely intellectual cognition. For clearly I may attend to a beautiful object, while I may not be seeking theoretically to understand and comprehend it. I may desire merely in a wide sense to apprehend the object, as when for instance I listen attentively to an air, or with attention observe the development of some pleasure or pain in myself.[2] The process in both cases is in a wide sense theoretical or ideal, because there is an object in it to which the whole process is referred as an adjective. The object preserves for me

---

[1] More accurately 'my end so far as attention is concerned'. My main end may be practical and may seek to alter the thing itself, and the ideal development of the thing in me may be a mere means involved in and consequent on this. See more below.

[2] So far as the pleasure or pain coming from an object qualifies as an adjective this object for me—or again is taken as an adjective qualifying my self—I can of course attend to it. Otherwise, and if the object merely gives pleasure, I can of course attend to the object, but so far not to the pleasure or pain since that is so far not 'objective'. Even if (to pass to another point) an object remains unaltered and does not change when maintained by attention, we may still properly call this permanence the ideal development of the object. The object preserves its ideal identity through the process of time and the change of context, and qualifies itself by that process. When Dr. Stout (*Manual*, p. 65; ed. 2, p. 71) makes attention aim at 'the fuller presentation of an object', I quite agree with him, if, that is, I may interpret 'presentation' in the sense of my text. I am not sure, however, that lower down in the same paragraph Dr. Stout does not teach a divergent doctrine. On the subject of attention I am indeed forced in some respects to dissent very strongly from some doctrines that have been urged by Dr. Stout, but I need not enter on that here.

its identity and unity, and develops itself in the process before me as an individual whole, a whole in which the beginning is qualified by the end, and where on the other hand my act does not make the object to be other than it is. Any such process must deserve the title of ideal or theoretical knowledge, if that is taken in a wide sense, and we need not go on to inquire here how it is related to understanding and truth and to a more strictly intellectual mode of cognition.

It may be objected here that in attention more is really done than to develop the object ideally. The object (it may be said) is always made more prominent and is strengthened by the process, and attention therefore alters the object as well as maintains it. To this I reply that I will ask later whether in attention the object is actually strengthened, and if so in what sense. But any such strengthening, even if it exists always in fact, is none the less, I would urge, accidental. It is an alteration of the object's psychical existence which falls outside the character of attention itself, and is as external to it as are again its physical effects. The only change in psychical existence which really belongs to the essence of attention is the maintenance in and for perception of the object itself. And the object itself, though developed by the process, cannot be taken as changed by it. And, if it is altered otherwise, its alteration must be regarded as accidental.

Attention is thus negative of any mere psychical interference with the object and its knowledge in me. And it might be said that attention therefore is directed not at all upon the object, but simply on myself. The essence of the process (it may be urged) is not to maintain the ideal development of the object, but merely to keep open my self to its appearance in me. Attention will thus consist in the suppression of any psychical fact which would interfere with the object, and its essence therefore is not positive at all, but merely negative. But any such view, though it perhaps might not take us wrong in practice, is really one-sided and in the end inconsistent with itself. And a true doctrine about the general nature of negation would assure us that any such view is false in principle. You cannot, in short, anywhere or in any way negate except from a positive basis. And you cannot suppress in particular whatever is to interfere with a special positive development, unless you have some idea as to what that development is and keep its requirements in mind. But if so, the process can be seen at once to be more than barely negative. If, in making attention to consist essentially in a mere alteration of yourself, you do not include in that alteration the end and object for which it is made, you clearly have not defined attention nor have you said what you must really have meant. But otherwise you have qualified the process essentially by the positive development of the object. The real development in an ideal form of the real object itself is in fact the positive end[1] which against hindrance is pursued in attention. Our scruples or our prejudices may not allow us to accept what I will call this evident doctrine. But, if so, we have preferred to make the general fact of knowledge and truth, I do not say inexplicable, but impossible. The merely negative character of attention would rest in short upon a superficial error.

Attention implies (we have seen) the ideal presence of an object, but it is not confined, we must remember, to thought in the narrower sense of that term. In what we call pure thought the object is not merely in some way developed without loss of identity, but it must itself seem to develop itself by a movement which, if not intrinsic, is at least ideal. On the other hand attention and knowledge are obviously not limited to this. For their result may come from observation and it may be given by sense-experience, and it may depend upon matter of fact without us or within us. At the same time we saw that an ideal synthesis is involved in attention, and the process may therefore be certainly said in a sense to involve thought. When I attend to a sequence of mere fact external or internal, there must be for me in the process a unity which

---

[1] Where not itself the direct end, it is included in the end as means and is so the indirect end.

is not merely given but is ideal. There is a single object which is qualified as a whole and at once by the series, and such a qualification cannot be merely given as a succession of facts. If we use in a wide sense the terms 'thought' and 'idea', attention always, we must say, in this sense involves thinking, and it involves a knowledge, the essential nature of which is to be held together by an idea.

But attention in the sense of *active* attention means more than any kind of mere knowledge. It implies (as we have seen) also a volition on my part, and we may with advantage once more here consider the actual facts. Suppose that I am sitting either listless or absorbed,[1] and that I see perhaps a rabbit move or a bird fly across the scene, do I necessarily give them my attention? If again I passively, as we say, accept the current and course of my own thoughts, must I be said also in every case to be actively attending to them? If we follow the usages of language I think we must deny this.[2] We cannot hold that in every such case my active attention must have been present, when nothing (as we should say) has excited and arrested it. Something necessary to make attention has been wanting, and that something is certainly not here the ideal identity of the object. For this may have been present, and may have been present even in a purely logical form, and yet attention itself may have been absent. And thus the reason why I have not actively attended cannot be that I have not

---

[1] These states are very far of course from being the same, and it would be a serious mistake for some purposes to confuse them. I think that they have been so confused with a bad result in connexion with the words *distrait* and *distraction*.

[2] My attitude towards the perceived activity of my own thoughts may in fact be often felt as disagreeably passive and as anything but active. There are statements made on this point which I read with astonishment. And to urge here that a feeling of my passivity must to some extent imply a feeling of my activity would in my opinion be indefensible, at least apart from an inquiry into the meaning of these terms. We want on this whole subject, I will venture to add, less prejudice and dogma and more inquiry, and I believe that in time we shall get it. The appearance of Mr. Loveday's interesting article, since these words were written, has tended to confirm this belief. See *M.* N.S. X. 455, 'Theories of Mental Activity', by T. Loveday.

thought. The reason is that I have not done anything myself to support and to maintain the object. There have been from time to time objects, each with an identity and an ideal development however short, but I on my part have done nothing at all towards actively developing them. The idea of the object was in short really not 'my idea'. It did not go before, and itself, directly or by implication, prescribe and bring about its own existence in me. There was, in other words, no will, and without my willing I do not actively attend. Even where, as in pure thought, an idea develops itself theoretically, we have not got will unless the foregoing idea of that development has itself been thus the cause of its own existence.[1] And where this feature is absent we assuredly have no active attention. In every observation and in all experiencing, if it is indeed actively attentive, we have, in however vague a form, the idea of my perceiving that which is to happen to the object, or we have at least an end which involves as means the ideal development of the object, an end which is felt in

---

[1] Cf. here *E.* xiv. 272–4. It may indeed be contended that *all* thinking does in the end imply will in this sense. Without pausing to discuss this view I will state in passing that I certainly cannot accept it. Of course, to pass to another point, I should agree that at first in the main the moving ideas in will are practical. The idea of myself, for instance, catching a beast causes me under certain conditions to keep still and to watch the movements of the object. And it can be argued that in the end every theoretical interest is thus ultimately practical. I cannot discuss such a large matter in passing, but I do not think that such a contention in its crude form is defensible. It is one thing to hold that no theoretical or aesthetic interest is in the end barely theoretical or aesthetic. It is quite another thing to propose to subordinate such interests to what is barely practical, without even asking whether a mere practical interest is not itself also in the end incomplete.

Since writing the above I have had the advantage of reading Professor Royce's interesting book, *The World and the Individual.* I hope that at some future time I may be able to discuss the doctrine there advocated with regard to the internal meaning and purpose contained in all ideas. As I understand this view, I however find myself unable to accept it. I cannot see how in the end and ultimately it is an idea which makes the selection which takes place in knowledge, and I have not succeeded in apprehending clearly the relation of thought to will as it is conceived by Professor Royce. I hope however to profit by further study of this volume.

that development to be carrying itself out. And this idea of end operates in determining the process in which itself ceases to be a mere idea and becomes actual fact. Active attention in short everywhere implies volition.[1]

But in what sense (this is now the question) does active attention imply will? We must here on each side be on our guard against error. In the first place attention is not the same thing as will. We have noticed already that in its absence volition may be present, and I shall hereafter return to this point. I shall therefore dismiss it here and ask how attention, itself not being will, implies will in its essence. I will begin by dealing with a mistake of a different kind. Attention certainly does not imply volition in the sense that all attention is willed directly. The attention itself is not always the aim of my will. It may or it may not be itself my end, according to the circumstances of the case, and the facts, as soon as we look at them, seem to put this beyond doubt. I may often of course have an idea of attending to this or that, and so go on to attend to it, but no one could say that apart from this there is no active attention. For, in carrying out some purpose without me or within me, I may be undoubtedly attending, and yet, having felt no tendency to wander mentally from my aim, I may as undoubtedly never have directly willed to attend. In short attention is a state which may itself be willed directly, but which certainly need not be so, and which far more usually is not so willed. Its essence is not to be itself an end and object of volition, and it is enough that it should be implied in an end and object which as a state of mind it subserves.

Wherever an end, external or internal, practical or theoretical,[2] involves in and for its realization the maintenance and support of an ideal object before me and in me—that is active attention. If I will to capture an animal, this purpose may imply the keeping of its movements, and

---

[1] The doctrine of an attention contrary to will, which is advocated by, for instance, Mr. Shand, in *M.* n.s. iv. 452, seems to me quite indefensible, if at least attention is to mean active attention.

[2] These distinctions, the reader should remember, are not the same.

perhaps also my own, steadily before me. If I mean to solve a problem, the idea of its solution entails my dwelling theoretically on the means. If I see and desire to go on seeing some show, that idea in carrying itself out involves my abstinence from distracting movements and thoughts, and it involves positively the keeping my eyes and mind open to the continuous perception of the object. In all these cases the attention comes from my will[1] and it is active attention, but you cannot say that the attending itself is itself that end which I willed. But it becomes this end, and it is this end, where the delay and the hindrance to the realization of my idea is apprehended as in some way consisting in my failing and distraction. The attention itself then goes on to be included explicitly in my idea of the end, and the state of attending is now itself directly willed, and not as before implied incidentally and even conditionally.

Active attention, we may say roughly, is the dwelling ideally on an object so as to do something practical or theoretical to that object or with regard to it. But this dwelling is certainly not always itself included in the idea of my end, it is certainly not always itself the direct aim of my will. If you take a state such as observation and active expectancy,[2] that state will without doubt always

---

[1] The reader will not forget that for me there is no will at all without an idea, and that volition is essentially the self-realization of an idea. Dr. Stout (*Manual*, pp. 248–51; ed. 2, p. 258) holds that we may have attention and even search without an idea of the object. I cannot agree that in any such case we have a right to speak of active attention, and if I agreed to this I can see then no reason why I should not descend even lower, and speak of attention being present even there where there is perhaps not even so much as perception. The pathological case, as Dr. Stout reports it, does not seem to me to show that the subject had in each case no idea (in fact I think it shows the contrary), but merely that his ideas were exceedingly vague and exceedingly restricted. But, if the opposite could in some way be shown, I should without the least hesitation refuse to admit the presence of either mental search or active attention in such a case.

[2] The assertion that all expectation implies will is in my opinion indefensible. What we call active expectancy and a sustained attitude towards the future does certainly imply will, but expectation is used also,

include attention, but it will not include in every case the will so to attend. My immediate end here is to get to know more about the object, to realize it ideally, with or without a further end theoretical or practical. In this direct end is implied the adoption of the necessary means; in other words, here my keeping the object before my mind and my assisting it to develop itself in me. But this assistance of mine is not in every case itself specifically willed. It is not itself directly willed except where its absence, actual or possible, has been brought before me. The delay or the failure in the realization of my object is one thing, and my failure in respect of this is another thing, and it is only the second of these which calls forth a direct will to attend.

Active attention may therefore be defined as such a theoretic or perceptive occupancy of myself by an object as is due to, and involved in, a volition of some sort directed on that object. The ideal development of the object in me is thus, directly or indirectly, the realization of my will. And whatever psychical support, positive or negative, is required to maintain this development, issues therefore from my will and must be regarded as my work. Wherever, on the other hand, an ideal content is so interesting in itself as of itself to produce, apart from my will, whatever is required for its own psychical maintenance, that maintenance is not active attention and cannot be taken as the work of myself.

The meaning so far given to active attention will, I think, be found in the main to agree with the ordinary employment of that term. The various divergent senses,

---

I should have said, with a wider meaning in which no will is implied. Expectation certainly need not always involve what we call observation. A mere suggestion as to the future or an anticipation of it on which I do not dwell, and again even a judgement about the future, need, I should say, none of them imply attention or will, and they clearly need not involve desire. Expectation, as containing essentially attention and a will to know, is used, in short, in a sense which is artificially narrowed (cf. *E*. xiv. 261–2). I have already mentioned that I cannot accept the doctrine that all interest is practical.

in which we commonly make use of 'attention', will be seen
by us to waver naturally and pass one into the other. And
that sense, which in the above account I have tried to fix and
define, hits, I venture to think, the point amid these variations which may be called their centre. In our ordinary
use the chief divergence is between active and passive attention. The latter seems equivalent to what may be called
the mere occupancy of myself.[1] A sensation or a feeling
or an idea, if these are sufficiently strong or sufficiently
influential, may be said to dominate me or engross me, or
also perhaps again to move me, in an eminent sense. Attention here, it will be seen, may be intelligent but is not so
essentially, and if, following this line, we make active attention to be the willed procurement of such an occupancy or
domination, the element of intelligence, of ideal dwelling
on the object, if present, is once more not essential. The
article which some years ago I published in *Mind*, xi, No. 43
[*E.* x] did in fact follow this line, and in the sense which it

---

[1] It would be a reasonable proposal to limit this wide use of 'passive
attention', and to apply the term only in cases where I am occupied by
an object before me. The fact that my organs and my mind are given
a certain 'direction' towards an object, may perhaps be taken as implied
in the ordinary use of 'attention'. To such a limitation I should not be
averse, so long as two points were kept clear. (i) In the first place the
aspect of exclusive domination is (we must remember) quite essential, and
this aspect is not contained in the mere fact that my mind possesses an
object. We have seen that, where I have a variety of objects before me,
I may be inattentive to some of them or even to all. (ii) In the second
place, even where an object occupies me and so I passively attend to it,
if its control over my mind comes from the activity of the object itself,
this control is not my work and there is no active attending. Now these
two essential features, first of domination and next of maintenance by
my activity, will tend, I fear, to be obscured by the proposed limitation
of 'passive attention'. For always, in having an object before me, my mind
naturally may be said in a sense to be 'active' and, if so, this mental
state naturally will tend to be called active attention. And it will be
called so where my mental state could not be fairly taken as my own
work, and it will be called so even where we have not the domination
which is involved in passive attention. Hence, in the presence of this
misleading tendency with all the confusion which it entails, I think it
safer to take the line which is followed in the text. But the limitation,
I agree, would keep us nearer to everyday usage.

gave to active attention it to some extent conflicts with the account I now offer. And this is a point which perhaps we must be content to decide arbitrarily, in whichever way we decide it. But with regard to attention, which is not active on the part of myself but consists in my domination or passive occupancy, the account which I have given above does not exclude such a meaning. Whether in psychology we are to use attention in this sense I do not attempt to decide, but I am sure that it is a sense, the existence of which we cannot afford to forget. Where an idea extrudes others and dominates me simply and so produces volition, my attention to the idea evidently will so far be but passive. Where after the advent of a sensation or a perception I act at once and without delay, my attention, so far as it exists, once more is passive. The action itself certainly is not an attending, and the action may even be not psychical and only physical. And we must decide in the same way where a sensation is, as we say, 'apperceived' and is modified by the activity of what we call a 'disposition'. This will not be my active attending unless I can be said as a result of my will to maintain and to dwell ideally on the object. Activity is present, if you like, and this activity again may be said, if you please, to cause in a certain sense attention to the object. But the attention once again, so far as it exists, will itself be but passive, and the activity, to whatever subject I refer it, will most certainly not be active attention employed by my self.[1] For we do not have that until, as we have seen, we have an idea and a volition.

I will now go on to show briefly how the main senses of attention pass naturally one into the other. If we begin with attention in the low and perhaps improper sense of psychical domination or occupancy, such a psychical fact must normally tend to become the object of a perception. And a prominent object of perception, even apart from its practical side, must tend naturally to become a thing to which I actively attend. It will probably, if it lasts, be

---

[1] I shall touch on this subject again lower down, and in the meantime may remind the reader that the activity here and the subject of it are taken by some psychologists to be simply physical.

dealt with in some volition theoretically or practically, and this will tend to imply a dwelling on it more or less directly, and an ideal maintenance and support thus proceeding from myself. For the suppression of conditions in myself hostile to the undisturbed presence of the idea seems involved in its continuance and development before me. And this suppression, we have supposed, will arise, not directly from the object itself, but at least in part from that object as a means to and as included in my end.[1] And with this we clearly have arrived at an active attending. And such attention tends to pass further into the attention which is itself the end and object of will. For so far as there is mental wandering the original purpose will tend to be frustrated, and hence the remedy of that frustration, if the purpose holds, will normally be suggested as a fresh idea. And this idea realizing itself is itself in general my will to be attentive actively. I do not think that any account of attention, which differs materially from the above, will be able in the same way fairly to do justice to the facts alike of language and of experience.

Active attention is not the same as thought or will, but in its essence it implies each, and it therefore possesses the characteristics of both while identical with neither. I will proceed at the cost of some repetition to enlarge on this thesis, using thought as before in a wide sense so as to cover the entire theoretical attitude.

(i) In the first place attention is not wholly identical with thought, and thought can certainly exist without active attention. Even if thought implied attention, the attention itself would be but one aspect of the thought,

[1] It may be asked whether that ideal development of the object, which is a means to my end, may not in itself become so interesting as of itself to engross me, and whether in this case we any longer have active attention. Any difficulty in answering this question arises, I think, from the difficulty of making in fact the abstraction required. So long as and so far as we take the end to remain dominant and controlling, we must speak, I should say, of an active attention. For, so long and so far, the repression of competing psychical factors is taken as coming, not from the mere idea itself, but from the end willed by me.

for the attention itself does not qualify the object. But it is not even true that all thought implies active attention, and it cannot be said that in all thought I actively maintain and support an ideal object. There must certainly in thought be on the positive side an ideal continuity, and on the negative side an absence of psychical interference. But no one would say naturally that in all cases I actively procure this result. We might perhaps as naturally say that in all thought I am passive, while the object itself actively produces the result in me. But neither of these extremes would really be tenable. (*a*) Let us consider first what happens when, as we say, my thought is concentrated and I am fully absorbed in it. Let us take the case of an intense intellectual or aesthetic activity, where the object seems to develop itself before us without help or hindrance. If you insist that here in all cases and throughout I myself am actively attending, I would ask you what it is that I myself am doing with or to the object or myself. And for myself I cannot find that I at least am *always* actively attending. For so far as the ideal development of the object is interesting in itself, the psychical control over my mind is naturally taken to proceed not from myself but direct from the object. (*b*) Let us examine next my state where, as we should say, I am inattentive altogether. Can we assert that in such a case there actually is no thought at all? My mind is wandering doubtless, and there is no one single object which emerges from the general background and develops itself ideally throughout. But are there no passsing objects here that develop themselves ideally before me even for a moment and to the very slightest extent? I cannot myself see how in the face of facts such a view could be sustained. (*c*) Where I am not (as we say) generally inattentive, but am occupied by, and am perhaps also actively attending to, one continuous central train of thought, is there outside of this central train not any recognition and judgement? It would be, I think, difficult to deny wholly the existence of such thoughts, however passing and sporadic, and yet, if we cannot, then apart from or outside of our active attending we shall once more probably have found thought, and shall certainly have found at least the fact of 'objective reference'. We may in any case rest our conclusion on the two previous instances, if about the third we are inclined to doubt. Thought may certainly exist apart from active attention, and attention itself is not wholly identical with thought.

(ii) Active attention (to pass to another point) is not the same as will, though it involves will in its essence. Will can undoubtedly exist in the absence of active attention, and, even where that is present, will must still in a sense be superior to it and prior. (a) Let us first take the case where, without pausing to think about my suggested action, I act at once. We are to suppose that there is present here an idea of what I am about to do, for without such an idea we should certainly not have volition. But in the case supposed the idea realizes itself forthwith without any further ideal development, and in such a case we have in the proper sense no attention. I certainly perceive an object, and that object may, as we say, violently strike me, and I may also be dominated and overpowered by the idea of my action on the object, but with all this, if I go on to act at once, I do not actively attend. My attention will under certain conditions, it is true, follow as a consequence, but it has so far had no time in which to develop itself, and so far in fact it is not there. (b) We may do well in this connexion to consider also the case where my attention is willed actually and as such. There is here a special will; a will, that is, to produce the state of attending. We have therefore present here the idea of myself attending, and this idea carrying itself out into existence is the special will to attend. But if any one maintained that this idea also itself must be actively attended to, he would be surely opposing himself to the evidence of fact. And if we keep to the facts, we must admit here the presence of a will which is itself certainly not attention but which on the contrary conditions it. The idea of myself attending dominates me, and the idea so produces the existence of my attention, but clearly I do not at the same time actively attend to my idea. That would require a further idea and a further volition, and we should thus be driven to enter on a fruitless regress. We assuredly never should arrive at an idea at once the ultimate condition of my attention and itself ultimately attended to. But probably no one could hold with us that will is implied in active attention and that an idea is essential to will, and at the same time maintain that this idea itself must be an object of attention.[1] If then our premises are right we may conclude that attention and will differ, and that attention implies, while on the other hand it is not implied in, volition. We must insist that without attention there may be will, and that where both are present both are not the same or even co-ordinate. Attention is an applied will, and it is therefore in this sense something clearly subordinate and lower.

(iii) We have seen that attention[2] is not the same as either thought or volition. But on the other hand, since it implies these, it will possess the characteristics of both, and I will go on to enlarge for a space on this head. I shall not attempt to exhaust the subject or in discussing it to follow a strict order, but I will offer some remarks which perhaps may be useful.

(a) Attention, we have seen, involves thought, if thought is taken in the general sense of the perceptive or theoretical attitude. Attention has always, in other words, an object qualified in me by ideal adjectives. And this attitude implies on my part a certain passivity. In attention I must be passive first in the sense that I do not go about to alter the object, but receive and accept it. And there is again beside this a further sense in which in attending I am passive. My self must more or less be occupied and affected by the object, and I (we may say) must suffer this object as mine and in me. And more or less clearly I must also feel and be

---

[1] If we believe that there is will and active attention without the presence of an idea, of course in that case the argument of the text does not apply; but I have already dismissed this doctrine. What in such a case the fact of a will to will really would mean I do not know, and it would be unprofitable for me to consider.

[2] The reader, I hope, remembers that apart from a special warning he is to take attention as *active* attention.

aware of this sufferance. In fact a feeling of this sort, which is present always in active attention, may go some way towards obscuring there my sense of being active. I shall very soon return to this and shall point out something which this felt passivity implies, but for the moment I will pass on to notice another mark of attention.

(*b*) Attention, being will, must of course give us, beside the sense of passivity, a sense also of being active, though this sense again can under certain conditions be weakened. And, as will, attention involves naturally the more or less clear awareness of my active relation to the object of my attention. The practical attitude implies always within what is experienced the opposition of my self to the not-self, and I must also be aware of these terms and of their relation. The same thing holds with a difference in the theoretical attitude, for there the relation and its terms must again be experienced, though not quite in the same sense.[1] I cannot properly attend without an experience of my self as passively affected and again as actively affecting. This awareness may be present of course in very various degrees of distinctness. It may be vague feeling or again it may be clear self-consciousness,[2] but it never fails to be present.

I will before proceeding lay stress on a point which I have mentioned already. We have, I presume, undoubtedly a sense and an experience of being active and passive, and I mean by this that we have an actual awareness of our selves in both these characters. But unless both self and not-self and their relation are actually experienced—and I mean by this are present within the experienced as parts or aspects or features of its content—I cannot see how a sense of activity or passivity, in attention or in anything else, is to be either explicable or possible. To be aware of activity and passivity without being aware of that which is active or passive, and without this also entering itself into

[1] I cannot enter on this matter here.

[2] I think that Mr. Shand is more or less exaggerating when (in *M.* N.S. iii. 459) he speaks of 'a clear awareness' in all attention. The awareness certainly always is present, but in what sense and to what degree can it be always called 'clear'?

the content of the experienced, is to my mind in the end a thing quite without meaning.[1] Others perhaps may understand how this is possible or at least may know that it happens, but in this understanding or knowledge they fail to carry me with them. And in their dealing, so far as they can be said to deal, with this fact of experienced activity, too many psychologists excite in me an astonishment which does not end in admiration. There is doubtless here, as we are told, a familiar distinction. There is the activity of a thing which is aware that it is active, and there is again the activity of a thing which has no such feeling and experience. We all in this latter sense should speak of the activity of a volcano or of a pill, and in this latter sense we may also in psychology make use of the term 'active'. And I might claim, even myself, without any very prolonged struggle to have possessed myself of this distinction. But having perhaps risen so far there remains a point at which I am still left behind. I fail to perceive how this distinction, even when we have attained to it, can either rid us of the fact of experienced activity or can entitle us to treat such a fact with neglect. I still do not comprehend how the knowledge on our part of this distinction—I do not even see how the ignorance of it on the part of others—can excuse us when we make apparently no attempt to find out what experienced activity contains. Such neglect still appears to me to be in short inexcusable, even though apparently its consequences with a little good will may conduct us to Theism.

In attention then I am practically related to an object, but this practical relation (I would once more repeat) is of a limited kind. Attention, being will, must involve the alteration of existence, but on the other side, as attention, it must not alter its object. The object, we have seen, is not changed by me, but develops and reveals itself within me. What then is that existence of the object which really is changed by attention? It is, we answer, the psychical existence which belongs to the ideal development of the object. In all perceptive knowledge there are these two

[1] Compare here the remarks in *M.* n.s. x [*E.* xxiii].

sides which are indissolubly united. And in active attention we have on one side the willed self-revelation of the
reality in and for me, and on the other side the psychical
existence and the alteration of that existence without
which the object cannot appear.[1] In attention you cannot,
as we have seen, leave out either of these factors. Attention does not merely consist in the alteration of my psychical existence, and again it cannot even by an abstraction
be regarded merely as the ideal movement of the object.

It is for this latter reason that we are not said to attend
to anything except what is 'presented'. Mr. Shand (*M.*
N.s. iii. 467) has noticed this usage, which appears to be
well marked, but he has not, I think, pointed out the principle and the reason which underlies it. But the reason is
that, being will, attention, like all will,[2] must be directed
on immediate existence. We cannot, as Mr. Shand remarks, properly attend to another man's thoughts or to
what is happening at the antipodes. And yet obviously I
can attend to an idea, say the idea of attention. I can attend
to it so far as it is taken as an idea existing now in and for
me, and is therefore in this sense 'presented'. But if on
the other hand you abstract from this side of the idea, I
can attend to it no longer. And in speaking of another
man's thoughts or of an event at the antipodes, you are
naturally taken for the purpose in hand to abstract from

---

[1] I may perhaps once more be permitted to remind the reader of a vital
point. That alteration of my psychical existence, which is involved in the
maintenance of the ideal development, must not, where we have active
attention, come direct from the object itself. For, wherever this happens,
it is the object which is taken to be active and not I myself, and naturally
with this we can speak no longer of my actively attending. In active
attention the ideal development issues from and is implied in my will, and
its maintenance also is thus taken to be willed and to proceed from myself.

[2] Mr. Shand would, I understand, not admit this. He adduces (*M.*
N.s. iv. 463) the fact of intention and resolve as a proof that will is
not always an action on immediate existence. But except so far as intention and resolve are or imply such an action, I cannot agree that they are
volition, and I think that when they are defined so as to exclude this aspect
no one would call them will, or would call them anything beyond *mere*
intention and *mere* resolve. I have touched on this subject in my *Appearance
and Reality*, 410 = 463, and I shall have to recur to it in a future article.

the existence of these things in my knowledge. Hence you cannot attend to them, since it is of the essence of attention to imply this aspect of psychical existence and its alteration. Whether we can will an event outside of and quite apart from our psychical existence, as we certainly can desire it (*E*. xiv. 267), I need not here discuss. But my willed attention to such an event is, as we have just explained, self-contradictory.

(*c*) I will now briefly indicate another feature which belongs to attention in its character of will. Attention may itself vary in strength, while its object either does not vary at all or becomes indifferently more or less.[1] In the first place I may be occupied and dominated more or less by an object, while that object, taken in itself, remains the same. The object may in a certain character and on a certain scale remain of the same degree, while the range and extent to which my self is involved and disturbed may change indefinitely. But that occupation and disturbance is of course not the same thing as my active attending. My attention will in the proper sense be strong or weak exactly in the way in which we speak of volition possessing these characters. The strength of a volition is a topic to which in another article I hope to return, but it consists, we may say briefly, in the strength of the idea with which the self is identified and the amount of tension and struggle set up between this idea and existence. The extent, up to which the whole self is involved in this idea and is excited by this conflict and is identified with one side of it, gives I should say, the degree of volition. With this of course is connected the felt amount of pleasure and pain. On the other hand the experienced strain on an organ, unless so far as it is included in the above, does not count towards fixing the degree of the tension. And my passive occupancy by the object once again is not a factor, except so far as it subserves and increases the struggle. I do not think that I can with advantage here enlarge on this subject.

---

[1] On the excessive ambiguity of a psychical 'more and less' see *M*. N.S. iv [*E*. xix].

We have perceived the essential nature of active attention, and have surveyed its main features from the side alike of volition and of thought. I have now to deal with some other problems, and in particular will discuss the meaning of the phrase 'object of attention'. But first I will glance at a question about attention's effects. Are we to say that it does or that it does not intensify its object? I could not here enter at length into this controversy, even if I were qualified to do so, but I will venture in passing to offer some remarks. Very serious ambiguity attaches not only to 'psychical intensity', but also, as we shall presently see, to attention's 'object'.[1] And without a previous inquiry into the meaning of these terms any discussion of the question, it seems to me, must in part lead to nothing. I should be inclined, if I might venture an opinion, to agree that attention does not *essentially* raise the strength of the object to which I attend, if and so long as this object is considered with reference to its own scale. If, that is, I am comparing one visual object with others, or even generally one psychical object with others, it is not of the essence of attention to raise in the scale one of these objects against another, so long as the scale enters into the whole object to which I really am attending. In other words, so far as you attend to a whole field of comparison, your attention does not essentially strengthen one part of this connected whole as against other parts. And, if this conclusion seems

[1] When Mr. Shand (*M.* n.s. iv. 464) says that, though attention does not arrest a disappearing sensation, will on its side may do so, I find the statement extremely ambiguous. If the will is simply to observe what happens within a certain field, the attention does not alter, or at least it ought not to alter, any one element in that complex. But on the other hand if the will is directed to an end which in itself involves a continued attention to some idea that naturally wavers—surely here the attention both can and often does arrest. From my point of view there would of course be no meaning in saying here that will can do that which attention cannot do. And so far as Mr. Shand understands by will an action that takes place without any idea of it, I radically dissent from any view of this kind. Mr. Shand's very interesting article is pervaded throughout by that ambiguity as to the nature of the 'object' which I am shortly to discuss. With regard to attention strengthening and not strengthening, the reader will find some instructive hesitation in Wundt, *Phys. Psych.*, chap. xv.

trivial, I can only reply by asking that it may at least not be forgotten. On the other hand I should agree that in general the effect of attention is to strengthen and to make clear,[1] and hence it may in fact incidentally falsify for the purpose of comparison some part of the object. I will not attempt further to enter on this matter, but before proceeding will offer a necessary remark. Attention is not something abstract and general, but is always individual and special. It is, we have seen, in effect a will to develop perceptively an object in me. And with regard to the nature of objects and their ways of development the greatest diversity prevails. And hence the strength and clearness which are essential to attention are not always one thing. They are in each case prescribed in amount and character by the particular matter and purpose. Whatever is enough to meet this particular demand will be sufficient, however little there may be of it, and only so much as this is really essential to attention. And a further end and purpose for which the attention exists, we must remember, is not the attention itself.

I will now proceed to an inquiry into the meaning of attention's 'object'. We can attend, as will presently be shown, to but one thing at a time. Except under certain abnormal conditions we may say that attention never really is divided, and before explaining this I will very briefly state why the fact must be so. There would be much more to say here if I had space at command, and I must content myself with giving what seems the main reason, while ignoring other aspects of the matter. Attention is single, we may say in a word, because will is single. And will is single not in the least because it is a faculty—there is too much of this kind of 'explanation' still on hand—but, we may say, because, if it were not single, it would have perished with its owners. Without the habit, and so in the end the principle, of doing and attending to one thing at a time, no creature could have maintained its existence and its race. This, I would repeat, is not offered as being by itself the whole reason, but it seems enough to show

[1] I cannot discuss here the meaning of 'clearness'.

why attention must normally be single. And with this I will pass on to inquire further about the 'object' of attention.

The object of attention, it will be said, is in fact very far from being single. And, it will be added, the object is so far from being one and not many, that authorities have differed and have even experimented about the extent of its plurality. And if the object really has all the time been one, this seems not possible. But it is more than possible, I reply, if the term 'object' is highly ambiguous, and if some psychologists have taken no account of its ambiguity. And I will forthwith state the main conclusions to which we shall be led. (1) There is in attention never more than one object, the several 'objects' being diverse aspects of or features within this. (2) Within the one object the unity is of very different kinds. (3) The nominal object and the real object may be very far from being the same, and the latter may contain within itself the former as a feature which is subordinated and even negated.

(1) The first of these heads I may pass over rapidly, since I can refer the reader here to the works of Professor James and Dr. Stout.[1] Apart from oscillation, and again apart from abnormal states, to attend to a plurality is always to attend to it as one object, and it is not possible to have really several objects of attention at once. The idea that we can do this comes from a want of insight into certain truths about the object, and I will at once, under (2) and (3), proceed to set these out. I would add that these truths have a wide and important bearing, and that any neglect of them can hardly fail to result in error.

(2 and 3) Attention, we all know, may in various degrees be diffused or be concentrated, but we may fail to perceive that this concentration and diffusion itself falls within the object and qualifies that. The extreme of diffused atten-

---

[1] Professor James, *Psych*. i. 405, ii. 569, teaches the right doctrine that there can be but one object. I do not know if it is quite consistent with this when, p. 409, he speaks of a plurality of 'entirely disconnected' systems of conceptions. Professor James's use of the word 'object' is however (i. 275 foll.) to the very last degree loose. As to oneness of attention, Dr. Stout teaches the right view throughout, *Anal. Psych*. i. 194, 211–12, 260.

tion would be, I presume, to observe impartially the whole
detail of a complex scene. Its aim would be to observe at
large everything which happens in and to this general object, to notice in other words any and every kind of change
which takes place before my mind. But even in this supposed extreme we should have the unity of my world, as
perceived here and now, and we should have the idea of
my noticing whatever may happen in this field; and thus
every diversity would be comprehended in and would be
subordinate to the unity of this general object. The plurality even here would be the adjective of one thing, but
the various features of this object would be of precisely the
same rank. They are thus taken as simply co-ordinate,
and they are coupled, we may say, by a mere 'and'. We
are to attend to an object, the several contents of which are
A *and* B *and* C, where A, B, and C are equal and all stand
on exactly the same footing. A case so extreme, I at once
hasten to add, cannot actually exist. If one is to observe
really and in fact, one cannot observe really at large, but in
order to act one must act, as we say, in a certain interest.
But this means that our attention is never equally diffused,
and that more or less we are compelled to select and to
limit. An animal that searches when hungry will search
not for anything and everything, but always for something more or less special while neglecting the rest; and
the animal must thus always select more or less from the
totality of what in general it perceives, and even from the
limited totality of that which it sees or smells. The extreme
of diffusion will therefore not be present actually and in
fact, since with regard to the whole object some neglect
and some selection is necessary.

There will in the first place be features of our scene, or
in other words of the total object before us, to which we
give really and in fact no attention at all. Our object is
thus so far divided into two fields, one of inattention, we
may say, and the other of attention. And passing by the
first let us look at the second, the field and object of attention. Will all the details of that object be without exception attended to equally? Is none relatively neglected

while another is in comparison more prominent? Is everything within attention's object still simply co-ordinate and
coupled still by a mere 'and', the one feature being no more
important and attended to no more than is the other? If
this is ever so, it assuredly is not so always, and, where it is
not so, we have even within the chosen field at least some
subordination. We find in short no longer a mere 'and'.
It is not a case of attending simply to A *and* to B, but of
attending to A while not omitting to notice B. And B has
with this become lowered to the rank of a condition or
circumstance. It is a mere adjective, a more or less subordinate detail in the object, and subordination once
begun can be carried to a great length. We may find in
short that in the end what we call attention's 'object'
may be very different from the true object and aim of
our attention. That true aim, that real object, may be even
the exclusion or the destruction of the nominal object of
attention.

We have in attention (*a*) that part of the whole object to
which we do not at all attend. This must be distinguished
on one side from all of the moment's feeling which is not
even an object, and on the other side from that part of our
whole object to which we attend. We have next (*b*) this
real object of attention with all its internal detail. And we
have last (*c*) the nominal object. The nominal object is that
part of the detail, or that aspect of the whole process, which
for some cause we select and call the object of attention.
And there is a tendency here to confuse, and to put this
nominal object, this mere fragment preferred mainly for
the sake of convenience, in the place of attention's real and
entire object. And from this origin rises a whole train of
more or less disastrous mistakes.[1] I will proceed to explain
and to enlarge on this statement.

[1] The metaphor of the visual field and focus, which in Wundt and his
followers appears as a doctrine, has, I venture to think, in its results been
decidedly mischievous. The metaphor appears in Lotze's *Med. Psych.*,
p. 505, and I should presume that Wundt owes the doctrine to Fortlage's
Psychologie, but he himself is, I suppose, responsible for its prevalence so
far as it has prevailed.

The 'object of attention', far removed from being a term clear and precise, is, as we have seen, a phrase full of ambiguity. But in too much psychology, as in common life, this phrase is used with no regard for its uncertain meaning. The 'object' of attention is in this respect like the 'subject' of a judgement. In a judgement the nominal subject may be something very different from that about which the assertion really is made, and the logician who fails to see this and to remember it will not avoid error. I will point out at some length this ambiguous character of attention's object. If we take such an instance as the pursuit of prey by a man or a beast, the real object of attention is not the mere animal pursued but the whole pursuit of that animal. And hence every detail in the scene which in any way bears on this pursuit, whether as contributing to it or as hindering it, is or may be included within the real object attended to. Or let us take the instance where a woman's object in going to some party is in fact to promote the success of her daughter. We might say here naturally that, apart from oscillation and failure, her daughter was throughout the time the real object of her attention. But this way of speaking, if convenient, is not correct. Her true 'real object' is the observing, the doing, and the preventing this and that thing with regard to her daughter, and, we must add, in a certain interest. And hence it is hard to say what detail in the scene may as a condition or circumstance fail to be included in the object which she pursues—to be attended to and to be contained in her attention's real object. And it is from this point of view that we must understand also the *diversion* of attention, for diversion once more is an ambiguous phrase. When we say that something occurs to attract the mother's attention to something other than her daughter, our meaning is doubtful. We may mean first that, for a longer or shorter period or periods of time, she does not think at all about her daughter or in any way notice her. And if so, during those periods her attention to her daughter has ceased, except in an improper sense to be noticed below. But on the other hand our meaning when we speak of diversion may be widely different. For the new pursuit and the old one may be co-ordinated in various ways into one whole object. And in this case the diversion of my attention from A will not imply that I cease to attend to A *because* I now attend to B. For I may attend at once to both B and A as coexisting adjectives in one pursuit or scene, or I may subordinate B to A in various ways as a more or less accidental detail, circumstance, or condition. The question is here not of 'Yes or No' and of 'Either one or the other'; the question is really about both, and it concerns the degree in which each is present, and again the relative position in which the one stands to the other. The diversion of attention, in short, takes place here within the attention itself. And hence the division and the diversion of attention are phrases, the meaning of which can never anywhere be assumed as known. The meaning will vary in different cases and it will vary perhaps vitally, and it must be investigated for each purpose in hand before conclusions are drawn. And I doubt whether even with the regenerate man of the psychological laboratory this necessary investigation has always taken place. The object of attention, even where our attention is concentrated, is not that aspect of it which for convenience we may abstract and may entitle the object. The real object is on the contrary always a process with this 'object'. It is a more or less systematic whole of action and scene in which the nominal object may be more or less reduced to a detail or condition. That which, for example, Mr. Shand has called the 'set of the interest' (*M.* N.S. iii. 454) is really an integral part of the attention's object, and this may be true again of the whole present scene with its background and environment. When I attend to the decay and to the disappearance of a sensation, this mere sensation is not the real object to which I attend. And the fact that I observe the cessation surely proves that any such view is erroneous. The object which I really observe is the sensation in its relation perhaps to a certain special system or scale, and at least in its more general connexion with a wider order and scene. And if we forget this, then, as we saw above with regard to the question of intensity, our inquiry may be ambiguous and our conclusions may be vitiated beforehand. In short between the real and the nominal object of attention the divergence may be vital. Our real object (as we saw) may even consist in the negation of what we call our object. I may thus be said to attend to a thought which persecutes me, while I really attend to the extruding of this thought from my mind. My object here is the process of extrusion together with all that this process implies. But I, taking into view the thing on which I am to act, for convenience call this my object, and I thus am led into error both in theory and practice. My real object, the process of extruding A, is a negation which, like all negation, involves a positive basis, and A itself is a detail which has no right to appear except as a condition thus positively negated. And if this essential subordination is for a moment wanting, and if A for one moment is set free, my object and my attention have at once been changed surreptitiously and radically. There are probably few of us who in practice have no acquaintance with this error. We have resolved to attend to the not thinking of something which tempts us. Our resolve here, if genuine, and our true object, is to drive out this idea when it occurs, and to do this by keeping our minds fixed on that which will extrude it. And the Devil, when he knows his business, induces us by some pretext to keep the temptation before us. He suggests that it is even our duty always to bear this temptation in mind, of course always qualified by the idea that it is a thing which we reject. And thus the idea naturally, by being held before us, tends to free itself at least in part from its mere subordinate phase, and so in the end acts positively and independently. And our object and our attention have in this way been essentially transformed. We may note again the same natural transformation in the case of repentance. The repentance, we may say, that allows itself ever to think of the past deserves to be suspected. And repentance, we might even add, is a luxury permitted only to those who are morally rich.

The bearing of this whole question is so wide and its

importance is so great[1] that I will ask the reader to delay
and to consider carefully a further instance. And I will
take this instance from Mr. Shand's article in *Mind*, N.S.
iii. 457. We can, of course, attend to a pleasure or a pain
and make it our 'object'. But the effect of our attention
upon this object may vary indefinitely and may go to
strengthen it or again to expel or to weaken it. And hence,
if in each case we assume that our object is the same, we
seem landed in a difficulty. But the real object, as we have
seen, is in each case not the same but different, and to
attend actively to a *mere* sensation or to a *mere* pain is in
no case possible. The sensation or the pain or the pleasure
never is and never could be the entire and real object. It
is but one feature in that larger object to which I really
attend and which in each several case may differ widely.
Thus with pain my true object may be the means which I
use to remove it, or I might possibly attend to the dwelling
on my self as a sufferer from this pain, indignant or un-
resisting or calmly resigned. My object and my attention
in each of these cases is something different, and, if the
effects vary, that result is surely natural. Again I may attend to a present pain not as to a thing by which I now am
perturbed, but as to a fact in which I take theoretical interest. I may wish to observe this pain as a given psychical
phenomenon, or I may wish to view it in its wider bearings
either as this pain or more generally, and in either case as
an element in the moral world or in the Universe at large.
The object even of such theoretical attention will not be
the same in each case. And even here the effects may be
more or less diverse, but the *general* tendency is here, we
may say, to subordinate the pain as now felt and so to
weaken it. From this I may go on to attend in a different
way. I may fix my mind on the pain as a thing which

[1] In the end it takes us back to the question of the true essence of negation, and I think that wrong views as to this have in certain points injured
psychology. The possibility of a negative will and the real nature of aversion are points to be discussed in a future article. For the second of these
see *M.* xiii. 21 [*E.* xiv. 268–9]. The doctrine of our text will be shown in
another article to have vital importance also with regard to the question of
mental conflict and of imputation.

should not be attended to except with contempt. Here my real object is the practical degradation or extrusion of the pain, and this negative process involves a positive object and a positive volition. My aim is to carry out that idea of my self which satisfies me and of which I approve, and such an object implies the negation of the pain. But there is, I think, no occasion to enlarge and to dwell further on this instance. Enough has been said to make clear the essential ambiguity of the 'object'. There is in brief never any presumption that what we are disposed to call attention's object is the real object of attention; and that real object may even on the contrary consist in the positive suppression of the nominal object. Hence every inquiry must begin with this preliminary question:—What in the case before us really is contained in the true object of attention?

I will now briefly touch on a point which I have noticed already, the meaning which should be given to a 'permanent attention'. We should all say naturally that perhaps for weeks we have been attending to something, and it is of course obvious that through all this time we cannot actually have attended. And in the same way we 'keep watch' where through all the time we have not been actually watching.[1] We mean, I presume, that we have had throughout a constant will to observe, and the sense to be given to a constant or permanent will can be best discussed further in a later article. But here as elsewhere, whenever we speak of attending, we mean a special attention with regard to a certain particular purpose. And if through any period our amount of actual attention has been sufficient for that purpose, we naturally express this by asserting that through all the time our attention has been there. It

[1] See here Professor James, *Psychology*, i. 420. There is no doubt that sustained active attention generally means a succession of willed acts, but it is not clear what are the limits of such an act. There must be an idea which realizes itself, and, when that is over, the act is over until again we have an idea, either the same or another. But suppose, e.g., I have willed to occupy myself with a subject and the occupation goes on, at what point does that occupation cease to be the realization of my idea and so to be my act?

has not really been there, but what has happened has been this. The idea of carrying out the proposed end has been associated with my inner and outer worlds in such a manner that, given the occurrence of any change sufficiently connected with this idea, my actual attention to the means will at once be aroused. And thus by a licence our attention is said to have been present throughout, since it has been present conditionally. And it has been actually present so far as our end and purpose requires, and everywhere the necessary amount of attention is and must be measured by the purpose and the end.

From this I will go on to offer a few remarks about the fixation of attention. If we remember that active attention involves will, and that will is the self-realization of an idea, we can at once reply generally to the question how attention is fixed. Active attention is fixed always by the idea of an end. The idea, we have seen, may be the idea of an activity which is no more than theoretical, but in some form the idea of an end is essential. Wherever it is absent, there at least for the time we are without active attention. We may be in a sense occupied and engrossed, we may be in such a state that whenever we deviate we are brought back, and hence, as we have just explained, attention is present in such a state conditionally. But, apart from an idea which realizes itself, we are not actively and in the proper sense attending. We may say, then, that always and in principle attention, in the sense of active attention, is fixed by an idea. And if we endeavour to pass behind this idea to a more fundamental attention, we are led either to a fresh and more remote idea, or to something which certainly is not active attention and will. We may doubtless ask a further question as to how ideas themselves become fixed, and this question is doubtless as important as it is wide and difficult. But I do not think that such a problem falls within the limited scope of this article, and at any rate it is impossible to deal with it here. A question which involves difficulties such as would be raised, for instance, by any discussion of what are called 'fixed ideas', deserves to be treated with some respect.

How and under what laws the idea acts in attention is again a question which I cannot attempt here to answer. Without entering on this I will briefly notice our employment of outward objects. As a help to concentration on an abstract problem we are used to gaze on something prominent in our field of vision and so to anchor our thoughts. This familiar process has two sides. It is in part negative and serves to inhibit distracting sensations and movements, but in the main and in principle it is positive. The outward object has itself now become part of the content of an idea, the idea of myself pursuing a certain end. And hence the object itself now on occasion re-suggests the pursuit and so resists deviation.[1]

I will conclude with some observations on a point which bears on the foregoing, the connexion between attention and what is called 'conation'. We have here again a term which is dangerously ambiguous.[2] Conation may be used for something which is either not experienced at all, or at least is not at all experienced as conation. But, passing by these senses, I should deny that conation is involved in attention, unless conation is used merely as a general head which includes volition. If it were used more narrowly and taken to imply an experienced effort or striving, we could not truly say that all volition and attention contain it. Attention, being will, must involve an opposition between existence and idea, but I cannot agree that this opposition must entail an effort and struggle. The resistance of the fact may be no more than what comes from inertia, and to remove it actually may cost little more than to anticipate its removal ideally. And if the alteration of existence implies always a struggle, I at least can often neither perceive this nor feel it. And hence I could not admit that, used in this emphatic sense, conation belongs to all active attention.

[1] On the unmeaning movements made in attention see Professor James, *Psychology*, i. 458. He however omits to notice that, beside 'drafting off', these movements, if monotonous, may fix positively. A movement with one character may serve as a fixed object. How far, if at all, without a fixed external world any attention and any self-control would in the end be possible, is an interesting question on which here I of course do not touch.

[2] With regard to conation I may refer the reader to *M.* n.s. x [*E.* xxiii].

It is true (to pass from this point which is of little importance) that our attention corresponds on the whole to our permanent interests. Our attention may be said to answer in the main to the felt wants and the unfelt needs of our nature and to conduce to their satisfaction. But to turn this broad correspondence into an essential unity, or even into a necessary connexion, is indefensible. It is an attempt to force a construction on the facts, against which the facts, unless we close our eyes, most evidently rebel. Thus to identify every 'disposition' with an actual conation is plainly unjustifiable, so long as we use conation for that which is experienced and of which we are aware. And if on the other hand we take it as something either not experienced at all as conation, or at all events not so experienced by that consciousness of which we speak, we should at least make clear what it is that we do and that we do not assert. But if, apart from such hypotheses, we go by the facts, one conclusion becomes plain. We may will and may attend actively because we have first been compelled to 'attend' passively, because, that is, we have been somehow impressed and laid hold of by an idea.[1] And if attention is used in this improper sense, we often will because we have attended, and do not attend in the least because we will. If one follows the known facts one must admit the existence of volition, where the idea realizes itself quite apart from any antecedent desire or conation, and where these have not even contributed to the origin and suggestion of the idea. We may end in such cases, and we probably do end, by attending actively to the idea; but we may do this because, and only because, the idea has laid hold of us passively. Thus our will to realize this idea in external action and in inward knowledge is but the self-realization of the idea which so has possessed us. And you cannot, if you keep to facts, maintain even that the suggestion holds us in all cases because it arouses desire or even pleasure. For in some cases these both are absent, at least from the known facts, while in other cases we may find even the

[1] 'Idea' here includes any suggestion even when coming straight from a perception.

presence of their opposite. In short the attempt to get rid of ideo-motor action, or to deny that at least some ideo-motor actions are volitions, is founded on error and leads to a conflict with fact.[1] The suggested idea which moves us does not, to repeat this, always move us because in any sense it corresponds to an actual conation, if, that is, conation means something which we know and experience. This idea may come from an association, or it may arise from some kind of external or at least sensational emphasis, or we may be unable in any way to assign to it a psychical origin. There are cases where all that we are aware of is that the idea somehow is there, and that in itself it does not please us nor do we desire its fulfilment. But the idea remaining there, and because it remains there, becomes insistent and goes on to realize itself, and in this way unfeelingly forces, we may say, our will and our active attention.

If it is urged that we have a general disposition to realize all our ideas, I have no wish to gainsay this. I am not, however, prepared to agree that such a disposition is ulti-mate, and in any case the assertion that it essentially de-pends upon pleasure or pain, or essentially answers to a conation, I must once more repeat, seems really contrary to plain fact. You may add again, if you please, that, with-out some special disposition in each case, no idea could hold and possess us. And once more, if you will not in every case assert the necessary presence of pleasure or pain, or of conation or desire, I am ready to accept and even to endorse this doctrine. But in some cases I must insist that this disposition is but physical, physical I do not say en-tirely but for the most part and in the main.[2] If you are true to facts, and if you keep to that individual soul with which alone you are here concerned, you cannot in all cases take the disposition as psychical. But to suppose that, with

[1] I hope to show this at length in a future article.
[2] What I mean is this, that, however right you may be in saying that for psychology a certain disposition is merely physical, you will never be right in asserting that its psychical result comes merely from it, and that psychical conditions have contributed nothing to that result.

a physical or with even a psychical disposition, a step has been made towards refuting the doctrine which we have advanced would in my opinion be most mistaken. It is a subject which, however, cannot be further pursued in the present article.

XXV

ON MENTAL CONFLICT AND IMPUTATION

[*First published in* MIND, N.S. xi, No. 43, 289–315. *July*, 1902.]

THE purpose of this article is very limited. It proposes to deal to a certain extent with the subject of divided will, the conflict in the mind of ideas generally, and specially of the ideas in desire and impulse. It will inquire into the alleged facts of action contrary to will with special reference to the general nature of volition. And its aim will be to point out the principles on which in practice we impute actions to our selves or again disown them. I have for some time desired to write this article, in order, while trying to throw further light on its subject, to defend and in part to supplement the account of Will which I gave in *Mind*, xiii [*E.* xiv]. And I was led to desire this largely in consequence of a very interesting 'Study in Involuntary Action' by Mr. Shand.[1] The proper course doubtless would be to treat systematically the whole topic of desire and volition, but that course (if I could follow it anywhere) is not possible here. Any paper of the present kind must at least endeavour to speak for itself, however narrow its limits, but I hope that it may find support in other articles that have preceded and will follow.

Volition I take to be the realization of itself by an idea, an idea (it is better to add) with which the self here and now is identified,[2] or it is will where an idea, with

---

[1] In *M.* N.S. iv. 450–71. Compare other articles by the same writer in *M.* N.S. iii. 449–73, and N.S. vi. 289–325, and one by Dr. Stout in N.S. v. 354–66. I perhaps may be permitted to say that I at the time wrote a brief reply to Mr. Shand's criticism. An unfortunate accident, however, prevented this from appearing at the proper moment, and so I thought it better to wait, not foreseeing the length of the delay. I have also made use in this paper of Dr. Stout's article, though I cannot assent to his definition of will. Compare also his *Analytic Psychology* and his *Manual*.

[2] In *M.* o.s. xiii [*E.* xiv] I left out this addition, not because I did not hold the doctrine, but because, having to treat a very large subject in a very small space, I tried, rightly or wrongly, to simplify the matter. The meaning of the phrase will be discussed in a later article.

which the self feels itself one, makes its own content to exist.

I hope on another occasion to explain this thesis more fully,[1] but I set it down here as that which the present discussion will in the main support and defend. I have not forgotten that Mr. Shand has written, 'It will be difficult for any one who has reflected on the type of abortive volition in involuntary actions to any longer maintain that the realization of the idea is essential to volition' (*M.* n.s. vi. 291). In fact, I may say that the study of his interesting papers has done a good deal to confirm me in my view. The one defensible account of will (I must hold) is that which makes it consist in the self-realization of an idea, and I cannot, even with Mr. Shand's help, perceive that a serious objection to this doctrine can be based on anything in those actions which he terms 'involuntary'.

I will at once proceed to state the objection urged against will being essentially the realization of an idea, the objection, that is, which Mr. Shand would base on the facts as he apprehends them. I will then try to show that, even when the facts are so taken, the objection will not hold good, and I will point out the falsity of that assumption which underlies it. I will then deal briefly with the nature of mental conflict and of action contrary to volition. And I will end by asking how the result gained will bear on imputation. But by imputation we are here to understand the mere fact that we accept or disown certain actions, and I shall not inquire if in thus disowning or accepting them we are morally right.

Will, we are told by the objection, cannot consist in the realization of an idea, since there are facts which are inconsistent with such a definition. And the fact, which we are here concerned with, is the alleged instance of action which realizes an idea but is contrary to will.[2] There may

---

[1] I may, however, in the meantime, refer the reader to *M.* o.s. xiii [*E.* xiv] and again to *M.* n.s. x and xi [*E.* xxiii and xxiv].

[2] Mr. Shand proposes to call this by the name of 'involuntary action'. I do not myself see how we can fix the sense of 'involuntary' as 'contra-voluntary', when the term has a wider meaning which is so well established.

be two ideas present, it is said, at once to the mind, two ideas which move us towards two incompatible actions, and which, so moving us, conflict with one another. Each of these ideas, it is added, is felt as mine, and is identified equally with myself. And we may take as an example the morbid desire for drink in collision with the effort after duty. When in the result an action comes in either direction, then by the definition either action alike should be will. But under at least some conditions when we have drunk we insist that we have not willed, but that our real will has been overpowered by the morbid idea. Hence the difference which constitutes the essence of will does not (it is objected) lie in an idea identified with the self. The difference must lie elsewhere, and Mr. Shand would appear to find it in an inexplicable Will.

Now I do not accept the above description of the facts as correct, for I cannot admit without very serious qualification the simultaneous presence of each idea. But before entering on this matter I desire to lay stress on another point. Even if it were true that the self is identified at once with two conflicting ideas, the self need still not be identified with them alike and equally. There may be a difference here which will amount to a distinction and to an alternative between Yes and No; and this difference will be a reason for our attributing the result of one idea to ourselves and for our disavowal of the other. To this aspect of the case Mr. Shand, I think, has not done justice. The difference here of higher and of lower, with the possible consequence of an alternative between will and no-will, is very far from consisting in the presence or absence of mere morality. A highly immoral act may in a sense be an act which is higher, and it may come in an eminent degree from my self and my will. And, in short, it is necessary to enter into an examination of the whole question from this side. We must ask in the case of ideas

I fear that the result of such a struggle against language must be confusion, and I cannot perceive that the struggle is necessary. I should add that I do not forget that Mr. Shand rests his case against the above definition of will on other grounds also. I shall deal with these on another occasion.

which move us, and again in the case of mental states generally, in what way one of these is higher and more mine than another. All of them are 'mine', we are agreed, but there may be a special sense or senses in which they can be distinguished also as more and less 'mine', and can even be distinguished as 'mine' and 'not-mine'.

1. We all recognize the distinction between on the one side our true self, or our self taken as a whole, and on the other side a lower and chance self of some moment. There is a central group and order of certain feelings, ideas, and dispositions, which we should call essential to our selves. And hence, when we fail to act in accordance with certain habits, interests, and principles, or even act in a way opposed to them, the self that is realized is felt to be accidental and other than our true self. This is all so familiar that it would be superfluous to dwell on it, and taking it for granted I will pass on to insist on a further point. This distinction does not rest on the interference of an inexplicable something which is called the 'Will'. For it holds, in the first place, obviously between one volition and another[1] as well as between volition and other aspects of our nature. And, in the second place, it holds in cases where no volition at all is present. And a distinction applicable between volitions, and applicable also neither solely nor specially to volitions, cannot reasonably, I submit, be based on an empty 'Will'. 'I was not myself when I could act in such a manner', 'I was not myself when I could so think of you', 'I do not feel myself at all to-day', 'It was not like him to make that stupid mistake'—we have here some ordinary examples. We do not find in all of these cases the presence of volition, but we find in every case alike the false or the chance self in opposition to the genuine self. I, in short, fail to see how volition can here be

---

[1] If the Will were taken as something known and possessed of a known character, then, of course, volitions could have more or less of this character, and so be distinguished among themselves. But if this same character were found also to exist in every part of our nature, there would be so far no reason for ascribing it to the Will. I am, however, in the text, speaking of a Will which, itself unknown, interferes from the outside.

specially concerned, since the same opposition seems on the contrary to prevail through every part of our being.

'But', it may be objected, 'this distinction after all is but an affair of more and less. Outside of morality we may have perhaps a self which is higher or lower, but we never find a self which is really mine against a self which is not-mine, and which stands on one side of the chasm which divides Yes from No.' An objection of this kind is common everywhere, but it seems really one-sided and superficial. Everywhere a difference in degree may amount to a distinction in kind. Everywhere, when you compare things with a view to some end, and so measure them by some standard, 'more' and 'less' may be opposed as what is right and is not-right. And in the narrow sense of 'moral' these distinctions are not all moral, and they are not confined to the moral world. Wherever in theory or practice one particular course must be taken, it seems even obvious that the course chosen, because it is better, will become for that reason the one course which is not bad. I am not at present raising any question with regard to imputation, and I do not say that everywhere the worse course, if taken, would be disowned by myself. This is a further question with which at present we are not concerned. What I wish to point out here is that everywhere and through all regions of our nature we find a distinction between the self which is, we may say, essential and the self which is accidental. And this distinction, however much it rests upon difference in degree, can and does come before us as a difference in kind between mine and not-mine.

It is the concrete matter and substance of our selves with which we have been so far concerned. And hence the distinction, so far as it has at present been drawn, may, if we please, be called *material*.

2. I pass from this to consider other ways of distinguishing higher from lower and mine from not-mine. There are several of these which in comparison with the foregoing may, if we please, be called *formal*. Everywhere the more universal, we may say, is the higher and more mine,

and it is on this principle that all our formal distinctions rest. But it was really this same principle which was involved above in our 'material' distinction. For, since our self is in its essence a system and concrete universal, the more general and the more material will in the end be identical. The higher, because it is higher, will for that reason be wider, and it will also be lower in the sense of being more deep-rooted and fundamental. But, though at bottom the same, these principles may diverge in practice and may even be opposed. The more general may often be only more abstract, and the increase in abstraction may be at the price of greater onesidedness and emptiness. Hence the higher will here be higher in one respect only, while viewed from another side it may be lower and worse. It is, in a word, but higher formally. On the other hand, that which is less abstract may often be really more universal. For it may extend far more widely, it may represent more of the whole, and, containing a greater amount of the essential matter, may so in the best sense be more material. But this opposition, we must remember, is not absolute, and whatever is higher materially would, if it became explicit, be higher also formally. On the other side, in practice there is a relative division and a divergence of two principles. And hence I will go on to point out some varieties of what may be called formal superiority. There are real differences between these, but the differences all come from one ground.

(*a*) In theory and practice alike a course will be formally higher when it explicitly and consciously asserts a principle instead of embodying it unconsciously. It is a higher thing, we may say, to act, knowing why we act, than it is to act simply. On the other hand, if you compare two actions while taking them as wholes, that which is conscious of no principle may, of course, really be the higher. For the principle asserted formally by the other action may be defective and narrow. In other words to act with a reason is, so far as it goes, higher than to act without one, but in any particular case the man who can give no reason may have more reason on his side. We know the one-sided theorists who always go upon a principle, and who usually go wrong, because their principle is too abstract or (it comes to the same thing) is too narrow. And on the practical side the same defect is familiar. When, to take an extreme case, I protest that 'I do not care what the thing is, I will do it because I have said so and because I choose'—such a course is in one sense extremely high. I am appealing to the idea of the self which is a law to itself and is a principle superior to anything in particular. On the other hand, I am applying this principle not as an individual system and whole, but as an empty abstraction. The connexion therefore between my principle and the particular act is accidental and external, and is perhaps supplied by the meanest and narrowest caprice. Still, if you consider it formally, my act is really higher and is more mine, than if without consciousness of any principle I had acted rightly. In the end there will be no divergence between what is best materially and best formally, but in any given case an opposition between the two may arise. And we must admit that to be conscious of a principle is, so far as it goes, a genuine superiority.

(b) I will pass on to another kind of superiority which also is formal, and which exhibits the same principle in a different application. We know, both in theory and practice, what it is to adopt a course at once and unreflectingly, and what it is, on the other hand, first to pause and then to say, 'Yes, I will take it.' I am not referring to the instances where incompatible suggestions leave us paralysed, and where, after oscillation or forgetfulness, one of these suggestions returns and determines our action. I am speaking of cases where we do not merely pause, but where we pause and reflect. We have a special end which is strong enough to prevent action until some course has been mentally qualified as its means. Or from the mere habit or, again, the idea and conscious principle of waiting, in the presence of a difficulty, until we have seen the thing from all sides—we in the presence of some suggestion or suggestions repress and suspend action. The suggestion or suggestions, whether in theory or practice, are, we may say, negated; they are for the moment alienated from my self and made into objects. This does not, of course, mean that they cease altogether to be felt, but it means that, in becoming objects and in being held before me, they tend so far to be felt less, and are kept in check by a principle with which the self is identified. These facts are so important that it is better to recognize them, even while ascribing them to a faculty or a miracle, than it is to ignore them altogether; but I cannot perceive that we are driven to a choice between such alternatives. In the earlier stages of the mind there is, of course, no reflection at all. Ideas which conflict in our minds leave us helpless and a prey to various kinds of oscillation. It is later, when possessed by some idea which we are unable to realize, that we make the means to this end, and again what opposes it, into the objects of our thought. And as the end becomes more generalized, and, we may say, pushed further back by conflict and competition among its details, the end naturally will come to hold under it a number of alternatives. And these alternatives are by the agency of this end, with which our self is identified, brought before us as objects. In this way arises the habit and the principle of suspending action in the presence of difficulty or doubt, and of considering the possible courses. But it is still and always that higher end, under which the alternatives fall, which is the fixed and active principle. It is the identification of my self with this higher principle, whether in unconscious habit or conscious idea, which checks the suggestions[1]

---

[1] I use the plural because I presume that, under normal conditions, if a suggestion in theory or practice really were and remained single, and strong enough to overcome what may be called my psychical inertia, I should certainly follow it. What restrains me is the presence in some sense of an alternative, and the only question is as to how general or how special this alternative is, and again at what point it is brought to consciousness. In connexion with the doctrine of the text I would advert to the phrase 'to collect oneself'. My self is dispersed by being identified with conflicting suggestions and scattered in their disorderly struggle. It is collected when the various incompatible courses are taken all alike as *not* the end, and as inferior to the end, but at the same time as possible means to the end. It is this which at once both negates and subordinates the suggestions, and, while checking their independent action, retains them as objects. And it is

and neutralizes them, while keeping them as objects before me and in a sense apart from me. And it is because my self is on the one side identified with this principle of a higher self, that a suggestion can be felt by it as on the other side embodying the lower self of the moment. And here in these cases we find the source of my felt constraint and self-alienation, and here is once more the reason of a further experience. When after reflection's pause a suggested course coalesces with the idea of my higher self, or at least ceases to arouse the opposition of a principle higher than itself, that course becomes, as we say, adopted. My self, before which the suggestion was held as something alien and incompatible, now feels itself one with the suggestion, and experiences that as its own self-assertion and development. Hence the process of the idea comes to me now as my truth or again as my reality that is to be. And it is because the possible alternatives have one and all been previously negated and so separated from my self, that my self is now free to discharge its collected and undivided energy in this single direction. And the coalescing of the self with that suggested modification of itself, which was for a time held aloof, naturally brings with it the heightened experience of reunion after estrangement. Here is the origin of that 'electric thrill' which Professor James seems to find inexplicable by psychology, and, if I may say so, endeavours to exploit for a mistaken end.[1] But, without

by identifying myself with this central principle that I become collected, and confront the detail as my property.

[1] The great reputation which Professor James deservedly enjoys as a psychologist compels me somewhere to notice his doctrine of moral responsibility. But even that very sincere respect and admiration which I feel for his work in psychology does not, I am sorry to say, make it possible for me to speak of this doctrine respectfully. When in the presence of two alternatives (so Professor James informs us), one of which is remote and ideal, while the other presses on me with sensational urgency, I will the former with an effort—this is something unaccountable. It is, among other things, an action in the line of the greatest resistance. It is also the real essence of volition, and, being an affair of the purest chance, is a conclusive instance of Free Will. And the fact that when I am tempted there is absolutely no reason why I will one thing and not the other—this fact, Professor James assures us, is a pledge that morality is not an illusion. But 'chance'

attempting here to dwell further on a large and interesting topic, we may pass to our conclusion. In theory and in appears with Professor James to have several senses. In his *Will to Believe* (p. 155) it is said to mean that under absolutely identical conditions the same result need not follow. This is, as I understand it, really to contend that the same A is at once and in precisely the same sense both B and not-B, a contention which obviously would destroy and remove the whole notion of truth. Every one who anywhere desires to ask and to speak about the true and the false, must begin by postulating in effect that any such contention is absurd. And even in the *Will to Believe* I find indications that such an undiluted absurdity is not what really is offered. There are signs, I think, that what Professor James actually means is that the two cases really do differ, but that, not perceiving in what without prejudice to his conclusion such a difference could consist, he has been led to deny its existence. There appears to me to be at any rate a very serious confusion in his *Psychology*. Professor James there states the alternative as being between Free Will and Determinism, so that whatever is not Determinism is *ipso facto* Free Will. He then seems to define Determinism as the doctrine which holds that the duration and the intensity of any effort, which we put forth, are 'fixed functions of the object' (ii. 571) or 'mathematically fixed functions of the ideas' before our minds (574). And any other doctrine but this (so I understand) is defined as Free Will. This is to say that in volition you are ordered to strike out (*a*) the influence of what is actually in the mind though not before it, and (*b*) the influence of everything in the shape of a disposition whether natural or acquired. You are to accept this mutilated view, which, not only in the case of volition but throughout psychology, you probably consider to be quite untenable—or else, according to the sense in which I am forced to understand Professor James, you are compelled to embrace the alternative of pure chance. And the only comment upon such an issue which I could offer would be this. I do not understand how any one with the abilities and knowledge possessed by Professor James could present such an issue to his readers, unless his mind were influenced by ideas extraneous to psychology. And when he himself appears to hold Determinism, as thus defined, to be for the most part satisfactory to himself, I can hardly suppose that I have rightly apprehended his meaning.

With regard to 'action in the line of greatest resistance', I will add a few words. We have here once again, as I understand it, the false alternative to a doctrine which itself is false, and the application to the soul of these mechanical doctrines is not likely to result on either side in anything satisfactory. The fact referred to, I presume, is this, that ideas and principles have not motive power in proportion to the amount of psychical perturbation which immediately corresponds to them. We therefore can choose the alternative which produces, and which we know will produce, most temporary trouble and unrest. But I am unable to perceive that this fact is in any way even abnormal—to say nothing of its supporting the worship of blind Chance. We find the same thing regularly in the world that is

practice alike a course that has been adopted after reflection will be so far superior. It will at least in one respect be a merely intellectual. Where I refuse to adopt a principle of explanation which would make things easier in a particular case, if to do this would conflict with my more general principles—this is to follow (if you *must* say so) the line of greatest resistance. But for myself I must decline to adopt metaphors which seem to me to be false and misleading (cf. here Dr. Stout, *M.* N.S. v. 354–66, and *Manual*, p. 596).

About the claim to base moral responsibility upon mere chance, and to make it literally an affair of sheer accident, there is but little to be said. And, again, whatever seemed called for from me has been said now a long time ago. I must be allowed to express my opinion that apart from its theoretical absurdity such a claim is morally revolting, or would become so if it really could be seriously urged. Professor James, it is true, seeks to attenuate this paradox. He limits, as I understand, my moral responsibility, and makes it begin and end with those cases where I decide with an effort in the presence of temptation. It is only here, he urges, or seems to urge, that my conduct is really a matter of pure chance, and that I, in consequence, am a responsible agent and not 'the dull rattling of a chain, &c.' (i. 453). But, if I had to choose, I should myself prefer the unlimited absurdity; for that is more consistent, and I cannot see that it is any more absurd. And if I am asked how, if these doctrines are really what I think them, they can possibly come to be upheld, I must answer as follows. I am forced to believe that these results are not got by an unprejudiced inquiry made direct into the real claims of our actual moral nature. Wherever they are reached, they appear to be reached by reasoning downwards from alternatives now long ago argued to be vicious. They come from our looking at morality while one eye glances at theological dogma. They are got, I must be allowed to add, by our neglecting to ask ourselves whether in the end what we mean is anything positive. If, in the presence of his moral experience, a man objects to every form of Determinism which he finds offered him on the ground that none of these forms is adequate to the fact—such a man may be mistaken, but he most assuredly is so far not irrational, and I at least so far could not refuse him my respect and even my sympathy. But if, assuming first (and it is a great assumption) that some doctrine capable of satisfying us wholly in this matter is possible, any one goes on to set up that which he takes (perhaps without sufficient inquiry) to be the opposite of Determinism, and then asserts this opposite without so much as asking if, considered morally, it is itself even tolerable—it is impossible for me to treat any such conclusion with respect. And I have thought it better, even at the risk of giving offence, to express in plain language what I think and feel on this unfortunate subject. Such thoughts and feelings are not very exceptional, and I should like to make it more difficult for any one quite to ignore them. And since Professor James has himself, as I think rightly, expressed himself freely on this matter, I am the more inclined to hope that I have not been wrong in doing so likewise. It is really the high standard which elsewhere

higher expression of my true self. The reason of this is that such a course has been separated from union with my self as the mere self of here and now. And it has been brought, consciously or unconsciously, under the principle of the self that is above the detail of one moment, and is in the best sense universal. But this formal superiority, we must remember, may be one-sided. It may on the whole be consistent with and may even conduce to failure. The self that has risen above the particulars of the moment's detail may remain idly suspended and incapable of re-entering them with collected force. Or, if driven into action, this self may be driven in the end by external accident and chance caprice, and the result will in the end really not have come from or depend upon the inner principle. And it is another case of the same defect where, without morbid suspension, the principle has been taken too abstractly, for here once more there will be no vital connexion with the particular result. Still, in one respect and in general, an act adopted after reflection will be so far higher and more mine.

(c) From this I will go on to consider another variety of formal distinction. When we have before us A and B, the ideas of two incompatible courses, we may or we may not recognize these ideas as in the proper sense alternatives. If we so recognize them, then each is qualified for us by the negation of the other. When, in other words, we think of A, we think of it as A which excludes B, and in the same way we qualify B by the exclusion of A. And, taken thus as alternatives, A and B are so far placed on the same level, and you cannot say that one of them is formally superior to the other. But the case is different where A comes before us as qualified by the negation of B, but where on the

he has kept before our eyes which has in a manner forced me to protest against what I cannot but regard as a dangerous lapse.

Nothing in the above remarks must, of course, be taken to apply to the theory of Pluralism as against Monism. It would certainly be quite incorrect to identify Pluralism with a doctrine of absolute chance, or with the claim that such an idea is the foundation of morality. On Professor James's doctrine of volition and consent I shall hope to comment in a future article.

other hand B is not actually thought of as excluding A. In this case B, however incompatible with A, does not come before us as containing the negation of A. And hence, taken formally, A and B are so far not on a level, since, as I think of them, while A embraces and subordinates B, B on the other hand does not contain any explicit negation of A. B is therefore, we may say, thought of as standing under and subject to A, while the subjection of A is not made any part of B's content. And A will therefore clearly so far be higher and will be so far more mine. It will be higher because it is wider and more inclusive, and is in this respect nearer to the idea of my true self as an individual and concrete whole. It is however scarcely necessary to point out that, here as before, a formal superiority may be barely formal, and may amount practically to nothing. But once again, so far as it goes, we are bound to recognize it. And trivial or trifling as this distinction perhaps may appear, we shall find that in its application it may possess great importance.

3. There remains a principle of distinction which, though connected with the foregoing, does not directly fall under them. An idea which is pleasant or more pleasant is so far higher and more mine, and an idea that is painful or more painful is, on the other hand, less mine and lower. In a given individual case this principle may of course prove one-sided and so far false, but still, as far as it goes, it will remain always true. And, taking the world as a whole, we have some reason to believe that any divergence between this principle and the foregoing principles is but local and relative. We make no assertions about the goodness or badness of pain and pleasure *per se*, and we leave that to the Hedonist and to others who insist on taking abstractions for realities. We find in fact that pain is connected with contradiction and defect, while pleasure on the other side goes with increase of being and with harmony. And if we are wise, we shall not seek forcibly to divide these aspects. We shall not attempt to derive the one of them from the other, or to make either of them in abstraction the absolute good. But, avoiding

this error, we may fairly say that the pleasant and the more pleasant are so far higher and more mine, while with pain the opposite is true. We might call this distinction material, on the ground that pleasure and pain are not forms, but are sensations or feelings. We might again, if we chose, insist that this distinction is but formal, since it to some extent varies independently of that which is material. But in my opinion we shall do better if we leave these terms alone. They are of little value anywhere, and used here they would probably even be mischievous.

I would, before proceeding, once more remind the reader that all these distinctions in degree may, under some conditions, amount to differences in kind. Everywhere that, which from one point of view is but more and less, becomes from another point of view right and wrong, and true and false, and mine and not-mine. The interval bridged by degrees becomes, in other words, the open chasm between Yes and No. And now, in view of the above distinctions, I would submit that, apart from mere morality, there may be differences between a higher and a lower self. To hold that, when my self is identified with ideas, these ideas must, outside of the moral sphere, all equally be mine is surely indefensible. We have found enough differences in the daylight, and have seen no need to invoke the darkness of an inexplicable Will.

I will pass on now to consider the actual facts of mental conflict and the struggle of ideas and desires to move me in opposite directions. And it will be convenient in this article to speak of these ideas throughout as being also desires, even where they really are not so.[1] It was, we

---

[1] The main difference here lies in the presence or absence of pleasure felt in the idea (see *M.* o.s. xiii [E. xiv]). I shall in the present article take some account of this difference with regard to imputation, and I hope to touch on the general nature of desire in a future article. It will be understood, of course, that I recognize desire nowhere where an idea is not present. The general head for me is that of 'moving idea', and 'desire' I take to be but one kind that falls under this head. It is merely for the convenience of the reader that in this article I make the two coextensive, and I would beg him, in justice to me, to remember this.

saw, maintained that I could have before me at once two incompatibly moving ideas, and that my self could be at once identified with each of these ideas as actually present together. And it was added that, though either of these ideas might be realized in fact, we had not in each case alike with this the presence of volition. And from this a conclusion was drawn as to the nature of will. On the other side, the reader will remember, I have already urged that, even from the ground of these alleged facts, the conclusion does not follow. And I will now give my reasons for not accepting the facts as alleged. The subject is of course a very old matter for discussion, and it must always remain difficult on account of the number of questions which it involves.

What in the first place, let us ask, are incompatible ideas or desires? They are such as, being diverse, would qualify the same point incompatibly.[1] But when we have such incompatible ideas or desires, we need not know them to be incompatible. We may have them, and know that we have them, and yet may be unaware that they are contrary. And in the first and in the simplest case of such unawareness the ideas have never as yet collided. They come before us as one single complex of idea and desire. They are, in fact, but diverse elements contained in one desire and one idea, and within this whole they are so far simply together, and coupled, we may say, by a mere 'and'.[2]

But as soon as action begins, these elements naturally prove incompatible. In their movement towards reality our ideas collide, and the 'and', which joined them in harmony, at once disappears. In our attempt to act we either altogether fail to produce an action, or, if we succeed, we succeed but in part, and perhaps with painful results. And, led thus to pause and to consider, we may perceive that our desires interfere one with the other.

---

[1] This means in the end that they would, being diverse, simply qualify the same point (see *A.R.* Appendix, Note A, 500 = 562).

[2] For a full explanation of this I must refer the reader to a former article in this series, *M.* n.s. No. 41 [*E.* xxiv].

Hence they are known now to be incompatible, and can no longer come before us as mere positive elements in one whole. And on this (*a*) one desire and one idea, as being far stronger than the other, may simply extrude it. The weaker idea may once and for all be driven out as an idea, and the result, which it leaves behind it, may be inappreciable, or at least too weak to reinstate it. And in this case the conflict of desires, in the proper sense, is at an end. But (*b*), if for any reason the desires are more equally balanced, such an extrusion will not happen, and in its stead a process of ebb and flow and of oscillation may set in. The ideas are not yet qualified for our minds explicitly one by the negation of the other, but practically, as soon as either begins to occupy us, the other also appears and struggles to expel its opposite. Each for the moment succeeding is in its turn forthwith driven out by the other, for neither by itself, or again with the other, can content us. In this alternation when, for a time, one idea is excluded, then for that time the desire which corresponds is in the strict sense at an end. But an idea, thus expelled after fluctuation, cannot fail more or less to survive in its effects. A mass of excited feeling which was joined with it will remain behind, and this feeling will be incongruous with, and will struggle against, the other idea which, for a time, has prevailed. The dog who, desiring to eat the forbidden, has been rebuked by his master, may for the moment have ceased in the proper sense to desire it. The idea of eating has been driven out, but the felt flow of saliva, with other elements of excited feeling, will remain. There is hence a psychical group incongruous with the idea of ready obedience, and struggling to restore its own opposite idea. And in the case of aversion the same thing will naturally hold good. We may have overcome our aversion in the sense that the idea of escape or destruction is banished. But none the less, feelings and movements which correspond to that idea may survive, and to an extent greater or less may strive against the prevalence of the counter idea. We may take as an instance of this the resolve to swallow some nauseous drug. We, in short, have not here, in the proper sense, the actual aversion or actual desire, but we still must be said to be averse or desirous.[1]

(c) What will be the end of this alternation of contrary desires? If the need for action is felt to be imminent, the chance pressure of some moment will force, we may say, accidentally one idea into reality. But, apart from this, the oscillation will tend normally to cease, as, from whatever cause, the excitement dies gradually down, and the ideas move us less strongly. We (i) may relapse into a state where we even forget the incompatibility and the conflict. And here, once again, we unite our opposite ideas and desires as elements in one positive whole, and simply re-join them by an 'and'. Or (ii) preserving some memory of their hostility, we may seek more or less unconsciously to reconcile them by an imagined harmony. We invent or we entertain the idea of some fancied situation, and, placed in this by a change or an addition of some element, our jarring fact undergoes an imaginary transformation, or at least tends, more or less unawares, to be ignored in a certain aspect. In this new complex, our contrary desires are both co-ordinated on equal terms, or again one of them becomes without negation in some way disregarded, or else taken as subordinate to and positively included in the other. Thus a man without conflict may desire both to remain in bed and to rise, because in some way his present does not come before him, altogether and without condition, as this 'now' that now is. Or, dreaming of how things might have been if he had married the woman that now is his neighbour's, he may succeed unrebuked by his conscience in desiring her sin-fully. What is done here is to imagine, more or less consciously, that some condition is added or removed, with the result that the case is altered, and is really no longer the actual case in hand. And so for the moment the in-compatibility, though in truth unremoved, is removed

---

[1] I hope to return to this whole subject. On the nature of aversion, I must, for the present, refer the reader to *M*. xiii. 21 [*E*. xiv. 268–9]. The ordinary doctrine on this head I still venture to think very seriously mistaken.

from the view, and the confused whole can be desired without collision.[1]

(d) We may, however, led by willing insight or driven by hard experience, have been brought to perceive that our two ideas A and B are really incompatible. And (i), in the first place, we may have qualified A by the idea of negating B, either in part or entirely, without at the same time qualifying B's content by the negation of A. B may be unable even to suggest itself as the exclusion of A, or, if so suggested, it may be unable to maintain itself as A's negative. On the other hand A, in its character of superiority to B, may perhaps be forgotten, but can never be consciously driven out or held in subordination by its opposite. And hence the conflict of desires is, under these conditions, at an end. For a desire in the proper sense is not present without an idea, and it is now impossible for the idea B to maintain itself in collision with A. B, in short, cannot as against A any longer appear as an independent idea. It can appear; but where A is present, it can appear only as held in subordination to A. It is so far, therefore, a mere element included now in A's content, and hence we must say that, as the idea B, it has so far ceased to exist. On the other hand, there may remain (as we have seen) a group of excited feelings and movements, which, if it could gain an independent expression, would be once more this desire and this idea of A's contrary. We may recall the instance of the dog, mastered but still hankering and licking his lips. So again in determinedly swallowing a nauseous drug there may be a struggle of hostile feelings and even movements. But so long as B,

---

[1] Cf. here James, *Psychology*, ii. 565. With this mode of removing practical conflict we should, of course, compare the theoretical solution of contradiction by way of distinction and division. In connexion with the doctrine of the text I should add that I, of course, reject the doctrine according to which the real and the imaginary can for me be distinct without an actual difference in their contents. While, e.g., I feel cold, I can certainly imagine that I feel warm, but certainly not without, in doing so, more or less abstracting from the conditions of my here and now. The widespread error on this subject makes, wherever it exists, a rational doctrine of belief and judgement impossible.

the idea of rejection, is not allowed to appear except as that which is to be and shall be crushed, it is held down as included in and subject to A, and hence, though in a sense averse, we actually have not the aversion B. It is so again when we start on some painful errand with the desire, first of all, to return home and to bid farewell. If this idea B, which in an independent form would be in actual collision with our starting, is subordinated to that idea and appears but as a thing which under the conditions is excluded—we have again no conflict of ideas or, in the proper sense, of desires. We have at most a hindrance and a resistance of elements which, so long as they are prevented from taking a higher form, fall short of a conflicting desire.

But, before proceeding, I would advert to a common error. It is absurd in volition to talk about the prevalence of the stronger motive and idea, before at least we have tried to make ourselves aware of the ambiguity of these phrases. And even to inquire whether our action takes the line of the less or the greater resistance, is, I will venture to add, in principle irrational. It is to discuss a problem, which to say the least is not merely mechanical, with a mind biased and in part blinded by physical metaphors. The defeated idea may survive, we have seen, in a mass of feeling hostile to our action. And in this case the volition may be made difficult, and the available energy lessened. But, upon the other hand, the result of conflict may on the whole be quite different, and the resistance, we may fairly say, has gone to increase the positive force. It is after all the whole self, and not the mere balance of its contents, which is realized in the act. And in many cases the excitement of the struggle, and even the very survival of the sensations and pains that belonged once to the defeated idea, pass to the credit of the idea with which the self is finally identified. The intensest volition, we might almost maintain, is that which has naturally developed itself from the smallest balance in the greatest sum of collision. Facts such as these will be for ever ignored by the crude gospel of Necessity, and for ever perverted into a plea for miracle by the blind apostle of 'Free Will'. They will be recognized as what they are by no one who has not rejected the prejudice on which both superstitions alike are based.

The idea B, though subordinated, as we saw, by its contrary A, may still be represented by a mental group which survives and struggles to restore it. And where decisive action is impossible, this group is a persistent source of constant danger to A. For, though B still may be unable to assert itself openly against A in the character of A's opposite, it may none the less, if for some moment its subordination by A is forgotten, assert itself independently and positively. And the result of this will naturally be a desire, and perhaps an act, contrary to A. We have already glanced at this perpetual origin of insidious self-deceit. It may be dangerous, even where you honestly disapprove, to dwell too insistently on disapproval. For the constant negation of B by A is in a sense after all the continual repetition of B. And B is an element which, though subordinated, is perhaps for ever struggling to break loose and to appear and act independently. And hence your supposed repetition of B's subjection may unawares have passed into the habitual toleration of its presence. You tend in effect to lapse into the holding of both ideas as positive, coupled with the mental proviso that the one is taken really as subjected to the other. And from this basis B may in the oblivion of some moment have gone on to become independent unconditionally, and, before you can take warning, may have suddenly realized itself in an act.[1]

(ii) But in the end A and B may become qualified explicitly each by the negation of the other. Each may possess so much mental support, whether direct or indirect, that we may have been forced or led to recognize them as equal and conflicting alternatives. The idea and the desire B will now explicitly include not-A in its content, while A is determined in like manner by the exclusion of B. And a question, we saw, was asked as to what will result when both of these opposites are present. But we must meet this question, for the present at least, by denying the fact which it assumes. These moving ideas A and B cannot, while

[1] Cf. here *E*. xxiv. 436.

really taken thus as alternative, be present together; and we are able to think this possible only because we really do not take them as opposites. We, for the moment, may merely ignore their reciprocal exclusion, or we more or less consciously may fancy some wider arrangement in which they cease to conflict. But while each appears simply and unconditionally as containing the negation of the other, I am confident that both practical ideas, as ideas, do not come before us at once. Apart from some compromise, in which they are more or less conditioned and modified, they cannot each at the same moment be identified with myself. One will banish the other, or they will oscillate in a wavering alternation. This process will be painful because of the excited group which supports each desire, a group which, itself unbanished and unsubjected, throughout struggles blindly yet insidiously, and moves to gain expression in an idea and a desire, and so to dominate in its turn. The pain of oscillation will indeed itself be a further motive for the self to terminate the conflict, and, where immediate action is not possible, to attempt at least to silence one claimant by a resolve. But each excited group, while it remains, will seek to recommence its struggle for a voice, and in the end for a despotism. On the other hand, as powers that openly assert themselves each as the opposite of the other, they cannot in this character both rise above ground and appear at once as possessors of the self.

We have been led to enter on an old and well-known problem, the question whether a man can knowingly and willingly do what is bad. It is possible, of course, to answer this question in the affirmative, and to explain the admitted fact rationally by the psychical weakness of one contrary (E. vi). But, if our foregoing conclusion was correct, such an answer will not wholly stand. We must deny the possibility of a volition where opposite ideas are present together, if it is true that these ideas cannot coexist where they actually are opposite. If 'bad' be taken explicitly as the contrary of 'good', and if both ideas are understood simply and unequivocally and without mediation and qualification, 'bad' and 'good' cannot coexist, nor can one of them be realized as against the other. And in the practical problem before us the meanings of 'good' and 'bad' are clearly fixed as so opposite. Since all will must be directed upon existence here and now, and is not possible except as a change in and of that existence,[1] an act proposed to be done, whether good or bad, will be good or bad for me now and here. And the 'here' and 'now' will inevitably force these terms to conflict as alternatives. Hence, if our view is right, they will be unable, as practical, to appear both at once, and the assertion of bad against good must be pronounced impossible. We fail to see this because the opposition tends unconsciously to be modified. The bad will become perhaps merely bad for others or, again, for myself at another time and place, or it may come to mean no more than what in general the world would mistakenly call bad. And so understood, the bad has of course become compatible with the good. In the same way when a man exclaims 'Though I know it is bad, I still do not care', or where he even experiences an added and evil pleasure in opposing goodness, he is after all not really doing the bad as bad. He is pursuing still and he always must pursue his own good. The bad in general, or bad for others, or bad conditionally, is now subordinated to his positive good, and is included in that. Wherever the opposite ideas, in short, are seen to be opposite unconditionally, there may be oscillation or extrusion of one by the other, but the presence of both practical ideas at once is not possible in fact.[2] We may conclude, then, that if I acted knowingly for the bad, the bad must *ipso facto* have become good, and otherwise (we shall hereafter see) the act would certainly not be my volition.[3]

[1] I shall deal with this point in a later article [*E.* xxvi].

[2] I am, of course, following here, as every one must follow, Aristotle, but how far at the same time I may diverge from him I do not inquire. His 'incorrigible man', at least as commonly understood, seems certainly an impossible monster.

[3] For this latter consequence see below, pp. 467–8. The reader may object that the doctrine of the text refutes itself by proving too much. By the same reasoning, he may urge, it would be impossible also to will the good knowingly as against the bad, and with this we should be brought into

There is, however, a possible objection which I will briefly notice before we proceed. 'If', it may be said, 'you cannot have at once two alternative desires and ideas, surely this will mean that you are unable to think at all of any contrary alternatives, and such a doctrine, it is evident, you cannot maintain.' To this I reply (a) that to entertain theoretically and to think of incompatible ideas is, in the first place, not the same thing as to have two such ideas tending to realize themselves as existences in our mental being. It is not even the same thing as theoretically to predicate these ideas of what we call *our* reality. That which makes an idea theoretical will tend to prevent its further realization in existence. And that again which makes it a 'mere idea'—an idea, that is, which is not judged to be true of *our* world—will once more tend to separate it further from our psychical being. And the failure to perceive this is at once a common and most mischievous error. In the second place (b) when, without judging them to be true of our real world, we entertain the ideas of incompatibles and reflect on their nature, it is not the fact that, as we hold them before us, these ideas are wholly and barely incompatible. On the contrary, the idea of them as co-existing in this other world of mere thinking seriously

collision with a large mass of fact. The answer is that, if the bad were present with the good as its independent opposite, in that case you certainly could not act for the good. But when the bad is not so present, but comes before you merely as negated by the good and as a subordinate element in that, the case is radically altered. You may reply, 'But then the same thing will hold with the bad. Where the good as an independent positive idea is absent, the good may on its side be merely subordinate to the bad.' Yes, but, I answer, you are now supposing what is downright impossible. The good, where I am conscious morally, cannot fail to be present as a positive idea. The good and the bad are certainly opposed, but none the less they do not stand on a level. The bad without the good would be nothing at all, but the good does not, except in a narrow and special sense, depend on the bad. The bad is, in short, essentially subordinate to the good. To call it a mere kind of goodness would certainly not be correct, but that would be far less false than to speak of good and bad as being two independent positive kinds. But I cannot, of course, enter into such a large subject here. We should be led once more to think of the self-contradiction inherent in the bad, and again to reflect on the absurdity of assuming that every idea has a legitimate contrary.

modifies their nature. Their transference to this other world removes the point of union through which in our world they conflict, and by a change of conditions it so far makes them actually compatible. And the thought that, if this condition were removed, A and B certainly would clash, is not the positive maintenance before us of A and B immovably in a state of clashing. It is rather the idea of the extrusion of their collision by and from the 'real' world into another world, where by a distinction this collision is prevented from taking place. With these too brief remarks I must pass from an important and wide-reaching subject.

We have now to some extent examined the facts of mental conflict and of what may be called divided will. We previously, as the reader may recall, laid down those principles on which one idea is judged by us to be higher and to be more mine than another. And we may now proceed to the question of imputation in connexion with the definition of will. But in speaking of imputation, I mean merely to consider the fact without inquiring how far it can be morally justified.

The results we have reached enable us to deal rapidly with the subject of action against will. We have seen that the alleged fact, as it was offered to us, does not really exist. If we use 'desire' in the proper sense in which it involves an idea, we cannot really have an actual conflict of opposite desires, and in the end we might insist that we cannot experience the presence of more than one desire at the same time. But apart from this we found at any rate that, while A not-b holds its place, we cannot have also the simple and unconditional appearance of B not-a. And, given two opposite ideas explicitly qualified as opposite, we certainly could not in fact go on to realize either in a volition. If, however, for the sake of argument we suppose that B (whether we take it as independent and merely positive or again as an independent B not-a) has actually realized itself in the presence of A not-b, that would be a case of volition. The act would be so far clearly my will, but for other reasons, we shall go on to see, I might probably disown it as really mine. But I must repeat that I cannot myself admit any such case to be possible.[1]

I am far from denying that, while the idea of A not-*b* is held fast, B in spite of this can in a sense realize itself and pass into act. In the case of abnormal ideas we must allow that, in a sense, this can happen. But as soon as we consider the real sense in which it happens, we must deny that an act of this sort is a volition. The act would be a volition if B had broken loose from its subjection to A, and had come before us as itself positive and without any reference to A. But as long as B is held subordinate and does not appear except as negated by A, a different answer must be given. You cannot say that a subjected element contained within an idea is itself an idea proper. And since you, therefore, cannot assert that an idea has, in the proper sense, here realized itself, you, by the definition, are unable to affirm the presence of will. In such an act we no more have a volition than in an analogous case we should have a judgement. If, while mentally holding fast the idea A not-*b*, I were somehow to give utterance merely to B, that utterance would be no judgement nor the true expression of any idea really in my mind. And in the same way the escape into act of a subordinate element contained under an idea is not in the proper sense the realization of an idea, and it is so, by consequence, no volition.[2]

---

[1] The reader must bear in mind that this case supposes that both ideas are held to the last clearly each in its own individual character. If that character becomes obscured or confused, then, whatever else happens, the idea B certainly will not have realized itself as against A not-*b*. If the two alternatives or incompatibles come in the act before the mind, as one inconsistent ideal whole, it is clear that such an idea as this is not the idea of either, and could not itself possibly pass into fact. The supposed case, in short, demands that each idea maintains its individuality and its relation to the other; and where and so far as these ideas work practically, I do not believe this maintenance to be possible.

[2] The same, I would repeat, must be said of the realization of one of the two struggling aspects of a self-discrepant ideal whole. That is not in any proper sense the realization of an idea, and it is, therefore, not will. In order for the volition of B not-*a* in the presence of A not-*b* to happen, what would be required would be the maintenance of each idea as at once distinct and as related to the other. And we have seen that for a theoretical purpose

Our conclusion, however, must be different if, as usually happens, there are opposing ideas which oscillate. In this case B for the moment may have broken loose from subordination to A, and may in its turn have subjected A to itself, or, as is more probable, for the moment B may simply have extruded A from the mind as an idea. Under these conditions, if B realizes itself in act, we have clearly got a volition, and I do not know why we should hesitate to assert this confidently. How far that volition may on other grounds be more or less disowned as mine, is again a further and a different question.

As long as we keep to theory and confine ourselves to that which is in general true, we can deal more or less satisfactorily, I believe, with any case that can be offered. It would be far otherwise if we attempted to lay down rules by which to settle particular cases in practice. We have already noticed a class of actions which, in theory not puzzling, would prove really intractable by any rules of art. There are cases, we saw, where the collision has been more or less unconsciously and surreptitiously removed. Neither of the opposite ideas has here been forgotten or openly extruded, but one or both of them has in some way been so qualified that they are conjoined together in one whole, and now coexist peaceably. The action that results cannot, of course, realize this inconsistent ideal whole, and the action, therefore, as failing at least in part to carry out its idea, will so far not be my will. If volition, it will be volition only to a certain extent, which will be different in each case.[1] But to know in each case what was actually in the mind of the agent, to find the degree of his illusion, and

these ideas can be so held before us. But the very condition which makes that possible is, so far as I see, removed *ipso facto* by the ideas becoming practical. In order to become practical they, in short, are forced in some way to change their character.

[1] The question would turn mainly, I presume, on the amount of connexion or disconnectedness between the elements of the ideal whole which is before the mind of the actor, and on what we are able to speak of there as one idea. We should also have to ask how far a volition can fail to realize itself and can yet remain a volition. This difficult question will be taken up in a later article [*E.* xxviii].

to estimate his responsibility, indirect and direct, both by way of commission and by way of negligence, is not a possible achievement. And to draw up rules for constructing such an estimate would at best be pedantry.

I will add another instance of this difficulty, mainly because it tends to illustrate the account which I have given of will. If I have the idea of another person as performing a certain act or as being in a certain condition, and if then the act or the condition really follows in me, this, to speak in general, would not be a case of volition. And we must say the same thing if I merely imagine myself as being in a certain psychical state, and if my imagination is thereupon realized in fact. The result will in neither case be volition, and it will probably fail of being so in two ways. The result in the first place may not have followed as a genuine consequence from my mental state, and, if so, it cannot be the self-realization of an idea. And, even if the result has so followed, it is still not a volition. For the idea of another's act, or the mere imagination of my own act, is obviously not that ideal content which the result has realized. For the idea in each case, as I held it, was modified by a condition which divided it from simple union with my self as existing here and now. And since this character is not and could not be carried out in the result, my actual idea has not been realized, and the result, therefore, is not will. That which has been carried out in act is no more than a partial aspect of my idea, and it therefore in the proper sense is itself no idea at all. On the other hand, if the qualification of my idea as alien or as imaginary for the moment lapses and falls out (and there is, of course, a tendency to this lapse), the case is altered essentially. The idea at once becomes a mere unconditioned idea of the result, and, if that result is as a direct consequence realized, we have genuine volition.[1] This distinction, taken in general, appears to be clear and simple, but to decide in

---

[1] It may possibly be objected that, unless I also believe that the result will take place, that result is not volition. But unless the term 'belief' is improperly used here so widely that the objection disappears, I cannot assent to this doctrine. I shall return to this point in a future article [*E*. xxvi].

detail on the point at which an idea has actually lost its qualification as merely alien or imaginary might hardly be possible. And the attempt in such cases to estimate by rule the amount of my responsibility for the result, in the case of that result being unwilled, or again being willed, would at best be useless. It would probably end in that which has too deservedly given an ill name to casuistry.

We have seen the general conditions, according to which the act which results from a mental conflict is either to be taken as a volition or disowned in that character. The alleged case of an idea realizing itself openly in the face of its opposite we could not accept. It is not a fact, but is a very natural misinterpretation of fact. But, if the reader decides to regard it otherwise, the principles we have laid down will still enable us to deal with it. By these principles I judge ideas and desires to be higher and lower, and to be mine and not-mine, and I can apply these distinctions to the alleged case in two different ways. I may narrow the definition of will so that the case falls outside and can be disowned as volition. And, if so, will is 'the self-realization of an idea with which the self is identified, provided that this idea is not too much opposed materially or formally to that which is higher than itself and is essentially mine'. In view of the ambiguity of language, such a proviso would, perhaps, be defensible, but for two reasons I do not propose to adopt it.

In the first place, I have convinced myself that the fact alleged is not really a fact, and in the second place, even if it were a fact, I consider that the proviso is not wanted. The idea realizing itself openly against its contrary would in this case be a volition, and we certainly must go on to allow that this volition would be mine. But with so much the question is very far from disposed of. The act would be my volition, but it need not be my volition in the sense that I should impute it to my genuine self, and consider that I on the whole was accountable for its existence.

I am not inquiring here as to what in the end can be morally justified, and I am not even sure that such a question is able to be answered. I am asking merely about the way in which a man naturally judges concerning responsibility. And when we view things so, we are led, it seems to me, to the following result. Human responsibility is not a thing which is simple and absolute. It is not a question which you can bring bodily under one head, and decide unconditionally by some plain issue between Yes and No. It is, on the contrary, if taken as a whole, an affair of less and more, and it is in the main a matter of degree. And not being simple, it cannot be dealt with by any one simple criterion, but must be estimated, as we have seen, by several principles of value. It is indefensible to insist that I am absolutely accountable for all that has issued from my will, and am accountable for nothing else whatever.[1] If I have willed anything, I am of course in a sense responsible for so willing, but what that amounts to on the

---

[1] This doctrine is open to question, not merely on its positive side, but also otherwise. To say that I am to think myself better or worse for nothing except what directly or indirectly has issued from my will, is to come into collision with a body of sentiment which is not easily repudiated. Any doctrine of this kind starts on a path which in the end leads to a choice between opposite abysses (*A.R.*, chap. xxv). On this subject of moral responsibility I must be allowed here to protest against the assumption that it is tractable only when you introduce theistic ideas. On the contrary, I submit that it is precisely the intrusion of these ideas which has turned the question into a battle-field for rival dilemmas. For myself, when I am offered the idea of a moral creator who tries to divest himself by some ludicrous subterfuge of his own moral responsibility, or the idea of a non-moral potter who seems to think it a fine thing to fall out with his pots—when, I say, I am offered these decrepit idols as a full and evident satisfaction of the highest claims of the human conscience, I am led to wonder if the writer and myself, when we use the same words, can possibly mean the same thing. It is even a relief to turn back to the old view that the Deity is a person limited like ourselves, a person face to face with mere possibility and with chance and change, and in truth, like ourselves, in part ignorant and in part ineffectual. Such a doctrine, I readily grant, need not interfere with our human morality, but I must be allowed to doubt if those who more or less consciously would seek to revive it, can realize what it means. It would in the end leave the limited Deity together and along with ourselves in a Universe, the nature and sense and final upshot of which would in the end be unknown. I cannot myself admit that non-interference with our moral distinctions need be bought at the price of such ignorance. And there are also those who, accepting a more unlimited ignorance, would, in my opinion, be found in a less irrational position.

whole is a very different question. Being so far responsible
I may on the whole be so little responsible for the act, that
without hesitation I disclaim it and disown it as mine. If
an abnormal idea, foreign both to my natural self as a whole
and to the self which I have acquired, becomes so intense
as for the moment to extrude or master opposite elements,
the result may be formally a volition; but to make me on
the whole responsible for such an act would be barbarous
pedantry. For legal purposes we are of course compelled
to do the best that we can. We have to abstract from the
individuality of each case, we are forced to apply hard distinctions and more or less to ignore what refuses to square
with them.[1] But when we try to judge morally, no such
abstraction in the end is permitted. And here the question
if an act is mine is very far from being simple. It must be
considered from various points of view, and the answer, if
we reach one, will be a conclusion drawn from more esti-
mates than one. It will scarcely rid itself of degree and of
'more' and 'less', and be able to arrive at a clear verdict of
'Yes' or 'No'.

There would be little advantage in our attempting to
enter further into this subject, and I will end by repeating
those principles which we laid down at the beginning of
this article. (1) If I can bring and retain A not-*b* before my
mind, and cannot do this with B not-*a*, A is so far higher
and is so far mine more truly than is B. (2) The same conclusion follows if, taken on the whole, A is more pleasant
than B, or less painful. And if any idea has moving force
out of proportion to its pleasantness or, again, to its freedom from pain, that is, to some extent and so far as it goes,
a sign of the idea's alienation. It is, so far as it goes, a
reason for taking the idea as not genuinely mine. This is,
however, a criterion which cannot be applied indiscrimi-
nately. In the first place, where an idea moves us at once

[1] Thus for criminal purposes, I believe, in at least most codes, a man
must be mad or not mad. But it is notorious that, apart from the difficulty
of such a clean division, moral responsibility can exist among the insane
in varying degrees. Responsibility in intoxication is again a well-known
puzzle which law must cut with a knife.

and before it is attended to, the criterion seems inapplicable, at least directly. And the ground which is here excluded is really large. And in the second place we must lay stress on the words 'taken as a whole'. It is too commonly forgotten that, when we are moved, the facts are often complex, and that it is a question not of either pleasure or pain but of a mixture of both. Thus any idea, no matter how painful, will, if it remains held before us, produce a feeling of self-assertion with a tension against fact, and so to some extent must become pleasant. The view that a man can will that to which he is averse simply, or even in the proper sense averse actually, is in principle erroneous. And when Dr. Stout (*Manual*, p. 604) adduces fascination as an example of the first kind, I must consider this indefensible. For if fascination is used negatively for paralysis, there is no act, while if it is used positively for attraction, the presence of some pleasure seems even evident. (3) If A is the outcome of and represents something like a deliberate choice, while this is wanting in the case of B, B is so far the lower and the less mine. And similarly (4) if A appears as falling under a principle, while B is taken as under a principle lower and less general, or as under no principle at all, A will again to this extent be higher, and will be so far more mine. (5) And last we come to that most important criterion of all, which consists in the material difference of content. If A represents some main interest of my being, and if this feature is not contained or is to a less extent contained in B, then, according to the degree in which it is more absent from B, B is so far lower and is not mine. I need hardly point out that this last principle has a very wide bearing. It is applicable where there has been no mental conflict, and where there has been no question about the presence or the absence of volition. And to some extent this remark will also hold more or less if applied to those criteria which precede. But to dwell on this point would perhaps not repay us.

Will may therefore be defined as the self-realization of an idea with which the self is identified, and we have found no reason for restricting or for modifying this account.

But the reader must remember always that a subordinate element contained in an idea has no right to be counted as an idea, if it is taken by itself. And in any case let us avoid anything like an appeal to an unknown Will. If we find facts which we cannot explain, let us by all means collect them and class them, and, if we think we are justified, let us again by all means set them down as inexplicable. But what in psychology is gained by referring them to an unknown power, by whatever name we entitle it, I am unable to perceive. On the other hand, I am persuaded that by our so doing a great deal may be lost.

XXVI

THE DEFINITION OF WILL (I)

[*First published in* MIND, N.S. xi, No. 44, 437–69. *October*, 1902.]

THE object of this article, and of two which follow it, is to explain and defend a definition of will, a definition which has been already laid down by me on various occasions.[1] The only proper explanation and defence of it would be a psychological treatment of the whole practical side of mind. I must content myself here with endeavouring in an unsystematic manner to advocate a view which, the more I see it criticized, strikes me more as the one view which is tenable. But the will of which I speak, is the will which is known and experienced as such. It is not something in a world beyond and behind the contents of our experience, something to be reached only by an inference valid or vicious. In other words we are to remain here within the limits of empirical psychology.[2]

A volition is 'the self-realization of an idea with which the self is identified', and in psychology there is in the end no will except in the sense of volition. We may speak of a permanent or standing will for a certain end, and may talk as if it existed there where at the moment no actual volition is present. In the same way we are said to have a permanent belief, or again a permanent attention, where for the moment we are not supposed to be actually attending.[3] But though a 'standing will' may be used with a legitimate meaning, there is in the proper sense no actual will except in volitions. Will therefore is action outward or internal, but on the other hand not every action is really will. You cannot even say that an action must be will in all cases

---

[1] *E.* xxiv and xxv. Cf. *E.* xxiii and xiv.

[2] Cf. *E.* xxii. The above statement does not mean that a volition may not be continued beyond the limits of what we experience. See below.

[3] *E.* xxiv. 438. The meaning of 'a standing will' is a point to be discussed in a later article.

where in some sense I impute it, or should impute it, to myself. But, wherever an action has the character laid down in our definition, I should impute to myself that act as a volition. Language and experience bear, I believe, an overwhelming testimony to this result, while upon the other side, apart from lax expressions which do not claim to be more than lax, I am unable to find more than misunderstanding and error. If in these articles I can remove some more or less serious mistakes, the doctrine which I advocate will, I hope, recommend itself to the reader.

A volition, I have said, is the self-realization of an idea with which the self is identified, and a volition is a whole, in which we may go on to find the following aspects. There is (1) existence, (2) the idea of a change,[1] and (3) the actual change of the existence by the idea to (4) the idea's content. And (5) in this change the self feels itself realized. The self is altered to something which before the change it actually was not, something which it felt to be its own proper being and existence. Up to what point, however, the actual realization of self must be felt, and again how far the self, beside thus feeling, must also perceive itself and so be self-conscious of itself as an object, are questions which will have to be discussed in their own place.

It is difficult in a series of articles to make a beginning except from some assumption. I think it best at present to assume provisionally the existence of what is called 'ideo-motor action', and to try to show that volition falls under this head. I shall therefore take for granted here the tendency of an idea to realize itself, and any question as to the existence and nature of this tendency must be deferred to another article. Let us then for the moment agree that ideo-motor action in general is a fact, and from this let us go on to consider in detail the aspects of volition which we have mentioned.

It may be convenient to take first the aspect of existence.

---

[1] Or we may prefer to say 'the idea of something different to what exists'. The precise content of this idea is a difficult question which will have to be discussed at length hereafter.

This calls, I think, here for but little remark, and any metaphysical discussion of its difficulties would be out of place. It is, we may say, the aspect of reality as opposed to anything that is merely ideal. It is the temporal series of events, external or inward only, when that is taken as an actual series; or again it is that which is now present to me, together with any actual prolongation which is continuous with and one with my present. How far the future, as well as the past, can be regarded in any sense as existing, I am unable here to discuss. Existence may be spatial also, and, as spatial, it will begin from my 'here' and will contain whatever is continuous and one with that datum. But I cannot myself agree that existence must always be spatial, unless I may add that it need not always be spatial directly. And there is no occasion, I think, at present for any further remark. The sense in which existence comes as a not-self in opposition to a self, as well as a reality over against an idea, will be dealt with hereafter.

Existence, then, is that actual series of events which is either (*a*) now and here, or is (*b*) continuous with my here and now. In volition (we must next proceed to note) this existence must be altered, and, further, the alteration must start directly from the existing 'now'. The change must begin on and from this 'present', and this present must be taken in its own character and unconditionally. But, while emphasizing this point, we must remember not to push emphasis into error. Volition certainly must begin from and on the 'this now', but volition as certainly is not confined within these limits. And it is wrong to deny that I can really will something to happen after an hour or after my death. I shall return to this error, but at present need insist only on the truth that, wherever volition ends, it must begin at once by an alteration of my present existence.

The reader may remember that this doctrine has been denied. It has, for instance, been objected that will does not always aim at an alteration of the present, for its end, we are told, may be a mere continuance and so an absence of change. But a continuance of the present in a certain character is, I must urge, if really willed, a real will for alteration. The present is taken here as naturally, and of itself, about to pass into a different character, and hence, if I will that it remain the same, I must will it to change from itself. And if this conclusion at first sight seems paradoxical, I think that on reflection the paradox may vanish.[1]

In volition there must be an alteration of existence, and of existence as such. The change, which comes in, must not merely be something which in some indirect way belongs to existence, and qualifies that so as to leave it, so far, unchanged as existing. On the contrary, the change must directly qualify the existence itself in such a way that, even as existing, it suffers that change. The alteration in other words must not be merely ideal. This is a distinction which within my present limits I cannot fully discuss, but a failure to grasp it would leave the reader at the mercy of error. Let us suppose, for instance, that what I have willed is to think and know this or that, the result of my volition will here have two sides which we must not confuse. The object has been qualified ideally, and this, again, is an event which has happened in me. My existence has, as existence, been changed by my will, but the existence of the object itself, on the other hand, has not been altered at all. It has become qualified not in fact but, as we say, ideally; while the actual change which has taken place belongs, we say, only to me. It is impossible to ask here what is the ultimate truth with regard to this distinction,

---

[1] Lotze, *Med. Psych.*, p. 300, gives the instance of a martyr whose will is directed on actual pain. But the martyr's will, I reply, has for its object the maintenance of a certain attitude with regard to the pain. He wills that the pain shall not move him, and this means that it shall not take the course which it naturally would take of itself. His real end is therefore to alter existence, to change it so that it will follow a different course. The willed maintenance of an attitude, in short we may say, is a perpetual willed alteration of existence. We may notice here another doubt which perhaps may be raised. Will is not always for something to come, it may be said, for I can will, however unsuccessfully, to alter my past. But, I reply, the fact that the change, when made, would lie behind me, is really irrelevant. From the point of view of the act itself the change is future, and the act starts from the present state of things and alters that. I shall consider later how far the fact of Resolve can be taken as an objection to the doctrine of the text.

but the distinction itself must be observed in psychology. If by your volition you have, for instance, produced truth and knowledge in yourself, you may by a legitimate abstraction neglect the aspect of its appearance in you, and so take the truth merely as being such or such in itself. But if, while still maintaining this abstraction, you attributed the resulting truth to your will—you would have fallen into a very serious confusion and mistake. At least for psychology the will to know cannot alter the real object known, and it cannot, in other words, make truth. Your will to know alters your actual existence, and with that there comes a changed appearance of the object in you, but the object itself is not thereby changed. The truth in brief has two aspects (I do not ask how they are connected), and it is only one of these aspects which can be produced by your will. The ideal qualification of the object has been a real change, but it has not, at least for psychology, altered the object as existing.[1]

From this I will go on to lay stress on another important point. Not only in volition must the existence be altered, but it must be altered to that character which was possessed by the idea. And not only must the existence suffer a change to this prescribed result, but the result must also be produced by the foregoing idea. The idea must itself alter the existence to its own nature, or in other words the idea must itself carry itself out into the changed existence. And, if all this does not happen, there is really no will, but at most a more or less explicable counterfeit and illusion. This point is so evident that I think it useless to enlarge further on it here, and will pass on to warn the reader against a dangerous misunderstanding. In insisting that the result in volition must come from the idea, I do not mean to assert that the idea must be the whole and the sole cause. This would be a doctrine which in my judgement could not possibly be sustained, and in short would involve a very serious mistake. I cannot here enter into the general subject of cause and effect, but for our present purpose I may perhaps express my meaning as follows.

[1] Cf. here *E*. xxii. 370 and *E*. xxiv.

The idea is certainly not that whole complex cause which goes before and issues in the effect, but the idea is a positive and necessary element within that complex whole. It is not a mere accompaniment or a mere *sine qua non*, however inseparable or even necessary, but it enters directly into the causal sequence so as to make a difference by which the effect is produced. I think that this justifies us in maintaining that the alteration is due to the idea, and without so much as this I would submit that there can be no real will.[1]

And for this reason a result, when it has only been expected, is not taken as willed. Expectation is not volition except to that extent to which it is a will for apprehension, and is a will so far for a change of my psychical existence. If I expect the arrival of a letter and the arrival in fact happens, my idea has certainly been realized, but the result is not attributed to my will. The cause of the letter's coming is not taken to lie in existence *plus* my idea, but in existence qualified by other and independent conditions. We may illustrate again by the case of a spasmodic movement which is expected but not willed. The whole question is in brief whether, and in what way, my idea contributes or does not contribute to the result.[2] We may

---

[1] A machine might be such that, say, its whistling might be the *sine qua non* of its work, since both in fact are effects from one and the same cause. If the machine took the whistling to be the cause of the work, that would be clearly an illusion, and if the idea in volition were a mere *sine qua non*, will would also be illusory. It may be urged on the other side that if the idea is but one element in the whole cause, we cannot say properly that the effect is produced by the idea. An objection of this kind, we must however not forget, has a very wide application. I think it perhaps enough to reply here that, where we consider that such an element has importance, and where we wish to insist that its presence really, as we say, 'makes the difference', we may fairly speak of the change as being produced by it.

[2] If I have not misunderstood the doctrine advocated by Professor Münsterberg in his *Willenshandlung*, he considers the mere precedence of the idea enough to produce the appearance of volition. Any such doctrine would, however, seem to be opposed to the plain facts mentioned in my text. Since writing the above remark, as well as the present and the two following articles, I have made the acquaintance of Professor Münsterberg's interesting *Grundzüge der Psychologie*. The account of our volitional consciousness seems considerably amended there (pp. 354–5), but it

illustrate this once more from the other side by a different example. If, instead of the arrival of a letter, we take the cessation of a pain, we may now be unable to decide as to the expected result having issued from my will. And the question here again will be whether and how far the idea itself contributed towards bringing about its own existence. I shall have in another article to enter more fully into the conditions of our perception of agency, and it is sufficient to insist at present on these two main points. On the one hand the existence must be changed so as to express the idea, and on the other hand this change must not come from the mere existence itself. If we do not take the alteration to be made by the idea, we are bound to deny the real presence of volition.[1]

remains, as I understand it, fatally defective. When a man expects to yawn, and then this happens, it surely does not by itself give him the consciousness of will. On the other hand it falls, so far as I see, within Professor Münsterberg's definition. But the problem, I venture to think, has been made hopeless from the first by more than one unexplained, if not arbitrary, assumption, and I must regret that Professor Münsterberg's great penetration and ingenuity have not been applied in larger measure to the work of making clear his principles.

[1] On Expectation cf. *E.* xiv. 261, 278 and xxiv. 417, note 2. I do not admit that in all expectation there must be will or even desire, but, so far as there is will, it is a will only for the ideal development of the object in and for me, and any other will, if present, falls outside the expectation itself. It is instructive to take a case where I both will a result and also therefore expect the result to happen. We have here (*a*) the existence as it is now, and (*b*) the existence ideally qualified for me by the result, when taken by me as subject to the condition of my idea and a time-interval. And so far there is no opposition between my idea and existence, and no awareness of will. For the actual volition we must have also (*c*) an awareness of the opposition of my idea of the result to the existence as it is now, followed by the attribution (in some sense) of the actual change as an effect to the idea. We need not stop to notice also the further possible attribution of my better apprehension of the result, when it arrives, to another volition. What we should observe in the above case is that, for actual volition to take place, the consciousness of the time-interval must for the moment lapse, or at least pass into the background, and that on the other hand this consciousness is essential to expectation proper. A thing may be desired and expected, and may even be willed and expected, but, so far as in the proper sense it is expected, we must add that, so far, it is not properly willed or desired. If you do not feel the idea of the change to conflict with the present existence,

I have now to some extent explained the sense in which volition is described as the self-realization of an idea, but I have so far said nothing on the meaning of the phrase 'identification with self'. I shall discuss this latter point hereafter at some length, but for the present it must be deferred. There are difficulties which still attach themselves to the former part of our definition, and I must endeavour in this article to remove them and to correct some mistakes.

It may be objected first that will cannot be the alteration of existence by an idea, since there may be a volition where the idea does not really carry itself out. And as examples of this may be adduced such cases as resolve and intention, will in paralysis, and again the facts of disapprobation or approval. I will discuss these objections beginning with resolve; and in connexion with this point I must deal with a matter of importance, the difference between a complete and an incomplete act of will.

If intention and resolve by themselves were really volition, why should we hear of a *mere* resolve or of a *mere* intention? The question is obvious and, I will add, it points to an evident truth. A resolve in its essence is not a volition, and, so far as actually it is will, it is so but incidentally. The moral chasm between the two facts often cannot be ignored. It is plainly one thing to be resolved beforehand, and another thing to act when the moment has come. And, if resolve were will, then to make a hero, or again a monster of vice, no more would be wanted than defect of imagination with ignorance and foolishness. But a resolve really is not volition, and the point of difference seems clear. A resolve is directed, and it must be directed, on what we know is not yet actual, and so is only ideal; while volition, as we have seen, must invariably begin with the present

you have no experience of volition, and, so far as the certain future is emphasized, this opposition disappears. On the other hand, in all expectation there is a tendency for this qualification by the time-interval to drop out. The moment that this happens there is an opposition between the existence and the idea, and desire and perhaps volition may in consequence be generated forthwith. Cf. *E.* xiv. 261.

'this'. Volition on the one hand is not confined within one moment, and yet on the other hand volition must start always from the actual present, while in resolve, if this could happen, the essential character would be lost. I do not mean that the existence which resolve confronts is always conditional, though, where this is so, resolve, we may notice, remains still resolve. Resolve may be directed on a prolongation of the present which, though ideal, is unconditional, but it never in any case is concerned directly with the actual 'this now'. Its object is sundered from the present by an interval, and is known to be so sundered; and if it were otherwise, and if to the smallest extent resolve could deal with the actual 'now', it would have evidently ceased to be resolve and would have passed into volition.

This to me seems clear, and I take the denial of it to be an obvious error, and it is therefore desirable to ask how such an error can have arisen. The doctrine of will, we may remind ourselves, is full of difficulty, and a readiness to grasp at anything which seems likely to help is a natural weakness. But apart from this there are various causes likely to create confusion about will and resolve. (i) Will may be taken in the sense not of actual volition but of standing tendency. (ii) Resolve in many cases involves the actual volition of a psychical state. (iii) There is an incomplete as well as a complete act of will, and, though resolve never can amount even to an incomplete volition, it can partake of its nature. For incidentally it consists partly in the same process and goes some length on the same road. But in resolve (I would repeat this) the existence to be changed by the idea is severed invariably by a gap from the actual present. I will now proceed to explain these three grounds of error, beginning with the last, and in connexion with this I must emphasize the distinction between complete and incomplete will.

With will taken in its full sense I agree that psychology cannot concern itself. My will is not completely realized until its end has been actually attained, even if that attainment does not take place until after my death. And for some purposes the confinement of will to a narrower meaning would not hold. But in psychology this complete sense is, I think, inadmissible, and the process of will cannot be taken as extended beyond the limits of my body. And even these limits, some would insist, are already too wide. If will is a psychical state, it cannot, they would urge, include a physical consequence; and even a psychical result must on the same principle be excluded from will. For a psychical fact, it can be argued, must in every case be defined as what itself actually is, and it is not characterized by anything beyond to which, however probably, it may lead. But I cannot for myself, even in psychology, accept on the whole such a limitation of will. I do not agree that, when a psychical process leads normally to a certain result in the individual's body or mind, the result can never be considered as part of the process. Such a question as how, for instance, I can will successfully to recall a word or to move my hand, must fall, I think, within psychology. I cannot naturally regard such results as events external to my will, and as additional consequences, the absence of which leaves my will unaffected. In volition the end anticipated in the idea is normally carried out into fact, and the process is normally recognized as a single movement of one and the same thing throughout. The removal of one part of this process leaves the whole incomplete, and to my mind modifies its character, and I cannot accept the mere beginning by itself as essentially complete.

Psychology, I agree, has to set bounds to its subject. The extent to which it can recognize physiological fact is limited. It will admit no more of this, in short, than it is forced to admit in order to justify its own account of psychical phenomena.[1] And psychology, I agree, cannot follow the process of will beyond the limits of the body, but on the contrary must take will as ended within them. While not denying, that is, the completer sense in which will goes

---

[1] On the one hand, physiological explanation and fact has, taken for itself, no place in psychology. On the other hand, if it is anywhere contended that a difference in the physiological explanation affects materially the psychological account, I do not see how such a contention can be on principle excluded.

on to a further end, the psychologist may fairly say that he is unable to consider it. And for certain purposes within psychology (as again within ethics) I agree even to a further limitation of will. The psychologist may narrow even further the meaning which he gives to the word, and may use it in a still more incomplete sense. He may take volition simply as that fact which at the present it is, without regard to anything physical, or even anything psychical, that we expect to result from it. Thus, if I will the movement of my hand, my volition, we may say, already is there, although my hand may perhaps in fact not actually move. And, if I will to recollect, then I may go on in fact either to succeed or to fail, but in each case alike my volition really is present. In this narrower sense we may for certain purposes take volition as actual. But I must insist that, however actual so far, my will so far is incomplete.

We may, in other words, distinguish roughly two periods or stages in volition. The first of these stages will consist in what may be called the mere prevalence of the idea, while in the second stage the idea will advance beyond its own existence towards its physical or psychical end. And I agree that in psychology we have a right to make use of these distinctions. On the other hand I urge that they everywhere involve some abstraction, and that this abstraction may be more or less artificial and vicious. There are cases where the action follows on the idea without hesitation or delay, and the stage of prevalence can hardly be said here to have an independent duration. And again the mere prevalence of the idea may itself go beyond the idea, for it may depend on the idea's carrying itself out to some extent into the fact. An actual movement of my body, however partial, may be the means by which the mere idea of such a movement prevails. On the other hand, in certain cases we may consider the whole process of will as roughly divided into two more or less separate movements. In the first of these the idea, we may say, merely as an idea gains possession of my mind, while in the second it advances further beyond itself to realize itself in the facts. And while I must insist that the first stage, if taken strictly by itself, is not a complete or even really an incomplete act of will, on the other hand, viewed otherwise and under some conditions, the prevalence of the idea does amount to an incomplete but actual volition.

But it will be objected that, if volition may ever be such an inward event, our definition of will is no longer tenable. Is not the prevalence of an idea, I may be asked, something different from its realization in fact? In order to answer this question we must inquire in what this prevalence consists. The point is difficult, and, in order to deal with all sides of it, I am forced in passing to anticipate a future result.[1] In the presence of a practical idea we have of course an ideal change of existence, and on the other side, against this, we have the actual existence itself, existence merely psychical or physical as well. But in the presence of an idea which is willed or desired, we have another feature also. The existence outward or inward, which is to be changed by the idea,[2] is also in a special sense a not-self opposed to my inner self; and this opposition, we shall hereafter see, is essential to will. This feature may be called in a sense the idea's prevalence. For the idea is felt as something which is in one with my whole inner self, and hence nothing in me can oppose it except some element which in a sense is excluded from my self. Prevalence in this sense may however belong to ideas which I should agree are not willed, and by itself therefore it evidently is not enough for volition. And there is no reason why we should further here concern ourselves with it.

We may pass from this to consider prevalence in another sense more material to our inquiry. If an idea is to be willed, it must not merely be felt as in one with my inner self. In order to be willed it must also dominate my psychical existence, and must banish or subject to itself whatever there is contrary to its being and progress.[3] Now

---

[1] The point has been noticed briefly, *Mind*, N.s. x. 446 [*E.* xxiii. 397–8; 398, note].

[2] We must never forget that the existence to which the idea is opposed may be merely psychical.

[3] I do not here discuss how this sense of prevalence is connected with the

prevalence, taken in this sense, is clearly a process, and it may develop itself to completion through various stages and degrees. Hence we may agree that, when the process is complete, we have reached volition, but on the other side must insist on an inquiry into its aspects and stages. For here once again we may verify the presence of will as the self-realization of an idea. (i) The idea, in the first place, has to banish or subdue any idea contrary to itself, and it has to overcome hostility or inertia wherever that is found in any other psychical element. And (ii) together with this the idea must develop its own content. It must to some extent go on to specify and to individualize further its own proper nature. As the idea, say, of striking prevails, it will become at the same time less general. It will become more and more the idea of a blow of this particular kind struck by myself in my present individual character. (iii) And in most cases, though perhaps not in every case, where the idea practically prevails, the specification of the idea will already include and consist in some part of its realization beyond itself. The prevalence of the idea, that is, implies, as already actual in psychical and perhaps in physical fact, a part of that change which it is the business of the idea to carry out into existence. We shall understand better the importance of these aspects, when we have examined some cases where will is alleged to exist apart from a realization of its idea.[1]

former one. We have, on the one hand, an unwelcome fixed idea which gradually dominates me, until, all opposition being overcome, it is identified with myself. On the other hand, we have a desired end which I feel wholly to be mine, and which yet cannot realize itself against some part of my psychical being.

[1] With regard to using the impossibility of recall as a mark of prevalence, I do not think that by this we should really gain anything. The prevalence of the idea certainly implies that the process must advance unhindered by 'me', the 'me' being here understood not to contain any psychical element to which 'myself' is opposed. But this prevalence, we have already seen, is not volition. On the other hand, the impossibility of recall, if taken in a fuller sense, would be deceptive, for it would depend on circumstances more or less accidental. To pass to another point, we may here notice the question whether an act which takes time is to be regarded as one will or as several. We may answer that, so far as the sequel does not follow auto-

I will, however, first ask generally in what sense and how far these three aspects of the idea's prevalence amount to its realization in fact. (i) In its subjugation or banishment of antagonists, and in its possession, as we say, of my self, the idea takes a step without which it could not advance to its end. If, however, by an artifice you consider this aspect by itself, it will belong to the progress of the idea as a necessary condition, and will not by itself be that actual progress. (ii) But with the specification of the idea's content the case is modified. Certainly in itself this internal development does not carry the idea out beyond its own being into fact. But on the other hand it is itself the beginning of one continuous process which beyond a certain point does so alter the actual existence. (iii) And at least in most cases the process of prevalence has already gone beyond that point. It does to some extent, as we saw, involve an actual change of the fact so as to correspond with the idea. And this alteration, however partial and slight it may be, carries, so far, the mere idea beyond itself into existence. A state of mind, possessing these three aspects, is a realization of the idea which we must admit is incomplete, but up to a certain limit it is an actual realization. The idea has actually moved in the strictest sense on its anticipated journey. And measured by our definition such an advance may be called an incomplete act of will. A prevalence, on the other hand, which remained ideal and failed to include this third aspect, I should myself refuse to term even an incomplete volition. It is an approach to will which has stopped short of the actual state, and how it can seem to have reached it I shall soon endeavour to explain.

We have now to some extent perceived the nature of complete and of incomplete will, and the degrees by which completion may be gradually approached. I have pointed

matically from the beginning, the act may be regarded as having both characters. Each new change in existence, which is made directly by the idea, may so far be regarded as a new volition. This point may become important where the idea has failed to anticipate features which arise in the actual execution, and where in consequence the will becomes, as we say, paralysed, or has to be renewed.

out how, even in a case of incomplete volition, the idea to some extent has carried itself out into fact. And where this feature is absent the idea may in a sense have prevailed, but I should certainly refuse to admit that volition has begun and that will is present. I can hardly hope that so far I have conveyed my exact meaning to the reader, but this meaning will, I trust, show itself in our examination of detail. And we may forthwith return to those cases where volition was alleged actually to exist, and where on the other hand the idea was asserted not to carry itself out. We may take first the objection which has been based on the fact of will during paralysis, and we may join with this an inquiry into what is called a 'will' for something not under our control. I shall then consider such an instance as our unsuccessful will to recall a name, and from that can pass to the claims of resolve and approval.

If a man's arm is paralysed so that in fact he is unable to move it, he is none the less able, we are assured, most fully to will this movement (see Professor James, *Psychology*, chap. xxvi). I do not question here the fact itself, but I should interpret it as follows. The patient perceives the existence of his limb as it is, and over against this he has the idea of its alteration. This idea possesses him, and, apart from the above perception of existence, it finds in him nothing which seems to oppose its complete realization. The idea starts unchecked on its anticipated course and becomes more particularized, and then, at a certain point beyond this, it ceases to advance. But, although the idea no longer goes forward, there is a sense of actual volition. Now, as I understand the facts, the idea, in most cases at least, succeeds to some extent in passing beyond itself into actual fact. It moves not the part required but other parts of the body (James, ibid.). And, where this is the case and where such an actual movement is also perceived, I take it to explain in accordance with our definition the conscious-ness of will. The idea has moved forwards towards the change of fact, not only, as we say, in its own character, but beyond itself into an actual movement of the body. And this movement will, I assume, be perceived as a continuance of its progress. And a process carried out to this point may, I think, be taken as a volition which is actual although incomplete.[1]

But, it may be urged, there are cases where the idea does not advance outwards even up to this point. In these cases the idea remains entirely within itself, and after all there is an actual experience of will. If this does not take place in paralysis, I may be told, it happens often elsewhere. It happens where I will, for example, the movement of something outside of and unconnected with my body, as, for instance, the arrival of a letter or a change of position in the furniture of my room. Now, with regard to this alleged fact, I do not dispute that in a sense it takes place, but as to what happens when it takes place I remain in some doubt. For myself, usually, where I will, let us say, a chair to transport itself across the room, I find that I connect this anticipated movement with some bodily act of my own. A fixed glance, an order uttered inwardly or some other slight movement, goes in most cases together with the 'prevalence' of the idea; and this actual movement, I believe, enters into the process of that idea's content. And, so far as this is so, the idea once more has carried itself out beyond itself. The idea has begun an actual change of the opposed existence, partial indeed and indirect, but enough probably to give the sense of its process having passed out into fact. And there is a further point which, in connexion with all these cases, I would recommend to the reader's notice. If I 'will', let us say, that a letter has arrived or that a chair

[1] The movement is not perceived as a complete carrying out of the idea. For in the first place the part moved is not that part of which the movement was willed. And in the second place, even if the two perceptions were to some extent confused, the absence of movement also in the required part, an absence which is perceived, would lead us to regard our volition as frustrated. On the other side our volition, though incomplete, will appear as actual. For the bodily movement, following in a continuous process on the prevalence of the idea, will naturally come to the mind as a sign that the idea has passed over into the body, however inadequately. And a process carried out to this point may in accordance with our definition be taken as will, as a volition which is not completed but which still is actually there.

of itself is to come towards me, I find that a vivid imagination of the event may be a condition of my willing it to
exist. I may have, that is, to view with my mind's eye the
letter now somewhere waiting for me, or I may have to see
in imagination the beginning of the chair's advance. And,
if I so help myself, I am able to reach an imperfect but
actual consciousness of will, and I admit that possibly I
may reach this in the entire absence of any bodily movement. This experience has perhaps an important bearing
on our problem. We have willed so often in fact that we
can will, as we say, in imagination, and while my hand is
stationary I can imagine myself producing its changes.
And let us for argument's sake agree that this may happen
without a muscular movement. We call this volition
imaginary because it is not directed upon our actual fact,
and because its change is not the movement in fact of my
real hand. But now suppose that, while I will in imagination some movement of my hand or of a chair, I have these
objects at the same time actually visible before me. Their
perceived rest must oppose the progress of my idea into
the fact now and here, but on the other side their imagined
motion will support its advance, and will so far give me the
consciousness of will. We have only then to suppose some
confusion between the object as perceived and as imagined,
and the door is opened to a more or less illusory awareness
of actual will. And this remark may have a bearing wider
than that which appears at first sight. Where a process is
familiar and where the beginning of that process is given,
it is possible to gain a premature and perhaps deceptive
awareness of the end. And in this way I think we may
sometimes create a more or less fallacious experience of will.

The conclusion then, which so far we have reached, can
be briefly resumed thus. An actual volition may certainly
be involved in the prevalence of an idea, but that volition
at the same time will be incomplete. But there will not be
in any case even an incomplete volition, unless to some
extent the idea carries itself out beyond itself. Where this
aspect fails there will at most be a doubtful experience, due

to a confusion between imagination and fact.[1] We may verify the same result again in such a case as our will to recollect.

The idea of recalling some name or some other circumstance may be suggested to my mind, and I may decide by an act of will to carry out this recall. But the attempt may fail in fact to succeed, though the volition has been actual, and the idea, it may be said therefore, has prevailed but has not to any extent realized itself. This is an interpretation which once more I am unable to accept. There may have been in the first place a successful will for some internal utterance, and, apart from this, we may notice another important feature in the case. A will to recollect is a will to effect a certain change in my psychical being, and, even where this idea fails to carry itself out to the end, yet in its prevalence it may make, as we saw, some actual advance beyond itself. The possession of myself by the idea of a name to be recollected involves to a certain extent in fact the actual process of recollection. The recalling consists, that is, in the recovery of contiguous detail, and, so far as I can judge, wherever the idea of such a recall has become prevalent, that detail is in every case actually restored up to a variable limit. If so, the idea, we must say, has to a certain point realized itself in fact. If we take on the other side a case where my inability is more complete, I cannot myself verify in such a case the experience of actual volition. I cannot, I find, 'will myself' to know something, if my ignorance is too complete. Where this ignorance extends beyond a certain degree I cannot myself find a place for the will in question. I must either imagine my case to be other than in fact it actually is, or again I must content myself with the volition of something like a form of words, or else, to speak for myself, I cannot arrive at any experience of will. And this, I think, is not because volition

---

[1] If the mere prevalence of the idea is looked upon as a step towards its carrying itself out, and if it comes to the mind in that character, some consciousness of will would naturally result. I could not myself, however, admit the actual presence of will, except so far as the prevalence of the idea incidentally involves its actual passage beyond itself as a mere idea.

depends on any belief as to possibility.[1] It is because the idea has failed to develop and to realize itself even incompletely, and has not passed beyond itself even in imagination. And hence, if my interpretation of this obscure fact is correct, it will fall once more under the principle which we have already laid down.

I will now return to consider further the case of resolve.[2] We saw that resolve is not volition, since will is directed always upon the present, while an actual aim at present existence must be excluded from resolve. On the other hand, there are several causes which may lead to a confusion between resolve and will. In the first place, my being resolved may be a state of standing or permanent will. We shall inquire later as to the proper meaning which belongs to this phrase, but a resolve so understood, though in a sense it is will, is clearly not itself an actual volition. In the second place, I may of course have willed to form some resolution, and in this case there is certainly an actual volition. But what has really been willed is the production of the mental state called resolve, and the volition here and the resolve itself are clearly not the same thing. And there is in the third place another reason why will and resolve are confused. The essence of a resolve, we have seen, divides it from volition, for it belongs to that essence that a resolve is directed on something other than the present. And yet incidentally it may imply an actual though incomplete will. The idea in a resolve may to a greater or less extent carry itself out at once into actual fact, and, so far as this process takes place, it will involve a real volition. Or, again, in resolve the idea may be realized in an imaginary existence, an existence more or less confused with actual fact, and, so far as this confusion happens, the resolve will be accompanied by some consciousness of will. But every such process falls, we must not forget, outside the resolve, when that is taken in its own true and special character. That character implies that the existence which is confronted by the resolve is distinguished from the existence

---

[1] This point is discussed later.
[2] Cf. here *A.R.* 410 [= 463], note.

which is present here and now simply. And, if this consciousness of difference lapses, and so far as it lapses, resolve has necessarily so far ceased to exist. In other words, when I resolve, I must take my idea as not to be realized at once now and here. And if the idea were not thus separated in my mind from a possible advance at once into the facts, resolve would have passed into will incomplete or complete. It is, we saw, not true that the existence aimed at by my resolve is always conditional. That existence may be taken as certain although lying in the future; but in every case necessarily it is regarded as sundered from the present. Resolve, on the one hand, is no mere contemplation of an anticipated or imaginary case. For there is an opposition of the idea to the contemplated fact, and a forward movement of the idea to alter this fact to itself. And we have seen that incidentally this advance may imply such a change in the actual fact as amounts to a real though incomplete will. But such a change, I repeat, is so foreign to the essence of the resolve that, if it were directly aimed at, the resolve would knowingly have passed beyond itself.

There are some additional cases where it is urged that volition can be present, although in these cases the idea fails to pass beyond itself. I must however defer the consideration of what Professor James has called 'consent', and the discussion of any argument based on Mr. Shand's 'types of will'. I shall explain hereafter why I am forced to reject these doctrines, and I must content myself here with some very brief remarks on the subject of approval. The approval or again the disapproval of a mere idea has been held to constitute will, and such a doctrine once more is in conflict with our account. There are two ways in which 'the idea' may be here understood. It may be taken as the idea of a change to be made in my present existence, and in this sense we have in effect discussed its claim already. There will be an actual volition so far as such an idea prevails, and so far as in its prevalence it also succeeds in carrying itself out. Apart from this process my approval certainly is not volition, and, where this process is present, my approval adds nothing to will. If, on the other hand, the idea were not an idea of a change here and now, volition so far would be even excluded by approval. To approve of things as they really are, or as they are imagined to exist, is to take an attitude in itself contrary to actual will. The subject of disapproval, so far as that requires any further treatment, must be deferred. Disapproval in itself is not will and, so far as it becomes will, it falls under negative volition. This is however a topic too obscured by error to be briefly discussed. I shall consider it hereafter at length when I examine some alleged irreducible types of will.

I have now dealt with several objections raised against our definition of will. They have been based so far on the assertion that the idea in will need not carry itself out beyond itself. And I have tried to show that such an assertion cannot be maintained. I must pass from this to examine some other views which in my opinion are mistaken, and we may begin with the alleged necessity in will for the presence of judgement or belief. But before I discuss this, I will remark on a point of importance.

We have seen that the idea in volition must prevail and dominate, and this in the end means that we are moved by but a single idea. I do not say that beside this one idea no other idea can be present in will, but, if present, no other idea can be the object of will or desire. It cannot be the suggestion of a change which, felt in one with my inner self, then moves itself towards its own existence in fact. So far as in volition we have the presence of two moving ideas, one of these, unless it comes as a not-self opposed to my inner self, must tacitly or explicitly be subordinate to and included in the other. It must enter the main process as a passive accompaniment or as an active factor, and it may contribute to the total idea positively or again by the way of its own subjection or banishment. I have explained the above doctrine in a former article and to this I must refer.[1] If in will there ever remains an independent prac-

[1] *E*. xxiv and again *E*. xxv.

tical idea which is not thus subordinated, that idea will belong to the not-self which is opposed to myself. There is not really a divided will and there is not even a divided desire, if these are understood as volition and as desire which actually exist. The plausibility of the opposite view comes mainly from a mistake as to what is meant by 'one idea', and this logical error has resulted in mal-observation of the facts. But I am unable here to do more than refer the reader to my preceding articles.

This doctrine of the idea's monarchy has another side which I will now proceed to notice. The idea which realizes itself in will must be the idea taken as unconditional and unmaimed. I do not mean that the incomplete realization of a positive idea cannot be will. Under some conditions I have agreed that an incomplete process may be an actual will carried out imperfectly. But under other conditions the passing into fact of anything short of the idea in its entirety must be denied to be will. And there are cases which exhibit strikingly the truth of this principle. If my idea contains the restraint of A, and if A then is carried out into fact unrestrained, my idea, it is clear, has not been realized. The same conclusion holds where my idea was to realize A modified and subject to a condition, and where in the actual process this modifying condition falls out. In these cases the result indubitably has not come from my will. And we must again deny will where my idea has indeed been actually carried out, but where the result follows not from the idea itself but from some other condition. The future application of these doctrines will show their importance, and I must content myself here with inviting the reader to notice them. I will however add an example which I have not invented. A priest in hearing a confession may himself pass into the fault reported by his penitent, and this result may be culpable, but presumably it is not willed. The idea, we will assume, has here carried itself out, but it has done this in such a manner as to lose its identity. Provided, that is, that the idea has remained qualified in my mind as the act of another, it cannot in its proper character, and as such, realize itself in my person.

Such an idea, while it maintains its integrity, cannot pass into will, and any consequence, therefore, in the strict sense is not an actual volition.[1]

I will proceed from this to examine the mistaken doctrine which I mentioned above. Beside the prevalence of the idea it may be contended that volition implies always a judgement or belief, a judgement, that is, with regard to my future or at least my possible action. This is a doctrine which I have never been able to accept. We may begin by distinguishing two senses in which judgement can be used. In its ordinary meaning a judgement about the future asserts its idea of my 'real' world, a world which includes everything which is taken as continuous with itself and in the same plane with its own 'reality'. But there is a wider sense also in which judgement may be taken. In this wider sense every possible idea is at the same time a judgement, and, in being entertained, is *ipso facto* used to qualify reality. The imaginary, the absurd, and even the impossible, are upon this view all attributed to the real, for all ideas in a sense, so far as we have them at all, are the predicates of reality. It is, however, not in this wider meaning that a judgement about the future is asserted to characterize volition. Indeed in this wider sense we should judge of the possible and the future as of something which *is*, and with this clearly we should have removed the distinctive essence of will. But in any case, I submit, it is not true that in volition the idea is always the idea that *I* am about to do something. I cannot admit that the qualification of the change as my act must always in volition form a part of the idea's original content. This is a point which I shall hereafter endeavour to make plain, and I can do no more here than recommend it to the notice of the reader. Its consequence, if made good, must be the rejection of the whole doctrine we are discussing, whether that is taken in a wider or in a narrower sense.

---

[1] This distinction between an unqualified and a qualified idea bears on the question why ideas do not always realize themselves. I shall deal with this point hereafter, when I have to show the means by which ideas carry themselves out.

The sense in which judgement has been actually claimed to be essential to will is the narrower meaning which it more commonly bears. And the claim so understood seems to me to be in collision with fact, and the origin of the mistake can, I think, also be shown. I will point in the first place to the collision with fact.[1]

The presence of a judgement in all volitions certainly cannot be discovered. You will not find it everywhere when, apart from theory, you examine the facts. If you take the case of actions where without delay the result follows the suggestion, no one, apart from theory, would deny that many such actions are willed. To suppose on the other hand that everywhere, before or even during such an action, there is a necessity for the judgement that I am about, or if possible about, to perform it, to my mind is indefensible. Unless you confine will arbitrarily to a certain number among reflective volitions, I cannot find this judgement, and I must express my disbelief in its existence. I will however not dwell on this point, but will leave it to the consideration of the reader. It serves, if made good, as a disproof of the alleged necessity for judgement.

I will however add to the above objections an additional difficulty. In a highly developed mind and under exceptional circumstances there may happen, I think, a case of the following nature. There may be present a judgement of the kind required, and then an act in which the idea is realized, and yet in spite of this there may be no real volition. I may have an impulse to sneeze where I have also a desire to restrain myself, and the impulse may induce a moving idea of its result, and even also the judgement that probably or certainly I am about to produce it. And yet, if the act follows, and is even the effect of the idea and the judgement, the act under some conditions must and would be denied to be a genuine volition.[2] I am aware that according to some writers such a complex case

[1] In the above I am taking belief throughout as identical with judgement, but for some purposes I should consider it needful to distinguish them sharply from one another.

[2] I have discussed these conditions in *M.* n.s. xi [*E.* xxv].

is not possible in fact, and, if the judgement amounts to
what we call a lively impression and a vivid belief, I am
inclined to agree with them. But otherwise I think a
judgement of the kind required may be present in the
case I have mentioned, and yet its consequence may be
evidently not genuine will. And I submit this objection to
the reader for whatever it may be worth.[1]

¹ Dr. Stout has adduced and discussed this instance (*M.* N.S. v, on
'Voluntary Action') and in connexion with it defends the doctrine criticized in the text. But the view which he advocates remains to me untenable and also obscure. 'Volition is a desire qualified and defined by the
judgement that, so far as in us lies, we shall bring about the attainment of
the desired end' (*l.c.* 356). The words 'so far as in us lies' may, however,
be understood in several meanings. They might be qualified either by the
addition of 'physically' or 'psychically', and, when we adopt 'psychically',
we may do this in more senses than one. We may take volition to be complete when there is a certain judgement about the future together with
desire, or we may mean that beside this a domination by the idea is required. But the discussion in the text provides, I think, for the whole of
these cases, since in the main it rests on the denial of a necessity for any
judgement at all. With regard to the presence of desire I shall hereafter
explain that in my view desire is most certainly not necessary for will.
But, to pass from this and to return to the instance of the unwilled sneeze,
I do not understand that Dr. Stout could deny the possibility here of a
desire for the result as well as of a judgement in the absence of will. And
I may perhaps urge this as an objection, although I could not myself admit
a desire here in the strict sense of actual desire. In addition I may remark
that in any case 'desired' must be understood as 'desired to be had here and
now', and the judgement must refer to an immediate production of the
result. If on Monday I have the belief or judgement that on Wednesday
I shall assuredly be tempted to realize an end which I even now desire,
and shall infallibly, 'so far as in me lies' and apart from interference, bring
about this result—such a state obviously need not already be an actual
volition, and it need not even amount to a resolve or intention. So far as
the desired end is viewed by anticipation as being realized by something
in the future, it is so far not willed or intended by me. You do not get
present agency unless my idea is opposed to fact, real or imaginary, and
against this present fact realizes itself and me. I have however already
explained this point in distinguishing expectation and again resolve from
will. But the words 'so far as in us lies' are capable of yet another interpretation. They might mean that, in order to be a genuine volition, an act
must proceed from my higher or true self, and that, if it is to a certain point
irrational, it must be denied to be will. I do not know how far I should
attribute such a view to Dr. Stout. It is a point discussed by me in *M.* N.S.
xi [*E.* xxv]. I may say in conclusion that I have considered the remarks

But if in truth no such judgement belongs to the essence of will, how, we may be asked, can a mistake of this kind have arisen? There are two reasons, I think, which have combined to make it plausible. (*a*) A judgement is the way in which we often and naturally express the fact of volition or resolve. It is not, however, a necessary expression or an unfailing accompaniment of this fact, and it may be so formulated as to become even incorrect and misleading. The judgement never is correct unless it refers to the volition as to a fact independent of itself. Thus 'I shall certainly do this' may mean that I am so resolved that on the occasion my volition will happen. Or it may refer to an actual volition already begun, and may assert that this process is about certainly to complete itself. But the resolve or the volition are here regarded as facts, the existence of which does not depend on my judgement about them. The judgement therefore, even when correct, is not essential. It is no more than an accompaniment, and, even as an accompaniment, it need not be there. And on the other side the judgement may take a form which is not even a tolerable translation of the fact. 'I want to do it, and so naturally I am sure to do it as far as lies in me,' would not be the expression of a present resolve or of an actual will. It is the voice of one who passively contemplates a future state of moral drift.

(*b*) There is another reason why a judgement has been supposed to belong to the essence of will. 'One cannot', it is said, 'will to realize an end which one regards as impossible, and in willing therefore one must judge that the end is possible.' But surely there is no force in this unless you assume the necessity for some judgement, and this assumption, I have pointed out, is opposed to the facts. We may, however, in this connexion inquire how far we can will the impossible.[1] We must, I think, assert or deny a will for that which is judged to be impossible, according to the

which (in *M.* N.s. vi) Mr. Shand has offered on Dr. Stout's doctrine of will. I cannot however say that in consequence I have been able to find this view clearer or more satisfactory.

[1] Cf. here Professor James, *Psychol.* ii. 560.

sense which is given in each case to these words. If the act is kept before the mind in the character of a thing which is impossible, no volition, I believe, can ensue. And the same conclusion holds if for 'impossible' we substitute 'doubtful'. I do not mean that an act cannot in some sense be judged to be doubtful or impossible and at the same time be willed; but an act cannot be willed if, in being willed, it comes before the mind as impossible or doubtful. If, that is, the idea remains actually conditioned in this manner, it does not itself issue in an act; and, if an action comes, it will certainly not be the volition of this idea. A judgement, we may say, that some end is impossible or doubtful prevents incidentally the prevalence of the idea in our minds, and so by consequence destroys the beginning of will. And this is true, but the more correct explanation is as follows. The idea of an action, if qualified as impossible or doubtful, is not truly and correctly the idea of that action. It is really a complex in which the simple idea of the act is an incomplete element. The act therefore, if it follows, is not the realization of the genuine idea, and so by consequence it is not so far a genuine volition. The idea of anything as doubtful, impossible, or imaginary, cannot as such become fact, and, if an action is to come from such an idea, that idea must alter its character. Its qualification may either pass wholly from before the mind, or it may be relegated to some other world remote from practice.[1] And, so far as this happens, the unqualified residue becomes and can work as the unconditioned idea of the act. Such an action, though it may be will, is not however the volition of the original idea, and I need scarcely add that it does not require and depend upon a judgement.

I will at this point very briefly notice several fresh errors. I cannot accept the doctrine that desire is essential to will.

---

[1] The extent to which such a division in the self can be carried is in some cases considerable. The subject is further discussed in *M.* N.S. xi [*E.* xxv]. The reader will notice that I treat as an obvious mistake the doctrine that the idea's content is not affected by a change in its modality. This mischievous error is far too prevalent.

Where volition follows on a suggestion and follows without delay, to assume that desire in any proper sense must
invariably be present seems plainly indefensible. I shall
however return to this point in a later article. Another
more palpable mistake is the identification of volition with
choice. The nature of choice is again a subject to be discussed hereafter, but, where choice is taken in anything
like a natural sense, it obviously is not coextensive with
volition. And this fact to my mind is so clear that I can
see no advantage in discussing it. I must again adopt the
same attitude with regard to attention. If attention is understood in the sense of an active attending, I cannot verify
its invariable presence in will. Such a claim, it seems to me,
disappears on confrontation with fact, and I have dealt
with it, so far as is required, in a former article, *M.* N.s. xi
[*E.* xxiv].

The objections, which so far we have considered, admit
the presence of an idea in volition, and have been directed
more or less against that idea's self-realization. I will proceed now to those which deny that an idea is essential to
will. There are undoubted acts of volition, it will be contended, where no idea of the end is even present. And such
a contention, if made good, would be a fatal difficulty, but
on the other hand I cannot doubt that it is opposed to the
facts. In every case of will I must insist that an idea is present; and, if an idea is not present, no one, I believe, apart
from some prejudice would call the act a volition. We
have in this connexion to deal with the actions which are
termed impulsive, and with these we may take acts from
imitation and from the word of command, and, generally,
whatever act is suggested by a perception. Mr. Shand,
again, would instance here the facts of what he terms 'negative' and 'imperative' will.[1]

The above objections are based in the main on one kind
of mistake, on a misconception, that is, with regard to the
real nature of ideas. When such misunderstandings are

[1] *M.* N.s. vi on 'Types of Will', to which article I refer the reader for
Mr. Shand's views in this connexion. They will be discussed hereafter.

removed it will be found, I think, that the objections are groundless. And I will endeavour to indicate the main errors on which they are based.

(i) An idea (I must insist) has not always a simple character, and what we term 'our idea' or 'our object' may be often the fragmentary aspect of a complex whole. To speak in general, our apparent idea and our real idea may fundamentally differ, and this difference, if unnoticed, may result in delusion. For what we call 'our idea' may in truth be incomplete or again irrelevant. I have had already in previous articles, as in the present, to call attention to this truth, and the neglect of it is a source of widespread error. An idea cannot be identified at pleasure with something less or something more than itself, and the question as to what in a given case is my actual idea, may entail a careful inquiry.

(ii) An idea may exist and may yet be unspecified and general. In order, for instance, to act on the idea of avoidance or injury, I need not have the idea of injuring or avoiding in some particular manner. The alternative, between the presence of an idea in a specific form and the absence of an idea altogether, is radically mistaken. I agree that something more particular than the general idea must exist in my mind, but I deny that this something (whatever according to the case it may be) must itself belong to the content of the genuine idea which I use. The whole assumption, if I may be plain, is the merest prejudice. In the course of the act itself the idea's content will in its process further particularize itself, but before the act the genuine content of the idea may be general. And it is perhaps sufficient here to call attention to what I will term this evident truth. Once assume that an idea must be specific or be nothing, add to this the assumption that whatever appears at first sight to be our end and object is always really and truly so—and you may be taken far, but unfortunately away from the truth.

(iii) An idea itself is not an image, nor is it always even based on an image as distinct from a perception. The denial of this truth is a prevalent error, and it underlies the mistake we have last noticed. But, so far as I can perceive, it is itself a mere prejudice. If a perceived object is to have a meaning and is to convey that meaning to myself, the meaning, I agree, has in a sense to be detached or loosened from the object. But this loosening does not imply always the existence of an image or images, separated from the object and maintaining themselves, for however short a time, as individual or particular. Such an assertion would not hold of our intelligence even when highly developed. Suppose that, in answer to the question What has he done? or What shall we do?, a feather flying in the air is actually shown, such an example to my mind is a conclusive refutation. It seems absurd to insist that here no idea and no meaning can be conveyed unless through the medium of individual images. Such images, separated from the feather and existing in a middle space *en route* until their fresh subject is reached, are to me mere inventions. The meaning in a more or less general form, is, I should say, conveyed direct from the feather to its new subject, and the necessary middle-space with its separable images is a creature of mythology. And such a doctrine at a lower level of mind would be still more inapplicable. When a breast appears to suggest sucking, or a fruit eating, or an enemy avoidance or injury, that doctrine would insist that in the absence of individual images, existing separated from the perceived object, there is no suggestion at all. But this to me is plainly untenable. The idea here is the perceived object, so far as that is qualified inconsistently, and qualified in such a way that its meaning in part is made loose from itself. This meaning can therefore be applied as an adjective to a fresh subject. And, in short, generally, the identification of the ideal with separate images, and the alternative between such images and no suggestion at all, may be set down as erroneous.[1]

If we return to the objections founded on the alleged fact of will without the presence of an idea, we may now discover them to be invalid. The removal of errors will

[1] On this and the preceding error cf. *M*. o.s. xiii. 23 [*E*. xiv. 269–70] and n.s. x. 5 [*E*. xxiii. 391].

have left them without plausible ground, and, confronted with the facts, they will, I think, disappear. These facts are in general the actions suggested by something perceived, and in particular they are the acts from imitation, from the word of command, together with the acts called impulsive. And with regard to these our position may be stated as follows. If in the act an idea is suggested and realizes itself, that act is volition, unless the idea in some way has lost its own character and has in effect carried out something which is not itself. If, on the other hand, no idea has been suggested, the act has not been really willed. This result I believe to be in accordance with the use of language and with popular opinion, and I do not suppose that it would be useful to dwell further on the matter. The appeal is to the reader who will carefully consider the issue. In every case we must ask whether a suggestion was or really was not made, and, if a suggestion was made, we must then go on to put further questions. What exactly was that suggestion, and did it carry itself out in the act, and did it realize precisely itself or, on the other hand, something less than or beyond its true meaning? I am content to leave the issue when thus defined to the reader's judgement.[1]

[1] There are a few points here which I would ask the reader to notice. (i) Will and volition are not taken to include what is called a standing will. (ii) To urge that the idea is often the creature of a blind impulse, which it does but passively translate, is quite inconclusive. If the 'impulse' is entirely without any consciousness of end, then, of course, so far it is not will. On the other hand, given the idea, the question of that idea's origin is by itself irrelevant, unless you are asking when and how the volition arose. The real question is whether in fact the idea, when it is there, carries or does not carry itself out in the act. The act is or is not will, according to the answer given to this question. (iii) I shall deal with any objection based on the alleged 'imperative' and 'negative' types of volition, when in their proper place I dispose of these doctrines. (iv) It may be instructive to quote from Mr. Shand's interesting article (M. N.S. vi. 290) what seems on another point a serious misunderstanding of fact. 'If we are angry with some one, ideas of hurting or paining him occur, and we sometimes find the pain or injury has been inflicted without any prior consciousness on our part that we were going to inflict it. If we are reproached for the action, we say we did not "mean" to do it.' This statement seems to contain more than one ambiguity, but I will confine myself to the words 'mean to

From this I will turn to an objection which may be urged from the other side. Your definition, it may be said, if not too narrow, is at least fatally wide. 'The self-realization of an idea with which the self is identified—this covers', I shall be told, 'facts which too evidently are not willed. When a man gesticulates so as outwardly to express his idea, this process by your account must be volition, while in fact it is not so. And you must include cases where by unconscious movement a man betrays that very idea which he is bent on concealing. Acts done in imitation will, at least sometimes, present the same difficulty, as will again instances where involuntarily we manifest our latent hostility or affection. Add to these the unwilled acts that result generally from a suggestion, if that is overstrong, or if on the other hand the mind is enfeebled permanently, or again temporarily as in hypnotic states. And the question surely, when you consider these cases, is settled. You have defined volition so as to bring this whole mass within its limits, and with such a result your definition has broken down finally.'

Before I reply to this in detail I will venture to recall the general position to the reader. I am not in these articles undertaking to cover the whole ground of psychology. I am offering a definition of will which claims certainly to hold good everywhere. It claims, that is, wherever it is applied, to remain consistent with itself and with the common understanding of the facts. Hence I consider myself bound to deal with any case that is offered me, if that case

do it'. Does the person using these intend to deny his volition? I should say certainly it is not so. He may intend to deny a deliberate volition or set purpose, but perhaps, and more probably, his denial refers to something else. He is saying that he did not mean to do, and so by consequence did not will, the particular act. He willed, that is, to injure in general but perhaps not to strike, he willed to strike but perhaps not with such a heavy stick, and at all events he did not mean that the blow should fall where it actually fell, and so did not will the particular result. The true question here is about the actual content of the idea, what that was, how unspecified it was, and how far the individual result can be taken as its proper self-realization. When the facts of the case are ascertained, and when they are approached in this manner, I cannot see that they really present any difficulty.

is so far defined that one could decide in practice whether it is or is not volition. On the other hand, I cannot fairly be asked to explain mental situations which are perhaps excessively obscure or otherwise difficult, merely because they are offered unexplained as an objection. I have to state the principles by which all such cases must be judged, and I am bound to show that when we judge them, and so far as we judge them, the principles hold good. But if a psychical state is so ill-defined that the person who offers it is not prepared exactly to describe it, or to decide if in practice it would be accounted a volition, I cannot be expected to discuss such a fact. Whatever psychical state, in short, is produced as an objection, must, so far as is required, be described by the objector himself. And I hope that on this point there may be a general agreement.

This being understood, I proceed to consider the instances offered above, and I find that I can at once dispose of a considerable part of them. The idea which in will realizes itself is the idea of a change to happen here and now in my existence. But it is obvious that in gestures, or in whatever may be called the mimic expression of an idea, the idea does *not* contain the element of my changed existence, and therefore in such a change the idea does *not* carry itself out. The gesture may as a gesture be willed, and if so we of course have volition, and a volition which exactly corresponds with our account. But, if the gesture is unwilled, the change in my existence is indeed caused by the idea, but on the other hand it never was contained in that idea. And, not being contained in the idea, it cannot have been carried out by it. The idea has not realized itself, and by our definition there has been therefore no will. The same thing holds of those movements by which I involuntarily reveal the place of a hidden object. These movements come from my idea and they betray it, and yet you cannot say that the idea has realized itself in them. For the idea of an object in such or such a place is not the idea of my change. The idea of my directing a person to the object, if that idea were unconditioned and so carried itself out, would by our definition be will. And the act would,

I think, be so accounted in practice. On the other hand, if the same idea is present in subordination to, or even coupled with, the idea of my preventing its result, then that result, if it happens, is not a volition. It has realized but a fragment of my total idea, and such a fragment, we have seen, is not my idea truly. So again with our involuntary instinctive movements of affection or hostility. If these do not in any sense come from an idea of their happening as a change in my present existence, they are not willed. And, even if they result from that idea, they are not willed, unless the idea became unqualified and expelled or subordinated its rivals. For otherwise it was a mere element in an ideal complex and was not properly an idea. But if the idea dominated, the act has been certainly willed, and in practice it could not be disowned as volition.[1]

With regard to acts done from imitation there is room for considerable doubt. But the doubt applies merely to the facts of each individual case and does not affect the principles on which our decision is formed. 'Imitation' I use here to cover cases where the perception of something done by or happening to another leads in me to the occurrence of the same action or state. And taken in this wide sense, imitation, I presume, must occur at a stage where the ideal suggestion can hardly be supposed to exist and carry itself out in the mind. Whether this wide sense should be narrowed we need not inquire, nor can I even touch on the difficulty which attaches to the beginnings of imitation. We are concerned here merely with the principles on which such acts are asserted or denied to be will, and about these principles I see no occasion for doubt. Where there is no idea of a change in my existence, there is by our definition no will, and the same conclusion is even more obvious where no idea at all is present.[2] And the

---

[1] I may once more remind the reader that this subject has been discussed by me in *M.* n.s. xi [*E.* xxv].

[2] We must not forget here that an ideal suggestion may come direct from a perception, and that usually, though not always, the presence of such a practical suggestion in me involves *ipso facto* the dropping out of the element of an alien personality.

result again is not willed if the idea does not of itself carry itself out. And once more, so far as the idea realized is but one element in an ideal complex, we must so far deny volition. The result from any idea which is qualified incompatibly with its own self-realization, we have seen, cannot be will. The priest who, hearing confession of sin, through that hearing sinned himself in like fashion, need not, we have seen, have actually willed this result.[1] In order here to pronounce on the presence or absence of actual volition, we must be further informed. The idea may have remained involved with another's personality, or may have freed itself from that condition, or it may again perhaps have turned that condition into an element in a new complex idea of sin. In the two latter cases the result presumably is will, while it is otherwise in the first case. But in view of the endless complexity of fact we may well qualify this sentence, and it is better to say that will is absent or present so far as each situation is realized. We must repeat this conclusion wherever an act is suggested by another's personality through imitation, through the word of command, or in any other possible manner. It is not enough to know that the result has arisen from an idea, and has even in a sense come from the idea of a change in my existence. We have in every case, before we pronounce, to ascertain the details more clearly. Was the idea qualified by a condition such as that of an alien personality, a condition which makes it impossible that the idea should as such be realized in me? The result, if so, has not realized the genuine idea and is so far not will. On the other hand, if the suggestion was freed from that alien condition, how far was it freed? The idea of another man striking, if as such it causes me to strike, is so far not a volition. And the same conclusion holds if the idea was of another desiring or ordering me to strike. The question of the idea's qualification in any given case is a question of fact, and, before that case is used as an objection, this question must be answered. And, however

---

[1] The reader will remember that I am not speaking here about degrees of responsibility. I am asking what I at least regard as a very different question, What is and what is not a formal volition? (Cf. *E.* xxv.)

it is answered, my difficulties are at an end, since they seem
to come solely from the obscurity of the individual case.
At the risk of wearying the reader, I will illustrate this
further by the case of action under threat. If for instance
a man signs a paper when threatened, is the act a volition?
In order to answer this question we must be informed of
his precise state of mind. Was he moved, in effect, by the
mere overpowering force of the suggested signing? Did
he, again, act on the mere idea of escape with momentary
oblivion of all else? Was it the idea of escape merely by
writing his name, or again by writing his name with a
certain meaning, and, if it was the latter, what was precisely the actual amount of this meaning? When these
questions are settled we may hope to decide as to the presence of a volition, and as to the limit up to which that
volition extended. But, while the fact remains obscure, it
is no fault in the principle if it cannot be applied. We may
give the same answer with regard to acts performed in
hypnotic states, whether natural or induced, and again in
madness and generally under abnormal conditions. The
question here as to the presence of formal volition is not,
I must repeat, the question as to the existence and amount
of responsibility. A man may will that for which he has
little or no moral responsibility, and he may be morally
responsible for that which he has not formally willed. But
as to the presence of volition we must be guided by the
principles already laid down. And these principles can, I
submit, be applied successfully to every case which has
been freed from obscurity.[1]

We have now, I hope, defended our definition from the
charge of undue wideness. It will include no consequence

[1] If the suggestion of an act remains so involved with another's personality that it does not free itself, or again become the idea of my doing the
act because of that other, the act is not volition. To take another case, if
the resolve for a future act leads to action immediately, the act is not will.
It fails to be will, because the idea was incompatibly conditioned. There
was at most a partial will in the sense in which that has been explained to
belong to resolve. The above doctrine as to a foreign personality raises,
I may remark, no real difficulty with regard to acts done in common.

which leads to collision with general usage. On the other hand, the denial of an idea in will, we have seen, can in no case be sustained. We endeavoured to explain the various points contained in the realization of itself by an idea, and argued that these points are without exception necessary to volition, while some other features, such as belief and judgement, are not essential. And we defended the distinction between a complete and an incomplete act of will. We have so far neglected the latter part of our definition, and have not discussed the sense in which the self is identified with an idea. In the following articles I shall endeavour to fix the meaning of these words, and in several points to make clear what may so far have remained doubtful. But, before proceeding, I will seek to remove yet another mistake.

It is often held that the genuine object which we desire, and which again we aim at in volition, must be something which when attained falls within our existence. The end, it is contended, must be realized for us, and it is so realized when our idea passes into a perception. And beyond such a perception, it is urged, we can desire and will nothing. I have some years ago remarked on this mistake (*M.* o.s. xiii. 21 [*E.* xiv. 267]), but I will attempt very briefly to deal with it here.

We have already noticed the view, according to which volition does not pass beyond the idea. The present doctrine is an error of a different kind, and it concerns the meaning contained within the idea itself. It maintains that I cannot even aim at anything which is not to be experienced by myself. And this doctrine, though based on a truth, is itself certainly erroneous. I will pass by that form of it which regards my pleasure as my one possible end, and will confine myself to the view that I cannot aim to realize anything unless that is to be perceived or experienced directly by myself.

If this were true, it would in the first place condemn some experience as illusory. No one, apart from theory, doubts that he can desire and will events to happen after his death. And the suggestion that his real aim is not those events, but is his own present certainty, would be dismissed as ridiculous. The objection, that after death a man's end cannot be realized for him, would be met by the reply that he never imagined his end could be so realized. An illusion, doubtless, is possible here and is sometimes present in fact, but it certainly does not exist in fact necessarily and always. It is, in short, the belief in this illusion which itself is illusory.

You may urge that a desire, which is not satisfied for my direct knowledge, must remain unsatisfied, and you may argue that in the end I can desire only that which would satisfy my desire. But in psychology, I reply, we can hardly insist on truth which is to be true in the end. And certainly we cannot assume as self-evident that all desires must be able to be satisfied, or identify my actual aim with whatever in the end that should involve or entail. You cannot argue, in short, that I have no desire for a certain object, if I perceive, or at least might perceive, that as such it would not satisfy me. For that personal relation to myself, which is implied in satisfaction, need not enter into the actual content of my idea. Desire is an inconsistent state, I agree, and its inherent contradiction, I agree, should be removed by satisfaction. But I cannot conclude from this that there is in fact no desire except for an end taken as attainable, and free from all inconsistency whether noticed or unnoticed. If you keep to the facts as observed, they are not in harmony with such a conclusion. And if you wish to make the mere existence of a mental state depend on its ultimate self-consistency, I cannot think you realize the effect and the ruinous sweep of your principle.

Volition (and in this respect it diverges from mere desire)[1] does imply a change to happen here and now in my psychical existence. And there is no will, we have seen, unless the idea has begun to carry itself out. This process so far may be said to turn my idea into a perception for me, and this perceived alteration may so far be said to be involved in the object of my will. But it is not true that the

[1] I shall return to this point hereafter.

process always must end at this point, and it is not true that the process is intended always to end there. If the idea of an event after my death is to be realized by my will, that process involves an immediate change in my perceived existence, and my idea so far must become a perception for me. But to maintain that no more than this was contained in my genuine idea, and that, with so much, my genuine idea has completely carried itself out, seems indefensible. The will is so far actual, but so far it is not complete, and it has stopped short of the goal which most certainly was aimed at. Psychology, we have agreed, may at a certain point cease to consider the process, but it must not, on this or on any other account, falsify the actual content of the idea. The general nature of that content is a difficult problem to be discussed in a later article, but we cannot take it as confined always within the limits of my perceived existence.[1]

[1] I do not here discuss another possible ground of the above mistake. This ground would consist in the doctrine that my psychical states, such as ideas and perceptions, cannot also and at the same time be more. On this point see *M*. n.s. ix. 5–7 [*E*. xxii. 369–71].

XXVII

THE DEFINITION OF WILL (II)

[*First published in* MIND, N.S. xii, No. 46, 145–76. *April*, 1903.]

WE have defined a volition as 'the self-realization of an idea with which the self is identified', and in the foregoing article we to some extent explained the first part of these words. I shall now proceed to show what is meant by a practical identification with self. I am in the present article still forced to assume the fact of 'ideo-motor' action, but the nature of this will be discussed on a later occasion.

To ask what is meant by the identification of an idea with my self, would in the end raise the whole question of the essence and origin of consciousness. We find that self and not-self are related both theoretically and practically, and we may inquire in general if these terms and their distinctions are original and ultimate. Or, if this problem is dismissed or is placed on one side, we may discuss the question of rank and priority as between perception and will. Since practice implies knowledge we may contend that the latter must come first, or we may on the other side reduce theory to a one-sided development of the practical process. We may insist again that neither attitude is higher in rank, and that neither taken by itself is original or prior. Both appear together, we may add, as essential aspects of consciousness, and we might go on to investigate their exact nature when first they appear, and attempt to trace their development from their earliest forms, if not from states which are neither. But in this article it is not my object to pursue such inquiries. I shall take the theoretical and the practical relation of the self to the not-self as facts of experience, and shall try to point out some aspects which are contained in both, attending specially of course to the practical side. Facts of experience the reader must understand to be experienced facts, and he must not include in these anything so far as, remaining outside, it appears in or acts on the experienced.

If in this way we examine the practical relation of the self to its world, we at once discover the features which were set out in our definition.[1] There is an existing not-self together with the idea of its change, and there is my self felt as one with this idea and in opposition to existence. And there follows normally the realization of the idea, and so of my self, in the actual change of the not-self; and this process must arise from the idea itself. And the process, at least to some extent, must be experienced by my self. In volition, if I attempt to find less than all this, I find that volition has disappeared. And, taking this for granted, I will go on to consider the practical relation in its distinction from mere theory, and I will try to indicate that special sense in which the self is practically made one with the idea.

(i) The not-self, we have seen, is an existence, and this existence is for me. It comes before me or comes to me as a perceived other or as an object. Now in the practical relation it is important to observe that this 'other' has two senses, and that only one of these senses is found in mere theory. It is in the sense common to theory and practice alike that I am going first of all to consider the object. The perceived object, we may say, on the one hand comes as something which *is* independently, and on the other hand it is felt as something which is for me. I am not attempting here, the reader will understand, to explain or to justify the apparent facts, but am endeavouring merely to describe them. The object *is* in a sense which is not applicable to the whole felt moment, for, while the object is felt, it is also experienced as other than the felt self. It is therefore for me as something which is not myself. But to say that its relation to me is an object, or that my passivity towards it is an object, would certainly be false. How far these aspects may become objects at a later time and for reflection, I do not here inquire; but at first and in their essence, while we confine ourselves to the theoretical atti-

---

[1] *M.* n.s. xi, No. 44 [*E.* xxvi]. The reader must also be referred here to the article on Conation [*E.* xxiii].

tude, they certainly are not objects. In the 'felt-mine' of
the moment the object appears as something other than
the rest, but its relation to the rest, if we are to speak of its
relation, is a matter of feeling.[1] That relation with both its
terms must fall within what is experienced, but only one
term of the relation is experienced as an object. The not-
self so far appears as an other, but not as an opposite.

(ii) In the practical relation the aspects we have described above are still to be found, but another feature is
added which transforms the character of the whole. This
feature is the opposition between self and not-self. In my
practical attitude I experience myself as something contrary to the object. I do not merely receive the object and
feel it as mine, although other than me, but I also feel myself as something which is opposite and struggles to change
it. And in this total feeling both the not-self and the self
are present now as contrary realities. The relation with
both its terms now appears before myself as two objects,
but in what sense I am an object to myself we must go on
to inquire.

In my practical consciousness there is a relation, we
saw, between the not-self and an idea. This idea is the
idea of a change in that object not-self, and the idea in its
conflict with the not-self is itself an object for me. Hence
a relation with both its terms is now before me as an object
perceived. But this relation on the other hand is not merely
a new perceived object. For I feel myself one with the idea
in a sense in which I am not one with that object which
opposes it, and therefore in and through this idea I feel
myself in collision with that object, which has thus become
in a further sense something alien and not-self. And my
felt oneness with the idea and felt contrariness to the conflicting existence are not two separate facts, but are inseparable aspects of one fact. Whether in any sense opposition
can otherwise be experienced and known I do not here inquire, but except through an idea there is no opposition if
that is really practical and means will. And this is a point

[1] I should perhaps remind the reader that I do not accept the restriction of 'feeling' to denote merely pleasure and its opposite.

which has perhaps been sufficiently discussed in previous articles. The practical relation depends on an idea, an idea with which in a special sense I feel myself to be one, and this idea is an object and it conflicts with an object. But, as for myself, I am not properly an object to myself except so far as I enter into the content of this idea. How far I must so enter is however a question which must be deferred for the present.[1]

(iii) This practical identification of self with the idea may be called specific,[2] and we cannot explain it in the sense of accounting exactly for its quality. On the other hand, we can indicate the distinctive feature which it adds to mere theory, and we can show some conditions which its presence implies. This may be done most clearly, perhaps, in reply to a possible objection. 'The self', it may be said, 'is identified alike with every one of its contents, and, as to the idea, you admit that the idea is an object and a not-self. Is not then the special oneness of the idea and the self something which in the end is meaningless?' In replying to this objection I shall have in part to repeat what I have put forward already.

In the practical relation we can find in the first place an existing not-self. There is an object, and it is felt as mine though as other than me. And we have in the second place an idea which conflicts with this existence. This idea once more is an object, and it is felt likewise as mine, and felt likewise again as other than myself. And so far we have no aspect, it may be said, which is not found in mere theory. For we have two objects in relation or two elements of one complex object, and each of these is mine and is not-mine in precisely the same sense. But we have so far left out of

---

[1] This is the question as to how far self-consciousness is present always in will.

[2] We must however be careful to avoid exaggeration on this head. I consider that, apart from the practical attitude, the self can be aware of the agreement or disagreement of its own felt content with that of the object before it. I think that such a sameness or difference may be felt, and the feeling then translated into a judgement. And if this were not possible, we should, I think, find it difficult to account for some aspects of self-consciousness. This is a matter, however, with which I cannot deal here.

sight the essential and differential feature of the case. The idea in collision with the existence, although it is an object and a not-self, is also, in its conflict with the existence, felt specially to be mine and to be one with myself. Hence this special feeling attaches itself to but one of the two objects before me, and it qualifies that one in its actual opposition to the other. The existence therefore, being opposed to what is specially one with myself, becomes *ipso facto* itself opposed and contrary to me. And I, in my union with the idea, am in conflict with existence. And thus by one and the same means the idea, though a not-self, is felt as myself, and the opposing existence becomes a not-self at a higher remove. It thwarts the self in the idea and is so experienced as in collision with me.

I have explained that I assume nothing as to any temporal or other priority, and I am far from maintaining the possibility in fact of a mere theoretical attitude. But to the reader, who will not forget this necessary warning, I will offer what follows as perhaps a help to a better understanding. Let us suppose a self with an existing object, and let us suppose that the contents of the self and of its object are discrepant. The felt content of the self will here be hindered in fact by the not-self, but the self so far will not know that itself is hindered. It will on the other hand feel the uneasiness of its checked expansion, and its object will become disagreeably qualified. But now let us suppose further that the main aspect, in which the self is hindered, itself qualifies the object inconsistently with the object's existence, and so itself becomes an idea for the self. With this the whole situation is forthwith changed. In this idea we have now an object in collision with existence and hindered by that. And the self now feeling itself to be specially at one with the idea, itself is hindered by existence and is aware of the hindrance. And the existence in this way has become not merely other but opposite. We in short have risen into the level of actual conation and will.[1]

(iv) The actual volition, we have seen, is the alteration

---

[1] I will once more here refer the reader to my previous articles. Cf. also *A.R.* 547–8 = 606–7.

of existence so as to agree with the idea. The existence, we may say, is changed by the idea to itself, and in the same process the self as one with the idea realizes itself in the not-self. This process of self-realization must, up to a certain point, be experienced as such by the self, and the self must become aware also, however momentarily, of the resulting harmony and peace. My world in a completed volition is not merely something which is there for me and which agrees with itself. My world has become so far the existing expression and realization of my own self. And, so far as this result goes, the not-self persists only as the medium and element, in which I have carried out and am satisfied with my being. It will repay us once more here to contrast the practical with the theoretical mode of con-sciousness. In the practical relation both self and not-self are alike qualified discordantly by the idea of the change. There is on each side a discrepancy between existence and idea. The idea both is and is not the adjective of the not-self; and the same thing again is true in the case of the self. From the one side as limited by actual existence I am not changed, and on the other side I feel that I am qualified by the idea of the change. I feel myself one with the ideal change in its opposition to the actual existence. Hence the process, which carries out into fact the content of the idea, realizes for me my inmost being which before was ideal. And because I am aware of the idea as itself making the change—a point which will shortly be discussed and explained—I am aware also that this change is the work of myself. In the result, therefore, I have expressed myself harmoniously on both sides of the relation.

The attitude of theory presents us here with an impor-tant contrast. The theoretical not-self, as we so far find it, may be discordant in various degrees, and the reality may more or less conflict with the idea which endeavours to express it. And in this discordance, since it qualifies me, I may suffer internally, and by its removal, so far as it is removed, I may feel myself expanded and satisfied. But the process here is experienced as in the main the self-realization of the object. The process can hardly be alleged to be made by the idea, and most certainly the process is not made by myself. My self in one with the idea is not opposed to the object, but on the contrary I follow the fortunes of the not-self, and receive from that inactively my part in its failure or success. I may will to think and to perceive, and in some thinking and in some perception there is doubtless will. But this will is not aimed at an alteration of the object itself. Its end is the appearance of the object in me as, apart from any will of mine, the object is real. And an attempt to make the truth other than it is by my will would at once subvert or at least transform my position as perceiving or thinking.

(v) There are several points on which I will now endeavour to obviate misunderstanding. The existing not-self is not always my external world, but may consist in any existence of and within myself which is opposed to me.[1] We have here within the whole, which is felt as my present being, the opposition of two objects. We have the idea of a change in some existing feature, and together with this first object comes the feeling of myself as specially one with the change. But, on the other side and as a second object, we have the actual feature of myself as I exist in fact, and this second object is a not-self which is opposed to the idea and to myself. And we have then the process in which the inner self carries itself out into this not-self. Everywhere, to pass from this special instance, we must bear in mind a general result. An element, which in one sense is a not-self, may in connexion with an act of will take a different position. And this is a point to which I must invite the attention of the reader. The not-self in a volition is always more or less particular and limited, and it is limited, we may say, for the purpose of the volition. Beside those internal feelings which have not even the form of a not-self or object, there will be tracts even of our outer world which for the moment will share their position. They will not make part of that not-self which opposes the idea and our volition. They will on the contrary fall back into that general mass which is felt as myself, a mass which in various

[1] Cf. here my *Appearance*, 83 = 97.

degrees qualifies me as in the idea I oppose myself to the not-self and so carry myself out. In will (to repeat this) the not-self which conflicts with the self is but one part of my world. The rest will lie within that self which is one with the idea, and will to a varying extent in the conflict support the idea and the self. On the whole, we may say, and in the main, there is between my world and my will no discrepancy, and, if it were otherwise, life could hardly be lived. Even the extreme case of suicide throws no doubt on this truth. For there is never, even there, an opposition between my world and the mere will for its negation. The conflict on the contrary is always between various elements within the self and its world, and it is this whole which in exceptional cases is distracted fatally. The same general result holds good also, but with a difference, in the case of the theoretical relation. The object for perception or thought is never the mere whole reality. Our object is a partial appearance, in which and as which the reality is for us, and in the end the opposition is between the concrete reality felt as a whole and this its partial appearance.[1] But in this conflict I, as distinct from my world, cannot actively take part. In will, on the other hand, the conflict is between myself, as expressing the main reality and the true self, and as identified in feeling with the idea of a change, and over against this some existing particular feature of the whole. And this feature, we have seen, as thus contrary to me is in a special sense alien and not-self.

(vi) I will pass on from this to emphasize two points of importance. In the first place both self and not-self must in volition have a concrete content, and both must be actually experienced in their own proper nature. We must have an experienced relation between two experienced terms, and, if it were not so, volition would not be 'a fact of experience'. If it were not so, an experience of activity or

---

[1] An idea is false, we may say, in so far as the reality cannot be expressed by it without conflict, and a will is bad in so far as the idea fails to express the genuine nature of myself. In this article I am concerned only, it will be understood, with the formal essence in which all volitions agree, and I pay no regard to any 'substantial' or 'material' differences between them.

passivity, or of self and not-self, would become unintelligible, if at least we mean by such an experience the awareness of these things in their own proper characters. We
should in each case be speaking of something, about which
by the conditions we could have no knowledge. And the
reply that other men, though not the present writer, can
distinguish between the fact of activity and the awareness
of that fact, is to my mind irrelevant. For it would hardly
follow that we may speak of activity and of will as existing
there, where by the conditions we could not possibly be
aware of their existence. Such a knowledge, if maintained,
seems at least to require some explanation. And it is surely
misleading, I would add, to term activity a fact of experience, if it does not itself fall within that which is experienced.

In will the terms and their relation and, in short, the whole
process is experienced, but this process in all its aspects is
not experienced in the same sense throughout. (*a*) The
existence and the idea of its change, we have seen, are both
objects. And the self is an object to itself so far as it is contained in the idea—a point to which we shall presently
have to return. And the self again, as itself carrying itself
out into fact, must to a certain extent be perceived as an
object. But however much these aspects of the whole come
before me as objects, they are none the less experienced
also as elements felt within the 'now mine'. And (*b*) this
experience of my total present is itself not an object, and
it cannot in the end even for reflection become an object
throughout. And (*c*) the same result holds of my identification of myself with the idea. The felt oneness of my
inner self with the idea of the change cannot become an
object, unless we go beyond and unless we so far destroy
will. It does not matter how much my self has passed beforehand into the content of the idea, and it does not matter
how much my self perceives itself as carried out in the act.
In the end my union with the idea must remain essentially
a felt union, and, so far as by reflection it becomes an object,
volition so far has been superseded and has ceased to exist.
I do not deny that this union, while being felt, can perhaps
to some extent also be an object, but it is merely as being

felt, I contend, that it moves. Its partial appearance in reflection, so far as it appears there, impedes it. And in the end no reflection can bring it before me in its experienced integrity. The same conclusion, I may add, holds good of self-consciousness in general. An exhaustive objectification of the present self remains in principle impossible; but this is a matter on which we are unable here to enlarge.[1]

I have now endeavoured to explain how in volition I am identified with the idea and opposed to the not-self. I have still to ask how far my self enters into the content of the idea, and together with this question I shall have to inquire into the experience of agency. But before I enter on this subject, I will endeavour to dispose of some remaining difficulties. I must deal briefly with the nature of reflective volition, and in connexion with this will remark upon Choice and Consent. And I will open the discussion of these points by stating a probable objection.

'Your account,' it may be said, 'whether so far it is satisfactory or otherwise, applies to will merely in its first and undeveloped form. But will in the distinctive sense is not found at that level. I do not really will until I suspend myself and consider my future course, and then assert myself in something like choice or consent. This is the essence of volition, and, however much your account may be laboured, this in the end falls outside your definition of will.'[2] Now I cannot here attempt even to sketch the development of will from its lowest form upwards. But in its highest form certainly no principle is involved beyond those which in our account we have set out already. And I will endeavour

---

[1] I cannot accept without qualification the statement that we are self-conscious in the practical attitude, and in the theoretical attitude no more than conscious. Not only, in my opinion, do we fail everywhere to be completely self-conscious, but I could not admit without some reserve the doctrine that all self-consciousness is in its essence practical. The above statement however expresses, if it exaggerates, an important truth.

[2] The same objection could be urged about our higher and lower will, our divided will, our attention, and so forth. I have already treated these cases so far as is necessary in *Mind*, n.s. xi, Nos. 41 and 43 [*E*. xxiv and xxv], to which latter article I may refer specially for some illustration of what follows.

very briefly to show how this is true. I will then point out the proper meanings of Choice and Consent, matters on which some dangerous confusion appears to prevail.

In the higher form of volition (so much cannot be disputed) we come upon a most important difference. Our will at this stage has become reflective. I do not here identify myself immediately with this or that practical suggestion, but on the contrary I regard these as things offered to me for my acceptance or rejection. This does not mean merely that I am inconclusively moved by conflicting ideas, and that I fluctuate and waver in their ebb and flow. And it does not mean that I am held motionless by balanced forces or paralysed by shock. The ideas are not mere forces which in me produce states of motion or rest. They are objects which I separate from myself and keep before me at will. The suggestions so far are mine, and again in another sense they are not mine, and their adoption in short lies entirely with myself. Of all the suggestions offered I may accept none, and, when I accept one, I do not merely become what is offered. I actively adopt the idea, I take it into myself, or, if you prefer the phrase, I put myself into the idea. This is a specific act, and with it comes a mode of feeling which is specific. And this by an exaggeration has been emphasized as a fact irreducible and unique.

The exaggeration being omitted I think the above statement is correct, but I claim that the facts are embraced by our definition of will. Indisputably the self is able to rise above suggestions. The self can in a manner alienate these from itself, and then, if it does not reject all, can adopt one of them formally. And it is desirable, I am sure, to lay stress on these facts. On the other hand I cannot take the facts as a kind of supervening miracle which, I know not how, is to prove something—it seems not easy to say what. The self can suspend itself, but, as soon as we inquire into the means, there is an end of the miracle. The means we can discover in every case to be a higher idea, and this higher idea, at least in one of its aspects, is the negation of the particular suggestions. It is with such an idea that in reflective will our self is identified. And the consequence, that has been described above, is the natural result. Given a further and a remoter principle, not in union with the suggestions offered, or not in union at once and immediately with these suggestions as they are offered, and the principle of suspension and of adoption is present. The idea may be of a special end which must be reached by some particular method, and cannot unite itself at once with two methods, however much both belong to it. Or the idea again may be a principle which is general and abstract, and it may, for instance, consist in a rule of not at once deciding on offered suggestions. But, whether more or less abstract, the idea always works in the same way. My self is identified with it, and is hence related to the detail which falls under it. And my self is related to this detail positively, and also, as we have just seen, negatively. Hence my self can confront the detail as a spectator and can hold itself aloof. Then, as soon as one particular (however this happens[1]) becomes superior to the rest, and appears as the means by which the principle can pass into reality, the situation is changed. The self, in one with the principle, comes together with this single particular, and it feels itself reunited with its object by an act of adoption. And here is the origin of that felt estrangement and aloofness and of the following awareness of reunion. These experiences certainly are specific, and it would be strange if they were not so; and you may call them irreducible, if you mean that from their conditions they could not wholly be constructed. But, unless the doctrine just advocated is seriously wrong, these experiences are neither unique nor exceptional.[2]

[1] This question is to some extent dealt with in a preceding article, M. n.s. xi, No. 43 [E. xxv].

[2] It would be well I think if those, who maintain that they are so, would explain how much in psychology is *not* exceptional and unique. We have again, with a difference, the same experience of alienation and reunion when after suspense and doubt an idea is accepted as true. The conditions here, as we have seen, are partly diverse. It is here the not-self which first rejects and then reunites itself with the idea, whereas in will this is done by the self which is opposed to the not-self. The conditions and feelings in both cases may be called the same generically, but not altogether. We

If we take our stand on the principle which has just been laid down, we may without difficulty apprehend the essence of choice and consent. Choice, to begin with that,[1] is (*a*) in the first place not merely intellectual or perceptive. A process which ends with a judgement, even if that judgement is about the means to an end, is so far, we must insist, not a genuine choice. The process is so far not choice, even if it leads to the conclusion 'I like this best' or 'this is nicer'. Distinction by a type and the selection by a type of one thing to the exclusion of another, if you take this process as issuing in a judgement, is, taken so far, not choosing. Choice in a word essentially is will. It may be incomplete volition in the same sense in which Resolve was incomplete will (*E*. xxvi), but a choice always and without exception is an actual willing.

(*b*) In the second place a choice must be made between at least two things which move me. It involves a preliminary suspension, however brief, and that suspension comes, at least usually, from conflicting desires. But choice always and without exception is between two or more moving ideas. I may indeed be ordered to choose before I begin to desire, and in this case the suspension may be said to start from the suggested idea. But the choice, when it takes place, takes place always in essentially the same way. The suggested idea moves me as I am moved by my own idea of an ulterior end, and in each case I have before me two opposite means which prevent instant action. The means in every case must be identified with the moving end, and, if you use 'desire' here in a widened sense, the means in every case must both be desired. The fact that, apart from this identification, they may be indifferent or even repulsive does not raise really the least difficulty.

(*c*) We have to choose 'between' things, and the 'between' implies that one thing is rejected. To say 'take one' and to say 'choose one' are different requests. Unless the

shall once more notice this difference when we deal with the subject of Consent.

[1] The subject of disjunctive volition will be briefly discussed in the article following this.

idea of rejection is implied, and unless for the chooser this idea qualifies the act, we cannot predicate choice proper. If, in short, the 'between' does not come or does not remain before my mind, I may take one out of a number but I most certainly do not choose it. But the 'between' may be present to my mind in various senses and degrees, and let us consider first an instance where it is highly developed and explicit. Here I desire an end to be realized in one of two alternatives which I recognize in that character. Each of these, therefore, is qualified to my mind by the exclusion of the other. I consider these first in relation to my end as contrary means to its attainment, and I then pass a judgement on both, and in consequence will one of them. But it would be absurd to contend that the whole of this is essential to choice. For there need be no judgement, there need be no idea of means in relation to end, and there need be no foregoing idea of an end. The essence of choice implies no alternatives in the sense of disjunctives, and I will now go on to seek the minimum which is really essential. In this minimum there must be two ideas which move me incompatibly so that neither is realized. In the second place, I must not merely oscillate from one idea to the other, but notwithstanding their discrepancy I must desire both objects at once. The main idea which moves me must be felt to be present in each, and it therefore, in relation to each, is a higher idea. If upon this follows my identification of myself with one of these objects, and so my volition, the act is choice if it is qualified by the idea of rejecting the other. If, on the other hand, any feature in the above account be wanting, I no longer in any proper sense have chosen. A child desires two lumps of sugar, and from some cause perceives that both at once are not possible. Each piece excites the pleasant idea of taking and eating, and both still do this when an attempt to take one piece has brought in, and checked itself by, the perception of losing the other. The impracticable 'both' which is desired is in fact the cause of a moment's suspension. Then, through the pressure of appetite or from some other cause, an action ensues, and the idea of taking now is actually realized. But whether the child has really chosen remains uncertain, and it entirely depends on the following condition. Was the idea of leaving one piece an element present in the act, or did for the moment the idea of this piece disappear simply? Choice in the latter case will be absent, while in the former it exists. There is choice because the idea, which acted, in the first place qualified both pieces, and then one piece with the aspect of leaving the other. And so much, I contend, is essential to choosing. On the other hand, there is contained here no idea of an end with its means, and certainly no judgement that one piece is nicer or is wanted by me more.[1] To resume, when I choose I must have before me two ideas under one head, and one of these ideas, when I act, must be qualified as excluded or at least as absent. If I merely lose sight of one idea, I have not really chosen. Hence choice cannot appear below a certain level of mental development, and most obviously it does not constitute the essence of will. Choice is perhaps not reached at all except in the case of human beings.

I will go on from this to remark upon the meaning of Consent. Professor James (*Psych.* ii. 568) has used this term to express the ultimate fact in action and belief.[2] I have already explained how far I can agree to call such experiences ultimate, and I will now point out why in the case of either action or belief the use of consent is really indefensible. In the first place my consent is given always to a foreign force, and in the end it is given always to a foreign will. In the second place consent is not my mere awareness that something is to come from this will, but it implies necessarily that to some extent I am responsible for the result. If, where I might have hindered another's act, I have not attempted to hinder it, I may be taken as a condition of the act and therefore so far as its cause. On the other hand, to call such consent my volition of the act would

---

[1] Mr. Shand, in *Mind*, N.S. vi, pp. 301 foll., appears to me to have seriously misapprehended the facts on this point.

[2] I do not know if this was suggested by Lotze's use of *Billigung, Med. Psych.*, p. 302. I have already remarked on Approval, *M.* N.S. xi. 453 [*E.* xxvi. 495].

be too untenable. And Professor James, excluding such tacit consent, finds the essence of will in the consent which is express. But while there is volition here certainly, so far as I will to express my consent, there is as certainly no volition of the act itself. And my consent never can amount formally to a volition of the act. Always in consent is interposed the idea of a foreign agent, and, however much by my consent I make myself a condition and so assume responsibility, I never, as consenting, am the real doer of the act in question. To give consent to an action, however expressly, stops short of uniting with another to will and to do it.[1] And consent is inapplicable to a common voli-

---

[1] Consent can of course be given in such a way that it amounts to an incitement, and it can be given in such a way as to have the opposite effect. But these effects, I submit, go beyond and fall outside of a bare consent.

A further inquiry into the nature of consent is not necessary here, but the following remarks may perhaps be of service to the reader. The difficulty of defining consent does not lie merely in the uncertainty of the particulars, but attaches itself also to the general idea. Consent is a positive attitude of mind which must exist positively to a certain degree. But on the other hand that degree is determined only by negation and by omission.

Consent is a mental attitude of one agent towards the act of another. The first agent must be aware of the act, and up to a certain point must share the sentiment from which it proceeds. That point is fixed by the presence of abstention from resistance to the act as proposed or from attempt to nullify it if existing. As consenting, I am dominated by a sentiment in accordance with the act, so far that either a feeling of hostility to it does not arise in my mind, or, if it arises, is prevented from carrying itself out. The result is that I do not oppose the act.

It is a further condition of consent that (*a*) the act must be taken by me as in some sense to concern me, and (*b*) some kind of opposition is in my power, or taken by me to be so. The act must fall within the region which I take to be the sphere of my will, and in this sense must interest me. And some kind of volition to oppose the performance or continued existence of the act is always possible here.

Consent must be distinguished from approval. Approval (*a*) extends beyond my personal concerns, and (*b*) involves some reference to a standard. In these two senses it is impersonal and disinterested.

Consent, in order to remain consent, must stop short at a certain point. If it becomes more than a positive state of feeling, measured and defined by abstinence, and if it passes into an attempt to further the act or commit it in common, it has ceased so far to be mere consent.

It is obvious from the above that the positive state of consent itself is not properly an act and is not itself willed. It might itself be willed as a

tion, because it implies that the actual will does not cease to be foreign. This idea of foreignness in the will from which the action proceeds cannot be removed from the meaning even of express consent. And hence as an expression for the essence of will consent is most inappropriate. My will is surely not the action of a foreign force in me, nor can it consist in my permission of such an event. Suggestions, we have seen, can in volition come before me as a not-self; but if, starting from this, I do not go on to make them mine, I have assuredly not willed. And in the presence of a great alternative, where I adopt one course with all the energies of my being, and throw myself, as we say, entirely into the carrying out of one event, to insist that all I do is to give an express consent to this event, somehow happening in me, seems really ridiculous.[1]

psychical effect, but as such it would be only the effect of a volition other than itself. On the other hand, the signification, to another or to my own mind, of my state of consent can obviously be willed. And that abstinence from opposition, which is one aspect of the consent, can itself again be willed. I can will to behave consistently as consenting without any ulterior end in view beyond this behaviour as following from the consent.

If on the other hand my behaviour, as consenting, or again as signifying consent, is willed as a means to the performance of the act in question, I have (as we have seen) passed beyond simple consent. I now have furthered by my act the act of another, and may even have joined with him in committing it. And the result here will be no longer the mere effect of my consent; it will be that effect as contemplated by me and set before me as my end. The mere foreseeing by me that in fact the effect will follow must be distinguished from this; and the difference between the two lies in the nature and action of the idea which in each case is before my mind.

Thus, even in theory, the mental state of consent is not easy to fix, while in practice the difficulty seems well nigh insuperable. The difficulty here lies mainly in knowing the exact nature of that to which at the moment consent is given. For the consent is given to something as it appears at one moment to the consenter, and as at that moment it is qualified by his feelings. But the exact nature of such an impression, as it happens in another, can be arrived at only by approximation and always presumptively. The difficulty again as to what is to be taken as and presumed to be a willed or unwilled indication or signification of consent, can only be disposed of roughly.

   [1] The reason why Professor James, with all his insight, is led to advocate this absurdity is, I venture to think, at once clear and instructive. Professor James, as I have noticed before (*M.* N.s. xi. 297 [*E.* xxv. 452, note]), seems

Consent, we have seen, does not go far enough for volition; but for belief, on the other hand, it goes a great deal too far. In the theoretical relation the object comes to me as something foreign, but I can hardly give consent to the object's being in character what it is. I accept the fact that the angles of a triangle are equal to two right angles, but to give my consent or permission is not in my power. It is a fact which I cannot help or hinder, and for which I have no responsibility. I can of course will the appearance of the truth in my mind, but I cannot will the actual truth itself to be this rather than that. The attempt would obviously at once destroy my theoretical attitude. And even my attitude, when I will to receive whatever is the truth in itself, cannot be defined as my express consent to that reception. For, if I actively will the reception, I do much more than consent to it. Consent in short for will is too little, and for mere belief is too much. Truth, I agree, is the satisfaction of a want in my nature, and the criterion, I agree, in the end may be called a postulate. There is no attitude in fact which is simply theoretical, just as there is no attitude in fact which is barely practical. But after all there is a difference between thinking and doing, and a difference which happily is ascertainable. And this ascertainable character on either side alike refuses to be described as consisting in consent.

We now approach a difficult part of our subject, the question how far in will the self enters into the idea of the change; and we may connect with this question a brief inquiry into the meanings of activity and agency. The

to approach the facts of the soul with a mind too much dominated by mechanical metaphors. What moves in the soul is forces external and foreign. And when in use such principles fail, and Professor James sees their failure, instead of rejecting them as disproved he attempts to help them once again from the outside. My will is more than the resultant effect of foreign forces, and it is therefore something inexplicable which supervenes and is added from the outside at a certain point. And, being merely added, it does not and it must not transform the external forces. Hence the special virtue of consent, which on one side makes an assertion of myself, and on the other side still leaves the forces foreign.

reader, if he is unable here to accept our result, will, I hope, at least find matter which deserves his consideration. We have seen that the end of will, when that is completely realized, need not involve throughout the knowledge or even the existence of the agent. The necessity for my awareness in all cases of my own volition cannot in short hold except of the beginning of the process. As that process starts from within, I cannot fail to experience it and to know in some sense that the process is my act. But up to what point this knowledge and experience will accompany the process, cannot be laid down in general. If, that is to say, you take volition as the complete process in which my idea reaches its end, my awareness is certainly not throughout a necessary accompaniment of my will. My will, we have seen, may even extend beyond my existence.

This being dismissed, we may enter on a more limited inquiry, and may ask first whether and how far my self must enter into the content of the idea. The idea, we have seen, is always the idea of a change in existence, and certainly in some cases it is the idea of myself making this change. I as realizing the end am in these cases an object to myself, and it is this idea of myself which here makes the beginning of the process. Now no one can doubt that such an idea is often present in will, and I am not concerned to deny that it is present usually. But I cannot agree that in will the idea does contain my self always, and I do not think that I as making the change must always be an object to myself in the idea.

This question taken by itself has but little importance. On the one hand, volition is the identification of my felt self with the idea, and this felt self, we have seen, is so far never an object. And, so far as it becomes an object, the felt self so far is not the self which actually wills. Hence the presence or absence of my self as an element contained in the idea can hardly be vital. On the other hand, in every case after the process has started, my self must perceive itself to some extent as entering into this process, and to some extent therefore my self must in every case become an object to itself.[1] And for this reason again the question, whether before the start I am an object to myself, does not seem in itself to be very material. But, since a confusion may give rise to dangerous consequences, the question, I think, must be briefly discussed.

I cannot admit that in all cases my self as changing the existence forms part of the idea's content. At an unreflective level of mind, whether in ourselves or in the lower animals, a suggestion, if it acts at once, need not be so qualified. The perception of another engaged, say, in eating or fighting may produce by suggestion these processes in me. And the result in such a case has on the one hand been certainly willed, but on the other hand the element of *my* fighting has not always been contained in the idea. An idea is present because the perception has for me qualified existence incompatibly with itself, and because this incompatible feature, opposed in me to the existing not-self, has then carried itself out. On the other hand, the idea is not the idea of the fighting of *another*, for this aspect of otherness drops out before the idea acts in me. And the question is whether the idea, in thus coming to me straight from the perception and in dropping out, as is necessary, some portion of that perception's content, must in part replace that omission by the insertion of my self. I know of no principle from which such a result must in all cases follow, and, as I observe the facts, the result in many cases is absent. The idea of fighting is felt in volition to be *mine*, but it need not contain *me* as an element in the ideal content. Neither the other nor myself need actually appear in that content, though the idea of fighting, freed from otherness, must be in relation with my not-self and must be felt as mine. Then, as the idea realizes itself, my felt self becomes in part also perceived, and in the actual process I acquire the experience of *my* fighting. And, if this is so, then in volition the idea is not always the idea of myself making a change.[2]

---

[1] This is a point to which I shall return very shortly.

[2] We must be careful not to assume that at an early stage the perception of another's fighting comes to my mind as something belonging to

It is difficult to ascertain exactly what in any case is contained in the idea at the commencement of the process. For the process itself necessarily is perceived when begun, and in that experience the idea goes on to qualify itself further. When the idea of the change begins to realize both itself and me, I perceive myself as moving in one with the idea. I am aware of myself altering the existence so as to correspond to the idea, and in this union with the idea I become an object to myself. The idea thus develops and qualifies itself in a continuous process, and on reflection we may naturally take its acquired character as there from the first. And it is easy in this way to assume that my self as acting is present always in the idea at its start. But though my self is thus present often, and I am ready to admit even usually, my self, we have seen, is not thus present always or even normally. Nothing is normal and necessary except that the idea of the change should be felt as in one with myself, and then that its actual process should be perceived as my making the change. My self, in short, as making the change, is not in fact always preconceived in the idea, and, whether this takes place or not, it is in every case external to the essence of will.

A confusion on this point may threaten danger to our whole doctrine of volition. 'Your view', I may be told, 'is entirely circular and so illusory. All that you have done is to take the fact of will as an unexplained mass. You then transfer that mass in idea to the beginning of the process, and the process therefore naturally appears as the realization of this idea. But the idea simply anticipates the actual process in an unexplained form, and you have therefore offered in fact no explanation at all. For it is will, you say in effect, when with will we have the idea of it beforehand.' But such an objection need, I think, not cause any serious

---

another. The perception will contain something like 'fighting there', and this, in becoming a suggestion, sheds the 'there', and in the action is perceived as 'fighting here' or 'me fighting'. At a still lower stage the 'here' and 'there' become even less specified, but, as long as we can speak of will at all, there is an incompatible adjective which is opposed to existence and which in this sense is an idea.

embarrassment. We do not in the first place admit that my self as acting must in fact be contained in the idea. And even if we admitted this, the conclusion which would follow really matters very little. For the conclusion which would follow amounts merely to this, that my perception of agency must come before volition in the proper sense of that term. This priority would, however, make little or no difference to our main result. The idea of a changed existence is suggested, is felt as one with me, and so carries itself out. And this process gives me, as we laid down, the experience of my agency; but the process so far, on the present hypothesis, would not amount in the strict sense to volition. On another occasion, however, this perception of my agency, which now is acquired, will or may be transferred to the idea as an element in its content. And the result will now follow from an idea which has been qualified as required, and the act will therefore now have become a volition proper. Hence, even if we accept a view which I submit is mistaken in fact, the alleged circle in our account is really non-existent or harmless.

In volition I must have, and must be conscious of, an object not-self, and I must be conscious again of an object idea. With that idea I must feel myself in a special sense to be one, and the idea must be qualified in its content by its relation to the not-self. Then, when the idea realizes itself, I perceive myself also as moving in the same sense, and up to a certain point in this movement I am an object to myself. And my self again in many cases, before the idea has even partly realized itself, is contained as an element in the content of the idea. But at the beginning of the act my self is not always so contained. And after a certain point the process, we have seen, may wholly pass beyond my knowledge and being.[1]

---

[1] We may ask whether the idea, *before* it realizes itself, need even be the idea of *my* future state. The idea must be felt inwardly as mine, and it must qualify the not-self which comes to me and which so far qualifies me. The idea must thus in its content be the idea of a change in me. But if you ask whether the idea is that of a change in myself as distinct from others, the question is different. The doubt is whether a change of my not-self, even where my not-self is in felt opposition to an idea felt as mine,

Then is the idea of agency, I may be asked, not essential
to will? This idea in my opinion is present usually, but I
do not think that it is essential, and I even think that in
some cases of will it is absent. We always experience
the process, when it happens, as our agency, but, before the
process happens, agency is not a necessary element in the
idea. In other words, the idea of an altered not-self, I think,
is enough, even if that idea does not contain the feature of
an active altering. Let us suppose that at an early stage
my self in some point has been expanded into the not-self,
and let us suppose that, without experiencing this process
as an act, I have perceived it as a change in which my self
has flowed over into the not-self. Let us again suppose
that later this same change is suggested in idea, and that
myself is felt as identified with this ideal change. The process which follows and realizes this idea will be experienced
as my agency,[1] and this process, I submit, is also an act of
volition. On the other hand, the element of agency was not
present beforehand in the idea. And if the process, being
without such an element in its idea, is denied to be volition,
this to myself, I would repeat, matters little or nothing.
The process in any case will give at least the perception of
agency, and on the next occasion that element, having now
been perceived, will tend to qualify the idea.

'But it is the perception of agency', I may probably be
told, 'which is here really in question. Agency and the experience of it are things one or both of which are ultimate,
irreducible, and unique, and in this inexplicable fact is contained the real essence of will. To make will consist in the
perception or in the idea of this fact is really circular. And
once more the perception like the fact is irreducible and
ultimate.'[2] Now, to confine my reply first to the objection

must therefore be qualified in the idea as a change of myself as distinct from
other persons or things. And I cannot maintain the affirmative here. But,
since the idea in its actual process at once goes on to qualify itself, the
inquiry, as I have explained in my text, seems to have no importance.

[1] It will be so experienced, that is, except under certain conditions discussed later in this article.

[2] I do not mean to imply that this objection as it stands would be offered
all at once by the same person.

based on the perception of agency, I am not concerned here to deny that such an experience is 'original' and 'ultimate'. Whether anything in our development precedes the practical relation and, if so, what precedes it, is a matter with which I am not here undertaking to deal. But I maintain that apart from the practical relation there is no will nor any perception of agency, and I insist that in this relation certain elements are essentially involved. And where these are wanting I utterly deny the presence of an experience of agency. On the one hand I do not assert that the elements can exist apart or that they precede the relation, and on the other hand I do not even maintain that with these the whole experience is exhausted. My perceived agency will contain usually, or perhaps even always, some psychical matter which I am not here attempting to detail. But this matter in my opinion most certainly is not essential, though it may give what may be called a specific character to the experience. What is essential is the presence of those several aspects which I have repeatedly described, and, where you have not these, you have not in fact, I contend, the experience of agency. But, in calling these aspects the essential conditions of the experience, I imply no conclusion with regard to their priority in time.

I will pass from this point to consider another mode of objection. 'The experience of agency', it may be said, 'falls outside your account of it. We might on your account of the matter perhaps perceive a change happening to the not-self, and we might also perceive a change happening to ourselves, but with this we should never get to perceive ourselves as making the change.' But for my part I cannot understand how this perception could fail. I feel myself one with the idea of a changed not-self, an idea opposed to the not-self which actually exists. And as this idea invades the not-self, I feel and I perceive that my self is expanded. The change of the not-self is perceived as my process of expansion, in which both that existence and myself become in fact what ideally I was. We have a change of existence beginning with its idea in myself and itself really ending in that which was ideal. This moving idea is

felt in one with myself, and my self thus is felt and is perceived as becoming actually itself. The process is experienced as beginning from within and as going continuously
outwards. And surely with this we must in fact have attained to the essence of agency.

There are fundamental difficulties, I admit, which I
must here leave untouched. The perception of succession
in general, and the qualification in any process of the beginning by the end, offer well-known problems which here
it is impossible to discuss. And the same remark holds, we
may add, of every kind of predication. But these difficulties
do not attach themselves specially to the perception of
agency in the self. They apply equally to the experience of
any change in outward existence. And these difficulties, if
so understood, furnish no ground for objection against our
doctrine of will. Such an objection is not grounded unless
these ultimate questions are answered in one special manner. It is possible to hold that in the self there is an agency
which the self knows in that character, and that this self-
conscious agency, while inexplicable itself and the essence
of will, serves to explain our perception of process in things,
and meets the difficulties which attach themselves to predication in general. I consider any such view to be untenable and to be in conflict with fact, but I cannot undertake
the discussion of it here. Whatever plausibility it may
possess comes I think from its vagueness and from its
inability to realize the conclusions to which its principle
would lead.[1] We must not confuse with such a view a
doctrine which differs from it vitally. This doctrine is alike
in holding agency and will to be itself inexplicable and ultimate, and to be on the other hand the main principle which
explains experience. It would however deny that this principle in its working is aware of itself. Or, if aware of itself
in any sense, the principle is at least not aware of itself in its
own proper character. If the agency in short is a 'fact of
experience', it is nevertheless not experienced in fact as an
agency. Such a principle however, it may be urged, is the

---

[1] The appearance of Professor Münsterberg's interesting volume since
these words were written has not inclined me to modify them.

real essence of volition. Once again it is impossible here to discuss such a doctrine, but such a doctrine may at once be dismissed as here irrelevant. For in these papers, I may remind the reader, I am merely concerned with what we experience as will. If indeed from such a principle you could account for this our actual experience, the case, I admit, would become very different. But for any satisfactory explanation on this head we should seek assuredly in vain. And we are really not concerned here even with 'a fact of experience' except so far as it either itself is an experienced fact or serves as a principle by which experienced facts are explained.[1]

It is better to leave an objection which, however fundamental, is far too vague to be discussed briefly, and I therefore will state in a concrete instance the former more definite argument. 'I may have a pain,' it may be objected, 'and the idea of its relief, and I may experience the tension of that idea against existence and may feel myself one with it. Then, when the idea is realized, I may experience, in and with this change of the not-self, a great expansion of my self. And yet with all this I may gain no perception of agency.'[2] But this is so, I reply, because the conditions are not fulfilled. The process is perceived as beginning from the not-self and as merely happening to me. Either from a general habit, or from the presence of some particular cause, the change does not come to me as starting from the idea in me. The realization of the idea on the contrary appears to begin with an independent movement of the

---

[1] I may refer here to *M.* N.S. ix and x [*E.* xxii and xxiii]. I have noticed for some years an increasing tendency in England to do what I must call to coquet with the doctrine of the 'primacy of will'. I do not, I trust, undervalue the lesson which is to be learnt perhaps most readily from Schopenhauer. But that lesson, I am sure, is much less than half learnt if we do not realize the difficulties which arise from anything like a wholehearted acceptance of the doctrine. Professor Münsterberg's important work should here prove instructive. I hope also that Mr. Schiller's essay, contained in *Personal Idealism* (which I have seen since writing the above), may in its way be useful, though one would seek in it in vain for any serious attempt to realize the meaning and result of that gospel which it preaches.

[2] Compare the remarks on Expectation (*E.* xi. 481–2).

not-self, and the process therefore naturally is viewed as the process of the not-self. I have the idea of relief and yet actually the pain remains. The idea changes in strength and fullness, and generally in the way in which it occupies my self, but on the other hand the pain remains unaltered. There is therefore no acquired tendency to connect actual cessation of the pain with its idea. On the other side, not only may the pain have ceased when the idea has been absent, but it may have ceased also when some prominent change of the not-self has been present, and this experience may have happened to me more or less frequently. We have, therefore, not only the absence of any acquired tendency to connect the change with the idea, but we may have a contrary tendency to view the change as beginning from the not-self. And this order again may be in general the more familiar way of our experienced world.[1] If then, in any particular case of relief from pain, there is nothing to suggest specially that the process has begun from the idea, we naturally fail to experience ourselves as active. And this failure is a consequence which serves to illustrate and to confirm our doctrine.

Let us now suppose, on the other hand, that the facts are altered. Let us suppose that relief from pain comes habitually when the idea of it is present, or when that idea to a certain extent has inwardly prevailed. And let us suppose that the respective increase and decrease of the idea and of the pain are in general related inversely. Under these conditions we should tend, I submit, to view the relief as ensuing from the idea, and in the process, when it happened, we should gain a perception of our agency. The relief in fact really might arise from another unperceived cause,

---

[1] A change ensuing on, and continuously following from, motion of some object not my body tends in general to be attributed to that object and not to myself. On the other hand, the origin of motion in my body, as coming from myself and proceeding outwards, is, I presume, the main source of our experience of agency. The perception of agency in my outward world, I should agree, is transferred, but, though transferred, it may have become a more familiar and natural way of apprehension. I do not however mean by this to imply that our experience of the order of the outward world begins with such a transferred perception of agency.

and our perception of agency would in this case contain an illusion—the same illusion which on one view makes the essence of all experience of will. But whether illusory or otherwise, the perception, I contend, would arise from these conditions, in the absence, that is, of other conditions which are hostile. If a suggestion is made to me that relief from pain comes from the idea, if this suggestion is not qualified in my mind by anything alien or foreign, but remains with me as a simple connexion of my ideas,[1] if then in the presence of the pain I have the idea of its relief, and the idea is realized in the actual cessation of the pain— under these conditions I shall experience agency and will. The experience may be illusory, we have seen, but that point is irrelevant or, so far as relevant, it is not an argument against our view. For we are asking merely as to the elements which are essential to our experience of agency.[2]

We have so far supposed as one of our conditions a special acquired tendency, a disposition, that is, to join the

---

[1] This proviso must be emphasized. If there is anything about the idea which makes it other than my idea simply, the act will so far not be experienced as my will. See the preceding article [*E*. xxvi].

[2] An unbiased inquiry into the conditions under which we get an experience of activity and passivity is a thing which, so far as my knowledge goes, is sorely wanted. I cannot think it satisfactory that two competent psychologists should in the case of some psychical process be clear, one that the experience of activity is there, and the other that it is not there. I cannot myself approve when I see such a difference end apparently with two assertions. But for myself, even if I were otherwise fitted to undertake this inquiry, it is plain that I could not be regarded as unbiased. In the main, however, and subject to some necessary explanation which is given below in this article, I find that the presence of the experience depends on an idea. If, for instance, my imagination is excited and I perhaps desire to sleep, I can view myself at pleasure as freely active in my imagination, or again as passive and constrained by the activity of a foreign power. And, as I view myself, so also I perceive and I feel myself. Similarly in a carriage or in a train I can regard and can perceive the movement as my act, or again as an alien force that actively sweeps me away either as merely passive or as unwilling. And I can even mix both experiences and can feel that it is at once my act and is also my fate which is taking me in each case to its end. The whole matter, I submit, is one for an unprejudiced inquiry, and I will venture once again, not without hope, to recommend this conclusion. Cf. *A.R.* 547 = 605.

relief with the idea as following after it in time. But such a particular connexion I think is hardly required. In any particular case a present emphasis may have the same effect as repetition and past conjunction. If, that is, the idea of relief is first opposed to the actual pain and is then realized, and if this experience throughout is prominent and is felt emphatically, we might, even in the absence of an acquired connexion between the relief and the pain, experience the process as our agency and will. I assume of course that there is nothing in the case to suggest the activity of the not-self. But it is not worth while to insist on a point which perhaps bears but little on our general doctrine. The reader will have understood generally that I am not offering an account of our psychical development, nor on the other side am I attempting an exhaustive analysis of the facts. There are psychical features, I would repeat, in our experience of agency, which, because I think them unessential, have been omitted altogether. And in the development of this experience the changes of my body, felt and later perceived in their felt unity with myself, are obviously a factor of primary importance. But our inquiry here must be limited to points which seem essential to the definition of will.

Before I pass from the subject of our experienced agency I must direct the attention of the reader to a remaining difficulty. Wherever you experience agency in the proper sense, there you have the experience of volition. Hence, if anywhere you perceived yourself as an agent in the absence of conditions which we have defined as essential to will, such a fact clearly would destroy our definition. Now, if we make no distinction between an awareness of activity and of agency, a contradiction of this kind is likely to arise, and I must therefore offer at once a brief explanation on this point. The question is, however, too fundamental to be discussed here in an adequate manner.

I will begin by noticing a doubt which may be forthwith dismissed. It might be contended that for an experience of activity and passivity it is not necessary to be aware of an other or not-self. But, when the not-self is understood so as to include my existence, so far as that existence is opposed to my idea, an objection of this kind at once loses plausibility.[1] We may therefore, leaving this, return at once to the more serious difficulty. If there is no difference in my experience between activity and agency proper, and if my experience of activity is possible without the presence of an idea of change, then it will not be true that an idea is essential to volition. And I will now proceed to draw out and to explain this objection. 'Even when idea is understood', it may be urged, 'as you have understood it,[2] I may perceive myself as active where no such idea can be found, or at least where no such idea carries itself out in existence. For I may perceive my self as it expands against and into the not-self, or again as it is contracted when the not-self advances into me. And this expansion or contraction may be experienced as my activity or passivity, without the presence in either case of any idea which realizes itself. If my self is written as AB and the not-self as CD, we may perhaps at first write their experienced relation as AB | CD.[3] Let us now suppose that this experience is changed to ABC | D, and that the process of this change, of myself from AB to ABC and of the not-self from CD to D, is perceived by me. And let us suppose also that there is no suggestion of this change having arisen from the not-self. In this case I become aware of myself as changing outwards from a narrower to a wider self, a self that has

---

[1] On this point see above, p. 521.   [2] E. xxiii. 391, and xxvi. 503–6.

[3] These symbols, of course, are miserably inadequate and may even mislead. I however offer them to the reader who is prepared to make the best of them. The vertical line which divides these groups of letters is of course not to be understood as distinguishing in the ordinary sense 'subject' from 'object'. The division holds merely within the content which is experienced in my whole self, and it is meant to distinguish those features in the object-world, which oppose and limit me, from the rest of my world, whether object or not, with which in feeling I am one. If we suppose a part of my body, which for the moment is out of gear and so prevents my ordinary feeling and perception of self, and if we then suppose that this restriction of myself is removed, such an example may perhaps explain the general sense of our symbols. Unfortunately, with the restriction and enlargement there goes also a qualitative change.

become more than what it was, and has become this at the expense of the not-self. The process into the not-self, if so, is referred to myself as a further quality; and experienced pleasure, though not essential, would contribute to my so taking it. There is here on the one side no foregoing idea which carries itself out, but on the other side there arises a perception of myself as active. So in the same manner my experience may change from AB | CD to A | BCD, this change being perceived as the invasion of me by the not-self. And here once again there will be no idea which realizes itself in the result. Hence without any such idea we have the perception both of passivity and of activity, and it therefore is false that without an idea there is no experienced agency or will.'

I can identify myself largely with this objection, but I cannot endorse it altogether. I do not think that in the absence of an idea I could possibly attain to the experience of agency. I should not under the described conditions either perceive myself as doing something or as having something done to myself. But if activity and passivity are used in a lower sense which stops short of agency, then under the above conditions I might be aware of myself as active or passive. And I should not myself object to the use of activity and of passivity in such a lower sense, at least so long as confusion is avoided. My perceived self-expandedness in what before was the not-self may thus, unless for some further reason the process is taken as be-ginning from the not-self, be regarded as the perception of my activity. And on the other side my self-contractedness, when my self is seen to become in part the not-self, may be an awareness of passivity; so long, that is, as the result is not made to appear as beginning from my self. And in neither case will such an experience involve an idea—an idea, I mean, which carries itself out in the result. But such a lower activity, whether on the side of my self or of the not-self, must be clearly understood not to amount to agency. It is not agency at all, that is, so long as it remains simply in its own character. On the other hand, it tends naturally to pass beyond itself and to become the experience of agency by a process of construction. And, since this tendency serves to obscure the distinction, I will ask the reader to pause and to consider its nature. The subject of the experience has perceived in fact merely his own expansion into the not-self or, on the other hand, the inroad of the not-self into his being. The process so far begins from one side of the relation, and in that character is regarded as belonging to that side. And with so much, I would repeat, we have not the perception of agency, since the process is not viewed as coming out of that which in its result it qualifies. But it is natural for the subject himself, or again for an outside observer, to make the addition wanted to produce the perception of agency. The result is transferred in idea from the end to the beginning, and qualifies that beginning as an element which lay within it and issues from it. And with this we now have agency and will in that character which our definition has ascribed to it. The above construction may be erroneous and may more or less misinterpret the facts, but at least in the subject of the experience it may develop itself into an actual perception. What was first perceived was in fact no more than a self-expandedness, and it is the presence of the idea by which it has now become a perceived self-realization and agency.

It may be instructive to dwell for a time on the above sense of activity and passivity, a sense in which as yet they do not imply agency and will. We must distinguish this again from feelings which, whether in idea or in actual time, are anterior to perception, and which in any case do not pass beyond their own lower level. These feelings of activity and of passivity of course exist at all stages of our development, and in some sense each, I should say, precedes its respective perception. But neither is in itself an experience *of* passivity or activity, if this means that, confined to them, we could be said to have any knowledge of either. Our first perception of activity or passivity goes beyond and is distinct from such feelings. It gives us the knowledge of something in the character of being active or passive, though this something is not yet qualified on either side by agency. I perceive myself first as passive when a change in myself is referred to the not-self as its process, when, that is, I become different and the object not-self becomes different, and the alteration is perceived as the increase of the not-self in me. This experience does not imply so far my practical relation to the object in the sense of my striving against its invasion. And again it does not imply agency on the part of the object. That agency and my struggle, I repeat, may perhaps in fact exist, but they are not contained so far as such within my experience. And I have feelings and those feelings may more or less qualify the not-self, but, once more, not so as to produce a perception of agency. We may find an illustration in my state as theoretical or perceptive. Where knowledge develops itself in me without effort or friction, my experience even here is very far from being simple. But my attitude, so far as I tranquilly receive the object's development, and so far again as that development is not viewed as its agency, is an example of what we mean by simple passivity.[1]

And we have a perception of activity which remains on the same level. In this, as we saw, I perceive my self to be enlarged at the expense of the not-self. But whatever feeling may accompany and may qualify this process, I do not perceive the not-self as striving or myself upon the other side as doing something to this not-self. Thus, in my theoretic attitude again, the unknown existence is beyond me as a not-self, and my knowledge of it can come to me as an expansion of myself at its cost. And yet my attitude so far involves no experience of resistance or of agency. We found another instance in what I may perceive on relief from a pain, although the cessation of the pain is not viewed as my doing. And we saw that activity and passivity in this lower sense are turned by a small addition into that which implies agency and will.[2] This addition in each case

[1] I refer to that state of mind in which the object comes to me as something which *is*, without my feeling at the time that it is *doing* anything to me, or I to it or again to myself.

[2] If we imagine a dog beginning to run, we may suppose that with this he gets at once a perception of activity (cf. *A.R.* 548 = 606). His experience,

consists in an idea of the result, an idea which, going before, carries itself out in the process.

These subtleties, however wearisome, cannot I think be safely neglected. We have often what may be called an awareness at once of both activity and passivity; but to take the two always here in the same sense and as exactly correlative might involve us in confusion and in serious difficulty. The practical attitude, we saw, involves in itself the attitude of theory, and without the perception of an object no will is possible. Now as receptive of such a not-self I have a sense of passivity, and we may regard this sense as in some degree present in will. But in will to take this perceived passivity together with our perceived agency, as at one and the same level of meaning, would not be defensible. It would be a mistake which might lead us to dangerous results.

Before I pass from this subject I must return to a final difficulty. 'It is impossible', I may be told, 'anywhere to understand activity in a lower sense, for activity and passivity are inseparable from agency both in fact and in idea. The distinction of self from not-self depends on the full practical relation, and apart from this relation there is neither in idea nor in time the possibility of an experience of anything lower.' This is an objection which obviously goes too far to be discussed in these pages, but I can at once make a reply which I consider to be here sufficient. The reader is at liberty to assume here for the sake of argument that our experienced distinction of self from not-self comes into existence with and in the experience of agency and will. I could not myself admit that before this distinction there is no experience at all. But for the sake of argu-

however, at first need not amount to agency proper. But the perceived expansion of self into the not-self will tend naturally to become an idea, and that idea of the result will tend to precede and to qualify beforehand the process. And, with such a self-developing idea of a changed not-self, the dog would have forthwith the experience of agency. The same ideal construction can of course be also made from the outside by a spectator, and can then be attributed, perhaps falsely, to the actual subject of the process. In the passage of my book to which I have just referred I have not distinguished between the two senses of activity referred to above.

ment I will admit that the practical relation, with its experience of agency, is the beginning of that consciousness which distinguishes not-self from self. Such an admission, I would however add, agrees perfectly with our doctrine. The practical relation still maintains that character on which we have insisted, and it involves always the self-realizing idea of a change. On the other hand we find in fact a lower perception of activity and passivity, just as in fact we still must find our theoretical experience and attitude. And such a consequence need entail no confusion or discrepancy. The practical relation, together with experienced agency, will be there from the first, and will remain the condition of our experience of any relation between self and not-self. But lower experiences of that relation may none the less actually be present. They will be present either as degraded forms of the practical relation, where one or more of its aspects have vanished in fact; or they will exist within the practical relation as dependent and subordinate features of that inclusive whole. In the latter case they will be abstractions on which our attention and our one-sided emphasis bestows the appearance of a separate existence. But this is a point with which for our present purpose we are not further concerned. And when this reply, together with what precedes it, is fairly considered, the objection to the use of activity in a lower sense may, I hope, be removed. And it will be impossible from this ground to argue against the presence of a self-realizing idea in our experience of agency.

I will end our inquiry into this difficult point by reminding the reader that in one sense I attach to it no great value. We have, I think, a natural tendency to make use of activity and of passivity in cases where the experience of agency is absent. And for myself I am ready to permit within limits and to justify this use, but on the other side I am also ready to condemn and to disallow it. But in the latter case, if we may not distinguish between activity and agency, we must at least distinguish both from a lower experience. There will be an experience, such as we have described, which falls short of agency, and which, if it is not to be called active and passive, must at least in some way be recognized. This lower experience, if left unrecognized in fact, becomes a dangerous source of confusion and mistake; but on the other hand the name which we are to apply to it is a matter of secondary concern.

We have now discussed the sense in which the self in will is identified with an idea, and in connexion with this have inquired into our experience of activity and agency, and we have asked how far these two should be regarded as distinct. Our space has been too short for a satisfactory treatment of such problems, even if otherwise such a treatment were within my power. There remain various questions with regard to the practical relation and its opposition of the not-self to the idea and to the self. I can however do no more here than notice some points in passing. (i) In the first place this opposition is, I should say, in no case motionless and fixed. The idea, if it does not at once realize itself, will ebb and flow, and, as against the not-self, will at its boundary more or less waver. There will be a constant movement, however slight, of passing forward into fact and of again falling back. (ii) The opposition of the not-self may again be so transitory and so weak that it fails to give us in the proper sense an awareness of resistance. The existence to be changed by the idea may be more or less isolated. It may find little support in any connexions with the self and the world, and its strength may be said to consist in its own psychical inertia.[1] And the extent of the existence and the inertia may be inconsiderable. In other words, the resistance to some special change may be no more than a resistance to change in general. But this resistance, it is clear, may in some cases amount to very little. (iii) We may have in volition a forecast and an expectation of the result, and this may be strong and may be definite in various degrees. And in some cases its strength and detail may tend to overpower the actual fact. The idea may, before the act, so prevail against the perceived existence as in part to suppress my experience of

[1] I shall return to the subject of inertia in my next article.

activity against an opposing not-self. I do not mean that this experience can in will be wholly suppressed, but it may be reduced in some cases to an amount which is hardly noticeable. In brief, within the act of volition our experience is both complex and variable, and to try to enter on these variations would be a lengthy task. But everywhere the main essence of volition remains one and the same, and that essence, I venture to think, has been described by us correctly.

In the next article I shall discuss the alleged plurality of typical volitions, and shall briefly deal with errors which prevail on the subject of aversion. Then, after disposing of some minor points, I shall finally inquire how and by what means the idea comes to realize itself in fact.

XXVIII

THE DEFINITION OF WILL (III)

[*First published in* MIND, N.S. xiii, No. 49, 1–37. *January*, 1904.]

IN some preceding articles I have defined will as 'the
self-realization of an idea with which the self is identified', and I have endeavoured to explain and to justify this
account. I have hitherto assumed the fact of what is called
'ideo-motor action', and I have still to show that the
assumption is warranted. But before I proceed to this
last part of my subject, I must attempt to deal with several
remaining difficulties.

The first of these is the question as to a plurality of
volitional types.[1] There is a variety, it has been urged, of
unique typical volitions, and each of these cases in the end
is said to be irreducible and ultimate. Will may be negative, or imperative, or hypothetical, or disjunctive; and
such types, it is added, will not conform to the general
account which we have given. Our best reply to this objection will be to exhibit briefly the true nature of these different types. We shall in this way reach the conclusion
that in every case our definition is confirmed. Certainly
these types are irreducible in the sense that, before they
were experienced, you could not in advance have anticipated their character. But everywhere, so far as they are
volitions, they consist in the self-realization of an idea, and
the main question is as to the exact nature of the idea in
each case. The types of will differ, in short, because in
each type I will to do something different. The difference,
in other words, lies in the diversity of the various ends, and
this diversity will in each case be found to consist in the
varying content of the idea which realizes itself.

(*a*) We may begin with a short account of 'imperative'
volition. In a true imperative I will the production of a

---

[1] Mr. Shand (*M.* N.S. vi. 289–325) has written a very instructive article
on this subject.

certain act by another, not simply, but in and through the manifestation of this my will to the other. In a true imperative the other's act must not come merely because I have willed it. It must come because I have also shown this my volition to the other, and, if the latter element disappears, there is no genuine order.[1] Since however this element has a constant tendency to be obscured or to vanish, it is often difficult in practice to decide if an imperative really is present. I will go on to illustrate this statement by several examples.

If, in walking with another man, I see him about to tread on some small living creature, I may will at once the prevention of this result. And I may execute my will in a number of ways. I may pull or push the person, or I may point to the object, or I may cry out 'There is something there', or 'look', or 'stop'. Now in any of these cases an imperative may be present or absent. If the manifestation of my will is included as a means in the idea of my end, we have in each of these cases a genuine imperative, and otherwise we have in no case an imperative volition. This is the principle, and all the rest is a question of fact to be decided in each case by a special observation. We may illustrate this again by what happens among some of the lower animals, where the mother is engaged in teaching her young. The tap, the push or the pull, the call or the warning sound, or the action set as an example, cannot in most cases, I presume, be regarded as orders.[2] They are not, in the proper sense, orders where they are done merely to produce the action of the other; for the idea of showing what is required seems essential to an imperative proper.

The instance of the sudden and instinctive imperative adduced by Mr. Shand (317) does not present us, I think, with any special difficulty. If we are to decide whether an

---

[1] I have of course always rejected the doctrine that a command must imply a threat. This fiction is as contrary to sound psychology as it is to plain fact.

[2] Whether the lower animals can use imperatives in the strict sense I do not here discuss. It is certain that they can behave in an imperative manner, and that this may be some evidence of their use of ideas I have long ago pointed out (L. 31–2 = 33).

instinctive act is in any case a volition, we have to inquire first if it is the result of a foregoing idea. And in the second place, if that idea is found and the action therefore is will, we have next to ask what precisely is contained in the idea. And according to the answer which we give to this question, we shall have to pronounce that a genuine imperative is present or absent. If I suddenly rise and ring the bell on the appearance of some danger or some want, such an 'instinctive imperative' (317) may perhaps be my willed order to a servant. But the act very probably is a volition which falls far short of this, and is no more an imperative than would be, for example, a movement to the door. And the act may possibly not even be the result of any volition at all. The whole question here is as to the presence and as to the nature of the idea, and, viewed in this way, the difficulty is reduced to a mere question about the particular fact.

In an ordinary imperative I will the real production of the act by the other, but it may be doubted if this feature belongs to the essence. The imperative consists merely, it may be said, in a willed manifestation on my part, and what lies beneath this appearance is not essential. But this is a subordinate point which we are not concerned to discuss, and, however it is decided, our main doctrine remains unaffected. And I do not think that we need dwell further here on the subject of imperative volition.[1]

(b) I must deal very rapidly with the alleged 'hypothetical' and 'disjunctive' types of will (Mr. Shand, l.c., 296–300). I cannot admit the existence of a conditional or an imaginary volition. We have to do in such cases, I should say, with an intention or a mere resolve, and how far this is will we have discussed in a previous article (see E. xxvi). So far as the idea really is taken as conditional or as imaginary, it is so far not willed; but it may at the

[1] The reader should recall in this connexion that in one sense my will is limited to my inner self, and in another sense it extends into the outer world. See E. xxvi. We may, in passing, notice how the use of an internal imperative to myself is possible only where I have two selves which are taken as alien to each other. To make the whole of morality coexistent with the actual use of an imperative is therefore a most serious exaggeration.

same time be willed in another character. And for an explanation of this I must refer the reader to our former discussion. The alleged 'disjunctive will' presents us with greater difficulties, but they are difficulties which do not seem to affect our account of volition. A disjunctive will, so far as it exists, must consist in the willing of a disjunctive idea, and the main question is about the real meaning of that idea. The question is difficult, and it is not possible to enter into it here, but I will very briefly set down what to my mind seems true. In determining (to use an instance given by Mr. Shand) to go to Paris by way of Calais or Boulogne, my state of mind is a compound of actual will and of mere resolve. I will unconditionally to go to Paris, and to go by a way which falls inside the space which is covered by both routes, a way which neither falls outside of them nor again falls within both at once. And so much as this I take to be unconditional and to be actually willed. But, to complete the disjunction of 'Either-or', a further meaning is required, and this meaning cannot be reduced to anything which is called categorical. It remains conditional, and it cannot therefore be actually willed, but, at least in its proper sense, it is but the object of a mere intention or resolve. In my opinion, therefore, a disjunctive will is not fully disjunctive, or on the other hand the object is not in the full sense willed throughout. But, if such a will exists, it is the self-realization of a disjunctive idea, and it falls under our general definition of will.[1]

(c) Negative volition must be discussed at greater length. The whole subject of negative states and of negative functions in psychology has, so far as I know, been treated unsatisfactorily. We had to enter this field in our inquiry into mental conflict, and with regard to some points I must refer the reader to that article (M. n.s. xi, No. 43 = E. xxv). But I should like to reprint here a passage from a paper published many years ago.[2] The doctrine contained in it has

---

[1] The nature of Choice has been discussed in the preceding article.

[2] Mind, o.s. xiii, pp. 21–2 [E. xiv. 268]. In this passage more stress should have been laid on avoidance and removal, as well as on destruction, as a form of negation. And again it might perhaps have been made clearer

not, I believe, so far been noticed, but I must hope that in its present context it may have better fortune.

'I will now glance briefly at a point far too negligently handled. What is the nature of *aversion?* First the object of aversion, like the object of desire, is always an idea. We may indeed *seem* to desire the sensations that we have, but our object is really their continuance or their increase, and these are ideas. And so it is with aversion. The mere incoming of the painful is not aversion, nor is even the fear of it, if fear is confined to mere contraction or again to aimless shrinking back. To me aversion seems positive, what we call 'active dislike'. It implies a desire for negation, for avoidance or destruction. And hence its object, to speak strictly, cannot be reality, since it implies negation, and that is an idea. But desire for negation is still not aversion, until painfulness is added. The object to be negated must be felt to be painful and may also be so thought of. Aversion then is the desire for the negation of something painful. It is not a negative kind of desire over against a positive kind, and I myself could attach no meaning to a negative desire. Aversion is positive, but its true object is the negation of that which is commonly called its object—a confusion which has arisen from taking dislike to be mere negative liking. Aversion has a positive character, or it would not be desire; but its positive side is variable. There may be a definite position whose maintenance we want, as when we are averse to the injury of something we love; or again, the positive may be left blank—something, anything, is what we want if it will serve to rid us of the painful. But again we may positively desire the act of destruction, with the agencies of its process, and so depend for the pleasures of life on our aversions. I hope this brief sketch may throw light on an obscure corner of our subject, and I will, in passing, advert to another mistake. Desire and aversion have been taken to be aspects of desire, since that is tension,[1] and (we may add) is to that extent painful. This is mere confusion, for all aversion has an ideal object.

that I do not deny the existence of negative desire, but only of desire which is barely negative.   [1] Volkmann, § 140; Lipps, p. 604.

Now the (painful) tension of desire is not an object at all. It may be made one, and so may give rise to an aversion. But this will clearly *not* be an aspect of the original desire, but will be a new desire supervening.'

What is negative will? It is a will to remove, to avoid, or to destroy. The idea which realizes itself in negative will is the idea of such a result. And negative will has a character of its own, which in one sense is irreducible and unique, but on the other hand most emphatically it is not co-ordinate with positive volition. It is subordinate, and is a specification of the main positive type. The idea which it realizes is never simple, but always implies, and always must imply, a positive basis and aspect. Thus the process of destruction or avoidance has an affirmative side, and without such an aspect of positive assertion all negation is meaningless. I will explain this doctrine by a defence of it against some objections.

'Your doctrine', I shall first be told, 'is contrary to fact. It would imply that with the negation of a particular A we have always a positive idea B, an idea which itself is particular and is co-ordinate with A. In other words, there would be no denying except on the basis of an explicit alternative between particulars. And any assumption of this kind would be contrary to fact.' But no such assumption, I reply, is involved in our doctrine. For the positive side of destruction or escape may remain unspecified and general, and certainly need not take the shape of a co-ordinate particular. In negative will, we may say, the affirmative is usually not specified. And to argue, 'Either no idea at all or an idea that is particular', would surely everywhere, and not only here, conduct us to ruin. On the contrary, I in fact may deny this or that without the actual assertion of any particular opposite. On the one hand, that which is to be removed must be specified always; but the positive aspect of the removal, although necessary, may be utterly vague. The thing in short is understood to be done somehow, but the positive 'how' is left blank.[1]

---

[1] It is in my opinion a mistake to hold that every positive term without exception must have a co-ordinate negative, and in the end this mistake

We may pass from this to an objection of a different kind. 'We can have negative will,' it may be said, 'where no idea at all is present; and this happens where we reject an offered suggestion and again where we disapprove.' But I find in these cases no special difficulty, except in discovering the precise fact which is offered. If, on its appearance, a suggestion is banished either because somehow it is incompatible, or again because it is incompatible with some known mental group, it seems absurd to offer such a fact as a case of volition. If the exclusion is simple we have surely so far no semblance of will.[1] On the other hand, if the suggestion, not being banished at once, is recognized as incompatible with a certain principle, and if the idea of the suggestion's banishment is excited and qualifies the principle—then I agree that the ensuing result may be a negative volition. But the nature of this volition now completely agrees with our definition of will. And the further instance of disapproval will certainly not shake us. For on the one side a disapproval is not in itself a volition, and on the other side it in no case is present without an idea. I will venture first to call attention to this latter point. The mere fact of a suggestion being in painful conflict with something either unspecified or again definite, even if this conflict results in the suggestion's banishment, does not by itself constitute a genuine disapproval. For, in order to disapprove, you must judge and must not simply eject, and you cannot judge unless you qualify your object by an idea. There must be a principle

would have a ruinous result. As to negative will Mr. Shand (pp. 292 foll.) appears to me to assume without inquiry that the alternative, 'Either a particular positive idea or none', is a sound one. He does not state whether he everywhere rejects unspecified ideas, and he does not explain how we are able to do without them, and how, for instance, we are to understand, say, the idea of an absence. I cannot agree with Mr. Shand that the psychology of negation has been injured by the transference from logic of ideas which there are true, but are inapplicable in psychology. I should say on the contrary that it is neglect of logic and mistakes in logic which have here injured psychology.

[1] There is here, we may say, no experience of agency proper, though there may be perhaps in a lower sense an experience of activity. See *M.* n.s. xii [*E.* xxvii].

or standard, however vague, with which the self feels itself one, and that of which you disapprove must be qualified by the idea of discrepancy with this standard.[1] Thus a simple inhibition or rejection may be a higher thing morally than the most explicit disapproval, but, considered psychically, it will stand always at a lower level. But in any case, to return to this, a disapproval is in itself no volition. I may have the idea of a principle in myself and its rejection of something which is offered, and I may feel myself one with this whole idea and may judge accordingly and so disapprove. But unless I have the idea of a change in immediate existence, and unless that idea carries itself out into the facts, however much I have disapproved, I have not actually willed.

An alleged negative volition, we have seen, is either not genuine will, and, when scrutinized, at once ceases to appear in that character, or else, if real, it does but specify our general account. It is a type which falls under and which confirms our definition of will. And we need, I think, consider no further these alleged types of independent volition. We have found that in every case, so far as it is a case of real will, we have an idea which carries itself out into fact. And the inability to verify the presence of this idea has, we saw, been due mainly to a failure to apprehend it in its proper character.

I will add some further remarks on aversion in its relation to positive desire. The extract given above contains, I believe, the main truth on this subject, but I will endeavour in certain points to confirm and to illustrate its doctrine. Aversion and positive desire certainly are not co-ordinate, any more than are denial and assertion in logic. And it is not difficult to show how the mistaken view about aversion has arisen; but I will first endeavour to remove some misunderstandings.

'All desire', it may be said, 'is and must be for change, and therefore all desire is negative; and on one side it must

[1] We saw in *M*. n.s. xi. 25 [*E*. xxiv. 436] that for this reason your disapproval may serve to retain the suggestion.

therefore consist in aversion.' But the premise from which this conclusion seems to follow is ambiguous. Desire is certainly for something which is not present, and it is a desire therefore for something else, and this naturally implies an alteration, and so in some respect a negation, of that which is. But in desire this negation is incidental, or at the very most is subordinate, while in aversion it constitutes the main and principal end. And 'change', we must remember, is a more or less equivocal phrase. A thing is changed by a subtraction which removes its positive character, but it is changed also by the mere addition to it of something positive; for the thing so loses the character which it had before, while it was not yet increased. If, for instance, I possess two sixpences, my condition is changed if you take away one, and my condition also is changed if, on the other hand, you give me a third. And if, having already two sixpences, I desire a sixpence, my desire implies incidentally the negation of the first two as two only. But you can hardly take this negation to be in all cases an actual constituent of my positive desire, and, even where it is present, you can hardly make it co-ordinate with my positive end. For I may have desired the third sixpence without any thought of or any reference to the first two, and, even if I desire to add to these, I obviously do not desire to remove them. Their change, so far as it is negative, cannot in short be regarded as my main object. It is an incidental result which is either not present in my end, or, if present there, has clearly a subordinate character. But in aversion the mere negation of what I change is my principal end, and any positive aspect of this main end is subordinate or even quite unconsidered. Positive desire, we may say, is for a specified something, and this implies the negation of some aspect of the world; but the aspect thus to be destroyed need not in desire be either specified or considered. But the aversion to something contains essentially and explicitly a destructive change of that something, at least in some aspect, while on the other hand the positive attendant or result of this negation need not be specified or even in any way considered.

Without refinements we may perhaps put the matter as follows. The negation in positive desire need be no more than indirect and incidental, and, even where it appears in the main end, it appears as subordinate. And in positive desire the negation need be neither specified nor considered. But in aversion it is the positive side which need be neither considered nor specified, and in any case that positive side is secondary and is not the main object. We shall realize this if we consider some instance of aversion such as the game-keeper's pursuit and destruction of vermin. This process of course has its positive side, and in this positive side the man may take pride and delight, and it is possible even that he may wish for no better employment. But with this we are concerned no longer with a simple aversion. We have a mixed state in which the aversion more and more is outbalanced. And by an increase of emphasis on the positive side, and by a subordination to that of the mere negative aspect, the aversion in the end might even become transformed wholly and lost. Once find a pleasure in the pursuit of an animal, however noxious, and more or less, according to the conditions, it tends to lose its character as an object of aversion.

We can now dispose of a difficulty which may seem to arise from the difference in the relations of aversion and desire to existence. The object of aversion, we may be told, must exist, while the object never exists in the case of desire. You cannot, in other words, desire that which is actual, while you can be averse to it. But there is a dangerous confusion here as to the meaning of 'object'. The object may mean either the existing not-self which is before me, or it may mean on the other hand my ideal end. Now in no case can my idea itself be something which actually exists; and on the other side, both in desire and in aversion alike, there is opposed to my idea something which I represent to myself as actually existing. This opposition of idea to fact holds even where the fact is imaginary. I can thus be averse to a calamity though I do not really expect it,[1]

---

[1] I am forced in this and some other points to dissent from Waitz, *Lehrbuch*, p. 444, by whose remarks I have however profited.

and I cannot desire to eat an imaginary apple unless for the moment, and as against the idea of eating, I regard it as actual. And there is no difference so far in principle between desire and aversion. They differ in principle through the diversity of that relation to existence which is not external, but is contained within their respective ideal ends. And it is contained, we must remember, in one case explicitly, and in the other case more or less by way of implication. Thus the negation of something taken to exist is the main end of aversion, while the appearance in existence of something positive is the main end of desire. And the further alteration of existence by this positive addition may be a result which in desire, we have seen, is not even considered. In any case, however, where negation is contemplated in desire, that negation is subordinate to the positive aspect. But it would hardly repay us, I think, to enlarge further on this head.[1]

The mistaken co-ordination of aversion with desire has arisen, I presume, in several ways. It has been helped perhaps by the confusion which we have just briefly noticed, and it is connected certainly with logical errors as to predication. But the mistake has come perhaps mainly from a natural but misleading parallel, and by a transference to aversion and desire of the opposition between pleasure and pain. Unless we separate pain from unpleasantness,

---

[1] Since this article was written I have made acquaintance with Dr. Pfänder's thoughtful essay, *Phänomenologie des Wollens*. Dr. Pfänder there (p. 71) criticizes the doctrine that aversion has a negatively determined end. He has however, I do not know why, understood negation here as bare privation or absence; and certainly, so understood, the doctrine he criticizes becomes untenable. In the presence of a painful noise, e.g., I may desire its absence, but that desire is not, as such, an aversion. It is not the mere absence, but it is the positive suppression or avoidance of what annoys me, that is really desired in aversion. Dr. Pfänder appears to me to be confused on this head, or to be dealing with some confused statement to which he does not refer. Again, pp. 109–11, he objects that a negative will may be a will for a bare not-doing. But unless my idea changes something which otherwise would be and is therefore taken to exist, I must insist that we have not a real case of volition at all. See *M.* N.S. xi. 440 [*E.* xxvi. 479–80]. And, again, the will to produce a state of privation is, as such, a positive and not a negative volition.

pleasure and pain are on one level. They stand to each other, we may say, as co-ordinate opposites. And since doubtless aversion has more to do with pain, and desire more to do with pleasure, one is led to assume that the relation between each pair is the same. And since from this there follows a variety of mistaken results, I must state briefly the connexion of pleasure and pain with desire and aversion.

In both desire and aversion, if we do not distinguish between pain and unpleasantness, we must to some extent have the presence of both pleasure and pain. The idea of the end must in positive desire be felt to be pleasant, and the same thing to a less degree will hold good in aversion. In both alike the whole state may, according to the conditions, be either pleasant or painful, though the latter case will more often be found to exist in aversion. But, since both are complex, we may have in each a preponderance of either pleasure or pain. In aversion the felt hostility of existence to the idea will be painful, but this same feature must appear also in positive desire. In both the felt tension of idea against existence will not fail to produce uneasiness, however slight that may be and on the whole outweighed. And thus the distinction, so far, may be said to consist merely in degree; but we must from this go on to take account of a further difference. In positive desire the idea of pleasure does not always qualify the object. In desire, that is, I must indeed always feel pleasure in the idea, but pleasure may either enter or not enter into the content of the end, and its entrance, where it enters, does not belong to the essence of desire. But in aversion, while in the same way to some extent I must with my idea feel some pleasure, on the other hand the internal content of my idea must be qualified by pain. Unless the painfulness of the object, upon which the process of negation is to fall, enters itself beforehand as an idea into my idea of this process, I cannot think that in the proper sense we have an aversion. We may again contrast here the desire to kill an animal for sport with the desire by any means to destroy noxious vermin. In the first of these cases we

have plainly no aversion. You cannot desire the mere negation of a thing unless that thing comes before your mind
as injurious and painful. For the positive side of such a
mere negation is not specified except as the removal of
that object to which we are averse. And, unless the object
were painful, its blank removal could not, so far as I see,
be desired. On the other hand, if the special process of
negation is itself directly desired, we are to that extent not
concerned with a pure aversion. Thus in all aversion the
positive aspect of removal must be desired; while on the
other side no aversion is pure unless the means of removal
are desired, not in their own character but merely as means.

Aversion and positive desire are thus in principle distinct. But in each the complication of pain and pleasure
may be great, and there is a tendency in each to transform
itself and to pass into the other. In many cases we find
them existing side by side in a mixed state, while in other
cases coexistence gives way to more or less complete
subordination. But a desire or an aversion, where completely subordinate, has ceased, we must remember, to
exist as an actual aversion or desire.

This last remark has a wide and important bearing (*E.*
xxv) and it leads us here to the discussion of a well-known
question. Can I will that to which, while willing it, I have
an actual aversion? If the doctrine laid down in the article
just referred to is sound, a volition of this kind will be
clearly impossible. Given an actual aversion, you would
have an idea which conflicts with the idea implied in your
will, and you would as a result have no action or, if an
action, no will. If, on the other hand, your positive idea
has prevailed over your aversion, the aversion has been
banished or else made subordinate. But in the latter case
it has been modified and has ceased to be an actual aversion. The will to do what I hate, although I hate it, must
imply that in some sense my hatred is changed. The negation has been turned into an element within a complex
positive idea. The aversion has lost its independence, and,
however painful, it is no longer an actual aversion. I am
still 'averse' in this sense that a mass of hostile feeling

remains, and this mass struggles, perhaps violently, against the realization of my positive idea, and it tends constantly to restore the independence of its own idea. But, so long as its idea does not break loose but is held as subordinate, there cannot in fact be an actual aversion. And in the same way, though desirous, I may fail to have an actual desire.

I shall soon return to this distinction between an aversion and a mere condition of averseness, but at present must remark further on the coexistence of aversion and will. The statement that I cannot desire and will that to which I am at the same time averse is seen, when compared with facts, to be clearly erroneous. The mistake arises partly from neglect of the distinction which we have just made, but it is mainly due perhaps to a failure in observation. The great complexity of aspects contained in aversion and desire, and the presence in each of elements, pleasurable and painful, which come from a variety of sources, is often not noticed. We have seen that a desire, when considered as a whole, may be painful, just as an aversion, when it is taken on the whole, may be pleasant. We may instance the desire of a mother to save her child when she fears that she cannot, and again the pleasure of destroying what we hate where there is not too much trouble or danger. And hence, though I can will that to which I am averse without also desiring it, I certainly on the other hand may desire it and desire it eagerly. The alternative which by itself excites our repulsion may, as an escape from the intolerable, be desired and may even be regarded with complacency. And we may be aware of this pleasure, or again, because the pleasure is outweighed by pain, we may, despite the actual fact, deny its existence. But I cannot here enter further into the detail of these complicated states.[1]

---

[1] Cf. *E.* xxv and *E.* xiv. 263. Mr. Shand (pp. 324–5) rejects the view stated in the text, but I must be allowed to doubt his having apprehended it rightly. He apparently fails generally to see how in desire pain and pleasure are mixed. An example of desire for a painful alternative is found in Claudio's mood of 'flowery tenderness' for death. And in De Goncourt's

I will now return to the distinction which we noted in passing. We may be desirous or averse although we have not an actual desire or aversion, and in the same way we can have a standing or permanent will to do something when the corresponding volition is plainly absent. I have had to refer to this point in a former article (*M.* N.S. xi. 26 = *E.* xxiv. 438) and a very brief statement here will, I think, be sufficient.

A state of desire or aversion, where the actual aversion or desire is not present, has two meanings, and these different senses may be conjoined or used separately. In the first sense I have a group of feelings, perceptions, and perhaps movements, such as belong to the actual aversion or desire, but, when taken by themselves, are incomplete and stop short of it. This group continually tends to produce the complete and actual state, and it may therefore be called its conditional presence. But even in the absence of such a group we may be said still to desire or dislike, if it is understood that, given the object, we should certainly assume that attitude towards it. And we may speak in the same sense of a will which is standing or permanent. We may mean by this the constant presence of actual feelings and ideas, such as go to make, let us say, a volition to injure, and such as, given the occasion, would actually produce the volition. And we have so far an habitual mood of a certain character. But again by a standing will we may signify no more than a general disposition to injure. Whatever may be in fact my present mood, and whatever may be the ideas and feelings which are now actually in my mind, I should, without regard to this, under certain conditions have a volition to injure. And since these conditions

Germinie, p. 15, we hear of 'une attente de la mort qui devenait à la fin une impatience de mourir'. The defect in Mr. Shand's account becomes visible from another side, when he fails to see that an act done from mere principle tends naturally to become an act done from desire (pp. 323–4). The pain caused by injury to the principle must tend to produce a desire for relief. I think that, if Mr. Shand generally had done more justice to the actual facts, he would have felt less need to betake himself to something inexplicable behind them. But, however that may be, his articles have not failed to throw light on the subject.

may be expected to occur in fact, my will to injure is taken already in some sense to exist. We noticed formerly the same use in the case of attention (ibid.). I may be 'attending' to a business although no actual attention is present. I am or I have something which on the occasion would turn to attention. And so, since I have all the attention which is at present required for my purpose, you may say that I attend really although no attention is there. In these cases we use a licence which not unfrequently degenerates into error, where the standing desire or will is assumed to be really an actual will or conation. But, when a man is reposing placidly with no idea or feeling except of tranquil enjoyment, to say of him that at this moment he has an actual conation or will to take revenge on his enemy would be surely mistaken. To assert this would be at least to take an undue liberty with language.

If you ask for the ultimate nature of a permanent disposition to act, I should myself decline in psychology even to entertain such a problem. But how the standing will passes into an actual volition is a question which on the whole is not difficult to answer. Apart from the oscillations of an habitual mood, which is a matter not here to be discussed, the actual volition in the main is produced by Redintegration. Something that occurs to us has a character which falls under the law of our disposition. The character may fall under that law directly, or again indirectly and through a further principle, and the connexion again may be positive or negative. In any case the disposition in this way becomes active, and brings into fact the further element which it ideally contains. But this is a point to which we shall very soon be compelled to return.

There are a number of questions about desire which I must here leave untouched,[1] but I will briefly notice the relation between desire and conation. Does all desire contain, or is it all identical with, conation and striving? An affirmative answer is common, but, I think, cannot be

---

[1] For some of these see *M. o.s.* xiii [*E.* xiv].

sustained if conation is to stand for the experienced striving of my self. But conation may be used besides in two different senses (*E.* xxiii). It may signify a striving which is not as such experienced at all, or is at any rate not so experienced within myself. Or, again, it may mean a striving which is actually experienced as such within me, and yet is the striving only of some psychical element, such as a fixed idea, and is not the striving of my self. I do not however propose to take further account here of either of these senses.

If then conation is understood as the experienced striving of my self, I cannot perceive that everywhere conation is involved in desire. It may be argued that without conation desire would not have begun to exist. Want and need, however urgently experienced, are not yet desire, since they lack the idea of an object which is opposed as an end to existence. And the argument would urge that, apart from movements which in fact realize the end, the end as an idea in desire would not have come into being. And the idea of these movements will therefore, it is said, qualify the end and object of desire. And apart from these movements, if the satisfaction could ever be gained, at least the idea of it could not possibly be retained by the mind. But the presence of these movements in idea will most certainly involve a conation. And this active attitude remains, it will be further urged, through all our mental development, and everywhere will qualify the object of desire, even in a longing, say, for warmth. Thus the desired object must contain always to some extent the idea of my actively getting it, and every desire therefore will essentially involve a conation. Now I admit the force of this argument, and I agree that, speaking broadly, desire will not be separate in its origin from conation. I could not maintain that without conation it in no possible case arises; but such an origin of desire, I admit, would certainly be in fact exceptional. On the other hand I cannot argue that, if in its beginning desire depends on conation, it therefore now must involve a conation in its essence. I do not see why the ideal element of my acting for some end should not in certain cases fall out of my idea of that end. And since in many cases I cannot discover that such an element now exists, I must reject the conclusion that in all desire a conation is involved.

And there is a counter-argument which to my mind has considerable weight. An intense desire for relief may be followed by an actual relief, and by a perception and a sense of complete satisfaction. But certainly in some cases the relief is not experienced as having been attained by my action, and, if all desire is conation, such a result seems to me hardly explicable. You may indeed contend that the experience required escapes my notice, although present in the result, just as, before the result, the conation was actual though I failed to observe it. But I prefer in each case to accept the evidence of the fact which I observe, and I must therefore deny that in all desire without exception a conation is implied. If it is to be always present it will be the conation of some psychical element not my self, or it will be the striving of something which itself does not enter into my experienced world.

I must go on from this to point out the distinctive character of Wish. Desire and wish tend naturally in fact to pass one into the other, and the distinction in language between them is at times not maintained. But this distinction exists, and it corresponds to a difference in principle, and on this point it is well to be on our guard against error.

In the first place a wish is not a striving or conation. It is, again, not the general head under which all desire falls,[1] nor can a desire be defined as a wish, the realization of which is judged possible. For no such judgement, we saw, is really involved in desire, nor in accordance with language can desire be taken to fall under wish. We shall find on the contrary that wish is a specialized development from desire. Further, a wish is not distinguished from a desire by its weakness. A wish, it is true, generally is inclined to be

[1] This untenable view is advocated by Professor Ehrenfels in his interesting study *Fühlen und Wollen,* and again in his *Werttheorie.*

weak; and, for a reason we shall point out, a wish cannot intensify itself beyond a certain degree without passing from a mere wish to become a desire. But, since desires are of all strengths, the essential difference could not lie in this point. Thus, when Professor Sully tells us (*Human Mind*, ii. 208) that wish 'marks off the *nascent* desires which are only momentary, being instantly dismissed *as futile*', I am myself unable to verify his assertion. For it seems in the first place obvious that wishes are not all momentary and instantly dismissed. And again, if wishes are taken to involve a 'nascent' desire, it is hard to see how that feature by itself is to serve as their differential character. To suppose that, wherever you have a 'nascent' and momentary desire, you have in the proper sense a wish, seems contrary to fact. And in short I do not see how Professor Sully would justify his assertions, unless through that virtue which evidently to his mind resides in such phrases as 'nascent' (see below, p. 574, note 2). To pass to another point, the difference of wish from desire does not lie in this, that in desire it is my action to which the real world is opposed, while in wish this world is contrary to something else. Desire we have seen does not in all cases coincide with conation, and again my desire for an end which is to be accomplished by another cannot possibly in all cases be termed a mere wish. The shipwrecked crew surely can be said to desire that the life-boat may reach them.

Wish is a desire which in a certain way has been specialized and limited. The idea of satisfaction has in a wish been broken from its connexion with my actual reality. The idea is disconnected, but at the same time it is retained, and its realization has been imagined in a world which is not the world of my reality. This world may according to the circumstances be more or less defined or indefinite, but it never ceases in a genuine wish to appear as imaginary. And hence the collision of the idea with fact can to a greater or less extent be suppressed. Wish is desire for an imaginary end which, because it is imaginary, can be regarded as attained. And hence a wish, so far as it is a desire which is imagined as satisfied, has in this respect passed beyond a simple desire. But in another respect a wish remains less than desire, since the imaginary object and its fruition are recognized as out of our reach. Our wish is therefore a *mere* wish, and it is an idea which is sundered from the real order. But since this absence of relation tends to come to us in experience as a relation which is negative, a wish entails logically, and it continually in fact tends to pass into, an actual desire.

The idea in wish is separated from our world by the perceived failure of means to its realization. And the failure may come to us as general, or again as conditioned by a special obstacle either negative or positive. This obstacle may consist merely in my fear or my scruple, but, so long as it qualifies the real world, it prevents the presence of my simple desire. If then I place my desire in an imagined world where this obstacle does not hold, I have a wish. And because this other world is recognized as not actually present, my wish does not lead me to an act or an attempt.[1] Being in a sense satisfied beyond the reality, it is so far removed from collision with fact. But, as we have seen, in so far as it is not actually satisfied, a wish tends to collide with the world and to become a desire.

Wish arises from the retention of the idea despite our inability to give it reality. The idea is retained by the persistence of the want which remains unsatisfied and compressed. And this want, we have seen, frees itself and expands into a heaven of its own. We have in wish a sense that fruition is at once more than possible and yet less so, according as we look first on one world and then on the other. A wish is innocent, because disconnected from the actual world. It is enervating, so far as it rests in enjoyment divorced from action. It is insidious, because its idea, being actually unrealized, tends to pass into simple desire.

The passage of mere wish into desire calls for little remark. The obstacle that bars our desired end may for a

---

[1] 'I wish you to do this' is less peremptory than a simple imperative, because it is hardly unconditional. But 'I wish that you would' is of course the correct expression of a wish.

moment be hidden from our sight, or it may pass from
our mind in a moment's forgetfulness. Or on the other
hand some unlooked-for means of realization may show
itself. In either case a tension between my idea and the
actual world is set up, and the old unsatisfied want now
breaks out into an actual desire. And if wish becomes
intense beyond a certain point, this result is inevitable.
For the ideal satisfaction becomes too shadowy, while on
the other side the idea, growing dominant, suggests forcibly
its own realization, even against the knowledge that this
cannot be attained. When thirsty beyond a certain point
a man cannot confine himself to a mere wish for water, and
the unfortunate lover is condemned not to rest in mere
wishes. This is the truth perverted into the doctrine that
wish consists in a weak desire. But because a mere wish,
if you intensify it, is transformed into a desire, you cannot
conclude that a desire, if you weaken it, will through its
weakness become a mere wish. For in one sense a wish, we
have seen, is more special and is more complex than desire.[1]

We now approach a part of our inquiry which perhaps
has been too long deferred, and must ask how it is that
in volition the idea realizes itself. That the idea does
realize itself is at least an apparent fact. And if this fact

---

[1] It will be instructive to note here the difference between wish and
resolve. In the first place a wish is for a mere result and does not essentially
imply agency on my part. In the second place my resolve is directed upon
the real world. In resolve this real world is not the world perceived as
immediately present, and in this point, we have seen, resolve is distinguished from will. On the other hand the world of resolve is not discon-
tinuous with my world as it exists here and now. There is no breach
between the two; for the present world is regarded as extending itself into
the future, and the present world is contemplated as itself actually there
before me in resolve, notwithstanding an interval and even perhaps a condition. And it is only because it is directed upon the real world, as in this
sense actually present, that my resolve is a volition, so far as it is one. On the
other side, in wish we have a world which we are aware is imaginary. This
world is therefore not contemplated as the prolongation of reality, but is
estranged from the real, and is sundered from it by a breach in nature. And to
throw a volition across such a breach does not even suggest itself as possible.
The subject of resolve has been discussed in *M.* n.s. xi, No. 44 [*E.* xxvi].

is mere appearance, then will assuredly has become an illusion. And the illusion remains an illusion, however great our success in explaining its origin. But on the other hand the belief in the existence of such an illusion rests, so far as I see, on misunderstanding and prejudice. I will here discuss this no further than once more briefly to point out what is meant generally by the action of the idea in volition. The idea is a cause of the result in which its content is realized, but it is not the sole and whole cause of that result. And if cause is to mean complete cause, you may maintain with us the reality of will, and yet may deny that your mere psychical state of the moment is the cause of what follows, or is even the cause of what follows merely on the psychical side. And still less can the idea, being psychically a mere element in your state, usurp the position of a complete cause. But the causality of the idea in will need involve no such meaning as this. The idea is a positive condition which is a genuine element in the actual cause, and it is a condition of such importance that we may fairly claim that its presence makes the difference to what happens.[1] And with anything less than this, I must repeat that will becomes an illusion. Even if the idea were necessary as an effect which is collateral with and so united to the result, that mere necessity would still turn will into a false appearance. For you seem once more to have denied that the idea actually goes to produce the result. And if you cannot affirm this, you cannot assert in any proper sense the existence of will.

Let us then proceed to ask in what way the idea realizes itself. We provisionally assumed the validity of ideo-motor action, but that assumption must now be allowed to drop. We must inquire, therefore, under what law or under what laws in psychology this fact of the idea's self-realization will fall. And I will begin by dismissing a view which is equally common and erroneous. A desire and a conation on this view are essential to will, and the presence of these together

---

[1] I cannot of course here enter into an inquiry into the exact nature of cause and condition positive and negative. I have already had to touch on the necessity for the idea's action in *M.* n.s. xi, No. 44 [*E.* xxvi].

with the idea explains the further result.[1] But if we look without prejudice at the facts no such doctrine can stand.

It is not the fact that desire and conation are to be found in all cases of will. Acts done at once from imitation or in obedience to an order, and generally acts which at once ensue from the suggestion of an idea, furnish instances which on this point seem really conclusive. No one, apart from theory, could fairly deny that of these actions at least some are volitions, or reasonably assert that in every case a desire or conation in any proper sense is present. When the sequence is delayed I admit that there is some ground for doubt. You may argue here that delay must cause necessarily a tension between the idea and existence, and that this tension must amount to conation and desire. But for myself I cannot accept even this modified conclusion. Where after delay volition follows from an unpleasant fixed idea, I cannot allow that in all such cases there is a desire or a conation of my self, and yet on the other side no one here, except to save a theory, would deny everywhere, where desire is absent, the presence of will. And where there is no delay, and where the result follows at once from the idea, the above contention, it appears to me, wholly breaks down. The existence need not be perceived in such a case as resisting the idea. On the contrary, all that is implied in such a case of volition is that the existing not-self should be felt as opposite to such an extent that its change is perceived as an alteration made by me. But this opposition need not amount to the tension involved in desire and conation. And again that felt pleasure in the idea which is certainly necessary for desire (*E*. xiv. 261–3) may be absent, it seems to me, in some cases of will. We must conclude, therefore, that conation and desire, even if usual in volition, cannot, if we respect the facts, be taken as essential and necessary.[2] There are actions—to repeat

---

[1] This matter is discussed further in *M*. o.s. xiii [*E*. xiv]. I do not propose to do more than mention the old mistake that the object of all desire is pleasure. We may fairly, I think, call this doctrine exploded.

[2] I cannot verify the presence of felt pleasure in the idea in all cases of volition, but this pleasure on the other hand (*E*. xiv) seems essential to

my argument—which cannot be shown in fact to involve
conation or desire, and some of these actions every one
apart from theory would call volitions. And according to
my definition of will such actions are volitions really. And
I urge this agreement of doctrine with usage as some evidence that the definition which I offer is true. Another
psychologist may reply that such actions cannot be volitions because they do not conform to his definition of will.
And this answer may stand so long as his account is neither
questioned nor denied. But afterwards, and when the very
point at issue is the truth or falsehood of his account, it is
obvious that any such position is fatally unsound.[1] If, in
other words, an objection against the view of will which I
adopt is to hold, that objection must be founded upon
actual fact.

But even if desire and conation were everywhere present
in will, their presence would supply no answer to the question before us. We want to understand how my idea is
able in each case to gain its own particular reality. And
when you point to conation and desire as that bridge by
which the passage is made, your answer, even if it were not

desire. It must be understood (I will repeat) that, in speaking here of
desire and conation, I am excluding the desire or conation of any mere
element in my self, or again any desire or conation which is not experienced
as such. On the alleged necessity for the presence of desire in volition the
reader may find it instructive, and perhaps entertaining, to consult Professor Sully (*Human Mind,* ii. 214 foll.). Professor Sully in my opinion
neither states fully nor indeed understands the case which it is incumbent
on him to meet, and even then, in his attempt to show the presence of desire
in all will, he begins even himself dimly to discover his collision with fact.
He is forced to substitute for 'desire' such phrases as 'analogue of desire',
'nascent desire', and 'rudiment of desire', and he is driven to speak of an
action as 'half-volitional'. But the seeking refuge in such unexplained, if not
meaningless, phrases is, I would submit, an unconscious admission of failure.
The only thing like an argument to be found in Professor Sully's pages is
the contention that pleasure and pain are of such importance in development that they must be regarded as even now essential to volition. I shall
deal with this point hereafter.

[1] This seems an evident truth, but it is too often not recognized in
practice. The case of 'disinterested actions' in Professor Bain's psychology
may perhaps be cited as a well-known instance of its neglect. But in other
forms this neglect is still too prevalent in the psychology of will.

contrary to fact, seems absurdly deficient. I may desire and I may strive (let us suppose) to skate or to play on the organ, or I may struggle to recall to memory some half-forgotten name, and yet, with no means of passage beyond a bare effort, my idea surely never would pass into reality. The passage from the idea to inward or to outward fact requires some particular bridge, and such a bridge is not given by the mere presence of a desire or a conation.

You may repeat your old song that the springs of action are pleasure and pain, and that, wherever I will, it is in the end these which produce my volition. But (*a*) in the first place, I may once more remark, your statement is contrary to fact. There are cases of rapid volition where such a doctrine is even seen plainly to break down. And (*b*) in the second place, to identify pain and pleasure with aversion and desire is surely to fall into a palpable and gross mistake. And it is not true even that pain and pleasure are always accompanied by aversion and desire. Nor in the case of pleasure do the facts allow us to admit even a tendency always to produce motion rather than rest.[1] But (*c*) in no case could pleasure and pain explain the particular detail of will. That which has to be explained is the passing, in a given individual case, of this particular idea to its own special reality. And even if against the facts we admit that apart from the influence of pleasure and pain there is in no case volition—even if we allow that everywhere in this sense pleasure and pain produce action—yet with this the essence of the volitional passage remains unexplained. We have not learnt how this idea, in distinction from that

---

[1] For a discussion of all these points I must once more refer the reader to *M*. o.s. xiii [*E*. xiv]. The existence of pleasures without want or desire is an old and well-known doctrine which I should have thought could not fairly be ignored; and in this opinion I am not shaken even by the following oracle, 'Wollen wir näher beschreiben, was wir denn bei Lust und Unlust in uns finden, so wissen wir dies nicht anschaulicher zu thun, als indem wir die Lust als ein Streben nach dem Gegenstand hin, die Unlust als ein Widerstreben gegen ihn bezeichnen' (Wundt, *Phys. Psych.* i. 589). I must be excused from any attempt to reproduce this sentence in English. I understand Professor Külpe to dissent from it (*Lehre vom Willen*, pp. 26, 49).

other idea, is able to realize its own special existence. The whip may start the horses, but the whip will throw no bridge across the stream. You must (we may put it otherwise) have machinery of a certain kind before you can set it in motion for a particular end. And I cannot see how by any stretch general pleasure and pain can be taken to serve as special machinery.[1]

Let us pass on to ask in what this machinery does really consist. Our answer to this question will traverse ground which is in the main quite familiar, and we may content ourselves therefore with a summary statement. We have in the first place a variety of special 'dispositions', and we have in the second place the presence of some ideal suggestion which is at the same time the presence of the starting-point of some one disposition. The consequent passage of this special disposition into act is, we may say, the bridge which carries our idea over into reality.[2] (a) As to the nature of these dispositions I can say very little. They either are simple, or else are complex wholes of more or less systematic detail. And they are native, or otherwise independent, or again on the other hand to a greater or a less extent have been acquired. On their origin I shall have, however, to say something hereafter. Dispositions again may be merely physical at first, or may later become so, and they may be physical wholly or merely in some part of their subordinate detail.[3] But, to serve in volition proper as a means of transition, a disposition must possess in all cases a psy-

[1] And we must of course say the same thing of Attention. The doctrine that attention is the essence of will was popularized by the late Dr. Carpenter (*Mental Physiology*, 1874), and I am personally indebted to him for having then forced that question into the front. Dr. Carpenter's work in psychology cannot, I imagine, be rated highly, but on one or two points he has not generally gained the credit which he seems really to have deserved. On the subject of Attention I must refer to *M*. n.s. xi, No. 41 [*E*. xxiv].

[2] I will ask lower down if there is any exception to this general law of will.

[3] By 'merely physical' I do not mean merely physical absolutely, but simply with reference to the consciousness of the subject. And again, when I speak of an aspect as psychical, I do not mean to deny that it possesses also a physical side.

chical aspect. The real essence of a disposition I make no attempt to explain, but in and for psychology it is a standing tendency or an individual law. Given, that is, one of two connected elements, physical or psychical or again possessing both characters, a disposition is the tendency for the other element to appear in consequence. And this second element itself may have a single or a double character. (*b*) On the other side we have an idea suggested in fact, an idea which is more or less identical in character with the first element of some psychical disposition. And this idea may come direct from a perception, or it may be suggested again in some other way. (*c*) The disposition in this manner is started into action, and the process which we have described is of course so far what is called Redintegration. (*d*) And at this point we may seem to encounter a difficulty. In will, as we know, the suggested idea is the idea of the end, and therefore the idea which is required in volition must be the idea of the disposition's result. But on the other side to start the disposition, and so to produce the actual result, what you want is the idea of the disposition's beginning. For dispositions, if they ever work in both directions, do not work thus in general. Let us suppose, for example, that the sight or the smell of a fruit has somehow—let us say through an original disposition[1]— produced the satisfaction of eating it. This experience, we may suppose further, has left behind it its result in a new and acquired disposition which at once is physical and psychical. The sensations and feelings, which accompanied the beginning of the process of eating, will now tend to bring in the actual continuance and end of that process. And there will be a tendency also for any suggested idea of the fruit to qualify itself further by the ideal sweetness of the fruit in my mouth[2]. But, it will be objected, this

[1] This original disposition will be physical in part or physical wholly. It is unnecessary for our present purpose to decide between these alternatives.

[2] I do not deny that, without any ideal modification of perceptions in themselves, there might up to a certain point be a development of diverse reactions corresponding to different perceptions. Objects, that is, not modified themselves ideally so as in this way to have acquired meanings,

ideal sweetness, however much present and desired, will not reproduce the actual process of taking and eating. For the sweetness, though identified with the result of the tendency, is not identified with that point from which the tendency starts. In other words, that idea of the end, which is essential to will, is useless for will because in short it is not the idea of the beginning.

To this objection I reply that dispositions are not merely successive.[1] The operation of seeing and eating the fruit is, for example, a connected series. It is a whole in which an identical character is maintained and developed. And the various stages of the detailed process, since they all qualify one whole, are connected with this whole; and they are connected, through this whole, with one another throughout. The sensations and feelings, which belong to the beginning of the process of eating, belong also to that same fruit which is connected with the taste of sweetness. And the idea of sweetness therefore, indirectly and by means of this unity, can ideally revive the felt aspect of the beginning. But, when this aspect is present, we have seen that the disposition to eat has now been supplied with the condition of its actual movement. And to object that a suggested idea, being a mere idea, is not the psychical fact required for this beginning would clearly be mistaken.[2] It is enough that you have something, whatever it may be,

might become associated through trials, through failures and successes, each externally with a diverse act. The connexions here would be external psychically, because the acquired dispositions would not be psychical. How far such a development is possible in fact I need not discuss, because I am unable to see how, upon this line, volition would ever be developed. I have found Dr. Stout's teaching on the nature of the 'disposition' left behind by practical experience not easy to understand. It is to my mind deficient in clearness. See *Manual*, bk. i, chap. 2, and bk. iii, chap. 1.

[1] I have already entered somewhat more fully into this very important matter in *M*. n.s. viii. 7 [*T.R.* 360–2], to which I would refer the reader. Cf. also *A.R.* 41 = 49.

[2] An idea, so far as referred away from my psychical moment to another subject, is certainly so far an abstraction from psychical fact. On the other hand, if confined to this aspect of itself, the idea could not be my idea at all. The idea in short, to be an idea, must have its own psychical existence, which existence is not referred away as above.

which possesses the right content. And it is an error to imagine in the soul a gulf fixed so that identity cannot traverse it.

The passage in volition from idea to fact, we said, was made by a bridge. And the bridge, we find, is a disposition, the latter element of which has through experience become qualified in idea by its starting-point. If in its origin the disposition is but physical, there is so far no will. But through experience of the process, both in its beginning and its result, we have now an acquired disposition which on one side of its working is psychical. The result is qualified in idea by those feelings which made part of the beginning, and there is a tendency for these feelings, when suggested, to pass into the actual result. And the suggested end, therefore, serves as the ideal beginning, and itself starts the machinery which bridges the passage into fact.

The new result, which in this way has been produced, need not of course reproduce the old result in every feature. The disposition, we must remember, is in itself always general. In our mental development dispositions are specified into subordinate varieties, but no disposition, however individual, can lose the character of a general tendency. And the present idea of the end coincides but generally with that disposition which it excites and which carries it into fact. It is the present situation which, we may say, selects through an idea the special tendency required, and then itself from that basis particularizes the actual result in accordance with itself. And there would naturally be room at this point for much discussion and comment. But the difficulty at this point, I would add, does not attach itself specially to volition, but belongs to the doctrine of reproduction in general. Within the limits of the present inquiry it would be difficult to enter further into the subject, and I do not think that here we are called on to do so.

I will now proceed to deal briefly with several objections. (a) 'There is a fatal defect', I may be told, 'in the account which has been offered; for it starts the disposition from its psychical side, and any such start is impossible. Even if we suppose that a psychical result could conceivably so follow, we must deny the sequence of a physical effect from a psychical cause or condition. You, it is true, do not take the psychical antecedent as bare; but, and this is the vital point, you regard it as active. But the soul and its states, if not inert altogether, are inert necessarily in relation to the physical series.' This objection, however, denies absolutely the real existence of volition, and when on the other hand we ask for its own foundation and basis, that basis is found to consist in mere prejudice.[1] (*b*) 'Your account', it may be said, 'conflicts with the course of fact as ascertained by physiology.' This is an objection into which my knowledge does not permit me to enter. But I know that for an outsider to assume the finality of such a physiological result, even if that result for a time had found a general acceptance, would be at least to desert the guidance of probability. I therefore do not think that we are called on to discuss what would follow in the event of such a final conflict.

(*c*) It may be objected that the above explanation, if correct in itself, is inadequate for its purpose. If no more than this were wanted in order for the idea to carry itself out into act, the idea of an action could never or seldom remain unrealized. But such unrealized ideas, upon the other hand, are a common experience. From which it follows that the essence of volition must consist in something other than ideo-motor action as explained above. But a sufficient reply to this objection is really not difficult. A

---

[1] On the connexion of soul and body see my *Appearance*. The above prejudice of course is widely prevalent. Professor Titchener for example, in his *Outline of Psych.*, p. 343, instructs the student that to suppose a causal connexion between physical and psychical, if perhaps not forbidden by 'metaphysics' is contrary to 'logic'. For myself I really do not know whether I am even permitted by 'logic' to hope that the student does not wholly depend for his information upon Professor Titchener. Since writing the above I have made acquaintance with Professor Münsterberg's interesting *Grundzüge der Psych.* No one who can appreciate good work would speak disrespectfully of Professor Münsterberg. At the same time I do not understand how he can think that those, who on the above point reject his conclusion, would accept the premises from which he draws it.

disposition, even where it is not a practical tendency, is something, the result from which is in any case conditional. And we have long ago seen that, for an idea to realize itself, that idea must be dominant. I will, however, add some remarks here by way of further explanation. (i) An idea has against it always the general inertia of my present condition (cf. James, ii. 526). This, to speak in the abstract, is an obstacle which is opposed to any possible change. Hence, if you take an idea, weak in itself and unsupported from without, my mere inertia is enough to prevent that idea's realization. Where I am resting placidly or again am mechanically employed, the bare irrelevant suggestion of a change, if that is weak, will by itself be ineffective.[1] (ii) Apart from some unusual strength, absolute or relative, an idea of change will not dominate unless it finds support in my present condition. There may be a present group of sensations in harmony with the beginning of the change, together with uneasiness and psychical movement in the direction required. And this may be assisted by the perception of some special object. And again a special disposition, or group of dispositions, connected with the idea may be predominant and explosive. And of course, *mutatis mutandis*, there is the same kind of support from the physical side. We may thus say generally that, apart from exceptional strength, an idea will not dominate except through the favour it receives. And, when it finds the mind engaged specially in an opposite direction, the suggested idea will under ordinary conditions fail to gain control. (iii) Up to this point we have considered cases where a genuine idea of change has been present, but where that idea has failed to dominate and move me. But the idea may have been qualified, so as itself not to be the idea of a change which is to happen here and now. The way of connexion with my real world may be seen by me to be absent, as where the suggested change is regarded as merely imaginary. Or again the idea of change may have become an element in some wider idea, a whole in which

---

[1] I should be inclined to illustrate here by the absence in general of actual movement in dreams. See *M.* N.S. iii [*E.* xviii].

it is taken as subordinated or even negated. We have in none of these cases the dominant idea of a change in my world, and, even if the change were realized, we should not have here a genuine volition (cf. *M*. n.s. xi, Nos. 43, 44 [*E*. xxv and xxvi]).

I will pass from these objections to deal with another kind of difficulty. Your account, it may be said, is based on redintegration, and yet that law, however valid, is certainly not final. The tendency of every idea to realize itself in existence is really more ultimate, and even beyond this we may find a law which is still more fundamental. Every psychical element by itself involves a more or less unnatural mutilation and sundering, and every such element seeks to repair its defect. It therefore tends to reproduce its complement and to restore itself to the full character of the whole. But (however that may be) I see no advantage in discussing such a doctrine here. For if the self-realization of an idea in will is an instance of this ultimate tendency, that in no way would conflict with our general account. And since an ultimate tendency does not realize itself, I presume, without particular machinery, we were right in any case to seek that machinery in dispositions and in redintegration. There is, however, a further point on which I admit that my account is inadequate. Redintegration works, I believe, in all cases of volition, and in most cases I think that its working suffices. But there are other cases which seem to call for an additional law. An idea has a tendency everywhere to reinforce that existence which possesses its content, and, where existence has a content which partly corresponds to the idea, the idea has a tendency to create in fact a completer agreement. It thus transforms the existence to its own character, and so realizes itself. Now redintegration, it may be fairly said, will here not wholly account for the result, and we must therefore admit a further law, say, of Fusion or Blending. This is a difficult point which I am not disposed here to discuss, but the suggested conclusion once more need occasion no difficulty. If we recognize a tendency which in the end falls outside of redintegration, and even if we go on to call that

tendency irreducible and ultimate, the doctrine of volition which has been offered remains unshaken. Volition
still will consist in the self-realization of an idea, and redintegration will still be the machinery which for the most
part brings about that result. Our account, in short, must
be modified merely so far that we have to admit the working to some extent of a further machinery.[1] There is
therefore no room at this point to intrude with a faculty
of Apperception or Attention, and to offer this as an explanation of the passage in will. For in any case nothing
can anywhere be really explained by a faculty. And if in
this case the faculty is offered merely as the compendious
statement of a law, it is still objectionable because probably it does not answer to the facts. It is either contrary
to the facts, or else idle, or else at least to myself it remains
unintelligible.[2] And any suggestion that in will sometimes there is no idea, or no idea which realizes itself, has
been disposed of long ago in preceding discussions.

We may thus conclude that will is a psychical process
certainly not original or ultimate or self-explanatory. It is
everywhere a result from that which by itself is not volition. The passage of an idea into existence, we found, is
the essence of will; and that passage, we have now seen,

---

[1] I assume here that redintegration cannot legitimately be reduced to
partial fusion. I should certainly myself not agree to speak of the fusion
of an idea with a disposition.

[2] It is contrary to fact that the tendency of an idea to realize itself
depends on pleasure or pain, and contrary again that it depends on my
attention to the idea. The assertion, again, that in volition the idea must
be 'apperceived' may perhaps be admitted if 'apperception' is used in a
very wide sense, but such an assertion is useless if offered as an explanation
of will. For whether in fact an apperceived idea realizes itself or not must
depend in each case on *how* the idea is apperceived. If it is apperceived
theoretically, that so far tends to prevent the realization of the idea in fact.
But as soon as you inquire about the nature of this *how* and this difference,
you are thrown back on the machinery which we have described in the
text. Into that which Professor Wundt calls 'apperception' I am unable
to enter. The limited time at my disposal would hardly justify an attempt
on my part to ascertain that exact meaning which for so many years
Professor Wundt has been endeavouring to expound or perhaps to discover.

depends on machinery. Thus in psychology the conditions of will come before will itself, and, at least in psychology, these conditions are in every sense more ultimate than their consequence. You may perhaps insist that the tendency of an idea to realize itself after all is original, and you may add that in this tendency you find the real essence of volition. But how and why one idea realizes itself in fact while another idea fails—this is the question, I submit, which we are called on to answer. And if the answer to this question falls outside of what you offer as the essence of will, your view, I must conclude, is certainly mistaken or at best defective. With regard to external will that doctrine which fifty years ago was advocated by Lotze[1] has remained, we may say, in principle unshaken and unanswered. And a like conclusion holds also in the case of internal volition. We have seen that in the main this also depends on dispositions and on redintegration, and thus results from machinery which pre-exists and is itself independent of will. There was a partial exception, we agreed, in some cases where the idea reinforces an element which is given in outer or in inner perception. And the exact nature of such cases we were obliged to leave doubtful. But we certainly in these cases should be wrong to assume that the idea works apart from a pre-existing disposition to the result.[2] In any case Fusion depends on the presence of an idea together with a given element which possesses in part the same character. And I do not see that such a fact, even if it had to remain unexplained, would support the doctrine that will is independent and original.

I may now proceed to touch very briefly on the development of will, but must first insist further on its connexion with pleasure and pain. I have declined to include either of these in the definition of will, but on the other hand I admit the importance of both. If I were writing a psycho-

---

[1] In his *Medicinische Psychologie*, 1852.

[2] To some extent these cases can be reduced to the support and liberation of a disposition previously held in check. And the idea itself, we must remember, may represent a disposition. I do not however (I must repeat) accept such explanations as quite adequate.

logical treatise and not a mere defence of a special definition, I should have to lay stress on pleasure and perhaps a
still greater stress upon pain. Apart from their influence
usually, we may say, an idea fails to carry itself out. It is
either banished from the mind or is at least held in check.
The unpleasantness of want suggests, and by persisting
maintains, the idea of relief. And, in the absence of want,
a suggested change is emphasized and supported by felt
pleasure, while on the other side felt pain or uneasiness
tends to bring about change.[1] And when we consider the
origin and growth of dispositions and habits, the selective
agency of pain appears as a prominent factor. I am ready
to agree that without pain and pleasure the will in fact
does not originate, and that without pain and pleasure, to
speak in general and in the main, it does not now exist.
But on the other hand, while I find actions which apart
from theory no one would deny to be volitions, but which,
so far as I see, do not issue from pain or from pleasure,
I cannot admit pain and pleasure into the essence of will.
I cannot in these cases find felt pleasure in the idea of
the change, or felt pain in the existence which opposes the
idea. And further I must insist once more that in pleasure
and pain you have not an explanation of the passage of the
idea to its reality. They are a means of selection among
various ways of bridging the interspace, but I could not
possibly admit that either itself serves as a bridge. The
bridge in short remains external to them as it is external
to the sundered idea. Thus, if pleasure and pain always
were present in will and contributed always to its existence, they could be placed in its definition as at most a
constant accessory in fact to its main essence. But since
the facts are otherwise, I have no choice but to exclude
them wholly. If I am to ignore or to override apparent
exceptions to their presence, I can do this only on the
strength of a necessary principle. But I have here looked
in vain for any principle or for any necessity.

From this I must pass to consider an objection based on
the development of will. 'Your account', I may be told,

---

[1] On these points I have enlarged in *M.* o.s. xiii [*E.* xiv].

'makes will rest upon dispositions. But dispositions in fact are made by and rest upon will. You have therefore turned in a circle and have explained will by itself.' An objection of this kind clearly opens a wide field for discussion. But we may perhaps deal with it sufficiently in a limited space if we keep in mind throughout some general considerations.

(i) It is not permitted in psychology to confuse the questions of origin and of essence. You cannot assert that a psychical fact now possesses a certain aspect, because you judge that at its origin this aspect was present and was even necessary. It is of course legitimate to argue that this aspect has not disappeared, if, that is, you are prepared to state the reason upon which your argument rests. But no man, who believes from observation that in some cases the aspect is absent, can accept your conclusion unless your reasoning, in short, is conclusive. And the general disposition to believe that what has been is, or that what is usually is always, cannot seriously be offered as a conclusive argument. Now in the present case, though it may well be due to my limited knowledge of the subject, I do not know of any attempt to offer a serious argument. If there is a conclusive reason why pain and pleasure cannot in some cases now be absent in fact from volition, I have not seen so much as an attempt to offer that reason. But I am too familiar with the argument that apart from pain and pleasure there is *never* volition, because the presence of these is *always* implied in will.

(ii) It is indefensible, we have seen, to confound origin with essence, and there is a further confusion under this head which should be banished from psychology. Let us suppose that in the history of the animal kingdom, or even in the history of the human race, certain dispositions have arisen as the result of pleasure and pain, or again as the result even of volition. And let us suppose that you are in a position to establish this origin. But to advance from this basis to an assertion now about the human individual, and to urge that in him these dispositions are to be taken as resulting from will, although you cannot maintain that they have arisen from *his* will—surely no leap of this kind is allowed in psychology. My will, whatever else I may inherit, is certainly my own, and the will of another that comes to me as a transmitted disposition is most emphatically not a volition of mine. And it is illegitimate to assume that, because a thing has happened in the history of the race, the same thing must repeat itself in the same way in the individual's development.

(iii) And on another point the reader must allow me to insist once more on the difference between assumption and proof. Suppose that you have shown (which I am sure you cannot show) that in every case dispositions are the result of pain and pleasure—you cannot, starting from this, affirm that dispositions originate in will, except on the strength of a further logical step. And, in the presence of a denial, to attempt that step by bare assumption is not permissible. Now I am forced to deny that the working of pleasure and pain is always volitional. When on the presence of a stimulus a reaction takes place, and when that reaction is maintained and intensified because it is pleasant, and in consequence tends now by association to be connected with the stimulus—this to me so far is not in the proper sense volitional. And when at the same level pain prevents the formation of some association, either through a counter-habit or simply by the removal of the painful—to speak of merely so much as being will, I must call indefensible. The doctrine that pleasure and pain imply, or even in all cases coincide with, conation or desire, at least in the sense of a desire or a conation of my self, we had to reject as contrary to irrefragable facts. And I must repeat even once again that the proof, if such a proof were possible, that dispositions originate through pleasure and pain, is not, taken by itself, a proof that they result from will. I am not of course speaking of proofs which seem to consist in mere verbal definition.

Having taken such a position I consider that in the main I am not called on to discuss further the argument from development. But for the sake of clearness I will try briefly to pursue this point further. There is an attempt, as I understand it, to show that will has no origin beyond itself, and that it does not contain and rest on passages which are given to it and which come before it in time. And in answer to the obvious objection that will depends upon given dispositions, an endeavour is made to show that dispositions, if you only go back far enough, themselves are a result which comes from will. Now if will is defined as we have defined it, such a thesis seems hardly to be arguable. And if will is identified with the working of pleasure and pain, the reader may now recall that we have rejected that assumption as contrary to fact. And we found again that, even if it were true that all dispositions are formed under the influence of pleasure and pain, it would hardly follow from this that pain and pleasure have made and produced them. You cannot, in short, to such an extent select and develop your means that you can maintain in the end that no means are presupposed.

There is, it seems to me, but one sense in which will could be really 'autogenous', and in which, as will, it would depend on nothing prior to itself. If you take your will to be a man who from the first possesses a certain character, and if you suppose that your development consists in the willed selection by this man of that material which suits with his nature, such a process, I agree, might perhaps be called the 'autogeny' of your will. At any rate your nature, so far as acquired, would have been acquired by your will, and certainly that result would have come from your volition. But no such doctrine, I presume, could be even so much as discussed in psychology. On the other hand, apart from an inadmissible view of this kind, I see no sense in which the will can be really 'autogenous'.[1]

If, however, within psychology we seek for a will which is before dispositions, it may repay us to see for ourselves how far a consistent view is possible. We must begin here

---

[1] I am far from denying that what is found to be true and beautiful and good is in the end so found because it is felt to answer the needs and express the character of the self. But I hardly think that psychology can concern itself even with this. And it would not lead to the conclusion that will is prior to psychical dispositions, or indeed is anything itself but a psychical result.

by enlarging will so as to include the results which in the widest sense are due to pain and pleasure. And we must go on to suppose a being which in its structure has no tendency to any special ways of reaction. From the stimulus of sensation, without regard to the sensation's quality, are to come diverse reactions which vary fortuitously according to the conditions of the moment. Or we may say that these reactions come only when pain and pleasure are added to the stimulus. This connexion of pain and pleasure with the stimulus is itself fortuitous, or else it itself must depend on an original disposition. And if diverse kinds of movement, such as contraction and expansion, follow specially from pain and pleasure, that would evidently once more presuppose a disposition. But, however the variations first arise, they are in some way supported or banished by pleasure and pain. And thus, by a natural selection which is also psychical, certain reactions are favoured and are developed into dispositions and habits.

How far we here have dispensed wholly with dispositions the reader must judge. But when we ask if such an account holds of the development of a human individual, the answer, I presume, must be a decided negative. Even if you add hypotheses with regard to his intra-uterine life, you cannot maintain that the individual to so great an extent is himself the immediate result of conditions and of fortunate survival. And, at least in human psychology, we surely in each case must begin with the individual. If on the other hand we go backwards in the development of our race and of the animal kingdom, we are met at a certain point by difficulties of a further kind. Let us suppose that at a certain point biology is willing to accept our being that has no special structural tendencies, yet at this point we perhaps have gone quite beyond psychology. How much in its psychical aspect can we say about a being such as this? If at such a supposed level it possesses any consciousness of its own, how far does that consciousness contain and depend upon pleasure and pain? I should have thought myself that, at least in the present state of our knowledge, it was not possible even to assert the existence of either pleasure or pain at the beginnings (wherever we place them) of psychical life. That all conscious life has its suffering and its enjoyment, we are prone to believe. We have some reason to think this, and to hope for a greater knowledge in the future. But on the other side to draw a necessary conclusion on this point seems certainly not warranted. And you cannot argue first that the will was such at the beginning because it is such now, and then, in the second place, when a man denies that the will really is so now, reply that it must be so now because it was such at the beginning. Further I may repeat that, even if the will at the beginning had really possessed a certain character, you cannot assume that in every respect this character has been preserved unchanged.

The effort to deny that will depends upon given dispositions, and the attempt to carry these dispositions back to a point where they originate in will, must end in failure. The will as an individual, who for private reasons or for no reason breaks out into definite action, seems hardly admissible. And again there is a wrong identification of will with the influence of pain and pleasure. There is a false assumption that such an influence, if original, could not later be dispensed with. And, lastly, by retiring backward in search of an uncontaminated beginning, you are threatened at a certain point by a formidable dilemma. You will reach a stage where there still are inherited dispositions, but where these dispositions now appear to have become merely physical.[1] And here, without finding what you seek, you will have been carried beyond psychology. Or on the other hand you will be forced to carry over into biology psychological doctrines which within psychology you cannot establish or justify.

'But no,' I shall be answered, 'you do not understand the logic of our argument. We take as a fact the actual formation of dispositions in accordance with our doctrine, and the fact therefore depends upon no preconception. For in our actual experience we can observe the production of

---

[1] Merely physical, that is, not absolutely, but from the point of view of any special science.

habits. Dispositions are made, and we ourselves see them made, through the influence of pleasure and pain. And hence we are able to affirm "This is how they are made", and we can therefore deny any other origin as unknown or rather as impossible.' Before I consider this denial, there are several points which it is desirable to recall. In the first place, unless a disposition has been made by my will, it is, I insist, external to that will in whatever way it has been made. The argument therefore must mean that in my own individual history I have made without exception all my dispositions on one and the same principle. And, if the argument begins to hesitate at this point, it has failed. And I may once more remind the reader that, where variations are selected under pleasure and pain, the selected variations do not cease to be external to these feelings. And at any rate in no case can all such selection be rightly called volitional. Whether in our experience no associations are formed in fact, except under the influence of pain and pleasure, seems to me a question on which, to say the least, some doubt is possible. For myself, while I here will not go beyond doubt, I certainly cannot accept the above assumption as true. I do not see how to deny, that is, that an association may arise from a mere emphasized or repeated conjunction and without the influence of pain or pleasure.

But it is time we turned to consider the negative side of the above argument. We know, it is contended, how in our experience dispositions are formed, and we therefore may exclude any other mode of origin as impossible. But such exclusion, I reply, if it is to be logical, must rest upon thorough knowledge. The excluded must be meaningless, or it must be self-contradictory, or it must be in plain collision with something positive which is itself clearly known.[1] Now can we say that the formation of dispositions within our own experience is known clearly? Is the influence of pain and pleasure a thing which we can call really understood? I do not myself see how any one can maintain that this is actually the case. How then can the formation of dispositions apart from this influence be

[1] I do not here ask how these aspects are connected.

taken to contradict our alleged fact of experience? To assert that no physical cause can produce anything like a disposition, and to say the same of any psychical cause other than that which is alleged, seems at least to me little better than an unwarranted and downright assumption. And thus the negative argument has only to be examined to be dismissed as untenable.

If you bring in metaphysics this result, it is possible, might be altered. You might contend that the minimum of reality in the end involves pain and pleasure, and involves what you call will. And you might go on to argue that to suppose the contrary even in a special science is not permissible. But, without attempting here to enter into your metaphysics, I must insist that to intrude such speculations into the sciences is not permissible. If a thesis is such that it cannot be justified on psychological grounds, that thesis, however admirable elsewhere, has no place within psychology.

I must conclude then that, even if action under pleasure and pain is wrongly identified with will, we cannot, however far we go back, get rid of external connexions. We must suppose that special dispositions everywhere precede and are the foundation of will. And, even if by retracing the history of the race you could free yourself at some point from given dispositions, yet, when you come to the individual, the difficulty returns. For if the will of the individual presupposes dispositions which by him are unwilled, his will originates in that which to it is external. And even if the origin of the individual will were in accordance with your doctrine, you could make no logical conclusion from the origin to the essence. It is bad psychology, it is no better than prejudice, to assume that a thing must remain all that it was. The fact is that the working of pleasure and pain is not all volitional, and, again, the fact is that some volitions do not involve any such working. And no mere argument from origin, even if it were well-grounded, can alter these facts. Hence pleasure and pain, however influential in general they may be, cannot be given a place in the definition of will.

With this conclusion I may perhaps bring these articles to an end. They have covered, I fear, so much ground as to unfit them each for a separate appearance. On the other hand they have neglected some parts of their subject, while what they have discussed has been treated too unsystematically. But they may serve, I hope, as some defence for that definition which they advocate; and, if they lead the reader once more to examine doctrines too lightly maintained, they will have satisfied at least the expectation of the writer.[1]

[1] I had hoped to have been able long before this to discuss the doctrine of will, which has been put forward by Professor Royce in his interesting and important work, *The World and the Individual*. I find to my regret that I can do no more than indicate very briefly the general attitude which, at least in psychology, I am forced to take with regard to it. (i) I could not agree that in psychology everything, which is felt as the satisfaction of my nature, can be taken as the realization of an idea or as willed. (ii) I must again dissent from the view that an idea is in itself so far the realization of a purpose or will. This is the case, I should say, only where there has been a will to have that idea, and in this case an idea of the idea must have preceded. (iii) I cannot make our intellectual and aesthetic self-realization subordinate to practice except in a sense and within limits far narrower than those assigned by Professor Royce. (iv) I cannot agree that in cognition the object is in the end selected by an idea. On the contrary I think that the idea is itself in the end 'selected' by something not an idea.

Generally I agree that the real is what satisfies, and that no other definition of reality in the end is so ultimate as this. But in psychology I certainly cannot say that what satisfies is or has been willed. And even outside psychology I cannot take reality as being merely, or even in the first place, a satisfied will. I am unable, that is, to regard will, either in myself or in the universe, as being more than one partial aspect of the whole. But I must hope to discuss hereafter some of the doctrines contained in Professor Royce's instructive work.

XXIX

THE EVIDENCES OF SPIRITUALISM

[*First published in* THE FORTNIGHTLY REVIEW, No. ccxxviii, N.S. December, 1885.]

'SPIRITUALISM, if true, demonstrates mind without brain, and intelligence disconnected from what is termed a material body. . . . It demonstrates that the so-called dead are still alive; that our friends are still with us though unseen. . . . It thus furnishes that *proof* of a future life which so many crave.'[1] The present article may be taken as a denial of these theses.

Three great gulfs, to be crossed by three separate labours, divide the spiritualist from his Land of Promise. His first task is to prove that the 'phenomena' are real. He must show next that they are not the abnormal work of human spirits. But, when these obstacles are passed, a third closes the way. He has to leap from the fact of non-human intelligences to the goal of immateriality and immortal life. It is this alone for which the common spiritualist cares, and my object is to show that, if all else were done, this at least is hopeless. Let us accept without question the phenomena as alleged. Let us admit that these 'demonstrate' minds extra-human and in communion with ours. But, arguing from these premises, we utterly deny the further conclusion. It does not follow that these minds have no material bodies. It does not follow that the dead are really alive. We have no right on this evidence to believe in any future; and, if we believed in it, then on this evidence we should be fools if we craved it; and, if the reader cares to traverse a dry chain of arguments, he will see with what poor fancies the spiritualist is fed.

I will begin at once with a fatal objection. In the premises of the spiritualist there is nothing at variance with

---

[1] Wallace, *Miracles and Modern Spiritualism*, p. 212.

the conclusions of a gross and thorough Materialism.[1]
The materialist regards souls as the adjectives of what is
senseless. They come and go with, and they depend on,
collocations of bare matter. But the spiritualist has found
souls not dependent on the matter which makes human
bodies, and he forthwith concludes that these souls are
bodiless or are clothed in 'ether'. He has argued in short
from a vicious alternative. He starts with 'Souls exist not
dependent on the matter connected with *our* souls', and he
rushes to 'Souls exist without anything that can be called
matter at all'. But now, suppose that there is matter different from ours, and which normally is not perceptible, and
we have a pitfall into which the spiritualist has fallen
blindly. He either has argued wrongly from his premises,
or else, where he knows nothing, has assumed omniscience.

As to what matter is we might dispute for an eternity
and fail to agree; and the difficulties are not simply made
by metaphysics, but obtrude themselves in forms like those
of 'fluids' and 'ether'. But by 'matter' we commonly mean
a reality extended in three dimensions, which can be moved,
and can move, and can cause sensation. And we are used
to suppose that there *is* no matter but that which we normally perceive, or which forms one system with what affects
our senses. But, if we reflect, we see at once that this sup-
posal rests on nothing. There is no logical objection to the
possibility of several kinds of matter, which, for us at least,
do not even form one system, which all have several spaces
of their own, and which do not move one another at all.
How, indeed, *could* we be sure that there is not matter
which fails to affect us, but which, if different ourselves,
we at once should perceive?[2] But, if so much is possible,
then I would suggest something else. This matter, which
usually is indifferent to our own, may under unknown con-

---

[1] In order to avoid misunderstanding I may say that I do not advocate
materialism. I might add, with some prospect of being misunderstood, that
I object to spiritualism because it itself is an outcome of materialistic tendencies. It is merely another sort of materialism.

[2] Mr. Wallace (*Miracles*, p. 45) agrees that there probably are 'forms of
matter and modes of ethereal motion' other than those which our senses
enable us to recognize.

ditions move and be moved by it. It may thus affect our organs as well as our environment, and again in its turn be affected by ourselves. But if matter of this kind were organized and so got souls, then these souls would depend on corporeal movements. They would be embodied, and yet, though commonly invisible, might in abnormal states communicate with us and produce all the facts ascribed wrongly to spirits. This hypothesis is consistent with a thorough materialism, but it covers every part of the alleged phenomena. And if the spiritualist retorts, 'It is an idle hypothesis'; not idle, we shall answer, if it accounts for the facts, and in itself entirely conceivable. But your naked spirit is perhaps not logically conceivable, and at any rate is also a mere hypothesis. And it is not the hypothesis which best accounts for the facts.

We ourselves have souls and bodies, and we perceive certain facts, assumed to be the effects of souls not our own, which yet, because like *our* effects, show that other souls exist. And we press on with this conclusion in spite of the fact that we have failed to find the intermediate bodies. Now we agreed to take this failure as evidence that the facts are not effects of *our* bodies; but the spiritualist wants to go much further than this. He argues, 'Not dependent upon *our* bodies, and therefore upon *none*, quite bodiless and "ethereal".' And this is irrational. For, in the first place, nothing excludes the idea that there are bodies not normally obvious to ourselves; or, in other words, such bodies are *possible*. And, in the second place, the evidence suggests that they are *real*. First, the analogy which we must use from the embodied soul is a ground, *a priori*, for expecting a body. And what is the evidence *a posteriori*? In the end it all resolves itself into effects on matter. There is not one shred, and there could not be one shred, incapable of being so interpreted. Nay, a great part, and apparently the part most relied on, could hardly be taken as anything *else*. Effects upon our matter have to be explained. Are they better explained by a different matter or by a naked ghost? Tables are moved, finger-marks and foot-marks are printed on sawdust, and furniture is shattered by a force of several horse-power. 'And what need', exclaims the spiritualist, 'of any further witness? Behold the manifest ghost, not corporeal nor corruptible, and a pledge of our immortality.' And here argument ceases. The analogy suggests and the evidence points grossly to another unknown body; and if the spiritualist still clings to his naked soul, yet he cannot call it the one hypothesis which is possible. He cannot deny that every particle of the evidence can be explained by a soul embodied in matter. Thus, if we allow that non-human intelligences exist and produce our phenomena, we are as far away as ever from bodiless spirits. These intelligences may depend upon material motions; the materialist will urge that they are corruptible and mortal, and that, whether better in other respects or worse than ourselves, they are alike in this, that they arise and perish.

But the spiritualist will reply, 'Your alternative is false. We are not forced to choose between matter and ghosts. The spirits are not bodiless any more than we are, but their bodies are higher and of ethereal substance. Thus though impalpable they are potent, and though active indiscerptible, and such bodies are a warrant of immortality.' For myself I must reply that if they were ever so thin, I do not see how that brings them nearer to spirit. If they are extended and movable they are probably discerptible, and most assuredly we have no hint that they are anything but mortal. The possibility that they are *not* so is an idle fancy, for which the facts alleged give no sort of excuse. This 'spiritual body' is a foolish imagination. It inhabits our space and yet is not material. It is attenuated to that degree that it passes through matter, and yet is indivisible and everlasting. It is not quite a solid and not quite a spirit, nor yet quite a gas. It is inexplicable and not wanted to explain anything else. Once admit that matter may exist and not normally be perceived, and then its thinness or grossness becomes irrelevant. Admit, on the other hand, it is thin past earthly thinness, and it still is material and still discerptible.

We have started by assuming the existence of active non-human intelligences, and we have so far seen that the

conclusions of spiritualism are not rational. There is nothing to suggest that these souls are bare of bodies, but the
evidence goes to show them both embodied and mortal.
And we saw that this result is in no way shaken by the
gratuitous chimera of a spiritual body. It may now, perhaps, be worth while to ask some questions as to the *nature*
of these souls. Like ourselves they have bodies, and these
bodies at least are presumably mortal, but can we know
more? Is there anything to tell us if, as compared with
ourselves, they are higher or lower, more or less spiritual?
If we consider first their material performances, it is clear
that they do much which we cannot do. And this certainly
has weight. On the other hand, when we ask if they can do
the things which we accomplish, the evidence fails us.
And if, further, we inquire if our ordinary life may not
seem to them extraordinary and even miraculous, we have
no information. We are not able to tie knots in an endless
cord, or to pass through a keyhole, and that is in their
favour. On the other hand, they have never made anything
useful or done anything great; and so far as we know, they
could not if they would. Again, living as we do in two
different worlds, what is common in one may be astonish-
ing in another. If they pass through our keyholes perhaps
we pass through theirs, and should bewilder them if, like
ourselves, they were wise enough to wonder, or if our high
matter could affect their gross bodies. But these are all
idle fancies, worthless imaginings. We have no evidence
which directly indicates that their bodies are either lower
or higher than ours.

But when we ask as to their souls, I think we get a little
light. When we weigh the probabilities, the balance does
move in a certain direction. There is reason to think their
souls *lower* than ours and, taken on the whole, less intelligent and feebler. Of course they perceive what we do
not perceive, but so, to some extent, do the lower animals.
That they perceive *all* that we perceive, or on the whole
more than we do, there is no evidence. The unusual need
not be higher, and to them we do not know what is unusual.
And it would never do to say, 'But we ask questions and

they none, and therefore they know.' They might ask no questions because they have no curiosity, no sense of defect or desire for knowledge. Hence, if we keep to simple power of perception, we cannot say if they are higher or lower. It is better to pass to what we can judge of—intelligence and general powers of reason. But when we judge by these, the souls we converse with are lower than ourselves, and we have no reason to believe in others which are higher. To the damning evidence of the so-called Spirit-Teachings no answer can be made. It would be unfair to say that the best of them are twaddle, and they perhaps may be compared with our own pulpit-utterances. They are often edifying, and often reasonable, and sometimes silly, and usually dull. Still, to mention them in the same breath with the best human work would be wholly absurd. And it is an inferior race which can produce nothing better. The spiritualist, of course, has met this fact with an hypothesis. Our means of communication at present are faulty, or as yet we have not lighted on the superior persons of the higher world. But these hypotheses are arbitrary. They are based on the prejudice which they are meant to support, and they have no other basis. But throw prejudice aside, and judge simply from the facts, and the result is otherwise. I do not mean that, like the spiritualist, we should treat the uncertain as if we had exhausted it, but I mean that, if we argue from what we do know, then the spirits are probably lower than ourselves, and we are offered no reason for belief in any other and higher spirits.

We have now seen that the spirits are probably embodied, and that their minds at least are inferior to our own. And like ours their bodies are too probably discerptible, and their souls, the adjectives of those physical aggregates, must too probably perish. And assuredly the materialist laughs in derision. You may count it a great thing that thought does not depend on the matter of the brain, but what if it rests upon something more coarse, something that you would hold still more despicable and vile? Your new revelation of these latter days has given us something to hope and something to live for. It has reinstated the soul and re-established religion. But in these latter days religion rests on converse not with spirit above us but with spirits beneath us; and our hope is one day to be made like these spirits. Such spiritualism is not spiritual, such religion is mere superstition, and it conflicts with the best aspirations of the soul in a way in which modern materialism does not.

Spiritualism, so far as we have seen, is exploded. Admit its facts and its conclusions do not follow. If there are souls, not ours, behind its phenomena, yet these souls are not bodiless nor are they immortal. And presumably they are inferior to our own; they give us nothing to admire and nothing to hope for. But the spiritualist will urge that I have left out of view a main part of the evidence. I have said nothing of the testimony borne by the spirits, and I have neglected the great fact of spirit-identity—the proof that our relations still are alive, and that therefore we shall live. The discussion of these points was put off for a time, since they involve some difficulties and require some patience. I will deal with them forthwith, and we shall very soon find that the testimony borne by the spirits is worthless. We shall go on to see that their identity is not provable, nor, if provable, a warrant of immortality, nor in any way comfortable. Let us first take their testimony.

From this we get information, edifying if not useful, as to the things both of spirit-land and of our own earthly life; but what specially concerns us is the assertion that after death we too go to spirit-land, and that life there is, or may be, much higher than here. Still testimony, as we know, may be false as well as true, and the question is whether in the case of a spirit we have got any reason for supposing it true. I am compelled to believe that we have simply no reason. We have control neither over the facts deposed to, nor over the mind and character of the witness. But under such conditions any testimony is worthless; and if the reader will have patience, I will make this point good.

Testimony, we must remember, does not supersede experience. It can never be an independent source of information, side by side and on a level with personal observation. For it must by its nature involve an inference, and that inference must be founded on our direct knowledge. It *is* an extension of our personal experience, but an extension that proceeds from and rests on that basis. We are indeed told that we have an instinct to believe, and that to take in mere assertion is to follow that instinct. And it is true that, when our mind is unformed and uncritical, the mere presentation of an idea to that mind is usually enough to generate belief. But then this is not the question. The question is not what we naturally do tend to believe, but what as rational beings we ought to believe. Should we accept anything and everything just because it is offered us by another intelligence? No one can maintain this. Well, but if we must discriminate and must use some criterion, what is it that we should use? Most palpably there is nothing but our own personal experience, and the inferences we can reasonably draw from that basis. And I think that every one in the end must take this view of the case, or find he is using words without a meaning.

What, however, do *we* mean? Do we mean that a man is to believe nothing but what he has seen, and nothing that runs counter to his private experience? We are far from meaning this. What we insist on is that our reason for believing the witness must come in the end from our own direct knowledge. It is not that we are confined to private experience, but that this experience itself must warrant our leaving it, by giving us a reason for going beyond. In the case of testimony what is this reason? It is an inference on our part to a mind in the witness which, first, is capable of having learnt the fact attested and, next, is able and willing to communicate the truth. We in short infer that the mind of the other may in these respects be treated as our mind; and in consequence we have merely to test its statements in the way in which we test our personal observations.[1] Thus, when Mr. A tells me of this or that event

---

[1] I cannot ask here how far the results of private experience may be set aside on the strength of testimony. I admit that in some cases they must be thus set aside. I have said something on this question elsewhere.

which lies outside the range of my own observations, what justifies my belief in him? It is, first, an inference to Mr. A's *ability*. He must have had a chance of observing, and must have used that chance rightly, from the proper point of view and without any bias. And how can I know this? Obviously from nothing beside my personal experience. Many links may intervene, but at last I must stand on my own knowledge of the world and of human nature. And it is the same when I ask about the truthfulness of the witness. I should not believe him unless I had reason to believe, first, that he can speak truth and, next, that he has no motive or unconscious bent towards deception.

Now the capacity and the desire of Mr. A to speak truth must rest in the end on my *positive* observation. But his absence of motive for untruth and deceit rests not only on that, but on something as well. It implies what may be called my *negative* experience, and it is based on an assumption. I assume that I know not quite *all* about the witness, but so much that, if he had a motive to deceive me, I should become aware of it. I assume that in my witness there exists no other life with other motives besides those which I discover. These, I think, are the criteria which we are forced to employ when we deal with unsupported human testimony. We do not always apply them with rigour and, where the testimony is supported by our own experience, we are, of course, not compelled to be so exacting. But where the gravest results follow from simple depositions, there we do and we must bring our tests to bear strictly. Without tests such as these (the defenders of miracles will endorse so far what I say) there is no reason why I should either believe or disbelieve.

If we apply our criteria to the teaching of the spirits, we gain at once a momentous result. Their assertions go beyond our personal experience, and their testimony is not supported. Hence our criteria must be applied with unsparing rigour. Let us make the experiment, and see if the spirit-witnesses are not turned out of court. In the first place, do the spirits know what they talk of, and have we got that assurance? I cannot think that we have. No doubt, being intelligent, they are aware of their immediate condition, but does their knowledge go much farther, and, if so, how far? May not much remain unknown to them which, if they knew it, would convict them of error? These questions cannot be answered, and hence (since we ourselves know nothing of spirit-land) we can in no way test the ignorance of our spirits, nor can we have trust in their information. This is enough, and yet even this is not all. We not only cannot gauge the defects of their observation, but we have a positive ground for distrusting their intelligence. From the data we possess we have been forced to conclude that the understandings of these spirits are lower than our own.

So far we cannot tell if the spirits are really well informed; and to this may be added a subsidiary doubt. When we communicate amongst ourselves we are sure that our system of signs is trustworthy. If it were not so the practical results must show it; and this is in the end the sole test that we have. But when we converse with spirits have we got that assurance; and if not, do we possess any other? I will only allude to this doubt in passing, and will proceed to state a more fatal objection. If the spirits really know and are able to communicate, does it follow that they are *willing*? May we suppose that they are truthful? We must not do so without reason, and have we any reason? With this question we arrive at a very noteworthy feature. It is admitted that some spirits are fraudulent and mischievous, but the spiritualist asseverates that others are sincere, and that *he* can winnow the false from the true. And, half dazed by his audacity, I can only reply, Produce your criterion.

Human testimony is sifted in part by our knowledge of the matters alleged, in part again by our experience of human nature, and by special information as to the character of this witness. The absence of a motive or a tendency to lie must either be shown or must else be assumed on a general presumption. And this is our criterion. But when we come to the spirits we can apply it no longer. We have no knowledge of our own by which to check their statements, and, what is worse, we know nothing about their characters. We do not know their moral natures; and whether they have or have not a motive to deceive us, we are utterly ignorant. It is not too much to say that if they were spirits of evil, whose happiness was staked upon fooling us men, we might (so far as we know) have no means for discovering it. Such an hypothesis is baseless, I quite admit that; but the hypothesis that the wish and the tendency of their natures is (where we are concerned) to speak what is true, is just as baseless, just as idle. We know nothing, and how then are we right to believe anything? We have no light and no test. 'But we are not to trust all spirits. There are good spirits as well as bad, and they tell us whom to trust.' *O sancta simplicitas*! It is always the vilest cheats who are the only honest men. It may be otherwise in spirit-land, but perhaps it is worse. And if there are good spirits, we at least cannot distinguish them. Nor would the idea of collecting a mass of spirit-evidence, and of so using false statements to eliminate each other, be any less fallacious. We do not know that our sources of evidence are independent, and, if they were, there might be tendencies which produce the same lies on different occasions. We need not dwell on these objections. The plain fact is this—that human testimony is received upon certain assumptions, and that with a spirit these assumptions can no longer be made.

But the spiritualist may deny that we have any need to make them. He may say that our experience gives us a test. The spirits tell us things that we ourselves verify. They are found intelligent and faithful in some things, and that gives us a reason to trust them beyond. But this conclusion is irrational. If a spirit perceives events through a wall and in the distance, if he sees what is hidden in the past or in the future, and we verify his competence, yet this, as we have seen, does not warrant him capable of any higher knowledge. He might yet be a witness not competent to speak of the things of spirit-land. His capacity is not established by the strange and unusual. It is when he proves himself our equal in the highest that we have, that

we should think him on our level. It is surely not by passing beyond my understanding that another goes the way
to convince me of his. And the same with their truthfulness. By what logic does it follow that, if they speak truth
in one thing, they will do it in another? That is the argument by which dupes are plundered perpetually. Suppose
a spirit ready to deceive (and we admit many are ready),
would he not first be found faithful so as to gain our confidence? It is only when we can assume that there is no
other side to the character, and no other motive lurking in
the background, that we can go from true in part to true
in everything. And of course with a spirit this assumption
is impossible.

To sum up the result:—When a spirit bears witness of
things beyond our world, we know neither his ability nor
his honesty, and we have no kind of presumption in his
favour. We have seen before that, apart from the testimony of the spirits, we must regard them as not bodiless
and may suppose them mortal; and their testimony also
has proved to be worthless. Nothing now remains save
the bulwark of spirit-identity, and if that goes, the last
defence of spiritualism has vanished. This bulwark at first
sight looks somewhat imposing. We recognize in the
spirits our dead friends and relations, and so are sure that
they survive. But if they survive, then we also shall not
perish. We are all immaterial and all immortal, and with
a destiny beyond the grave which may fill us with hope.
But, unfortunately, the edifice has no foundation. We do
not know that these spirits really are our friends, nor can
we hope in consequence ourselves to survive. And if we
knew this, yet our friends may be material and mortal, and
our heritage not joy but sadness and foreboding.

It would be a task alike ungrateful and useless to argue
against that which some of us call 'instinct', against the
assurance of love and the impulse of affection. And to
those who are persuaded that they converse with their dead
my reasonings are not addressed; but to others I must
show the flaws in the evidence. Even here amongst ourselves and in the daylight of the sun such a proof is not

infallible. If, in spite of evidence, the mother can find her long-lost son in the gross palpable impostor, that I think should make us hesitate. In the deceitful twilight of spirit apparition we must not hope that our instinct will be proof. To satisfy others we must admit the chance of illusion and reasonably discuss the case on its merits. I will attempt to lay down the tests we should apply. Identity is a subject not easy to handle, and the identity of a spirit with a deceased human being presents several difficult questions. And the spiritualist has, I think, advanced gaily on the surface without much thought for the pitfalls which make it unsound. Hence I must ask the reader once more to have patience, for, if we hurry the discussion at this point, we are lost.

How do we know here on earth that the man whom we recognize is really our relation? And, first of all, how should we prove it in a law court? We should show in the first place the identity of his mind, as evinced by memory and by sameness of habits, and in the second place we should point to the identity of his body; but on reflection we see that this latter carries everything, and that the sameness of body is the goal of our argument, to prove which indirectly or directly they all would be aimed. And the reason of this is (as we shall see lower down) that we cannot show, except by way of the body, the continuity of the soul. If the body exists it must exist continuously; but the continuous existence of another man's soul can be shown, if at all, only by a circuitous process. I shall return to this hereafter, and at present will but point out that for legal purposes the identity of the body proves the sameness of the man. Now the body is, of course, a material thing, a thing differing from other things, and puzzling us much by its change and its sameness. But we need not notice the special problems which it offers, and may confine ourselves to the question, how we show the identity of a material object. Is it enough to make out that it seems to our tests just the same as it was? No, that is not enough, for it shows no more than sameness of *description*. The identity of this or that material object depends also on the continuity of its existence. If, for instance, we could know that a coin or a diamond had been ⟨temporarily⟩ removed from our universe, then no test we could apply would ever prove it was the same and not another just like. It is unbroken existence, undivided persistence, that makes the identity of a material object.

Hence if we proved the continuity of our relation's body we should prove his identity. But strictly to prove continuity is impossible, and we must content ourselves with a certain probability. We try to show that at the end of various intervals a body like our relation's was present in the world, and that if, during those intervals, the body had been changed, we must have been aware of it. We try to prove that the facts are in favour of continuity, and that nothing suggests an opposite hypothesis. But we may meet a great obstacle, for throughout some part of the time in question we may be able to get no sort of direct evidence. Still our case is not hopeless. We are able to add an indirect argument. First, our relation is not known to be dead or elsewhere, and the man before us is like what our relation would have been, and his story is credible— hence he *may be* our relation. And now, secondly, we produce our indirect proof. There is no one save our relation who could appear so like him, and therefore our man *must be* the person we seek. This decides the question.

Now our *must be*, it is obvious, rests on an assumption. We suppose ourselves to have such a knowledge of the world that we can be sure there is no facsimile of our relation, or, if there were, that we should get to know it. We see the nature of our argument if we take the case of twins, so like as hardly to be known apart. If these twins, A and B, had been absent for even a moderate time, then, if no evidence could be got to show continuity, it might be utterly impossible to prove the identity of A or B. And this shows us the assumption which we commonly use. No one save a near relation could ever be so like, and, in this case before us, no such person is possible. Our assumption, perhaps, may be no more than probable; but we must employ it, or have no opinion at all. And, whether probable or certain, it rests entirely upon our experience of this world.

If we now return to spirit-identity, we shall find that we have got an important result. We cannot use for a spirit the same sort of proof that we use for a man. Continuity of body cannot be shown where no body exists, or where it exists ethereally and not in our world. And to argue from the exclusion of all other bodies is equally impossible. Hence, where we have no body material as mine is, the legal evidence for identity is quite out of place. This, I think, must be admitted, and the question is, Have we among human beings any *other* way of proving identity? I confess I cannot find one. Let us suppose that A and B have two wives C and D, and, though the bodies of C and D seem still the same, that their souls are transferred. In this (impossible) case could we get to know the identity of their souls? I do not think that we could. A man might say, 'This woman C is no longer my wife; she is at present not the same with the woman I married.' But nothing could entitle him to find the soul C in the body D. For myself at least, I do not see what evidence could establish that point. And if so, we must say that without the same body the same soul is not provable.

We have so far made good that the identity of a spirit is not capable of the proof which we use amongst men. That, however, may not matter. The removal of the body removes a difficulty. 'Our relation's soul is hard to recognize, when we know that his body is possibly elsewhere, and itself with a soul. But death strikes out the old body, and simplifies the question, so that knowledge becomes possible.' A spirit appears to us like our relation in appearance, disposition, and knowledge of facts. That is really all the evidence, and is it enough? If we strike out the body it is the same evidence that we used to establish human identity, and so far it is valid. But unfortunately it stops at a fatal limit, for it wholly leaves out the indirect proof. We assume with a man that no other could resemble him, since we know our own earth and the nature of its people. Without this assumption the inference is broken, and with a spirit the assumption would rest upon nothing.

The identity of an individual, corporeal or otherwise, does not consist in sameness of present description. If the same soul lived twice at the interval of a century, would it really be the same? Or must we not add continuity of history? But how with a spirit is such evidence possible? Shall we venture to assert that none could really be so like unless he were the same? Think for a moment of the unknown region of spirit-land, and then judge if such assumptions are better than fancies. It would be easier if we knew that no spirit was anything but a man deceased. It would be easier, but still unlawful. For to us the other world is buried in darkness, and we know nothing of the dead, how they are changed (it may well be) and sadly translated. The proof that we seek for would have to lie in this, that after certain signs we should be forced to exclaim, 'My kinsman or the devil.' And we cannot reach this alternative. And moreover, even if the alternative were reached, we could not exclude the latter supposition. 'The spirit may be a devil . . . and abuses me to damn me.'

We are too ignorant to assume that from spirit-land no counterfeit would come to mock us. We cannot tell that no spirit save the soul of the deceased could so put on his knowledge and wear his semblance. It is all wild imagination. If I asserted that each man has got his double in spirit-land, sometimes seen during life, and which, lingering after death, amuses his kinsfolk, I should say it on grounds to the full as convincing. We cannot tell that no spirit is like our relation; we cannot say that no spirit is able to personate. But would they do it if they could? Well, we do not know their motives, and we cannot say they would not. Nay, there is some evidence that they do. The spiritualist himself teaches counterfeiting spirits, fraudulent and mischievous. True, he adds that we detect them by their own non-success, and by the help of those others, not fraudulent or (perhaps) still undetected. But, as we saw, this is illusory. Since we know nothing beforehand, the chances seem even that *all* of them are fraudulent;

against the admitted fact that at least *some* do personate I
see nothing to be set, and I will leave the reader to draw
the conclusion. Nor will it avail to urge the extent of the
deception, and to object that the scale is too large for
treachery. It may be, for all we know, easier to cheat many
than one. And if, finally, I am met by the personal appeal,
Would not you after continual intercourse, after constant
communion, be satisfied yourself that you held converse
with the dead?, I must reply that I cannot say what would
stagger my reason and break down my intellect. But that
is really not the question. The question is, what is reasonable for a man to believe; and I have tried to show the
conclusion which reason will justify. I do not despise feeling, but I cannot argue against it.

We can never know that we really converse with our
relations, and hence we cannot tell that we ourselves shall
survive. But even this is not the end. If we did recognize
in the spirits our friends that are dead, that would not prove
them or us immaterial or immortal, or exempt from worse
than earthly afflictions. It would not prove them wholly
immaterial, since they probably, as we have seen, have
material bodies. Nor would their identity weaken that
probable conclusion, for a soul might have one body and
then, again, another, possibly without any loss of identity;
or, if identity were lost, yet at least to us the appearance
would remain. 'Do you say, then, you admit that the soul
is transferred, and is therefore independent?' Nothing
need be transferred. The materialist holds soul to be a
function of the body. Well, then, obviously if you were to
destroy my body, and after a thousand years make another
one like it, my soul must (so far as my consciousness is
concerned) start afresh without a break and maintain its
identity. When the pressure of the bone is removed from
the brain, the consciousness begins from the moment of
the blow; and if the patient were not trephined but destroyed, and ten thousand years hence a man like him were
made, then, after an operation ten thousand years hence,
the consciousness would start from the moment of the injury. You may object that the soul would not really be

the same, and I will leave that undiscussed, but it would seem to you the same, and it would reply to the tests to which your 'spirit' replies, and after all you would be wrong if you called it immaterial. And I argue from this that you are likely to be wrong when you deny that the spirit has a perishing body. You have given nothing to weigh against that general probability, which we saw was against you. Another body like in function explains all the facts, and a bodiless principle seems no better than a phrase.

Hence our relations are material, and are probably mortal, and we can draw no hope from their existence after death. They may say that they progress, but why should we believe them? In the first place, we have seen and conversed with but a fraction, and the rest are not known. Then, again, we cannot tell that our witnesses do not lie. And if they speak what they believe, how much do they know? How much of their own prospects, how much of all those creatures whom perhaps they never see? Their own intelligence is not high, perhaps now it is decaying, and their own degraded future they cannot forecast. Were they doomed to extinction, to mouldering dotage, even to something unspeakable, why suppose that they would know it? And there is an ominous circumstance. The souls of great writers, when called upon, indite, if not fustian or drivel, the saddest commonplace. And we reject them as counterfeit, but perhaps we are wrong. Perhaps our Shakespeare after all and our Bacon and St. John were the genuine men, travelling ignobly through decrepitude to final dissolution. This is a fancy, but not more fanciful than the rest. And so we must say that, if our apparitions are really the deceased, they do not open the future nor give us hope that their lives will be long or desirable. And in the face of this result (if that were all that we had) there would be comfort in the death which gives peace in the grave. It is much to know the worst, and if we can say, 'They are not troubled, for their poor private selves death is sleep everlasting, and the higher life which they lived lives on through their labour', then that worst is not bad. But to be sure that they exist, but not for how long, really to know nothing of the what and the how—it is this which makes death hideous. We are a prey to each 'lawless and incertain thought', and, indeed, 'it is too horrible'.

Let us collect the result of our long discussion. We have seen that, even if we hold converse with the dead, yet that gives no hope of bliss beyond the grave, either for ever or even for a very little while. And we have no right to believe that we hold this converse. And, if we commune with intelligences, yet we have no right to take anything from them on trust. Further, though we may admit an intercourse with souls, yet these souls are not any more spiritual than we are, nor are they any less material or more immortal; nor again are these objections dependent one upon the other, but any one by itself is dangerous to spiritualism. Still, I fear that the result may be a feeling of too much. I fear the spiritualist may reply to these doubts by a counter-charge of general scepticism. I have indeed laboured to distinguish our ordinary inferences from the reasoning employed to establish the spirits, and it is on those distinctions that I would take my stand. Still, that the spiritualist and myself may each understand the other, I will endeavour to meet a possible objection. 'On your showing,' I may be told, 'though the spirits did exist and with a message for ourselves, yet they would have no way of delivering their tidings—or rather, though they delivered them, we never should be sure of it, or at least ought never to accept their testimony. And this position is absurd and is palpable scepticism.'

I answer that I fail to perceive the absurdity; and while I defend an opinion, not formed for an occasion, but embraced long ago and tried by some wear, I would beg for a little the attention of the reader. I deny utterly the right claimed by the beings of one sphere to hold communion with those of another. I see no reason to expect any converse of the kind, nor is it incredible or unlikely that, if such converse took place, there should exist no means for the accrediting of testimony. We must not first make our fancies the measure of the universe, and then exclaim that the facts are absurd and impossible.

There is, of course, a prevalent and obstinate idea that signs and wonders can accredit a messenger, and that marvellous works can entitle a spirit to claim our belief for his depositions. The idea is most natural, but is a mere anachronism. No revelation can be authenticated by miracle or testimony, or by anything else but internal evidence. I do not mean that, if in England there now were a spirit both able and willing to be in earnest with miracles, to strike dead his detractors, to send disease on the unfaithful, and prosperity and health upon all his worshippers— that such a spirit ought to fail in establishing a following. For he could not fail, and religion (in this sense) would be rational, and atheism would be folly, and indeed would not exist. But then this is not the question. The question is whether anything which that spirit could do would make him a witness whom we ought not to doubt. When he told us of things quite beyond our experience, could we ever have a right to accept his bare word? And, if we reflect, we are compelled to answer in the negative. For in the first place we have no means of checking his account, and in the next place it is impossible to be sure of his mind, his ability and his desire to tell us the truth. It is impossible, since we see (or can know that we see) but a fragment of his nature, and the inference from this fragment to the whole of his being is quite illegitimate. And if I am told, 'But we know that his strength is irresistible, and we therefore should believe', I can only reply that this is barbarous and childish, a survival from the logic of the primitive savage. If we believe this, we should hold that Mahometan fire-arms are a proof that Gabriel's feather wrote the *Koran*, or that the Athanasian Creed may be demonstrated by the power of Cockle's pills. But what is good for the negro is not so good for us.

No convincing revelation can now be made to us which is to stand on anything but internal merit. A revelation of this sort is by no means incredible, but what does it mean? It means that our souls are so assisted and enlightened that we perceive of ourselves that the testimony is true. The testimony, in other words, is not taken *as* testimony, and may not even bear that character, but is held on its merits as evidently true or certainly to be inferred. That is not impossible, nor unreasonable, nor even improbable. But an external revelation is a mere anachronism; it may weigh with the foolish and may persuade the superstitious, but others will not easily come to embrace it. And if religion is to depend on external evidence, then there can never be a religion for the most educated men.

Against the religion of the spiritualist, if we take it at its best, against his conception, that is, of the true aim of the soul and of its duty towards God, I have nothing to say. He stands far above the common level of orthodox Christianity, and if I thought that this article would weaken his persuasion, that would cause me regret. And I wish the spiritualist to understand that my objections are not aimed at his practical doctrines. They are directed against his forecasts of our personal future, which, if true, could make no difference to our duties, and which he rests upon evidence entirely worthless. His premises could never establish his result. It is not his fault or his spirits' fault, but it lies, I am convinced, in the nature of things, that no proof of the kind which he attempts is possible. And if he replies that a religion must be something for the people, and that what to me is but a puzzle to them is demonstration, I must answer that I could not even for the sake of religion take part in his deception.

I will not assert, if we were quite sure of the truth, and were sure that our fraud would but tend to support it, that then we might not say, 'Since the people must be deceived, be it ours to deceive them wisely and well'; but since the case is far otherwise, and since our fraud would take its place amid the uncleanly struggle of superstition and priestcraft, we ourselves must be defiled if we countenance deceit, and admit bad evidence for true conclusions. This in any case must be true, and there is something besides. Who is able to guarantee us against these spirits? They are not saying to-day what they have sometimes said before, and who knows but hereafter they may say something else? I do not trust these spirits however fairly they may speak.

And I confess when I look back upon the annals of the supernatural, I cannot feel quite easy. It may be very well to say, 'I have found no devil yet. I have no fear of bogie.'[1] The orthodox 'Bogie', I agree, if alive, is now quite decrepit; but we should remember from whence he had his origin. There are still terribly low strata in our poor human nature, and in the end I am afraid they might light upon a stratum of answering spirits. From the cold fires of the defunct some devilish phoenix might arise to hinder us, and to force us to victories which are too like defeat. We have a great deal to do, a great deal to make war against, and we feel that we have had enough of spirits. So long as any human duties are left to us, we are something too high to be their battle-field or their play-ground. But if we dally once again with superstition, if we leave the honourable daylight and once more follow after voices from the dark, then the sun has gone back on the dial of humanity.

Spiritualism has had so far a very easy game to play. Its facts have been canvassed much more than its inferences, and it has for the most part enjoyed a monopoly of interpretation. But when its data are established (if they ever are established), that monopoly will go, and it will, point by point, have to battle with rival hypotheses. I shall have succeeded in my purpose if I have shown that that battle is hardly begun.

Note

The following extract from a letter written by the author on February 1, 1922, may be of interest.

'I don't want to write about spiritualism generally. What I want is to correct a mistake which I made in writing, as if what is called spirit-identity could not be shown to exist by *any* evidence. I have written for myself an abstract of what I think is correct now, but I can't, I fear, make this interesting generally, and doubt if I shall now try to do more. Certainly I dislike spiritualism very much, but of late years there has been evidence of much better character, though I have read little of it. I cannot see any reason to think that any new religion can ever be built on spiritualism.' The

[1] *Spirit Identity*, p. 97.

'abstract' was begun, but not continued, and is too fragmentary for publication.

Another reference to this subject will be found in *Essays on Truth and Reality*, 440, footnote, where he says:—

'What I myself wrote on this head some time ago (*Fortnightly Review*, 1885) is, I recognize, one-sided and unsatisfactory; but it contains doubts which are far easier to ignore than to remove. For instance, to discuss the question of the identification of a "spirit", without any regard to what is involved logically in the identification of a man, seems to be still the common way, and to myself it still seems to be ridiculous.

XXX

ON THE TREATMENT OF SEXUAL DETAIL IN LITERATURE

Note. The following article was written in 1912, at a time when the flood of erotic novels had not yet swept over the English reading public. Some harsh and, as he thought, unjust strictures on certain books had called the author's attention to the subject, and he thus briefly recorded his own views.

On re-reading his article some years afterwards, when already a change had taken place in current literature, he thought it necessary, in order to guard against misconception, to add the Note which is printed below (see pp. 626–7).

THE question as to the right of the novelist to present and dwell on sexual detail has, I understand, begun to trouble us. In this dispute it is only too easy to take a side, but to judge intelligently requires more than mere personal bias. And if we are to form a reasonable decision, we must at least make some attempt to understand. It is in aid of any such attempt that these pages have been written. To freedom from bias on my own part I make no pretence at all. I should be false to all the tradition of my life, such as it has been, if I were not wholly on the side of liberty in science, literature, and art. The feelings which I entertain towards any part of the public, which I am forced to regard as enslaved and hypocritical, I need not express. My object here is, so far as I can, to set out the principle on which any rational discussion must be based.

I will for the moment imagine myself to be a novelist attacked and blamed for treating of sexual matters. And I will first state briefly, and merely in general, the real essence of the attack, and next will explain the proper line of defence. The attack will be developed not quite as it is usually made, but as it must be made, if it desires to be logical and consistent.

(1) It is a recognized law that all ideas have a tendency to work themselves out into personal emotion and action. This law obviously holds good in the case of amatory sexual

ideas. However they are suggested, these ideas tend to develop themselves within me into emotional disturbance, and this disturbance tends to carry itself out in action. Hence, except possibly in some situations of actual married life, no amatory suggestions of any sort or kind can fail to be dangerous, and therefore none can be allowed. And it is not novels merely which here are concerned. All study of anything sexual, even in science, must provisionally be held suspect. If for medical purposes such study is permitted, even this, except so far as necessary, is not excusable. But, in any case, for any one of the general public all scientific knowledge of sexual matters must be forbidden, whether in anatomy and physiology or even in the natural history of animals.

Next, everything in sculpture or in pictorial art which portrays, or even suggests, anything amatory must be excluded. The nude figure tends to become a mere pandering to lust. Further, in poetry no sexual love may be introduced, except perhaps in a guarded way the love of husband and wife, and possibly the amours described so chastely in the Song of Solomon. As for the novel (the theatre need not even be mentioned), we have something here worse even than poetry, because nearer to actual life. The novel, if not (like the *Morte d'Arthur*) full of 'bold bawdry', is at least replete with pernicious suggestion, witness Paolo and Francesca, and all those others whom romances have led to sin and to death spiritual if not bodily. And music so far as it is 'the food of love' should be peremptorily silenced.

The attempt to distinguish between loves of diverse kinds must be repelled as insidious. If the love is sexual, it is sexual; and sexual emotions and ideas tend normally to one end. They lead to desires which, except in matrimony, cannot be gratified without sin. Even though resisted, such ideas must unsettle or corrupt. And the one remedy is to banish whatever tends to excite them. Hence everything, everywhere, which suggests amatory ideas, must in principle be forbidden.

I have stated the objection to the treatment by the

novelist of sexual themes, in the form in which to my mind it is consistent and honest. As we usually find it, however, the objection seems to be more or less inconsistent and hypocritical. And before proceeding I will ask the reader to pause and to consider how far the above objection to sexual ideas has removed perhaps the greater part of our spiritual life. Seeking to cast out one evil spirit, is there no danger that we have left our soul well nigh blank, an empty space ready to receive other visitors?

(2) For indeed such is the result, to which the attack on novels seems necessarily to lead. And I will now go on to ask where the process, which has taken us to such a conclusion, has been mistaken.

Is, in the first place, its foundation, the general law of the development of ideas, to be condemned as an error? No, we must answer, the law in itself is perfectly true, but here it has been misapplied because misunderstood. For what the law really states is merely a tendency. Suggested ideas *tend* to develop themselves in me and with personal consequences. This, however, is only true so far as taken conditionally. It should mean simply that the ideas produce a certain result where they are not interfered with, so far, that is, as they are not obstructed by other ideas or contrary feelings and sensations, and not subordinated to impersonal interests. Obviously there are various ways in which to prevent undesirable disturbance of my personality by, for instance, sexual ideas. And obviously one way will be to embody these ideas in some impersonal setting, to attach them, that is, to an object or world of objects other than, and beyond, my mere individual life.

An idea associated with an interest which transcends my mere being, as this or that human animal, this or that creature as it lives and feels at this or that moment—will develop itself accordingly. The movement of the idea will take the direction of the interest. But this will, so far, prevent the idea from discharging itself in mere personal emotion and action. In short, so far as the mind is full of independent interests, these will attract ideas amatory or otherwise within their circle, and will so control them. It is in the empty mind that ideas find room to work themselves out into personal disturbance.

What, we may now ask, are these interests of which we have spoken? We have first the habit of mind which is called scientific, the set desire to know and understand, and everywhere to arrive at truth. And it is surely beyond doubt that, where sexual matters are attended to in this way, whether in anatomy, physiology, medicine, the history of animals, or again in anthropology, the result, to speak in general, is not libidinous. All such studies of course *can* be used improperly and wrongly. But then, as so used, they certainly, so far, have ceased to be scientific.

Let us consider in the next place pictorial art. So far as this art really is pursued and loved as art, and not as something which is different, the same principle holds. The interest in the artistic effect controls the tendency of amatory subjects to disturb the personal state of the man who studies the picture. There is in the picture, to those who can appreciate it, the victory of the master over all the difficulties of composition and technique. And to the public in general there is visible, at least in some measure, the achieved beauty of the result. And beauty, as beauty, is always outside of and above and beyond any mere personal feeling. Beauty is not something which remains within me, as a mere condition and state of myself. It is there, whether in motion or at rest, as an object outside me and for me, or else it fails to be beauty. My interest therefore in what is beautiful must, if it is genuine, so far prevent any amatory ideas from taking in me what we have called a mere personal direction.

There are times, we must admit, where at least in the case of certain persons art fails to achieve its end, and then may in consequence merely disturb and excite. Art again *can* be even intended and used to produce this result. But here assuredly, so far and to this extent, we have not to do with genuine art.

When we pass on to poetry and to the novel, our general principle still holds, though it is more difficult perhaps here to apprehend it clearly. In poetry and in novels (it will be urged) the reader is compelled to sympathize. If you do not actually have certain emotions, you have not understood. With amatory subjects, for instance, you have to feel yourself into the characters and the situations, and you have to feel yourself in them. Hence your own state will be amatory, and must so develop itself in you. If you think otherwise, it is because you merely deceive yourself. So runs the objection, but our answer is ready. It is true that you do, in reading, have to some extent amatory sentiment and sensation, but the extent and the power of this is bounded by a principle. The interest of the poetry as poetry, or of the novel as a novel, should dominate your feelings. It uses these as its material, it diverts, it limits and directs them to subserve its own purpose. And hence the subordination of the amatory ideas to an object beyond your mere personality controls (to repeat this once more) their development within yourself. The ideas are checked at a certain point, and are prevented from issuing in personal emotion, disturbance, and conduct.

With poetry, in contrast to the novel, it is far easier to realize this truth. The whole situation described in the poem may be said usually to be set in a kind of frame apart and remote from my actual life. Even where the poetry is lyrical, the emotion is felt to be idealized, raised above the being of the mere moment, and so made impersonal. I have never heard Tennyson, for example, denounced as a carnal poet. And yet he could write:

> Last night, when some one spoke his name,
> From my swift blood that went and came
> A thousand little shafts of flame
> Were shivered in my narrow frame.
> Oh love! Oh fire! Once he drew
> With one long kiss my whole soul thro'
> My lips, as sunlight drinketh dew.

If here you cannot recall or imagine, and so feel the sensation more or less, the poetical effect is wanting. But if your ideas and emotions stray beyond the vision of Fatima's passionate heart and burning flesh, if they begin to wander and to turn to a mere something in yourself—it is because you have lost hold of the poetry. The beauty which transported you beyond your private being, and which held and purified your individual feelings, has vanished. But it is by your own default if that, which in yourself has taken its place, has harmed you.

You may in this connexion recall the erotic sentiments warbled by young ladies in drawing-rooms. These flames have indeed in *one* sense tortured many, but I do not suppose that they have often inflicted moral injury. The imagined situation is detached from the actual environment. Whatever ideas and feelings are excited are felt to belong to another world, the region of 'mere music' and of 'only poetry'. The ideas and emotions therefore qualify and are appropriated by this other world, and their downward and outward irradiation and development in the singer and the audience are checked.

When we pass to the treatment of sexual matters in the novel the same principle which has guided us, still keeps its force. But not so (it will be urged), since the novel differs essentially from poetry, because it has to keep closer to ordinary life. In reply I might indeed ask where there is any fixed border-line between some poetry and romance in prose. But I prefer to deal more directly with the main point at issue. I insist that everywhere in literature, enjoyed as literature, our principle is valid. We have everywhere what we have called the impersonal direction and set of the interest. We are absorbed not in ourselves but by an object before our minds. It is this object which our ideas and our feelings colour, and by this object they are dominated and held. So being controlled, their development within our personal selves is obstructed. Detached from our own life they go on to realize themselves in that world which we only contemplate. And in this detachment lies the freedom which is bestowed on us by every form of genuine art.

To inquire into the nature of all that interest which is satisfied by the novel would carry us far. It is a question too wide for our present discussion. In a prose romance, beside beauty of style we have the sense of adventure, the development of incidents and character, we have psychological study, we have the individual presentment of idealized human types, we have all that is meant (and I cannot here ask how much is meant) by the words comic and tragical. Into this new-born world which moves before us our thoughts and feelings are carried. The ideas and emotions that are aroused live not merely in ourselves. They are beyond us as the souls of those figures, whose acts and sufferings, whose sorrows, sins, and delights are for the moment more real to us than anything of our own. What we feel into those creatures we feel out of ourselves. And the tendency of our emotions and ideas to realize themselves to the end in our own minds and bodies is at a certain point limited. Our sympathetic entrance even into the last mysteries of carnal and aberrant passion should leave our hearts still pure. For we are in the hand of that Ideal which, so long as we can serve it truly, will hold us unharmed.

It is possible, we all must agree, for an artist not to succeed. The painter, the poet, or the novelist, in introducing sexual material, may have failed to keep the detail duly subordinate. Hence, instead of qualifying the main interest, this detail may break loose. It may remain no longer bound to the service of the artistic purpose. And, thus set free from the object before us, the sexual ideas and feelings, no longer checked, may develop their natural process in ourselves. Such a result, however, where it happens, is due not to art but to art's failure.

But more commonly, far more commonly, the failure is in ourselves. To take and to enjoy art and literature for what they really are, is not given to all of us. During early life (I cannot here ask why) this defect may more or less be expected. The outbreaks, for instance, caused in boys by the reading of tales of piracy and of other criminal adventures, are things of constant occurrence. And too many persons, in the same way, remain through all their lives children. The detachment of personal feeling, and its location beyond us in another world, is for such minds not possible.[1] And reading of those who 'loved not wisely but too well', the result to those unfortunates may be the production of personal excitement and trouble, followed perhaps by a burst of indignation against the corrupt art and the immoral aims of the writer. For such persons the avoidance, perhaps the more or less wholesale avoidance, of painting, of poetry, of romance, and above all possibly of music, may be a moral necessity. Even for the average man there may be special forms of literature and art, the enjoyment of which should be deferred until he has taught himself to appreciate their true character. But what is not tolerable is that stunted natures should set up their defects as a standard. It is an outrage, it is sheer blasphemy, when they bring the divine creations of literature and art to the touchstone of their own impotence, their own animalism, and their own immorality.

Which is the higher being? Is it the man who strives to empty his mind of all that is sexual, to banish from his life all the beauty and all the romance that, based on sex, carries sex into an idealized world? Is it he who thus leaves his own nature at best vacant and starved, or opened perhaps to the inroad of that which turns it into 'a cistern for foul toads to knot and gender in'? Such a question surely cannot be answered in the affirmative.

The higher man surely is he who, loyally accepting his whole nature, seeks a positive remedy for its weakness. Such a man will know that his safety lies not in vacancy but in fullness. He brings, so far as in him lies, the entire tendencies of his being as an offering to that which is more complete than himself. He seeks generally to identify all his energies with a higher purpose. And in science, in art, and in literature, by setting even the lowest recesses of his nature before him as an object, he aims at personal free-

[1]   Sprüh'n einmal verdächt'ge Funken
            Aus den Rosen—sorge nie!
            Diese Welt glaubt nicht an Flammen
            Und sie nimmt's für Poesie,
so writes Heine in addressing a lady. The reverse process, alas! is but too familiar. There are too many who, understanding nothing of literature or art, degrade their pure radiance into personal inflammation.

dom. Those feelings and ideas, without which he would cease to be human, he transfers so far as he can to the keeping of the Ideal. In that all passion, every idea and emotion, becomes a thing sanctified and hallowed. They all are lifted into the realm of truth and of immortal beauty —and the man himself follows them. He rises, at least for that moment, into a sphere removed from the sway of those elements, which experience has perhaps taught him to fear as a mere part of himself.

A Note—added at a later date

Such is the justification in principle for the use of sexual detail, and all that remains is to guard against certain misunderstandings.

I have already explained that certain persons are not fit to appreciate art or literature where sexual detail comes in. The detail to them becomes something other than art or literature. Again some persons are inclined both in their lives and elsewhere to give too much attention to passionate sexual love, and still more persons to romantic love. Now even in the form of art and literature it is better for some of these persons not to have their attention too much centred on this subject. And it must be admitted against the novel that, retaining to a greater or less extent the aspect of a tale of adventure, it, to speak in general, is prone to exalt the adventurous aspect of sexual love, which is not really the aspect which in life possesses most moral importance. So that while it is perfectly true that literature, like art, can and does free us from personal desire, it is true nevertheless that, if one-sided, it does or may tend to exalt one-sidedly one side of human nature, and possibly depress others.

So much for the reader. And for the writer, while it is impossible to say that any subject is incapable of literary or artistic treatment,[1] some beyond doubt are excessively difficult to treat. And, while success in art justifies itself and is subject to no dictation from the outside, on the other hand there are subjects where failure is disastrous. The art that has failed to be genuine art can hardly be justified merely by its own good intention. The writer or painter who has aimed at his highest, and done his best to reach it, is justified, that is, morally, whatever he has done or failed to do. But he is justified only as a man and as to his own conscience, and his actual work may not be justified aesthetically or morally.

[1] e.g. Balzac's *La Fille aux yeux d'or*, and perhaps *Une passion dans le desert*.

Subject to this explanation I hold unreservedly to the position set out in the above article. I am wholly on the side of freedom in art and literature, and against those who would adapt them to the weaknesses, real or supposed, of young persons, or estimate their character by its effect on their own uncultivated or perhaps vicious personality.

XXXI

RELATIONS

I

Introductory Note.

BETWEEN January and April 1923, and again during the first four months of 1924, Bradley was at work on the subject of 'Relations'. His original intention was to put what he wished to say into the form of an article for *Mind*.[1] But the work grew far beyond these limits;[2] and in February 1924 he decided to divide his treatment of the subject into two parts, so that it might be published in successive

---

[1] Compare the following extracts, all from letters to his sister:—

'I am decidedly better . . . and have been doing a very little work in arranging my ideas with a view to an Article in *Mind* perhaps . . .' (Weston, 17 January 1923.)

'The Article I want to write would have done well as another Terminal Essay in the Logic, only I wanted to get done with that. . . . It contains nothing really new, but its object is to insist on the ultimate unsatisfactoriness of any "relational" stage of experience—however necessary.' (Weston, 25 January 1923.)

'This thing I am preparing to write as an Article for *Mind* is logical and metaphysical. It is on the nature and position of "relations". . . . I am not ready to write yet, but am making an outline and notes. . . .' (Weston, 1 February 1923.)

'I am writing, as a preliminary, a full abstract.' (Weston, 1 March 1923.)

'I am writing a full sketch . . . I hope to have got this done in a day or two now. . . .' (Weston, 19 March 1923.)

'I have finished an outline and notes for that Article I want to write.' (Weston, 23 March 1923.)

[2] 'I have been looking . . . at the Sketch and Notes that I made at Weston, and rather fear that it will turn out a bigger job than I thought.' (Oxford, 9 April 1923.)

'I have been going over the notes of what I wanted to write when here last year. There is a good deal too much stuff, I fear, for an Article in *Mind*, unless I can cut it down—which I may be able to do.' (Weston, 8 January 1924.)

'I have too much material (which I got together last winter) and find a difficulty in dealing with it, apart from the actual difficulties of the subject.' (Weston, 4 February 1924.)

numbers of the journal.[1] He began to carry out the new plan and, though much interrupted and delayed by illness, had written 'about 20 pages' of the first part by April 8th.[2] But, after writing eight or nine more pages, he was forced to postpone further work on 'Relations', and turned his attention during May and June to the preparation of a new edition of *Ethical Studies*. He left England for a holiday in Switzerland at the end of June, and died on September 18th, shortly after his return.

Thus the projected article remained unfinished. The major portion of the first part (probably about three-quarters) exists in the draft referred to above. The manuscript (hereafter called C) fills twenty-eight and a half pages of a 'memorandum tablet'. Though much corrected in places, it is very nearly in final form, and is printed without substantial alteration below. But the second part of the article was never written, and not even a rough draft or outline of it exists.

Prior to his change of plan, however, Bradley had accumulated a quantity of valuable material in preparation for the *undivided* article as originally designed. Most of this preparatory work is contained in a black quarto notebook (hereafter called A). There are, besides, twenty pages of a manuscript (B) enclosed in an envelope, on which the author has written 'MSS. & Notes for Article'; and, lastly, a few entries in a red quarto notebook (W) to which both A and B occasionally refer. Many passages, taken from these sources (A, B, or W), are reproduced in the Appendix (pp. 653–76), and arranged, so far as possible, as notes supplementary to the text of the first part of the *divided* article (pp. 630–50). Nearly all the selected passages do in fact throw further light upon various points in this completed portion of the projected work; and many of them sketch problems which the author intended to discuss in the second part, and even foreshadow to some extent the arguments he would probably have used.

[1] 'I am arranging to make the whole thing divisible into two parts so as to be able to appear in *Mind*—to do this I am putting off the discussion of some serious difficulties to the latter part. The risk here is that I *may* find that I shall have to alter the first part after I have tackled the second.' (Weston, 17 February 1924.)

[2] 'I have done a little more and have actually written about 20 pages; but the subject extends itself, and, unless I limit it arbitrarily and unsatisfactorily, will become unmanageable in anything short of at least 50 or 60 pages, to say nothing of the difficulties. I may however be able to limit it so as not to be ashamed to publish, and this I must try to do.' (Weston, 8 April 1924.)

II

Unfinished Draft of the First Part of an Article on Relations

WE all, I think, are agreed that the question as to relations, their nature, truth, and reality, is both central and difficult. To deal with it and all that it involves within the space of an article is certainly not in my power. But the main view as to relations which I advocate I will attempt so far as I can in what follows to make intelligible.[1]

If 'relation' is not used merely as a vague term for any sort of connexion or union of that which is both one and many, but is employed in a stricter and more limited sense, then to me relations do not in the end as such possess truth or reality. Experience, so far as in a proper sense relational, I take to be in no sense either primary or ultimate. Such experience is necessary and is justified as a way of advance in knowledge; and if we fail to recognize this, we are led into fatal error. On the other hand, any relational view involves self-contradiction in its essence. It rests on a form of experience which is more primary and, in a sense, more ultimate—which form, though vitally implied in itself, it attempts to leave behind and supersede. And thus the relational view, while justified and more than justified in advancing, must fail in the end to reach full reality or truth. Its essential presupposition and support remains, we may say, throughout infra-relational, while the higher stage of a unity which at once includes and transcends mere relations is reached by no relational experience so long as that remains itself. Such experience, then, I take to be a makeshift aiming unawares beyond itself at an end, fulfilled in which it must lose every claim in its own right to truth and reality.

This consummation (I may perhaps be here allowed once more to insist) I take as an experience neither one-sided, nor abstract and negative. It is the complete realization of all our desires for truth, beauty, emotion, sensation, and activity.* It is not in detail knowable and it remains, if you please, inexplicable. But in its main positive character, as the fulfilment of every end and the complete reality of all partial existence, it is both knowable and certain. And since it is beyond any one kind of experience—feeling, thought, and intuition, sense, activity, and will—while it positively includes each and all of these, to identify it with any single one is of course ridiculous. Hence, when those who hold to an Absolute such as the above are set down as mere Intellectualists or as seekers in vain to find a universe in the blank nothingness of abstract identity, I must be permitted to doubt whether we have anything here which deserves the name of criticism.[2]

Relational experience, to return from this digression, is to my mind in no sense either primary or ultimate. It presupposes and rests on another mode of experience which, though itself also imperfect, has a better claim to such titles. And I will now proceed first to describe and contrast the main characters of each; and then, after entering into fuller detail, endeavour to deal with some points of difficulty.

The primary form of experience may, I think, be best called 'immediate experience' or 'feeling', and with regard to this I may be allowed to refer to what I have written elsewhere.[3] To limit the meaning of feeling to pleasure and pain I must take as quite indefensible. And if there ever is such a thing as one simple feeling, I will put that here on one side. I mean here by 'feeling' such a mode of experience of sameness and difference in one as is an awareness direct and non-relational of that which is at once one and many. If we may permit ourselves to speak here prematurely of a whole and parts, then in immediate experience the whole qualifies every part while the parts qualify all and each both one another and the whole. Thus extension and colour as they come first are not given as related. They are both in one, just as the contents of every 'this', 'now', and 'mine' come in one and make one with the

* [The MS. reads 'truth beauty sensation and emotion and activity'. The reading given above is taken from earlier drafts in A and B.]

pleasure and whatever else belongs to their moment's feeling. And if we mean by 'given' here to imply a relation of object to subject, then we must certainly avoid the word 'given'. For immediate experience, taken strictly, is free from every kind of relation. The diversity contained in it directly qualifies and is qualified by the unity,* just as throughout each single feature makes a difference to any other of the rest. We have here a mode of union where the category of Whole and Parts cannot as yet properly be applied, and where even the form of Predication must be used subject to serious reserve. But on the other hand we are in possession here of what to my mind is, so far as it goes, an indubitable fact.

There are some real difficulties to which later I shall have to return, but my next task is to show how the form of relational experience differs essentially from feeling. There are, however, some misunderstandings which, before proceeding, I will attempt to remove. I do not suggest that what I call feeling is in every sense ultimate, and that we can take such a mode of experience as itself, in short, absolute Reality. On the contrary, such a doctrine would be to my mind a radical and fatal error. The ultimate reality of the universe is not something merely below or above what appears. It must on the contrary hold within itself every variety of fact and experience; and wherever you can even suggest a more, you have failed to reach what is really ultimate. And so, dismissing the above error which in another form I have noted already, I will go on to mention some points where I am met by real difficulty.

Are we to maintain (i) that, in the race and in the individual, the stage of mere feeling is prior in the sense of coming first in time? Can we again (ii) say that at any time feeling did, or does, come to us pure—and by 'pure' I mean verifiable as such internally throughout each detail comprised in it? Obviously we can see at once that often, if not usually, this is not the case. Our feeling is one and is a whole, but none the less may contain pieces of relational

* 'the [total] unity' [MS.]

matter, inside which the form of feeling is certainly not dominant. If we may so express ourselves, we here have clots present and contained in and belonging to a liquid whole, the general nature of which fails to rule within the limits of each. Within a state of feeling you thus often, if not usually, may have details which, though felt, are internally far beyond being merely felt. And hence to treat them as exhibiting throughout the general nature of feeling would be certainly wrong. Our one feeling taken therefore as mere feeling, we may say, is not pure, since its mere general nature fails to dominate pervasively. And I fully agree that the above doubts as to the priority and purity of feeling are a matter which will call later for further discussion.[4]

But what I fail to understand is the position of those who seek apparently to deny or ignore the very existence of what I call 'feeling'—an experience, that is, which, being more than merely simple, holds a many in one, and contains a diversity within a unity which itself is not relational. To take an ordinary sense-perception—say, for instance, that of a green leaf—as a unity which consists in one or more relations is to me to go counter to the plainest fact. And the same result to my mind is obvious when we look at some experience which is aesthetic or consider again any, no matter what, emotion. To attempt to deny that an emotion is one whole, or to treat its unity as consisting in no more than some relation or relations, I cannot but regard as really monstrous.*

Or take that experience which at any and every moment, however little we attend to it, comes to us as the world in its character of 'this', 'now', and 'mine'. Is it possible to deny that we have here a feeling which contains a diversity in unity, however vague? Is it possible to maintain that this unity is no more than merely one or more relations? Obviously and undeniably, on the one hand, we can and do and must transcend the above unity. But, on the other hand, ⟨in order⟩ to be actual and real, surely there is nothing which can fail in some sense to be contained in it and

* [The author intended to add a footnote with references.]

to belong to it, however much within its own further character it must also pass beyond. Thus every relation, to be even possible, must itself bear the character of an element within a felt unity—and apart from that is an abstraction which by itself is nothing. And feeling, we thus may insist, if not all in all, is the base and condition of the whole universe; and to fail to recognize this may be ruinous.[5] To forget on the other side to ask, with regard to every element in the world, in what way and how far, within its own special character, it passes beyond that existence which it shares with all else that is felt—may bring equal disaster whether in theory or in life. Here and everywhere the worst way in which to seek an escape from error is to throw oneself into the arms of some counter onesidedness.[6]

Dismissing now for a time any doubts or difficulties with regard to feeling, as the immediate experience of many in one, I will go on to show the main difference when we pass to an experience which is relational. Both are alike in being ways that hold a diversity in unity, but in feeling the whole and the parts (if we may use that expression) qualify (we have seen) one another throughout. But such qualification, where you have relations, ceases in part to be possible. The diversity here, while still forming a whole, has hardened itself into a plurality of terms, each so far independent as to have become an individual with a being and character of its own. And hence to say anywhere here about the parts and the whole that any one thing really is the other leads to obvious contradiction. A relation (we find) holds between its terms, and no term (we find) can itself simply be or become a 'between'. On the contrary, in order to be related, a term must keep still within itself enough character to make it, in short, itself and not anything diverse. And again, while the relations are not the terms and the terms are not the relations, neither the terms nor the relations can make that whole, in which nevertheless we find them. For the terms and the relations (we have seen) cease as such to exist, unless each maintains

itself against whatever is not itself but is outside. And
the attempt to find the required unity and totality in the
terms and the relations taken somehow together must end
obviously in failure. For this 'together' must bring in
something more than, and going beyond, the experience
if (*ex hyp.*) that is taken as relational. Or else, to gain our
required 'together' and the fact of 'relatedness', we shall
have fallen back on the old unity which we found in feeling. But such a mode of unity (we have seen) no longer
holds when once our experience becomes relational.[7]

Relational experience must hence in its very essence be
called self-contradictory. Contradiction everywhere is the
attempt to take what is plural and diverse as being one and
the same, and to take it so (we must add) simply or* apart
from any 'how'. And we have seen that without both
diversity and unity the relational experience is lost, while
to combine these two aspects it has left to it no possible
'how' or way, except one which seems either certainly less†
or certainly more than what is relational.

Whether immediate experience, as feeling, itself already
involves contradiction in its essence is a question with
which later I shall endeavour to deal.[8] But I prefer first to
set out more in detail the discrepancies inherent inseparably in all that is relational. Relational experience on the
one hand is, I agree, unavoidable and is fully justified in its
own place as a way of life and knowledge. But on the other
hand I have to urge that it can claim no title higher in the
end than that of a necessary makeshift.

In the detailed criticism, which now follows, the reader
must expect to find little more than what already, I hope,
has been in principle laid down.

(i) A relation both is and is not what may be called the
entire relational situation, and hence in this respect contradicts itself.

(*a*) A relation, to be experienced and to be actual, must
be more than a mere abstraction. It must be an individual

* 'or [Ref.] apart' [MS.].
[Cf. Note A in the Appendix to *A.R.*]
† 'which seems [whatever else it may be] certainly either less' [MS.]

or particular fact, and, if less than this, it cannot be taken as itself.* Now the experienced relational situation must —to speak loosely—be viewed as a whole which has parts. And on examination we find that the relation itself cannot be something less than the above whole and all the parts of the whole. For it is not merely the terms or merely a bare form of union between them. Merely with either of these, or again with both of them in the sense of each one, the actual relation is not there. What is still wanting to it to make it itself is what has been called 'the fact of related-ness'. A relation to be actual cannot itself be less than all and everything that makes the entire relational fact.

(*b*) This on the other hand must be denied. For a rela-tion *is* not its terms, but, on the contrary, it is between them. And though the terms may 'enter into the relation', yet, if they were nothing beyond it, they obviously would no longer be terms. A term (we have seen above) is as such not a quality. On the contrary, anything, to be a term, must itself be a particular or individual.

Certainly every content and aspect of the relational situa-tion as an experienced fact may and must be taken as quali-fying in some sense the situations as a whole; and, without so much as this, we cannot have a relation at all. But you cannot take the particular terms as thus qualifying the relation, even if you could take them, so far as they are particular or individual, as thus qualifying the whole. In short, to experience a relational situation as one whole and one fact, you must take it so that, as relational, the whole is not, and cannot be, qualified by its aspects or parts. The relation, as soon as and so far as the whole situation has become relational, has become no more than one of the parts. And to regard this part as itself the entire whole is an obvious absurdity.

Every actual experience is a unity of the diverse and may, speaking loosely, be taken as a whole with parts. But the unity, so far, is merely that which belongs to immediate experience or feeling, and taken so far is no more than

* 'as itself—[any more than if you tried to take it as without any terms.]' [MS.]

what may be called qualitative simply. And it is only when taken as no more than this, that you are able to assert the whole of its contents and its contents throughout of the whole. And the moment anything contained here is viewed as what is individual or particular, to that extent the above unity has been removed. But to have an experience as relational, you must have terms which are individuals and which therefore cannot qualify the former unity, but on the contrary so far destroy or supersede it. But when you ask for the unity, which in relational experience has come in and has taken the place of the unity so superseded—you find that there is no answer. There is no unity left, except by a tacit and illegitimate appeal to that which the relational view has discarded. You can have the terms, without which you cannot have the relation, only so far as (in order to have the relation) you abstract from the former mode of unity, on which (to keep your relation, which requires some unity) you are forced vitally to depend. And this is a contradiction in its essence insoluble, except by a further development of experience,* and by the rejection of any claim made on the part of relations to possess ultimate reality or truth.

You cannot escape here from contradiction by an appeal to what may be called the diversity of respects. It is idle to urge that the terms are individuals only in respect of their relation and so far as they are related, while none the less, so far as they are taken otherwise, they still remain mere aspects of, and mere qualities in, the one whole situation. This attempt but transfers the dilemma into the bowels of each particular term. For, with such an internal diversity in each term, either the term has been broken and destroyed by the loss of its unity, or else, seeking to preserve that and so keep the diversity of respects together, you are none the less ruined. For you have now fallen back on what holds within the stage of mere feeling, and which has ceased to hold so far as the situation has become relational.

* 'experience [into that which supersedes what can be called merely relational], and' [MS.]

And the failure only becomes worse if, for the plurality of respects in the situation itself, you seek to substitute the various ways in which we can look at it and regard it. For not only is the real fact itself given up here apparently as lost, but the problem of the unity of these diverse ways, in which one or perhaps a number of persons choose to regard the fact, still remains on our hands. And once more here covertly to fall back on an experience, which is itself not relational, is but once again, and in an aggravated form, to renounce all attempt at real consistency.

The whole result, which so far we have reached, may perhaps become even more visible when we pass on to consider another form of the same fundamental discrepancy.

(ii) Every relation does and again does not qualify its terms, and is and is not qualified by them. To state this otherwise, and in a way to which I will return—the terms and the relation must 'enter' one into the other, and yet again are ruined if they do so. You cannot (this is the point at present) alter one or both of the terms and leave the relation unaltered, or alter the relation without making a difference to the terms. But on the other hand unless, and except so far as, you are able to do this, you cannot think relationally. And to combine the above requirements without contradiction is impossible so long as relations are accepted as something which is ultimately real and true.

After what has gone before, we need not, I think, develop the above discrepancy in detail. A relation as actual is not a mere abstraction. It means a relational situation, which is an individual and unique fact. It means a unity qualifying and qualified by the diversity which it contains and which, like itself, can and must be called unique. But on the other hand, unless allowed to abstract from the above fundamental fact, no experience, which is in the strict sense relational, can exist. And to the question how the abstraction is compatible with the individual unity, which is no less essential, the relational experience has no rational answer. It claims tacitly a right everywhere, so far as a present purpose is served, to ignore some vital aspect of its whole being, while attributing to some other aspect an independent reality. And its practice is to treat at its discretion anywhere as the essential fact what elsewhere, and to suit another end, it disregards and in effect banishes as something that does not exist. Relational thinking is and remains (I would repeat) a method which is legitimate and is necessary for our understanding of the world. But it pays for every advance by an inconsistency which is irremovable so long as we insist on its ultimate truth and reality.

We are not called on everywhere (I also am sure) to emphasize the difference between our abstractions and the concrete fact. It would be stupid, I agree, to insist everywhere that, with a relation and its terms, a change made on one side makes also a change on the other side. Any one, I suppose, can see, and can maintain* that a man can still be the same man, though one or more of his relations have become different. And none of us, I presume, seek in practice to deny that a relation may remain the same, though those who entered into it, and still remain in it, have more or less modified their characters. For such alterations may—or again they need not—change what we are taking as the vital point here in some entire situation. But, on the other side, all of us (I hope) may agree, whether in theory or in life, that there is something which is too often forgotten. We tend to forget that, whether we like it or not, we have to deal with abstractions and to take our stand on partial aspects; and that these, however proper and right in one connexion and in one place, may none the less in another place be ruinously false.

Our one way of safety, whether in theory or in life, is (I presume) more or less to keep in mind the danger inseparable from our use of abstractions. Everywhere, I presume, when so called on, we should be ready to consider, and perhaps to agree that we are leaving out something required to make the whole and real truth—and to do this even where we cannot show and specify what particular aspect in a given case is lacking. Everywhere, in short, we

* 'maintain [be ready to assert]' [MS.].

should be ready to recall that our judgements fall short of, and are subject to correction by, the entire truth and whole reality—however much for our present purpose we have a right to believe that such a correction would not be material.

I am not to be moved here by the charge of an insult offered to Common Sense. For not only in speculation, but in life, we must all be ready to affront that which somewhere, perhaps, in the name of Common Sense may claim our respect. Common Sense certainly should consist, and at its best certainly it does consist, in the emphasis everywhere, whether in theory or in conduct, on what may be called the main view—the view, that is, which mistrusts and keeps furthest from mere abstractions, and comes nearest on the whole to that which is entire and is sane. But Common Sense, taken (as too often it may be seen) at its worst, is in its essence a one-sidedness, which we must not be afraid to mark as stupid or even, perhaps, to denounce as immoral.

Concrete individuality, the ultimate inseparability of identity and difference, is in my view everywhere the character and the test of reality and truth, and no other view in the end but this to my mind is tenable. A sameness where there is no kind of difference has in the end no right to its name, and a diversity not based on identity is nowhere a fact. A distinction without some difference is neither actual nor possible, even if we hesitate to add that there is no difference without a distinction.*

A sameness or a diversity which is merely 'numerical' is no better than an abstraction which is permissible only so far as it is found to be useful. And the same conclusion holds of an otherness, which denies that in the end its other is 'another of the same', and assumes that others are possible (and even exist) which differ in no respect but their otherness. Such abstractions, I would repeat, we have a right and a duty to use, if and so far as they help us. But they are indefensible, and they may be dangerous, if and so far as we mistake them for genuine truth and reality.[9]

* I shall return to this point hereafter. [*Note by the author.*]

Reality, as the concrete identity of sameness and difference, offers a problem not soluble by any relational thought.
We find there no rational answer to our inquiry of 'how
in the end'; but we find there the question forced on us,
only to leave us, if we accept relational truth as final, turning hopelessly in a blind maze of unending regress.* Our
dilemma as to terms and relations has been, I hope, so far
both established and explained.† We have a right everywhere to make and to employ whatever assumption seems
to aid us most to a better understanding of the world.
Our assumption has been shown in the present case to involve a contradiction in its essence, and hence to admit of
no defence if offered as ultimately true. For in the end it is
not true that a sameness and difference in our terms and
relations can be one-sided, separable, and independent.
But I would repeat that, understood and used as a makeshift, good for a limited purpose, our assumption can claim
what it is perhaps best to call 'relative truth'.

(iii) I will now deal briefly with relations, taken as what
may be called 'external' or 'internal' merely. And, though
at the cost of some repetition, I will show how such a
distinction, if we insist on it as ultimately valid, involves
us again in contradiction. It exhibits once more the discrepancy inseparable from all relational thought.

Every relation (unless our previous inquiries have led
to error) has a connexion with its terms which, not simply
internal or external, must in principle be both at once.
And, if so, the above distinction, if you take it as absolute,
will be plainly untenable. On the other hand, if understood and applied as no more than a useful makeshift, the
above distinction may stand. When it has ceased to claim
more than what may be called 'relative truth', it may be
accepted as true.

I will first of all consider relations, taken in an absolute

* See my *Essays*, pp. 240, 264 note. [*Note by the author.*]

† For comment on the attempt to escape by an appeal to the plurality
of respects, or of the diversity of 'ways in which you can look at it', I would
refer the reader to what has been already said on pp. 637 and 638. [*Note
by the author.*]

sense as merely external or internal; and will then deal
with the same distinction as confined to what is but relatively true.

What should we mean (I will ask first) by a relation
asserted as simply and barely external? We have here, I
presume, to abstract so as to take terms and relations, all
and each, as something which in and by itself is real independently. And we must, if so, assume that their coming
or being together in fact, and as somehow actually in one,
is due in no way to the particular characters of either the
relations or the terms. From neither side will there be
anything like a contribution to, or an entrance into, the
other side—or again to, or into, that union of both which
we experience as a relational fact. Undeniably the fact is
somehow there, but in itself it remains irrational as admitting no question as to its 'how' or 'why'. Or, if you insist
on a reason, that would have to be sought neither in the
terms nor the relation, but in a third element once more
independently real and neither affecting, nor again affected
by, either the relation or the terms. This, I suppose, is the
way in which relations have to be understood, if you take
them as external merely and also as ultimately and absolutely real.

What (I ask next) should, on the other hand, be meant
by a relation viewed as absolutely and merely internal?
You, I presume, still in this case would continue to take
the terms each one as, so far, in and by itself real, and as
independent absolutely of any whole that could be said to
contain them. And you would go on to attribute to the
particular characters of the terms, as so taken, some actual
relation or relations which you find, as you say, to fall
between them. Something like this, I suppose, is or ought
to be meant by a relation which is asserted to be real ultimately and internal merely.

The idea, I would add, that I myself accept any such
doctrine as the above seems to myself even ludicrous.* And
to whom, if to any one, it should be attributed in fact, I will
not offer to discuss. In any case, to assume it as the necessary

* ['seems baseless' is written above 'even ludicrous' in the MS.]

alternative, when the mere externality of relations is denied, is (I submit) an obvious, if perhaps a natural, mistake.[10]

Such, if the above statement is correct, should be the meaning to be given to mere external or internal relations. And it remains now to show briefly that, if taken as valid ultimately, such relations must be rejected. For in both cases we are met by a fatal inconsistency. We rest, in each case alike, on abstractions which refuse to come together so as to realize that diversity in unity which belongs in fact to the relational experience. And, in each case, if we are to regain this admitted fact, there must be a covert appeal to an experience which is in principle non-relational.

With mere external relations (to take these first) it should be clear that what we have to start with are no more than abstractions. The terms, each as real by itself, are not actual facts; and the relation taken by itself is but one more abstraction. And from terms taken as in themselves unrelated, and from a relation not taken as itself their relation, there is no logical way to the union present in, and required for, the relational fact. What has to be accounted for has hence so far been simply ignored. And while we keep to our terms and relation* as external, no introduction of a third factor could help us to anything better than an endless renewal of our failure. Without a diversity in unity, we must remain for ever outside of that which, on the other hand, we must admit as the relational fact. Or, to regain this, we may fall back blindly on a form of experience which in its essence is not relational. We may rest on a covert appeal to experience in the form of mere feeling, to help us beyond our mere abstractions to the result which we need. But any such appeal must be at once illegitimate and suicidal. For the unity of feeling contains no individual terms with relations between them, while without these no experience can be really relational. And, committed to external relations with a necessary 'between' and a no less essential 'together', we end in a bankruptcy, from which we seek in vain to escape by suicide.[11]

Passing on now to consider relations taken as internal

* relations [MS.]

merely, we can reach no better result. The terms here once again are no more than abstractions. Taken each as real independently, and apart from some whole, they are things which cannot be found to exist in any actual experience. And once viewed as real, each in and by itself, there is no way in which they could pass or be carried beyond themselves so as to generate a relation.

An actual relation, we may remind ourselves, must possess at once both the characters of a 'together' and a 'between', and, failing either of these, is a relation no longer. Hence our terms cannot make a relation by passing themselves over into it bodily. For in that event their individuality, and with it the required 'between', would be lost. All that we could have left would be another form of experience, now no longer relational, qualifying which directly our terms would have ceased to be terms. On the other hand, if, to remain themselves, our terms retain their character as individuals, there is no legitimate way (we have seen) to their union in fact. We are without the 'together', which (like the 'between') is essential if any relation is to be actually there.

And it is idle here once again to fall back on a real distinction to be found in our terms, and to seek once more to solve our problem by a division of respects. It is useless to urge that the terms really in one respect can pass beyond themselves, and by that self-surrender make the unity required for the relation, while none the less in another respect the same terms save the relation's character by still each preserving its own. Any* such plea, we have long ago seen, would be futile (pp. 637–8). Far from solving the problem offered, it is but the transference of that problem still unsolved into the nature of the individual terms. The diversity between, and the union together, of the 'respects' taken within each term raise the old dilemma, still insoluble and still unavoidable if we keep to relational experience. And no attempt to show there how the same thing can at once remain within, and still pass outside, itself can in the end avoid self-contradiction—while to fall back on a covert

* But any [MS.]

appeal to what holds at the stage of feeling is once more illegitimate and useless. It is, as we have seen, an attempt to meet the just claims of relational experience by a fraudulent offer of drawing on that which only within a non-relational experience can be valid.

Mere internal relations, then, like relations that are merely external, are untenable if they make a claim to ultimate and absolute truth. But taken otherwise, and viewed as helpful makeshifts and as useful aids in the pursuit of knowledge, external and internal relations are both admissible and can be relatively real and true. And the distinction made between what is intrinsic and extrinsic, or between what we call essential and (on the other side) accidental only,* may not only be legitimate, but can in various degrees have genuine importance. The relations, obviously, in which a man stands, can be taken as due to his own character or ascribed, again, more or less to external facts and events. And to object to such a distinction, when confined within its proper limits, would be obviously mistaken and even ridiculous.

But the distinction holds just so far as we are able in practice to take the nature of our individual term as double. A term in the end (we have seen) can stand in no relation into which it itself does not enter. But on the other side, if the relation is not to be destroyed, the term's entrance cannot (we have also seen) be entire and made bodily. It must be no more than partial and confined to what we call 'a certain respect'. But the question as to how that part of the term which enters in is related to that part which remains outside leaves us (we may remind ourselves once more) with a final contradiction.

Still in practice, and for a limited purpose, you can divide your individual term, and take one part as what you call 'essential'. And so far as this division is made, the distinction between intrinsic and extrinsic relations will hold. Wherever that part of your term which you select as

* [The MS. here is very much corrected. It is possible that we ought to read 'or between what we call "really essential" and (on the other side) "accidental only and circumstantial"'.]

its essence remains outside of some relation, into which the
individual term enters, the relation so far is extrinsic. And
on the other hand, where the entrance of the term includes,
and carries into the relation, the essence also as in one with
the whole term, the relation here is intrinsic. But no such
distinction, if I may repeat this, can have more than relative
validity.

Your individual term is an abstraction always. It implies what we may call a selection from the concrete fact of
the whole and entire experience. And the* question in
every case is as to how far your selection has been carried.
How much of the fact, that is, has it abstracted and fixed
within an individual term, and secured so that you can take
it as your term's essence?† Any relation involved in‡ that
result will be intrinsic. And on the other hand, where
any§ relation goes beyond that special limit,‖ it will belong
to the term only so far as that is taken as in one with the
whole relational fact, and will so far be but external. But
the above abstraction, however much it may serve, must
remain in the end indefensible.

Every term in every possible relation¶ is due to, and
involves, abstraction. And the idea that, apart from its
implication beyond itself in some whole, you could possibly,
starting from any kind of term, pass in any way beyond its
limits is to me a radical error.** And a hard division, made

* 'the [crucial] question' [MS.]
† 'essence? [What is the extent of that which has thus been made the
essence of your individual term?] [omit?].' [MS.]
‡ 'involved in [and to be recovered from]' [MS.]
§ [Or 'where the relation'. Neither alternative is struck out in the MS.]
‖ 'limit [made by your abstraction]' [MS.]
¶ 'relation [such at least is my view]' [MS.]
** *Footnote on Similarity.*
The above will hold even in the case of suggestion by similarity—where
from one idea we are supposed to pass directly to another idea like it, which
it excites by similarity.

In the first place, the exciting idea (taken by itself) is not a fact, but an
abstraction; for it comes and must come to us only as in one with the whole
comp⟨lex⟩ psychical fact of the moment.

And, in the second place, it is only because of the identity between itself
and what it excites—an identity present as what we call a 'disposition' left

anywhere between what is internal merely and what is
external only, together with the distinction anywhere
drawn between (on the one hand) essence and (on the
other hand) mere circumstance or mere matter of fact,
cannot in the end be accepted. It may be justified in
practice, I agree; but it cannot, I must insist, be offered
as anything which possesses ultimate truth and reality.[12]

(iv) I will next take the question whether a relation is
essentially single or plural, and will further ask if in any
case its plurality can be more than dual. Deferring this
latter point, we may anticipate the answer that a relation
must be both single and plural, though to reconcile these
characters without a contradiction is in the end not
possible. And when we recall our previous result—that in
every relational experience there must be terms and also
their unity, and that this experience (we had to conclude)
cannot in the end be justified—our present question may
seem perhaps unnecessary. But the discussion of it may
in any case, I hope, direct attention to problems at once
difficult and important.

How far, and in what sense, does every relation (we may
ask) involve what may be called a 'passage'? We have
seen that a relational experience, taken in its strict sense,
is beyond the stage of mere feeling and of mere'inherence',
and is in its essence discursive. It has to contain terms and
a 'between'; and must it not also (we have to ask) involve
a 'way' and a 'passage' in the sense of a going actually from
one term to another? In the case of some relations an
'order' and 'direction' we find admitted to be essential,
though in others this feature seems at least to be non-
essential and at first sight even quite absent. Still, considering further, we are led to ask with regard to every
relation, no matter of what kind, whether for its existence,
if not also for its essence, a passage always is required, and
what a 'passage' in the end must be taken to mean. Does
it, not to mention anything more, involve at least the

by previous experience—that we are able to pass to the excited idea. The
connexion once more will be through an implied totality. Refer to my
Logic. [*Note by the author.*]

element of time, if not also of space; and are we to say that apart from at least one, or both, of these characters there can exist in the proper sense no relational experience—even if in what we call the 'essence' of the relation these characters can be ignored?

Such questions, we may all perhaps agree, are not easy to answer; and for myself they raise a further difficulty as to the precise form in which what is temporal and spatial appears, while experience is still at the stage of feeling and is below the level at which relations in the proper sense are developed. I cannot, however, even attempt to deal here with these problems, the importance and the difficulty of which I certainly recognize. And for our present purpose an answer to this question as to the final nature of that which in a relation we have called 'passage' is (I venture to think) not necessary.

We may content ourselves here by repeating that a relation in the strict sense is always an abstraction. The relation itself is not the entire fact of the relational situation, as actually experienced, but in every case omits and ignores more or less of what there is contained. And in the amount omitted relations can differ. Some can make a complete abstraction from what is implied in the aspect of passage with its order and direction, while in other relations more or less of this aspect is to be found, and is taken as essential to, and as meant by, the relation itself. But since the relation in no case offers us unabridged the entire fact of the relational experience, we here, I think, can leave unanswered this question as to the ultimate meaning and sense of 'passage'. For some feature, which we take the actual experience to contain, can fail (we have seen) more or less to appear in, and make part of, the relation's 'meaning' and 'essence'.[13]

And in any case our former difficulty will remain unremoved. Every relation must contain a diversity in the form of individual terms; and, on the other hand, unless the relation is one, the relation is destroyed. And there is no way, we found, in which these characters can legitimately be combined. And we hence must here accept the result that a relation must certainly be both single and plural, though to assert this conclusion as an ultimate truth is not permissible.

We may pass on to deal with a further question as to a relation's plurality. We* have seen that, since there must be two terms, a relation at least must be dual. But a relation's plurality, it may be contended, in some cases is more, and can amount to what is called 'multiple'. But before I discuss this final point, I will ask leave, at the cost of a digression, to notice an objection which has been urged against what is called Monism. In at least some relations we find (it is agreed) an order, and a direction which is not reversible; and this admitted fact, since inexplicable by any Monism, raises against it an objection which admits of no answer.

The objection seems however, so far at least as I am concerned, to rest on a grave misunderstanding. It stops, in the first place, short of that, to which in principle it should be led. For not one kind of relation, but every and any relation, if taken as an ultimate reality, would (on any view such as mine) be fatal to Monism. And, apart from this, the objection seems to assume not only that all Monism is based on the fact of 'simple inherence', but that it also implies that in this experience we are to find ultimate and absolute reality.

Now, so far as my Monism is concerned, I take an opposite view. Simple inherence, if relational, is to my mind self-contradictory. And, taken as non-relational and in the form of mere feeling, any such experience must on my view fail to reach ultimate truth and reality. For nothing, I have urged, which is not all-inclusive and complete, can satisfy that want and demand, in which we find our criterion of Reality—a want and demand which to me obviously and plainly cannot be satisfied by mere feeling. Reality on my view is doubtless infra-relational, but doubtless again it is relational, and in neither of these characters is it ultimate. It is only in what is super-relational, and is at once neither and both of the above, that we can find,

* And we [MS.]

I think, a Reality which is ultimate and absolute. And of course, if this conclusion is erroneous, my Monism is wrecked. But to ignore this conclusion, or to exclude it by some bare assumption, seems to myself not permissible.

And if I am told that in any case Monism, if it is to stand, must be able to explain, and to exhibit more or less in detail, the positive 'how' of the universe—that again is what I deny. On no conceivable view can, I should say, the world become explicable throughout; and some feature of the world left unexplained can serve to refute a general view only so far as it can be shown that, if that view were true, this particular feature should be explicable.* But, once again, this is not a matter for sheer assumption.

And if it is urged, finally, that since relations of every kind are, in the end, no more irrational than is everything else there can be no reason for not accepting them all as ultimately real—I am at no loss for a reply. I have shown in the first place that relational experience has to fall back on a non-relational form of unity, and is therefore not ultimate. And even experience in the non-relational form of feeling I myself do not accept as ultimate reality. Nothing to myself is real ultimately but that super-relational unity of the One and Many, which is at once the consummation and the pre-condition of all and everything.[14]

To return from what I fear has been too long a digression, I will notice a further question as to the sense of a relation's plurality. This, we have so far seen, must at least be dual. But it has been urged by Mr. Russell that, beyond mere duality, we must accept relations which are multiple. Such a conclusion I have however not found myself able to accept.†[15]

* * * * *

* *App.*, Index, *s.v.* Inexplicable; and p. 556 [9th impression, p. 494]. [*Note by the author.*]
† See my *Essays*, the Index, *s.v.* Relations. [*Note by the author.*]

III

APPENDIX

Note on the Sources:—

THE following account of A, B, and W is inserted here, since all the passages quoted in the present Appendix have been drawn from one or other of these sources. References to the original paging are given throughout for the convenience of future students who may desire to examine the manuscripts, should the latter eventually be accessible in the Bradley Library.

(1) 'A' contains about forty-six closely written pages. After an Index, the first entry begins on a page numbered 'p. 6', and seems in fact to be the continuation of three loose sheets of manuscript which were enclosed in the book.[1] This entry—obviously a rough draft of the beginning of the article —is interrupted on p. 14 by a note on the 'intuitive understanding' (a subject dealt with again on p. 43 and pp. 46–7). On p. 15 there is a draft for the treatment of a difficulty in regard to the primitive form of temporal and spatial experience, so as to meet a possible objection to Bradley's view (stated on pp. 11–14) that relational experience presupposes feeling.

Then follow entries (isolated or loosely connected with one another) which together cover all or most of the topics to be discussed in the article. Thus pp. 16–17, 22–4, and 34–45 are drafts (in different stages of completion) for the treatment of the distinctions between 'external' and 'internal', and 'extrinsic' and 'intrinsic' relations. On p. 24, and again on p. 45, there are drafts for a discussion (in connexion with 'extrinsic' and 'intrinsic' relations) of Hume's distinction between 'relations of mere ideas' and 'matter of fact'. Then, at the end of the entry on 'extrinsic' and 'intrinsic', there is a Note (p. 43, and again on p. 47 with a reference to the earlier page) that the article is to conclude 'with some general remarks about the relational view as valid, though not ultimately true, and how it is to be transcended', or whether the ultimate result is 'Scepticism'. On pp. 18–21 Bradley, starting with a quotation from Professor Alexander's *Space Time and Deity*, develops some of the main contradictions involved in relational experience, justifies his own description of it as a 'makeshift', and sketches and defends his conception of the 'one individual which is real and true'. There is a reference back to this passage on p. 55, where Bradley refutes the suggestion that asymmetrical relations disprove Monism. Pages 24 *a*, 25, and 26 show that every relation is both single and dual (involving a 'passage') and discuss whether (or in what sense) relations can be 'multiple'; and another treatment of the same subject occurs on pp. 32–3. Lastly, there are two different drafts (the first on pp. 27 *a*, 29, and 31, and the second on pp. 27, 28, and 30) for a discussion of the question whether relations differ in degree.

---

[1] These loose sheets are numbered on both sides (1, 2, 2, 3, 4, 5), but one of the sides numbered '2' is a first draft of pp. 4 and 5.

Towards the end of A—possibly, though not certainly, later in date than the rest of its contents—there are two Sketches for an outline of the article.[1] Sketch No. 1 (pp. 49, 48, 51 *a*, and 51 *b*) is confined to the opening section —i.e. covers what would probably have constituted the first third of the *undivided* article. Sketch No. 2 (pp. 57, 58, 59, and 60) in some respects goes further. So far as concerns the opening section of the article, No. 2 is more elaborate than No. 1, mapping out in greater detail the questions that are to be discussed in regard to 'feeling'.[2] Further, No. 2 contains an explicit statement that the contradictions in relational experience are to be 'drawn out in detail later' (p. 58). And it ends with a 'Recapitulation' (reproduced below, Note 8, p. 658) which is clearly intended to summarize the entire contents of the *undivided* article.

(2) It is possible—on the whole, perhaps, even probable—that in B we have a rough draft of the *undivided* article, to be identified with the 'outline', 'full abstract', or 'full sketch' mentioned in Bradley's letters of 1923 and 'finished' by March 23rd of that year.[3] B presupposes and uses most of the contents of A—even, apparently, the two Sketches at the end of the book.[4] It seems to cover more or less the whole ground of the *undivided* article, though in two respects it fails to follow the order of exposition which the 'Recapitulation' implies.[5] For (i) B *ends* with the detailed criticism of relational experience—whereas the author's intention (to judge by the 'Recapitulation') was to revert to the question of the 'purity' and 'priority' of feeling, and to conclude the article with a re-statement of his view that 'what is ultimately real must contain, and also go beyond' both feeling and relations. And (ii) the passage in B (pp. 6–10) showing that, and why, feeling 'does *not* (as it is) contradict itself' comes *after* the general exposition of the self-contradictions inherent in relational experience—not *before* it, as the 'Recapitulation' would lead us to expect.[6]

But the identification of B with the 'outline' mentioned in Bradley's letters is far from certain. For a comparison of B with C[7] shows that nearly all the contents of the former are reproduced in a fuller and more final

---

[1] There are four unmistakable references to B in these Sketches, viz. on pp. 51 *b*, 57, and 58 (*bis*). But the exact date of B is uncertain; and in any case the references may have been inserted long after the Sketches were written.

[2] Some of these questions are dealt with in an entry on pp. 52 and 53; and the author has inserted cross-references between these pages and pp. 58 and 59 of Sketch No. 2.

[3] See the extracts quoted in the Introductory Note (above, p. 628, n. 1).

[4] In spite of the references to B, which these Sketches contain (see above, n. 1).

[5] There is nothing to suggest that the 'Recapitulation' is of later date than the rest of Sketch No. 2.

[6] See below, Note 8, pp. 658 and 659.

[7] C is the unfinished draft of the first part of the divided article: see Introductory Note, p. 629.

version by the latter. It is true, no doubt, that nothing is said in C to show why it is impossible for 'finite beings in a world of change' to rest satisfied in feeling; that certain 'doubts as to the purity and priority of feeling', as well as the question whether it 'involves contradiction in its essence', are set aside in C for later discussion;[1] and that, on the other hand, these subjects are sketched, more or less fully, on p. 4 and pp. 6–10 of B. But these omissions or postponements are obviously not incompatible with the view that B is simply an earlier draft of C—in other words that B is an 'outline' not of the *undivided*, but of the first part of the *divided* article.

(3) W, or 'MS. Book W', is the latest of a series of notebooks which Bradley used to record the results of his philosophical reading and reflections. The earliest entry in W presupposes the publication of *Essays on Truth and Reality*, i.e. is later than 1914; and the book was still in use. The paging is on both sides and is continued to p. 78; and about seventy of these pages are filled with entries, closely written and remarkably free from erasures or corrections. There are notes amongst the entries, and drafts for the discussion and solution of problems drawn from almost every field of philosophical inquiry—psychology, aesthetics, ethics, logic, metaphysics, and philosophy of religion; and, in addition, critical studies, e.g. of Russell's *Analysis of Mind*, Alexander's *Space Time and Deity*, Sir Henry Jones's *A Faith that enquires*, and Professor Parker's *The Self and Nature*.

There are references in A and B to pp. 22, 23, 43, 45, and 71–73 of W; and pages 43 and 45 are reproduced in Notes 11 and 12 below (pp. 665–7).

NOTE 1

The question of relations, their ultimate nature and place in the world of reality and of knowledge, is obviously so large and so central that to deal with it satisfactorily would involve a treatise. This I naturally am not attempting in the present article. My object here is to be allowed not so much to justify as to explain. I find myself with a view as to relations for which I claim no originality, and which seems to me the only tenable view. . . . Even if faulty, that view, I venture to think, is instructive. And I hope that an explanation, however defective and even dogmatic, may be excusable.   [B, p. 1.]

NOTE 2

This perfect experience, which is absolute truth ⟨and⟩ reality, cannot (as I have so often urged) be fully realized intellectually either by the understanding or by any form of intuition. It is the complete union not of one side but of every side of our being and experience. It is feeling, will, sense, and understanding in one. And though from any one side it can be approached and enjoyed, it cannot be fully there except from all sides at once in a way which, in

---

[1] Cf. above, p. 633 and p. 635; and below, Note 8, pp. 658 and 659.

and for finite beings, is not possible. But this is the one 'ultimate' and criterion of truth and reality. And in this sense neither feeling nor relational experience is ultimate and final. But if you ask whether each alike is fundamental, a different answer must, I think, be given. For relational experience involves and depends on feeling in a way in which feeling does not imply or depend on relational experience. [B, p. 9.]

NOTE 3

I will first explain briefly what I mean by immediate experience or feeling. I have dealt with this in *Appearance*, *Essays*, and *Logic*, to the Indexes of which I would refer the reader. [B, p. 2.]

NOTE 4

I myself venture to think that everywhere, in the individual as in the race, this stage ⟨viz. feeling⟩ comes first in development. And I think that, as it comes first, it is free throughout from relations and so may be taken as pure. An awareness, say, of temporal and spatial diversity, as it comes first, does not to my mind wear a relational form.

This seems evident, if we agree that in relations in the proper sense a passage to and fro between the terms is implied. And to maintain that this is to be found in the first awareness of temporal and spatial diversity seems an untenable view. Hence, though to be clear as to the undeveloped form of space and time is (I admit) difficult, I consider this to be the more acceptable alternative.

If however we hesitate to affirm this, we must admit that, so far, where these ⟨spatial and temporal diversities⟩ are present, the whole experience cannot throughout be called pure. There will, that is, be parts of it where, within each, the character of the whole awareness will not be carried out fully. Of course I do not mean that the character of the whole is thereby vitiated throughout, for that would destroy it. What I mean is that within the fluid whole there would be clots, inside which the character of the whole would fail to be there—and something further would be there, though (apart from their 'insides') these, as all else, would be contained in and qualify the whole, and it them. [B, pp. 2–3.]

And if a difficulty is raised as to temporal and spatial experience, and how this can be there in a non-relational felt form, I admit the difficulty—as to this form. But that at worst only shows that the felt is never pure throughout. The oneness of the felt whole remains; only in it are diversities which *internally*, when you consider that aspect of them, are not concordant with the general character. They, however, *as wholes* are so, and *are* felt detail each as a whole —the internal discordance being ignored.   [A, p. 15.]

[For the 'passage' implied in every relation, see above, pp. 647–8.]

NOTE 5

If you ask for reality, you must have that ⟨i.e. feeling⟩ at least, however much else you also have. The 'this', 'now', and 'mine' are irremovably there, or the 'real' is not there. This to my mind is so plain, that I don't know how to argue for it. Of course it is transcended, but still remains contained in whatever transcends it—so that the universe, if it could cease to be 'mine', however much else it is, would become unreal except as an abstraction.

From this we can arrive at once at a conclusive result. If the contents of feeling have the form that I have described, and if a relational fact has also the form I have shown, then a mere relation cannot be immediately experienced. Relations of course, like everything else, that is, are immediately experienced, but never as relations in the proper sense, simply and merely as such. Relations are nothing if not conjunctive; but what is merely conjunctive so far does not belong to immediate experience, and cannot in that character enter into feeling. And yet, since it is nothing if not felt, a relation enters into immediate experience as a self-contradictory abstraction.

Hence to talk about immediate experience of mere relations of various kinds as fact is to me absurd. The felt unity is there, and hence the *mere* experience of relations is not there as fact, but as an abstraction made by the understanding.

This view may be wrong; but to ignore it, and to talk about relations as given directly in our immediate experience, without (apparently) an idea that they [i.e. those who use such language] can be held to mistake abstractions for given reality, seems to me really remarkable.[1]   [A, pp. 48–9.]

NOTE 6

I have taken, and must take, as a fact the immediate non-relational experience of diversity and oneness in unbroken union. There are those, I know, who at least seem to deny this and to

---

[1] On the position taken here by Professor James I have remarked in my *Essays*, pp. 149 ff. To these pages I would venture to invite an attention which I think they have never received. [*Note by the author.*]

maintain that all unity of diversity is in the end relational; and that, except perhaps as a mere illusion, the above fact is not anywhere experienced. But, since to discuss rationally one must first understand, I cannot attempt to discuss their position. . . . I do not understand how any thinking person can maintain that in the objects, which in sensuous perception we take as one, the unity is throughout experienced as relational and that, say, in a green leaf the greenness and the other perceived qualities are not unified apart from relational couplings. I do not understand how emotional wholes are not experienced as one, or how their oneness can be reduced to experienced interrelation. I understand of course the thesis that all reality at bottom and in truth is relational, and that any experience to the contrary is in the end more or less illusory. But that the illusion should as an actual experience be apparently denied or ignored, this I confess is beyond me. And I must with regret so leave the matter.

I do not mean that the holder of a thesis is bound to explain everything which seems to look like an experience to the contrary. This is not my opinion. It is the apparent refusal to recognize any such experience, even as an experienced fact, [1]which I cannot think justifiable.[1]

I had hoped at least to learn from Mr. Russell's *Analysis of Mind* what view he takes as to an actual or possible experience of a non-relational union of oneness and diversity. But this hope ended for myself in complete disappointment. Mr. Russell does not even raise the question whether everything distinguishable has, in and by itself, reality. He seems to start, on the other hand, with the assumption that every mental fact can be analysed in the sense of being shown to be a relational complex—where, that is, it fails to be an atomic unit whether as a sensation or a relation. And of this enormous assumption he appears to be so sure that, when it fails to work in his hands, he (in this respect unlike J. S. Mill) believes that with another man it might work and that the fault so far is his own.

With regard to 'feeling' used to designate some whole of which we are directly aware—the contents of which whole are not unified by a relational framework, but qualify one another and their whole immediately—Mr. Russell feels himself justified apparently in treating any such view as negligible, even to the extent of ignoring its existence as an actual error. But in his own use of 'feeling' Mr. Russell not only seems to my mind to be inconsistent but even,

[1-1] which I think needs to be justified. [*Correction added in pencil by the author.*]

where convenient, to lapse into the very view which he appears to regard as a negligible error.

The question as to what makes the togetherness of this or that relation with these or those sensations (where they happen to be together in fact) is naturally ignored. But what surprised me was to find that Mr. Russell apparently fails to perceive that what has been called 'the problem of Inherence'—the question, that is, of a non-relational qualification—arises even with regard to the atoms themselves. Whether diversity and similarity, or either of them, are 'relations', I am unable to say; but, so far as they are such, they can hardly qualify the units except relationally and from the outside. But passing this by, if we aim at consistency we seem forced to take the ultimate units, whether 'terms' or 'relations', as simple—as mere 'qualities', free from the least internal diversity. But how a relation (or all relations) can be so taken as merely simple, I do not understand. And with regard to 'sensations', if these possess themselves either feeling-tone or strength (which apparently is the case), we have to ask if this diversity can qualify the simply one. If you take the qualification as internal and as non-relational, the whole ultimate assumption as to analysis seems forthwith wrecked; while, if you take the diversity as relational, and as so stuck on to the simple unit from the outside, you are in collision with what seems to be plain experience—to say nothing of the hopeless difficulty which arises with regard to the relatedness in fact of this or that relation with these or those units, of whatever kind they may be.

For myself, I consider that the use of fictions, however indefensible ultimately, is justified in psychology—so far as, and provided that, they work in explaining the facts. But I regret to add that I cannot find that, even if Mr. Russell were content to justify his analyses on this ground, there has been any success gained by the use of his principles such as seems to justify their ultimate unsoundness. [A, pp. 6–8.]

NOTE 7

Take a relational situation and examine it.[1] You cannot say that the terms are the relation or the relation is the terms. And you cannot say that the real fact is the relation and the terms; for obviously that is not enough, since the fact goes beyond a mere 'and'.[2]

[1] Ref. to *Appearance*. [*Note by author.*]
[2] 'Relatedness' here. Ref. for 'And' to *Logic* and *Appearance*. [*Note by author.*]

The relation (even if it is one of diversity) must be between, and must couple, *these* terms; and the terms must enter into *this* relation, which so far makes them one. But when you ask as to the where and how of this unity as a fact, you find no real answer except a tacit reference back to that unity of immediate experience, where many-ness and unity are one, and to remedy the failure of which the new view came in. And when you go to the terms, you fare no better. You certainly cannot say that they are the relation; and you cannot even say that somehow they 'make' the relation, any more than you can say that the relation somehow 'makes' them. And it is not even true that *they* enter into the relation; for, as individuals, while enter-ing into what is 'between', they must, to save the 'between', no less remain outside. . . . [B, p. 5.]

NOTE 8

Note by the editor:—

According to the original plan of the article, it is clear from both A and B, this question would have been treated here. Thus (i) there is in A the draft for a 'Recapitulation' (cf. above, *Introductory Note*, p. 652) which runs as follows:—

'We have seen what is meant by immediate experience or feeling, taken as union of one and many. We have described its nature and shown that it exists unquestionably.

'We have seen that ⟨it⟩ is not an ultimate answer to ⟨the⟩ ques-tion as to what is real in the end. It does *not* (as it is) contradict it-self; but it, as such, cannot keep its place. In finite beings in time there tends to be a clash; and when we try to mend this theoretically, then feeling does and must contradict itself, because it can't supply its "how"—even apart from practical collision.

'Hence relational experience. Its nature has been described, which does and must contradict itself since it depends on a unity, which is not relational, and hence itself by itself fails to be anything as a whole. It is a necessary and useful way of advance, but remains a makeshift.

'Feeling is more ultimate; but whether prior in time we agreed to leave doubtful, as also whether it ever was or is pure. Usually it is not pure, but contains relational matter—as "clots" merely.

'Hence neither is ultimately real. What is *that*, must contain, and also go beyond, both. This we may and do aim at, but cannot throughout verify in detail as fully reached and the sole reality of everything.'

And (ii) *approximately* the same order of treatment is followed in B, where the question 'whether feeling involves contradiction in its essence'

is discussed (and answered in the negative) not indeed—as the 'Recapitulation' in A implies—before the 'abstract' or general exposition of relational
experience, but before the detailed criticism of the discrepancies it entails
(cf. *Introductory Note*, p. 652).

But the author's decision (cf. letter of 17 Feb. 1924 quoted above, p. 629,
Note 1) to divide his material, so as to make of it an article in two parts, led
to a modification of the original plan. It became necessary to put off 'the
discussion of some serious difficulties to the latter part'—and amongst them,
no doubt, *this* 'difficulty' about feeling and its essential freedom from contradiction. Unfortunately, the second part of the article was never written;
but the following extracts from A and B may be taken as rough indications of
the lines along which his treatment of this 'difficulty' (and of other connected
difficulties in regard to feeling) would probably have been developed.

What is to 'understand'? It is to have the real as something before
us as an object, so that our mind can pass, as to its diversity, from
one of the many differences to another, and from each and all to the
One, and from the One to each and all—and do this without thereby
altering the real so as to make it to be another one and cease to be
the same, in the sense of becoming a fresh one generally, or (more
specially) by causing it (as we take it) to show a jar and a break in its
continuity. . . .

But in what is felt, or experienced immediately, there is no question so far of 'understanding' in this sense. If we have one simple
feeling (I do not ask if we ever do or can) no diversity would be there
or could even be suggested. And, given that diversity, we may have,
in feeling, so far no object and in any case no passage from this
feature or aspect to that. We have simple qualification of each by
the other, and all by the whole which they qualify, and there is hence
no question of any intellectual contradiction nor any inquiry as to
'how'. And if we reflect on this, still, so far as we keep to it, we
meet with no difficulty. If and so far as we take it as it comes and is,
the felt is ultimate and real. And it is 'unintelligible', so far, only
in the sense that to try to understand it is to transform it into something beyond itself and something not itself.

I will not ask here whether, and how far, and in what sense the
apprehension of a change in reality, the mere presence of an object
for a self, and the experience of passivity and activity (these cannot
be divided) already involve a transcendence of the level of mere feeling. What we are assured of is that practical collision, and struggle
in what is felt, is what forces reflection, and makes it impossible
merely to take as it comes the union of sameness and difference, the
one and the many. And when change is felt as alteration, the passage beyond mere feeling has been made. That something should be

itself and yet not itself, and be both at once and in one, and combine the 'here' and 'now' with the 'there' and 'gone'—cannot be taken as real just as it comes. We have passed beyond simple apprehension. . . .   [A, p. 2 and pp. 4–5 on loose sheets.]

Feeling satisfies us as long as it keeps its form and does not clash. We should never ask for understanding if it didn't clash. But it does clash, and therefore to seek a remedy by going beyond it is necessary. How and why does it clash? It clashes practically in life, and it must do ⟨so⟩ because we are finite beings in a world of change.

But is it even satisfactory as to its form? No: when we reflect on it, we see that it is not so, because its matter and form are not really connected, but only so in form. Hence it does not contradict itself while it remains mere feeling, but it does so when we have taken the way of ideas and ask for truth—*then* we see that, even internally, there was a necessity for a clash.

Contradiction proper may be said to belong only to the world of ideas and truth. It is the failure to take Reality as an ideal union of the One and Many without an internal collision. . . . Our remedy by ideas succeeds only so far as we do this, and we never succeed in doing this except partially—though partial success is a necessary way of advance. We seek also to remedy our failure by construction of beauty, but this is *not* truth. And we seek again to do this in and by intuition—but that again fails, except partially.

But in feeling there is no contradiction, because there is no attempt at analysis—with its separation of the One and Many, and the attempt to rejoin them otherwise (i.e. by ideas and truth), and the opening of the question of 'how' and 'why' and the problem of mediation. On the other hand in relations in the proper sense this analysis and abstraction are necessarily involved, and the question of contradiction is raised and must be faced. [A, pp. 51 *a* and 51 *b*.]

Experience (to repeat this) as immediate union of one and many (as above described) so far as it goes is ultimate, both as being there and as being irremovable. . . . And, so far as it goes, it is satisfactory. Unless, that is, . . . the diverse contents are or become such that they refuse to comply with the form, no criticism is possible. There is no self-contradiction, because there is no question of any 'how'—⟨how⟩ this can be that and the whole everything. The 'is' is final and, so far as it goes, is enough.

But in the confusing[1] detail of finite existence, its medley and its refusal in practice to comply throughout with the form, a struggle

---

[1] ['Confusing' seems to be the word intended.]

must ensue, in which the form of immediate experience is helpless. And to live we are forced beyond it, and led to adopt more or less a relational way of knowledge. And this, though necessary and the one way of advance, is (I shall now go on to show), if you take it as ultimate truth, a self-contradictory makeshift.   [B, p. 4.]

Well, but why not agree (i) that the mediated or relational view depends in the end for its unity on the unity of an immediate felt whole, and so far rests upon that; and yet (ii) like the immediate whole may and must be taken as an ultimate fact, with regard to which to ask if it contradicts itself is unnecessary and improper? Why not swallow also and equally this second undigested vital necessary? . . .

Now what I have said is that the felt as it comes, and so far as we keep to it, is real undeniably. It is not self-contradictory, nor is it unintelligible in the sense of refusing to be understood or as itself at once implying and frustrating a claim of the intelligence. It has (where not simple—if it ever is so) the features or aspects (or call them what you will) of diversity and unity in one. And you may attend to these, so as to recognize them as there, without altering them and without any analysis in the sense of applying the category of Whole and Parts. You can say that the felt combines unity and diversity, and does not do so analytically—but somehow otherwise, though positively.

At this stage (I have agreed) it is impossible to remain. This union of one and many (I have shown) is broken and torn in practical conflict and then theoretically. And so far as this happens, it becomes self-contradictory and (as above) unintelligible . . . and (if you will) no better than the relational view which follows. The difference is that this second view cannot be called a felt fact. The felt so far as relational (time and space) is not felt in a relational form, while the second view is obviously an attempt to satisfy a claim which it admits. It is provoked by the break-down of feeling in its unreflect-ing discord. It is an attempt, by analysis and the application in some sense of Whole and Parts, to take the immediate union in the felt *otherwise*, so as to satisfy our intellectual want—which it therefore recognizes and admits as a criterion of reality. This the first view does not do, so long as it is true to itself.

I agree that, so far as you describe the felt so as to analyse it and make a claim to have understood it (and to describe it, without so doing more or less, is not possible—though it is possible provision-ally and subject to understood negations), the felt has ceased to be a felt fact. It has, so far also, itself become a self-contradictory attempt to be intelligible and is on the same level, so far, as the relational view—i.e. the level of makeshift and fiction. But then it need not so be taken. It can be taken otherwise and yet as positive, whereas the relational view cannot be. *It* is an attempt to satisfy the understanding—or it is nothing—and, as such an attempt, for *it* to rest in the end on the mere felt is suicidal. But the first view (while, as a theory, it is equally suicidal) has behind it in a non-theoretical form the immediate fact; and so far as it keeps to that as merely immediate, as combining ('how' it does not understand) certain recognizable aspects, it is not suicidal, because making no claim to satisfy an understanding—the need for, and nature of, which it does not even (so far) recognize. . . .

[A, pp. 11–12.]

Feeling . . . combines the two aspects of 'one' and 'many' so as not to contradict itself nor to be rejected as unintelligible; but this holds only so long and so far as it remains pure and non-relational and non-reflective. I do not hold that, when and so far as we reflect on feeling, it can stand that[1] in theory, any more than it can remain in finite beings whole and secure in practice. I mean that, while it is merely itself, it makes no claim to be understood. It does not offer itself as intelligible, and so does not at once imply and ignore, and admit while in fact refusing to satisfy and frustrating, a demand of the intelligence—since, where there is as yet no question of any 'how' or 'why', and where and so far as there is no attempt to predicate,[2] there may be jar and struggle, but there can be no self-contradiction in any strict sense.

As soon as you analyse the felt, you so far destroy it as such. And in any attempt to describe it in words we tend perforce to adopt the attitude of analysis, and to surrender ourselves to the necessary form of the discursive understanding and apply to some extent the category of Whole and Parts. But this tendency can be resisted. We can attend to the diversity of its aspects (in union), and apprehend and recognize this as a positive fact,[3] and set this fact down truly and in a sense describe it. We can, that is, while describing, at the same time warn ourselves that our description must be taken throughout

[1] [After 'that' there is an illegible word of four letters (? 'long') in the MS.]

[2] [Cf. 'There is in the strict sense no predication here' (i.e. in immediate experience) 'for that implies a relation—just as, taken in the full sense, even distinction does so' (B, p. 2).]

[3] [The author may have intended the sentence to run: 'We can attend to, and apprehend and recognize, the diversity of its aspects (in union) as a positive fact.']

with, and subject to, a reserve. We thus can recognize in feeling taken as prior to distinctions and relations, already there that positive concrete character, that unity of the one and many, which distinction and relation and the whole way of ideas and discursive intelligence attempts to attain and carry out in its own manner, and at its later stage and level—though never in the end with complete success.

Thus the mode of union in immediate experience of sameness and diversity, of the one and the many, of the ideal and the real, can be taken as fundamental. It is not ultimate in the sense that we can remain there and be satisfied. But it is not as such false, because as such it makes no claim to be true; and as it ignores any question as to 'how' and 'why', it so far cannot fairly, while it remains itself, be rejected as unintelligible. You may say that it is, so far, not so much above or below, as it is outside of, falsity and truth.

It is otherwise with experience that is relational. That (we have seen) is beyond the stage where this can simply come to us as also that, and both diversities as One while their One is what it is as being each. It has become in essence reflective in the sense that, aiming to remedy a failure, it in effect admits the demand to reach truth; and because, offering an answer, it has raised the question of mediation and of 'how' and 'why', and has offered itself not merely as there, but as intelligible. It is inconsistent because (as we have seen), while it claims to have superseded and remedied the felt, it still rests upon that—or is dissipated, in the absence of any real Oneness[1] (*a*) within the relation itself or (*b*) within the terms which it unites. And an attempt to swallow whole a mass thus bristling with contradictions and falling asunder must thus end in failure.

[B, pp. 7–8.]

NOTE 9

Nothing in the end is real but the individual; and the individual is unique and (at least in my opinion) there is in the end but one individual which is real and true. And it is individuality that everywhere we seek, and with this alone can be satisfied more or less perfectly in so far as its realization is more or less complete. And individuality means the union of sameness and diversity, the presence in all of the One and of the One in everything, with the qualification of each by the other throughout and of the whole by all and everything—so that there is no actual or possible other than

---

[1] [Below 'Oneness' the MS. has 'individuality', which may have been intended as a correction.]

the One and, within the One, nothing can to anything else ever actually or possibly be merely other. And here, and here alone, can we escape from that self-contradiction which, everywhere short of this, is in varying degrees inseparable from our attempt to make the world intelligible. This is the claim inherent in feeling or immediate experience—a claim which we saw was not, could not be, there completely realized. And it is not merely to remedy our practical failure, but in the end to satisfy the same claim, that we are led to enter on the relational and discursive way of knowledge. Here we gain truth not merely useful, but real and increasing indefinitely—but never in the end free from self-contradiction, and stopping always and everywhere by its own nature necessarily short of that truth which has ceased to be other than, and different from, the true Reality.

[A, p. 20.]

. . . I would repeat first that every case of terms in relation is an individual and unique 'situation'—a whole, where any alteration on either side must affect the whole throughout and not leave that anywhere unaltered. There is no valid process, by which the opposite of this principle can be justified in the end. You can abstract legitimately, wherever such an abstraction is required as being serviceable; and any such abstraction is justified relatively and for its purpose, but not as such ultimately and absolutely. Of course it seems monstrous to say that the same relation cannot hold where the terms have become different, or that the same terms cannot as such acquire some altered relation. And it would be monstrous to insist on such a principle in practice, and to refuse everywhere to agree to what rests on a necessary abstraction.

And of course, again, to show in detail everywhere how the above principle holds of terms and relations alike, is, I agree, quite impossible. But once again I have to insist that an inability of this kind is not a ground of disproof, unless you assume that differences nowhere may be asserted unless the exact and particular point of diversity can be specified—an arbitrary assumption, the results of which have not, I imagine, been faced.[1]

To my mind there are in the end no such things as sheer sameness or mere diversity. And to my mind, again, every actual relation is a situation, which is an individual whole—which any kind of analysis and abstraction must, in the end, more or less falsify as such. On the other side, if we are to understand, the way of abstraction and analysis is necessary, and it is justified or not in any particular case according to what we gain or lose by it theoretically. And hence I

---

[1] See *Appearance*. [*Note by the author.*]

see no advantage in taking cases, where identity or difference between relational wholes is on either side denied or insisted on. The answer in every case is the same—that whatever serves best is justified, and may be taken as true relatively and so far as it serves best for a certain purpose.   [A, pp. 22–3.]

Note 10

Relations would be merely internal if, the terms being taken as real independently, each in itself, the relations between them (as a class, or in this or that particular case) in fact arose or were due merely to the character of the terms as so taken.

Such a view has truth in it, so far as it denies mere externality and, again, recalls the fact that every relation rests on a unity taken as an immediate whole, and again insists that any change in the internal character of the terms must (in some sense) alter also the relation. But, in going further and in denying wholly the external character of relations, it obviously to me either ignores or denies wholly the fact of relational experience—or else, while keeping it ostensibly, asserts of it what involves a destructive self-contradiction.

How far such a view has ever in fact been advocated, we need not consider. The attribution of it to Hegel rests, I should say, on a misinterpretation. We meet it nowadays as the consequence taken to follow from a foregone alternative between external and internal relations, the idea of neither being in the end true being at the same time ignored.

[A, p. 39: the first sentence has been inserted, in accordance with a note by the author, from an earlier draft in the same notebook.]

Note 11

'Relations are external only in abstract mathematics, in which the terms can be ranged side by side, and united by a sign which symbolizes their relation, without in any way modifying them. The number 8, for instance, will always remain the same number in all the relations in which it can be placed to other numbers: 8×4, $8+3$, $8-5$, $8 \div 2$, &c.' (Aliotta, *The Idealistic Reaction against Science*, pp. 336–7.)

This, if I remember rightly, is a going back to Hume's relations of ideas and matter of fact.[1] It's obviously plausible, and yet is untenable. The '8' remains the same number only so far as you abstract it—that is, if by 'same' you mean '*not* different' simply. The real difference is that in some cases you cannot show that

[1] [Cf. Note 12.]

and how a number, or a body in space, is altered by change of relation, and in others you can. In the first of these classes you can only prove that it must be so because the opposite is not possible.

In ideal construction you say that $6+2$ and $9-1$ are the same, and that 8 and 9 are different. The identity and difference are relations. Are they merely external? Then why one and not the other? Is it mere chance? And, if so, how and why predicate the result of the terms? Are they merely internal? Then how and why can you have the terms without them; and how and why one special arrangement rather than another, and apart from all the rest that are possible? You must have at least an ideal 'And' or 'Together', and that is external.

You cannot *show* the difference to the terms, but you prove it thus:—

Is there a difference or not? If none, the result is nothing. If any, where does it fall? If outside the whole, then (once more) nothing. If inside, then *where*? You cannot say. But, if inside and not elsewhere, then surely in the terms. And, if not, by what right do you predicate it of the terms? The conclusion therefore is that there is always a difference, and one *to* the terms; but that in some cases you can for certain purposes abstract from it more or less wholly, and can in other[1] cases more or less *see* it as affecting the terms.   [W, p. 43.]

To appreciate the doctrine of 'external' relations, take the case where you have identity or equality, or more and less or inequality or diversity in general. Say you have '$5+1=6$', or '6 does not equal 7', &c., &c. Here the relations are to make no difference to that of which they are predicated.

If so, is it a matter of pure chance *which* you have? Why one here, and not the other? Why not both at once? How can contraries exclude or be incompatible, if they make no difference—if one being there makes no difference to anything? And is it not monstrous to predicate, if this (whatever it is)[2] makes no difference to anything?

The answer is: 'But where *is* the difference? After all, 6 remains 6 throughout all its diverse contexts—one and unaltered.'

I reply: 'Yes, so far as you abstract and keep to your abstraction; but this is *(ex hyp.)* just what you *don't* do when you predicate. And so far as you *don't*, it's false that the "6" is one and the same simply.' To reply, 'If so, analyse and show exactly how it is affected (i.e. abstract the various affections, and show them as abstracted)', won't

---

[1] some [MS.]
[2] if this whatever it is (or *all* is) makes [MS.]

do, because I don't pretend to be able to analyse anything without residue.

And if you object 'Yes, but you admit yourself that there is an identical "6" in itself, of which you predicate alteration', I reply that I don't do this. There is no number at all apart from the context of other numbers—the whole world of number. And, more generally, no abstract element is anywhere as such real apart from some context ('And', 'Together', &c.).

And if you urge 'But then the "6" actually *is* whatever you can anywhere predicate of it'—this is not so. It is so, if you take the whole world of its possible predicates as actual. This is another further question I don't raise here. But what you predicated *as actual* was of the '6' *here*, under such and such conditions, *as actual* (whether as the abstract '6', or the '6' as specially here in '$5+1=6$'). Actual and possible have got to be distinguished.

Of course all the above becomes far worse, if a term can be related to itself. [W, p. 45.]

NOTE 12

No relation is *merely* intrinsic or external, and every relation is both. A relation may be called one or the other, according as its 'why' is supposed to be present and known or not; according as we have the individual whole, in and by which the relation holds, or fail to have it; and according as (to put the same thing otherwise) we can suppose the relation possibly absent. The appeal may be to a given perceived whole, or to an understood one. In neither case can it be sufficient to make the relation merely 'intrinsic'. [W, p. 43.]

Every relation . . . is both external and internal, and cannot be merely either. But still, taken relatively, this distinction is tenable as extrinsic and intrinsic, or as accidental and essential. (See Alexander, *S. T. and D.*, vol. i, pp. 249 ff.)[1]

It is tenable just so far as we are able to presuppose an 'individual' with a certain character, and ⟨depends upon⟩ whether in this character the relation is taken as included or is only super-imposed and contingent. It is plain that, in one case, for an individual to enter into certain relations belongs to his character and that, in[2] others, the entry depends on circumstances which fall outside that. But obviously this distinction holds just so far as you are able to take in the individual a double nature—an essence and accidents. *He* must everywhere go into the relation—that is clear—but he may go in different respects, and so be affected, but *not* in his essence.

[1] For this distinction I refer to Alexander, though I do not agree with him wholly. [*Note by the author.*]   [2] with [MS.]

But this distinction is not tenable ultimately. For it goes back to the distinction of ⟨the⟩ original nature and the nature as qualified by the relation, with its two 'respects' and 'in so fars'. . . . ⟨And⟩ the problem of a term with two 'respects' we found was insoluble. They can't qualify the term immediately; and, otherwise, the relational trouble breaks out insolubly inside the term, in the question how the part that goes into the relation is related to the part that stays outside.

[A, pp. 23-4. Some sentences have been inserted from p. 43 in accordance with references given by the author.]

This distinction ⟨of Extrinsic and Intrinsic, Accidental and Essential, &c.⟩ underlies Hume's distinction of relations of mere ideas and of matter of fact. In the first, you go from the mere ideas themselves to the relation, which therefore doesn't depend upon circumstances. In the second, you have a set of circumstances, in which you find a relation—which, therefore, you may or may not find in another and different set. Now it is not true that from two mere ideas you can logically develop a relation between them; for that conclusion requires a further premise, in the form of a whole to which they belong. And it is not even true that, without a further premise, you can even analyse, and show a relation within, one single idea.[1]

What is true is that, in one (*first*) case, you have all you want for a valid conclusion in the abstract and that, in the other (*second*) case, you have not—since 'matter of fact' implies always the presence of that which defies complete analysis, and leaves your further process at the mercy of some unknown and irrelevant factor. [A, p. 24.]

Recall here Hume's view. This is false on both sides. It is true that with mere ideas you may have all the knowledge you want, and with matters of fact not so. But it is false that you ever can go anywhere from one idea or more as simply themselves. Everywhere (*a*) a whole is involved, and everywhere (*b*) you abstract and your conclusion is abstract. It never can reach ultimate truth and reality. It never is true of *that*, since that is individual. And what in that falls outside your conclusion will therefore, so far as unknown, remain mere 'circumstance', 'matter of fact', and (if you will) mere conjunction. And so far as you abstract, you *can* go from 'matters of fact' to others—and you can't go otherwise. What is once true is always true, and otherwise is *not* true. But with matters of fact it's harder to abstract from mere circumstances, as you can't construct.

In both cases alike you are therefore left in the end with mere

---

[1] See my *Logic*. [*Note by the author.*]

circumstance and conjunction, because you cannot fill in *all* the conditions in either case. Even when you construct, you don't know exactly what 'whole' you use, and can't say exactly *how* your conclusion is real. Intellectual intuition seems (even so far as possible) no solution, as it remains ideal only and therefore abstract and therefore subject to circumstance and conjunction.[1] The only absolute truth is in an Absolute Experience which goes beyond truth.

[A, pp. 45 and 47.]

NOTE 13

Some relations (we naturally say) are the same each and either way. Others not so. This raises ⟨the⟩ question whether for a relation proper a 'way' is needed or not. If you say 'Yes, a relation is essentially discursive', then what is the 'way'?

(i) It seems certainly, so far, temporal. A relation seems to imply a passage, and a passage 'between'. Then, is there a backwards and forwards, and ⟨are there⟩ two directions, in *every* relation? Clearly so. Yet not in the same sense, since we have two classes of relation called 'symmetrical' and 'asymmetrical'. We may say perhaps that, while in all relations a passage is ⟨involved⟩,[2] yet in at least some relations the idea of passage and direction disappears, since that is not essential. In 'the relation' we abstract, and 'the relation' is an abstraction from our actual experience, and the temporal is dropped out.

(ii) But is every relation spatial? The question of how in the end we come to perceive the diversities in spatial perception comes in here, and is extremely difficult. Still, where order and direction essentially come in, is the difference here always spatial as well as temporal?

Perhaps *for reflection* some spatial schema is used in every case; but I should say ⟨it⟩ not only is not, but never was, involved everywhere.

(iii) Then, again, is the difference of what comes in and what goes out in the self with its felt expansion and contraction to be considered as a possible ground of diversity—and also the teleological character of this (*Essays*, pp. 308–9)? I am inclined on the whole to say that not every relation involves a *spatial* character, except when in a highly reflective form. But *temporal*—otherwise.

[A, pp. 25 and 24 *a*.]

[1] [Facing this sentence, on the opposite page (p. 46) of the Notebook, the author added: 'An intellectual construction or intuition can't stand simply in its own right as there, and as being and containing all that's wanted for ultimate truth and reality.']

[2] concerned [MS.]

It is true that relations can be divided into two classes, and that in one of these classes order and direction are taken as implied while denied of the other. But in the end passage (and, with passage, order) must be taken as present in all relations.

In the class where passage is denied it is still present; and, though ignored, we abstract from it and it is still there. It belongs (we should say) to the situation, only when you take that as psychological; and it does not make a part of 'the relation itself'. But, when we ignore or abstract from what here is irrelevant, we have 'the relation itself'. And that contains no passage, and is single—in its character (that is) of an abstraction.

In the other class such an abstraction is not admitted or admissible. From the passage and order, taken as merely psychological, we still of course continue to abstract; but we none the less assert their[1] presence in the relation itself. And here obviously the relation itself is admitted to be dual—whether we still do or do not also attempt to maintain that it is single.   [B, p. 19.]

There remains the interesting question as to how far the passage essentially involved in all relations is merely temporal, or whether it also everywhere must be spatial. This question would involve a discussion of the ultimate nature of the order and direction in time and space, and of the character of time and space as each first appears in experience. And even if I felt myself competent to deal with these problems, the space here would be lacking. But in any case I venture to think that our result as to the fundamental inconsistency of all relations would continue to stand.   [B, p. 20.]

Note 14

I will take here (as instructive) an argument against Monism.

Asymmetrical relations are said to disprove Monism, because Monism rests on *simple* inherence as the only way in which there is ultimate reality.

The argument, if right, is improperly limited—because *any* relations, *if so*, disprove Monism.

But Monism does not rest on simple inherence as the one form of reality. It even (in my case) says that that form is unsatisfactory (see *Appearance*).

Monism (with me) starts with the above form, but shows that it does not satisfy a want, which is to be satisfied only when the above imperfect solution is developed so as to be made perfect.

Of course also it is possible to base Monism on a given ultimate

---

[1] its [MS.]

principle (such, e.g., as the identity of thought and will or, again, time and space in one) which will contain, as already there, all that is implied in asymmetrical relations. That, however, is not my view.

Again, if it is meant ⟨that⟩ Monism must be prepared to explain everything—that I reject altogether. There is no view, I think, which conceivably could explain everything in detail—and no reason why it should do so, in order to be true.

Again, if it is said that at any rate asymmetrical relations are as ultimate as anything else, I dissent. *They* imply inherence, which does *not* imply them. Feeling *contains* everything, which clearly asymmetrical relations do not. Even if you urge that in all feeling there is change and so asymmetrical relation (at least implicit), in the first place I deny the fact; and, next, in any case the feeling of change is subordinate to the whole felt aspect of oneness.

Of course, if there is no unity which is non-relational or super-relational, then (I agree) there is no final unity of any kind and no Monism. But what a monstrously false assumption!   [A, p. 55.]

Of course I agree that to take the one reality as merely felt, or merely at the stage where qualities inhere non-relationally in their subject, is a fatal error. Obviously with this not merely one kind of relation, but every kind is left outside the real, and Monism therefore is impossible. But the assumption that every Monism in this way must commit suicide is to my mind untenable. Why, beyond the stage of relational development, there should not be a higher and all-inclusive reality, in which all contradictions are made good, I have always failed to understand. The demand to find this completed reality as a fact, and produce it and show it as fact to any kind of perception, to my mind is irrational. The criterion to my mind consists in the satisfaction of a demand. This is the criterion we all use, and all must use—unless we prefer to rest on arbitrary private liking. And if our main demand is satisfied by such an ultimate reality, and is not satisfied otherwise, that to my mind is enough. To object that it and its 'how' in detail are inexplicable is no refutation, unless you choose to assume that whatever is inexplicable is so far unreal—an assumption probably in your case inconsistent, and in any case arbitrary. If you could show that such a reality fails in its general character to meet and satisfy our ultimate demand, or again collides with that in principle, the case would be altered. But I have asked in vain for any evidence that such is the fact.   [A, p. 21.]

Professor Parker, in his interesting and instructive chapter on Relations,[1] while pointing out that relational unity everywhere (*a*) presupposes and rests on pre-relational unity, contends, I understand, (*b*) that the relational experience is not in the end self-contradictory, because, while resting on the former unity and not superseding it, it is a fresh development beyond it and equally true. The reader will see that, while largely agreeing with Professor Parker, I am unable to follow him to his conclusion. For me, while the relational experience is less fundamental, yet neither of the two ways of taking the One and Many as one is in the end true and real. The contents of the feeling experience refuse to answer to the form; and, as we have seen, we are forced to transcend it.

And I may be permitted, perhaps, here in this connexion to notice the objection, adopted in the main from Mr. Russell and urged by him[2] as fatal to every kind of Monism. He assumes that every Monism must take the universe as throughout a simple unity of qualities or adjectives in and of a whole which completely determines them, and is bound (I understand also) in this way to account for and explain all its contents—which it obviously cannot do in the case of 'asymmetrical relations'.

Now nothing, I agree, can be more obvious ⟨than⟩ that not only some, but any form of relational experience is, on such a view of Monism, impossible, while (as a fact) it is undeniable. But for myself (if I may speak as a Monist) this from the first has been obvious, and I do not take the ultimate reality as above, and I had hoped that so much was clear; and further, as to claiming or admitting that Monism has to 'explain' everything, nothing could be further from what I hold. Such a contention to myself is ridiculous.

Hence, when it is objected against me as a Monist that all that I as such have a right to is the terms and the whole, while the order or direction is in neither—my answer is that *no* whole is really a simple whole, and in every whole are always conditions unexpressed, and that in these conditions falls the difference required here, and here is the reason why A R B and B R A are incompatible (that is, *when* and *where* they are so). In short, far from admitting that Monism requires that all truths can be interpreted as the predication of qualities of the whole, Monism with me contends that all predication, no matter what, is in the end untrue and in the end unreal, because and so far as it involves always and ignores unexpressed conditions.   [B, pp. 10–11.]

---

[1] [*The Self and Nature*, by De Witt H. Parker, chapter ix, pp. 212–73.]
[2] [i.e. by Professor Parker, cf. pp. 233–7.]

Note 15

Note by the editor:—

At this point C breaks off. On the subject of Multiple Relations, however, there are two drafts, one in A and the other (containing a reference to the first) in B. Both drafts are reproduced below, since taken together they may serve to indicate the lines which Bradley would probably have followed in C.

Although the question of 'multiple relations' is referred to as 'this final point' (above, p. 649), there is some ground for thinking that, had C been completed, it would have included the discussion of one more subject. For in B (p. 4) the author draws up the following Plan or List of Headings for his treatment of relational experience:—

' (*a*) State relational view abstractly.
 (*b*) Show contradiction in detail.
 (*c*) Show how it stands on immediate experience, while attempting to supersede it.
 (*d*) Show how it can't be taken (as immediate experience is taken) as not unintelligible and not self-contradictory.
 (*e*) It is not another ultimate form of unity (Parker).

Then, more detailed questions about it—

 (i) Every relation is and is not the whole situation (Alexander).
 (ii) Every relation does and does not qualify its terms, and so also reciprocally.
 (iii) A relation may therefore be multiple indefinitely.
 (iv) Every relation is (*a*) both external and internal, and again (*b*) may be intrinsic or extrinsic.
 (v) Every relation is, and is not, capable of degree.'

Now this Plan is carried out in B (pp. 5–20), though not without considerable modification. Thus the treatment of the more general topics, (*a*)–(*e*), is run together. And, as regards the 'more detailed questions', No. iv (the treatment of which is in B far less adequate than in C) is merged with No. ii (and Bradley has accordingly corrected the 'iv' into 'ii' in the Plan); the treatment of No. iii is expanded so as to include a discussion of the singleness and duality of every relation; and No. v is omitted altogether. But, as the reader will have observed, the treatment of the 'more detailed questions' in C follows the Plan very closely—the only modification being that No. iv precedes No. iii. And since there is no evidence to show that the omission of No. v in B was intentional, we may reasonably conjecture that the First Part of the Article would have included a discussion of the question whether relations differ in degree. Accordingly the later and better of the two drafts, which A contains on this subject (cf. above, p. 651), is reproduced below.

I. *'Multiple' relations.*

Of course, if we assume that every unity of one and many is a relation, then (*a*) on the one hand we may go downwards, and—where we obviously have qualities united non-relationally, as (say) in a perceived green leaf—we may insist that one or more relations, though against all appearance, are there. Or (*b*) in the other direction we may insist that, since the unity of every kind of 'whole' is relational, therefore every complex is a relation; and (no matter how many terms and relations of however many kinds it may contain) it is, and must be, itself therefore *one* relation, to be called 'multiple'—e.g. jealousy.[1] Referring to my *Essays* for further detail,[2] I will only say that the initial assumption made here is false. We have seen that, so far from all unity being relational, a relation everywhere depends for its unity on what is not relational. And as to the conclusion, it seems to me not merely false, but to be in monstrous collision with obvious fact. [A, p. 26.]

Of course, if every complex must have some kind of unity, and if there is no unity beyond what is relational, and if a mere plurality of several relations is not a unity—it follows that the required unity of the diversity is one relation, which therefore is called 'multiple' because of the diversity which it unites.

The relation obviously is taken as the whole relational situation, in which also it is contained as a part, or again as a member of parts. And such a result, I submit, involves a self-contradiction. . . . Of course I agree that, in a relational situation, the same relation may recur (more or less) throughout, and may be called 'pervasive' and 'distinctive' and, if you please, 'dominant'. And, further, to call this a 'multiple relation', and take it as what gives unity to the whole situation, may perhaps (I am prepared to believe) be useful in practice—and, if so, I agree should be used. But that we have here an idea, which (however useful) is in principle self-contradictory, I hope to have made evident. [B, p. 18.]

II. *Every relation is, and is not, capable of degree.*

Do relations differ in degree? We have here, I think, once more to say 'Yes' and 'No', and to both assert and deny. The cause of this is the ambiguity (essentially inseparable from the idea of relation) which we have found meeting us everywhere.

A relation may mean the whole relational situation, or it may

---

[1] [Cf. Bertrand Russell, *Philosophical Essays* (1910), pp. 177 ff.]
[2] [Cf. *Essays on Truth and Reality*, pp. 303 ff.]

mean an abstraction from that; and the two are in principle so inseparable, that we are led blindly to identify them and so to contradict ourselves; or, by ignoring one, to embrace the other—whichever it is that we prefer.

And ⟨so⟩ to the above question my answer is both 'Yes' and 'No'. If you mean the 'situation'—*that* is certainly capable of degree. If you mean the mere relation, abstracted from the situation, my answer is 'No'.

One's first impression, no doubt, may be 'Yes'. For take (with Mr. Russell) similarity and difference, say between colours or shades of colour. The difference or similarity, when we pass from one to another, may in diverse cases be more or less; and, since these are relations, our conclusion seems proved. But on the other hand take equality (which also is a relation), and it is disproved. Or let us take adultery and homicide, each of which (like jealousy) is a relation, and note the more and less prevalence of each in various countries as a proof that both must have degree, though this is only recognized in one. And, finally, let us take two mixed collections of coins, and note that in one we have more cases of equality—which therefore shows that equality must be there in a higher degree.

But I submit that, whenever we speak of more and less, there is an underlying 'what', of which we assert this more and less. And for any rational discussion this 'what' must be ascertained.

And (to repeat the result anticipated above) I should say that, if this 'what' is taken as the relation in the narrower sense (as abstracted from the situation), the answer is that it is everywhere incapable of degree. It is there, or not there—and not more or less of it there, or even (in strictness) there more or less. And otherwise it is of course capable.

Let us take some cases of this 'otherwise', and ask there for the 'what'.

(i) This may be merely psychical, as say (*a*) the relative frequency of occurrence, or (*b*) the relative occupancy of my mental space or strain of my attention, or ⟨(*c*)⟩ the general emotional disturbance (shock), or generally the kind of emotional tone.

These (we should all perhaps agree) are not degrees of the abstract relation itself, and should not be taken as belonging to it properly.

⟨(ii)⟩ Take, then, the passage from one shade of colour to another, or from one colour to another, and the diversity in various cases of the degree of likeness or difference. Of what is this predicable except the relation itself?

I answer:—there is always an underlying identity there, though not always explicit. When I pass from one red to another, there may be no difference in respect of colour. There are two cases and not two degrees of redness. When I pass from a pure to a dulled or whitened red, I pass from more to less red; and the 'what', of which there are degrees, is the red which underlies the process and the relation. When I pass again from red to purple, I can carry with me ⟨more and⟩ less of red, and there is more and less of diversity and likeness; but it is a more and less of red, and not of the mere relation —unless you take that as essentially qualified by the situation.

The same thing holds when I pass from one colour to another, where the underlying identity is colour, which may be present or absent in some varying degree. And, in the end, the 'what' underlying the change (whatever it may be) is always there; and it is that, and not the mere relation itself, of which there is more and less.

And we may (if we think it worth while) also note that a sense of change, and of resistance to change, may be more or less there at a stage when no relation in the proper sense is as yet experienced.

In short, when and so far as you do not (consciously or unconsciously) identify the relation with the relational situation, you have no right to speak of more or less of it. On the other hand, and so far as you do identify it, you certainly may do so. But whichever of these courses you take, you fail . . . to reach any view which is consistent with itself.   [A, pp. 27, 28, and 30.]

XXXII

REPLIES TO CRITICISMS, AND NOTES

INTRODUCTORY NOTE

It has been decided, though not without some hesitation, to reprint the following *Replies to Criticisms*.

Polemics of every kind were increasingly distasteful to the author as life went on; and, though formidable as an opponent, he was only induced to enter the lists when he considered that not only his own reputation but some vital point or principle was attacked. It was then that often, in a few trenchant sentences, his own views came more clearly to light, or were at times more fully developed.

Chiefly for this reason, and for the sake of completeness, but partly also because old misinterpretations tend to recur, it has been thought well to reprint the following *Replies*.

1. MR. SIDGWICK ON 'ETHICAL STUDIES'

[*First published in* MIND, o.s. ii, No. 5, 122–5. *January*, 1877.]

IN the last number of *Mind*,[1] Mr. Sidgwick did me the honour to review my *Ethical Studies*. His remarks were on the whole welcome to me, for they showed clearly the necessity there was, and is, for some work of the kind. I am not surprised that my reviewer did not *see* that necessity: that he *felt* it I think his article shows. 'Really penetrating criticism, especially in ethics, requires a patient effort of intellectual sympathy', and I am sorry that such an effort should be made in vain. But that in this instance it has been so I should like to be allowed to show. I am prepared to go through the article point by point, but cannot

[1] *M.* o.s. i, No. 4, 545–9.

ask from the readers of *Mind* so much space for matters partly personal. Indeed, if the reviewer had confined himself to remarks of a personal or generally depreciatory nature, I would not have trespassed on their forbearance at all. As it is, I must ask leave to correct some misunderstandings which are calculated to prejudice my views by representing them to be other than they are.

And (1) I must impress on the reader that I disclaimed the attempt to solve the problem of individuality in general; and in particular that of the origin of the Self in time, and the beginning of volition. But so far as I have said anything, I will endeavour to show that it is not incoherent, as soon as objections against it are distinctly formulated. I cannot do so before. However, I may say that I have no quarrel with Determinism if only that view will leave off regarding the Self as a collection, and volitions as 'resultants' or compositions of forces, and will either reform or cease to apply its category of cause and effect. The problem, as Mr. Sidgwick states it, on p. 46 of his *Methods of Ethics*, I consider to involve a false alternative.

(2) The fact that when I speak of self-realization 'we naturally think of the realization or development into act of each one of the potentialities constituting the definite formed character of each individual' is not surprising, until we have learnt that there are other views than those which appear in the *Methods of Ethics* (72 ff.). And this we very soon do if we proceed. I have written at some length on the good and bad selves (*E.S.* vii); and on p. 161 = 146, I have repudiated distinctly Mr. Sidgwick's understanding of the term. I thought that I had left no doubt that characters might be partly bad, and that this was *not* what I meant by self-realization as = end.

(3) 'We may at least say that a term which equally denotes the fulfilment of any of my desires by some one else, and my own accomplishment of my duty, will hardly avail us much in a definition of the Highest Good.' Perhaps. But I emphatically repudiate the doctrine that the mere bringing about by some one else of anything desired by me is my self-realization. If the reviewer wishes the

reader and myself to believe that I put this forward, he owes us a reference. If it be meant as a *deduction* from my premises, he owes us an argument. He has given us neither; and, as I think, nothing but a sheer misunderstanding.

(4) Mr. Sidgwick must be aware that I have endeavoured to define self-realization as = end. He proceeds to remark, 'the question then is whether we gain anything by calling the object of our search " the true whole which is to realize the true self" '. I think we do: but then I have not left the matter here as my reviewer seems to indicate. That point of view is reached on p. 73 = 67, and the whole remainder of the discussion down to p. 81 = 74 is quietly ignored by him. I call particular attention to this.

The passage on Hedonism which follows I will take hereafter.

(5) I do not know whether in what is said about Kant there is an objection to my views, nor, if so, what that is; but when the reviewer says of me, 'he accepts a merely relative universality as a sufficient criterion of goodness', I must remark that this is what I do *not* say. I say relative *and* absolute (192 = 173–4); and this appears even from my reviewer's next page.

(6) 'Mr. Bradley, I think, has not clearly distinguished this view from his own; and the effectiveness of his argument against Individualism depends chiefly on the non-distinction.' The view is 'the old doctrine . . . that the individual man is essentially a social being'. But (*a*) if my view is partly the same as another, what is that against it? (*b*) If Mr. Sidgwick will point out confusion, I will admit it or answer it. I cannot do either until he does. (*c*) At any rate, 'that the individual man is essentially a social being' *is* my view, and is *not* my reviewer's. If it be 'a vague and barren ethical commonplace', yet in his book he must be taken to deny it, for he finds the end and, I suppose, the essence of man by examining a supposed 'single sentient conscious being'.[1]

(7) 'He allows . . . even that "open and direct outrage

[1] *Methods of Ethics*, p. 374.

on the standing moral institutions which make society and
human life what it is" may be "justified on the plea of
overpowering moral necessity".' Here I must earnestly
beg the reader to consult the context in my book (226–
7 = 204–5). I cannot ask for space to quote it. The
question I was discussing was the extent to which *in theory*
we must hold that collisions may proceed (cf. 157 = 142).
On pp. 158–9 = 143 I distinctly denied that 'moral
theory' is 'meant to influence practice' (cf. 227 = 205
footnote). And I do think this ought not to have been
ignored.

(8) My reviewer continues—'But here he plainly comes
into conflict with "unsophisticated common sense": and
surely, if that authority be thus found *falsus in uno*, it must
be at least *fallibilis in omnibus*: and thus we have still to
seek for some criterion of the validity of its dictates.' First,
I must ask for a reference for 'unsophisticated common
sense'. It is given as a quotation from me, but I do not
recognize it. Next, I have maintained that I do *not* really
come into collision with common morality, but, when
understood, am at one with it (226 = 204, cf. 157–
8 = 142–3). And my reasoned exposition, ignored by
the reviewer, may stand, I hope, against his 'plainly'.
Thirdly, he argues, What is *falsus in uno* is *fallibilis in
omnibus*. The falseness in this one thing I deny. Next, if
I admitted it, I should like to see the steps by which the
conclusion follows. Next, I have never hinted that the
moral consciousness is *not* fallible in particulars. Mr. Sidgwick really should give references for what he attributes
to me. Next, I deny that it is fallible in all points. Lastly,
even if it were false throughout, I say we have *not* 'to seek
for some criterion of the validity of its dictates'; for none
is possible.

This is all I think it necessary to say in answer to that
which my reviewer has urged against the doctrine I have
put forward. The rest, which I have not noticed, I must
not be taken to admit. And now, seeing that a large part
of my book was directed against Hedonism in general, and
one or two pages even against Mr. Sidgwick in particular,

I naturally hoped for some discussion of the matter. This is all I can find. 'The notion of Maximum Pleasure is certainly sufficient for systematizing conduct, as it gives us a universally applicable standard for selecting and regulating our activities. But it does not give us an end which can ever be realized as a whole, in Mr. Bradley's sense, that is, all at once: for obviously there is and can be no moment at which a "greatest possible sum of pleasures" can be enjoyed.'

First, as was said above, the reviewer ignores my interpretation of self-realization. Next, he suggests that my argument against Hedonism is that pleasures cannot be enjoyed all at once. True, that is *an* argument; but is it possible that Mr. Sidgwick can really believe that in other respects Maximum Pleasure answers to my conception of the end? This is so wholly at variance with the doctrine I hold that I confess I was not prepared for it. Thirdly, that the notion of Maximum Pleasure can systematize conduct and give a standard is a proposition I have formally contested. Mr. Sidgwick not only gives me an assertion for an answer, but by the way he introduces the assertion suggests to the reader that I believe it myself.

I can find no other defence of his opinions but the (unsupported) charge against me that I use rhetoric for argument, and that my apprehension of the views which I assail 'is always rather superficial and sometimes even unintelligent'. Those views I think should be securely founded, if they are to bear being defended in this way.

2. A REPLY TO A CRITICISM

[*First published in* MIND, N.S. iii, No. 10, 232–9. *April*, 1894.]

THE long 'critical notice' of my volume[1] in the last number of *Mind*[2] hardly pretends, I suppose, to be an ordinary review. It seems not to be an account or estimate of my work, but a mere attack on what the writer takes to be its

[1] *Appearance and Reality.*
[2] *Mind*, N.S. iii, No. 9, 109–25, by Professor James Ward.

fundamental errors. I am sorry for this, and I do not see what good can come of it. From a criticism which would teach me to question what wrongly I have assumed, or which from an admitted basis would point out my inconsistencies and defects, I have, I am sure, much to learn; and for any such criticism I am sincerely grateful. But an assault which is based tacitly on assumptions which I have rejected, or which consists in the mere assertion of doctrines such as I cannot fairly be taken either to be ignorant of or to hold—how is anything like this to be of use to me or indeed to any one? With this reflection I enter on the profitless task of a reply.

There are first (109) some prefatory statements about method which to me seem erroneous, but which, being mere assertions, I leave to themselves. Then, on p. 111, the actual attack is begun. The general nature of Reality as held by myself is called in question. My critic starts from a tacit assumption as to 'purely formal' truth. He seems unaware that any one could regard his doctrine as an exploded fallacy, or could hold that a truth, if purely formal, would be no truth at all. But on the same page he has also, I observe, made a reference to Hegel. He then (112) proves that the universe need not be 'an absolute unity', and that I at least have no right to say more than that it 'is'. The sequence of ideas seems here obscure, and the meaning may have escaped me, but I must deal with the arguments as rightly or wrongly I understand them.

First as to the 'is', my critic appears to assume that 'all determination is negation', and that hence I must qualify the universe negatively or merely by 'is'.[1] He does not ask if I share this belief about negation; and, to speak broadly, I do not, nor do I know why I should be taken to do so. My critic fails to seize the distinction between further determination within a universal and its limitation from without. And he brings out the familiar dilemma between what is 'conditioned' and what is 'clear of condi-

---

[1] I do not attribute to Mr. Ward the assertion that that which has no competing predicate must be simply 'is'. That of course would be a bare and naked *petitio*.

tions'. But of course the Absolute is that which contains its conditions, and in this sense only is unconditioned. So much at present for the mere 'is'.

Then as to the oneness of the universe I argued in this way. Here is the world before us and in us, a world full of content and diversity. To try to explain this away would clearly be foolish, but, as we take the world up, it contradicts itself. In that character, then, we must assume that our world is not true or real; and yet, because it is, it must somehow with all its diversity be real. But (I argued) it cannot be plural, for that is self-contradictory, and every division and distinction pre-supposes and rests on a unity. Hence we are forced to take the whole mass of facts as all being one in such a way as *also* and *without abridgement* to be free from discrepancy. And as to the *word* 'unity', that of course matters little or nothing. Now, how does my critic meet this position? His statement is so obscure that I must quote it.

'It would be absurd, no doubt, to talk of two universes, but the denial of plurality is only tantamount to the affirmation of unity when we are dealing with the discrete. To this, whether as one or many, the continuous is opposed. Thus it may be absolutely true that the universe is, and still remain an open question whether it is an absolute unity and not an indefinite continuum. No doubt the latter alternative is cheerless enough; but Mr. Bradley seems to be more or less vaguely aware that it is there.'

The statement about the denial of plurality looks rather like a naked *petitio*, but I pass this by. We have to deal (I have urged) somehow with the given mass of facts. Everything discrete or otherwise, the whole world of things and selves with all their contents and relations, we have on our hands. And Mr. Ward seems to assert that all this can, without any self-contradiction, be 'an indefinite continuum', that it is cheerless, and that of this I seem more or less aware. But what, as I understand it, has no meaning, has no power to trouble me. And the idea that the universe is 'an indefinite continuum' is to me meaningless or self-discrepant. A continuum, not one and identical in its diversity and diverse in its unity, is, in the first place, to my mind, no continuum at all, nor do I quite understand how my critic is able to be unaware of this. As to 'indefinite'—whether it is meant to deny distinctions or limits or something else—we are not informed; but in any case it seems to increase the internal discrepancy. And, since this possible alternative to unity, which is to ruin my doctrine, is not brought into the light, I must without more detail dismiss it as self-contradictory or meaningless. The further remarks as to 'logical principles' seem merely to repeat the same dogma about 'form', or to imply further that I have assumed, without any argument, that there are not many Realities. This latter implication would of course be incorrect.

Passing next to the doctrine that Reality is one experience, my critic tries once more to show that for me Reality = 'is'. And the process is very simple (113). He finds that Reality and Being are at times not distinguished by me, and he concludes that *therefore* Reality (proper) cannot possibly mean more than Being (proper). But the principle which underlies this wonderful argument he does not state.[1] The notion that an idea can be taken as internally filled in, and that conceivably his author might hold this view, seems not to have occurred to him.

I have contended also that the universe is a perfect individual, perfection including a balance of pleasure, though as to the pleasure I pointed out that doubt is not quite excluded. My argument, right or wrong, was simple and an extension of what went before. If all phenomena, without abridgement, are to be consistent and one, then (I urged) they must be a complete individual and this whole must be perfect; because want of harmony between idea and existence, and again pain, must mean discord and so contradiction. Now with this argument, good or bad, I cannot find that my critic deals anywhere at all. He flies off instead (114) to a discussion on the ontological proof. The position I have given to this in my work, and the way in which I have treated it parenthetically, should have

[1] The assertion that for me the 'real' or the 'experienced' = 'that' seems to me baseless.

warned any one that I could not intend to rest my case on an argument in this form. All that I feel called on to say is that what I have written on this proof my critic does not appear to have understood, and that my plain argument, so far as I see, he has totally ignored. After some remarks on pleasure, the bearing of which I have been unable to perceive, he asserts that the identity of idea and existence does *not* mean 'the attainment and consummation of all ideals and ends'. Well, so far as the whole is concerned, I have tried to reason that it does and must. And until a better way is shown me, I have no choice but to put reasoning, even my own, before the mere assertion of however great a metaphysical authority.

The conclusion so far, that Reality is a perfect individual experience, is naturally abstract. It certainly, if true, has cleared away a large mass of competing theories, though my critic appears never to have looked at the matter from this side. But the conclusion is abstract and so far not satisfactory. On the other hand, it is a principle applicable (I have argued) to every part of the universe. The idea of individuality, I have contended, can be, and is, used as the criterion of reality, worth, and truth. Since everything which at all exists must fall within Reality, everything in some sense is an element in a perfect individual. And individuality, we can observe, shows itself variously through the facts of appearance, and is found in varying degrees. From the space and atoms of matter to the highest life of the self-conscious self we can perceive a scale of individuality and self-containedness. Realized perfectly in no one part of the universe, the Absolute still is realized in every part, and it seems manifest in a scale of degrees, the higher of which comprehends the lower. And the system of metaphysics (I have added), which I have not tried to write, would aim at arranging the facts of the world on this principle, the same principle which outside philosophy is unconsciously used to judge of higher and lower. If this doctrine is not true, most assuredly it is not new, and some knowledge of it, I suppose, may fairly be demanded from any one who comes forward to speak on metaphysics. Nor, again, do I perceive, when this principle is worked through the various aspects of the world, how within metaphysics we can look for anything more concrete.

But my critic urges that such a principle remains 'purely formal', 'the matter remains absolutely indeterminate and the form is a purely logical framework' (114), or this 'absolute knowledge is form simply'. And he implies that such knowledge is not knowledge of the universe. If I had said that Reality was a perfect Will containing somehow within itself a plurality of finite wills, and if this principle were argued to be applicable to the various aspects of the world—would that also, I wonder, have been formal merely? But I am not told what it is that my critic expects from metaphysics. So far as I see, he argues downward from two assumptions.

He seems to believe that, without applying it to the concrete facts of the world, I ought to deduce straight from some abstract principle my ultimate conclusion. But he does not exhibit any warrant for this bare preconception. And when (113), after a sort of appeal to Hegel, my critic assures me that to 'place the spirituality of the real beyond question ... is what we want as a first step towards idealism', he seems, in criticizing me, to bear witness against and to judge himself. For he appears to start from a sheer *a priori* construction of 'idealism'.

And the assertion as to pure form is surely once again the merest dogma. Mr. Ward seems to offer a dilemma. Absolute truth (apparently) is to be a 'determinate positive knowledge' which has to 'co-exist along with' finite truth (115), or else it is 'form simply' and 'a purely logical framework'. But this division of form and matter is precisely that which he has to prove against me, and to urge it as if in philosophy it were an undisputed axiom seems a strange procedure. Does the physical analogy from a material frame and what fills it hold good? Are the general character and the detail two factors more or less indifferent to each other, and of which either can be anything apart from the other? Is it conceivable that knowledge could be made up of two coexisting morsels? Is God (if we like to put it so) *either* an indifferent 'framework' in which individuals are somehow stuck, *or else* one 'morsel' in an undigested mass which somehow coexists in (or without?) some stomach? And would it not be better if my critic addressed himself to the discussion of such points, instead of simply assuming against me as true what he surely might know that I reject? To me the idea that detail is *not* determined by its general character is irrational, that finite truth or being should 'co-exist along with' what is absolute is unmeaning. To me, of course, there is *no* truth which is not the knowledge which the Absolute has of itself. The distinction which I have drawn in my last chapter amounts to what follows. *All* truths are in various degrees imperfect. Finite truths have other truths falling outside which modify them; and, however much knowledge is organized, it never can be the perfect systematic totality of its detail. But the general character of the whole has, on the other side, no truth falling outside it. It is not one member in a disjunction, because any disjunction must be the specification of itself.

Now this whole doctrine may of course be mistaken in principle. I have failed, I know well, to grasp it and carry it out as it should have been carried out. Nay, if I had been able to keep closer to a great master like Hegel, I doubt if after all perhaps I might not have kept nearer to the truth. But when I am assailed to-day with the same dogmatic alternatives, on the criticism of which long ago Hegel based his system, and when these seem blindly urged as axioms removed from all possibility of doubt, my own doubts are at an end. For even if Hegel's construction has failed, Hegel's criticism is on our hands. And whatever proceeds by ignoring this is likely, I will suggest, to be mere waste of time.

From this point onward I can deal more briefly with my critic's objections. I showed that in our psychical experience the various aspects point to a superior whole above relations, and that this whole in an imperfect form appears before, and still persists below, the relational consciousness.

I was certainly wrong in employing (I hope not more than once or twice) the word 'intuition'. It was a misjudged attempt to assist the reader, and I left no doubt that the whole was not merely perceptual or theoretical.

My critic meets me (116) with bare assertions. Feeling could only be mere being without diversity, it could suggest only continuous change—both of which assertions I of course deny. It could not always be called 'a finite centre of experience'—to which I of course assent if he means *for itself*. Then Mr. Ward seems surprised and shocked that a principle in development should appear first in a less differentiated form. Then he states that for me differences are absorbed by an empty Reality, as, on the next page, he asserts that for me all finite content is destroyed in the Absolute—ignoring the fact that I, rightly or wrongly, have at least insisted on the opposite. Then I am assured without a reference (117) that I make mind a mere logical *summum genus*. And, because I say of the theoretic and other aspects that they are factors among which none has supremacy, and, speaking of the Absolute, add 'how these various modes can come together in a single unity must remain unintelligible', I am asked 'How can we talk of life if there is no supremacy and no subordination, or if its unity is to result from "factors" *coming together* for the purpose?'[1] But this question (so far as I understand it) does not seem to concern me. And when Mr. Ward proceeds (apparently) to take my words 'and how . . . unintelligible' in the sense of *that . . . inconceivable*, I confess that once more I am at a loss for a suitable reply.

We come now to the connexion of finite centres of experience with the Absolute. The introductory paragraph (118) seems obscure, and I cannot pretend to have understood it, and it is therefore most unwillingly that I am forced to notice it. So far as it means that there is a serious difference between finite centres on the one hand and mere aspects of one centre on the other hand, I naturally assent to it. But the paragraph appears to imply very much more

[1] The italics are Mr. Ward's.

than this. I of course should not admit that unity and identity are mere relations, or that unity is possible without identity. But I do not know if either of these statements is implied. The questions asked as to the identity of and difference between the universe and reality and experience I have failed to understand. Perhaps they put once more the points which I have dealt with already; and in any case from my point of view they seem to be meaningless. But all that I am certain of is their great obscurity.

Then follows a supposition as to what I hold concerning finite centres. It is not a correct supposition, nor does it even seem to be offered as correct, and I am hence not forced to examine it closely. It involves what the reader of my work can see I regard as contradictions. There is, however, a statement (119) which I cannot pass over. 'To all finite centres, it will be remembered, there pertains a felt reality; and *that is not appearance*.'[1] Mr. Ward has misconstrued the passage to which he refers, and surely I have committed myself fully to the doctrine that without exception every element in the finite is appearance. Anything like an acceptance of the reality of Monads would, I believe, reduce my work in principle to a mass of inconsistency. 'Ideality', I think, and 'appearance', I am sure, are used against me in senses different to that which I have given them. And when I 'admitted' (*A.R.* 430 = 485) 'that some appearances really do not appear', what I admitted was that I (like many others) use the word 'appearance' in a sense which (if you please) is arbitrary, and that to appear does not necessarily imply appearance to some percipient. The passage is a reply to a criticism made, I think, by Lotze, and I am not convinced that it is really very hard to understand.

Passing on I find my critic still astonished. If appearances apart from Reality are nothing, and if in the end the 'how' of appearances is inexplicable, he urges that they cannot be the 'revelation' of Reality. But I am not aware that revelation must mean total manifestation perfect in

[1] The italics are Mr. Ward's.

every point where the whole is revealed. And if Mr. Ward will make inquiry he will find, I think, that he is merely trying to strain language. But he seems to approach the whole matter with fixed preconceptions. I have mentioned ($A.R.$ 458 = 517, 415 = 469) various facts which in the end I cannot explain. Amongst these the fact of finite centres takes a place, though not the only place. And this, I suppose, is contrary to what my critic feels he has a right to expect. I have argued that a mere inability to explain in the end 'how' a thing can be forms no valid objection to our assertion 'that' it is, if we have good reason on our side and on the other side nothing. Of this vital and reiterated argument Mr. Ward takes absolutely no notice. He doubtless finds it easier to refute me by distorting my meaning, and by taking 'how' at his pleasure in the sense of 'that'. That a revelation can be imperfect and yet genuine is to him a thing strange and unheard of. And he seems possessed by the idea that I am bound to explain and deduce everything. But I cannot consider myself in any way responsible for his disappointment.

On the next page (120) my critic pursues the same path. After some statements and some implications as to the process in Reality, parts of which are incorrect, he urges that process within the Absolute is but appearance, not true as such, and he asserts that *hence* it is 'pure illusion'. I have of course argued that appearance, though error, is partial truth, and is therefore *not* pure illusion. This contention doubtless may be mistaken, but a criticism which ignores it is surely not criticism at all.

The following page repeats with variations the same idle procedure. I have tried to show that time and change in their own character are appearance, but that (how in detail we do not know) they are corrected and preserved in a higher whole to which they minister. Once more, totally ignoring that on which I have insisted, my critic represents me as holding that time and change are reduced to zero. And, not content with this, he even allows himself strange liberties with my statements. The extract from p. 194 = 220 taken from one context is without a word applied to another. And when (with a reference to $185 = 210$) I am said to make an attempt which I myself style illusory, I reply by asking the reader to see for himself what attempt I really spoke of, and to save me the task of qualifying Mr. Ward's method of attack.

The mere illusoriness of phenomena (which in fact I do not hold) I might, it seems, have avoided, if I had not strained myself to escape from the pre-eminence of will (122). The history of philosophy since Kant does not wholly tend to support that hypothesis. And I am offered a dilemma between something like the pre-eminence of will and a belief that all changes 'are but events and not acts'. This ready-made alternative (we have known for years) exhausts for Mr. Ward all possibilities. He is forced to see, and he even admits, that I do not assent to it, and yet he has no resource but, without any discussion, to charge me with incoherence. But is it criticism to judge an author from preconceptions which he is admitted not to accept? And then my critic seriously represents me as holding a doctrine quoted as to goodness and immortality, when on the same page ($382 = 432$) I plainly disconnect myself from it, and in part criticize it again on p. $450 = 508$. That this extract from my work, the only one quoted for approval, should be put forward in spite of myself as my doctrine is characteristic. It is even more significant that, *if* this doctrine *were* mine, I should be blindly re-asserting it in the face of Hegel's elaborate criticism. But what pleases me is that in my volume ($450 = 508$) this criticism actually is referred to.

On p. 123 the remark following the extract from my p. $29 = 34$ may be commended in passing to the reader's attention. And, coming to that essential inconsistency of thought which I have tried to prove, my critic prefers to stand outside the discussion and once more merely to assert. And when (124) he crushes me with 'in what sense can a system be perfect, harmonious, and complete, when every constituent is not only partial but defective?' —he seems never even to have heard of the doctrine that, *unless* partial constituents *were* defective, they never could be elements in a system at all (see my p. 374 = 422). But, even if that view could elsewhere be taken as unknown, or as what might fairly be ignored, it is here the very view which Mr. Ward is undertaking to criticize.

At the end of his attack (124) my critic remembers that something has been forgotten, the chapter on degrees of truth and reality. He has never understood that an appearance is rejected as simply false, only so far as it offers itself as simply real. He seems ridden by the notion that between appearances and the real there is a sort of wall. The idea that nothing is or exists at all, except so far as it is the one Reality, that this Reality appears and shows its character everywhere in a more or less imperfect form, and yet that nothing taken by itself can claim to be the Reality —any such idea plainly has never entered Mr. Ward's field of vision. And hence he is staggered to find that appearance after all has degrees. He asks in amazement how finite spirits are to use absolute Reality, as if finite spirits could possibly use or could be anything else, as if outside the finite the Absolute were anything at all, and as if a principle must be employed explicitly or applied in a perfect form, or else, failing that, not applied and not used in any way. He once more roundly asserts that, when the whole is qualified non-relationally, this means that the relations are not added to, but extinguished. He does not anywhere even mention the fact that I at least insist on the opposite. And he ends with a sketch of my mental characteristics, which I am led to infer must be such as to account for and justify anything. When a man does not understand me at once, it is because I am unintelligible; when his statement as to what I hold contradicts itself, that is because I am incoherent; and when, suppressing one part of what I teach, he presents a fragment as the whole, he but does me the service my unhappy nature prevents me from rendering to myself. And this is all possible, but after all there is another possibility. If that idea could have been able to suggest itself to my critic's mind, we might perhaps have been spared a controversy which (so far as I can judge) is wholly futile.

3. NOTE, IN ANSWER TO ALFRED SIDGWICK

[*First published in* MIND, N.S. xiv, No. 53, 148. *January*, 1905.]

In the last number of *Mind* Mr. A. Sidgwick complains that he has suffered injustice. His attitude towards the new Gospel, it seems, has been misrepresented, and he seeks to deny my statement that he claims to be the champion of philosophic scepticism. As to the first point, how far he has been misrepresented the reader may decide; but on the second point perhaps I should offer a few words. In the article to which I referred (*M.* N.S. iii. 336–47) the reader, I think, will find that Mr. Sidgwick unquestionably takes the field as the self-elected representative of philosophical scepticism, and the doubt is merely as to the meaning to be given to this term. Certainly Mr. Sidgwick explicitly there rejects scepticism in one sense, and explicitly defends it in another special sense which I have noticed elsewhere. But these special senses, and in short the ambiguous detail of the article, are, I submit, here irrelevant. The words 'philosophical scepticism' were used by me in their ordinary meaning. And the real question is whether the scepticism which Mr. Sidgwick champions does or does not imply scepticism in this general sense. Does he or does he not advocate the main sceptical conclusion that no positive doctrine in philosophy is theoretically indisputable? As to his acceptance of this conclusion the reader, I submit, is left no liberty to doubt (see more particularly p. 339). And I thought it well perhaps to remark on the apparent coexistence of this position with a benevolent interest in our new philosophical creed.

If Mr. Sidgwick's intention was not to accept the main doctrine of scepticism, as commonly understood, he has of course only to state this, if indeed he is in a position to do so. And as his attack on myself showed to my mind little comprehension of my meaning, there is no reason, I presume, why I may not on my side have failed to understand his. But as to the person who in that case is most to blame for the wrong of which Mr. Sidgwick complains, the reader must judge, if he thinks it worth while to do this. I should be sorry to have contributed to injustice, but on the other hand I could not accept responsibility for any divergence between Mr. Sidgwick's literary intentions and their execution. I should add that practically I am acquainted only with those writings of Mr. Sidgwick to which I have referred. And I must end with an apology to the readers of *Mind* for intruding on them with matters which perhaps have little but a personal interest.

4. NOTE, ON AN ARTICLE BY H. V. KNOX
(in *M.* N.S. xiv. 210–20).

[*First published in* MIND, N.S. xiv, No. 55, 439. *July*, 1905.]

MAY I be allowed to make a brief statement in reference to the article by Mr. Knox in the last number of *Mind*? This article purports to criticize my views on certain ultimate questions. The discussion of such final difficulties, and the attempt to solve them, is naturally to be found mainly in the latter part of my book. On the other hand, in the above article I see no reference to any page beyond the first quarter of the volume, and I discover no acquaintance with anything that comes later. To speak in general, where I have raised a difficulty and offered a solution, my discussion is not condemned as worthless (as perhaps it is), but seems taken as if it possessed no kind of being.

Out of several instances I will point to the most obvious. I published in *M.* N.S. v,[1] an examination of the nature of Contradiction. This (with omissions) was reprinted some eight years ago in my book, and, under the heading 'Contradiction and the Contrary', its existence is visible in the table of contents.[2] But in the article, in which Mr. Knox now controverts my view of Contradiction, I find no

---

[1] ['The Contrary and the Disparate'].   [2] [*A.R.*, p. 500 = p. 562].

reference to that which presumably he must know is my professed discussion of the topic. Its contents and the very fact of its existence seem taken as things which are nowhere in the world. See especially pp. 213 and 218.

I could adduce other instances of what appears to be the same procedure, but one perhaps is enough. And to myself, though possibly not to others, the whole thing is inexplicable. I am not, I hope, under much illusion as to the defects of my volume, and on this special subject it will be a disappointment to me if it has to contain my last word. On the other hand, I perhaps need explain no further why, without denying the merits of Mr. Knox's article, I have been unable to find in it much which concerns me personally.

5. A DISCLAIMER

[*First published in the* JOURNAL OF PHILOSOPHY, vol. vii, p. 183. *March*, 1910.]

THE too flattering notice of myself by Professor James, in the *Journal* (January), contains a statement which I think I should ask leave to correct. Professor James credits me with 'breaking loose from the Kantian tradition that immediate feeling is all disconnectedness'. But all that I have really done here is to follow Hegel. In this and in some other points I saw long ago that English psychology had a great deal to learn from Hegel's teaching. To have seen this, and to some extent to have acted on it, is all that common honesty allows me to claim. How far Hegel himself in this point was original, and how again M. Bergson conceives his own relation to post-Kantian philosophy, are matters that here do not concern me. I write merely to disclaim for myself an originality which is not mine. It belongs to me no more than does that heroical perversity or perverse heroism with which I find myself credited.

6. A REPLY TO A CRITICISM BY E. H. STRANGE
(*M.* N.S. XX. 457–88).

[*First published in* MIND, N.S. xxi, No. 81, 148–50. *January,*
1912.]

I CANNOT but feel honoured by the space which is given
in the last number of *Mind* to a criticism of my views. And
I should like to be permitted to offer some remarks on this
criticism. I find myself, however, here in a difficult position. So far as my own views have been misapprehended, I
could hardly make this clear otherwise than by an attempt
to re-state them throughout. And again so far as Mr.
Strange argues from a position which I reject, I should not
feel myself justified in dealing with that position as it is left
in his article. All that I can do, therefore, is to attempt to
indicate briefly a series of apparent misconceptions with
regard to the doctrines which I hold.

(1) Mr. Strange apparently takes me to identify feeling
with reality. Everything, I understand him to say, arises
out of feeling and returns into it. This, of course, is to me
a fundamental mistake for which I am in no way responsible. The mistake runs through and vitiates a large part
of Mr. Strange's criticism. It is another side of the same
error when I am told that for me feeling is indisputable
and beyond criticism. I am unable to do more here than
once more to express my surprise.

(2) I am further taken to limit the actual to a series of
momentary and fleeting psychical events. I cannot think
that my critic has the least idea of what to me is the position of events in time, or again of psychical existence and
mental facts of the moment, and of how all this to me
depends on ideal construction from the basis of immediate
experience. He evidently takes mental facts as being for
me something which in their own shape are ultimately real
(488). The only answer which I can make here is a general
reference to what I have written on the subject. Again
(482) I am offered a dilemma on the ground that I deny
'that the soul is existent'. I however thought that what I

held was that the soul is existent, and that its existence involves inconsistency. How could I possibly deny the existence of the soul?

(3) The assertion that I identify feeling with 'the self or individual' (464–5) once more causes me surprise and prepares me for anything or everything in the way of a conclusion. But I pass from this to notice the argument (465–6) that, if my doctrine as to feeling were true, I at least could not know this. Mr. Strange is apparently unaware that I have myself raised this objection and tried to deal with it (*A.R.* 79–80 = 93, 95 = 110, and *Mind*, No. 69).[1] What I have written here may be worthless, but how can my critic claim a right to treat it as having no existence?

(4) With regard to my alleged failure to recognize any act or subject in judging, and my inability to distinguish myself from other selves, I will merely refer to what I have written on these heads,[2] and will pass on to another misunderstanding. When I speak of using content as 'loose', Mr. Strange takes me to mean that this content in fact is removed and that the actual fact is destroyed (472–5). He does not argue that this is what I *ought* to hold, but treats me as holding it. I am aware of no justification for this interpretation except that the result is of course ruinous to myself.

(5) On page 478 there is a passage which I notice because it exemplifies a common misapprehension. Mr. Strange, like some other advocates of realism, fails to understand the position which he is anxious to attack. The contention which he has to meet is this, that he is taking a mere abstraction for reality, and that the burden of showing that what we contend is an abstraction is really more rests properly with him. Such an idea seems not to have occurred to him, but he will find that it is perhaps more worth his attention than the ingenious arguments which, I must acknowledge, he does *not* attribute to myself. In the same way I would add (though this has no

---

[1] [*M.* n.s. xviii. 40–64 = *T.R.* chapter vi.]

[2] On the second of these I have touched recently in *Mind*, No. 74, pp. 155–6 [see *M.* n.s. xix. 153–85 = *T.R.* chapter ix].

reference to Mr. Strange) that it is idle to advocate the ultimate reality of change, unless you at least consider the view that mere change is no more than an abstraction.

The above misconceptions, it seems to me, leave little value to Mr. Strange's article as a criticism of myself. Certainly my views may be no better than those which he has attacked, but at least they are different. But there are doctrines which Mr. Strange has incidentally laid down, which, if they were tenable, would render detailed examination of what I hold quite superfluous. As to that I am entirely of one mind with Mr. Strange. But he does himself here, I must think, a most serious injustice when he speaks (479) of his having 'tried to elaborate' his doctrine. That is precisely the thing which on the contrary I would invite him to do, for, as he has left it, I feel that I could not in common fairness to himself attempt to criticize his position. I wish to keep in mind that, if a view opposed to my own is untenable, it does not follow that I myself am not equally wrong; just as the pointing out of misconceptions may, I know, do nothing to remove real difficulties. But if Mr. Strange would seriously apply himself to such a statement of his doctrine as would enable the reader to see how it can hold against familiar objections, I venture to think that, far from losing his time, he would produce something which would be read with attention and interest.

BIBLIOGRAPHY

BOOKS

1876. Ethical Studies.   *E.S.*
1927.   ,,   Second Edition, with Notes.
1883. The Principles of Logic.   *L.*
1922.   ,,   ,,   Second Edition, Revised, with Commentary, and Terminal Essays.
1928.   ,,   ,,   Corrected Impression.
1893. Appearance and Reality.   *A.R.*
1897.   ,,   ,,   Second Edition. (With an Appendix.)
1930.   ,,   ,,   Ninth Impression. (Corrected.)
1914. Essays on Truth and Reality.   *T.R.*
1930. Aphorisms.
1935. Collected Essays.   *E.*

PAMPHLETS

1874. The Presuppositions of Critical History.   *E.* i.
1877. Mr. Sidgwick's Hedonism.   *E.* ii.

ESSAYS

1877. Mr. Sidgwick on *Ethical Studies.*   *M.* o.s. ii = *E.* xxxii. 1.
1883. Is Self-sacrifice an Enigma?   *M.* o.s. viii = *E.* iii.
  ,,   Is there such a thing as Pure Malevolence?   *M.* o.s. viii = *E.* iv.
  ,,   Sympathy and Interest.   *M.* o.s. viii = *E.* v.
1884. Can a Man sin against Knowledge?   *M.* o.s. ix = *E.* vi.
1885. The Evidences of Spiritualism.
            Fortnightly Review, No. ccxxviii, N.s. = *E.* xxix.
1886. On the Analysis of Comparison.   *M.* o.s. xi = *E.* ix.
  ,,   Is there any special Activity of Attention?   *M.* o.s. xi = *E.* x.
1887. On a Feature of Active Attention.   *M.* o.s. xii = *E.* xi.
  ,,   Association and Thought.   *M.* o.s. xii = *E.* xii.
  ,,   Why do we remember forwards and not backwards?
                                      M. o.s. xii = *E.* xiii.
1888. On Pleasure, Pain, Desire, and Volition.   *M.* o.s. xiii = *E.* xiv.
  ,,   Reality and Thought.   *M.* o.s. xiii = *A.R.* ch. 15.
1893. Consciousness and Experience.
                  M. N.s. ii = *T.R.*, Appendix to ch. 6.
  ,,   Professor James's Doctrine of Simple Resemblance (I)
                                     M. N.s. ii = *E.* xv.
  ,,   ,,   ,,   (II)
                                       M. N.s. ii = *E.* xvi.
  ,,   ,,   ,,   (III)
                                       M. N.s. ii = *E.* xvii.

1894. Some Remarks on Punishment.
                    International Journal of Ethics, April = *E*. vii.
  „   The Limits of Individual and National Self-sacrifice.
                    International Journal of Ethics, October = *E*. viii.
  „   Reply to a Criticism. (James Ward on *Appearance and Reality*).
                                    M. N.S. iii = *E*. xxxii. 2.
  „   On the Failure of Movement in Dream.   *M*. N.S. iii = *E*. xviii.
1895. What do we mean by the Intensity of Psychical States?
                                    M. N.S. iv = *E*. xix.
  „   On the Supposed Uselessness of the Soul.   *M*. N.S. iv = *E*. xx.
  „   In what sense are Psychical States extended? *M*. N.S. iv = *E*. xxi.
1896. The Contrary and the Disparate.
                        M. N.S. v = *A.R.*, Appendix, Note A.
1899. Some Remarks on Memory and Inference.
                        M. N.S. viii = *T.R.*, ch. 12.
1900. A Defence of Phenomenalism in Psychology. *M*. N.S. ix = *E*. xxii.
1901. Some Remarks on Conation.   *M*. N.S. x = *E*. xxiii.
1902. On Active Attention.   *M*. N.S. xi = *E*. xxiv.
  „   On Mental Conflict and Imputation.   *M*. N.S. xi = *E*. xxv.
  „   The Definition of Will (I)   *M*. N.S. xi = *E*. xxvi.
1903.   „   „   (II)   *M*. N.S. xii = *E*. xxvii.
1904.   „   „   (III)   *M*. N.S. xiii = *E*. xxviii.
  „   On Truth and Practice.   *M*. N.S. xiii = *T.R.*, ch. 4.
1905. Note (in answer to Alfred Sidgwick).   *M*. N.S. xiv = *E*. xxxii. 3.
  „   Note (on an Article by H. V. Knox).   *M*. N.S. xiv = *E*. xxxii. 4.
1906. On Floating Ideas and the Imaginary.   *M*. N.S. xv = *T.R.*, ch. 3.
1907. On Truth and Copying.   *M*. N.S. xvi = *T.R.*, ch. 5.
1908. On Memory and Judgement.   *M*. N.S. xvii = *T.R.*, ch. 13.
  „   On the Ambiguity of Pragmatism.
                    M. N.S. xvii = *T.R.*, ch. 5, App. I.
1909. On our Knowledge of Immediate Experience.
                        M. N.S. xviii = *T.R.*, ch. 6.
  „   On Truth and Coherence.   *M*. N.S. xviii = *T.R.*, ch. 7.
  „   Coherence and Contradiction.   *M*. N.S. xviii = *T.R.*, ch. 8.
1910. A Disclaimer.   *Journal of Philosophy*, vii. 183 = *E*. xxxii. 5.
  „   On Appearance, Error, and Contradiction.
                                    M. N.S. xix = *T.R.*, ch. 9.
1911. On some Aspects of Truth.   *M*. N.S. xx = *T.R.*, ch. 11.
  „   On Professor James's *Meaning of Truth*.
                        M. N.S. xx = *T.R.*, ch. 5, App. II.
  „   Reply to Mr. Russell's Explanations.
                    M. N.S. xx = *T.R.*, ch. 9, Supp. Note 3.
  „   Faith.   *Philosophical Review*, xx = *T.R.*, ch. 2.
1912. Reply to a Criticism (by E. H. Strange). *M*. N.S. xxi = *E*. xxxii. 6.
  „   On the Treatment of Sexual Detail in Literature (hitherto
            unpublished).   *E*. xxx.
1924. Relations (hitherto unpublished, unfinished).   *E*. xxxi.

INDEX

Roman numerals in black type refer to the numbers of the Essays.

Existence, *v.* Idea (self-realizing), Ideal content, Fact, Psychical fact, &c.
— for volition, 477 ff.
Expansion, 248–52, 256, 262, 281–4.
Expectation, 261–3, 417 n., 481–3, 550.
Experience, 18, 115, 396 ff.
— immediate, 205, 206, 366, 376. Cf. Feeling, Relational experience.
— personal, 19–20, 25, 30, 64–5, 67, 69–70, 602–3.
— philosophy of, 12.
— the experienced, 369, 378–82.
Experiment, 21–2.
Extension, **XXI**.
— perception of, 223 n., 357.
Extensity, 357–63.
Extent, 361–2.

Fact, 11, 13, 23, 31, 41–2, 48, 49, 51, 64–6. *v.* Event, Psychical fact.
— and theory, 17.
Fear, 259.
Feeling, 13, 14, 78–82, 183, 185, 197–8, 216–18, 220–5, 263, 369, 377 n., 378–9, 381, 394, 396–8, 517, 523, 631 ff., 688, 696, 697.
— and consciousness, 80, 81.
— and contradiction, 635, 653, 658–63.
— Cf. Relational experience, Experience (immediate).
Finite centres, 688–9.
Foreknowledge, 5.
Fortlage, 211 n., 433 n.
Freedom, 23, 87.
Fusion, *v.* Blending.

'Geschichte', 8.
Gibbon, 63.
Given, the, 312, 331–2, 632. *v.* Psychical fact, 'This now', 'What' and 'That'.
God, 472 n., 687.

de Goncourt, 565 n.
Good, the, 72, 79, 85, 87, 92, 117, 122–3, 126, 150, 678.
— the common, 121 n.; **VII** *passim.*
— and bad, 464–6.
Green, T. H., 125.
Grote, J., 133, 134.

Hallucination, 351.
Hamilton, W., 182 n.
Happiness, 79–81, 85 n., 87, 92.
Harmony, 248–51, 256, 283–5.
Hatred, 136, 137.
Hedonism, **II**; 285–6, 456, 681.
Hegel, 296, 665, 682, 686, 687, 691, 695.
Heine, 625 n.
Hellenism, 150.
Herbart, 209, 213, 214.
Herodotus, 63.
History, **I**.
— limitation of, to human tradition, 35.
— material of, 35, 45, 46, 48, 49.
— and natural science, 21–3, 32–7, 41–5, 60–2.
Holsten, 52 n.
Horwicz, 135, 214 n., 247 n.
Humanitarianism, 167–9, 172.
Hume, 665, 668.
Hypnotism, 277, 279, 303, 304. *v.* Mesmerism.

Idea, 178, 183–92, 254, 392, 504–5. Cf. Attention, Image, Object of desire, Pleasure, Psychical fact, Volition.
— aesthetic, 386.
— as event, 369. *v.* Psychical fact, &c.
— self-realizing, 192 ff., 264–6, 273–4, 277 ff., 618–20.
— — in volition (q.v.), 409 n., 415 ff., 438 n., 439, 441, 444–6, 451 ff., 467–71, 474, 476 ff., 572–93.
— — in volition, identified with self, **XXVII**.